Prosper Mérimée

Mérimée in 1866

Prosper Mérimée

A. W. Raitt

Mieux vaut être amant sans être aimé –
qu'amant aimé, puis trahi ensuite.
Sérénade d'un berger de Zicavo,
Notes d'un voyage en Corse

Charles Scribner's Sons · New York

Contents

5

Illustrations

7

Acknowledgements

The author and publishers would like to thank the following for permission to use copyright material:

His Excellency the Duke of Alba for plate 4a; Her Excellency the Duchess of Alba for 4b; Archives Photographiques for frontispiece; the Bibliothèque Nationale for 9b, 11b, 11c; Collection Paul Prouté for 3b; Éditions Champion for 1, 2a, 2b, 3a, 5a; Éditions Payot for 6a; Marquis Carlos Muñoz de Laborde for 6b; the Mansell Collection for 7a, 8a, 9a; the Musée Carnavalet for 11a; the Musées Nationaux, Versailles for 5b, and endpapers; the National Portrait Gallery for 8c, and Radio Times Hulton Picture Library for 7b, 7c, 8b. The drawings reproduced as plates 10a, b, c, d, are in the possession of the author. Plate 12 is taken from M. Tourneux. *Prosper Mérimée, Ses Portraits. Ses Desseins. Sa Bibliothèque*, Paris, Charavay, 1879.

Note on the Endpapers

These show the Reception of the Siamese Ambassadors in 1861 at the court of Napoleon III. Mérimée stands to the left of a guard and just above the head of the second Siamese ambassador. He described the occasion in a letter to Mme de Montijo (29 June 1861, *C.G.* Vol. X, p. 312):

The three ambassadors with their retinue lay flat on their stomachs as soon as they entered the great hall of Henri II, where Their Majesties' throne had been set up. Imagine a man as ugly as an ape, bedecked in gold brocade, wearing a picador's hat surmounted by a sort of gilt cone, crawling along on his elbows and knees, and holding in both hands a vase containing the letters from his sovereigns. At every movement the vase shook and the hat wobbled as though it was about to fall off. The whole retinue advanced in the same way, each one crawling more or less gracefully, the second having his face up against the first one's backside, so that every time the moving column came to a halt, all the black faces bumped into the brocaded bottoms. Despite the ludicrousness of the ceremony, there was something degrading in the sight of these human beings, supposed to be the owners of immortal souls, imitating grasshoppers in this way.

Introduction

On 23 September 1970, it will be exactly a hundred years since Prosper Mérimée died at Cannes. During that time, his reputation has undergone many vicissitudes, but he has never ceased to be one of the most widely read authors of his period. In English-speaking countries especially, his popularity has remained constant, both in the original and in translation. Yet this fame has a surprisingly narrow base: to most people, Mérimée is known only for a handful of short stories, while his achievements as an historian, as an archaeologist, as a translator, as a dramatist and as a letter-writer are largely ignored. Nor has his life attracted much attention outside France. There have been two biographies of Mérimée in English, it is true, but both were written before the publication of Maurice Parturier's magnificent edition of his *Correspondance générale*, which has completely transformed our understanding of him as a man. The moment thus seems opportune for a reassessment in English of Mérimée as a writer and as a personality, and that is the aim of this book.

The biographical chapters are intended both to present a chronological account of an unusually crowded and fascinating existence, from the Romantic *salons* of the 1820s to the Court of Napoleon III, and to give some insight into a complex, contradictory but profoundly human character. Too often the coldly hostile gaze which Mérimée turned on the outside world has been taken as the symptom of a sterile, desiccated nature; in reality, it was the means by which an almost morbidly sensitive heart tried to protect itself from wounding contacts. The critical chapters contain analyses of all Mérimée's major writings, in the manifold domains in which he made his mark. I have tried to take a fresh look at works which have not always been accorded their due of critical examination, either because their apparent straightforwardness seemed to obviate the need for close scrutiny, or because they have simply not been very much read, at least outside France. A first appendix gives the text of some unpublished Mérimée letters which have come to light during the course of research for this book, and a second reproduces the text of a forgotten article on Mérimée (including some translations) by Mary Shelley, the poet's widow, whom he had briefly courted. All the text of the book and the quotations in it are in English, but, for those to whom it may be useful, the original French is preserved in a third appendix.

I am happy to record my debt to those people whose kind co-operation has done so much to make my work easier and more fruitful. My thanks are due especially to those who have granted me permission to make use of unpublished documents: to Professor Egon Pearson, owner of the Sharpe papers, and to the Librarian of University College, London, where they are now housed, for two letters from Mérimée to Sutton Sharpe; to the Librarian of University College, London for three letters from Mérimée to Lord Brougham and two from Mérimée to Mrs W. Brougham; to the Librarian of the John Rylands Library, Manchester, for a letter from Mérimée to H. Bellenden Ker. I am very grateful also to Mr E. J. Miller of the British Museum, author of an admirable biography of Mérimée's great friend Panizzi, for his help in enabling me to find four letters from Mérimée to Lady Holland and one to W. E. Gladstone. My friend and colleague Dr Angus Macintyre has answered the many questions I put to him with as much patience as erudition, and Dr Enid Starkie generously lent me unobtainable books. In addition I have received valuable help by correspondence from the National Library of Scotland; the Library of the University of London; Mr H. M. C. Baillie of the Historic Manuscripts Commission; the Archivist, Broadlands; the Marquess of Northampton; Lord Ashburton; and the Warden of St Deiniol's Library, Hawarden.

Prosper Mérimée

Chapter 1

Boy

Nous, qui avons eu le malheur de voir dans notre enfance, des
Cosaques aux Champs-Elysées. . . .
'Les Cosaques de l'Ukraine et leurs derniers atamans',
in *Mélanges historiques et littéraires*

Autumn 1803: after the collapse in May of the uneasy Peace of Amiens,
the most brilliant period of the Napoleonic era was beginning. Soon
to be metamorphosed from First Consul into Emperor, Napoleon was
massing his forces to crush his enemies both inside and outside France.
The breaking of the Cadoudal conspiracy and the execution of the
Duc d'Enghien were to establish him firmly as the master of his
country, and although English sea-power was to frustrate his schemes
for a cross-channel invasion, it was not to be long before his armies
surged across Eastern Europe. These were stirring times for every
Frenchman, memorably evoked many years later in Alfred de Musset's
Confession d'un enfant du siècle (*Confession of a Child of the Times*).

It was the air of this immaculate sky, in which so much steel sparkled,
that was breathed by the children of those times. They well knew that they
were destined for sacrificial slaughter; but they thought that Murat was
invulnerable and the emperor had been seen to cross a bridge with so
many bullets whistling round him that no one knew if he was mortal.
And even if one had to die, what did it matter? Death itself was so beautiful
in those days, so great, so splendid in its steaming crimson cloak! It looked
so much like hope, the young corn it reaped was so green, that it was as
if it had become the very stuff of youth, as if no one believed any longer
in old age. Every cradle in France was a buckler; so was every coffin; in
truth, there were no more old men, only corpses or demigods.[1]

Yet there were many areas of life in France to which the echoes of
these martial exploits scarcely penetrated, in which life continued much

[1] Alfred de Musset, *Confession d'un enfant du siècle*, Paris, Garnier, 1956,
pp. 2–3.

as it had done before Napoleon. One such sheltered haven was the academic art world of Paris, and in that world, one of those who were too immersed in the day-to-day business of life to pay much attention to outside events was Léonor Mérimée, a respected teacher and artist in his mid-forties, living comfortably if not opulently in the Carré Sainte-Geneviève, near the Panthéon.

Léonor Mérimée came of a family of Norman lawyers and had been born in 1757 in the castle of the Duc de Broglie, to whom his father was factor. While at school at Caen, he had developed a taste for both literature and painting, and shown sufficient talent to be sent to study in Paris at the École de l'Académie, first with Doyen, then with Vincent. Years of hard work gave him more competence than brilliance, and when in 1787 he competed for the Prix de Rome, the annual awards designed to send France's most promising young artists to live and paint in Italy, he came second, and in 1788 third. Perhaps discouraged by this honourable failure, he took off instead to Holland, but by the end of 1788 had turned up in Rome, where he was charitably assigned a room in the Mancini Palace, the official residence of those who won the prizes which had eluded him. There he persisted in his studies, earning from the Director of the French Academy in Rome the commendation of being 'very honest and very worthy'.[2] The outbreak of the French Revolution and the hostility it aroused soon drove most of his fellow-students back home, and by the time Louis XVI was executed, Léonor was one of only four young painters left at the Mancini Palace. Perhaps his stubbornness in staying on was due to his having liberal and free-thinking convictions which made him loth to desert his post; perhaps an amorous attachment kept him in Rome; perhaps he was simply too single-minded to be easily deflected from his chosen way of life. At all events, when the Republic was proclaimed, he and his colleagues were given a single night in which to paint the Republic's new arms on the French Consul's house. The Italian mob then invaded the Mancini Palace; Léonor escaped in order to warn a friend and had to be hidden by his Italian *inamorata*. In the street below his hiding-place the rioters lynched a young secretary from the French legation with Léonor looking on. Eventually, after having done his best to help others to freedom, he was imprisoned and lost all

[2] Quoted by G. Pinet, *Léonor Mérimée (1757–1836)*, Paris, Champion, 1913, p. 11.

his possessions. But he was soon released and managed by mid-1793
to make his way back to Paris via Florence and Naples.

After this hectic interlude, in which he revealed unexpected courage
and loyalty, Léonor returned quietly to his career as a painter, indemni-
fied for his losses and granted lodgings in the Louvre by the grateful
Republican authorities. His reputation was growing, both for his portraits, such as that of the Lebœuf family, and for his picturesque mytho-
logical canvases in the classical manner, of which the best known were
*The Discovery of the Remains of Milo of Croton, Bacchant playing with a
little snake, Venus wounded by touching Cupid's darts, Daphnis and Chloë
in the Cave of Philetas* and *Vertumnes and Pomona*, which now hangs in
Montpellier Museum. In 1802 he was commissioned to execute a wall-
painting for one of the exhibition rooms in the Louvre; his composition representing *Hippolytus recalled to life by Aesculapius* is still to
be seen there. All these works, conceived in the mannered and sentimental style of late eighteenth-century classicism, show that if Léonor
Mérimée was by no means devoid of talent, especially over detail, he
lacked vigour and originality. Little of his work survived, and no doubt
little of it deserved to; in any case, several of his paintings perished when
his son's flat was burnt in 1871. Of these, the most curious was the
obscure allegorical piece *Innocence feeding a serpent*, which used to
hang in Prosper's bedroom. Exactly what Léonor intended it to signify
is unclear, but its dark warning against the dangers of naïveté must have
appealed to his son's sardonic sense of humour as did his choice of
hanging.

Though his pictures won him a modest celebrity Léonor was too
level-headed to harbour illusions about his own skill: there is no sign
of a fine frenzy in his attitude to art. It was thus natural for him, soon
after his return to Paris, to take on jobs which would keep him in
contact with the world of painting without compelling him to rely on
his own creations for his bread and butter. In 1795 he became an
assistant drawing master at the École Polytechnique, and it was generally thought that he would become head of the art department there in
1808, when Neveu the previous incumbent died. However, with typical
modesty he withdrew on hearing that more distinguished men were
candidates, and, with equally typical loyalty, continued to serve as
assistant. In the end, only the political upheavals of the Restoration
brought his tenure of office to an end.

Momentarily brushed aside in 1814, he was finally obliged to resign after the Hundred Days. He had not paraded his anti-royalist convictions with any vigour, but he had been indiscreet – or pigheaded – enough to leave a laurel-crowned bust of Napoleon dominating his office.[3] Some years later, he commented ruefully but without rancour: 'I was rather badly done by in 1815. A man with a post that carried a salary of a thousand crowns was bound to be denounced, and I was.'[4]

But by then he had other posts too. In 1804 he was appointed assistant to the aged Renou, the first permanent secretary of the School of Fine Arts in Paris, and when Renou died in 1807, Léonor Mérimée succeeded him, and remained in office until his death. The post was an important one, since the secretary was in practice the administrative head of the school, responsible only to a council of professors, and Léonor obviously ran the school efficiently, since he was even allowed to remain in 1815. He supervised two moves to new premises, and took a deep and practical interest in the nature of the teaching there. Always concerned with art in its relationship to material matters, he joined enthusiastically in the activities of the Society for the Encouragement of National Industry, writing regularly for its *Bulletin*, investigating new techniques, experimenting with new inventions, studying new discoveries, prompting officialdom to make French industry more modern and French art more useful. It was partly the report he wrote in 1817 after being sent to London to examine English industry that led to the setting up of a French industrial exhibition, to the main jury of which he became secretary. His services were rewarded in 1820 when he was made a Chevalier of the Legion of Honour.

His insatiable curiosity and severely practical nature led him to take an interest in topics as diverse as the weaving of cashmere shawls, steel-making, dyeing, cutlery, papermaking, lithography, and the mechanism of the harp – in these latter fields, he conducted experiments and perfected inventions of his own. At the same time, he was particularly concerned with the technical problems of the conservation of paint, and for years discovered all he could about the early history of the

[3] Prosper Mérimée, *Correspondance générale*, ed. M. Parturier, P. Josserand, J. Mallion, Vols. I–VI, Paris, Le Divan, 1941–7; ed. M. Parturier, Vols. VII–XVII, Toulouse, Privat, 1953–64 (hereafter referred to as *C.G.*); Vol. I, p. 68, n. 1.   [4] Pinet, *op. cit.*, p. 40.

manufacture of oil paints, perusing ancient treatises, corresponding with chemists, and carrying out researches of his own. Eventually in 1830 he published his *Treatise on Oil-painting or, The Materials and Methods used in this type of Painting from Van Eyck to our own Times*. Its learning, its careful investigations and its well-motivated judgements made it for long the standard work on the subject; had Léonor never had a son, it would still give him some claim to fame.

Not surprisingly these multiple activities almost put a stop to Léonor's career as an artist, and from 1802 he hardly painted at all. This caused him little regret and in 1821 he wrote to a friend: 'I am busy all the time, and never paint; there is no harm in that, since I have no ambition; I am far from displeased with my lot.'[5] Of an even-tempered, frank, amiable and kindly disposition, he was universally popular, and, as he himself said, his greatest desire was to leave 'a fine epitaph in golden letters'[6] in the hearts of his friends. He liked helping his pupils and chatting with them; they in return worshipped him. Too much aware of his own limitations to be jealous of his more celebrated contemporaries, he remained on excellent terms with many of them, and numbered among his friends Ingres (who has left a drawing of him), Baron Gérard, the actor Talma, Ampère the scientist and various English writers and artists, including Holcroft and Copley Fielding, and William Hazlitt, the essayist, who visited him in 1802.

Always cautious in his opinions, Léonor held fast to classical tenets, sternly recommending the study of nature and the old masters, insisting on exact and careful detail, urging mistrust of popular favour, and ironically mocking the innovatory pretensions of Delacroix and his disciples – 'The Romantic School is losing something of its credit,' he noted with satisfaction in 1835; 'one always comes back to those good people who are true to life.'[7] In his youth he had espoused the cause of liberty; in later years, he seemed disillusioned and sceptical: 'When I see the people of Paris massacring a dozen men because they think the government wants to reduce the population by putting poison in the wine; when I see them convincing themselves that the doctors began the cholera epidemic, I have little faith in government by the multitude.'[8] As Prosper was later to say: 'my father was not credulous

[5] Pinet, *op. cit.*, p. 33.   [6] Pinet, *op. cit.*, p. 85.
[7] Pinet, *op. cit.*, p. 71.   [8] Pinet, *op. cit.*, p. 86.

and his habit was to examine everything before accepting it as true'.[9]
This prudence is apparent in his modest yet questing approach to the
problems of oils:

> If I have failed to attain the goal which I set myself, at least I shall have
> drawn attention to it. I shall have opened up a useful path, along which
> others may tread with greater success [. . .] I have confined myself to ex-
> plaining what people did without pretending to draw up precepts.[10]

A contented, resigned, unambitious man, interested in scores of different
topics; friendly and helpful; humorous and sceptical, but never cynical;
intelligent, cultured, practical, eager to think for himself and find out
for himself; a rare combination of artist and bourgeois, the one side
of his character constantly tempering the other: such was Prosper
Mérimée's father.

Léonor Mérimée was by no means insensitive to the charms of
women, and his son later suspected him of having had more than one
adventure. But his wild oats were all sown before his marriage, which
did not take place until he was forty-three, in 1800. His bride was
Anne Moreau, like him of solid middle-class stock and like him deeply
involved in the fine arts. Anne Moreau, who was twenty-five when she
married, was born in Avallon and counted among her forbears Mme
Leprince de Beaumont,[11] author of children's stories including *Beauty
and the Beast*. Anne's mother, who had seven children and was the
widow of a military surgeon, kept a boarding school in Passy where
Léonor Mérimée taught drawing, and Anne herself was a portraitist
of some talent, whose sitters were chiefly children but also included her
husband's nephew, the scientist Augustin Fresnel, and Prosper's friends
Victor Jacquemont and Sutton Sharpe. Her character seems to have
been sharper and more marked than that of her husband. An unbeliever
too, she was more combatively Voltairean and boasted that she had
never been baptised. Scornful of convention, she had a mind of her
own and a vigorous, cutting sense of humour with which she appears
to have delighted in disconcerting people. Stendhal judged that she

[9] *C.G.*, Vol. II, p. 91.
[10] *De la peinture à l'huile*, Paris, Huzard, 1830, pp. x and xxii.
[11] Not 'la princesse de Beaumont', as Robert Baschet inadvertently calls
her (*Du Romantisme au Second Empire. Mérimée*, Paris, Nouvelles Éditions
Latines, 1959, p. 11).

was full of French wit and had a superior intellect, but was 'capable of feeling emotion once a year'.[12] If she disdained to wear her heart on her sleeve she was devoted to her family. Like her grandmother she had an inexhaustible talent for story-telling and used it to keep her little models still during sittings. Sometimes her disregard for formality verged on eccentricity. It is said that when she was nursing Prosper, an English visitor arrived unexpectedly for tea (her family had lived for years in England, and her mother's wedding had taken place in London); undeterred by finding that there was no milk in the house, she surreptitiously used her own to fill the visitor's cup.[13] In later years, she would sit in a vast armchair, surrounded by cats, and invariably dressed up in odd old-fashioned clothes – a white frilly bonnet, a shawl crossed on her breast and mittens on her hands – with beside her a chased silver bowl filled with rose-petals into which from time to time, she would spit with – one hopes – unerring precision.[14] Despite their difference in age she was happy in her marriage and found the same undemanding contentment with her life as Léonor: 'My husband is ever plump and rosy-cheeked, kind and calm[. . .] For the time being I am as happy as one can be when one has neither ambition nor tastes which have to be satisfied.'[15]

After three years of marriage, Anne Mérimée bore her husband a son on 28 September 1803 at No. 7, Carré Sainte-Geneviève. The infant was called Prosper, a name which its owner was subsequently to find an embarrassing oddity. His only consolation was that he had narrowly escaped the even worse fate of being called Zéphyrin.[16] Probably the child was not baptised; certainly he was brought up without religion.[17] Although they were devoted to the boy, the parents thought it sensible not to lavish on him the overpowering affection in which only children are sometimes submerged. Young Prosper was

[12] *Souvenirs d'égotisme*, in *Œuvres intimes*, ed. H. Martineau, Paris, Bibliothèque de la Pléiade, 1961, p. 1467.

[13] Marie-Louise Pailleron, *François Buloz et ses amis. La vie littéraire sous Louis-Philippe*, Paris, Calmann-Lévy, 1919.

[14] Pailleron, *op. cit.*, p. 259.

[15] Pinet, *op. cit.*, p. 117.   [16] *C.G.*, Vol. VI, p. 163.

[17] His contemporaries certainly believed that he had never been baptised, and no record of a baptism has ever been found, but, according to Dr Parturier (*C.G.*, Vol. XIV, pp. 44, n. 1), the question remains open.

consequently treated rather as a miniature adult, whom one did not cosset, with whom one talked as an equal and who had to learn the lessons of life the hard way. One incident resulting from this left such an indelible mark on him that the memory of it was still sharp in the last years of his life, more than half a century later. Prosper, who was a self-willed and occasionally bad-tempered child, had been playing in his mother's studio when for some offence he was severely scolded and sent out. Returning some minutes later, he apologised with such transports of remorse and mortification that his mother burst out laughing, at which Prosper, humiliated beyond measure at having been taken in by her previous display of anger and at having made a fool of himself by his exaggerated pleas for forgiveness, swore never to be duped again.[18] The incident is revealing of a permanent trait of character rather than productive of a sudden change; but it typifies Mérimée's lifelong reluctance to lay bare his emotions for the possible amusement of others.

Once he started school, the fear of mockery continued to haunt him. His parents, Anglophiles both, dressed him in the English style, which brought down on him the jeers of his fellow-pupils at the Lycée Napoléon, which he attended from 1812: his cousins the Fresnels appear to have been particular tormentors. It is difficult not to see an autobiographical reminiscence in these lines from his sketch of Saint-Clair in Le Vase étrusque (The Etruscan Vase):

> He was born with a tender and affectionate heart, but at an age when it is all too easy to contract impressions which last for a lifetime, his over-expansive sensitivity had drawn upon him the mockery of his school-fellows. He was proud and ambitious; as children do, he cared about the opinion which others had of him. From then on he was careful to hide all the external marks of what he regarded as a dishonourable weakness. He achieved his aim, but his victory cost him dear. He managed to keep the feelings of his excessively tender soul concealed from others, but by shutting them up inside himself, he made them a hundred times more cruel.[19]

---

[18] There are at least three versions current of this story. One is told by Sainte-Beuve, quoting Mérimée's mother in 1841 (Les Cahiers, Paris, Lemerre, 1876, pp. 11–13). Another comes from Hippolyte Taine in his preface to the Lettres à une Inconnue (Paris, Lévy, 1874, Vol. I, p. ii). The third is quoted by Dr Parturier in his edition of Mérimée's Romans et Nouvelles, Paris, Garnier, 1967, Vol. I, p. 602. The details vary somewhat, but the substance is the same in each case.

[19] Romans et Nouvelles, Vol. I, pp. 353–4.

It must have been about the same time that Mme Mérimée painted a portrait of her son, which is now lost but known from a copy. It shows a little boy with wavy fair hair cascading down to his shoulders and dressed in velvet, lace and frills. But already in the eyes there is the melancholy disenchantment of someone much more experienced, and around the sensuously curved lips there plays a faintly malicious smile. It is the face of a child old beyond his years, lively and intelligent, but already aware that the world is a harsh and often unfriendly place.[20]

At the Lycée Napoléon, Prosper was a diligent but unexceptional pupil. When he was only eleven, his mother, never over-indulgent, informed her elder brother Paul: 'He is very anxious to do well; but he is bad-tempered and so cheeky one could hit him; his health isn't bad, but he is as thin as a lath.'[21] He won a few prizes in Latin and Greek; at home, he was taught English, and his father inculcated into him the rudiments of Italian, which he spoke fluently after his five years in Rome; he also began to read Spanish for himself. Living constantly in contact with artists and with a father and mother who both painted, the boy naturally tried his hand at that too. Léonor was amused by his eagerness and helped him at first, later allowing him to take lessons with Simon Rochard, an anglicised Frenchman who was a close friend of the family, and, after 1815, with the English artists who came to study in Paris. But Léonor, circumspect as usual, harboured no high-flown ideas about his son's capacities. In 1817, he told Rochard: 'Prosper still amuses himself by daubing away from life, and he fondly hopes that he will some day be able to dash off sketches like yours and those of English artists [. . .] The main thing is that, without spending much time at it, Prosper should acquire sufficient skill to enjoy himself.'[22] Ten years later, Léonor was still aware of his son's inability to draw correctly, even though he had a gift for colour: 'the stimulus you gave Prosper is still just as strong and his greatest joy is putting paint to paper. Unfortunately, unlike you, he hasn't got a solid grounding; he can't draw an eye, and he has never in his life studied the joint of a wrist.'[23] Until his death painting was to remain one of Prosper's favourite pastimes (as well as a useful skill in his archaeological career),

[20] The portrait is reproduced in Pinet, *op. cit.*, p. 91.
[21] Pinet, *op. cit.*, p. 98. An emended text is published in the catalogue of the Bibliothèque Nationale exhibition on Mérimée (Paris, 1953, p. 16).
[22] Pinet, *op. cit.*, p. 99.   [23] Pinet, *op. cit.*, p. 100.

but while he had a higher opinion of his talents than did those friends on whom he sometimes inflicted unwanted gifts of garishly coloured landscapes, he never seriously considered art as a career.

As Mme Mérimée taught art to young ladies, Prosper soon found himself exposed to the pains and pleasures of love. Among his mother's pupils was a Mlle Dubost, with whom Prosper became infatuated when only seven. His tender years did not prevent him from showing unusual strength of feeling, and when Mlle Dubost married a Dr Régnier, young Prosper was so jealous that for years he refused to speak to her husband. Stendhal later reminded him ironically: 'Where on earth were you in 1810? In the arms of Mme Régnier the doctoress.'[24] As Mérimée was to pay frequent visits to the Régniers at their home in Coulommiers in the 1820s, one wonders whether the relationship was resumed in a less juvenile context.

Also among Mme Mérimée's pupils were two young English ladies, the Misses Fanny and Emma Lagden, whose parents had been friendly with Mme Mérimée's mother in London. Not much is known of the Lagden sisters, who remain shadowy figures in the background of most of Mérimée's life. Fanny, the elder of the two, was born in Little Abington, near Cambridge, on 7 May 1797;[25] her sister Emma was two years younger. At some stage before 1822, they came to live in the rue de Fleurus in Paris with their aunt Mrs Beans, an Englishwoman who during Revolutionary times had married a French prisoner of war named Béens and had subsequently settled in France.[26] Quiet, pious, self-effacing, Fanny was probably Prosper's first mistress; that is perhaps why her body rests in the same grave as his at Cannes. Many years after the death of both of them, Emma handed over to a friend the letters which Prosper had written to Fanny; the friend records that, as they were going through the documents together, Emma suddenly gave a cry of horror at the sight of an ardent love letter and exclaimed: 'I thought so, but I was never sure!' The next day, she burnt the incriminating paper, but not before her friend had noted its contents:

[24] Stendhal, *Correspondance*, ed. H. Martineau and V. del Litto, Paris, Bibliothèque de la Pléiade, 1967, Vol. II, p. 181.
[25] Hilda Dale, 'Note sur Fanny Lagden', *Revue de Littérature comparée*, xxviii, 2, avril–juin, 1954.
[26] Introduction to Prosper Mérimée, *Lettres à Fanny Lagden*, by Georges Connes and Pierre Trahard, Paris, Boivin, 1938.

'In my heart, in my soul, in my body you are everything, my beloved Fanny. Now you are mine and I am yours for ever. I swore it to you yesterday and I say it again: I love you, I adore you for life.'[27] Though this passionate declaration cannot be dated, it probably took place while Prosper was still an adolescent: later he learnt to be more discreet and more reticent. But if he scarcely kept his promises to Fanny, she remained loyal to him to his dying day, and while her sister married a Mr Ewer in Shoreditch in 1825, Fanny increasingly devoted her life to the humble and selfless service of her dear Prosper. What may have been at the outset no more than the first sexual adventure of an enterprising and precocious youth thus formed the basis of a relationship on which the grown man became more and more dependent.

In the meantime, Prosper's studies were continuing their appointed course. Only in 1819 did he seem momentarily to flag in his regular, disciplined work, but this was not so much laziness or rebellion as the pursuit of a new interest: magic. Hostile as he was throughout his life to organised religion, and little inclined to mysticism as he may have been, Prosper nevertheless traversed an adolescent crisis, in which, with characteristic thoroughness, he investigated esotericism as a more exciting alternative to orthodox dogma. Twenty-five years later, he remembered how enthusiasm and scepticism had mingled in his researches:

> Many years ago, about the time when I was leaving school, I read books on magic, and for six months I studied the subject as I should have studied maths. Despite the ardour with which I plunged into that mass of confused idiocy, I could never find anything in it except intellectual amusement[. . .] After reading for quarter of an hour, my imagination became sufficiently heated for me to espouse the author's ideas: but a quarter of an hour after I had laid the book aside, I thought that he was a madman and I was a fool.[28]

The experience sufficed to convince him that religious belief was an impossibility for him; it also equipped him with a fund of recondite lore culled from such works as Della Porta's *Natural Magic*, Don Calmet's *Treatise on Apparitions* and Bekker's *Enchanted World*. In addition, he was left with a residual doubt about the supernatural; though he could never bring himself to believe in it, especially in its more

[27] Connes and Trahard, *op. cit.*, p. xx.
[28] *C.G.*, Vol. VIII, p. 183.

generally accepted manifestations, he was unable to rid himself of a sneaking suspicion that there might be something in the visions of the occultists. He freely admitted to being superstitious and always attached significance to portents and talismans, even if he simultaneously laughed at his own folly. Sainte-Beuve admirably summed up his attitude: 'Mérimée does not believe that God exists, but he is not altogether sure that the Devil does not.'[29]

Mérimée made many firm friends while he was at school. Anxious for companionship and intellectual stimulation, he found several kindred spirits among the brilliant young men who attended the Lycée Napoléon (or Lycée Henri IV, as it became after the Restoration). Most prominent among these was Jean-Jacques Ampère, son of the scientist who was a close friend of Léonor Mérimée. When they met, Prosper was twelve and Ampère fifteen. Unlike the prosaic Mérimée, the older boy was passionately and idealistically inclined towards poetry and was immersed in the composition of a poem about Attila and a tragedy. According to Mérimée's later recollections, Ampère at this time was 'very quick-tempered, even violent, very decided in everything',[30] but lost all the sharp edges of his character once he had had the misfortune in 1820 to fall hopelessly in love with Mme Récamier, Chateaubriand's middle-aged Egeria.[31] Mérimée deplored Mme Récamier's influence which continued until her death in 1849; 'he came into the world with the most virile temperament and was castrated by an old coquette'.[32] Ampère's intellectual curiosity was voracious if disorganised: literature, music, science, mathematics, history, philology – the list is almost endless. Untidy and short-sighted, he came to present almost a caricature of donnish absent-mindedness, capable of continuing to discourse wildly even when covered in a coating of white ashes after an unruly gesture had sent a dustpan flying. His romantic enthusiasms, his frank and open character, his lofty intelligence and vast erudition delighted Mérimée, and may well have helped to turn his interests from painting to literature, since it was with him that Mérimée first read Ossian in the original in 1820 – Ampère wrote to Jules Bastide (another pupil at the Lycée Henri IV, later to achieve brief distinction as Foreign Minister in 1848): 'I am continuing with Mérimée to learn

[29] *Les Cahiers*, p. 39.   [30] *C.G.*, Vol. XIV, p. 82.
[31] Cf. L. de Launay, *Un Amoureux de Mme Récamier. Le Journal de J.-J. Ampère*, Paris, Champion, 1925.   [32] *C.G.*, Vol. XIV, p. 84.

the language of Ossian, and we have a grammar. What joy to be able to give an exact French translation, with a naïve rendering of the inversions and the images!'[33]

Another school friend was Charles Lenormant: like Ampère and Mérimée, Lenormant was highly intelligent, brimming over with intellectual curiosity and imbued with a spiritual restlessness that made him too into an indefatigable traveller. An excellent linguist, an efficient administrator, a distinguished numismatist and archaeologist, Lenormant perhaps lacked the quirks of originality which gave Ampère's character its charm, and it was Ampère to whom Mérimée was from the beginning more closely drawn. But the three of them shared too many interests and too many talents not to benefit enormously from each other's society, and the excitement over things of the mind which they encouraged in each other probably has much to do with each of them, in their different ways, going on to brilliant careers as men of learning.

Two further members of the same group were Albert Stapfer and Adrien de Jussieu. Stapfer, bilingual, serious-minded and intelligent, was to win fame at the age of twenty by producing the first French translation of Goethe's *Faust*, but a premature retirement from public life in 1835 meant that his early promise never came to public fruition. Adrien de Jussieu, the son of a famous scientist, was slightly older, having been born in 1797; he rapidly made his own reputation as a botanist, succeeding to his father's chair in 1826, and is still remembered today for his work on plant life.

At school Mérimée, like all his generation, was brought up on the stilted rhetoric and narrow taste of what passed for classicism in the late eighteenth century. But encouraged by adventurous friends and parents whose attitudes were broad-minded and cosmopolitan, he busied himself with more exciting and exotic fare. Byron was soon one of his favourite authors, avidly read and discussed with other Anglophiles; no doubt Byron's example is partly responsible for Mérimée's pose as the disdainful English dandy, breaking hearts all round him but himself remaining mysteriously unmoved. Shakespeare too attracted him, at a time when the French were gradually coming to realise that the tragedy of Racine and Corneille did not constitute the sole pattern

[33] A.-M. Ampère and J.-J. Ampère, *Correspondance et souvenirs de 1805 à 1864*, Paris, Hetzel, 1875, p. 160.

of dramatic excellence. Sir Walter Scott was arousing enthusiasm in France in the 1820s, and Mérimée shared this feeling, though his admiration soon yielded to a preference for Bulwer Lytton. Indeed by 1832 Mérimée was announcing with disgust: 'That Scotsman certainly pulled the wool over our eyes. The fact is that he only cares about making money.'[34]

The Spanish theatre delighted him, with its rapid movement, its changes of mood and its violent passions, nor can he have escaped knowing something of modern German literature, especially with Ampère and Stapfer among his friends. But he never felt much sympathy for the German mentality; like Stendhal, he preferred Mediterranean light and clarity to the misty darkness of the North.[35]

There is not much evidence that he greatly cared for his compatriots who were the leading figures in the new modern literature; there was too much religiosity in Chateaubriand, Mme de Staël or Lamartine, and he abhorred the unnatural elevation of lyrical prose. The visits which he paid to Mme Récamier's *salon* in the 1820s were undertaken reluctantly, at Ampère's behest, and he cordially detested both the lady of the house and Chateaubriand complacently sniffing up the incense of praise burnt at his altar by adoring acolytes. No doubt he felt more at home with the lucidity and the incisiveness of the writers he met in the liberal *salons* – Benjamin Constant, whose disillusioned clear-sightedness is not far removed from his own, Paul-Louis Courier the satirist, or Béranger, the composer of so many irreverent, amusing and sentimental ditties. But already Mérimée was preferring to walk in paths where not many could follow him, and it flattered his sense of lonely superiority to neglect the authors whom everyone could read in favour of those who, at least in the original, were only accessible to the happy few.

[34] *C.G.*, Vol. XVI, p. 34.
[35] He once averred: 'No reasonable idea ever came from the mind of a German, which is a chaos of obscurity' (*Journal de Prosper Mérimée*, in *Lettres à Francisque-Michel*, ed. P. Trahard, Paris, Champion, 1930, p. 170).

Chapter 2
Youth

Les impressions de l'adolescence sont ineffaçables.
Histoire de Don Pèdre Ier roi de Castille

When Mérimée left school in 1819, he gravitated, like most clever and well-educated young men of his time, to the study of law at the University of Paris: it was the universal passport to a post in the liberal professions, in teaching, in government service, in politics or in diplomacy. There was no disagreement over this between Mérimée and his parents; they were and remained a remarkably united family. Guided by the example of his father, who had succeeded admirably in combining a love of the arts with a secure and ordered position in society, Mérimée felt no need to kick over the traces and rebel against the boredom and discipline of parental or social authority. In 1821, Léonor wrote to a friend: 'I have a big son, eighteen years old, whom I should like to see as a lawyer [. . .] Always brought up at home, he is well-behaved and well-educated.'[1] Mérimée's docility was later rewarded when his father, far from raising objections to his literary activities, encouraged him.

His legal studies lasted four years, from 1819 to 1823, and were pursued regularly though without brilliance. One suspects that Mérimée already had that lucid and incisive intelligence, that faculty for the rapid assimilation and evaluation of great masses of material which was to mark his later contributions to scholarship, and that he saw no reason why he should not coast easily through his training in law. His thesis (which has never been found) was, paradoxically enough for one who showed such permanent distaste for marriage, entitled *De Matrimonio*. Patently, he attached no great importance to it; his only reference to it in later years was to poke sardonic fun at the bad Latin of one of the examiners who at the viva had asked him: 'Quid est nuptiae?'[2]

[1] Pinet, *op. cit.*, pp. 99–100.
[2] 'Le Procès de M. Libri', *Revue des Deux Mondes*, 15 avril 1852

During this period Mérimée first began to appear in society, at balls and in the *salons* which his father visited. The sector of society was that of the liberal-minded and cultured upper middle class, often connected with banking and often Protestant by faith. Hostile to the reactionary régime of the Bourbon restoration, with its strong clerical bias and its preference for the landed aristocracy, the people whom the Mérimées frequented were essentially those who were to supply the motives for the 1830 Revolution and to take the power out of the hands of the old élite of blood and breeding into those of the new élite of finance and education. It is the milieu which Stendhal was to depict in *Lucien Leuwen*, in the pages of which we may recognise many of Mérimée's friends and perhaps even something of Mérimée himself.

His first recorded appearance in a *salon* took place in 1821; the lady of the house was a Mme Davillier, whose husband was an industrialist. The *salon* was a distinguished one, graced by the presence of the great men of the Liberal party: La Fayette, whose name had become almost synonymous with the pursuit of liberty; General Foy, the orator and leader whose death a few years later was to form the pretext for one of the most massive demonstrations of anti-Bourbon feeling; and Béranger whose vast following and facile satirical verses made him a permanent thorn in the side of the régime. Young Prosper, who was said to look like a German student, seems to have been far from overawed by the company in which he found himself and delivered some observations 'of striking temerity'.[3] He also showed off his remarkable memory by providing instant answers to recondite historical questions posed by his father.[4] His temerity perhaps also extended to casting his roving eye over the young and attractive Émilie Lacoste, Mme Davillier's niece and wife of one of Napoleon's ex-officers. But if there were stirrings of feeling then, her departure for America with her husband the following year put a stop to them, and it was only on her return in 1827 that their relationship was to blossom violently and dangerously.

A less overtly political setting was provided in the *salon* of Philippe-Albert Stapfer, father of his friend Albert, a Swiss pastor and teacher, and one time Minister for Art, Science and Public Works in Switzer-

[3] G. Girod de l'Ain, 'Une Muse romantique: Émilie Lacoste', *Revue des Deux Mondes*, 15 septembre 1954.
[4] *C.G.*, Vol. IX, p. 221, n. 1.

land, who had settled in France in 1803. He was at home on Wednesday evenings to a varied and cosmopolitan society, mostly of liberal inclinations and including several well-known travellers and men of learning such as Bonstetten, the Swiss statesman and writer, and Alexander von Humboldt, the naturalist. Two other *salons* both used to take place in the same house in the rue de Chabanais. Emmanuel Viollet-le-Duc, who occupied a post in the King's Household, received his guests on Friday evenings; the political tenor of the gatherings was liberal, but in literary discussions strict classical principles held sway, which was not much to the taste of Mérimée, whose views on literature were already advanced and aggressive. But his contacts with Viollet-le-Duc were to have unexpected consequences twenty years later, when he was responsible for launching his host's son Eugène on his controversial career as a restorer of ancient monuments.

The atmosphere was more congenial in the attic quarters of Étienne Delécluze, Viollet-le-Duc's brother-in-law, an indulgent middle-aged bachelor, mild-mannered and somewhat melancholy, who liked to collect young people around him and argue gently with them about politics and literature.[5] Timid and eclectic in his own tastes, he rather enjoyed being shocked by the paradoxes of bolder spirits, and under his benevolent eye there took shape in the 1820s a liberal wing of the growing Romantic movement, much concerned with historical realism and simplicity of expression, and almost as suspicious of the monarchistic, Catholic Romantics led by Hugo, Lamartine and Vigny as it was of the classical conservatives.

Mérimée first visited Delécluze in 1825, but they had already met several years before at Stapfer's and Viollet-le-Duc's. They got on well together. The older man recognised the budding talent of the young Romantic and was amused by his irreverent wit; Mérimée found in Delécluze a sympathetic listener, a sage if timorous counsellor and an occasional collaborator in the practical jokes which he was beginning to perpetrate on the public. The diary which Delécluze kept assiduously and his memoirs, which still retain their interest today, show that they met frequently in the mid-1820s, sometimes to dine together at the Frères Provençaux or with Mérimée's parents, to exchange hints about new materials for water-colour painting, to visit a carnation-grower, or

[5] Cf. Robert Baschet, *E.-J. Delécluze témoin de son temps (1781-1862)*, Paris, Boivin, 1942.

to read English poetry, notably Byron's *Don Juan*. It is Delécluze who has left the best portrait of Mérimée at this period:

> Mérimée, when he was twenty-two or three, already had strongly marked features. One's attention was the more readily drawn to his sharp, furtive glances as the young writer, instead of having the casual, laughing confidence usual at his age, was as sparing of words as he was of gestures, and only allowed his thoughts to show by the often ironic expression of his eyes or lips [. . .] Mérimée is by nature little inclined to talk much, so he took small part in the arguments which regularly arose, except by throwing in some phrase or reflection, usually witty and comic, accompanied by that look and that ironic smile which contrast so strongly with the normal immobility of his features.[6]

Drawings of Mérimée at this time show a tall, well-built young man, dressed with taste and sobriety, clean-shaven but with thick, wavy hair, heavy, arched eyebrows, a mocking, sensual mouth, a large nose with wide nostrils and a curiously squared-off end, and eyes that seem somehow serious, sensitive and yet evasive. The expression is that of someone outwardly confident in his own superiority but inwardly much less certain; one feels that the pseudo-English impassibility, the slightly dandyish elegance are part of a carefully chosen and maintained façade designed to keep the world at a distance. The full lips are held tightly closed, and there is an ironic curl to them; the eyes look as though they would be swiftly averted if you were to try to see through them to the soul behind.

Intellectually, Prosper Mérimée was probably more like his father; in personality, more like his mother. He had Léonor's thoroughness of method, his breadth of interests, his empirical approach to problems, his clear-headed organising ability; perhaps too in his manner one may recognise something of Léonor's sober ponderation of character. But he resembled his mother in his sharpness of tongue, his aggressive anticlericalism, his love of story-telling, his disconcerting wit, his reluctance to indulge in public displays of emotion, his enjoyment of the unease which a deliberately unconventional attitude could bring to others. From both he acquired a systematic incredulity, a love of the arts, both painting and literature, which was nevertheless integrated into a healthy respect for the bourgeois comforts of life, and a stoical

[6] E.-J. Delécluze, *Souvenirs de soixante années*, Paris, Lévy, 1862, pp. 223 and 227.

undemonstrativeness that hid a temperament capable of deep feeling
and extreme sensitivity.

In the *salons* Mérimée acquired habits that were to leave their mark
on his character. He learnt the pleasures and benefits of conversations
with people of distinction and intelligence; the precocious ripening of
Mérimée's intellect, already started by an enlightened upbringing and
an extraordinarily talented set of school friends, was furthered by his
regular contacts with older and more worldly-wise men. He also joined
a prominent liberal milieu, staunchly opposed to the influence of the
clergy and the nobility, emancipated in its philosophic opinions, dedicated in politics to the cause of personal liberty but repudiating the
excesses of republicanism, and open in literature to the examination
of new ideas, if not always to their adoption. Though Mérimée was not
in these years a very active politician, he clearly identified himself with
a particular segment of opinion, and much of what he wrote had a
much stronger political slant than might now be apparent. In 1825,
he was one of the pall-bearers at the funeral of General Foy. Had
Mérimée not thus made common cause with the Liberals under Louis
XVIII and Charles X, it is doubtful whether he would have been so
readily taken into government service after 1830 and achieved such
rapid promotion to the Inspectorship of Historic Monuments. On the
debit side, the taste which these *salons* gave him for the social whirl and
which he retained throughout his life (even when he grumbled bitterly
about its inconveniences and obligations) was in the long run detri-
mental to his art, perhaps even to his character. The need to preserve
a superficial veneer of politeness, to avoid an open break with convention, to flatter the habits and prejudices of a small audience, to hide
one's innermost feelings lest they prove upsetting to others – all had
an inhibiting effect on Mérimée as man and artist. No doubt he would
have been prone to such a development anyway; but Stendhal,[7] Sainte-
Beuve[8] and Renan[9] all regarded the *salons* as having had a debilitating
influence on him.

[7] Cf. *infra.*, p. 115.

[8] *Mes Poisons*, ed. Victor Giraud, Paris, Plon, 1926, p. 98: 'Mérimée: at
bottom a bit of a *man of fashion*, which makes the artist in him cold and circumspect'. p. 100: 'Mérimée, too much a man of the world to be altogether an artist'.

[9] *Souvenirs d'enfance et de jeunesse*, Paris, Calmann-Lévy, 1953, p. 197. 'Méri-

The decisive event of the early 'twenties for Mérimée was a meeting
which occurred one summer day in 1822 in the garden attached to a
ground-floor flat belonging to one Joseph Lingay. Lingay, then aged
about thirty, was a curious and rather shady figure who, after being a
teacher, had become a journalist and civil servant, mainly in the police
department. His political allegiances seem to have been variable, since
his attachment to various Royalist ministers did not prevent him from
becoming speech-writer to Casimir Périer and then Soult under the
July Monarchy; in all probability, he knew too much for any régime
to be able to dismiss him. Mérimée probably knew him through
Léonor's connections with the Duc Decazes, the police minister whose
confidential minion Lingay was at the time, and appears to have
regarded him as a mentor in literary affairs – he addressed him as 'mon
cher Maître' and took care to inform him of the progress of his own
writings. Sometimes Mérimée would go and drink beer with him in
the garden in the rue de Caumartin, served by a tall, attractive woman
whom Lingay had acquired as mistress when her husband, a printer,
had defaulted with a large sum of Lingay's money. On one such
occasion, another of the guests was a plump, talkative, excitable man
of about forty: Henri Beyle, later to become better known as Stendhal.
Beyle's first reaction to Mérimée was one of strong antipathy – 'a poor
young man in a grey frock-coat, so ugly with his turned-up nose.
About this young man there was something insolent and extremely
unpleasant. His expressionless little eyes always had the same look in
them and that look was spiteful.'[10] But this unfavourable impression
did not last long, and the two men soon discovered that they had much
in common – a vigorous, independent temperament, a love of shocking
people, a joyously irreverent anticlericalism, a deep admiration for
energy and violence, an epicurean attitude to physical pleasures, a strong
inclination to liberalism in politics and Romanticism in literature, an
instinctive fear of making themselves ridiculous in the eyes of others,
a determination to strip life of its disguises and see its unadorned truth,
an insatiable curiosity about human beings and their idiosyncrasies.

---

mée would have been a man of the first rank if he had had no friends. His
friends took complete possession of him.'
[10] *Souvenirs d'égotisme*, in *Œuvres intimes*, p. 1466.

1 Mérimée, aged five, from a portrait by his mother

2b Léonor Mérimée, Prosper's father, from a pencil drawing by Ingres

2a Anne Mérimée, Prosper's mother, from a portrait by Picot

So many shared interests, prejudices, ideas and feelings made them firm if uneffusive friends for the next twenty years.[11]

Not that they always saw eye to eye. Stendhal was as spontaneous and voluble as Mérimée was reserved and deliberate; Stendhal was prepared to carry his ideas to their logical extreme of absurdity, whereas Mérimée was never able to rid himself of a discomfiting caution; Stendhal believed passionately in passion, while Mérimée harboured a deep-seated mistrust of strong emotion. The result was that they regularly wrangled with each other, that they disagreed bitterly, that they criticised one another mercilessly and that each had serious misgivings about the character of the other. Stendhal clearly saw the danger that pedantry and irony would dry up the wells of feeling in Mérimée's nature; Mérimée seems to have thought that Stendhal was mildly and amusingly mad. Stendhal noted, after visiting Mérimée in 1829: 'I have often found less charm in his person than in the omnibus which takes me to his house,'[12] and a few years later: 'I'm not too sure of his heart, but I am sure of his talent.'[13] On the other side, Mérimée's letters and the articles he wrote after Stendhal's death show no sign that he recognised his friend's genius: they treat him as an amiable and highly entertaining paradoxer. But as their relations were based on total and reciprocal frankness, these disagreements, far from growing into rifts, may well have reinforced their friendship; the mutual exasperation was proof of mutual confidence.

It is difficult to know how far Mérimée was influenced by Stendhal.[14] Sainte-Beuve declared that Mérimée was Beyle's only faithful disciple;[15] subsequent critics have been much less affirmative. Mérimée himself varied in his assessment of what he owed to the older writer. On the one hand, he affirmed that he and Stendhal did not have a single opinion in common;[16] on the other, he admitted that his own ideas had

[11] The best summing-up of the relationship between Stendhal and Mérimée is that given by J. Boulenger in . . . Mais l'art est difficile, 2e série, Paris, Plon, 1921.

[12] J. Boulenger, Candidature au Stendhal-Club, Paris, Le Divan, 1926, p. 135.

[13] Souvenirs d'égotisme, in Œuvres intimes, p. 1466.

[14] Cf. notably Pierre Trahard, La Jeunesse de Prosper Mérimée (1803-1834), Paris, Champion, 1925, Vol. I, pp. 69-75.   [15] Les Cahiers, p. 142.

[16] Notes et souvenirs, in Portraits historiques et littéraires, ed. Pierre Jourda, Paris, Champion, 1928, p. 169.

B

been 'singularly coloured' by Stendhal's.[17] The two things are not necessarily incompatible: it is possible to find oneself profoundly swayed by views with which one vehemently disagrees. Relatively little is known of what Mérimée thought and felt before he met Stendhal, so it is hard to say how far his mature personality might in any case have been predicted from his adolescent attitudes. Equally, there must have been affinities between the two men, or they would not have become such inseparable companions: how is one to say now what is affinity and what is dominance of one personality over the other? But if one takes into account the fact that Mérimée was not yet twenty when they met, that Stendhal was a man of mature years, of a certain reputation (though his main works were still to come), and of what now seems indisputable genius, it is surely to be expected that the one should succumb, however reluctantly, however circumspectly, to the other's magnetism. It is certain that, immediately after their meeting, Mérimée enthusiastically took up Stendhal's theories on drama and, in *Le Théâtre de Clara Gazul* was the first to put them into practice. But in the long run, it was on the deeper level of a new understanding of the secrets of the human personality that Stendhal's example affected him. Mérimée followed Stendhal in refusing to believe that the most authentic tendencies of our real being could find adequate expression in the hypocritical climate of conventional society, and in looking with nostalgia at more primitive and more passionate states, in which the individual asserted his identity with blithe disregard for civilised moral codes or public opinion. But, more prudent and more down-to-earth than the volatile, imaginative Stendhal, Mérimée could never quite convince himself that it was safe to repudiate the values of modern civilisation, and he was never really sure that Stendhal was right to prefer his beloved Renaissance to the cramping confines of the nineteenth century. Thus in Mérimée's novels, historical works, and letters, in his discussions with friends, there is a continued questioning of standards which he could neither wholly accept nor wholly reject. Again and again one finds Mérimée hesitating over the wisdom of releasing the dangerous forces which each of us holds imprisoned within himself, and in the end no definite answer is provided. Stendhal, on the other hand, bolder, more original, more whole-hearted in his enthusiasms and aversions, had no such doubts, and it is this quality

[17] *C.G.*, Vol. VI, p. 348.

of spiritual adventurousness which makes him a great novelist. But without the stimulus, one might almost say the irritant, of Stendhal's ethos, it is doubtful whether Mérimée would have become the man and writer he was.

When they met in 1822, Stendhal had only recently returned to France after some six years spent mostly in Italy. He had published a *History of painting in Italy* and *Lives of Haydn, Mozart and Metastasio*, and was working on his treatise *De l'Amour* (*On Love*) as well as on his pamphlet-manifesto in favour of Romantic drama, *Racine et Shakespeare*. He and Mérimée, who had published nothing (perhaps indeed not even started to write), were thereafter regularly seen together, at Delécluze's, where Stendhal was the great man (rather to the irritation of his timid-souled host, who thought him an eccentric bore); at the house of the opera-singer Judith Pasta, where Mérimée had his first introduction to a rather more bohemian section of society; in the so-called 'tent' at the Jardin des Plantes, a curiously draped room at the end of a line of book-strewn apartments where the zoologist Cuvier received his friends on Saturday evenings;[18] at the *salon* of Baron Gérard, the painter and old friend of Léonor Mérimée's, and at the home of Jacques and Virginie Ancelot, a slightly comical but good-hearted couple, mediocre authors both but expert in academic intrigues in which Virginie usually took the intiative, even succeeding in the end in having her dull but worthy husband elected in 1841.[19] In these surroundings, Stendhal would hold forth irresistibly, watched, with a quizzically cocked eyebrow, by his disrespectful young friend, who delighted in bursting the bubble of his lyrical fantasies. Mme Ancelot described how Stendhal would be perturbed by the casual and slightly mocking silence which Mérimée maintained while he chattered on exuberantly;[20] Delécluze likewise noted that Mérimée would 'laugh up his sleeve, without saying a word, at Beyle's sudden harangues'.[21]

It was also under Stendhal's aegis that Mérimée made his debut as an author. In the spring of 1822, he began a tragedy entitled *Cromwell*; the subject, which also attracted Hugo a few years later, accorded

[18] Cf. Louis Royer, *Stendhal au Jardin du Roi*, Grenoble, Arthaud, 1930.
[19] Cf. Henri Martineau, *Stendhal et le salon de Mme Ancelot*, Paris, Le Divan, 1932.
[20] Mme Ancelot, *Les Salons de Paris, foyers éteints*, Paris, Tardieu, 1858, p. 63.   [21] *Souvenirs de soixante années*, p. 233.

well with his anti-royalist opinions and he appears to have treated it in conformity with Stendhalian views on the abolition of the unities, the use of prose, the presentation of action on the stage and so on. Even at this stage, he was his own severest critic and almost threw it away after re-reading the first draft, but, encouraged by Stendhal and Lingay, he persevered, and towards the end of the year, gave a reading of his play, in the *salon* of Viollet-le-Duc or Stapfer, to an audience including Delécluze, Ampère and Stendhal himself.[22] Mérimée was always nervous when he had to speak in public, and Delécluze relates that he read so fast and with so little expression that he was very difficult to follow:

> . . . only observing those pauses rendered indispensable by the divisions of the sentences, but without raising or lowering the tone of his voice, he read the whole of his play without changing his intonation, even in the most exciting parts. The uniformity of this long cantilena made the reading rather cold.[23]

Those present, with the exception of Stendhal, who congratulated him warmly, were somewhat taken aback by this perverse refusal to woo their favour; perhaps their lack of enthusiasm prompted Mérimée to leave the tragedy unpublished and turn to other things. The text has not survived and little is known of the play itself; Delécluze found the action dramatic and the dialogue natural, but complained of a lack of unity;[24] another spectator remembered years later that the players were puppets in a fairground booth, representing historical figures;[25] Mérimée himself told Lingay that it was too long and that the public would dislike it because they would be unable to sympathise with any of the characters.[26] In all this, one may discern features of Mérimée's later art: concentration on action and realism, inability to organise a large-scale work around a single centre of interest, deliberate insistence on the illusory nature of art, reluctance to identify himself completely with the people he depicted. But while the play was one of the earliest attempts at Romantic drama in France, posterity has probably not lost

[22] Baschet, *E.-J. Delécluze témoin de son temps*, pp. 160–2; *C.G.*, Vol. I, p. 2, n. 1.
[23] *Souvenirs de soixante années*, pp. 223–4.   [24] *Ibid.*
[25] According to Stapfer, quoted by Maurice Tourneux; cf. P. Trahard, *La Jeunesse de Prosper Mérimée*, Vol. I, p. 141.
[26] *C.G.*, Vol. I, pp. 2–3.

much by its disappearance, since none of those present in 1822 remembered it very clearly.

Mérimée next turned to narrative fiction. While staying with the
Régniers at Coulommiers in September 1823, he started a novel, helped
by the Marquis de Varennes, a young friend with whom he remained
vaguely in touch for many years. Only one rapid and rather incoherent
episode of this has been preserved; it is probably all that was written.
It has to do with a duel in which a young officer is killed in the 1780s,
but it is too brief and sketchy to provide any indication of what the
completed novel might have been like.[27] A few months later, in April
1824, Mérimée wrote out another military anecdote, entitled *La
Bataille* (*The Battle*), recounting the story of an American officer who
won glory while fighting against the English in 1812, had a bad
tragedy of his own produced as a result, and then married a Quaker
girl. It is puzzling in that it seems to have no particular point and to
belong to no particular genre; there is a characteristic acerbity in the
writing, with one or two effective satirical touches, but otherwise it
simply whets our appetite without satisfying it.[28]

However, Mérimée's first publication, four articles which appeared
in *Le Globe* in November 1824, betoken the discovery of a new and
richer field to prospect: the Spanish theatre.[29] Spanish was one of the
languages, along with English and Italian, which Mérimée had been
learning in time stolen from his law studies, and for some while he
had been particularly interested in Spanish drama, reading Calderón,
Lope de Vega, Tirso de Molina and Moratin in the original. These
Spanish plays, along with Shakespeare and Schiller, were, for the young
Turks of 1820, one of the prime incitements to abolish the irksome
restrictions of neo-classicism and found a freer and more vital drama-
turgy, and it is no surprise that an admirer of Stendhal's 'espagnolisme'
should investigate their attractions. The four articles, unsigned, deal
mainly with the Spanish actor Mayquez, praising his natural diction
and commending the Spanish tradition of historical subjects and lifelike
dialogue in the theatre. Revelatory of Mérimée's preoccupation with
realism in art, they are not in themselves of any great consequence and
passed unnoticed by his friends. But they would probably never have

[27] *Romans et nouvelles*, Vol. II, pp. 569–77. [28] *Ibid.*, pp. 578–82.
[29] *Le Théâtre de Clara Gazul*, ed. P. Trahard, Paris, Champion, 1927,
pp. 11–31.

been written had Mérimée not for some years been working on his own modernised version of Spanish drama, *Le Théâtre de Clara Gazul*.

The idea of writing a series of plays to be attributed to a fictitious Spanish actress had occurred to him at least as early as 1823, and by September of that year he had composed the prologue and *Une Femme est un diable* (*A Woman is a Devil*), and was consulting Lingay on the historical background to *Les Espagnols en Danemarck* (*The Spaniards in Denmark*).[30] The project was allowed to mature, and it was not until March 1825 that Mérimée, escorted by Ampère and another young friend, the ill-fated publisher Sautelet, who committed suicide a year or two later, gave a reading of these two plays at Delécluze's – again galloping through the text so fast as to render it almost unintelligible.[31] Perhaps it was for this reason that a few days later a repeat performance of *Les Espagnols en Danemarck* was given by Ampère, this time followed by *Le Ciel et l'enfer* (*Heaven and Hell*) and *L'Amour africain* (*African Love*). By now, though the staid Delécluze was inclined to think that Mérimée was too much concerned with the seamier side of life, his circle of friends was clearly realising that these short plays heralded the birth of a new and powerful talent, and the series of readings was continued with a further one-man performance of *Le Ciel et l'enfer* by Mérimée on the afternoon of Easter Day, a repeat at the home of Cerclet, a friend of Delécluze, on 9 May, and then, at Delécluze's again on 29 May, a reading of *L'Amour africain* and *Inès Mendo, ou le Préjugé vaincu* (*Inès Mendo, or Prejudice Overcome*) which reduced the ladies to tears.

At the same time as Mérimée was successfully publicising his works at Delécluze's *salon*, he was making arrangements for their publication. Here, perhaps spurred on by Stendhal's incorrigible love of pseudonyms and aliases, perhaps anxious to be able to disclaim responsibility for plays which expressed sentiments at once markedly liberal and violently anticlerical, perhaps, too, obscurely impelled by a desire to use an *alter ego* so as to reduce the hurtfulness of adverse criticism, he resolved to publish the plays without mention of his own name. They were to be presented as the work of the actress Clara Gazul, introduced by a Frenchman ironically named Joseph l'Estrange. Delécluze, titillated by the daring of the enterprise, was commissioned to provide

[30] *C.G.*, Vol. I, pp. 4–5.
[31] *Souvenirs de soixante années*, pp. 272–3.

a portrait of the supposed 'Clara', which was done by the simple expedient of drawing Mérimée wearing a mantilla, a necklace and a frilly dress. At the end of May 1825, the book appeared, with Sautelet as its publisher and Delécluze's portrait as frontispiece. It was extremely well received by the liberal press. Loudest of all in his praise was Stendhal, who at the time was acting as Paris correspondent for two leading English periodicals. In the *New Monthly Magazine*, he proclaimed ecstatically that the volume was 'incontestably the most original and genius-like production that France has witnessed for many years' and that it would without doubt 'operate a revolution in the dramatic literature of the country, and rescue it from the reproach only too justly cast upon it, of servile and spiritless imitation, and sickly sentimentality'.[32] In the *London Magazine* he was just as enthusiastic, analysing the plays in detail, inducing the editor to take the exceptional step of including a translation of the whole of *Les Espagnols en Danemarck*, and returning in a second article to 'the eulogy of the youthful genius, who conceals himself under the name of Clara Gazul'.[33] No doubt it was this blaze of publicity which tempted an enterprising English publisher to issue a complete translation of the plays before the year was out.[34]

In *Le Globe*, which was liberal in politics and open-minded on literary matters, and which in any case had many of Mérimée's friends among its contributors, Ampère respectfully saluted the new dramatist (not without hints that Clara Gazul was not all she seemed), tempering what might otherwise have seemed too friendly an article by a few mild reservations on the excessively schematic and swift-moving nature of the plays. *Le Globe*, obviously eager to do all it could for one of its own protégés, a few days after published a second article, this time anonymous, reproaching Ampère with having been too lukewarm in his praise and proclaiming proudly that the author was, 'with Walter Scott, the most eminently truthful of modern writers'.[35] The *Revue*

---

[32] *New Monthly Magazine*, August 1, 1825. Stendhal's articles in the English press are reproduced, translated back into French, in the *Courrier anglais*, Paris, Le Divan, 1935-6. The text given here is that printed in the original publication.

[33] *London Magazine*, July 1825.

[34] *The Plays of Clara Gazul*, London, Wittaker, 1825. The translator's name is not given.   [35] Quoted in *Le Théâtre de Clara Gazul*, p. 513.

encyclopédique, La Pandore, Le Journal des Débats and *Le Mercure du XIXᵉ siècle* all joined in the chorus of appreciation, most of them stressing the boldness of the author's realism and some of them seeing in the plays the model for a regeneration of the theatre. But the highest accolade came when Goethe, the grand old man of European letters, bestowed his warm approval, telling the faithful Eckermann that Mérimée was one of the 'great talents, who have their foundation inside themselves and hold aloof from the fashion of the day'.[36] When Ampère and Stapfer visited the sage of Weimar in the spring of 1827, the conversation frequently turned on Mérimée, for whom Goethe expressed 'much admiration'.[37] Unfortunately, Mérimée was much less generous in return, becoming progressively more sarcastic about the German's writings until, near the end of his life, he exclaimed with vexation that Goethe was 'a great humbug, who is only good at making up riddles which have no answer'.[38] Though the general public was little touched and the book sold slowly, Mérimée could be more than satisfied at its reception. He was recognised, by those whose opinion counted (for 'Clara Gazul' deceived few people), as one of the brightest hopes of the nascent Romantic movement and as a budding dramatic genius; he had even laid the foundations of a European reputation. At one stroke this young man of twenty-two had stepped (albeit backwards, so that his face might not be seen) into the limelight of literary fame.

It was clear that Mérimée was going to be a man of letters, even if he never intended to make a living from his pen. For the time being, neither he nor his parents saw any reason why he should take a job; there was sufficient money to support him at home, and his father looked favourably on his literary ambitions. In 1827, Léonor Mérimée wrote to Prosper's teacher, Rochard:

> I confess that, if he had begun sooner, I should have liked to see him splashing paint around; but since he has taken to literature and has made quite a good start, I have the feeling, when I see him spending a whole

---

[36] J. P. Eckermann, *Gespräche mit Goethe in den letzten Jahren seines Lebens*, ed. H. H. Houben, Wiesbaden, Brockhaus, 1949, p. 173.

[37] *Correspondance et souvenirs*, Vol. I, p. 442.

[38] *C.G.*, Vol. XIV, p. 300.

morning painting, that he is wasting his time. However, there is inexpressible pleasure in doing what one doesn't have to do.[39]

So he stayed at home, sometimes helping his father with his research and reports for the Society for the Encouragement of National Industry, reading as widely and attentively as ever, going to balls and the opera, dining out with Stendhal and his friends, and continuing his assiduous round of the *salons*. At first, it seemed as though his creative activity had slackened after *Clara Gazul*: 1826 saw only a preface for a new translation of *Don Quixote*, a commission presumably inspired by his supposed competence in things Spanish and doubtless engineered by his friend and publisher Sautelet. This *Historical Account of the Life and Works of Cervantes* is lively but unoriginal, and is interesting for us chiefly in its contribution to the campaign which Mérimée was continuing to wage, in alliance with Stendhal, against the outworn conventions of classical drama.

> Passion always demands the exact word, even if it is vulgar, and does not the distinction, which in this country people insist on so imperiously, between words which are poetic and words which are not, produce absurdities just as nonsensical as the conceits of which we have just been speaking?[40]

But at the same time, Mérimée was working on a more ambitious scheme, springing from his abiding interest in folk-poetry. The revival of folk-poetry which had begun in England and Germany in the latter half of the eighteenth century had been late in reaching France, but the great popularity of Ossian (which Mérimée studied with Ampère in 1820) had created a curiosity about the folk-songs of other lands (though a prejudice against the naïveté of French folk-song meant that the native heritage of France itself derived little benefit from this new-found interest). One of the outstanding figures in this revival was Claude Fauriel, born in St Étienne in 1772, the son of a master carpenter, who had become an outstanding authority on European poetry and literary history, to be rewarded in 1830 with the first chair of foreign literature at the Sorbonne. In 1824 and 1825 he had published, with immense success, two volumes of translations of *Folk Songs of*

[39] Pinet, *op. cit.*, p. 101.
[40] *Histoire de Don Quichotte de la Manche*, translated by Filleau de Saint-Martin, Paris, Sautelet, 1826, p. xvi.

Modern Greece, and it was shortly after this that Ampère took Mérimée to see him. Fauriel received Mérimée with a blunt injunction: 'Here are two volumes of Serbian poetry that I have just had sent to me. Learn Serbian.'[41] Mérimée did not take his advice (he subsequently regretted it), but his interest in Illyria was awakened, and with Ampère, he began to wonder how he might visit the country. Finding that his resources would not stretch so far, he decided to compensate for his disappointment by composing his own collection of Illyrian ballads, with at least as much local colour in them as the country itself would have provided: if he managed to sell it, it might pay for his voyage, especially if Ampère abetted him by producing their travel recollections in advance. So, while on holiday in the autumn of 1827, he tossed off a ballad a day until he had enough to make a volume of respectable size.[42] So at least runs the story that Mérimée himself propagated about the origins of *La Guzla* (*The Guzla*) – so-called from the name of the Serbian musical instrument. Probably the whole project was a good deal more serious than his flippant tone suggests – as always, he tried to forestall criticism by disparaging his own works.

Mérimée took much greater care over this second hoax than over *Clara Gazul*, where most of his friends had been in the secret from the outset. This time, not only did he hide behind the double mask of Hyacinthe Maglanovich, a redoubtable Dalmatian bard-cum-outlaw, and his putative discoverer, an unnamed Italian traveller, but he also saw to it that mystery surrounded the actual publication. Lingay was charged with finding a publisher, and the book was printed, almost clandestinely, at Strasbourg, where it appeared in July 1827. Press criticism was favourable again, but on this occasion no one appeared to suspect that the book was anything other than what it purported to be. In Germany, *La Guzla* received an even more flattering reception. Wilhelm Gerhard, a friend of Goethe, who was busy preparing his own collection of Serbian poetry under the title *Wila*, was so delighted with Mérimée's pastiches that he promptly translated them into German and incorporated them into his book. In England, the compositions of the supposed Maglanovich received benevolent attention from the *Monthly Review* and the *Foreign Quarterly Review*, and completely

[41] *C.G.*, Vol. XIV, p. 82.
[42] *C.G.*, Vol. I, p. 375; cf. also Mérimée's 1840 preface to *La Guzla*, ed. Eugène Marsan, Paris, Le Divan, 1928, pp. 3–6.

deceived the slavophile John Bowring, a cloth merchant and M.P., who himself dabbled in second-hand translation from Serbian; Mary Shelley, the poet's widow, also praised them and produced English renderings of three of them.[43] A few years later Pushkin was translating *La Guzla* into Russian, while the poets Mickiewicz and Chodzko translated some of them into Polish. The success of Mérimée's ruse was very nearly complete and his little book was being read with pleasure all over Europe.[44]

Only two illustrious contemporaries were not deceived: Goethe and Hugo. After Goethe's generous praise of *Clara Gazul*, Mérimée doubtless thought that it would not be seemly to trick the old man and so sent him a copy of *La Guzla* inscribed: 'In homage from the author of *Le Théâtre de Clara Gazul*.'[45] This was rewarded by a favourable notice in an article in *Art and Antiquity* in March 1828, in which Goethe unveiled the secret of the mysterious Illyrian bard. As for Hugo, with more humour than one might have credited him with, he noted enigmatically on the flyleaf of his copy 'M. Première Prose' – which is a not inappropriate anagram of 'Prosper Mérimée'. It was probably

[43] It has long been suspected that Mary Shelley had translated part of *La Guzla*. As early as 1832, the critic Gustave Planche, in an article on Mérimée, said that 'several pieces from *La Guzla* have been put into verse by Mrs Shelley, almost without alteration' (article collected in *Portraits littéraires* Paris, Charpentier, 1848, Vol. I, p. 189). But attempts to find these translations failed (cf. Voyslav M. Yovanovitch, '*La Guzla*' de Prosper Mérimée, Paris, Hachette, 1911, p. 496; and Dennis McNeice Healy, *Mérimée et les Anglais*, Paris, André, 1946, p. 68), and it was thought that they were lost, if they had ever existed. In fact they were included in her article 'Illyrian Poems – Feudal Scenes', which appeared in the *Westminster Review*, Vol. X, n. xix, January 1829, pp. 71–81. Planche is wrong in suggesting that they are in verse; otherwise his information is correct. As he was friendly with Mérimée at that time (cf. Maurice Regard, *L'Adversaire des Romantiques. Gustave Planche*, Paris, Nouvelles Éditions Latines, 1956), it may have come from the author himself, since there cannot have been many people who knew of the existence of such translations. These poems have never before been reproduced, so they are given in full in an appendix to the present volume.

[44] Cf. Yovanovitch, *op. cit.*, and R. Maixner, 'Quelques victimes de la Guzla de Mérimée', *Revue de Littérature comparée*, xxx, 3, juillet–septembre 1956.

[45] Yovanovitch, *op. cit.*, p. 467.

Hugo who spread the news of the true authorship of *La Guzla* around Nodier's *salon* late in 1827; certainly most people in the French literary world knew fairly soon – but not before Mérimée had savoured the mischievous pleasure of listening to them lauding the genuineness of his fake.

So by the end of 1827 Mérimée was firmly established as a young author of notable promise and substantial achievement. One of the most prominent of the liberal Romantics, he had conquered a position for himself in elegant society as well as with the reading public; he was on familiar terms with many of the best-known political and artistic figures of the times; the most prominent critics had paid tribute to his originality and his boldness. Outwardly at least, fortune was smiling on him, and if inwardly his solitary and susceptible nature prevented him from finding total satisfaction in his situation, he allowed little of this to show to his friends.

Chapter 3

Romantic

Il n'y a pas un très-grand mérite à exciter une impression
d'horreur, et [. . .] on y parvient par des moyens tout à fait
étrangers à l'art.
'Salon de 1853', *Le Moniteur Universel*, 5 juin 1853

Le Théâtre de Clara Gazul, as published in 1825, consists of a prologue
in dramatic form; two three-act plays (*Les Espagnols en Danemarck* and
Inès Mendo ou le Triomphe du préjugé); and three one-act plays (*Une
Femme est un diable, L'Amour africain* and *Inès Mendo ou le Préjugé vaincu*
which is in reality a prologue to the longer play about Inès Mendo). To
appreciate this little collection of plays, none of them more than about
fifty pages long, one must see them in their literary and political context:
in both contexts they appear as belligerent and provocative works.

Five years before the performance of Hugo's *Hernani*, despite years
of bitter quarrels, the Romantic drama existed only in theory; the
stereotyped five-act verse tragedy, set in Greece or Rome and obedi-
ently conforming to pseudo-classical unities, still reigned supreme on
the stage of the Comédie française. The public stayed away or went,
slightly shamefacedly, to the blood-and-thunder offerings of the so-
called 'Boulevard of Crime', where most of the melodrama theatres
were situated; but the pundits held firm: there was no salvation without the unities. The protestations of Mme de Staël and of Benjamin
Constant had some effect in making people aware that in other countries they ordered these things differently; Shakespeare and Schiller
were widely read, and a long series of *Masterpieces of the Foreign Theatre*
in translation sold well in the 1820s. But putting them on the stage was
a different matter – for all the popularity of Schiller, his plays had to
be either toned down to regular five-act tragedies or enlivened to
lurid melodramas before they could be acted, and when in 1822 a
foolhardy troop of English actors tried to produce Shakespeare in
English at the Théâtre de la Porte Saint-Martin, the audience, in a

frenzy of hysterical xenophobia, hooted them off the stage to cries of: 'Down with Shakespeare! He's one of Wellington's aides-de-camp!' Cavalry had to be called out to keep order in the streets. Indigenous attempts to reinvigorate tragedy were conspicuously absent. One or two of the less hidebound practitioners hazarded a few timid innovations – but these merely alienated the Classics without satisfying the Romantics.

It was in 1823 that Stendhal, incensed by the treatment of the English actors, fired a resounding broadside at the enemies of progress in his swashbuckling pamphlet *Racine et Shakespeare*. Abolition of the unities, action on the stage, French historical subjects, removal of restrictions on style, disregard of the traditional distinctions of genres, sweeping away of the cramping, stilted alexandrine: such was Stendhal's programme for modern tragedy. Not all these ideas were new and some of them, notably the attack on the alexandrine, were unacceptable to the poetic wing of the Romantic movement, more concerned with lyricism than with naturalness – in 1827, in that much overrated manifesto, the Preface to *Cromwell*, Victor Hugo was to deliver a condescending but firm rebuke to those who imagined that even a Romantic tragedy could be in prose.

Mérimée at this stage was pugnaciously on the side of the Romantics, arguing fiercely with the retarded provincial upholders of classicism whenever he stayed at Coulommiers with the Régniers,[1] and his friendship with Stendhal undoubtedly had much to do with his ardour. The failure of his own *Cromwell* did not deter him from continuing their joint campaign in favour of a radical reform of the theatre – indeed, for one brief moment, they even thought of writing a play together[2] – and *Le Théâtre de Clara Gazul* is the product of their years of unremitting propaganda. It is the first published attempt in French to create plays which would exemplify the new aesthetic, antedating Hugo's *Cromwell* by two years, Dumas' *Henri III et sa Cour* by four

[1] *C.G.*, Vol. I, p. 3.
[2] Cf. *H.B.*, in *Portraits historiques et littéraires*, p. 155. This project mentioned by Mérimée may be the same as that outlined to him by Stendhal, under the title *La Cheminée de marbre*, in a letter written in April 1830 (Stendhal, *Correspondance*, Vol. II, pp. 181–3). The plan is examined by Henri Martineau and François Michel in *Nouvelles Soirées du Stendhal-Club*, Paris, Mercure de France, 1950.

years, and Hugo's *Hernani* by five years. In retrospect it appears – as
it did at the time to a small but influential body of literary opinion – as
a date in the history of the French theatre.

Mérimée himself takes care to draw attention to the boldness of
his experiments. In the prologue, Clara gaily discards the unities:

> To decide whether a play is good or bad, I don't ask whether the action
> takes place in twenty-four hours and whether the characters all come to
> the same place, some to conspire, others to be murdered, and others to
> stab themselves over the dead bodies, as is customary on the other side of
> the Pyrenees.[3]

There are ten scene changes in *Les Espagnols en Danemarck*; in the
second part of *Inès Mendo*, we move from Estremadura to Elvas and
thence to Badajoz, and the play covers a period of weeks if not months.
Even the one-acters (with the exception of *L'Amour africain*) contrive
to shift from place to place. Clara also underlines the modernity of
the subject-matter of *Les Espagnols en Danemarck*, which is based on
events which took place as recently as 1808. To the poet, who is
shocked that the characters have not been dead for four hundred
years, Clara rejoins: 'And if they had only been dead for three hundred
and fifty years, couldn't the play be good?'[4] Equally spirited is the
defence of the freedom of the language, which is earthy and uninhibited: a note to *Une Femme est un diable* explains, with mock
naïveté:

> Ladies may perhaps be shocked by certain expressions in the role of
> Antonio. The author begs them to remember that this unfortunate young
> man had seen nothing of the world and had read no books save the Scrip-
> tures, in which everything is called by its proper name.[5]

As for action on the stage, even the most bloodthirsty spectator ought
to be satisfied: there are six murders in full view of the audience, one
death from natural causes and a man chopping off his own right hand.
Verse of course is proscribed; so are flights of poetic fancy. As the
preface to *Inès Mendo* says: 'We should be grateful to the author for
not having copied the *culto* style, so wearisome to present-day readers.'[6]
French notions on the inviolable barriers between genres are dismissed.
The supposed Joseph l'Estrange explains that 'Clara Gazul has the

[3] *Théâtre de Clara Gazul*, pp. 49–50.   [4] *Ibid.*, p. 52.
[5] *Ibid.*, p. 168. The note was only added in 1830.   [6] *Ibid.*, p. 189.

habit of using the word *comedy*, *comedia*, applied by Spanish poets in olden times to any dramatic work, whether comic or serious',[7] and at the end of *L'Amour africain*, Mojana talks of the play as a 'comedy, or, if you prefer, tragedy, as they say nowadays.'[8] All the plays have swiftly changing moods, switching almost without warning from witty buffoonery to death and catastrophe: indeed, Mérimée's juxtapositions of contrasting scenes are bolder and more brutal than those of any other French Romantic. Local colour is laid on thickly, and Mérimeé loses no opportunity to insert an exotic touch, whether it be the Moorish customs of *L'Amour africain*, the point of honour in *Inès Mendo*, the inquisitional setting of *Une Femme est un diable*, the dagger in the garter in *Le Ciel et l'enfer* or the constant interpolation of Spanish words and phrases (there are three times as many Spanish words in these short plays than in the whole of Lesage's vast novel *Gil Blas*.)[9]

So *Le Théâtre de Clara Gazul* is designed to shock: it is full of aggressive iconoclasm directed at the outworn forms of the classical theatre. From this point of view, the pretext that the plays are the work of a Spanish actress is a mischievously cunning device: if the public of the time accepts that a Spaniard has a right to his own dramatic system, why should it object when it discovers that the Spaniard is a Frenchman?

The plays are equally explosive in the political climate of the mid-1820s. In 1820 a revolt had broken out in Spain against the absolutist rule of the Bourbon monarch Ferdinand VII, and a sporadic civil war between the liberal constitutionalists and the monarchist *serviles* had followed. The French government, prompted by Chateaubriand, who was Foreign Minister at the time, decided in 1823 to intervene by sending an expedition to restore Ferdinand to his throne, a move which enraged those French liberals already alarmed by the increasingly authoritarian tendencies of the Bourbon régime in their own country. Mérimée was furious at the unexpected success of the French force, and on hearing of the fall of Pampeluna relieved his feelings by belabouring the unfortunate nag on which he happened to be trotting round the countryside near Coulommiers.[10] In these circumstances,

---

[7] *Théâtre de Clara Gazul*, p. 158.   [8] *Ibid.*, p. 183.
[9] According to Pierre Trahard, *La Jeunesse de Prosper Mérimée*, Vol. I, p. 199.   [10] *C.G.*, Vol. I, p. 5.

attributing his plays to a Spanish actress of the liberal persuasion driven into exile by the monarchists was an act of defiance and bravado.

These combatively liberal opinions are from the outset paraded with the same ostentation as his Romantic convictions. In the prologue to *Les Espagnols en Danemarck*, the Grandee sighs nostalgically for pre-constitutional times: 'In France ministries are always given to great nobles; whereas in this country nowadays . . .'[11] In *Une Femme est un diable* and *Le Ciel et l'enfer* the Church and especially the Inquisition are ruthlessly mocked. In the former play, Fray Rafael and Fray Domingo are stupid, corrupt, hypocritical, sadistic and lecherous, while Fray Antonio is a tormented fanatic; in the latter, Fray Barto-lomé is gluttonous, unscrupulous and cunning. These are caricatures in the tradition of the most scurrilous eighteenth-century anticlerical-ism, unconvincing no doubt, but effective by the very zest of their exaggeration. In the first part of *Inès Mendo*, the prejudice which is defeated is that of class distinction; the aristocratic Don Esteban defies convention to marry Inès, the executioner's daughter. More even than the other plays, *Les Espagnols en Danemarck* is ingeniously conceived to discomfit French right-wing opinion. It deals with a famous episode of the Napoleonic wars when in 1808, a Spanish division stationed in Denmark under the command of General La Romana, hearing that Napoleon proposed to instal his brother on the Spanish throne and transform Spain from an ally to a subject nation, was spirited away by the English fleet and returned to its native country to fight against the French. The heroes are the Spaniards who, out of love for their own land, are determined to take up arms against France; the villains are the French who, by all manner of treacherous schemes, try to prevent their departure. This is a logical position for the Spanish Clara, but it is a disturbing experience for the French public, all too conscious that French interference has once again thwarted the will of the Spanish people, to be forced to watch its own representatives making odious fools of themselves while the Spanish characters ardently extol the virtues of patriotism and independence. This plea for the recognition of the rights of other peoples, with its biting criticism of narrow-minded jingoism, has lost little of its actuality today, and Louis Aragon, the Communist writer, has rightly seen in it an exemplification of 'true

[11] *Théâtre de Clara Gazul*, p. 50.

patriotism, the patriotism which refuses to allow one's country to become an accomplice of crime'.[12]

Mérimée is out to stir up controversy: he wants to demonstrate the merits of a dramatic system as yet untried in France, and to discredit the social and political views of the conservatives. But what is the value of Le Théâtre de Clara Gazul for a twentieth-century reader? Can one still derive pleasure from it now, or has it, like so many literary landmarks, crumbled away into an insignificant heap of rubble?

That it has its defects and weaknesses cannot be denied. Mérimée's predilection for action rather than talk brings him at times to the verge of melodrama. The end of the first part of Inès Mendo is an extreme example: Mendo the executioner is about to behead his daughter's lover but instead brings the axe down on his own hand with a shout of 'I am no longer the executioner!'[13] Inès mounts the scaffold beside Don Esteban, the crowd acclaims them, and the king rides in to pardon them both. It is all done with such off-hand laconicism that the reader might be pardoned for thinking that there was a whiff of parody about it, an impression likely to be heightened if he remembers that 'Joseph l'Estrange' had presented the play with these derogatory words: 'This strange comedy was written by Clara Gazul to please a friend of hers, a lady with a passion for sentimental and improbable novels.'[14] Similarly, the characters are sketched in rather than portrayed in depth, a reproach which Mérimée seems to have foreseen when he makes 'L'Estrange' explain that Clara, striving to imitate old Spanish playwrights, has deliberately adopted 'their usual defects, such as excessive rapidity in action, lack of development, etc'.[15] The changes of heart of the two bosom friends in love with the same woman in L'Amour africain are so swift and so radical as to be incredible; the struggle between fanatical asceticism and lust in Antonio, the main character of Une Femme est un diable, is of such perfunctory simplicity that the didactic and satirical intention becomes far too clear. Delécluze was justified in finding these plays schematic;[16] they sometimes read more like scenarios than finished works. The local colour is laid on heavily and attracts too much attention to itself; moreover – Mérimée know-

---

[12] Louis Aragon, La Lumière de Stendhal, Paris, Denoël, 1954, p. 194.
[13] Théâtre de Clara Gazul, p. 219.
[14] Ibid., p. 189.   [15] Ibid.
[16] Souvenirs de soixante années, pp. 272–3.

ing Spain only from books – it is not always accurate, and one may criticise the implausibility of a Spanish grandee insulting his ancestors or the visibly confused account of the workings of the Inquisition. Mérimée's determination to avoid flights of lyricism or unnatural grandiloquence led him to adopt a style which can seem strangely flat at moments of tension: Don Juan's patriotism in *Les Espagnols en Danemarck* is disappointingly lacking in eloquence, and some of the monologues meant to be expressive of unbearable emotion read more like the agenda for a committee meeting.

Yet the plays are anything but boring. They move rapidly, they are full of surprises, there is continuous dramatic conflict, and they come to the point with refreshing directness and efficiency. Even the two longer plays have a clarity and simplicity of structure not often met with in the exuberant confusion of Romantic drama. One senses in them the touch of the future master of the short story. Secondly, the psychology of some of the characters, where Mérimée is not concerned with lampooning those of whom he disapproves, has its merits. Don Juan Diaz, the hero of *Les Espagnols en Danemarck*, stands out because of his casual bravery and his capacity for combining outward flippancy with great depths of feeling; Mme de Coulanges, the unwilling spy exploited by her degenerate mother, is far more convincing than the declamatorily repentant courtesans of later Romanticism. The hesitations and contradictions of Doña Urraca in *Le Ciel et l'enfer*, as she wavers between denouncing the lover whom she believes to be unfaithful and trying to save his life, show a sure sense of the frailties o human love, as does Don Esteban's growing disenchantment with his rustic bride when prejudice triumphs in the second part of *Inès Mendo*. Passion is depicted as a brutal, violent and destructive force; it may not be analysed with any great subtlety, but it is presented with sombre vigour.

The language too is vigorous; the characters speak with a terseness, a directness and an expressive earthiness that is much more true to life than the verbal attitudinising and irrelevant lyricism in which Mérimée's contemporaries tended to indulge. It is at its best in the racy coarseness of characters like the adventuress Mme de Tourville or her soldier son in *Les Espagnols en Danemarck*, with their concrete vocabulary, their bold images, and their forceful interjections – Mérimée always liked the vividness of popular diction and nothing he wrote is more powerful than the story of Carmen told in the simple, military words of Don José. But his incisive and irreverent wit also sparkles in some of the comic passages of the shorter plays. The atmosphere is living and much of the detail carefully and exactly chosen for effect. Mistakes there may be, but the background of *Les Espagnols en Danemarck* is indicated with that sureness of information which was to characterise Mérimée's later work as a historian. There is no danger of confusing the setting of one play with another, though all are Spanish: the soldiers of 1808, the Inquisition during the War of the Spanish Succession, the Moors of Cordoba, Galicia in 1640, an elegant *salon* at an unspecified time are all sharply differentiated and conjured up with admirable clarity.

Perhaps most remarkable of all is the evocation of the Spanish temperament. Natural affinities no doubt play a part here; the punctilious observance of a code of personal honour, the torrid violence of passion, the contemptuous rejection of conventional opinion are all elements which drew Mérimée towards things Spanish long before he had seen the country. Later he was to become one of the most eminent Spanish scholars in France; but now he relied on travel-books, Spanish authors and perhaps a few hints from friends. Yet he somehow divined the Spanish character with much more penetration than anyone else in his time: to quote one student of the image of Spain in French Romanticism, Mérimée 'is alone among his contemporaries in having really understood the genius of Spain'.[17]

Le Théâtre de Clara Gazul raises one problem of interest for an understanding of Mérimée's creative activity: the author's attitude to his own work. How seriously is Mérimée himself involved in these plays? The element of hoax and pastiche suggests a certain distance between the writer and the drama. But the device of the non-existent Spanish actress justifies the departure from the canons of French dramatic practice and makes the French public see its own prejudices with the unbiassed eye of an outsider; it is also true that Mérimée did not try seriously to keep the pretence up for long. But by attributing the plays to a fictitious character Mérimée is able to escape responsibility for them. If we think they are by Clara Gazul, Mérimée is exempt from our criticism; if we discover them to be his work, he

[17] Ernest Martinenche, *L'Espagne et le Romantisme français*, Paris, Hachette, 1922, p. 101.

can still elude our grasp by claiming that they are merely imitations, a game which he has played with no other aim than that of simultaneously hoodwinking us and entertaining us.

A curious feature common to all the plays deliberately reinforces the impression that they are not meant seriously. This is Mérimée's deformation of the ending typical of the old Spanish theatre, in which one of the characters announces that the play is over and asks the audience's indulgence for the shortcomings of the author. But whereas playwrights like Lope de Vega or Calderón simply tack on a perfunctory last phrase as a polite salute to the spectators, Mérimée ironically uses the convention to discredit the illusion which his play has produced. For instance, at the end of *L'Amour africain*, Nouman stands in despair over the bodies of his friend Zain and his mistress Mojana, both of whom he has just killed; at this point, a servant comes in to say that the play is over and supper ready, Nouman says cheerfully: 'Ah! that's different',[18] the 'corpses' stand up, and Mojana delivers a little homily on literary realism. Similarly, at the end of *Inès Mendo*, the heroine has just died of grief and her father has shot her faithless husband, whose dying gesture is a noble exhortation to the old man to flee. But Mendo transforms pathos to bathos when he replies: 'I shan't budge, seeing that the play's over. Yes, ladies and gentlemen, that is the end of *Inès Mendo, ou le Triomphe du préjugé*'. Whereupon his dead daughter jumps up to say: 'The author has told me to come alive again to crave your forbearance; and you can leave with the satisfaction of knowing that there won't be a third part.'[19] To end on this jarring note is to make the reader feel uneasily that he was perhaps foolish to take seriously what has gone before. If the author makes light of his plays, ought we not to do the same?

Yet we have seen that Mérimée does care about what happens in them. He cares about their literary form, their political message, their satirical impact, their documentation, their verisimilitude, their characters and their portrayal of passion. He is unmistakably present when Don Juan cries: 'Shoot them! shoot them! shoot them! men are all knaves who are worth no more than a bullet to carry them off to the other world!';[20] when Don Esteban tires of his humble Inès and prejudice begins to reassert itself; when Fray Antonio, surveying the

[18] *Théâtre de Clara Gazul*, p. 185.
[19] *Ibid.*, p. 273.　　　　　[20] *Ibid.*, p. 133.

wreckage of his life, exclaims: 'In an hour I have become a traitor, a fornicator and a murderer';[21] perhaps most of all when Don Esteban, faced with certain death, tries to whistle to show his indifference but stops in case nervousness makes him sound a wrong note. This is humanity as Mérimée saw it: riven by irresistible, disruptive feelings, frail, changeable, selfish, cowardly, trying desperately to keep its courage up in face of the black truth about life. Here, no matter what he may pretend, he is exposing his inmost feelings about the world, and, though his insights may as yet be relatively crude, it is this which gives the plays their individuality and their lasting value.

Why then does Mérimée take such pains to decry his own efforts? The answer lies in a defence mechanism which is to operate almost throughout his career. He was always a painfully vulnerable man who had soon learnt to protect his sensitivity by building round it a shell of hard indifference. At the same time, his inner life craved the expression which he gave it through literature and a voluminous correspondence, thus producing the paradox of someone unable to resist the baring of his soul and yet ever anxious to avoid contacts which might bring him unbearable torments. To quote the pithy summing up of one critic, 'he needs a disguise to dare to be himself'.[22] This is why he writes plays which spring from the innermost wells of his being, and then tries to pretend that he cares nothing for them. Only thus can he satisfy both the impulse towards self-expression and the need for self-protection. Such ambivalence is one of the hallmarks of his work and, in different ways, we shall see it affecting his creativity, until in the end it inhibits it completely.

Mérimée later wrote two other plays which were then added to subsequent editions of *Le Théâtre de Clara Gazul*, as well as a third which dates from the same period and inspiration. These are *L'Occasion* (*The Opportunity*) (1829) and *Le Carrosse du Saint Sacrement* (*The Carriage of the Holy Sacrament*) (also 1829), and *La Famille de Carvajal* (*The Carvajal Family*) (1828). The dramatic techniques are the same and the settings similar, though instead of Spain we are now in South America – a change no doubt brought about by Mérimée's conversations with Dr Roulin, his mother's physician, who in 1827 returned to Paris after

[21] *Théâtre de Clara Gazul*, p. 167.

[22] L. Dugas, 'La Timidité de Prosper Mérimée', *Mercure de France*, octobre 1920.

several years' residence in Peru.[23] The plots of the plays too are recognisably by the same hand – there is the same urgency of action, the same violent brutality, the same sudden reversals of feeling, the same bitter humour, the same acid mockery of priests. But there are differences too, and it is these differences, allied with the persistence of existing qualities, which make two at least of these plays into Mérimée's most satisfying and durable dramatic achievements.

The third play, *La Famille de Carvajal*, is an enigmatic work. Openly based on the tale of Beatrice Cenci, a favourite subject for the more lurid-minded Romantics throughout Europe,[24] it portrays the incestuous passion of the villainous Don José for his daughter Catalina, which leads him to murder his wife before attempting to rape the girl. Catalina stabs him in self-defence, is accused of parricide, and in despair disappears into the jungle. This singularly horrible drama is prefaced by two letters, patently faked by Mérimée himself; one is from a buccaneer who claims that he and his crew need something really spicy to stimulate their jaded palates, and the other supposedly emanates from a prim little girl at a convent school, who asks for 'a very dark, very terrible little novel or play, with a lot of crimes and love like in Lord Byron'.[25] Combined with the paroxysmal violence of the subject and its undeniably melodramatic treatment, these spoof letters have led most critics to suppose that *La Famille de Carvajal* is a parody, designed by its very exaggeration to pour ridicule on the horrific excesses of Gothic Romanticism.[26]

[23] Cf. Marguerite Combes, *Pauvre et aventureuse bourgeoisie. Roulin et ses amis, 1796–1874*, Paris, Peyronnet, 1929.

[24] Apart from Shelley's *The Cenci*, one might instance Stendhal's *Les Cenci* in the *Chroniques italiennes*. In his *Candidature au Stendhal-Club*, Paris, Le Divan, 1926, Jacques Boulenger attributed to Mérimée a brochure entitled *Histoire de la famille Cenci*, published in 1825. But Dr Parturier has shown that this suggestion is groundless ('Stendhal, *Le Masque de fer*, et la famille Cenci', *Le Divan*, avril 1936).

[25] *La Jaquerie. La Famille de Carvajal*, ed. E. Marsan, Paris, Le Divan, 1928, p. 288.

[26] For instance, P. Trahard, *La Jeunesse de Prosper Mérimée*, Vol. I, pp. 335–49, and Eugène Marsan, in his preface to *La Jaquerie. La Famille de Carvajal*, pp. xii–xiii. A different view is taken by Maxime Revon in his edition of the *Théâtre de Clara Gazul*, Paris, Garnier, 1928; he argues that it presents 'the pathological study of a case of morbid perversity' (p. xvii).

But while Mérimée insinuates by his preface that the play is not meant seriously, in essence it differs little from the more extreme scenes of *Une Femme est un diable* or *Inès Mendo*. Only the particularly repugnant nature of Don José's obsession brings it closer to the point at which horror is laid on so thickly as to become comic. Otherwise Mérimée has studied Don José's case with clinical accuracy; as a detailed portrayal of a sadist uncontrollably gripped by incestuous lust, the play is a convincing and effective essay in psychopathology. That Mérimée should then have attempted to disguise his interest in such a hideous aberration is entirely in character. But when one remembers Mérimée's fascination with love as a terrifying and fatal power, from *La Vénus d'Ille* (*The Venus of Ille*) to *Lokis*, it is scarcely surprising that he should wish to investigate the destructive effects of a passion for a close relative – Don José's lust for Catalina is no more scabrous a topic than the murderously bestial consummation of Szémioth's passion for his bride in *Lokis*. *La Famille de Carvajal* is best seen as another example of Mérimée's sombre view of love, this time carried to such extremes of terror and perversion that he is afraid to admit he meant it in earnest.

Even so, it must be allowed that, as a play, it is little more than a literary curiosity. Whatever the merits of Mérimée's depiction of Carvajal's warped mind, the events and emotions of the drama are so far removed from normal human experience that our sympathy is repulsed rather than enlisted, the more so as his usual insistence on the revelation of character almost exclusively through action brings it very close to melodrama.

Much more impressive is *L'Occasion*, the story of Maria, a young boarder at a convent school who falls head over heels in love with a priest, only to discover that he is in love with another pupil. Maria resolves to sacrifice herself by giving the lovers enough money to flee together and then committing suicide, but at the last moment, in a fit of jealous rage, she allows her friend to drink the poisoned lemonade which she has prepared for herself. What makes this play so moving and so telling dramatically is the depth of psychological insight which it reveals. Though Maria's final act comes swiftly, suddenly and without any commentaries, it has been much more carefully and fully prepared than similar crimes in the earlier *Clara Gazul* plays. Maria, Francisca and Fray Eugenio are all allowed time to establish themselves as rounded and subtly delineated characters. They talk to each other at length, and Maria soliloquises with a minuteness that Mérimée has hitherto avoided. No longer do we feel that people in his plays can only express themselves with telegrammatic brevity; here their emotions, especially those of Maria, grow and change with a fineness of texture that only a more sensitive style and a less schematic understanding of temperament could bring. There is even an unwonted touch of lyricism when Francisca describes her secret meetings with Fray Eugenio under the old tree in the moonlit courtyard, and for the first time the reader senses that Mérimée, without losing any of his accustomed incisiveness, is seeing into the complexities of human behaviour. The tone of the play, too, is more tender: Fray Eugenio is not a philandering Tartuffe but a lovelorn young man who had only been made to embrace the priesthood out of a sense of filial duty. Nor is there any of that caustic, grating humour which had character- ised the 1825 plays and often detracted from their tragic impact: in *L'Occasion* – except for the usual flippant last line – Mérimée does not seek to palliate the seriousness of what is happening, and the play consequently gains in depth and in unity. It is one of the few Romantic dramas which are still alive and stageworthy today.

The same is true of *Le Carrosse du Saint Sacrement*, save that this is a comedy. The tale of the Viceroy of Peru who was induced to hand over his new carriage to his actress mistress, who then donated it to the Church so as to carry the sacraments to the dying, is based on fact: La Périchole flourished in the middle of the eighteenth century, and the carriage incident is reputed to have taken place in 1761 – Mérimée had doubtless heard of it through Dr Roulin.[27] Surprisingly enough, he treats the subject with a light, amused touch, far removed from the grim and indignant lambasting of the clergy which had been so prominent in *Une Femme est un diable* or *Le Ciel et l'enfer*. It may well be, as he subsequently claimed, that in 1829 it was an act of courage to make fun of a bishop and a representative of royalty,[28] but that is not his main aim here. He is much more interested in depicting the foibles and inconsistencies of human nature than in satirising professions or institutions, and the play is above all concerned with the comic potential of a vain, pompous, incompetent and weak-willed old man in love with a woman who is vulgar, unfaithful, unscrupulous, cunning

[27] Cf. Combes, *op. cit.*   [28] *C.G.*, Vol. V, p. 393.

and impulsive. The scenes in which the viceroy's jealousy is aroused by his secretary's insinuations and then allayed by La Périchole's magnificently histrionic performance are excellent psychological comedy, as wittily written as they are acutely observed. The dialogue is free-flowing and natural, matching the constantly entertaining evolution of the characters' emotions, and because the humour springs essentially from the vagaries of personality, there is less insistence on twists of plot or on physical violence. Indeed, one almost feels that Mérimée, very much contrary to his usual practice, has taken so much pleasure in recording the conversations of his characters that they have been allowed to run on longer than is strictly necessary. But that in itself is a welcome departure from the drily schematic compression of the earlier plays.

Alone among Mérimée's plays, these two works have had some lasting success on the stage. *Le Carrosse du Saint Sacrement*, though it was a failure when first produced in 1850, has more recently been accorded a permanent place in the repertoire of the Comédie française and in the 1950s inspired *The Golden Carriage*, one of Jean Renoir's most sparkling films. Since the last war *L'Occasion* has also found favour with some theatre managers. Neither of them, in terms of dimensions or profundity, could be accounted a major achievement, but their sureness in the understanding of human behaviour, their easy, pointed dialogue, and their constant sense of dramatic effect make one regret that reluctance to curry approval from a fickle and vulgar public turned Mérimée away from the theatre. He certainly had in him the potential of an expert stage writer – much more so than any of the other French Romantics except Musset and, on a lower level, Dumas. But as he explained to Turgenev many years later, writing for the theatre required two qualities: '1) Guessing the tastes and susceptibilities of the public, what are called stage effects 2) Having inexhaustible patience, firmness and resignation to get the actors to do what you want. Even if I had No. 1 which I completely lack, I know that I could never stand the boredom of a rehearsal.'[29]

La Guzla, like *La Famille de Carvajal*, is a work which defies categorisation. Nominally, it is a *Selection of Illyrian poems collected in Dalmatia, Bosnia, Croatia and Herzegovina*; in reality, only one of its thirty-two

[29] *C.G.*, Vol. XIII, p. 29.

supposed translations is genuine – the others are all Mérimée's invention.[30] The pastiche is clever and highly effective, and, whatever Mérimée may later have pretended, it depends on careful documentation and on a considerable familiarity with the themes and techniques of European folk-poetry. The typography and the critical apparatus are based on Fauriel's *Folk Songs of Modern Greece*, and the skill of Mérimée's imitations is attested by the number and quality of those they deceived. Experts can find faults which give the game away; we are told that Serbian folk-songs are not divided into stanzas, as most of Mérimée's are, and that vampirism and the evil eye, two of his favourite themes, occur in Serbian legends but not in poetry.[31] But almost all of Mérimée's contemporaries enjoyed it in the belief that it was genuine. If all Mérimée wanted was to perpetrate a practical joke, then he undoubtedly succeeded.

But *La Guzla* is more than the schoolboyish hoax which Mérimée himself suggested it was in a preface written in 1840, and which has been called 'a second hoax grafted on to the first one'.[32] In this, after an amusing if improbable account of how it came to be composed, he says that the book, born of fascination with local colour, had revealed to him that local colour was such a simple trick that he ended by doubting its value.[33] In 1835, he had been even more categorical when writing to his Russian friend Sobolevski, averring that the work was intended 'to make fun of the local colour into which everyone was diving head first about the year of grace 1827'.[34] But it is obvious that Mérimée himself remained fascinated by local colour – *Colomba* and *Carmen*, both written in the 1840s, are there to prove it. Moreover, Mérimée had worked too hard at the picturesque details of *La Guzla* for their intention to be purely parodic. He once said himself: 'I do

[30] The one genuine translation is 'The Sad Ballad of the Wife of Asan-Aga', which had already appeared several times in French, German and English (cf. Yovanovitch, *op. cit.*). 'Milosch Kobilich', added to the 1842 edition, is neither Mérimée's invention nor a genuine folk-poem: as Mérimée says in a note (*La Guzla*, p. 185), it is based on a poem found by Count Sorgo, a Ragusan diplomat living in Paris, who was himself probably ignorant of its origins (cf. Yovanovitch, *op. cit.*, and R. Maixner, 'La Retraite parisienne d'Antoine Sorgo-Sorkočević', *Revue de Littérature comparée*, juillet-septembre 1966). [31] Cf. Yovanovitch, *op. cit.*

[32] Augustin Filon, *Mérimée et ses amis*, Paris, Hachette, 1894, p. 37.

[33] *La Guzla*, p. 6. [34] *C.G.*, Vol. I, pp. 375-6.

not deny the pleasure which a hoax can give its perpetrator; but the
first essential for it to be successful and complete is that it should not
cause him too much trouble',[35] and *La Guzla* certainly required considerable trouble. No doubt Mérimée was delighted when so many
eminent critics were taken in, but that does not prove that his intentions stopped there – indeed, one may well suspect that he is never
more serious than when he appears most flippant.

Pastiche, when it is successful, implies a certain community of spirit
between the imitator and the imitated, and Mérimée was well attuned
to the charms of primitive poetry. To modern poetry he was indifferent
to the point of philistinism, scorning verse as a useless adornment to
thought and a great obscurer of ideas, suspicions which he voiced when
writing about Pushkin, who, with Béranger, was almost the only
contemporary poet to appeal to him. According to Mérimée's jaundiced view, a poet 'will be content with sounds instead of thoughts,
and will think that he has reached the summit of art when he has
pleased the ear by a melody which only a few connoisseurs can appreciate. It happens not infrequently that, when an instrument has
reached the peak of perfection, the player is led astray into the minutiae
of puerile experiments. Many a poet mistakes confused images for
ideas and over-refines his work to the point of unintelligibility.'[36] But
the greater directness and spontaneity of primitive poetry escapes this
reproach, as Mérimée explains in a revealing article on a collection of
Rumanian Folk-songs and Ballads:

> I like the popular songs of all countries and all periods, from the Iliad to
> the romance of Malbrouk. To tell the truth, I cannot imagine – and this
> may be a heresy – I can hardly imagine poetry except in a state of semi-
> civilisation, or even of barbarism, to be perfectly frank. It is only in that
> blessed state that the poet can be naïve without being silly, and natural
> without being trivial. He is then like some delightful child stammering
> out songs before being able to put a sentence together. He is always enter-
> taining and sometimes sublime; he moves me, because he is the first to
> believe the tales he tells.[37]

---

[35] *Notes d'un voyage dans le Midi de la France*, Paris, Fournier, 1835, p. 454.
[36] *Études de littérature russe*, ed. H. Mongault, Vol. I, Paris, Champion,
1931, p. 6.
[37] 'Ballades et chants populaires de la Roumanie', *Le Moniteur universel*,
17 janvier 1856.

Mérimée is thus led, by his mistrust of the superficiality of civilised values, into a hankering after a primitive simplicity of mind which alone can produce poetry without affectation.

But of course moderns can only achieve such a state by a conscious act of identification with the mentality of unspoilt societies. According to Mérimée a boldly imaginative use of language in elevated form is natural only to the uncivilised mind; in a more advanced state of civilisation, verse is inimical to naturalness. Driven as usual by what he himself called 'the great fear of ridicule which I, as a Frenchman, naturally have',[38] Mérimée thus steered very clear of poetry, eyeing it with evident suspicion – except when it was folk-poetry, when he revelled in it. Throughout his life he was an enthusiastic collector of folk-poems, continually pestering friends in distant lands – Albania, Corsica, Russia, Greece[39] – to send him new specimens; he regularly reviewed or even prefaced volumes of folk-poetry;[40] he even sat on a committee formed by Napoleon III with the ambitious aim of constituting a corpus of French folk-poetry.[41] In the light of this deep and durable interest in balladry, *The Guzla* may not unreasonably be regarded as an attempt to strip off the personality of civilised man and recapture the inspiration of a wilder and more authentic nature. How far it may perform the same service for the reader is doubtful; he will always be more aware of Mérimée in it than of any real community of feeling with primitivism.

On the other hand, he may well savour the dramatic effect of these little ballads, most of which have a narrative content typical in its startling vividness of later Mérimée techniques. He may, too, appreciate the distinctive quality of a tense yet heightened style which admirably captures the flavour of poetry translated into prose. *La Guzla* indeed marks a significant stage in the evolution of the prose poem

[38] *C.G.*, Vol. I, p. 441.

[39] At different times, he enlisted the help of Grasset, Turgenev and Gobineau, among others.

[40] Apart from the already-mentioned article on Rumanian folk-song, one may note 'De l'origine des Albanais', *Revue contemporaine*, 31 décembre 1854, and his introduction to Marino Vreto's *Contes et poèmes de la Grèce moderne*, Paris, Audois, 1856.

[41] Cf. Julien Tiersot, *La Chanson populaire et les écrivains romantiques*, Paris, Plon, 1931, pp. 317–24.

as a literary genre in France; Suzanne Bernard, the most authoritative
historian of the genre, has pointed out that the form of the prose poem
is established by *La Guzla* and that Aloysius Bertrand in *Gaspard de la
Nuit*, the most famous example of the genre before Baudelaire's *Petits
Poèmes en prose* and Rimbaud's *Illuminations*, simply follows Mérimée's
formal devices while introducing new subject-matter.[42] The unique interest of these works is thus midway between short stories and poetry,
with the additional complication of some specious local colour and a
deliberately misleading attribution. Their subtitle of 'Illyric poems'
may be a pun [43] – certainly it is characteristic that Mérimée's embarrassment over the idea of poetry should have led him to approach it by
such an oblique and mysterious route. But perhaps the last word on
this elusive subject should be left with Goethe, who spoke of the young
Mérimée with almost uncanny penetration:

> These poems are full of all manner of gruesome themes such as cemeteries,
> crossroads at midnight, ghosts and vampires; but none of these horrors
> touches the poet's inner nature; rather does he treat them from a certain
> objective distance and so to speak ironically. He sets about it just like an
> artist who enjoys trying something of the kind for once. [. . .] Of course,
> Mérimée is a fine chap! It takes more power and genius to deal objectively
> with a subject than people think.[44]

---

[42] Suzanne Bernard, *Le Poème en prose de Baudelaire jusqu'à nos jours*, Paris,
Nizet, 1959, pp. 45–7.
[43] So Jean Dutourd suggests in *Le Fond et la forme*, Paris, Gallimard, 1958.
[44] Eckermann, *op. cit.*, pp. 578–9.

Chapter 4

Suitor

J'ai passé ma vie à être loué pour des qualités que je n'ai pas
et calomnié pour des défauts qui ne sont pas les miens.
                                    To Jenny Dacquin, 2 December 1842

In the late 1820s, Mérimée was rarely out of Stendhal's company. Sometimes they turned up in *salons* together; sometimes they met privately and argued about literature; sometimes they went out to paint the town red. It was in those years that there grew up a group of like-minded friends who dined once a month in some elegant restaurant before going on to less respectable forms of amusement elsewhere. Apart from Stendhal and Mérimée, the most regular diners included Eugène Delacroix, the Romantic artist; young Alfred de Musset, already brilliant but already wedded to a life of pleasure; Baron Adolphe de Mareste, a close friend of Stendhal to whom is attributed (wrongly) the famous dictum that 'bad taste leads to crime'; Horace de Viel-Castel, an impoverished nobleman who later achieved eminence as an archaeologist and museum curator; Dr Koreff, an extraordinary expatriate German Jew who dabbled in mesmerism, played a large part in publicising in France the works of his friend Hoffmann, and was probably engaged in mild forms of espionage;[1] and Édouard Grasset, who had spent five years in Greece fighting with the rebels and who in 1830 was to become involved in a celebrated elopement scandal.[2]

Viel-Castel was later to affirm that 'we enjoyed ourselves greatly, we talked long and wittily, and we didn't get drunk'.[3] But if the first

[1] Cf. Marietta Martin, *Un Aventurier intellectuel, le docteur Koreff*, Paris, Champion, 1925.

[2] Cf. Dr Parturier's edition of Mérimée's *Lettres aux Grasset*, Paris, La Connaissance, 1929.

[3] Horace de Viel-Castel, *Mémoires*, ed. P. Josserand, Paris, Le Prat, 1942, Vol. I, p. 75.

two propositions are true, the third is more than doubtful. The party usually managed to collect a few chorus-girls from the Opera, or else set off for establishments where – at a price – they were sure to find female companions. Mérimée gives a staggering account of one such evening a year or two later, when Musset, having had too much champagne, offered to demonstrate his sexual prowess by candlelight, only to start finding objections and eventually succumbing to a nose-bleed when pressed to carry out his project; the other members of the party were consoled by 'gymnastic exercises by six young ladies *in naturalibus*'.[4] Mérimée himself was addicted to the company of *grisettes*, *rats* and other varieties of easy-living ladies, partly because his sexual appetites were imperious, partly because he relished the contrast with the polite society which he frequented, and perhaps most of all because of the amused interest with which he contemplated yet another category of humanity. There was a good deal of sharing and exchanging of mistresses among the group – Stendhal once nearly lost Alberthe de Rubempré to Mérimée who, however, agreed to refuse her attentions, having been put off by the sight of her stockings wrinkled round her legs.[5]

One of the gayest and most prominent members of the party, when he was in France, was Sutton Sharpe.[6] The son of a prosperous business-man, Sharpe was a successful lawyer, a militant liberal and a passionate lover of the good things of life, which he found in ample measure in Paris every summer. According to Mérimée 'he would earn 150,000 francs in ten months, then spend two more months among the Opera chorus-girls'.[7] Highly intelligent, hard-working, amiable, witty and artistic, Sharpe had much in common with Mérimée, and, together with Stendhal, the two saw as much of each other as they could, whether in Paris or in London. Mérimée's first journey to England was made during or before the summer of 1825,[8] when he had visited the watchmaker Benjamin Vulliamy, a friend of his father, and he had returned for a longer stay in 1826, interrupted by a brief return to Paris in midsummer. On this occasion, he was with Delécluze, Duver-

[4] *C.G.*, Vol. I, p. 122.

[5] *Souvenirs d'égotisme*, in *Œuvres intimes*, pp. 1443–4.

[6] Cf. Doris Gunnell, *Sutton Sharpe et ses amis français*, Paris, Champion, 1925.

[7] *C.G.*, Vol. III, p. 334.   [8] Cf. *C.G.*, Vol. XVI, p. 3

3b Mérimée as a young man, from a study by Deveria

3a Victor Jacquemont, a portrait by Anne Mérimée

4a Madame de Montijo with her two daughters, Paca, later Duchess of Alba, and Eugenia, later Empress Eugénie of France, painted by Blaize in 1837

4b The Montijo house at Carabanchel, a painting by Mérimée

gier de Hauranne and Baron Gérard, and painting was one of their main preoccupations. He spent some time with Simon-Jacques Rochard and through him met Sir Thomas Lawrence, whose technique and temperament made a great impression on him – Lawrence's precepts had much to do with the practice which Mérimée later adopted in art of centring his compositions on some significant detail.[9]

In Paris, too, Mérimée liked to keep in touch with English-speaking society. One of the *salons* where he appeared most regularly was that of Mary Clarke, an Irishwoman who had come to live more or less permanently in France after 1814.[10] Mary was the sort of woman whose company Mérimée always enjoyed: lively, clever, amusing, sociable, talkative, unconventional and capable of deep feeling. The great drama of her life was her long affair with Claude Fauriel, who was much older than she was and with whom she fell heavily in love in 1822. At first, Fauriel was on the point of marrying her, but then the habits of bachelordom reasserted themselves, and, to her fury, he preferred to keep their relationship on the basis of a permanent but unacknowledged liaison – this lasted until his death in 1844. Her great admiration for Sir Walter Scott may have helped to orientate Mérimée's curiosity in that direction; her *salon* provided yet another opportunity for him to meet eminent liberal politicians and historians – Thiers, Mignet, the Thierry brothers, Victor Cousin – and distinguished Anglo-French figures like Louise Swanton Belloc, the authoress whom Stendhal suspected of having an illicit affair with Mlle de Montgolfier.[11] It was Mérimée who first introduced Hugo there and was responsible for his meeting Benjamin Constant, 'by then a white-haired old man, carelessly dressed, with a tired, venerable face'.[12]

[9] Cf. Mérimée's article on Lawrence in *Le National*, 24 February 1830, reproduced in *Pages retrouvées de P. Mérimée*, ed. H. Malo, Paris, Émile-Paul, 1929. The impact made by Lawrence on Mérimée is discussed by P. Trahard, *La Jeunesse de Prosper Mérimée*, Vol. I, pp. 254–5 (but at the time when Trahard was writing, Mérimée's authorship of the *National* article had not been established). It is also mentioned by R. C. Dale, *The Poetics of Prosper Mérimée*, The Hague–Paris, Mouton, 1966, p. 46.

[10] Cf. Mary Elmina Smith, *Une Anglaise intellectuelle en France sous la Restauration, miss Mary Clarke*, Paris, Champion, 1927.

[11] *Œuvres intimes*, p. 1429.

[12] *Victor Hugo raconté par un témoin de sa vie*, Paris, Hetzel-Quantin, n.d., Vol. II, pp. 238–9.

c

More important still in Mérimée's life was the salon of the Misses Julia and Fanny Garnett.[13] They came of an English-American family who had set up house in Paris after the death of their father, and their drawing-room attracted celebrated international figures, including La Fayette, Washington Irving, Charles Wilkes and that eccentric liberator of American slaves, the Scotswoman Fanny Wright, foundress of the Nashoba settlement in Tennessee. Stendhal and Mérimée found their way there in 1826 or thereabouts, and Mérimée almost immediately fell in love with Julia Garnett who was some ten years older than he was. At this stage, though he had already contracted the habits of sexual licence which were to remain with him until old age damped his ardour, Mérimée was far from having developed the aversion to marriage which he was later to display so brazenly, and on more than one occasion in the late 1820s, he would have been only too ready to marry, had not circumstances thwarted him. As much inclined to idealised passion as to more or less sordid debauch, he saw no incongruity in separating the satisfaction of the senses from loftier aspirations, and his brief encounter with Julia Garnett was probably the first occasion on which a serious emotion might have led him to matrimony. But unfortunately for his hopes, the habitués of the Garnett *salon* also included a German historian and archivist, Dr Georg Heinrich Pertz, later to win fame as editor of *Monumenta Germaniae Historica*, and it was he whom Julia chose to marry in September 1827. Despite Mérimée's secretiveness, his passion for Julia was known to at least some of his friends. Delécluze teased him about it,[14] and Stendhal commented, on hearing of Julia's wedding: 'What grief for a tender heart!'[15]

[13] Cf. J. F. Marshall, 'Les Dames Garnett amies de Stendhal', *Le Divan*, oct.–déc. 1949.

[14] At least it may have been about Julia Garnett. On 8 January 1826, Delécluze noted in his diary that he, Sautelet and Ampère had been teasing Mérimée 'about a young Englishwoman with whom he has been very much smitten and who has recently married, leaving him with memories which make him jealous' (*Journal*, ed. R. Baschet, Paris, Grasset, 1948, p. 296). But it seems that Julia did not marry until 1827. There remains the possibility that Delécluze confused engagement with marriage (cf. Dr Parturier's note in *C.G.*, Vol. XVII, pp. 67–8). Otherwise the young Englishwoman might conceivably be Emma Lagden, who was married in 1825 – save that all the evidence is that Mérimée was far more interested in Fanny than in her younger sister.   [15] *Correspondance*, Vol. II, p. 128.

The circumstances in which Mérimée heard of the impending marriage were particularly taxing to his self-control. A lady who thought he already knew about it said to him: 'You know that Julia Garnett is marrying Dr Pertz?' In a tone of utter indifference, Mérimée replied: 'No, indeed I didn't,' but at the same time he flushed so violently that those present thought he was about to have a fit.[16]

But consolation of a kind was not far away. Émilie Lacoste, whom he had met at Mme Davillier's in 1821, returned from America in the spring of 1827.[17] In the meantime, she had become the mistress of Joseph Bonaparte, Napoleon's elder brother, former King of Spain and her husband's patron in New Jersey, and had had a son in 1825, tactfully called Félix-Joseph to placate both the real and the putative fathers. When his business failed in 1826, Félix Lacoste, to the displeasure of both his wife and Joseph Bonaparte, decided to return to France, and Émilie had no option but to follow. By the end of 1827, she had given herself to Mérimée, who was blissfully unaware of her association with Joseph Bonaparte, and an ardent affair was soon in progress. However, in January 1828, Félix came across an unequivocal love letter from Mérimée to his wife, and, having first prudently ascertained that the lover's status and means were insufficient to allow him to draw the same sort of benefits as he had from his wife's adventures with Bonaparte, he challenged him to a duel. Young Prosper, ignorant both of Émilie's chequered past and of Félix's sordid cupidity, decided to be quixotic, and, when the duel took place, allowed his adversary to shoot him down without attempting to fire in reply. The result was a severely wounded left arm, which remained weak for some years, and an increasingly Don-Juanesque reputation. When Mérimée reappeared in his usual haunts towards the end of January 1828, he explained the fact that his arm was in a sling with his customary discretion: to some, he said he had fallen while getting out of a carriage,[18] to others, he

[16] The story is told by Paul Stapfer, son of Mérimée's friend Albert (cf. C.G., Vol. XVII, p. 68).

[17] Cf. the article quoted above by G. Girod de l'Ain; also P. Arbelet, Trois Solitaires, Paris, Gallimard, 1934, and A. Lelarge, 'Une Amie de Mérimée: Mme Lacoste', Bulletin de la Société de l'histoire de Paris et de l'Ile-de-France, fasc. 2, 1935.

[18] For instance, to Mme Ancelot: C.G., Vol. I, p. 23.

blandly (and truthfully) stated that the injury had been caused 'by a gentleman who didn't like my prose'.[19]

The incident brought Mérimée face to face with death for the first time. Nearly forty years later, he recalled standing by a moat while a 'frightful cuckold aimed at [him] a pistol which he handled with great skill'. But he was intrigued to find that his reaction was not fear, but worry lest he should 'fall in the shit, if you'll forgive my saying so, for the moat was full of it'.[20] Instead of putting an end to his affair with Émilie, the duel gave it a new lease of life. She refused to return to America with Lacoste, and remained Mérimée's mistress until somewhere about 1832, when the arrival of a new admirer caused her abruptly to dismiss him.[21] Their affair remained tempestuous throughout. Despite her frequent lapses from grace, Émilie was devout and spent much vain energy trying to convert Mérimée; echoes of this are perceptible in the relationship between Mergy and the pious but sensual Diane de Turgis in Mérimée's historical novel *Chronique du règne de Charles IX* (*Chronicle of the Reign of Charles IX*). Moreover, the impressionable Mérimée was not spared the torments of retrospective jealousy. When he first fell in love with Émilie, he knew nothing of her connections with Joseph Bonaparte, until a chance word dropped by a friend at dinner, and he then found himself in the invidious position of Saint-Clair in his story *Le Vase étrusque*, granted the lady's favours but violently jealous of her past.[22] It is small wonder that, at the height of his relations with Émilie, the amiable

[19] This is reported both by the Count d'Haussonville in *Prosper Mérimée. Hugh Elliott*, Paris, Calmann-Lévy, 1885, and by M. C. M. Simpson (quoting Mary Clarke) in *Many Memories of Many People*, London, Arnold, 1898, pp. 292–3. D'Haussonville adds that the husband asked in which arm Mérimée preferred to be hit, and that Mérimée replied: 'The left arm, if it's all the same to you.'

[20] *C.G.*, Vol. XIII, p. 59.

[21] The new admirer was Louis-Edmond Anthoine, to whom Mme Lacoste clandestinely bore a son in June 1833. The son was later to achieve fame as a novelist under the name Duranty, and Mérimée was often credited with his paternity. But it has been proved beyond doubt that Duranty was Anthoine's son (cf. M. Parturier and A. de Luppé, *La Naissance de Duranty* (*fin d'une légende*), Paris, Giraud-Badin, 1947; also M. Crouzet, *Un Méconnu du Réalisme: Duranty (1803–1880)*, Paris, Nizet, 1964).

[22] G. Girod de l'Ain, *art. cit.*

Mme Ancelot should have remarked slyly: 'M. Mérimée is the un-happiest happy man that I ever saw'.[23]

Clearly with M. Lacoste still alive, there could be no question of marriage, even assuming that either would have wanted it, which is doubtful. But before his arm was fully healed, Mérimée was trying his luck elsewhere, apparently with matrimonial intentions and once again in the Garnett salon. This time, it was a distinguished visitor who set his heart aflame: Mary Wollstonecraft Shelley. Well known as an author in her own right, as well as the daughter of one famous man and the widow of another, she came to Paris in April 1828 to see her friend Julia Robinson and perhaps also to give some lectures.[24] But she was immediately stricken with smallpox and forced to remain in bed for three weeks. Then she courageously decided to hasten her convalescence by appearing in society, and was taken to the Garnett salon by Fanny Wright, who had the previous year tried to enlist her support for emancipating negro slaves.[25] Though her illness did not leave her permanently scarred, it dimmed her usual radiance, and she was agreeably surprised to find herself the object of the pressing attentions of 'one of the cleverest men in France, young and a poet'.[26] So rapid and violent was the upsurge of his passion that before the end of May Mérimée had penned a burning declaration of love to her, probably including a proposal of marriage. But although Mary was not so devoted to the cult of her dead husband that she would neces-sarily have turned down a sufficiently brilliant match, she felt that neither Mérimée's constancy nor his resources were equal to his literary genius, and rejected him. His love letter was sent back to him with a firm but kindly note, couched in idiosyncratic French, in which she informed him that she was reluctant to keep evidence of feelings which he might later regret having expressed, and that he could always be sure of her friendship – so long as he showed himself worthy of it.[27]

[23] Doris Gunnell, *op. cit.*, p. 244.

[24] Cf. Mrs Julian Marshall, *The Life and Letters of Mary Wollstonecraft Shelley*, London, Bentley, 1889.   [25] *Ibid.*

[26] To Isabel Booth, on 16 June 1828: *The Letters of Mary W. Shelley*, ed. Frederick L. Jones, Norman, University of Oklahoma Press, 1944, Vol. I, p. 377. It is true that Mary does not name the young writer in question, but as we shall see, there are excellent reasons for thinking it to be Mérimée.

[27] The letter, without the name of the addressee, was first published by

Mary was undoubtedly flattered, and immediately on returning to England set about composing an article to celebrate his fame. This essay, full of high praise for *Clara Gazul* and *La Guzla*, of which three poems are reproduced in translation, appeared in *The Westminster Review* in January 1829.[28] In his turn, Mérimée must have been flattered that such a distinguished and beautiful lady should publicly have paid tribute to his 'spirit, originality, and fire', to his 'mind, imbued with grand and unsophisticated imagery', and even to 'the force of the genius' that he displays. But would Mary Shelley have noticed, had Mérimée not declared his love for her, that there ran throughout the rugged poems of *La Guzla* 'a vein of sweetness [. . .] that lends to each a particular charm'? Mérimée bore Mary no ill-will. She may even have been right in suspecting the permanence of his feelings for her; there was perhaps more dazzlement by her good looks, intelligence and reputation than genuine love in his declaration. They remained for some years in amicable correspondence and he may have

---

D. M. Healy, 'Mary Shelley and Prosper Mérimée', *Modern Language Review*, xxxvi, 3, July 1941. Cf. the same author's *Mérimée et les Anglais*, where the question is also discussed. But that Mérimée was the recipient was a supposition based on the presence of the original among the papers of Esprit Requien, Mérimée's autograph-hunting friend in Avignon, to whom Mérimée was known to have sent an autograph of Mary Shelley (*C.G.*, Vol. I, p. 386). When one reads this letter in the context of Mary's correspondence and articles, that supposition becomes a virtual certainty, since Mérimée is the only man she mentions meeting in Paris and since she clearly had the highest regard for his talents. Whether his declaration to her included a formal proposal of marriage is unclear from the terms of her reply, but it is by no means impossible.

[28] This article (cf. pp. 375–82) was not commissioned by the *Review*, but offered, in pressing terms, by Mary herself to Sir John Bowring, the editor (oddly enough, himself a victim of the *Guzla* hoax). On 11 June 1828 she wrote to him: 'I have also a request to make of you. You know and I believe think well of the two works the "Comedies of Clara Gazul" and the "Guzla" – Merrimée [*sic*], the author of these, is now bringing out another publication, which he will send me as soon as it is printed – I expect it daily – If I write an article on his works, will it prove acceptable to the W[estminster] R[eview]? – I should very much like so to do' (*Letters of Mary W. Shelley*, Vol. I, p. 376). Patently, Mary was at this time most enthusiastic about Mérimée.

called on her on one of his subsequent visits to England.[29] It is fascinating to speculate what progeny the inventors of *Frankenstein* and *La Vénus d'Ille* might have produced together, but their temperaments were in fact too far apart for any lasting relationship to have blossomed.

It may well be that the catalogue of Mérimée's sentimental disappointments in the late 1820s is still incomplete. There are hints of yet another distressing episode connected with the beginnings of one of the most significant if short-lived friendships in his life. In June 1825, Delécluze noted in his diary that, after dining at the Frères Provençaux, he had gone with Mérimée to present a copy of *Clara Gazul* to the singer Adélaïde Schiassetti, 'with whom, by the way, I think he is rather in love'.[30] But Mérimée was far from being the only young Parisian to have fallen for the celebrated contralto; one of her most lovelorn idolaters was Victor Jacquemont, a brilliant scientist and explorer whom Mérimée had met in curious and unpromising circumstances a few months previously.[31] Mérimée arrived one evening at either Gérard's or Delécluze's salon having stepped in some dirt; Jacquemont, who did not know him, unwisely made some humorous remark, and was astonished the next morning to receive a visit from Mérimée, accompanied by his seconds, and ready to fight a duel because of the imagined insult. But once Jacquemont had apologised, the susceptible Mérimée calmed down, and the two men became close friends – both were liberal and anticlerical, reserved and ironic, critical of official hypocrisy and artistic conformism, and stoical in the face which they showed to the rest of the world.

Jacquemont was so hopelessly smitten with the haughty Schiassetti that, after a year of vain but earnest attempts to win her favours, he was sent off to America by his parents so that he might forget her. Whether Mérimée was seriously attracted to her it is impossible to say; it would at any rate be wholly in accordance with his generous

[29] Mérimée mentions having received a lot of letters from Mary (*C.G.*, Vol. I, p. 386) and he certainly wrote to her several times – Mrs Marshall (*op. cit.*, Vol. II, p. 305) refers to letters which she had seen. Unfortunately, it has not been possible to trace any of these letters.

[30] *Journal*, p. 30.

[31] Cf. Pierre Maes, *Un Ami de Stendhal. Victor Jacquemont*, Paris, Desclée de Brouwer, 1936, pp. 127–32; also Pierre Josserand, 'Jacquemont et Mérimée', in *Jacquemont*, Muséum d'Histoire naturelle, 1959.

character to have withdrawn so as not to interfere with his friend's chances. Certainly Mérimée's admiration for Jacquemont's character and intellect was extreme; in later years, he was to say of him:

> Victor Jacquemont was one of the most remarkable men I ever met, the one who in my eyes came closest to the ideal of the Greek stoic, but amiable at the same time, and full of elegance and gaiety. Whenever I am in an awkward situation I always think of him and of the advice he might give me.[32]

The similarity of their temperaments is brought out in an article which Mérimée wrote near the end of his life.

> I never came across anyone with a more sensitive heart than Jacquemont. His was a loving and a tender nature, but he took as much trouble to hide his feelings as others do to disguise evil inclinations. In our youth, we had been shocked by the spurious sentimentality of Rousseau and his imitators, and there had come about a reaction which, as often happens, went too far. We wanted to be strong and we made fun of tearfulness. Perhaps Victor, without knowing it, was giving way to that tendency of his generation.[33]

In his innermost thoughts, Mérimée had much to contend with in the late 1820s: rejected by two women whom he wanted to marry, wounded in a duel over a third who continued to cause him torments of jealousy, possibly sacrificing his pretensions to a fourth in order not to offend a friend, his hypersensitive temperament was severely bruised. Yet none of this deterred him from pursuing his literary career.

After the success of *Clara Gazul* and *La Guzla*, he turned his attention to yet another genre, that of the 'historical scenes', practised with some success by Ludovic Vitet in *Les Barricades* and *Les États de Blois*, which were read at Delécluze's salon in 1826 and 1827. This hybrid form consisted of historical subjects treated in sequences of dialogue, but much more episodically than in a regular drama, and without any thought of stage performance. Mérimée's preference fell on the fourteenth-century peasants' revolt in Northern France, and after reading Froissart and later historians, he proceeded to write *La Jaquerie* early in 1828. This time, he made only the most perfunctory attempt to conceal his identity, signing himself 'the author of the *Théâtre de*

[32] *C.G.*, Vol. XIII, p. 698.
[33] *Portraits historiques et littéraires*, p. 104.

Clara Gazul', and publicised the work in advance by giving a reading to a group of friends including Stendhal and Jacquemont, now returned from his American voyage, and allowing a scene to appear in the *Revue trimestrielle* in April 1828. The volume itself was published in the summer; it also included *La Famille de Carvajal* and was probably the outstanding book printed by Balzac during his disastrous venture into publishing. The critics received it respectfully, but with manifest reservations: *La Jaquerie* was generally felt to be diffuse and disconnected, while *La Famille de Carvajal* shocked nearly everyone by the scabrousness of its theme.

Still, Mérimée was only experimenting, and *La Jaquerie*, with its overt imitation of Scott, Shakespeare and Goethe's *Götz von Berlichingen*, had at least revealed to him the rich resources to be derived from the imaginative exploitation of history. So he next moved on, like so many of his contemporaries, to the historical novel, and, before the year was out, was well advanced in the composition of what he called, with his usual self-deprecatory flippancy, 'a bad novel that bores me stiff, but that I want to finish because I have a lot of other ideas in my head'.[34] In fact, *1572, Chronique du temps de Charles IX*, as it was first called, was his most ambitious work to date, necessitating considerable historical research and obviously being planned and written with some care. Stendhal, perhaps surprisingly, disliked it when he read the manuscript in December 1828, and told his friend, with savage frankness, that neither *La Guzla* nor *La Jaquerie* had been up to the standard of *Clara Gazul* and that he would consequently be well advised to forget all about the novel for a year – too summary, too casually written, insufficiently logical, lacking in tenderness.[35] But Mérimée – who had been just as ruthless in his criticisms of Stendhal's *Armance*[36] and was to be even more harsh about *Le Rouge et le Noir*[37] – was not put off by

[34] *C.G.*, Vol. I, p. 33.   [35] *Correspondance*, Vol. II, pp. 152–4.

[36] On 23 December 1826, Stendhal wrote at length to reply to Mérimée's criticisms (*Correspondance*, Vol. II, pp. 96–9). But Mérimée's original letter is lost, and all that remains is a fragment of a later letter written some time in 1827 (*C.G.*, Vol. I, p. 20).

[37] 'In Julien's character there are some revolting features which everyone recognises as accurate but by which they are horrified. It is not the object of art to show that side of human nature. Remember Swift's portrait and the awful line with which it ends: *But Delia pisses and Delia shits*. Agreed, but

these misgivings, and had the novel published in the spring of 1829. It created much more of a stir than *La Jaquerie* had done, and elicited high praise from eminent critics: Sainte-Beuve wrote to an acquaintance that 'Mérimée, [. . .] who is a great friend of mine, has published a delightful book, half novel and half chronicle, on the Court of Charles IX',[38] and even Stendhal relented far enough to admit that it was 'full of Voltairean wit'.[39] American and German translations appeared almost at once,[40] and there were regular re-editions throughout Mérimée's lifetime.

Mérimée's situation in the literary world was by now an enviable one. One critic saluted him as 'the Mazeppa of an army of which M. Hugo is the Charles XII',[41] and Hugo himself somewhat fulsomely dedicated one of his books to him in these terms: 'To M. Prosper Mérimée, the master of us all'.[42] Although he was avowedly Stendhal's disciple, he was rapidly extending his friendships on the Hugolian side of the movement. Hugo himself he had known for some years, having been one of those favoured in 1829 with an invitation to be present at a reading of *Marion Delorme*, after which, forthright as usual, he had remarked that it served Didier right to be killed, having been so hard on the unfortunate Marion.[43] Though he mistrusted the great man's lyrical pomp, he was for the time being ready to make common cause with him against the Classicists, and helped to recruit Romantic troops for the first night of *Hernani*. Occasionally he dined with the Hugo family at their home, and won great credit by producing a dish of *macaroni à l'italienne* when asked to show off the culinary talents of which he

---

why say so? You are full of odious truths of that sort' (*C.G.*, Vol. I, pp. 83–4). A few months later, Mérimée accused him of having written about an impossible character (*C.G.*, Vol. I, p. 89).

[38] Sainte-Beuve, *Correspondance générale*, ed. J. Bonnerot, Paris, Stock, 1935, Vol. I, p. 128.

[39] *Correspondance*, Vol. II, p. 165.

[40] The German translation was published by Cotta in 1829 (P. Trahard and P. Josserand, *Bibliographie des œuvres de Prosper Mérimée*, Paris, Champion, 1929, p. 43). The American translation is mentioned by Mérimée in 1830 (*C.G.*, Vol. XVI, p. 13).

[41] Charles Magnin, in *Le Globe*, 30 May 1830.

[42] R. Baschet, *Mérimée*, p. 49.

[43] Sainte-Beuve, *Correspondance générale*, Vol. I, p. 251.

was proud.[44] On another evening Hugo introduced him to Liszt; in return, Mérimée took Hugo to the Clarke salon. He also got on well with Sainte-Beuve; the two men understood each other, sharing many of the same strengths and weaknesses of character – some of Sainte-Beuve's articles on Mérimée are among the most penetrating and judicious criticism of his works ever written.[45] As for Musset, he was a regular member of the group with whom Mérimée went out wining, dining and whoring, but he also impressed the older man by his precocious literary talent: Mérimée was one of those present at Musset's reading from the *Contes d'Espagne et d'Italie* on Christmas Eve 1829,[46] and alone among the young poet's friends encouraged him when another reading of his plays fell flat in 1832.[47] Only the aloof Vigny and the pious Lamartine seem at this time to have had little contact with Mérimée.

Whether it was out of a genuine desire to bring about a rapproche-ment between the leaders of the two main Romantic factions, or merely out of a mischievous delight in trying to mix two incompatible temperaments, Mérimée even saw fit to invite Hugo and Stendhal to dine together at his parents' flat in January 1830. Sainte-Beuve, who was present, has left an amusing account of the two men spend-ing hours in exploring their reciprocal antipathy, 'on the defensive, like two stray cats from opposing alleys, their fur bristling and taking in-finite precautions before sheathing their claws'.[48] Though Stendhal a few weeks later joined Mérimée at the premiere of *Hernani*, he was unimpressed, complaining the next day that the play and the cham-pagne he had drunk had given him indigestion.[49] Mérimée, who can scarcely have hoped that Hugo and Stendhal would unite in a marriage of true minds, was amused by their hostile incomprehension of each

[44] *Victor Hugo raconté par un témoin de sa vie*, Vol. II, p. 238.

[45] There is a brilliant summing-up of Mérimée's literary character in the article Sainte-Beuve wrote for *Le Globe* in January 1830 (cf. *Les Grands Ecrivains français. XIXe siècle. Les Romanciers*, Vol. II, ed. Maurice Allem, Paris, Garnier, 1927).

[46] Paul de Musset, *Biographie d'Alfred de Musset*, Paris, Charpentier, 1877, p. 91.

[47] P. de Musset, *op. cit.*, p. 109.

[48] A. Billy, *Sainte-Beuve. Sa vie et son temps*, Paris, Flammarion, Vol. I, p. 122.

[49] Henri Martineau, *Le Cœur de Stendhal*, Paris, Michel, 1952, Vol. II, p. 152.

other, but continued to prefer the novelist's astringent lucidity to the poet's grandiose visions.

1829 and 1830 were productive years for Mérimée. In addition to *Chronique du règne de Charles IX*, he began publishing the short stories for which he is best known today; he added several new poems to *La Guzla*; he wrote *Le Carrosse du Saint Sacrement* and *L'Occasion*. He was one of the coming men whom travellers in Paris were most eager to meet. Lady Morgan, for instance, the Irish novelist, regarded him as the most charming conversationalist she encountered there: 'Easy, simple, gay, humorous, and natural, indifferent to, or unconscious of, his superior talent, speaking many modern languages, and knowing all well – Mérimée is an epitome of the European youth of the present day.'[50] Such was his prestige that the detested Mme Récamier decided that he ought to be given a post in the diplomatic corps (which was probably already his secret ambition) and in October 1829 persuaded the Duc de Laval, who was about to leave for London as Ambassador, to offer to take Mérimée with him. But Mérimée felt that his freedom as a militant liberal and as a quasi-polemical writer would be compromised if he accepted such a post under the reactionary régime of Charles X, and he declined, citing, somewhat maliciously, the example of Chateaubriand, who had just resigned his ambassadorial post because the government was too liberal![51] Mérimée's patience was to be rewarded in 1830 when he was able to demonstrate his consistent loyalty to the ideas for which the new constitutional monarchy of Louis-Philippe stood.

But these successes were not enough to compensate for the increasing disarray of his private life. After the dashing of his hopes with Adélaïde Schiassetti, with Julia Garnett, and with Mary Shelley, Mérimée was approaching one of the bitterest disappointments he was ever to experience. One of the neighbours of the Mérimée family in the rue des Petits-Augustins was a celebrated physician and author of medical treatises, Dr François-Joseph Double, who had a daughter named Mélanie, slightly younger than Prosper. Mélanie appears to have attracted him from about 1825, to judge by a letter written in 1828, in which Stendhal, the great authority on love, solemnly pronounces his diagnosis on the young man's case and advises him to make Mélanie

[50] Lady Morgan, *France in 1829-30*, London, Saunders & Otley, 1830, pp. 24-5.   [51] *C.G.*, Vol. I, p. 51.

jealous. 'Jealousy only kills love in the cold and despairing heart of someone aged forty. This jealousy will etch your name for ever in M's heart. The crystallisation may be slow. You can hasten it by six months (+ or —) if you say to her: "I have worshipped you for three years, but my income is only 1,700 francs and I cannot marry you. I didn't want to die mad." No more and no less. Leave her heart to do the rest.'[52] Evidently these tactics were either not put into practice or failed to work. At all events, there was such a social and financial barrier between the Doubles and the Mérimées that soundings in view of a possible engagement came to nothing: Dr Double wanted his daughter's future husband to have a settled position in society as well as substantial wealth.[53] When at the beginning of 1830 it became clear to Mérimée that he had not the slightest prospect of gaining the consent of Mélanie's parents, his first reaction was to try to persuade her to elope with him.[54] Then he was overcome by scruples about his own motives and about the sacrifices which he would be imposing on the girl – perhaps in this he was influenced by the sorry example of his friend Édouard Grasset who in January 1830 had fled to London with Mary de Neuville, niece of an ex-minister, only to see her returning to Paris, disillusioned and humiliated, a month later. Torn between love for Mélanie and anxiety about its consequences, in the end he said nothing to her, but suffered immeasurably at his renunciation – so much so that his father and mother got together enough money to enable him to make a prolonged trip to Spain, which he had long wanted to visit.

Mérimée's attitude over this affair is not without nobility, even if a man of more spontaneous character might simply have spoken up

[52] *Correspondance*, Vol. II, p. 153. Stendhal only uses the initial M., but it seems reasonable to assume that he is referring to Mélanie, given that the question of Mérimée's income being too small to permit a marriage is exactly what caused the break with Mélanie. H. Martineau's identification of Stendhal's M. with Mme Lacoste is untenable: M. was not her initial, by December 1828 she was already his mistress anyway, and there could be no question of marrying her since her husband was still very much alive.

[53] Cf. what Dr Parturier says in his edition of the *Romans et nouvelles*, Vol. I, p. ix.

[54] The letter to Jenny Dacquin referred to in the next note is clearly alluding to the idea of an elopement: Mérimée talks about the girl having to give up everything in exchange for his affection.

and taken the risk of later complications. In the discreet account of the episode which he later gave to Jenny Dacquin, there is a resigned sadness which shows how profoundly it had scarred him.

> I couldn't fall in love again, because my illusions have brought me so many *desengaños* on love. I was about to fall in love when I left for Spain. It was one of the good deeds of my life. The person who was responsible for my journey never knew anything about it. If I had stayed here, I might have done something very stupid; to a woman worthy of all the happiness possible on earth, in return for the loss of everything she held dear, I would have offered an affection which I knew myself to be inferior to the sacrifice she would have had to make. You remember my motto: 'Anything can be excused by love, but one must be absolutely sure that love really is there.'[55]

So on 27 June, Mérimée set off for Spain, charged by his father with investigating Spanish museums on his behalf and financed by the money his father had earned by inventing a cartridge-paper for naval use.[56] Mélanie, ignorant of the silent conflict which she had provoked in his heart, remained in Paris and two years later married a lawyer called Athénodore Collin. But twenty years later, Mérimée's chivalrous devotion to her was to cause a second crisis in his life when he resolved to spring to the defence of her second husband, the notorious Libri.

On his way to Spain, Mérimée stopped at Bordeaux to visit Léon de Laborde, member of an old and distinguished family of bankers under the *ancien régime*, and for the time being an officer before becoming a diplomat, archaeologist and art historian. Laborde was greatly impressed by Mérimée's wit and erudition.[57] From there Mérimée went

---

[55] *C.G.*, Vol. I, p. 184. Mérimée is too reticent to name the woman, and there has been much speculation about her identity. Of all the possible candidates, Mélanie seems by far the most likely. Mérimée could not marry her because her parents objected, but could easily have considered persuading her to elope with him, being deterred by the fact that she would have lost all that her father's wealth had accustomed her to. The tone of high respect scarcely accords with what Mérimée must by then have known about Émilie Lacoste, who in any case had a husband already. Moreover, by 1830 he either was or had been in love with her; he certainly was not on the point of falling in love. The only other person of whom one might think is Fanny Lagden, but there is no reason for believing that there was any special crisis in her relations with Mérimée in 1830.

[56] *C.G.*, Vol. IX, pp. 5–6.   [57] *C.G.*, Vol. I, p. 69, n. 2.

on to cross the frontier, not without some slight apprehension lest his reputation as a dangerous radical should cause him to end up inside a Spanish gaol. His progress through Spain was leisurely and discursive. Both for his own sake and in order to assist his father's researches on painting, he visited as many museums as he could, taking notes as he went. But of more interest to him than either the landscape or the art were the people themselves. Indeed, he must in later years have been somewhat embarrassed at the vehemence with which he had disavowed any interest in archaeology: 'Antiquities, especially Roman antiquities, leave me cold [. . .] I have no set aim in my travels; I am no antiquary.'[58] He rapidly decided that he had a natural affinity with the raw energy of the lower classes in Spain and took every opportunity to frequent them.

Among those with whom the hazards of travel brought him into contact was a Spaniard who had been a guerilla lieutenant and who, suspicious of the politeness of a countryman, had had him strung up from the nearest tree in case he should be a spy.[59] On another occasion, on the road between Granada and Baylen, Mérimée and his guide struck up an acquaintance with a man who turned out to be a convict on parole; they all drank wine out of the same goatskin, and Mérimée paid tribute to the convict's courtesy and friendliness.[60] His great hope was to meet a real brigand, but though he never tired of listening to tales about bandits and smugglers, especially the famous José-Maria, the nearest he got to them was when his coach was stopped near Ecija by a ferocious-looking band of armed men, who however proved to be only the local farmers on their way to market.[61]

Local customs and superstitions excited him just as much as the picturesque inhabitants. On an excursion to Murviedro, on foot and in scorching sunshine, he was much intrigued when his Valencian guide refused to go with him into a wayside inn for a drink of water and a plate of gazpacho, served by an attractive dark-skinned girl called Carmencita. After they had set off again, all the guide would say was: 'A bad house!'

'Bad! Why? The gazpacho was excellent.'

[58] Mosaïque, ed. Eugène Marsan, Paris, Le Divan, 1930, p. 332.
[59] P. Mérimée, Histoire du règne de Pierre le Grand, ed. Henri Mongault and Maurice Parturier, Paris, Conard, 1947, pp. 303–4.
[60] Mosaïque, pp. 304–8.   [61] Ibid., pp. 312–14.

'That's not surprising; it may have been the devil who made it.'

'The devil? Do you say that because she puts too much pepper in it, or has the good woman hired the devil as a cook?'

'Who knows?'

'So . . . she's a witch?'[62]

The picture of the raven-haired beauty with the sinister reputation was to remain with Mérimée for many years until it eventually assumed literary form in *Carmen*. In Valencia, Mérimée watched the public hanging of a condemned man. As usual, his curiosity was directed as much to the reactions of the spectators as to the principal events, but he was first moved by the splendour and solemnity of the religious ritual surrounding the gruesome act: 'in truth, I like these Catholic ceremonies, and I wish I believed in them'.[63] In one of the four *Letters from Spain* which he sent back for publication in the French press, the moment of the execution is described with remarkable virtuosity:

> I heard a soft voice beside me say *Amen* with feeling; I turned round and saw one of my pretty Valencian lady friends with the blood mounting to her cheeks and her fan fluttering wildly. She was staring attentively at the scaffold. I looked in the same direction: the monk was coming down the steps, and the condemned man was hanging in the air, with the hangman clinging to his shoulders and the assistant pulling on his feet.[64]

No one but Mérimée could have presented the awesome climax to the spectacle with such precise and succinct baldness, which is far more effective in its simplicity than all the rhetoric of Hugo's *Dernier Jour d'un condamné* (*Last Day of a Condemned Man*).

Some of his other distractions during the three weeks he spent in Valencia were of a more cheerful kind. 'I had four girls on active service, all four called Vicenta, St Vincent being the town's patron saint. So as not to get mixed up, I had Vicenta 1 and Vicenta 2, then Vicentita 1 and Vicentita 2, an easy classification to remember.' He was favourably impressed by the low cost of a pretty girl of fifteen; even a guaranteed virgin, so he said, cost only 42 francs.[65]

Bull-fights naturally exercised a particular fascination over a man so preoccupied with savagery and human attitudes towards it. To begin

---

[62] *Mosaïque*, pp. 338–9.

[63] *Ibid.*, p. 298.

[64] *Ibid.*, p. 302.

[65] *C.G.*, Vol. XVI, p. 89.

with, Mérimée was worried lest his own softheartedness should betray him:

> The first time I went to the arena at Madrid, I was afraid that I would be unable to stand the sight of the blood so freely spilt there; above all, I feared that my sensitive temperament, in which I had no confidence, would make me ridiculous in the eyes of the hardened devotees who had given me a seat in their box.[66]

But he soon took to it with enthusiasm:

> Now I feel ineffable pleasure when I see a bull stuck with darts, a horse disembowelled, or a man sent sprawling. At one of the last bull-fights in Madrid, I shocked everyone. I have been told, but I can hardly believe it, that what I applauded so furiously was not the matador, but the bull, as he tossed man and horse on his horns.[67]

Mérimée's excitement was due in part to the fact that bull-fighting combines the high emotions of tragedy with the authenticity of what is real as opposed to what is invented. He twice makes the point explicitly. 'No tragedy in the world had ever gripped me so much', he says,[68] and later relates an anecdote about the actor Maiquez insulting a matador who had hesitated in the presence of the bull; 'You see, Señor Maiquez,' the matador replied, 'here it's not all make-believe like it is on the stage.'[69]

Mérimée's most significant meeting occurred when he found himself sharing a stagecoach[70] with a middle-aged Spanish aristocrat, an ex-officer of liberal persuasion who lost his right eye fighting in Napoleon's armies, had had his left arm maimed at Trafalgar and had also suffered a wound in his right leg. This was Don Cipriano Guzman Palafox y Portocarrero, Count of Teba, currently in disgrace after becoming involved in the purges following the 1823 restoration of the Bourbons. He took to his young travelling companion, who shared his political opinions and who no doubt reminded him of the years he

---

[66] *Mosaïque*, p. 259.
[67] *C.G.*, Vol. I, p. 72.
[68] *Mosaïque*, p. 259.
[69] *Ibid.*, p. 278.
[70] On the road between Granada and Madrid, rather than the opposite direction, as Harold Kurtz says in his otherwise impeccable account of the incident in *The Empress Eugénie*, London, Hamilton, 1964, p. 13. After Don Cipriano's banishment came to an end in 1830, the family left Granada and resumed residence in Madrid in the Calle del Sordo, until they moved to the Montijo house in 1836.

had spent as Colonel Portocarrero bearing arms in the service of the French, with the result that Mérimée was invited to his home in the Calle del Sordo to meet the Countess and their two daughters Paca and Eugenia, aged five and four respectively.

Manuela, his wife, was a handsome, strong-willed woman of Scottish and Belgian parentage, intelligent, cultured, ambitious and ill-reconciled to the obscure position to which her husband was relegated, while his elder brother, the Count of Montijo and a loyal supporter of the Bourbons, lorded it in luxury in Madrid. She and Mérimée at once became firm friends, without there ever being any danger of their falling in love. Some time later, he affirmed to Stendhal – and why should one not believe him, since he was much more inclined to overstate than understate his amatory exploits? – that 'she is a wonderful friend, but there has never been any question of sex between us'.[71] Mérimée even got on well with the two little girls, to whom he started giving French lessons; like many confirmed bachelors, he was an ideal avuncular figure, constantly keeping his small friends entertained, treating them with unpatronising comradeship, and effortlessly winning their lasting affection. Thus began one of the most durable friendships of Mérimée's life, destined one day, when Eugenia had become Empress of France, to work a complete transformation in his existence and providing him with a constant fund of kindly feeling on which he never called in vain.

Mérimée spent about six months in Spain in 1830, travelling right across the country from north to south, and then over to the east coast, with two spells in the capital. Though the journey brought him a continual enrichment of his artistic experience, his knowledge of human nature, his delight in exotic places and customs, his devotion to friendship, it did not wholly cure him of the pessimism which had settled on him like a black cloud after his disappointments in love. In 1831, Stendhal referred to him as 'the profound and gloomy Mérimée',[72] and on another occasion dubbed him 'the melancholy young man',[73] and there is no doubt that he had resolved never again to expose himself to the agonising rebuffs and uncertainties of attempted marriage. Already accustomed to putting on a show of sardonic superiority,

[71] *C.G.*, Vol. II, p. 60.   [72] *Correspondance*, Vol. II, p. 205.

[73] Count J.-N. Primoli, 'L'Enfance d'une souveraine', *Revue des Deux Mondes*, 15 octobre 1923.

he now accentuated his cynicism and treated women as objects of mockery, as prospective mistresses, or at best as companions and confidantes. Marriage was never mentioned save to revile it as a repellent and embarrassing institution, and the habits of debauchery contracted in the 1820s became for a time an obsessive necessity, as if the image of an ideal love could only be forgotten by degrading it and trampling on it. For some years at least, and perhaps even permanently, his character had been coarsened by repeated disillusionment; there is a hint of desperation in the wild life of pleasure into which he plunged on his return to France, in the frightening obscenity of some of his letters and conversations, in the biting misanthropy of his attitudes.

But in his absence, political changes had occurred which completely altered his situation and prospects in other ways. Not long after his departure, the increasingly autocratic behaviour of Charles X had culminated in his notorious 'Ordonnances', which provoked the 'three glorious days' of July 1830 which saw his overthrow and the installation on the throne of Louis-Philippe, King of the French people rather than of France and pledged to govern according to a constitutional charter. This at last was the liberal régime for which Mérimée and his friends had so long been clamouring, and there was every chance that, as one of the most brilliant young men of his generation, he would be given that post in diplomacy or in government service which he coveted. His friends, notably Mme Ancelot, were afraid that his absence abroad might harm his interests,[74] but Mérimée, with a dandyish display of indifference, declined to hasten his return, complaining only that he had been deprived of an interesting spectacle: 'I cannot get over having missed a show that is only put on every few centuries. I have missed two performances now, one because I was born slightly too late, the other (a charity performance specially for us) because of this unfortunate trip to Spain.'[75]

[74] In Stendhal, *Correspondance*, Vol. II, p. 852. But perhaps by talking about the dangers Mérimée would run by staying in Spain, she means hostility to liberal Frenchmen from Spanish reactionaries.

[75] *C.G.*, Vol. I, p. 71.

Chapter 5

Historical Novelist

> ... remarquons seulement à quelles absurdes et dégoûtantes
> exagérations s'abaissent les hommes dans leurs querelles
> religieuses.
>
> 'Les Mormons', *Études anglo-américaines*

La Jaquerie (the usual spelling is *Jacquerie*, but Mérimée's version is an uncommon alternative rather than a mistake by Balzac's type-setter) has not found much favour with critics. Even the author's friends were lukewarm: Stendhal regarded it as a falling-off from *Le Théâtre de Clara Gazul*, and Mary Shelley complained that 'we feel the want of one prominent character to concentrate the interest'.[1] Lack of plot and unity, dispersal of interest, characters who are little better than types, excess of melodramatic devices, crudeness and confusion of local colour, inaccuracy of historical background – these are but a few of the reproaches heaped on a work which has only rarely been reprinted since 1828. Yet when one reads it nowadays, it is strangely fresh in its appeal; that it has shortcomings is undeniable, but taken for what it is, it is more successful than some of Mérimée's detractors – and even some of his supporters – are inclined to allow.

La Jaquerie bears the subtitle *Scènes féodales* (*Feudal Scenes*) and this indicates the way in which he proposed to handle his investigation of the fourteenth-century peasants' revolt in Northern France. Following on the vogue for Scott's novels, for Shakespeare's chronicle plays, for the picturesque evocation of the past by historians like Barante, Mérimée's aim was to make a violent and critical period of French history come alive in the mind's eye of his readers – since there was never any question of staging this sequence of thirty-six separate scenes, with its immense cast, its surging battles, its decapitations and mutilations, and its broad sweep over time and space. Encouraged by the example of Vitet and of Dittmer and Cavé (the authors of the

---

[1] *Art. cit.*

popular *Soires de Neuilly*), he wanted to use dialogue form not so much for specifically dramatic purposes as to give a greater sense of immediacy to the unfolding of a historical perspective. This is why he declines to allow a single figure or group of figures to dominate his pictures; sometimes we follow the fortunes of Frère Jean, the plebeian monk who agrees to lead the revolt when he fails to gain election as abbot of his monastery, sometimes we are more concerned with the unfortunate Pierre, educated above his station and languishing with unrequited love for the lady of the castle, sometimes we even find ourselves sympathising with d'Apremont, the local lord who, cruel and unfeeling though he may be towards his serfs, nevertheless displays in adversity a stoical courage and a respect for the laws of chivalry which are far from despicable. If any one of these characters were visibly to become the hero, we should see these scenes as a play, whereas they are meant as an imaginative re-creation of history.

For the same reason, Mérimée evolves a technique of character formation which was to stand him in good stead in the *Chronique du règne de Charles IX* and later in *Colomba*: that of envisaging individual psychology above all as the embodiment of the main features of a given time or country. The active, practical, earthy Frère Jean and the pious, unworldly abbot represent two aspects of the medieval clergy. The brutal, ignorant but courageous d'Apremont, his sadistic son Conrad, his haughty and beautiful daughter Isabelle and her coarse fiancé Montreuil stand for the nobility, blinded by prejudice, shackled by rigid rules and customs, scarcely aware that the peasants are human. The peasantry have as their spokesmen the honest Simon, the vengeful Renaud, the cowardly Morand, the drunken Gaillon, pushed beyond endurance by the harsh rapacity of their masters, capable of bravery as well as savagery when they rise in defence of their lives but too stupid and selfish to see where their true interests lie, and eager only to get back to the harvest once their immediate objectives are attained. Then there are those who stand for the disruptive forces outside the feudal system: the so-called Werewolf, the ex-blacksmith who has taken to the woods with a band of ravening outlaws, Siward and Brown, the English soldiers of fortune, ready to sell their swords to the highest bidder until hostilities between England and France are resumed. It was not Mérimée's intention that these people should emerge as rounded individuals; the function of each is to have sufficient character to distinguish him as a human being while primarily embodying one or other of the forces at work in a particular historical situation. No doubt a Shakespeare or a Scott can achieve both aims simultaneously; Mérimée does not rise to those heights, but he does present a singularly clear and convincing picture of a historical process in motion.

As for the interpretation of history itself, Mérimée was, for his time, reasonably well documented on what remains an obscure episode. He had read Froissart, Buchon's *Chroniques*, Lacurne de Sainte-Palaye's *Mémoires sur l'ancienne chevalerie* and other historians,[2] and though he undertook no research of his own he could justifiably feel that his knowledge of the subject was a thorough one. It is however true that in the *Jaquerie* he made no effort to keep strictly to known historical fact: all the characters and most of the places mentioned are fictitious, and there is no reference to such important figures as Guillaume Karle, the main leader of the *Jacques*, or Étienne Marcel, who at first fostered their rebellion as a means of increasing his own power. With the information in his possession, Mérimée could undoubtedly have been more accurate, in terms of facts, than he was; but instead he chose invention. The reason for this deviation probably lies in the compromise which historical fiction always forces on its practitioners. The following year, in the *Chronique*, Mérimée was to show himself well aware of the dangers of centring a historical romance on well-known characters, rightly preferring the freedom of invented figures and sniping mercilessly at Vigny for having adopted a different system in *Cinq-Mars*. In *La Jaquerie*, he consequently deals exclusively with people who, because he can mould them to his will, more clearly exemplify what he regarded as the outstanding traits of the whole revolt. The verisimilitude of the general colouring takes precedence over particular detail, and in that respect, Mérimée's understanding of what the Jacquerie involved seems lucid and convincing.

In choosing that moment of French history, he was of course once again demonstrating his radicalism. Under the reactionary monarchy of Charles X, to give a sympathetic analysis of the uprising of the lower classes against the oppression of the clergy and the nobility was the act of a militant liberal. Mérimée's picture of the savagery, the ignorance, the lawlessness, the corruption of the Middle Ages stands in deliberate

[2] Cf. Trahard, *La Jeunesse de Prosper Mérimée*, Vol. I, pp. 297–335.

and violent contrast to the idealised image of medieval piety, courtliness and feudal virtue propagated by Chateaubriand and the devotees of the 'troubadour style'; he declares uncompromisingly in his preface: 'I have tried to give an impression of the horrifying *mores* of the fourteenth century, and I believe that I have lightened rather than darkened the colours of my picture.'[3] Never one to allow illusions to subsist unchallenged (especially when they ran counter to his own opinions), Mérimée takes a positive pleasure in emphasising the greed of the clergy, the cruelty of the nobles, the poltroonery of the middle classes. Yet he has too sombre a view of human nature to allow his work to degenerate into a propaganda exercise on behalf of the victims of tyranny. The peasants may have a just cause, but their behaviour is ferocious, inconsistent, cowardly, undisciplined, naïve and confused; it is inevitable that they should in the end be betrayed, outwitted and defeated. When the English soldier Brown exclaims with disgust: 'That's what all these Frenchmen are like. They're always complaining and they never have the courage to set themselves free',[4] one may well hear Mérimée speaking directly to his fellow-countrymen in 1828; but when one sees the eventual fate of the revolt, one realises that Mérimée had too little faith in the quality of the masses to believe that revolution could lead to anything but chaos and suffering.

La Jaquerie is no masterpiece, but like everything Mérimée wrote, it is remarkably readable, and it contains a salutary dose of realism about a period which his contemporaries were all too liable to idealise. Moreover, it combines two qualities not often found conjoined. On the one hand, by its concentration on details, short scenes, intimate events, numerous characters, it brings the reader into immediate contact with the life of the Middle Ages in its most concrete form: its directness makes us relive the tragic adventures of the revolt as if we had been there. On the other hand, its discreet use of types imperceptibly makes us aware of what social and other forces lay behind the rebellion of 1358, and at the same time presents us with a characteristically grim and unadorned vision of humanity. It has the strong, harsh flavour of much of Mérimée's most effective writing, and it deserves a more honourable place than it is usually given.

If *La Jaquerie* is often underrated, there is little danger of the same

[3] *La Jaquerie*, ed. E. Marsan, Paris, Le Divan, 1928, p. 3.
[4] *Ibid.*, p. 39.

happening to the *Chronique du règne de Charles IX*. It has always been one of Mérimée's most popular works; translated into German within months of its publication,[5] more than once used as an opera libretto,[6] it ran through several editions during its author's lifetime and has never been out of print since – it has even survived being prescribed for generations as a school text. Critics are not entirely of one mind about its merits (they rarely are with anything Mérimée wrote); one would see it as his masterpiece,[7] another as the greatest French historical novel of the Romantic period,[8] while some are displeased by its structure, its style or its attitudes.[9] But few would be prepared to dismiss it as negligible, and hardly anyone could fail to derive pleasure from reading it.

In conception, it springs from the same area of interest as *La Jaquerie*: the imaginative recreation of history in the wake of Sir Walter Scott. But the semi-dramatic form of the earlier work is now abandoned in favour of full-scale narrative fiction. Superficially this might betoken a movement nearer to the pattern of the Waverley Novels; in fact, Mérimée, who was already beginning to look askance at the Scottish author's talent, only adopts what appeals to him and ostentatiously rejects the rest. Like Scott he bases his story on solid and minutely documented historical fact; like Scott, he is careful to assign only subsidiary roles to well-known historical figures; like Scott, he aims to give a vivid and convincing picture of the inner and outer life of a distant period; like Scott, he makes his dialogue as rich, as varied and as realistic as he can. The resemblance stops there, and Mérimée takes care that we should notice where he differs. In an interpolated *Dialogue between the Reader and the Author*, he makes fun of the over-elaborate portraits and interminable descriptions in which Scott and some of his imitators indulge, and suggests that anyone who wants to know what Charles IX looked like should go and inspect his bust in the Angoulême

[5] Cf. p. 74.   [6] Notably for Hérold's *Le Pré aux clercs*.

[7] Maurice Rat, in his introduction to an edition of the *Chronique* (Paris, Garnier, 1949).

[8] Louis Maigron, *Le Roman historique à l'époque romantique*, Paris, Champion, 1912.

[9] E.g. Eugène Marsan, in the preface to his edition of the *Chronique* (Paris, Le Divan, 1928), and Trahard, *La Jeunesse de Prosper Mérimée*, Vol. II, pp. 10–62.

Museum. He avoids philosophising and moralising, which is all the more notable a feat as the subject would have lent itself to the sort of discursive generalisation to which Scott is prone. And there is no need to point out that his view of passion is much earthier than Scott's. Above all, the speed of his narration is far greater than the sedate progress of Scott's massive volumes. The result is that the *Chronique* is as picturesque and evocative as anything Scott wrote, but with the additional virtues of a more realistic picture of humanity, a more impartial attitude, and a much increased liveliness of tone and pace.

That Mérimée should have chosen to build his novel around the Massacre of St Bartholomew's Day in 1572 is entirely typical. In the first place, it was a favourite topic for liberal and anti-Catholic authors under the rule of Charles X, and though Mérimée successfully resisted the temptation to make a propaganda piece out of it, his work is clearly intended to remind his contemporaries of the dangers of fanaticism and religious persecution (one of the most controversial pieces of legislation enacted under Charles X provided that anyone guilty of sacrilege might have his hand cut off). Moreover the *Chronique* follows *La Jaquerie* in examining, with fascinated horror, the peculiar savagery inherent in civil war. Already Mérimée seems to have had premonitions of that dread of violent strife within France which, after 1848, was to make him such a staunch upholder of the Second Empire as the only bulwark against chaos. Nothing is more effective in the *Chronique* than the grisly account of the mass slaughter of 24 August 1572, its hideous aftermath, and the subsequent resumption of the Wars of Religion, and Mérimée is undoubtedly, if reticently, moved by this appalling spectacle.

Most of all, his choice of subject is symptomatic of a growing preoccupation with the sixteenth century as a time when men were less afraid to be themselves than in the modern era. This preoccupation was fostered by his friendship with Stendhal, who regarded the Renaissance, especially in Italy, as one of the most attractive periods in history. According to Stendhal, passions ran high, and crime was consequently rife; but men were filled with a vigour and a confidence which produced greatness and which have sadly atrophied under the pressure of conformist civilisation. Mérimée was much less sure of his ground. Allured by the frankness and the vitality of the sixteenth-century mind, he was disturbed by the violence which accompanied it, and constantly debated with himself – as no doubt with Stendhal – the question of whether it would or would not have been preferable to live three centuries earlier. The issue is raised, rather tentatively, in the preface: 'I find it intriguing to compare this way of life with our own and to note that in the latter vigorous passions have decayed, to the advantage of peace and quiet, and perhaps of happiness.'[10] In a later article on Henri de Guise, he is somewhat more affirmative: 'I am on the whole inclined to think that the sum total of vice and virtue has always been the same; consequently I do not believe we are any better than our forefathers, though we murder less. Murder was one form of their passions; their passions are still ours, but they have different forms; but I think we must congratulate ourselves on living in a time when these forms have become appreciably less harsh.'[11] This same point recurs in his 1858 edition of Brantôme, one of his main sources for the *Chronique*: 'We are not among those who think our ancestors were much better than we are; nor do we think that we are greatly superior to them in morality.'[12] These hesitations in the end redound to his advantage as a chronicler of the sixteenth century: he feels an instinctive sympathy with the men and manners of that period which enables him to write about them with insight and conviction, but at the same time he remains sufficiently detached to present them coolly and in perspective.

His knowledge of the times is extensive. In the preface, he indicates the part played by reading in the genesis of his novel:

> I had just been reading a considerable number of memoirs and pamphlets relating to the end of the sixteenth century. I decided to produce an extract from my reading, and here it is.[13]

His own footnotes and the researches of scholars confirm the thoroughness of his investigations. Among his main sources were the works of Brantôme and of Agrippa d'Aubigné (both of whom he read with great relish and of whom he was later to produce enthusiastic studies), as well as Pierre de l'Estoile's *Journals*, and other authors he consulted were Montluc, Tavannes, La Noue, de Thou and Arcère. Most of these were contemporary accounts – Mérimée always preferred to turn to first-hand sources of historical scenes, and the effect is to put the reader squarely among the characters he evokes. As in *La Jaquerie*,

---

[10] *Romans et nouvelles*, Vol. I, p. 11.
[11] *Portraits historiques et littéraires*, pp. 27–8.
[12] *Ibid.*, p. 82.   [13] *Romans et nouvelles*, Vol. I, p. 11.

he achieves an immediacy of impact which is most effective, as well as being highly praiseworthy in its fidelity to the general lineaments of the epoch. Though Mérimée was not yet a professional historian, the qualities of precision, vividness and penetration revealed by the *Chronique* demonstrate that he was already well on the way to possessing the method and equipment of a specialist. The historical side of the *Chronique* is undeniably far superior to that of the novels of Vigny, Hugo or Dumas – not until Flaubert wrote *Salammbô* is there another novelist who takes his duties as a historian so seriously.

This is not to say that his account is above reproach. In the preface, he argues ingeniously (though his case has not convinced modern historians) that the massacre of the Huguenots was the unforeseen result of a variety of chance circumstances, with the Duc de Guise inciting fanaticism in order to secure his own precarious position. In the novel itself, however, it appears that the massacre was premeditated by the king himself. Why there should be this discrepancy between novel and preface is unclear; probably the story was written first with the traditional explanation in mind, and the alternative interpretation only occurred to Mérimée when he was summing up his ideas. There is also one notable anachronism: the emphasis placed on duelling among the *raffinés*, the young bloods of the period. In reality, the *raffinés* and the vogue for duelling belong to the reign of Louis XIII in the next century. Mérimée was confused by his reliance on d'Aubigné, who talks about both periods. Most damaging, however, is Mérimée's inability to evaluate the religious feeling of the time. Himself remote from religious belief, he fails to convey anything of the inner motives or experiences of those with strong faith. To him, convinced Protestants and Catholics alike are potential fanatics, and he can identify himself only with George de Mergy, the elder of the two brothers around whom the novel is built and who has been aptly described as 'a Voltairean in the wrong century'.[14]

George's attitudes are certainly Mérimée's. In the following conversation, George, who has nominally become a Catholic, explains to his brother Bernard why he cares nothing for either religion.

'Papists! Huguenots! It's just superstition either way. I cannot believe what my reason tells me is absurd. Our litanies and your psalms are

---

[14] A. Filon, *Mérimée et ses amis*, Paris, Hachette, 1894, p. 44.

equally worthless nonsense. The only thing is,' he added with a smile, 'that there is sometimes good music in our churches, whereas in yours it's torture for sensitive ears.'

'That's a fine advantage for your religion – just the sort of thing to convert people to it!'

'Don't call it my religion; I don't believe in it any more than yours. Ever since I could think for myself, ever since I could call my reason my own . . .'

'But . . .'

'Ah, that's enough preaching. I knew by heart all you could say to me. I too have had my hopes and fears. Do you think that I haven't made strenuous efforts to preserve the happy superstitions of my childhood? I have read all our sages to try to find in their works some consolation for the doubts that terrify me, but all I did was increase them. In a word, I couldn't believe and I still can't. Belief is a precious gift which has been withheld from me, but I would never dream of trying to deprive others of it.'[15]

This resigned scepticism is Mérimée's last word on the subject. Acutely alive all his life to the perils of fanaticism, Mérimée was profoundly mistrustful of those who confidently asserted that they alone possessed the truth in religious matters; in 1859, he still felt as he had in 1829. 'In practical terms, I consider that doubt has fewer drawbacks than belief. There is nothing more terrible than a man who is sure of himself, when he goes in for reasoning and starts from a false premise.'[16]

Under the circumstances, it is hardly surprising that Mérimée showed more sympathy for the persecuted than the persecutors. Not only were the Catholics the perpetrators of the massacre, they were also the most powerful and hence to him the most dangerous religious group in his own day. Moreover, Mérimée was friendly with many Protestants – Stapfer, the Lagdens, Cuvier, the Delesserts among others – and eventually died as a Protestant (though it would be exaggerated to speak of a conversion). So in the *Chronique* the Catholic party appears as the more fanatical, the more ferocious, the more unscrupulous, and events are seen almost exclusively from the Protestant side. But Mérimée nevertheless makes it clear that, given the opportunity, the Protestants would be just as intolerant as their opponents. In the last scenes of the novel, a Catholic monk and a Protestant minister fight

[15] *Romans et nouvelles*, Vol. I, pp. 61–2.
[16] *C.G.*, Vol. IX, p. 271.

over the dying body of George de Mergy, who rejects them both. Ultimately, the enemy for Mérimée is not Catholicism, but fanaticism, whatever the flag it flies.

But these overtones scarcely obtrude themselves in the book. What concerns Mérimée is the depiction of human behaviour. He defines his own interests with admirable clarity in the preface.

> In history, I only like anecdotes, and among anecdotes I prefer those where I think I can find a faithful portrayal of manners and characters in a given period. It is not a very noble taste; but I admit, to my shame, that I would willingly exchange Thucydides for the authentic memoirs of Aspasia or a slave of Pericles; for memoirs, which are intimate conversations between author and reader, alone provide those portraits of *man* which entertain and interest me.[17]

This conception of history (which continued to inform his historical works throughout his life) leads him to construct his novel around a series of characters and incidents designed to throw into relief the most picturesque and typical features of life in the 1570s. Both plot and psychology are very much subservient to this intention. None of the characters is very complex: Bernard is the naïve young man learning wisdom in a hard school, George is the unhappy apostate who would prefer not to have to commit himself to either side, Diane de Turgis (who owes much to Mme Lacoste) is the beautiful seductress who combines piety and sensuality in equal measure. The others, whether real or invented – Hornstein, Comminges, Coligny, Charles IX, Béville, Vaudreuil, La Noue – are no more than vigorously drawn sketches. Nor is the plot very prominent. Simple in outline and episodic in nature, its function is to provide a pretext for a series of brilliant *tableaux de genre*, not all of which are even strictly necessary. The incident at the inn, when Bernard loses his horse and his money to the thieving German mercenaries, has little relevance to the main action, but it enables Mérimée to give a vivid and exciting depiction of the *reîtres* who were such an important adjunct to the Protestant forces, and similar reasons govern the inclusion of set-pieces like Frère Lubin's rollicking sermon or Bernard's duel with Comminges. With consummate skill, Mérimée has arranged his plot in such a way that the reader is carried from one such scene to another, led on by the interest which he is made to take in the principal figures but which is never

[17] *Romans et nouvelles*, Vol. I, p. 11.

allowed to obscure the fact that the novel really exists to display the backcloth against which the action is played out.

There are of course disadvantages in this system. The novel does give the impression of a piece of intricate mosaic work rather than an integrated whole; it has no clear centre; the main characters do not always marry happily with the background. But as with *La Jaquerie*, these shortcomings seem insignificant when one realises the true purpose of the work as an imaginative evocation of the past. Seen in that light, Mérimée's unobtrusive choice of the significant detail culled from contemporary sources is nothing short of masterly. Whether in scenes, in costume, in vocabulary, in habits or in attitudes, he shows a remarkable gift for selecting the salient trait which remains in the memory and typifies a man or an era, and this confers on his novel a striking vividness and clarity – Coligny's toothpicks, the king's shifting eyes, the woman whose skirts catch on the beams of the bridge as her body is flung into the Seine, the soldier who is roasted to death when his bulky armour wedges him in the window of a burning mill. Mérimée may mock historical novelists who cannot resist the temptation of lengthy portraits and descriptions, but he himself takes care that the reader should be able to visualise with great immediacy all that he needs to make the scene present to him. However, the curt incisiveness with which he does it avoids any sense of gratuitous word-painting. Here for example is Dietrich Hornstein as he sits carousing in an inn:

> Before an oak table, blackened with grease and smoke, was seated the captain of the *reîtres*. He was a tall, burly man of about fifty, with an aquiline nose, a fiery complexion, thin greying hair which did not hide a broad scar beginning near his left ear and disappearing beneath his thick moustache. He had taken off his breast plate and helmet, keeping only a doublet of Hungarian leather, darkened by the rubbing of the arms he carried and carefully mended in several places. His sabre and pistols were placed on a bench within easy reach, but he still wore a broad-bladed dagger, a weapon which a wise man only removed when he was going to bed.[18]

Such lightning sketches are frequent; they are always rapid, picturesque and telling, and they always make the reader feel that he is an eye-witness to the events. This effect is heightened by a style which

[18] *Romans et nouvelles*, Vol. I, p. 23.

never draws attention to itself. Stendhal thought Mérimée's way of writing was commonplace; Mérimée thought much the same of Stendhal's. In fact, each of them possesses the cardinal virtue of naturalness, and it is this which makes their French so much more pleasant to read nowadays than the dated rhetoric of those of their contemporaries who were forever striving after grand literary effects. Mérimée was the first to practise the precept he gave years later to an aspiring young author:

> You will soon get used to expressing your ideas easily and naturally. Without those two adverbs it is impossible to write French [. . .][19] Write everything as you would a letter, and remember that between high style and familiar style the greatest difference is not in the words but in the ideas.[20]

In the *Chronique* the free-flowing, urbane style not only keeps things moving with commendable alacrity, but by its coolness, its moderation and its humour allows events to speak for themselves. The massacre is of itself so horrifying, the siege of La Rochelle so dramatic, that Mérimée has no need to heighten tension by stylistic devices, and the matter-of-fact tone of his account leaves the reader to react to facts rather than authorial virtuosity. This is how he relates one of the most poignant climaxes of the book, the shooting of George in an ambush commanded by Bernard de Mergy.

> The captain with the red plume turned his head, and Mergy recognised his brother. He stretched out his hand to push aside his neighbour's arquebus; but, before he could reach it, the shot had been fired. The horsemen, surprised by the unexpected volley, dispersed and fled into the countryside; Captain George fell to the ground with two bullets in him.[21]

Mérimée sometimes goes further than this to keep the temperature down. Determined not to be visibly moved by what he writes, he injects into it humour, not only in the numerous comic scenes such as Mergy's discomfiture at the inn, Diane's mystification of her suitor, Frère Lubin's grotesque sermon, or the rich episode where two fake monks are made to baptise two chickens 'carp' and 'perch' so that a band of hungry miscreants can have a good feast on a Friday, but also in lightly ironic comments or in interpolated quotations from Molière, Saint-Évremond or Rabelais.[22] In two places he even reverts to the

[19] *C.G.*, Vol. V, p. 324.
[20] *Ibid.*, p. 328.
[21] *Romans et nouvelles*, Vol. I, p. 221.
[22] *Ibid.*, pp. 54, 71, 223, etc.

deflationary tricks he had employed in *Clara Gazul*. One is the notorious eighth chapter, in which he blandly interrupts his story to discuss with an imaginary interlocutor the aesthetics of the historical novel; the conversation ends with the reader exclaiming in disgust: 'Ah! I see that in your novel I shall not find what I wanted,' to which the author calmly replies: 'I fear so.'[23] The other concludes the novel with the same reference to its fictitious nature that one finds in the Gazul plays: 'Did Mergy get over it? Did Diane take another lover? I leave it to the reader to decide, so that, however he feels, he will be able to make the novel end as he wishes.'[24] The flippant tone of the last sentence is intended, as usual, to indicate that, whoever else may be taken in by his fiction, the author certainly is not.

All in all, the *Chronique* is a considerable achievement which has stood the test of time much better than the other historical novels of the period. It has a fresh and frank air about it which, allied with its vivid directness, makes reading it an invigorating experience. That it is carefully built up as a patchwork of details and separate scenes is therefore anything but a disadvantage; we ourselves live through the events of 1572, like contemporaries, seeing the effects rather than the causes, not always able to discern a meaningful pattern in them, swept along by the course of things without time to reflect or moralise but aware that, below the surface, there is much to be learnt from them. The dispassionate manner of narration and the almost constant presence of humour keeps us at arm's length from the narrator, just as it keeps him at arm's length from the frightening reality which he describes: perhaps it was this which led Walter Pater to call the *Chronique* 'Mérimée's one quite cheerful book'.[25] But the cheerfulness is only the barrier which holds passion at bay; the picture of humanity which emerges from the novel is as grim and as disturbing as that which the rest of Mérimée's work gives us. The combination of ironic detachment and powerful emotion is one of the hallmarks of Mérimée's art, and the *Chronique* represents one of his most successful fusions of these two elements. It would be misleading to place it on the same level as the great masterpieces of the novel in nineteenth-century France –

[23] *Romans et nouvelles*, Vol. I, p. 88.
[24] *Ibid.*, p. 231.
[25] *Studies in Modern European Literature*, Oxford, Clarendon Press, 1900, p. 40.

Balzac's *Cousine Bette*, Stendhal's *Le Rouge et le Noir* or Flaubert's *L'Éducation sentimentale*. After all, it is the first attempt at narrative fiction by a young man of twenty-five, and it is not surprising if its psychology is not particularly deep, its construction somewhat loose, and its philosophy of tolerant scepticism of no great originality. It remains nevertheless one of the outstanding successes of its notoriously difficult genre and by its keen observation and telling use of detail it looks forward both to mid-century realism and to Mérimée's own later distinction as a historian.

D

Chapter 6

Good-For-Nothing

Il se peut que je sois né avec quelque chose d'exploitable dans la tête. Mais [. . .] au moment où j'avais le plus de cœur à cette exploitation, une révolution s'est faite dans mon pays, dont le résultat le plus net a été de me tenir pendant mes plus belles années de verdeur et de jeunesse à l'attache dans un ministère.

To Ivan Turgenev, 27 January 1865

Mérimée was too prominent a supporter of those who now formed the ruling party and too well known a name to be passed over in the distribution of the spoils of victory, and it was not long before he was snatched from the life of leisured if not moneyed ease which he had been leading ever since he completed his studies. When he got back to Paris from Spain early in December 1830, he was immediately drafted into the National Guard, the middle-class militia which was called out in civil emergencies. As the ministers of Charles X were on trial at the time, its presence was required in case of riots, and Mérimée found himself in the fourth artillery battery, known as 'The Killer' not because of its warlike propensities but because of the number of doctors serving with it. One of his comrades-in-arms was Alexandre Dumas, with whom he discussed art and literature while on guard;[1] another was Alexandre Bixio, doctor, co-founder of the *Revue des Deux Mondes*, agriculturalist and politician, with whom he became firm friends after they had accidentally exchanged muskets.[2] Mérimée's part in the repression of disorder was confined to catching a cold through staying out all night in bad weather.[3]

After the July Revolution, there had naturally been a large-scale distribution of government posts to the young men of liberal opinions who had, by their hostility to Charles X and his policies, paved the way for the new régime. Many of Mérimée's closest associates had

[1] Alexandre Dumas, *Mes Mémoires*, Paris, Cadot, 1854, Vol. XIX, p. 135.
[2] *C.G.*, Vol. I, p. 81.   [3] *Ibid.*, p. 82.

already profited from such appointments or promotions, Stendhal, Mareste, Vitet, Rémusat and Lenormant among them. Mérimée himself by the end of the year was unofficially acting as private secretary to Comte Apollinaire d'Argout, Minister for the Navy. He probably owed the post to the fact that d'Argout's wife was Mareste's wife's cousin and to d'Argout's long-standing friendship with Stendhal; moreover, at least two ministers in the new government were supporters of his – Adolphe Thiers, for whose newspaper *Le National* he had written a number of articles, and the Duc de Broglie, with whose family the Mérimées had been closely connected for more than one generation.[4] Mérimée's aim in accepting the job was not to become a permanent desk-bound civil servant, but to use it as a stepping-stone to the diplomatic service, an ambition he had harboured for some time but which he had not pursued so long as Charles X was in power. He told Stendhal that he would remain in charge of the minister's staff until he was promoted to the next administrative grade of *maître des requêtes*, after which he hoped to move to a post in an embassy.[5] Clearly, he was now embarking on a new career of a very different kind.

Not that Mérimée had ever wanted to earn a living as a writer. 'Authorship, in him, is a vocation, not a profession', said Lady Morgan,[6] and, like his father, he had no desire to cut himself off from the security of a regular income and a settled existence. Up to this time, there had been sufficient money available from his parents and from his publications to make it unnecessary for him to take a job, and though he was not wealthy, he had never run short of funds. He had turned down one tempting offer of a diplomatic post, partly out of principle, but partly too, one may suspect, because he knew that his avowed liberalism would prevent him making much headway under the Bourbon monarchy.[7] So he bided his time, meanwhile acquiring fame if not riches as a man of letters, and making large numbers of well-connected friends who would be extremely useful at the right moment. That

[4] Mérimée's appointment is often attributed to the Duc's influence. But in October 1832, Mérimée told Grasset that he scarcely knew the Duc, who had a very low opinion of him (*C.G.*, Vol. I, p. 194). So it is likely that his other protectors (maybe his father's friend Decazes as well) were active on his behalf.　　　　　　　　　　[5] *C.G.*, Vol. XVI, p. 15.

[6] *Op. cit.*, Vol. I, p. 324.　　　　　　　　[7] Cf. p. 76.

opportunity had now come. Mérimée's father was growing old and he himself was twenty-seven, so that his parents must have been glad to see him launched on what seemed a promising course, even if it was not the diplomatic post he had hoped for. 'My son wanted to go in for a diplomatic career [. . .] Now his literary activities have been interrupted, but in the Civil Service he will acquire new ideas that will stand him in good stead later,' Léonor Mérimée wrote to a friend in April 1831.[8] Everyone was satisfied with the new arrangement.

After a few weeks of unofficial attachment to d'Argout, Mérimée's position was regularised by official decree on 5 February 1831. The opposition press did not miss the chance of sarcasm at his expense:

> M. Prosper Mérimée, author of the *Théâtre de Clara Gazul* and several other distinguished works, has just been appointed principal officer of the General Secretariat of the Navy. There is said to be a vacant place in the literary department of the Ministry of the Interior. We hope it will be given to a naval officer.[9]

But Mérimée had no intention of treating his post with anything other than the utmost seriousness. He had a solid legal training, an exceptionally clear mind, a vast capacity for hard work, some experience through his father of the technique of administration, and a systematic way of setting about his tasks. D'Argout, a financier as well as a politician, was the most caricatured minister of Louis-Philippe's reign because of the imposing dimensions of his nose, but, despite the ruthless mockery to which Mérimée subjected him in his letters, he was a sensible and cultured man who realised that his private secretary was both a talented administrator and a writer of genius: it is entirely to his credit that in 1832, he should have written to Mérimée to say that he knew well that his young protégé's name would still be famous long after his own had been forgotten.[10] That he thought highly of Mérimée's efficiency is shown by the fact that he retained his services when he moved from the Navy Ministry to the Ministry of Trade and Public Works in March 1831, and again when another cabinet reshuffle took him to the Ministry of the Interior at the end of December 1832.

Mérimée's tasks during this time were numerous and varied. He

[8] Pinet, *op. cit.*, pp. 101–2.   [9] *C.G.*, Vol. I, p. 87, n. 2.
[10] Catalogue of the Bibliothèque Nationale exhibition, p. 20.

was dealing with the telegraph service, the fire brigade, and fine arts (this was much to his taste, as it took him behind the scenes in the state-subsidised theatres), and during the terrible cholera epidemic of 1832 he was special commissioner for sanitary measures. The latter involved him in frequent visits to hospitals filled with highly infectious patients; he carried out his duties with stoical courage, making light of the dangers and telling Stendhal that the best way to avoid cholera was 'not to give a damn about it, never to fornicate after dinner, and to keep the stomach warm'.[11] He thoroughly detested his fellow-bureaucrats, to whom he never referred without biting scorn: 'I hate and despise all that scum as much as they hate me.'[12] Most of his work (except when he was dealing with the fine arts) bored him intensely; he complained that he was 'dying of boredom and fury'[13] and that by seven o'clock he was too exhausted to do anything interesting. Conscientious as he was, he gave a great deal of time and effort to it; this was the quality which in later years was to make him such an indispensable member of important committees. Indeed, tempting offers were several times made to him by Thiers, who in October 1832 invited him to become his private secretary, with a salary of 10,000 francs, his own carriage, the title of *maître des requêtes* and the powers of secretary-general of the Ministry.[14] But Mérimée preferred to remain faithful to d'Argout, as he did again three months later when d'Argout and Thiers changed posts, despite the latter's renewed blandishments.[15] Recognition of his considerable administrative ability was in any case not long in coming; the cross of the Legion of Honour had been bestowed on him in May 1831, and in December 1832 he at last gained the coveted title of *maître des requêtes* – news which he claimed to have received with his 'old philosophy of *nil admirari*'.[16]

This new way of life resolved itself into a time-consuming and tiring succession of chores, which did nothing to lighten the depression into which he had sunk before his departure for Spain. To deaden the pain of his past disappointments and to relieve the monotony of his life in the office, Mérimée threw himself into an existence of pleasure with more abandon and more cynicism than ever before. His letters at this time are often of incredible crudity, but it is a crudity without gaiety;

[11] *C.G.*, Vol. XVI, p. 35. [12] *C.G.*, Vol. I, p. 90.
[13] *Ibid.*, p. 113. [14] *C.G.*, Vol. XVI, p. 40.
[15] *Ibid.*, p. 53. [16] *C.G.*, Vol. I, p. 54.

he seems to want to exaggerate the obscenity of his stories in order to forget that anything nobler exists. Among the diners at Véry's restaurant, even in the absence of the ebullient Stendhal, now a consul in Italy, there reigned an atmosphere of frenetic enjoyment, and once Mérimée's professional obligations gave him an entry into the theatrical world, it was even easier than before to find willing actresses and chorus-girls to add spice to the party. Unable to take his conquests to his parents' home, Mérimée arranged to borrow Édouard Grasset's flat when necessary.[17]

How many transient mistresses he had during these years is of course impossible to guess; but the number was considerable. Among them for a period in 1832 was one Pauline, a girl from the colonies who sang in the chorus at the Opera; Mérimée met her on a boating expedition in the Seine and was only dissuaded from taking her by force while she was changing her wet clothes by the promise that he would enjoy it more if he waited until she wanted it too – a promise that was duly kept.[18]

A more lasting attachment was with another singer and actress, Céline Cayot, who took Mme Lacoste's place when Émilie dropped Mérimée some time after his return from Spain.[19] Céline's detractors alleged that her style was vulgar and her voice unmusical. But she was pretty, cheerful, lively and uninhibited, and there seems to have been some affection on Mérimée's part. He always spoke of her with a certain comradely friendship during the years they were together, and remained vaguely in touch with her almost until his death. He was much upset when in 1866 it was rumoured that she had been drowned in a shipwreck: 'She was a very strange person, virtuous in her way, who remains in the memory of the many men she made happy.'[20] He was always eager to defend the character of girls of this type as against women of conventionally correct behaviour, and told Stendhal that Pauline had enabled him to make some interesting observations on the hearts of chorus-girls and their like. 'I firmly intend to write a fine dissertation on the subject, when I have time,'[21] he added, and indeed,

[17] Cf. *C.G.*, Vol. I, p. 194.   [18] *C.G.*, Vol. XVI, pp. 41–3.
[19] On Céline Cayot, see M. Parturier's introduction to Mérimée's *Lettres aux Grasset*, Paris, La Connaissance, 1929, and the same author's 'Précision sur Céline Cayot', *Le Divan*, janvier–mars 1946.
[20] *C.G.*, Vol. XIII, p. 265.   [21] *C.G.*, Vol. XVI, p. 43.

with numerous reminiscences of Céline, did so a few years later in *Arsène Guillot.*

This intensive pleasure-seeking was not a compulsive necessity for Mérimée; part of him remained detached from it and unsatisfied by it. Curiosity, too, played a large part:

> I can only stand bad company at long intervals, out of an inexhaustible curiosity about all the varieties of the human species [. . .] I just like to see different manners and different faces, and to hear a different sort of conversation.[22]

That overstates the case, since Mérimée's intense sexual needs had to be satisfied. In the bluntest terms, he once told Grasset that the way to be perfectly happy was to love and be loved and not sleep with the woman; he himself fornicated without loving or being loved, 'and I'm bored.'[23] Subsequently, he commented on his years of profligacy: 'The strange thing in my life is that, having become a great scamp, I lived for two years on the good reputation I had before, and that, now that I am very moral again, people still take me for a scamp. The truth is that I don't think I was one for longer than three years, and I didn't do it from the heart but solely out of sadness and perhaps out of curiosity.'[24] One need not take him absolutely at his word; three years is an understatement, and some of the habits of the early 1830s persisted for years afterwards. But one may accept that the intensity of his preoccupation with frivolous enjoyment at that time was primarily the result of boredom, discouragement and cynicism.

Without doubt the strangest episode of his life as a scamp was his brief encounter with George Sand in 1833.[25] George Sand was already

---

[22] *C.G.*, Vol. I, pp. 174–5.

[23] *Ibid.*, pp. 254–5.   [24] *C.G.*, Vol. III, p. 207.

[25] Mérimée's short affair with George Sand has had much written about it, but the details are the subject of some dispute, the main points at issue being the date at which it took place, whether or not it was prolonged after the initial *fiasco*, and the circumstances under which it came to an end. Mérimée himself appears to have told the story in full to at least three people. One was Chancellor Pasquier, who immediately noted his words, with great precision, in the margin of his manuscript copy of *H.B.*; this version was published by M. Parturier in his entertaining account of the affair, *Une Expérience de Lélia, ou, Le Fiasco du Comte Gazul*, Paris, Le Divan,

as well known for the eccentricities of her behaviour as for her novels, and by the beginning of the year Mérimée was taking a pressing interest in her. It was probably in February that they first met,[26] and Mérimée lost no time in making clear to her what his intentions were. George was in a depressed condition, unhappy in her marriage, convinced of her own frigidity, and at first she repulsed his advances. But Mérimée won her over by carrying her daughter Solange on his shoulder one night when the little girl had gone to sleep at the Opera,[27] and one

---

1934. Another was a friend of Count d'Haussonville (perhaps even d'Haussonville himself, since he once wintered at Cannes with Mérimée); this is reported in d'Haussonville's *Prosper Mérimée*. *Hugh Elliot*, Paris, Calmann-Lévy. The third recipient of Mérimée's confidences was another of Mérimée's friends in Cannes, Dr Maure, who repeated the conversation to Juliette Adam, who recorded it in one of her volumes of memoirs, *Mes Premières Armes littéraires et politiques*, Paris, Lemerre, 1894.

There is not much documentary evidence about it, which is scarcely surprising, save in George Sand's letters, notably to Sainte-Beuve, to whom she poured out her heart in despair after it was all over (cf. George Sand, *Correspondance*, ed. Georges Lubin, Vol. II, Paris, Garnier, 1966). Apart from that, there is little to go on except more or less well-informed gossip by contemporaries. This account is pieced together from a collation of these diverse sources.

[26] In *Une Expérience de Lélia*, M. Parturier suggests that they may have met in December 1832. But it appears from George Sand's correspondence that in January 1833 she was still anxious to make his acquaintance and had deputed one of her lovelorn admirers, the critic Gustave Planche, to arrange a meeting. A first attempt to do so on 28 January fell through because Mérimée was otherwise engaged. So it was probably only in early February that they were introduced to each other (cf. G. Sand, *Correspondance*, Vol. II, p. 244).

[27] This at least is the story put about by another contemporary critic, A. de Pontmartin, who knew Mérimée quite well (*Mes Mémoires. Seconde Jeunesse*, Paris, Calmann-Lévy, 1886, p. 66). If he is to be believed (and he appears well informed about the whole business), the opera being performed on that occasion was Meyerbeer's *Robert le Diable*, in which case the Opera archives suggest that the most plausible date for the incident is 22 April. M. Lubin also argues that a letter from Mérimée paying court to George Sand, which M. Parturier tentatively dates February 1833 (*C.G.*, Vol. I, pp. 228–9), belongs in fact to the month of April, since only then was her husband Casimir Dudevant – whose presence is referred to by Mérimée – in Paris (G. Sand, *Correspondance*, Vol. II, p. 295, n. 2).

evening as they were walking by the Seine along the Quai Malaquais, she yielded to his entreaties and said:

Very well, all right; let us do as you wish, since it gives you so much pleasure, for as far as I'm concerned I have to tell you that I'm quite sure it will give me none.[28]

So they went up to her flat together, where George made the great mistake of allowing her fastidious suitor to be present at a lengthy and intimate toilet. As a result, when they eventually got to bed, there occurred what Stendhal called a *fiasco*: nothing happened. Both grew impatient, and George in the end bit Mérimée sharply on the shoulder. The next morning, they parted with a good deal of coolness on both sides. Legend, variously embellished, has it that that was the end of their affair, but the evidence is that neither partner was prepared to leave it at that, George because she had genuinely fallen in love, Prosper because he wanted no aspersions cast on his virility.[29]

[28] Quoted verbatim by Pasquier: cf. Parturier, *Une Expérience de Lélia*, pp. 16–17.

[29] As Östen Södergård has pointed out ('George Sand et Prosper Mérimée', *Revue des Sciences humaines*, oct.–déc. 1959), George Sand's letter to Sainte-Beuve is categorical in affirming that she did indeed become Mérimée's mistress.

M. Lubin quotes a letter from George to Mérimée, in which she begs him to come to see her, saying: 'I am more resigned than you think. I have improved a lot since yesterday. No, I protest that I am not mad. I should not be ashamed if I were, but I don't even feel very hot-headed' (G. Sand, *Correspondance*, Vol. II, pp. 295–6). M. Lubin's hypothesis is that this letter was written on April 20. In fact, assuming that the *fiasco* occurred in late April or early May (at any rate after the performance of *Robert le Diable* on 22 April), it looks as though the letter ought to be assigned to a slightly later date: it appears to refer to George's distress at that humiliating failure and is intended to make it clear to Prosper that she is nevertheless determined to persevere with him. The only specific clue to its date is the heading 'Saturday'. Rather than 20 April, one might propose 27 April or 4 May. According to the Pasquier account, it was 'on a fine summer evening', that George agreed to sleep with Mérimée, so that choosing a later date for their first night together tends to fit rather better with the recollections of the principal protagonist.

M. Lubin also draws attention to the reputed existence of a love letter, since destroyed, from George Sand to Mérimée (G. Sand, *Correspondance*,

Shortly afterwards in fact she did become his mistress and remained so for two or three weeks.[30] Then, one morning when Mérimée had called on her and was waiting for her to get dressed, he picked up a page of notes she had left lying around, describing the actress Marie Dorval, with whom she was reputed to have a lesbian attachment. 'How can you be on friendly terms with Mme Dorval?' Mérimée asked through the bedroom door, at which George began to defend herself volubly. While she was talking, he started to read the next sheet, which opened with the words: 'P.M. is five feet ten inches tall . . .' At this point George shot through the door and snatched the

---

Vol. II, p. 296, n. 2). What is certain is that even as late as 29 June George was still making efforts to be friendly towards Mérimée, since on that day she wrote to congratulate him in the mistaken belief that he had been appointed to a post at the embassy in Madrid (*Correspondance*, Vol. II, p. 344). Pontmartin, who first met Mérimée in 1834 in Avignon and may well have heard the story from his own lips, or perhaps through the intermediary of Mérimée's friend Esprit Requien, said years later that George Sand's detestation of Mérimée was born of her resentment when he abandoned her: 'Alone among those who adored her in her palmy days, Mérimée, after two or three days, had taken the initiative in breaking with her, and women in love cannot bear to be left' (*Souvenirs d'un vieux critique*, 3e série, Paris, Calmann-Lévy, 1883, p. 7).

All these pieces of evidence tend to discredit the legend that theirs was simply a one-night affair which stopped short after a single unsatisfactory experiment. There are very good grounds for thinking that, after the *fiasco*, George became his mistress for some time, and that Mérimée then broke it off, against George's wishes, partly because he was furious at her indiscretions and partly because her submissive attitude disappointed him.

[30] A friend of Sainte-Beuve named Charles Didier noted in his diary in June 1833 that he had been told by the critic that George had given herself to Mérimée and that it had lasted twenty days. There are two different transcriptions of this nearly illegible and somewhat enigmatic entry, one by Maurice Regard in *L'Adversaire des Romantiques. Gustave Planche. Correspondance*, Paris, Nouvelles Editions Latines, 1955, p. 75, n. 2, the other by Georges Lubin in the already quoted volume of Sand's *Correspondance*, p. 321, n. 1. M. Lubin's interpretation is that Mérimée had had to wait twenty days before George would consent to go to bed with him, and that this extended suspense was the cause of the *fiasco*. It seems more likely, in view of the other evidence, that Didier simply meant that the pair were lovers for three weeks.

paper out of his hands, but not before he had seen that it went on with some other measurements of a much less flattering kind.[31] This was more than he could stand, and though the complete break still did not come until later, when he discovered that she had spread the news of his momentary failure among her friends, it was obvious that they were not going to be able to form a permanent relationship.

For Mérimée, this was no more than a misadventure, an experiment which had failed. He had thought that George Sand had something of his own adopted character – that of someone capable of governing their own emotions – and preserving an icy calm, even in love. 'In her there was nothing, absolutely nothing, of what I had expected to find. Sentimental, docile, she offered herself up to slavery.' So he had repulsed her roughly: 'but even then, instead of curses and hatred, I was merely faced with a woman who had lost yet another illusion and was weeping over her shattered dream'.[32] For George Sand, on the other hand, it was a crushing blow which left her – so she said – on the verge of suicide. Already in low spirits before they met, she had persuaded herself that Mérimée was capable of changing her life.

> On one of those days of boredom and despair, I met a man free of doubt, calm and strong, who had no understanding of my character and laughed at what grieved me. The power of his mind completely fascinated me,

---

[31] This is the story reported by d'Haussonville, pp. 14–15. M. Lubin (op. cit., p. 321, n. 1) refers to the version quoted by Dr Parturier as though it had been dictated to d'Haussonville. But while M. Parturier does not directly identify the author of the marginal annotations to the *H.B.* manuscript, he does allude to him as 'the highest magistrate in the kingdom', which can only mean Pasquier, who had been Chancellor of France.

[32] Juliette Adam, op. cit., pp. 358–9. The quotation is admittedly second-hand. But Mme Adam is generally a reliable memorialist, and what she was told by Dr Maure corresponds remarkably closely with what George Sand herself confessed to Sainte-Beuve about the psychological background to the affair.

The only detail in what she says which is visibly unfounded is the claim that Mérimée's interest in George Sand was awakened by reading her novel *Lélia* – in reality, *Lélia* did not appear until the beginning of August 1833. Indeed, the completion of the novel was delayed by the agonies of the ignominious collapse of her affair with Mérimée (cf. Pierre Reboul's edition of *Lélia*, Paris, Garnier, 1960, p. xli), and it is possible that the character of Trenmor owes something to Mérimée.

and for a week I thought he had the secret of happiness, that he could teach it to me, that his disdainful indifference would cure me of my childish susceptibility. I thought he had suffered like me and that he had overcome his outward emotions. I still do not know if I was wrong, if the man is strong because he is great or because he is poor. I am still inclined to believe that the former is true [. . .] In short, a girl of fifteen would have known better than to behave as I did at thirty; I committed the most incredibly foolish act of my life: I became Mérimée's mistress. The experiment was a total failure. I wept with suffering, disgust and discouragement. Instead of finding an affection to sympathise with me and console me, I only encountered bitter, frivolous mockery.[33]

It was in this mood of black despair that, a month or two later, she fell violently in love with Musset, setting in train one of the most celebrated and dramatic of literary love affairs.

George Sand's indiscretions to Marie Dorval had been repeated to Alexandre Dumas, who thought it all a huge joke and added his own embroidery, spreading the story all round Paris.[34] Mérimée took his revenge in kind, excusing himself with the explanation that rumours about his sexual inadequacy could do him irreparable harm among the chorus-girls of the Opera.[35] To Viel-Castel, for example, he said that George Sand was 'a woman whose debauchery was coldly deliberate – the result of curiosity rather than temperament'.[36] She was even more acid about him. In 1839, for instance, it came to Mérimée's ears that, when someone had told her that the popular novelist Eugène Sue was an atheist, she had said he was like Mérimée. 'Yes', replied her interlocutor, 'but he has a filthy mind.' 'In that case, he is exactly like Mérimée.'[37] When Maxime du Camp asked her about him, she replied with a shudder: 'Never mention that man to me, I loathe the very memory of him.'[38] For years they never met and it was not until

[33] G. Sand, *Correspondance*, Vol. II, pp. 374–5.

[34] It was partly because of Dumas' coarse and indiscreet joviality on the subject that a hapless admirer of George Sand, the critic Gustave Planche, thought it incumbent upon him to challenge Dumas to a duel in June. In the end, matters were smoothed over without bloodshed, and Planche was made to look a fool (cf. M. Regard, *L'Adversaire des Romantiques. Gustave Planche*, pp. 115–16).   [35] Cf. *Une Expérience de Lélia*, p. 25.

[36] H. de Viel-Castel, *Mémoires*, Vol. I, p. 243.

[37] *C.G.*, Vol. II, p. 302.

[38] Maxime du Camp, *Souvenirs littéraires*, Paris, Calmann-Lévy, 1882–3,

1848 that an English friend of Mérimée, ignorant of their previous relations, invited them both to lunch; there was a moment of embarrassment, but it soon passed,[39] and Mérimée, who was not a rancorous man, later did his best to get the Academy to give her a prize.[40]

Another strange affair, of a very different but much more durable kind, got under way about the same time. In October 1831, Mérimée had received a flattering letter in English, signed 'Lady Algernon Seymour', and had become involved in a friendly correspondence with his aristocratic English admirer, through the intermediary of a Mme Lemaire of Calais. Intrigued by the mystery surrounding this new acquaintance and further attracted when his friend Vulliamy in London, on whom she had called, informed him that she had 'a splendid pair of black eyes',[41] Mérimée pressed the lady to meet him. Alternately enticing him and rebuffing him, she refused until in the autumn of 1832 Mérimée went on a semi-official journey to England. On his way back, he was told that, if he called on Mme Lemaire in Calais she would arrange an interview in Boulogne. But Mme Lemaire, to his astonishment, then revealed that 'Lady Seymour' was in reality the daughter of a Boulogne lawyer, that she had written to him at first only as a way of getting an autograph, that she had now fallen madly in love with him, that she and her mother beseeched Mérimée to see her and cure her of her passion. Mérimée, more intrigued than ever, agreed and set off for Boulogne – with a swordstick in case it turned out to be a trap.[42] Instead, he found himself in a dimly lit room with an attractive young lady, whose well-turned ankle, as he said, caused an insurrection in his trousers.[43] At first inclined to attempt an immediate seduction, Mérimée desisted when he saw how troubled the girl was; this was just as well, as he subsequently discovered that her mother was listening from the next room.[44]

The young lady was Jeanne-Francoise Dacquin, born in 1811, and

---

Vol. I, p. 329. Du Camp, it is true, was a bitter enemy of Mérimée and may be suspected of exaggeration.

[39] The story is related by Alexis de Tocqueville, who was another of the guests, in his *Souvenirs*, ed. Luc Monnier, Paris, Gallimard, 1942, pp. 133–4. Mérimée himself mentions his mixed feelings on seeing her again on that occasion (*C.G.*, Vol. V, p. 304).   [40] *C.G.*, Vol. X, pp. 285–6.

[41] *C.G.*, Vol. XVI, p. 44.   [42] *Ibid.*, p. 63.

[43] *C.G.*, Vol. I, p. 226.   [44] *C.G.*, Vol. XVI, p. 49.

known in her family as Jenny.[45] She was well-educated, intelligent, independent and determined, and had already published prose and verse pieces under a pen-name – some of them in the same volume of the *Annales romantiques* in which Mérimée's *Federigo* had appeared. A woman of principle, she had no intention of entering into any relationship with Mérimée other than platonic friendship or marriage; he, on the other hand, was impressed by her personality, amused by her wit, attracted by her beauty and irritated by her adamance. Thus there grew up between them a curious mixture of love, comradeship and exasperation which lasted literally until Mérimée's dying day. Whether she ever became his mistress is open to question; if she did, it was not until many years later. In the meantime, they wrote to each other regularly, sometimes affectionately, sometimes in anger, sometimes to argue, sometimes to agree. Jenny never married, and her life seems almost to have revolved around her friendship with Mérimée. As for him, though he was baffled and often furious at her attitude to him, he set great store by her friendship, and despite the threats and complaints which run through his letters, never broke off a relationship which came to be one of the most stable elements in a disturbed emotional life.

At the same time, Mérimée, who always had several irons in the fire, was pursuing yet another amorous interest which had been preoccupying him for some years. In 1829, his friend Sophie Duvaucel, Cuvier's stepdaughter (and yet another woman with whom he had conducted a prolonged flirtation), had introduced him to someone with whom she sat on a committee for orphanages. This was Valentine Delessert, née Laborde, and sister of the Léon de Laborde whom Mérimée was to visit in Bordeaux the following year.[46] In 1829, Valentine Delessert was twenty-three and had been married for five years to Gabriel Delessert, a man much older than she was, a prosperous Protestant banker and a leading supporter of the Orleanists, the party of the constitutional monarchy.

She was generally agreed to be intelligent, imaginative, artistic and

[45] On Jenny Dacquin, see A. Lefèbvre, *La Célèbre Inconnue de Prosper Mérimée*, Paris, Sansot, 1908, and M. Parturier, 'Jenny Dacquin ou l'Inconnue mieux connue', *Le Figaro littéraire*, February 14, 1959.

[46] *C.G.*, Vol. I, p. 55. On Valentine Delessert, see M. Parturier's introduction to Mérimée's *Lettres à la famille Delessert*, Paris, Plon, 1931.

well-read, as well as very attractive; it was also known that she was not very happy with her middle-aged husband, who carried earnestness and integrity to the point of dullness. Her *salon*, a centre of Orleanist intrigue, was full of talented and ambitious young men, and the only question appeared to be which of them she would take as her lover. Mérimée entered the lists at an early stage, but found the coquettish and hard-headed Valentine anything but an easy prey. His changing relations with 'Mme Sypas', as he called her in his code language with Stendhal by an anagrammatic rearrangement of Passy, where she lived, were to keep him on tenterhooks throughout the early 1830s. In March 1831, he was consulting Stendhal on the legitimacy of committing adultery with her or alternatively despatching her husband in a duel;[47] a week or two later, he was congratulating himself on not having gone too far with her: 'Taking everything into account, I think I was a muggins with her, but I think I gained more in her estimation than I would have done by treating her like a needle.'[48] After another few days, he was convinced that she looked on him with favour,[49] but by the end of year he had almost fallen out with her.[50] By October 1832 he had decided that she was worthless:

> I had a superb jewel, well cut, shining, sparkling, admirable in every way. I thought it was a diamond that I wouldn't have given for the Grand Mogul's – not at all! Now it turns out to be just a fake. A chemist I know has just analysed it for me. Imagine how downcast I am. I have spent many hours thinking of this supposed diamond and how lucky I was to have found it. Now I shall have to spend just as many (even more) convincing myself that it was only a fake.[51]

What lay behind this momentary disillusionment is unknown; probably Valentine seemed to be preferring some other suitor.[52] At all events, the unfortunate Mérimée was too deeply entangled to forget her, and through all the manifold complexities of his love-life in

[47] *C.G.*, Vol. I, p. 93.   [48] *Ibid.*, p. 105.
[49] *C.G.*, Vol. XVI, p. 18.   [50] *Ibid.*, p. 26.
[51] *C.G.*, Vol. I, p. 190. Mérimée does not name the person concerned, and the spurious gem has consequently exercised the ingenuity of commentators. But in 1832 Valentine was probably the only woman about whom he had sufficiently strong feelings to express himself in this way.
[52] Again the allusion is discreetly ambiguous, but it is reasonable to relate it to Valentine.

those years, he never lost sight of his ultimate aim of conquering her. One has the impression that from the outset she was aware of the power she had over him and that he was too fascinated by her strong personality ever to break loose from her bonds.

Mme Delessert, Jenny Dacquin, George Sand, Céline Cayot, Mme Lacoste, Pauline – even this list is not exhaustive. During his visit to London in 1832, Sutton Sharpe, in exchange for similar services in Paris, put Mérimée in touch with young ladies of easy virtue, including one Trench, a dark-eyed beauty not unlike Jenny.[53] At another point, Mérimée was consoling himself with a mulatto woman:

> When one's heart is heavy, one can only produce an effect on the animal part of one's nature by some kind of monster. Mulatto women are excellent for that. The pleasure they give rises no higher than the pit of the stomach.[54]

Other allusions in his letters, almost always plaintive, refer to various losses or disappointments in love; the confusion is inextricable. Clearly Mérimée was at this time an unhappy and dissatisfied man, seeking to forget his cares in an unthinking whirl of superficial affairs and entertainment – and signally failing to do so.

Given the heavy pressure of his work and the hectic activity of his social life (which continued, too, in the elegant *salons* of literary and political society), it is no wonder that Mérimée's artistic production practically dried up in the early 1830s. Apart from the belated publication of his *Letters from Spain*, a single obituary article and, in 1833, a long story entitled *La Double Méprise* (*The Double Misunderstanding*), nothing new came from his pen during this period. But early in 1833 he decided to gather together the tales and assorted short pieces which he had been publishing at intervals since 1829, and in June there appeared the brilliant but heterogeneous volume entitled *Mosaïque* (*Mosaic*), which enjoyed considerable success.

Mérimée was now no longer the committed Romantic he had been before 1830. The evolution of the movement towards either morbid extravagance or social commentary, the development of his own art towards greater sobriety and control, the increasing maturity of his personality, all contributed to making him a much more solitary figure than he had been before. Now that the battle against the Classi-

---

[53] *C.G.*, Vol. I, p. 227.   [54] *Ibid.*, pp. 239–40.

cists could safely be said to be won, Mérimée was no longer interested in supporting the victors, especially as he had never had much more in common with them than opposition to the same enemy. This dis-affection showed itself above all in a mounting hostility towards Hugo. The sardonic detachment of the one and the visionary grandiloquence of the other had never gone well together; now Mérimée waxed more critical with each successive work by the poet. Of *Notre-Dame de Paris*, he said: 'I should be in despair if that were the sort of thing this century wants,'[55] and he noted without regret the failure of *Marie Tudor*.[56] The final break came when Hugo accused Mérimée, who was then at the Ministry of the Interior, of having had a hand in the banning of *Le Roi s'amuse*. Mérimée was able to clear himself and Hugo somewhat grudgingly apologised, but the damage was irreparable.[57] Long after, Hugo dated their mutual antipathy to this period:

> When I was very young, I had some regard for Mérimée. I began to despise him the day I saw him come running when M. d'Argout rang a bell. 'Aha!' I said to myself, 'he's a lackey.'[58]

In politics, too, Mérimée cooled off noticeably. Like other reformers before and since, he found his radicalism seriously modified by the responsibilities of office, and he was soon using the word 'liberal' as a term of opprobrium.[59] Moreover, his experience of parliamentary democracy in France and England brought him a disappointment bordering on disgust. He was sent to England as an observer at the 1832 elections, but his greatest pleasure was seeing someone fling a dead cat at one of the candidates for Westminster, and he related with satisfaction that, at Hertford, a candidate had stopped one of his hired bullies from beating up a voter with the words: 'Don't you see you are knocking down the wrong man?'[60] His opinion of French politicians, with whom his work brought him into daily contact, was equally uncomplimentary, and his persiflage of the worthy d'Argout was inexhaustible. Now that Bourbon absolutism had been laid low, Méri-

---

[55] *C.G.*, Vol. XVI, p. 19.

[56] *C.G.*, Vol. I, p. 260.

[57] Hugo's letter is reproduced in *C.G.*, Vol. I, pp. 203–4.

[58] Quoted by François Michel, *Fichier stendhalien*, Boston, Hall, 1964, Vol. II, p. 628.

[59] *C.G.*, Vol. I, p. 198.   [60] *Ibid.*, p. 212.

mée was discovering that Orleanist constitutional rule was just as ridiculous, if slightly less odious.

Even diplomats were viewed with scant respect. The aged Talleyrand was Ambassador in London when Mérimée went there in 1832 – Chateaubriand, who loathed him, said viciously: 'his mummy, before being lowered into its crypt, was briefly exhibited in London as the representative of the corpse-like royalty which rules over us'.[61] Mérimée was above all intrigued by the extraordinary spectacle which Talleyrand offered at the end of an official banquet, as the old man noisily sniffed two glasses of water up his nose and spat them out of his mouth. When Lady Jersey tactfully observed that it must be a very healthy habit, Talleyrand replied brusquely: 'Oh, very dirty, very dirty!'[62] At another dinner a few days later, Talleyrand kept all the guests waiting for the news of the siege of Antwerp which they knew he had just received (a French expeditionary force was in Belgium maintaining the country's independence against Dutch intervention). Eventually, unable to bear the tension any longer, one dowager said loudly that France might well have to raise the siege, at which Talleyrand remarked with mischievous satisfaction: 'That is indeed what has happened, gentlemen: Antwerp has been ours since yesterday.'[63]

Mérimée's friendships changed somewhat during these years. Stendhal had succeeded in getting himself drafted into the consular service immediately after the July Revolution, and before Mérimée's return from Spain set off gleefully for Trieste, where he hoped to enjoy riches, pomp, power, and easy living. Unfortunately for him, the Austrian government refused to countenance the presence on their territory of such a subversive influence, and he was transferred to the much less attractive post of Civitavecchia, where he was to remain for years, quarrelling with his chief assistant, alternately neglecting his duties and pursuing them with confused zeal, and perpetually preoccupied with thoughts of promotion and decoration. Except for three months' leave in Paris at the end of 1833, he saw nothing of Mérimée, but they exchanged a series of bawdily entertaining letters – so bawdy, in fact, that those of Mérimée were for long only published in clandestinity.

[61] *Mémoires d'Outre-Tombe*, ed. Maurice Levaillant and Georges Moulinier, Paris, Pléiade, 1952, Vol. II, p. 904.

[62] *C.G.*, Vol. I, p. 210.   [63] *Journal de Prosper Mérimée*, p. 165.

Here is a representative example of Mérimée's bawdy which has been left in the original French as it loses its flavour in translation:

Je vais vous écrire une histoire bien salope qu'on m'a racontée à Madrid. La reine saxonne que Ferdinand a épousée, était une princesse confite en dévotion, et si chrétiennement élevée, qu'elle ignorait jusqu'aux choses de ce monde les plus simples, et que savent en Espagne les petites filles de 8 ans. C'est un ancien usage, lorsque le roi épouse une princesse présupposée vierge, que la princesse du sang mariée la plus proche parente du roi, ait avec la reine un entretien d'un quart d'heure pour la préparer à la cérémonie. A défaut de princesse du sang, la Camarera mayor est chargée de cette instruction. Or la saxonne étant venue, la belle-sœur du roi, femme de l'infant D. Carlos, et sœur de la feue reine Marie-Isabelle, à qui la reine saxonne succédait, déclara tout net que pour rien au monde elle ne mettrait cette allemande en état de remplacer sa sœur. D'autre part la camarera mayor, vieille putain dévote, protesta qu'elle n'avait jamais fait assez d'attention à ce que son mari lui faisait, pour pouvoir l'expliquer à d'autres. Il en résulta que la reine fut mise au lit sans aucune préparation. Entre sa Majesté. Représentez-vous un gros homme à l'air de satyre, très noir, la lèvre inférieure pendante. Suivant la dame de qui je tiens l'histoire, son membre viril est mince comme un bâton de cire à la base, et gros comme le poing à l'extrémité, d'ailleurs long comme une queue de billard. C'est en outre le plus grossier et effronté paillard de son royaume. A cette horrible vue la reine pensa s'évanouir, et ce fut bien pis quand S.M.C. se mit à la farfouiller sans ménagement. (N.B. La reine ne parlait que l'allemand dont S.M. ne savait pas un mot.) La reine s'échappe du lit et court par la chambre avec de grands cris, la roi la poursuit, mais comme elle était jeune et leste, et que le roi est gros, lourd et goutteux, le monarque tombait sur le nez, se heurtait contre les meubles. Bref il trouva ce jeu fort sot et entra dans une colère épouvantable. Il sonne, demande sa belle-sœur et la camarera mayor, et les traite de P. et de B. avec une éloquence qui lui est particulière, enfin il leur ordonne de préparer la reine, leur laissant un quart d'heure pour cette négociation. Puis en chemise et en pantoufles, il se promène dans une galerie fumant un cigare. Je ne sais ce que diable dirent ces femmes à la pauvre reine, ce qu'il y a de certain c'est qu'elles lui firent une telle peur que sa digestion en fut troublée. Quand le roi revint et voulut reprendre la conversation où il l'avait laissée, il ne trouva plus de résistance, mais à son premier effort pour ouvrir une porte, celle d'à côté s'ouvrit naturellement et tacha les draps d'une couleur toute autre que celle que l'on attend après une première nuit de noces. Odeur effroyable, car les reines ne jouissent pas des mêmes propriétés que la civette. Qu'auriez-vous fait à la place du roi? Il se sauva en jurant et fut 8 jours sans vouloir toucher à sa royale épouse.[64]

Stendhal was anxious that a diplomatic post should soon remove Mérimée from what he regarded as the deleterious influence of the *salons*. To Mareste in 1831 he confided that he thought it high time that 'Clara' (his nickname for Mérimée) went abroad:

> I should prefer him to be in the same position as me. Parisian society, I fear, is fatal for a young writer; he sees that it is perhaps more dangerous to rise above mediocrity than to sink below it. Then he is seized by disgust. As far as disgust is concerned, Clara is already a man of forty-five; so, Consul at Cagliari or Salonica.[65]

The surprisingly decorous timidity which Mérimée showed in his judgement of *Le Rouge et le Noir* must have done much to strengthen Stendhal in his opinion. So unbridled and unconventional in his correspondence, Mérimée had professed to be shocked by the novel. But as he grew older, Mérimée's opinions on literature became progressively more classical and more conservative.

Another absent friend was Jacquemont, who in 1828 had set out for a voyage of exploration in India, with Mérimée's copy of *Tristram Shandy* in his pocket as a memento. News from him reached Paris at intervals, but by April 1833, after no letters had arrived for some time, there came rumours of his death. These were confirmed all too quickly: Jacquemont had died in Bombay of an abscess on the liver in August 1832. Mérimée was greatly distressed at the loss of someone to whom he had been profoundly if undemonstratively attached, and one may take him at his word when he said he found Jacquemont's last letter 'heart-rending'.[66] A paradoxical proof of the depth of his emotion lies in the obituary notice which he wrote for the *Revue de Paris* a month later.[67] If it is stiff, formal and impersonal, it is because Mérimée was so moved that he was afraid of letting his feelings run away with him if he once started to express them. This is amply demonstrated by the much warmer essay he wrote many years later, when the pain had subsided

---

[64] To Stendhal, December 1830; *C.G.*, Vol. 1, pp. 85–6.
[65] Stendhal, *Correspondance*, Vol. II, pp. 240–1.
[66] *C.G.*, Vol. I, p. 234.
[67] It is reproduced in *Portraits historiques et littéraires*, pp. 93–9.

and he felt strong enough to expose his real affection for Jacquemont without losing control.[68] In the meantime, Jacquemont's death was a heavy blow to him amid all the other losses and disappointments which made him regard 1833 as a 'fatal' year,[69] coming close to fulfilling a fortune-teller's prediction that it would be his last.

One of his distractions in this gloomy period took the form of practical jokes. Mérimée had a highly developed sense of humour, and even his most despairing letters usually contain a note of comedy. Moreover, he took a perverse delight in mystifying people and disconcerting them, especially the pompous – there were those who were perpetually on their guard against his irony. The brother of the composer Meyerbeer was so wary that, if Mérimée passed him the vegetables at dinner, he would say: 'Spare me!'[70] He was not above posing as someone else, and once solemnly allowed Koreff to introduce him to some eager lion-hunter as Alfred de Musset. On another occasion, he and his friends went around Paris writing 'The late Duponchel' on the walls, having the unlucky victim's door draped with black and sending out notices of a mock funeral.[71] These irreverent pranks were a taste which he never entirely lost. Something of the same attitude is detectable in his lifelong predilection for telling dirty stories with impassive composure. His motives were, at least in part, both to puzzle everyone about what sort of man he really was and to remind them crudely of their own animality. Charles du Bos said of him: 'No one ever took a more secret delight in letting people down than Mérimée.'[72] Putting them in a position where they did not know what to make of him is one aspect of this, as well as yet another way of protecting his inmost nature from unwelcome contacts. It was about this time, too, that Mérimée accentuated the English style of his dress, getting Sutton Sharpe to do his shopping for him when he could not visit London;[73] that he assumed that cold, distant manner towards strangers or chance acquaintances that some found so repellent; that he affected more than ever an unchanging, impassive air; in short that he completed his pose

[68] *Portraits historiques et littéraires*, pp. 100–10.
[69] *C.G.*, Vol. I, p. 40.
[70] *C.G.*, Vol. XI, pp. 326–7.
[71] *C.G.*, Vol. I, p. 259.
[72] *Notes sur Mérimée*, Paris, Messein, 1920, p. 73.
[73] Cf. for instance *C.G.*, Vol. I, p. 248.

as an unostentatious but unmistakable dandy. Musset is reported to
have said of him:

> It's no use his wearing tight gloves and having his clothes tailored in
> England, he'll never be a perfect dandy; the back of his head will always
> look like a peasant's, and his hands and feet are those of a common fellow.[74]

But to others the illusion was complete: phlegmatic, imposing, laconic,
Mérimée cultivated an opaque exterior which disguised his true self all
too well.

Hard, cynical, coarse, debauched, foul-mouthed – superficially the
portrait of Mérimée in these years is anything but sympathetic, and it
is not even redeemed by the production of major literary works. Even
his diplomatic ambitions had petered out, and when in 1833 Stendhal
asked him when he was going to join the corps, he replied: 'I'm not
cautious enough for that. I'm too fond of my own comfort, and laziness
has made me rather brazen.'[75] However, two features modify the picture
and make him a more human and more interesting figure. One is his
inner aloofness from this way of life. Amid all his licentiousness, he
preserved a detached stability which made him as much a spectator as
an actor. He never succumbed to the lure of compulsive debauch as
did Musset; he could hold back from the worst excesses and even
withdraw from such a life when he judged it opportune. The second
is his own very real unhappiness. Embittered by disappointment, he
flung himself into a pit of sensuality as a way of forgetting, as a way of
insulting the hopes and ideals which had hurt him so unbearably. No
one reading the letters he wrote at that time can fail to hear, among the
cacophony of scandalous gossip, violent blasphemy, deliberate crudity
and cynical egotism, a recurrent note of extreme pain. To Jenny
Dacquin, Mérimée said he was spiteful when he was suffering,[76] and
throughout much of his life his hypersensitive temperament made him
suffer agonisingly. He told her that she was too young to have a
heart.

> Wait a little longer. When you really do acquire a heart, you can tell me
> how it feels. You will regret the happy days when you only lived through

---

[74] Auguste Barbier, *Souvenirs personnels et silhouettes contemporaines*, Paris,
Dentu, 1883, p. 293.

[75] *C.G.*, Vol. XVI, p. 58.

[76] *C.G.*, Vol. I, p. 188.

your mind, and you will see that the pains from which you suffer now are mere pinpricks compared to the dagger thrusts which will rain down on you when the time of passions arrives.[77]

This is what underlies the apparent hardness of Mérimée's character in the early 1830s: an excruciating torment which could only be borne by stifling it beneath a mass of triviality.

[77] *Ibid.*, pp. 196–7.

Chapter 7

Story-teller

. . . mon défaut à moi a toujours été la sécheresse; je faisais des squelettes.

To Ivan Turgenev, 6 December 1865

Mosaïque, as its name indicates, is a patchwork of heterogeneous elements, composed of short narrative and semi-narrative pieces which Mérimée had been writing since 1829.[1] Apart from seven tales, some of which are among the most celebrated in world literature, it contains a satirical playlet entitled *Les Mécontents* (*The Malcontents*), a handful of pseudo-ballads in the manner of *La Guzla*, and three belated *Letters from Spain*, in which he recounts his adventures in 1830 (a fourth, on *Spanish Witches*, did not appear until after the publication of *Mosaïque*[2]).

[1] The dates and places of publication are as follows: *Mateo Falcone*, *Revue de Paris*, 3 May 1829 (there is a manuscript dated 14 February 1829); *Vision de Charles XI*, *Revue de Paris*, 26 July 1829; *L'Enlèvement de la redoute*, *Revue française*, September 1829; *Tamango*, *Revue de Paris*, October 1829; *Le Fusil enchanté* (one of the Illyrian ballads), *Revue de Paris*, October 1829; *Federigo*, *Revue de Paris*, November 1829; *Romances* (*La Perle de Tolède* and two Illyrian ballads), *Revue de Paris*, December 1829; *Le Vase étrusque*, *Revue de Paris*, January 1830; *Les Mécontents*, *Revue de Paris*, March 1830; *La Partie de tric-trac*, *Revue de Paris*, June 1830; *Letters from Spain*, *Revue de Paris*, January and March 1831, and August 1832.

[2] In the *Revue de Paris*, December 1833. This is not all that he produced during that period. He omitted from *Mosaïque* a little anecdote of brigands entitled *Histoire de Rondino* which appeared in *Le National* on 19 February 1830 and of which Stendhal said to Sophie Duvaucel: 'It is the exact truth. The fish-man [a nickname given to Mérimée because he used to sketch fish in the aquarium] has, if anything, lessened the beauty of the character. He has taken away some of his *élan*' (*Correspondance*, Vol. II, p. 176). Nor did he include various critical studies: a review of the *Mémoires de Lord Byron* (*Le National*, 7 March 1830), *Réclamations contre les Mémoires de Lord Byron* (*Le National*, 6 June 1830), *Sir Thomas Lawrence* (*Le National*, 2 February 1830) and an article on the Madrid Museum (*L'Artiste*, March 1831).

Letters from Spain are among the most attractive and personal of Mérimée's writings. The colour and clarity of the scene-setting, the sinewy vigour of the narrative sections, the unobtrusively elegant style, the sudden glimpses of the author's enigmatic personality, combine to constitute unusually lively and original vignettes of travel in Spain. The light they throw on Spanish life in the early nineteenth century and the insight they afford into some of Mérimée's secret predilections make them gripping miniatures, as effective now as they were when they first appeared. Only their fragmentary nature, their brevity and their overshadowing by the tales which accompany them, have prevented them from taking their rightful place with the classics of travel literature.

Of the ballads, there is little to be said. *La Perle de Tolède* (*The Pearl of Toledo*) transfers to a Spanish setting the hot-blooded passions and imitation folk-song techniques of the *Guzla* poems, and is neither better nor worse than they are; the others too continue the same tradition. Nor does *Les Mécontents* add much to Mérimée's reputation. Nominally set in 1810 but in fact aimed at the ultra-royalists of 1829, it is a caricatural attack on reactionary nobles who dabble in amateur political conspiracies – to that extent it may be compared to parts of Stendhal's *Le Rouge et le Noir*, but it is infinitely less telling and less convincing. This is partly because the characters are little more than lay figures, partly because the plot has the simple obviousness of a music-hall sketch, partly because the satire itself lacks real bite. The only two characters who flicker into life are Édouard, the brusque and naïve young officer, who joins in the plot to please his beautiful if scatter-brained cousin, and Bertrand the peasant, rough, ill-mannered, courageous and bluntly ready for action where his aristocratic patrons are merely playing games. The schematic nature of the playlet deprives it of either human interest or comic force: it cocks a mildly amusing snook at a section of society which had never reconciled itself to the loss of its privileges under the *ancien régime*, but it does no more than that, and is notably inferior, even as liberal propaganda, to some of the pieces in the *Théâtre de Clara Gazul*.

The stories in *Mosaïque* are much the most successful and most significant part of the volume. Mérimée's progress towards the short story had been gradual but, at least in retrospect, inevitable. In his plays, he had concentrated on action; in his fake translations, he had built the poems round a narrative framework; in his one novel, he had preferred stringing together separate episodes to developing a broad theme. All that he had written thus sprang from the seed of brief sections of narrative fiction; once he had realised that these seeds were themselves viable works of art, he had only to offer them to the public without further adornment to produce masterpieces of the short story. That he should do so in 1829, when he was still in search of the genre best suited to his talents, is natural too, since that was a year when the Romantics, having discovered the fantastic tales of Hoffmann, were becoming especially interested in the potentialities of the form he had popularised.[3]

Certainly the brief tale proved much more suitable for Mérimée's special requirements than either the novel, the prose poem or the drama. He was never able to master the problem of imposing unity on diversity in a longer work of imagination, and the more ambitious his intentions were, the more he was liable to end up with a series of juxtaposed but disparate elements. As Pierre Trahard has pointed out, in his early years Mérimée practised a 'divergent aesthetic', which led to fragmentation and disunity; in 1829 he realised the virtues of a 'convergent aesthetic',[4] and by restricting his canvas to small dimensions, was able to impose on it a coherence and a density which had hitherto escaped him. Thereafter almost all his imaginative writings were brief narratives. He had discovered the form best attuned to his own temperament and was thereafter little inclined to go outside it.

There are many reasons why Mérimée felt so much at home with the short story. Compared with the novel, it gives little scope to a writer whose view of the world is broad and complex. On the other hand, by its very compactness, it offers excellent opportunities to anyone who is more concerned with effects than with causes, since a point can be made effectively without the necessity for those preparations and explanations which the novel normally requires. Thus that inveterate scepticism which made Mérimée suspicious of all generalisation tended to unfit him for novel-writing, while pushing him towards a reliance

[3] On the great vogue for Hoffmann which began in 1829, see P.-G. Castex, *Le Conte fantastique en France*, Paris, Corti, 1951, and Elizabeth Teichmann, *La Fortune de Hoffmann en France*, Geneva, Droz, 1961.

[4] *La Jeunesse de Prosper Mérimée*, Vol. II, Chap. 2. Cf. by the same author *Prosper Mérimée et l'art de la nouvelle*, Paris, Nizet, 3rd ed., 1952.

on individual facts that corresponded exactly to the bounds of the short-story form. Indeed, Mérimée's reluctance to visualise happenings on a large scale is one of the defects of a work like the *Chronique*. Moreover, his predilection for sudden, violent action, unencumbered by lengthy dialogue or diagnosis, sorted well with a genre which, by definition, demands concision. The pressure of strong emotions, which sometimes makes his longer works appear schematic in their succession of unexpected events, produces an intensity of feeling in the short tales that is perfectly expressed by a single dramatic act. Even Mérimée's style lends itself admirably to short-story writing: the urgent, clipped tones, the blunt statements of fact, the direct assault on the reader's sensibility are the ideal instrument for the tale as Mérimée conceived it. As early as 1831, Sainte-Beuve provided this penetrating summary of the qualities which drew Mérimée to the short story:

> the broad view of things does not suit him, his mind is too positive to believe in it; he believes in clearly defined, circumstantial facts, each carried to the logical conclusion of its special form of passion and of its expression in physical reality; the rest strikes him as so much smoke and cloud.[5]

The result is that when Mérimée first tried his hand at a short story early in 1829, he achieved mastery at one stroke. How far this success was brought about by deliberate calculation and how far it was an instinctive divining of a new technique it is hard to tell. Mérimée only rarely indulged in theorising about literature, and that for the most part in the later years of his life, when he drew on his own experience to appreciate the skills and problems of other authors.[6] What is certain is that his handling of the short story owes little to any of his immediate predecessors in France. One has only to look at the works of Charles

[5] Originally published in *Le Globe*, January 1831. In Sainte-Beuve, *Les Grands Ecrivains français. Le Dix-neuvième Siècle. Les Romanciers*, Vol. II, p. 283.

[6] For a stimulating study of Mérimée's thought on aesthetic questions, hitherto almost totally neglected, see R. C. Dale, *The Poetics of Prosper Mérimée*, Paris–The Hague, Mouton, 1966. But it would be difficult to argue that the ideas which one finds expressed with some consistency in the last twenty or thirty years of Mérimée's life were necessarily in his mind in the late 1820s and early 1830s, which was much the most productive period as far as works of imagination are concerned.

Nodier, the acknowledged master of the short story in the 1820s (and whom Mérimée was to succeed in the Academy in 1844), to see how vast is the gulf which separates the tales of *Mosaïque* from the great majority of earlier French stories. Where Nodier narrates slowly, amiably, digressively and verbosely, Mérimée strips his tales down to their bare essentials, makes every word and every detail count, and drives the action forward with relentless energy. In this way, he ensures that the short story acquires an identity and a character of its own – to quote one historian of the form,

> unhampered by tradition or the urge to write novels, he became the first French writer to treat brief fiction as more than a dehydrated novel or a miniature long romance.[7]

Their hallmark is that they could neither be expanded without a damaging dilution of their effects, nor reduced without a serious loss of substance and credibility. But this is the very quality of exactly adjusted economy by which we have come to recognise the best short stories written since Mérimée's time. Before him, only Diderot saw the necessity for packing a short narrative with as much explosive matter as possible if it was to produce its most devastating impact.[8] After him, most composers of short stories, from Maupassant to Camus, have regarded it as axiomatic that the unity of extreme compactness should distinguish the short story. Mérimée's tales, and foremost among them those in *Mosaïque*, are an unmistakable landmark in the history of the French short story.

Oddly enough, those tales which most strongly indicate this development are those written first, in 1829 – *Mateo Falcone*, *La Vision de Charles XI*, *L'Enlèvement de la redoute* (*The Storming of the Redoubt*), *Tamango* and *Federigo*; the two which date from 1830 – *La Partie de tric-trac* (*The Game of Backgammon*) and *Le Vase étrusque* – deal with more complicated psychological states and consequently require a more

[7] A. J. George, *Short Fiction in France 1800–1850*, Syracuse, Syracuse University Press, 1964, p. 132.

[8] Tales like *Les Deux Amis de Bourbonne* are among the few examples from earlier centuries which appear to conform to the same conception of the short story as that held by Mérimée. It is by no means impossible that Mérimée owes something to Diderot: such at least is the opinion of P. Trahard, *La Jeunesse de Prosper Mérimée*, Vol. II, pp. 47–57, who regards Diderot as one of Mérimée's early guides in the art of realism.

circumstantial mode of narration. The earlier group deals largely with the uncomplicated natures of brutal primitives – a Corsican peasant, a West African negro chief, soldiers in the thick of a murderous battle – whereas the second investigates the subtler reactions of a more civilised milieu (though violence is no less present here). It is the preoccupation with the spontaneous urges of people whose natural reactions are not stifled by convention that enables Mérimée to treat his subjects with such exemplary succinctness. The more delicate and profound the psychological dissection is to be, the more time the author needs for the operation, and the general direction of Mérimée's art after 1830 is consistently towards greater finesse and precision in the analysis of motive and feeling. Thus the extreme compression of *Mateo Falcone* and *L'Enlèvement de la redoute* is more of a starting-point than a fixed formula. Paradoxically, having demonstrated by his first essays in the genre the virtues of rigorous concision, Mérimée evolves towards a somewhat less restrictive art.

For the moment, however, his conception of the short story depends above all on compression. In nearly all these tales, he concentrates on a single situation of crisis and omits all description, comment or character-drawing which is not directly relevant to it. In *Mateo Falcone*, the action obeys the unities as strictly as any classical tragedy: the peasant's son betrays the bandit he has hidden, the father returns, discovers the boy's treachery and shoots him. In *L'Enlèvement de la redoute* all the glory and savagery of 1812 is condensed into a rapid account of one short but bloody combat. In *La Vision de Charles XI*, the king's sinister prophetic vision is related as abruptly as it happened. In *Tamango*, though the action covers a longer period, there is an equal sense of precipitancy in the story of the negro slave-trader who is shanghaied by an unscrupulous French captain, succeeds in rousing the slaves to massacre the crew, only to see them all perish when they find they cannot sail the ship. *Federigo* has a more complicated anecdote about a scamp who ingeniously tricks both God and the Devil, but Mérimée did not take it very seriously – he hesitated before including it in the collection and then excised it from subsequent editions. Even the two tales written in 1830 do not allow their slightly looser form to detract from their confinement within the strict bounds of economy and unity. Roger's remorse for having caused a man's death by cheating in *La Partie de tric-trac*, Saint-Clair's unreasoning jealousy and its fatal consequences in *Le Vase étrusque* may be more complex emotions than Mateo's cruel sense of honour or Tamango's animal cunning, but they are depicted with the same deft attention to detail and the same swiftness of movement.

Perhaps the most telling feature of Mérimée's art in the laconic concision of these tales is his brilliant use of the significant detail to enlist belief, to concentrate interest and to provide a concrete image for the mind to fasten on. From his earliest critical writings to his late literary studies, Mérimée regularly stressed the importance of singling out the one detail which would give the whole work, whether in fiction, in painting or in architecture, a centre and a term of reference. After his visit to Lawrence's studio, he noted that the painter had been accused of an excessive neglect of accessories, but that Lawrence deliberately dimmed out non-essentials:

> like Reynolds, he believed that *slackness* in the background brought out the *care* taken over the faces,[9]

and years later, he remembered hearing Lawrence say: 'Choose one feature in the face of your model, and copy that faithfully . . .'[10] He felt this meticulous selection of concrete detail to be especially important in tales of the supernatural. 'Never forget that, when you are recounting something supernatural, you can't have too many details of material reality. That's the great art of Hoffmann's fantastic stories.'[11] Elsewhere, writing about Pushkin, he makes his thought clearer; it is not the amount of detail which counts but its proper choice:

> The fact is that there has to be a little obscurity in any ghost story. Notice too that in all of them there is some striking, unforgettable feature: the problem one has to solve is finding the right feature [. . .] Any big lie requires some highly circumstantial detail to make it pass muster. That is why our master Rabelais left us the admirable precept that 'one should always use odd numbers when telling lies.[12]

---

[9] *Sir Thomas Lawrence*, in *Pages retrouvées de Prosper Mérimée*, ed. Hector Malo, Paris, Émile-Paul, 1929, p. 10.

[10] *Ivan Tourguénef*, in *Études de littérature russe*, ed. H. Mongault, Paris, Champion, 1931, Vol. II, p. 242.

[11] *C.G.*, Vol. V, p. 238.

[12] *Alexandre Pouchkine*, in *Études de littérature russe*, Vol. I, pp. 12–13.

This principle is much in evidence in the *Mosaïque* stories. The cupidity of young Falcone when the sergeant bribes him to reveal the whereabouts of the bandit he has hidden is given a palpable physical presence by the shining watch which is dangled in front of his face as a reward:

> meanwhile the watch was swinging to and fro, and sometimes bumped against the end of his nose. At last, little by little, his right hand rose towards the watch: the tips of his fingers touched it; and all its weight was resting in his hand, though the sergeant-major still held on to the other end of the chain. . . . The dial was sky-blue . . . the case newly polished . . . in the sunlight it seemed to be on fire . . . The temptation was too strong.[13]

In *La Vision de Charles XI*, one might suppose that the king's sanguinary vision was a mere hallucination – save that there remained on his slipper a bloodstain from the severed head. *Le Vase étrusque* is at the heart of the story named after it: the thought that it had been given to his mistress by a former admirer excites Saint-Clair's jealousy; the sight of it is a continual torment to him; and Mathilde has to smash it before he will believe her assurances of innocence. Other details have a similar function. The description of the maquis at the opening of *Mateo Falcone* is indispensable to an understanding of the privileged status of outlaws in Corsica and almost every reference to dress or customs has its place in evoking the unique atmosphere of the island, without which these events could never have happened. The West African local colour of *Tamango* likewise serves to define the uniqueness of the events recounted: unobtrusively woven into the narration, it becomes less a backcloth than an integral part of the story itself. What we have no need to know is omitted. Of the lieutenant who relates *L'Enlèvement de la redoute* we learn only that it was his first taste of battle. If Mateo Falcone is described at somewhat greater length, it is because the shooting of his son would be neither comprehensible nor credible without some knowledge of his pride, his ruthlessness, his autocratic single-mindedness. Mérimée always regarded word-painting for its own sake with withering contempt – he said of Renan, with amused superiority: 'instead of getting on with his story, he describes the woods and the fields'.[14]

But Mérimée is also a master of the apparently inconsequential touch or unnecessary piece of information which carries conviction precisely

[13] *Romans et nouvelles*, Vol. I, p. 247.   [14] *C.G.*, Vol. XIV, p. 530.

because it is there for no visible reason. The endings of his tales illustrate this. *Mateo Falcone* concludes, not with the death of the boy, but with the father saying: 'Send a message to tell my son-in-law Tiodoro Bianchi to come and live with us,'[15] thereby indicating that the tragic death of the child is only an incident in a continuing sequence of existence, that the waves of time will soon wash away the name written in sand. In *Le Vase étrusque* the hero Saint-Clair is killed in a senseless duel which he provoked when he was jealous of his mistress's past. But we only hear of this at second hand, in a conversation between two of his friends, who are more concerned with irrelevancies like the way in which the body had fallen or the unfortunate damage to the butt of his expensive pistol than with the snuffing out of a human life. Saint-Clair will soon be forgotten; his mistress will pine away; the world will continue as if he had never loved and died. The most brutal intrusion of an indifferent reality comes at the end of *La Partie de tric-trac*. The story is being told by the captain of a ship lying becalmed somewhere at sea. Just at the moment when he is about to describe Roger's death, he is interrupted by the sighting of a whale, breaks off his tale and thinks only of the new diversion which has presented itself. Mérimée concludes laconically: 'I was never able to find out how the unfortunate Roger died.'[16] The reader is at once impressed by the air of honesty and naturalness which emanates from this admission, and disturbed by the coolly ironic detachment of an author who can bring a moving story to such an incongruously abrupt close. Credibility and impersonality are equally served by this highly sophisticated technique of assumed casualness.

The style, too, by its precision and its sobriety, creates an impression of truthful frankness. Mérimée has often been reproached with having a colourless style.[17] To the extent that he cultivates no rhetorical effects,

[15] *Romans et nouvelles*, Vol. I, p. 253.   [16] *Ibid.*, p. 346.

[17] Cf. for instance these annotations by Jean de la Varende, the contemporary novelist, in his copy of Mérimée's *Nouvelles*: 'One of the things that astonishes me – and there are quite a few of the same sort – is Mérimée's reputation as a stylist. Never mind how arid and fleshless his writing is – that's ghastly, but one can find excuses for it; but what about that lifeless prose, that heavy, ill-conceived composition? . . . Oh yes, the style is bare all right – as bare as a skinned rabbit' (from an autograph catalogue by Michel Herbert, II, rue de Vaugirard, Paris. I am indebted to M. P.-E. Artur for drawing my attention to this quotation).

that his sentences are simple and direct, that his images are neither frequent nor original, that the tone is generally conversational, there is something in this criticism. But the very absence of poetic flourishes, emotional tirades or elaborate convolutions makes his language the ideal vehicle for short stories which aim both to convince and to shock. 'My antipathy for stylistic brilliance is so strong that I kill it off wherever I find it',[18] he declared in 1831, and the fact that he writes with such anonymous detachment gives his tales the dry crispness of the reports of a trained observer, concerned only to present a factual statement of events. But Mérimée did not seek the same kind of impersonality as Flaubert. He makes no attempt to disguise the presence of a story-teller or to avoid the introduction of phrases expressing personal opinions: several of the tales in *Mosaïque – Mateo Falcone, L'Enlèvement de la redoute* and *La Partie de tric-trac* – are told in the first person, and the others contain frequent authorial interjections. However, this serves to create a distancing effect – the narrator of *Mateo Falcone*, for example, has such a shadowy existence that the author's personal involvement is decreased rather than enhanced by his presence, and the officer and the ship's captain in the other two stories simply make it clear to us that Mérimée is repeating hearsay for which he accepts no responsibility. The creation of a false identity behind which he can shelter unseen is a device which he will use to even greater effect in *La Vénus d'Ille* and *Carmen*. Similarly, when in *Le Vase étrusque* Mérimée uses autobiographical material which for him carries an unusually high charge of personal emotion, he deliberately affects a tone of almost supercilious amusement to describe his hero, Saint-Clair.

These effects of aloofness and impassiveness damp down any pathos latent in the subject-matter of the tales – to see just how much Mérimée has left unspoken, one needs only to glance at Balzac's *Un Drame au bord de la mer* (*A Drama by the Seaside*), in which the theme of a father killing his son to redeem the family honour is treated with heavy stress on the horror of the deed and the remorse it would later inspire.[19]

[18] *C.G.*, Vol. I, p. 98.
[19] Cf. *Un Drame au bord de la mer* in Balzac, *Short Stories*, ed. A. W. Raitt, London, Oxford University Press, 1964. The same conclusion emerges if one looks at Adalbert von Chamisso's German versification of the tale entitled *Mateo Falcone, der Corse* or at Flaubert's juvenile imitation *Matteo Falcone, ou Deux Cercueils pour un proscrit*. Both authors strive for Mérimée's economy,

E

Yet the events of all these brief anecdotes burn with a white heat of passion. Mateo's fierce pride compels him to destroy what he loves most dearly; Roger's shame at having caused a man's death by cheating at backgammon is so overwhelming that he courts and finds death in action; Saint-Clair is consumed by silly, pointless jealousy until he too is killed by it. The savage instincts of Tamango, the horror-stricken shudder of Charles XI, the unreasoning actions of soldiers in the heat of battle, all reveal the same view of humanity as constantly shaken by feelings and appetites which it cannot control and which defy rational analysis.

As G. Hainsworth has pointed out,[20] the contrast in *Tamango* between those reputed to be savages and those reputed to be civilised is instructive. Mérimée (who as a good liberal, a friend of Fanny Wright and a frequenter of the Stapfer salon was accustomed to hearing slave-trading indignantly condemned as a degrading and inhuman practice) begins his story with a series of sarcastic digs at the hypocrisy of dealers in black ivory: the ironically named Captain Ledoux generously allows a space of five feet by two for each negro during the six-week voyage, ' "for the truth is", as Ledoux told the shipowner to justify this liberal measure, "negroes are, after all, human beings just as much as white men" '.[21] But as the story develops it becomes clear that it is anything but abolitionist propaganda. A kindly interpreter turns loose a few slaves, 'who ran off in all directions, completely at a loss to know how to get back to their homeland two hundred leagues from the coast',[22] and those who try to seize their new liberty are, like Tamango himself, selfish, brutal, and above all stupid. 'The sum of the tale, clearly, sets in parallel savagery and civilisation, to the greater glory of neither.'[23] Human nature is shown as never far from the basic animality of passion, and Mérimeé takes sardonic pleasure in demonstrating that the elegant and sophisticated Saint-Clair is just as much the plaything of his unstable emotions as an uneducated primitive like Tamango.

It is this combination of highly controlled narrative craft and un-

---

but neither can resist the temptation of interpolating words or phrases to stress the vileness of Fortunato's betrayal and the pathos of his death.

[20] G. Hainsworth, 'West African Local Colour in *Tamango*', *French Studies*, January, 1967.   [21] *Romans et Nouvelles*, Vol. I, p. 286.

[22] *Ibid.*, p. 290.   [23] Hainsworth, *art. cit.*

controllable feeling which gives Mérimée's tales their unique flavour. Keeping the tightest possible rein on his own reactions, relating events with the imperturbable technical mastery of a born *raconteur*, never allowing the tone to rise above that of urbane conversation, Mérimée brings us to the very edge of the abysses which open up within our very being, allows us a terrifying glimpse into their depths, and then, with an off-hand shrug, returns us to the apparent security of ordinary existence. Just as in his own life, Mérimée protected himself against the ravages of a hypertrophied sensibility by cultivating intellectual detachment and humorous deprecation, so in his tales he hints at the proximity of what Theophil Spoerri calls 'the blood-crazed elemental nether regions'.[24] He makes the techniques of restraint, so essential to a good short story, not merely an artificial foreshortening of perspective but an indispensable instrument for viewing realities which would be too terrible to be borne if they were seen in their full, stark truth.

Which of the tales is most effective is ultimately a matter of personal choice. Certainly none makes a more powerful impact than *Mateo Falcone*. The story itself is not new; a good half-dozen versions were already in print.[25] Nor can Mérimée be given much credit for the details of local colour, since he had culled them all from various guide-books and historical works about Corsica[26] (after he had himself visited the island in 1839, he corrected some of the more glaring inaccuracies and removed the subtitle of *Mœurs de la Corse* (*Corsican Manners*)[27] which in the meantime had become sadly dated). But if

[24] Theophil Spoerri, 'Mérimée and the Short Story', *Yale French Studies*, 4, 1949.

[25] Much has been written about the sources of *Mateo Falcone*. The main articles are Max Kuttner, 'Die korsischen Quellen von Chamisso und Mérimée', *Archiv für das Studium der neueren Sprachen*, Vol. CXI, 1903; G. Courtillier, 'L'Inspiration de *Mateo Falcone*', *Revue d'Histoire littéraire de la France*, avril–juin 1920; Gustave Charlier, 'La Source principale de *Mateo Falcone*', *Revue d'Histoire littéraire de la France*, juillet–septembre 1921. Two full recent studies sum up the present state of knowledge. These are Maria Kosko, *Le Thème de 'Mateo Falcone'*, Paris, Nizet, 1960, and A. Naaman, *'Mateo Falcone' de Mérimée*, Paris, Nizet, 1967.

[26] The most useful of the works he consulted was Feydel's *Mœurs et coutumes des Corses* (1799, 2nd ed. 1802).

[27] Cf. Maurice Souriau, 'Les Variantes de *Mateo Falcone*', *Revue d'Histoire littéraire de la France*, avril–juin 1913.

Mérimée's imagination invents little it excels at the selection and rearrangement of given materials and the vivid immediacy of *Mateo Falcone* is utterly convincing. Hastening through a series of linked crises – the arrival of the hunted bandit, the vain search by the troops, the bribe and its acceptance, the return of Mateo, the shooting of the boy – it maintains an almost unbearable tension. Few lines in French literature deliver a more stunning blow with simple means than the famous sentence relating the boy's death: 'Mateo fired and Fortunato fell stone dead.'[28] The total absence of moral comment or inner psychological analysis concentrates attention exclusively on the action itself, but that is so carefully prepared and so full of emotive force that further explanations could only seem superfluous. The exact adjustment of outward deed or gesture to inward states of mind is always one of the great strengths of Mérimée's art. Here the contrast between the awfulness of the killing and the author's rigid refusal to capitalise on it conveys a sense of icy sobriety which fully justifies Walter Pater's description of *Mateo Falcone* as 'perhaps the cruellest story in the world'.[29]

La Vision de Charles XI, Mérimée's first attempt at the ghost-story, seems somewhat less effective, perhaps because he himself surpassed it so brilliantly in later works, perhaps because the Gothic horrors of the vision barely escape meretriciousness. Its most interesting feature is the care taken to persuade us of its authenticity. Mérimée's claim that it is based on attested documents is not without justification (though in fact the papers in the Swedish archives to which he refers were apocryphal),[30] and he adopts the calm, impartial style of a historian whose sole aim is to set out established facts. Moreover, the non-hallucinatory nature of the vision seems to be guaranteed by the bloodstain which remains on the king's slipper after the gory phantoms have faded – but that is a detail of Mérimée's own fabrication. In this story Mérimée deploys his gifts of minutely convincing narration to instil in us the same sense of uncomprehending unease as overcomes the supposed participants in the vision. Perhaps for the first time, a French writer has sought to use the supernatural, not as fantasy, as entertain-

[28] *Romans et Nouvelles*, Vol. I, p. 252.
[29] *Prosper Mérimée*, in *Studies in Modern European Literature*, p. 45.
[30] Cf. Roger Peyre, 'A propos de *La Vision de Charles XI* de Mérimée', *Revue d'Histoire littéraire de la France*, janvier–mars 1914.

ment, as allegory or as a scarcely credible embroidery on reality, but as something which can inexplicably but incontrovertibly intrude into the fabric of ordinary life. If at the end of the tale we are uncertain whether or not to believe him, his purpose has been achieved. His own attitude to the occult is compounded of approximately equal parts of credulity and scepticism, and if he can insinuate the same doubts into the minds of his readers, he has effectively demonstrated to them how frail and unsteady is the position humanity holds in the universe.

L'Enlèvement de la Redoute has, from its publication, ranked with *Mateo Falcone* as a masterpiece of the short story. It has the same background of real or assumed authenticity as the two earlier tales,[31] the same streamlined economy of execution, the same urgency of style, the same insistence on violence as an essential part of human life. Yet many readers would sense in it, as André Gide did in *La Partie de trictrac*, 'an intolerable impression of useless perfection and well done homework'.[32] No doubt it is an astonishing feat to have condensed into half a dozen pages the whole atmosphere of Napoleon's Russian campaign, but one wonders whether it was worth performing: inevitably, the epic sweep is missing, and no great human interest compensates for its lack. Technically, the tale is impeccable, but once that has been said, there is little to add.

Tamango is a more complex and a more disturbing work. Again Mérimée has documented himself thoroughly, and skilfully used his knowledge to authenticate the strange events which constitute his story.[33] But here his ulterior motive, never clearly indicated though

[31] Cf. Lucien Pinvert, 'L'Enlèvement de la redoute', *Revue des Études historiques*, mai–juin 1914. The redoubt of Schwardino, which Mérimée calls Cheverino, was captured on 5 September 1812, after a violent combat. The involuntary deformation of the name tends to confirm Mérimée's assertion that he heard the story from a lieutenant who was present at the battle; if he had had a written source, there would be no reason for the spelling to be wrong. Cf. also Col. Ferron, 'A propos d'une nouvelle de Mérimée (*L'Enlèvement de la redoute*. Deux épisodes de la bataille de la Moskowa)', *Carnets de la Sabretache*, décembre 1960.

[32] *Journal 1889–1939*, Paris, Bibliothèque de la Pléiade, 1939, p. 277.

[33] Cf. especially Léon Vignols, 'Les Sources du *Tamango* de Mérimée et la littérature négrière à l'époque romantique', *Mercure de France*, 15 décembre 1927; Alexander Haggerty Krappe, 'Notes sur les sources de Mérimée',

always implicit in the progress of the action, is, as we have seen, to set the savage beside the civilised man and to give an equally bitter picture of both. The irony which runs through the story serves not only this misanthropic end, but a variety of subsidiary purposes: to expose the horrors of the slave-trade, to ridicule the myth of the 'good savage', to give a grim reminder of the futility of unplanned humanitarianism, and generally to deride human folly, human greed and human ferocity. Little that Mérimée wrote has quite the same note of unrelieved pessimism as *Tamango*; its dark colours are enhanced by an acid humour in the style, which culminates in the ultimate incongruity of Tamango's career:

> The colonel of the 75th noticed him and took him on to play the cymbals in the regimental band. He learned a little English; but he never talked much. On the other hand, he drank rum and tafia to excess. He died in hospital of an inflammation of the chest.[34]

Federigo has never enjoyed the popularity of its fellows, and Mérimée himself was unsure whether to include it in the collection. Yet this slight anecdote of a reprobate who by his cheerful trickery outwits both God and the Devil has an unpretentious charm of its own. How much this is due to Mérimée's own ingenuity is unsure, since the source of the story has never been clearly identified – but there is no reason to doubt his word that it derives from an old Neapolitan legend. The tone is light and unassuming, as befits a folk-tale which neither author nor reader takes very seriously; at most, one might see in it a vague prefiguration of the theme of *Les Ames du Purgatoire* (*The Souls in Purgatory*), Mérimée's version of the Don Juan story, which it resembles in that both treat the theme of the rogue who seeks to escape retribution for his misdeeds. But it would be going too far to diagnose it as a twinge from the conscience of an author who was well aware of his own transgressions of the conventional moral code; it remains no more

---

Revue d'Histoire littéraire de la France, avril–juin 1928; G. Hainsworth, *art. cit.* Another article by L. Vignols on 'Une Version remaniée et inconnue du *Tamango* de Mérimée', *Revue d'Histoire littéraire de la France*, avril–juin 1927, may safely be ignored, since it is highly unlikely that Mérimée had anything to do with the text in question, which appears to be an unauthorised plagiarism.

[34] *Romans et Nouvelles*, Vol. I, p. 307.

than an amusing recital of a blithely and harmlessly irreverent folk-tale.

Le Vase étrusque, on the other hand, bids fair to be considered as one of his greatest achievements. Based as it is on Mérimée's tempestuous affair with Émilie Lacoste,[35] it contains in Saint-Clair a discreet but extremely revealing self-portrait which renders it doubly precious to his admirers. This current of genuine personal emotion, though half-hidden by the froth of surface frivolity, gives it a tragic colouring and a power to move which Mérimée is inclined to forfeit elsewhere by a too rigid refusal to admit any sympathy with his characters. The vacillations of the morbidly sensitive hero are portrayed with a re-markably delicate touch, and though Mérimée still prefers to reveal emotion through gesture and action rather than through abstract categorisation, the greater complexity of Saint-Clair's reactions induces him to treat the subject more spaciously than he had done with the relatively simple natures of Mateo or Tamango. Indeed, the long conversation at the stag-party during which Saint-Clair's jealousy is first aroused, though an outstanding example of natural and lifelike dialogue,[36] moves sinuously through areas of no great relevance to the central topic. Mérimée, incorrigibly attracted by local colour, even manages to bring it into this Parisian tale (with a wry smile) by means of Neville's account of his travels in Egypt. But all this accentuates the essential intimacy of the tale. As in the two plays which were added in 1829 to the *Théâtre de Clara Gazul*, Mérimée has become fascinated by the tragic inconsistencies of human feelings, and these he traces with profound skill and insight. The agony of suspicion in a proudly solitary mind leads to a fatal petulance which is as pointless as jealousy of a dead man had been in the first place. The tragedy of *Le Vase étrusque* is all the more moving for being so unnecessary. It is perhaps Mérimée's harshest lesson on the fragility of human happniess.

Like *Le Vase étrusque*, *La Partie de tric-trac*, while not quite attaining its emotive force, is a telling study in the destructive effects of a momen-tary impulse. Just as Saint-Clair's life is lost because in a fit of pique he

[35] Cf. pp. 67–9.
[36] Attempts have been made to identify the participants as various friends of Mérimée – Stendhal, Jacquemont, Mareste and so on. But it is far more likely that all the portraits (including even Saint-Clair, who resembles Stendhal and Jacquemont as well as Mérimée) are composite.

insults a friend, so Roger's life is wrecked because in a fleeting second of weakness he cheats at backgammon. Mérimée, typically, refuses even to allow him the excuse of having love as the spur:

> When I cheated that Dutchman, all I was thinking of was winning twenty-five napoleons! I had no thought of Gabrielle, and that's why I despise myself . . . . That I should hold my honour worth less than twenty-five napoleons! . . . What vileness![37]

This debasement of motivation is matched by a devaluation of the whole story when the captain breaks off: 'A whale!' cried the captain, overcome with joy and forgetting all about his tale; 'Quick! Lower the longboat! Lower the yawl! All the longboats! Harpoons, ropes, etc., etc.'[38] Probably only Mérimée would have dared to use 'etc.' as an anticlimax to such a dramatic sequence of events, but then only Mérimée would want to show us how trivial the most appalling disasters may seem in perspective.

The tales of *Mosaïque* constitute one of the most remarkable collections of short stories ever assembled. Models of a genre which was still far from maturity, they retain today all of their whiplash force, and not even Maupassant has surpassed the best of them. Their qualities make them read as though they were still fresh from the press; even what might seem shortcomings are converted by Mérimée into positive elements in their success. It may well be that Mérimée did not have it in him to produce a great novel, but in the more modest genre of the short story, he undoubtedly ranks with the world's masters.

[37] *Romans et Nouvelles*, Vol. I, p. 343.

[38] *Ibid.*, p. 346. In 1828, Mérimée had visited his cousin Jean-Auguste Marc, who was a naval officer; this may account for the presence of two seafaring tales in *Mosaïque*. There is no known source for *La Partie de tric-trac*.

Chapter 8

Inspector-General

Pourquoi, dans ce siècle de spéculations, n'en ferait-on pas
une pour la recherche des monumens antiques?
Notes d'un voyage dans le Midi de la France

In April 1834, in one of those ministerial crises which have always been
a feature of French parliamentary democracy, the Duc de Broglie was
eliminated from the government and with him, Mérimée's patron
Count d'Argout. At first, Mérimée feared that his own future might be
jeopardised, but a few days later, when the diminutive though irrepressible Thiers took over the Ministry of the Interior, he was offered
the post of Inspector-General of Historic Monuments, which he
accepted with alacrity: 'it's just the thing for my tastes, my indolence
and my desire to travel'.[1] The official announcement of his appointment, at a salary of 8,000 francs, appeared on 17 May, heralding the
start of a new and totally different life for him.

At first sight, Mérimée's qualifications for the job might have
seemed insignificant, and there were those who poked fun at his total
lack of experience in archaeological matters. Alexandre Dumas, for
instance, remarked that Mérimée would have to begin by learning
what he was expected to teach others.[2] In reality, Thiers's choice was a
remarkably shrewd one in the circumstances, which were anything
but the same as those which would attend such an appointment today.
It was only in 1830 that Guizot, himself a professor of history, had
created the post for Ludovic Vitet, a friend of Mérimée, an ardent
liberal politician, an author of historical plays, and one of the leading
figures on the review *Le Globe*.[3] Until then, although since the turn
of the century the state had taken an occasional interest in the preserva-

---

[1] *C.G.*, Vol. I, p. 275.

[2] Quoted by A. de Pontmartin, *Mes Mémoires. Seconde Jeunesse*, Vol. II,
Paris, Calmann-Lévy, 1886, p. 62.

[3] On Vitet, see M. Parturier's introduction to Mérimée's *Lettres à Ludovic
Vitet*, Paris, Plon, 1934.

tion of old buildings, no arrangement had existed for it to accept any general responsibility for their upkeep.[4] In the 1820s, accompanying the great renascence of historical studies, there was heard an increasing outcry against the neglect of the country's architectural heritage, in which Hugo and Montalembert denounced vandalism with particular vehemence,[5] while Baron Taylor and Charles Nodier began publicising the forgotten artistic riches of the provinces in a celebrated series of travel-books.[6] In order to join in the movement the new-born July Monarchy instituted various ambitious measures, of which the most important was perhaps the creation of the post of Inspector-General of Historic Monuments.

Vitet, who counted among his manifold accomplishments a sound knowledge of archaeology and the history of art, had in four years done much to define the duties of the post, to establish the techniques necessary to carry them out, and to give his small department a recognised place in the complicated machinery of the civil service. He had laid it down that his two overriding tasks were to list all the outstand-

[4] The definitive work on the history of the conservation of ancient monuments in France is P. Léon, *La Vie des monuments français*, Paris, Picard, 1951. In this large and lavishly illustrated volume, there is an authoritative account of Mérimée's activities as Inspector-General. It may be supplemented by the history of 'Le Service des Monuments historiques', P. Verdier, in *Le Congrès archéologique de France*, 97, Paris, Picard, 1936, Vol. I. Much of the background information to the present chapter comes from these two works. In addition, the reader may consult the first section of P. Trahard's *Prosper Mérimée de 1834 à 1853*, Paris, Champion, 1928, and A. Hallays, 'Mérimée Inspecteur des monuments historiques', *Revue des Deux Mondes*, le 15 avril 1911, as well as other articles mentioned below. Despite the value of these investigations, there is still room for a full-scale study of Mérimée's contribution to archaeology and to the cause of ancient monuments.

[5] Hugo's *Guerre aux démolisseurs!* and above all *Notre-Dame de Paris* in 1830 are powerful pleas for respectful treatment of old buildings. Montalembert's campaign, inside and outside the French parliament, was long and vigorous, including works with titles such as *Lettres sur le vandalisme*, *Le Vandalisme en France* and *Du Vandalisme et du Catholicisme en France*. Both men played extremely active parts on the various official committees concerned with ancient monuments. Cf. J. Mallion, *Victor Hugo et l'art architectural*, Paris, P.U.F., 1963.

[6] The *Voyages romantiques et pittoresques dans l'ancienne France* were started in 1818 and went on appearing until 1878.

ing buildings in France and to ensure their preservation, and had himself undertaken tours of inspection in Provence and the South-West
of France. But active commitment to politics prevented him from
devoting all his time to the post, and when in 1834 his close friend
Tanneguy Duchâtel became Minister of Trade, Vitet was offered and
accepted the job of Secretary-General of the Ministry. Vitet's achievement was as nothing compared with what had still to be done to save
the rapidly decaying heritage, and there was no obvious successor.

Thiers, who had always felt considerable respect for Mérimée's
talents, saw that he possessed unusual qualities for the post. Deeply
interested in things artistic, familiar with the world of artists, endowed
with apparently endless energy, a conscientious, skilled and experienced
administrator, Mérimée was also a man of sufficient fame and personal
authority to lend a fairly novel position something of his own prestige.
That he had no specialised knowledge of the subject was of no great
moment: in those days few people had, since interest in the conservation of historic buildings, especially the medieval, was very new. What
mattered most was that Mérimée had a keen sense for historical research, a real if unostentatious love of beauty, and a proven ability to
master quickly the intricacies of any subject which might be thrust
upon him. This was what he now set about doing before embarking
on his first tour of inspection. Naturally he enlisted the help and advice
of Vitet; he wrote to eminent archaeologists and antiquaries such as
Arcisse de Caumont, founder and president of the Society of Antiquaries in Normandy and perhaps the most illustrious French archaeologist;[7] he borrowed notes from Baron Taylor.[8] No doubt, too, with
his usual scrupulous respect for exact information, he spent as much
time as he could reading in libraries and consulting specialists in the
capital.

Nevertheless, it was after only two months' preparation that the new
Inspector-General departed on 31 July 1834 for the South of France,
on what was to be the first of a long and arduous series of tours of
inspection. For the next eighteen years, he was to set off every summer on
similar pilgrimages to the four corners of France, visiting ancient ruins,
recording his discoveries, assessing the relative merits of claims on his
limited funds, supervising repairs and restoration, conferring with

[7] Cf. *C.G.*, Vol. I, p. 287.
[8] Cf. M. Parturier, introduction to Mérimée's *Lettres aux Grasset*.

local dignitaries and politicians, trying to find competent architects, sculptors and stonemasons, sorting out delicate legal, aesthetic and structural problems, endeavouring to reconcile conflicting interests, and indefatigably combating vandalism, ignorance and negligence wherever he found it. At first, these tours usually went on for several months – in 1834, his journey through Burgundy and Provence lasted until December; in 1835 he was in Brittany and the West from July until October; in 1836 he spent three months in the eastern provinces; in 1837 he travelled for the same length of time in Auvergne and the centre of France; in 1838, he left for the West and the South-West in June and returned in mid-September; in 1839 an unusually long peregrination through Provence and on to Corsica kept him away from Paris from June until December.

Later, once he had familiarised himself with each region and its particular problems, his travels tended to be shorter and his annual tour was often over in less than a month. But there were many brief trips at other times to special destinations – for instance in December 1834 to Saumur, at Thiers's behest, to examine the tomb of Richard the Lionheart, which called forth from him the cutting verdict that 'your tomb of Richard the Lionheart is just a bad joke, not worth making a poor devil catch a cold to go and see it'.[9] Moreover, he often found himself travelling over bad roads in decrepit coaches, living in flea-ridden inns, spending interminable evenings of boredom in sleepy provincial backwaters, obliged to see every supposed ancient monument or disinterred relic with his own eyes and to send back elaborate reports and recommendations to his Minister in Paris. The extent and conscientiousness of his investigations is almost incredible.

On these tours, his double mission was to list and describe the often unknown architectural treasures of France, and to save them from ruin or desecration. The first task took more of his time on the early tours; the second task predominated in later years, once the initial prospections had been completed. The dangers to ancient monuments were multiple. For centuries, Gothic architecture had been disdained as barbaric by both architects and public, brought up in a narrowly classical tradition, and little had been done to protect medieval buildings against the ravages of time. Their parlous state had often been worsened by the vandalism of the Revolutionary mobs and the

[9] *C.G.*, Vol. I, p. 370.

fanatical anti-Catholicism of Revolutionary authorities. More insidious and frequently more irreparable was the damage done by incompetent restoration and embellishment. Left to their own devices, local priests and church councils had covered medieval frescoes with flat washes of cheap paint,[10] knocked down rood-screens and porches that hampered processions, thrown away stained-glass windows that did not let in enough light, replaced priceless tapestries and pictures with cheap modern works so as to keep up with fashion, tampered recklessly with the structure of buildings already nearing collapse. Ancient monuments in private hands had been converted into shops, barns or warehouses, or even demolished to provide stones for new constructions. Government departments had taken over churches, castles and palaces and ruthlessly mutilated them for their own purposes – the abbey on Mont-Saint-Michel was a prison and the Palace of the Popes at Avignon a barracks. Local authorities likewise put medieval relics to incongruous purposes, allowed parasitical structures to be erected all round them, razed them to the ground to accommodate schemes for road widening, hacked them about or destroyed them in the great expansion of urban development which was beginning in the nineteenth century. By the 1830s, when Gothic architecture started to arouse a quite new enthusiasm, the situation was desperate, and the difficulties facing the Inspector-General redoubtable.

First of all, the law was neither clear nor helpful. The principle of state protection of historic monuments was such a recent innovation that the *locus standi* of the Inspector-General was anything but certain. It was possible for him to have a building classified as an ancient monument, but that did not confer on him any very effective rights. After 1833, expropriation became possible in certain circumstances, but it was such an extreme and costly step that it was rarely taken.[11] Otherwise only the provision of subsidies for repair and restoration

[10] From the outset, this was – understandably – one of Mérimée's hobby-horses. Ever since his visit to Spain in 1830, he had been furious at the idea of slapping paint over old murals or decorations, and even before it was officially his business, he had persuaded d'Argout, as Minister of the Interior, to send out a circular forbidding the practice (cf. *C.G.*, Vol. I, pp. 289–90).

[11] Mérimée used it to help clear the amphitheatres at Arles and Orange of the houses which had been built there. But it was so onerous and so productive of ill-will that he preferred to keep it in reserve as a threat.

gave him a firm responsibility for the work to be done. But this provision of course was in itself a major issue. When Mérimée became Inspector-General, the government was making annual *ad hoc* payments of up to 100,000 francs for the upkeep of historic monuments. But though he succeeded in inducing the government to give him a regular budget of 120,000 francs in 1836, to raise it to 200,000 francs in 1838, 400,000 francs in 1840, 600,000 francs in 1842 and 800,000 francs in 1848, these increases always lagged behind the magnitude of the expenditure, even allowing for the voting of supplementary credits for special projects like the restoration of Notre-Dame de Paris in the 1840s. As Mérimée added more and more buildings to those worth preserving, so his funds fell more and more short of what was needed. It was his responsibility to advise on their allocation, and it was a heavy burden to respect simultaneously the national interest, local susceptibilities, political pressures and practical possibilities.

In addition, Mérimée's work was seriously handicapped by lack of trained staff. Not only was it impossible for him to delegate responsibility for the inspection of the monuments, but it rapidly became apparent that there were very few architects to whom delicate and complicated tasks of repair could be safely entrusted. No one had specialised in the difficult task of conservation – the technical and aesthetic peculiarities of the Gothic style were ignored in architectural schools; many provincial architects were no better than clumsy amateurs. Mérimée soon found that it was folly to allow local architects to supervise major programmes such as the preservation of the church at St Savin with its magnificent wall-paintings. When Mérimée returned there in 1840, he was horrified by the ignorance of the architect in charge of the repairs:

> He asked me if St Savin was a Gothic church, and seemed to be living in the pious belief that Gothic and Romanesque were contemporary with each other, something like the Ionic and Corinthian orders, and that people sometimes built in one way, sometimes in the other, according to taste.[12]

After 1840 he preferred to send trusted specialists from Paris to take charge of important projects in the provinces, but as late as 1846 he was complaining to Vitet that 'it gets more obvious every day that we have only three or four architects on whom we can rely'.[13] Once

[12] *C.G.*, Vol. II, p. 372.   [13] *C.G.*, Vol. IV, p. 482.

Viollet-le-Duc's work at Vézelay and on Notre-Dame in the 1840s had established him as a national figure, the situation improved, since he attracted disciples and emulators, as well as evolving new techniques of preservation. But until then, Mérimée had to spend almost as much time checking the effectiveness of the architects he employed and correcting their blunders as he did in assigning them their tasks in the first place.

Administratively, too, Mérimée's position was fraught with perils. Many ancient monuments, even those officially classified as such, fell within the sphere of some other government department: the Ministry of Ecclesiastical Affairs dealt with churches in so far as they were considered as places of worship rather than works of art, the Ministry of War was responsible for the many historic buildings which it occupied, the General Council for Civil Buildings looked after the upkeep of other official buildings belonging to the state. Each authority was inevitably jealous of the others and clung desperately to its own powers, prerogatives and finances, with frequent demarcation disputes as a result. The body to which Mérimée owed allegiance was at first the Historical Committee for Arts and Monuments, founded by Guizot as part of a grander Committee for Letters, Philosophy, Science and Art, but in 1837 a separate Commission for Historic Monuments was instituted, with Mérimée as its secretary, and Vitet and Taylor among its members. This Commission still exists today, and owes much of its organisation and principles to Mérimée's work. But it was far from easy for him to pick his way through the labyrinth of inter-departmental rivalries, divided responsibilities, inadequate resources, clashing interests and procedural pitfalls. For years, he attended innumerable committee meetings in Paris, kept the minutes, prepared reports and estimates, argued with ministers and deputies, stimulated the activities of honorary correspondents in the provinces. There is no doubt that he was working with the same unflagging assiduity in Paris as on his provincial tours, and his published works, his letters and the archives of the Commission for Historic Monuments bear witness to the efficacy with which he discharged, almost single-handed, the enormous duties which were laid upon him for nearly twenty years.[14]

[14] There are numerous quotations from these archives both in the book by P. Léon mentioned above and in the notes to M. Parturier's edition of the correspondence.

Relations with local authorities often presented an even more thorny problem. The basis of the quarrel is defined by Mérimée himself:

> Unfortunately, though I have encountered provincial patriotism everywhere, in my experience, it rarely takes the form of caring for or being interested in those works of art which do most honour to the region.[15]

Local councils tended to care only about money and to resent interference by gentlemen from the capital, however exalted their station. Mérimée was obliged to undertake long and wearing conflicts with a whole series of municipalities – with Saintes to prevent the demolition of a Roman arch, with Tours to try to get the town to buy the Abbey of St Julien, with Avignon to protest against the planning of a railway which would have wrecked the ramparts and the famous bridge, with Orléans to condemn the pulling down of the old Hôtel-Dieu. In 1847 he said resignedly: 'I'm already at war with so many towns that one more or one less doesn't worry me much.'[16] Sometimes he came out victorious, as in Saintes and Avignon; sometimes, as in Orléans, he had to stand by in powerless fury while the vandals had their way. Paris itself was perpetually on bad terms with Mérimée and his Commission, since the city wanted to keep independent control over its monuments, and indeed for years largely succeeded in doing so.

In all these tribulations, Mérimée manifested in a high degree qualities of firmness, judiciousness, diplomacy, stoicism and intelligence. Viollet-le-Duc, perhaps better placed than anyone to assess the reasons for his success as Inspector-General, has given this penetrating summary of his talents:

> Mérimée had an eminent gift for captivating people – when he bothered to try – and was admirably equipped to make them take notice of what he said. His measured tones, with their serious inflexions, his large, gentle eyes, to which attention was irresistibly drawn by his bushy eyebrows and the profundity of his gaze, his expression in which kindness mingled with irony, his coaxing way of asking questions, everything about him took possession of you and won you over. Without even noticing what was happening, the person to whom he was speaking was induced to give him all the information he wanted, to confess everything to him. He would have been the most amiable examining magistrate one could imagine. At

---

[15] *Notes d'un voyage dans l'Ouest de la France*, Paris, Fournier, 1836, p. 194.
[16] *C.G.*, Vol. V, p. 157.

the same time, he was a good diplomat and a clever politician [. . .] Although he was an outstandingly kindhearted man (as he many times proved), it was a rule with him never to allow the slightest derogation from the authority which he represented, and woe to anyone, whatever his position, who behaved incorrectly towards him: the offender was called to order with a firmness of touch which left a lasting impression.[17]

His habitual reserve made him all the more intimidating when he did decide to show anger;[18] equally, he sensed with the greatest accuracy when it was advisable to use flattery or sympathy to win his point.[19] In the innumerable committees on which he sat, he was indispensable if he cared to be, speaking briefly and without eloquence but always to the point, always clear and practical, always defining the issues and suggesting solutions with more vigour and lucidity than anyone else. He knew he could be a formidable opponent when roused, and for that very reason took care never to show feeling save over vital matters.

Everyone knew too that he was a man of absolute integrity. Though hot-headed provincials occasionally charged him with bad faith, ignorance or even theft (a scandal broke when in 1835 he was wrongfully accused of having stolen a Breton manuscript)[20] those who dealt with

[17] E. Viollet-le-Duc, 'Prosper Mérimée et les monuments historiques', *Revue de Paris*, le 15 novembre 1895.

[18] Letters such as Nos. 1187 bis and 1195 bis (*C.G.*, Vol. XVI, pp. 230 and 235) are written with a cold, stinging irony and an implacable logic which must have caused their recipient to quail. But they are rare exceptions: in professional matters, Mérimée was able to exert his authority without recourse to extremes.

[19] One amusing example of this: in January 1835 Mérimée was privately pouring scorn on Guizot for the lavishness of his promises: 'At the first meeting, M. Guizot told us we were to catalogue *all* the monuments existing in France today. When I objected, he said: "Bear in mind that you will have all the time and money you need." This reduced me to silence, and my neighbour, the worst sort of man, wrote on a scrap of paper: "Time? In three months he won't be a minister. Money? He's already spent every penny of the 120,000 francs voted for 1835" ' (*C.G.*, Vol. I, p. 387). But in 1839, in a letter to the press, the same incident is recalled in positively fulsome terms: 'We have already been told by a minister to whom historical studies are eternally indebted that we have no need to worry about the question of time and money' (*C.G.*, Vol. II, p. 226).

[20] Cf. *C.G.*, Vol. I, pp. 471–4, and Vol. II, pp. 1–2 and 7–8. Cf. also G.

him regularly never questioned his reliability. It can be shown from the archives of the Commission for Historic Monuments that he never claimed a penny for travelling expenses that he could not justify. In archaeological matters, he was sometimes wrong,[21] but very rarely for a man who had had to learn his trade in a few weeks when he was already over thirty – in fact, barely a year after his appointment, he was publishing lengthy and authoritative accounts of the monuments he inspected. Archaeologists, historians, architects, civil servants, politicians, all soon found that Mérimée was highly proficient in their own various specialities and that his opinion could never be dismissed lightly. His command of detail, his clear-headed, systematic approach to problems, his questing and sceptical intelligence made him an invaluable adviser on an extraordinary range of subjects.

Mérimée's ideas on the principles of the preservation of ancient monuments were from the outset sane, firm and lucid. Bad restoration was the greatest enemy. As he wrote to Thiers when he was setting off on his first tour of inspection,

> the lack of taste which has presided over most of the repairs which our medieval monuments have undergone in the last two hundred years has left perhaps even more deplorable marks than the devastation caused by our civil wars and the Revolution. The Protestants and the Terrorists were content to mutilate a few statues and destroy a few ornaments, whereas the repairers have often changed the whole appearance of the building they were trying to restore.[22]

Gourvil, 'Voleur sans le savoir. Prosper Mérimée et Gwenchlan en 1835', *Nouvelle Revue de Bretagne*, mars–avril and mai–juin–juillet–août 1949.

[21] For instance, part of his *Notes d'un voyage dans le Midi de la France* was attacked in the *Publicateur du département des Pyrénées-Orientales* by one Pierre Puigarri in January 1836. Mérimée was put out by this but had to admit that 'the worst thing about these criticisms is that they are true' (*C.G.*, Vol. II, p. 14). However, he took his revenge by caricaturing Puigarri as M. de Peyrehorade in *La Vénus d'Ille*.

[22] *C.G.*, Vol. I, p. 291. Cf. also this quotation from his study of the paintings of St Savin: 'I have no hesitation in saying that neither the inconoclastic fury of Protestantism nor the stupid vandalism of the Revolution has left such deplorable marks on our monuments as the bad taste of the eighteenth and nineteenth centuries. The barbarians at least used to leave ruins; the so-called repairers have only left us their own sorry work' (*Études sur les arts au Moyen Âge*, Paris, Lévy, 1875, p. 58).

Restoration required the utmost caution:

When there is some certainty about what remains there is not the least objection to repairing it, or even rebuilding it, but when it comes to *supposing*, to adding, to recreating, in my opinion one is not only wasting one's time but also running the risk of making serious mistakes and causing others to make them as well. Note that as a science archaeology is still in its infancy [. . .] At the present moment I believe it unwise to try to reconstitute something which has totally disappeared.[23]

To these rules, which correspond very closely to modern attitudes, Mérimée adhered strictly throughout most of his career, and any architect who indulged his own whims in restoration was roundly upbraided. In 1844, for example, visiting St Savin with Viollet-le-Duc, he discovered that a lot of unauthorised painting had been done. 'For a good quarter of an hour, I was struck dumb. Then I got my voice back and flew into such a rage that Leduc was afraid that at any moment I might disappear through a hole in the scaffolding.'[24] Only later did he tend to relax his views, when architects like Viollet-le-Duc, having demonstrated their prowess in restoration, began with overweening confidence to replace missing parts, to imagine plausible decorations, to complete buildings left unfinished by their medieval founders. But by that time Mérimée was no longer in active charge of historic monuments; there is in any case more to be said later on the controversial question of his patronage of Viollet-le-Duc.

In the allocation of his limited funds, Mérimée adopted the principle that priority should be given to those buildings which were most representative of a given style or period, and sensibly held that it was pointless to divide up the available money into a multitude of small sums: far better to concentrate it on the most urgent and important cases, and leave those that were either past help or only in need of minor adjustments. When he appealed to the state or to local authorities for increased subsidies, he used a double argument: a duty to preserve the treasures which the past had bequeathed to the present, and enlightened self-interest. In the conclusion of his *Notes d'un voyage dans l'Ouest de la France* (*Notes on a Journey in the West of France*), he puts his case with great persuasiveness:

The time is not far distant when ordinary resources will be quite inadequate to repair the damage to which the passage of time and a fatal lack

---

[23] *C.G.*, Vol. III, pp. 9–10.   [24] *C.G.*, Vol. IV, pp. 145–6.

of foresight are adding every day. Then we shall have to ask ourselves whether it is right that at one and the same time there should disappear all the relics of our history, all the monuments created by our ancestors, all those noble edifices which bear witness to the genius and splendour of past centuries. Some will remain indifferent to their passing and will say that one can pray to God just as well in a vast shed as in a Gothic cathedral, and that so long as we have canals and railways, it matters little if all works of art perish. But I have too high an opinion of our country to believe that it could so coldly resign itself to the loss of such a great part of its glory. If enormous sacrifices become necessary, I should like to believe that we will agree to make them; but today, at less expense, we could indefinitely postpone the day of universal ruin which is drawing near. There is still time to stave it off, and rapid, immediate help would be less costly than belated restorations forced on us by ineluctable necessity.[25]

Knowing that it might be useless to appeal solely to the artistic sensibilities of materialists and philistines, Mérimée always reinforced his aesthetic arguments by carefully calculated demonstrations of the financial insanity of allowing fine buildings to go to wrack and ruin. He would for instance point out that restoration provided employment for the indigent, that it kept old crafts alive, that it was likely to inspire new artists, that, without art, industry would languish, even that the danger of revolutions was reduced by keeping workers busy in the countryside, rather than allowing them to congregate in the poverty of big cities. His propaganda in favour of paying to save ancient monuments lacks the pathos of a Chateaubriand or an Hugo but by its sober practicality was perhaps in the end more efficacious.

Inevitably, despite the immense services which Mérimée rendered his activities have not escaped criticism. His own preferences were relatively narrow, and late Gothic held few charms for him. In 1837, he wrote:

If on entering a Gothic church, we admire the boldness of the vaults, the loftiness of the columns, in a word its airy structure, to use M. Dusommerand's very apt expression, when we see it from afar we experience the painful impression aroused by the sight of some collapsing ruin shored up with props.[26]

---

[25] *Notes d'un voyage dans l'Ouest de la France*, pp. 428–9.
[26] *Études sur les arts au Moyen Age*, p. 48. Cf. a similar view expressed in conversation: 'Viollet and I disagree about flying buttresses. It's madness to put up walls so high that they have to be supported on crutches. But this

Romanesque and early Gothic architecture attracted him, but the ornate style of the late Middle Ages offended his rationalism; for him, the reason for the existence of each part of a building had to be apparent, and gratuitousness was something he mistrusted:

> Every time I see these thistle leaves, these Gothic canopies, these pinnacles which are so slender and so delicate that they scarcely seem part of the stone, I cannot help thinking how vexed the artist would have been if he had absent-mindedly hit them too hard with his hammer. But in those days artists were never absent-minded, and I suppose they took pleasure in these marvellous trifles. But is that the aim of art?[27]

He was even more severe on seventeenth-century architecture. At Candes, he noted:

> the wall of the façade shows signs of having been very clumsily repaired at some unknown date, possibly under Louis XIV; but I only put that forward as a timid guess, for, as I loathe the architecture of that period, I am perhaps over-inclined to attribute to it all the barbarism which has disfigured so many fine medieval monuments.[28]

He was not a man for undiluted enthusiasm, and there is some truth in Vitet's remark that 'Mérimée admires beautiful monuments, but he has never felt his eyes brim with tears when he saw them in ruins'.[29]

On the other hand, there is no evidence that his personal taste influenced his decisions as to what to restore and what to abandon, and there was certainly something to be said for having an Inspector-General who was not liable to be carried away by uncritical excitement. Mérimée's ingrained scepticism stood him in good stead in assessing the value of new discoveries or new theories, and he rightly scorned those of his contemporaries who practised what he called 'sentimental archaeology'.[30] Amused by the lucubrations of those who sought fanciful explanations for Breton dolmens, he explained: 'I am

---

disagreement stems from the criticism which I make of the Gothic style, generally. Viollet tries to justify it, but it offends my common sense' (Ferdinand Bac, *Mérimée inconnu*, Paris, Hachette, 1939, p. 138).

[27] *Notes d'un voyage dans le Midi de la France*, Paris, Fournier, 1835, pp. 69–70.

[28] *Notes d'un voyage dans l'Ouest de la France*, p. 362.

[29] Quoted by M. Parturier in the *Lettres à Ludovic Vitet*, p. lii.

[30] *Notes d'un voyage dans l'Ouest de la France*, p. 190.

totally sceptical when it comes to monuments of that sort; I do not even believe in my own theories about them.'[31] On the origins of the Gothic arch, his caution brought him closer to modern ideas than the ambitious theorising of men like Arcisse de Caumont.[32] Moreover, Mérimée could be moved by architectural beauty. Admittedly, like his official reports, his four volumes of *Notes* on his travels adopt a largely factual tone, suited to architectural guide-books, but when he is struck by some particularly magnificent building, his prose has a note of lyrical emotion, all the more impressive for being so rarely sounded. Here, for instance, is how he tells of his first sight of the Pont du Gard.

> The Gardon, swollen by prodigious rains, had broken its banks, and as its waters rolled with a frightening roar under the arches of the aqueduct, they were the colour of coffee; the sky was stormy, but through a break in the clouds, the sun gilded the edifice which seemed to sparkle with light; the wild setting, the utter solitude of the place and the noise of the torrent lent a sublime poetry to the imposing structure which I saw before me.[33]

No less expressive are his descriptions of Vézelay seen in the misty sunlight of dawn,[34] of the lonely bay of Paimpol,[35] or of the picturesque lines of stones at Carnac and Erdeven.[36] Mérimée may not have worn his heart on his sleeve about architectural beauty, but there can be little doubt how deeply he came to care for it and to respond to it.

Another criticism sometimes made of Mérimée is that he had a mania for centralisation and that he picked unnecessary quarrels with those whom he suspected of trampling on his preserves. He was certainly eager to carry off provincial treasures – manuscripts, paintings, tapestries and the like – to museums in Paris.[37] But one can hardly blame

---

[31] *Notes d'un voyage dans l'Ouest de la France*, p. 31.

[32] Mérimée's ideas on the origin of the Gothic arch are to be found both in his *Notes de voyage* and in his *Essai sur l'architecture religieuse du Moyen Age, particulièrement en France*, collected in the *Études sur les arts au Moyen Age*. Cf. P. Trahard, *Prosper Mérimée de 1834 à 1853*, pp. 51–7.

[33] *Notes d'un voyage dans le Midi de la France*, pp. 316–17.

[34] *Ibid.*, pp. 28–9.

[35] *Notes d'un voyage dans l'Ouest de la France*, pp. 134–5.

[36] *Ibid.*, p. 237.

[37] He himself makes it clear that he regarded this as a matter of deliberate policy: 'I think it is indispensable to take their manuscripts away from little

him when one learns of the appalling carelessness with which such relics were kept. When he visited Tournus in 1834, he came across a precious early manuscript of the life of St Valerian.

> The library at Tournus is in the greatest disorder. In days gone by, it had quite a lot of rare books; most of them have been lost. No record is kept of books lent, and in the last few years several valuable volumes have disappeared [. . .] It is highly desirable that this manuscript which no one in Tournus is capable of reading should be sent to Paris. If it has to be left in that library, it is as good as lost.[38]

Mérimée's desire to concentrate art treasures in Paris was not mere acquisitiveness; it was a sensible precaution at a time when competent specialists in the provinces were rare and when local museums were often in such chaos and disrepair that it was dangerous to leave valuable objects in their care. It is true, too, that Mérimée jealously guarded the privileges of the Commission for Historic Monuments and that it was, for example, perhaps unnecessary for him in 1837 to be so suspicious of the French Archaeological Society founded by his erstwhile mentor Arcisse de Caumont.[39] When he was on his way to consult the antiquary Auguste Grasset in 1834, Édouard wisely wrote to warn his brother that 'Mérimée is touchy'.[40] But Mérimée was striving to establish a new department, to give it prestige and a firm base, to protect it and the cause it served from interference and disdain, and he could not have done this without occasionally standing on his dignity. He had at heart not personal vanity, but the best interests of the French cultural heritage.

The charge most frequently levelled at Mérimée is that he is to blame for the misdeeds of his protégé Eugène Viollet-le-Duc, who under his aegis became the most powerful and celebrated restorer of ancient monuments in France and who was ever more inclined to substitute

---

provincial towns; no one knows what to do with them and they only stay there until some collector comes along and steals them' (*C.G.*, Vol. I, p. 321).

[38] *Ibid.*, p. 318.

[39] He ungratefully accuses his erstwhile mentor of provincialism, of overweening ambition, of biting off more than he can chew, even of 'charlatanism' (Vol. II, p. 87).

[40] Quoted by M. Parturier in his introduction to the *Lettres aux Grasset*.

invention for restoration.[41] To quote one of his harshest critics, 'Mérimée and Viollet-le-Duc, who are inseparable, carry the crushing responsibility for the false witness unwittingly borne by the most venerable monuments of French art.'[42] Mérimée certainly launched Viollet-le-Duc on his long and controversial career, but a fair appraisal of his share in the younger man's activities demands a closer look at the facts. Mérimée had known him as a boy in his father's flat in the Rue de Chabanais and had later taken a friendly interest in his architectural studies.[43] When in 1839 Mérimée was looking for an architect to take on the restoration of Vézelay, a task so daunting that even the most eminent practitioners in the country had turned it down,[44] Étienne Delécluze suggested to him that he might try Viollet-le-Duc, then aged only twenty-six. At first Mérimée was reluctant, lest a failure, however honourable, should irrevocably compromise the young man's future, but in the end he agreed, and the Commission gave Viollet-le-Duc the job early in 1840. Two years later, after what was for its time one of the most brilliant and original feats of repair ever undertaken, the church was saved, and Viollet-le-Duc had proved himself a master, a reputation consolidated a year or two later by the equally outstanding restoration, carried out jointly with Lassus, of Notre-Dame de Paris. From that time onwards, no one doubted that Viollet-le-Duc was by far the most gifted specialist in France for the restoration of medieval buildings, and the most spectacular and arduous tasks were regularly assigned to him – especially under the Second Empire, when he became a personal friend of the Imperial family.

Mérimée was aware from the beginning that Viollet-le-Duc, who was inspired by an unshakable faith in his own genius, had a dangerous tendency to innovate. In 1842, in a letter to Vitet, he reproached Viollet-le-Duc with having surrounded the church at Vézelay with a frieze for which there was little archaeological justification: 'it must

[41] On Viollet-le-Duc, cf. P. Gout, 'Viollet-le-Duc', *Revue de l'art chrétien*, Supplément 3, 1914.

[42] Y. Christ, 'Chronique du règne de Mérimée', *La Table Ronde*, mars 1962.

[43] Cf. *C.G.*, Vol. I, p. 424.

[44] So great was the risk of failure that even Caristie and Duban, the two architects who sat on the Commission, both refused to have anything to do with it.

have cost a lot of money and adds nothing to the quality of the restoration'.[45] Thereafter, it is true, he kept to himself any misgivings which he may have felt about Viollet-le-Duc's ever-growing reliance on his own imagination. At most he allowed himself some ambivalent comments in private conversation. In later years, the Empress once asked him what he really thought of Viollet-le-Duc's riotous treatment of the Château de Pierrefonds, which he had restored at her command. 'It is a piece of work before which I feel absolutely crushed . . .' said Mérimée, to which the Empress replied gratefully: 'Thank you, you are a true friend.' Mérimée then regretted having allowed ambiguity to go too far.[46] But Viollet-le-Duc, whatever his faults, was a remarkably accomplished architect, a man of immense erudition, a fantastically skilled technician, and a dominating personality, imbued with a strong sense of mission. Moreover, his worst excesses only occurred after Mérimée had relinquished active control over historic monuments; his early work not only demonstrated unique brilliance of technique, but was also relatively sober in execution. Mérimée may have given him his head, but after Vézelay it would have been difficult to do anything else. Just as the balance of praise and blame for Viollet-le-Duc's work must be a matter of dispute, so must it be for Mérimée's championing of him. At least it should be recognised that Mérimée has more to do with the discovery of a young man whose unique talents saved scores of priceless monuments from destruction than he had with the same man's later aberrations of taste.

Against these few criticisms of Mérimée's long tenure of office, the credit side is almost incalculable. Under steady pressure from him, the state increased the money available for ancient monuments almost tenfold during his term of office; between 1831 and 1853, government expenditure on historic buildings (excluding the Inspector-General's salary and expenses) totalled over nine million francs. By 1849 nearly 4,000 buildings had been classified as historic monuments, the great majority of them on Mérimée's personal inspection and recommendation; about a third of these were in receipt of subsidies from funds allocated by Mérimée. With very little administrative assistance, Mérimée organised the work of the Commission for Historic Monuments for over eighteen years, saw it solidly established as a respected

[45] C.G., Vol. III, p. 182.
[46] Ferdinand Bac, *Mérimée inconnu*, p. 86.

and important government department, gave it a network of provincial correspondents, developed for it a specialised corps of architects and artists, defined its principles and its tasks, and ran its day-to-
day affairs with smooth efficiency and remarkably little friction. By
his tireless journeying through France, his voluminous writings, his
personal influence on ministers, deputies, prefects, local worthies and
the public at large, he made an enormous contribution towards turning
the preservation of historic monuments into a popular and reputable
cause.

The list of buildings which would have been mutilated or destroyed
but for his personal intervention is almost endless: among the most
outstanding are Vézelay, the Palace of the Popes at Avignon, the
Roman theatres at Orange and Arles, the cathedrals of Laon and
Strasbourg, the church at St Savin, the abbeys of St Denis, Charroux,
and Fontgombault, the castles of Blois and Chinon. Among towns
which would be architecturally much poorer today without his help
are Poitiers, Saintes, Angers, Caen, Avignon, Bourges, Loches, Tours,
Saumur, Vienne and Vaison-la-Romaine. All over France there are
churches which were saved, sometimes even discovered, by Mérimée.
It is impossible to imagine that, in his time, anyone could have been a
more active, more intelligent, more devoted custodian of a corpus of
fine buildings which is among the richest in the world. 'He deserved
well of the France of olden times; he has a right to the gratitude of
France today.'[47]

[47] P. Léon, op. cit., p. 200.

Chapter 9

Lover

Malgré toute l'expérience que l'on peut avoir des effets des-
tructifs du coït sur l'amour, le coït est toujours impérieux
et veut être satisfait.
To Édouard Grasset, 24 December 1833

Consideration of Mérimée's role as Inspector-General of Historic
Monuments has carried us further forward in time than the point at
which we saw him taking office, so we must now return to him as he
was in the mid-1830s. His appointment in 1834 changed not only his
way of life but also in some ways his character. The necessity for
frequent long absences from Paris helped to break up some of the habits
acquired in the preceding years, especially as he was now an official
personage, a public figure obliged to preserve at least the outward
appearances of dignity and decorum. Though he often grumbled at
having to suppress his natural inclinations, he undoubtedly derived
pleasure from being someone whose opinion counted, whose social
position was assured, whose movements were respectfully reported by
the press, who was received as an honoured guest wherever he went,
who was able to wield substantial power in a domain which meant
much to him. Mérimée may not have been an ambitious man in the
usual sense of the word; his disdain for worldly honours was sincere, for
he knew all too well that his inner needs were too profound to be
satisfied by such things. But that never prevented him from applying
both skill and vigour to the pursuit of them, because they helped, at
least superficially, to reassure him against the irrepressible doubts which
beset him.

So when he went on tour, he was careful to impress his provincial
hosts with his icily correct behaviour, even when his one desire was to
discover the whereabouts of the local brothel. To his friends in Paris,
he confided his frustration:

The truth is that the life I lead is absolutely exhausting. When I'm not
travelling around by coach, I get up at nine, have breakfast, then give

audience to librarians, archivists and others of the same ilk. They take me
off to look at their wretched ruins, and if I say they're not Carlovingian,
they look on me as a blackguard and start intriguing with the local deputy
to get my salary reduced. Caught between conscience and self-interest, I
tell them their monument is marvellous and that there's nothing in the
North to compare with it. Then they invite me to dinner, and the local
paper says I'm a devil of a clever fellow. They beg me to inscribe a sublime
thought in an album; I obey with a shudder. At the end of the evening,
they ceremoniously accompany me to my hotel, which prevents me from
indulging in vice. I go back to my room worn out and sit up putting together notes, drawings, official letters, etc. I wish those who envy me could
see me then.[1]

Often he endured agonies of boredom at interminable dinners with
enthusiastic but incompetent amateur antiquaries. At Apt, he claimed
that the inhabitants had led him off to see a 'druidic monument' which
turned out to be a foxhole and a '*Syriac* inscription' which was just
bad Latin.[2] Nor did his notorious anticlericalism make for good relations with the numerous priests whom his work compelled him to
meet, especially if they had been indulging in what he regarded as
their favourite hobby – spreading thick coats of cheap paint over
medieval wall-paintings. Even publicly, he found it difficult to contain
his indignation at their misdeeds, as witness these angry questions from
the *Notes d'un voyage en Auvergne*:

How long are bishops and the clergy to be allowed to spoil our finest
edifices by clumsy restorations or additions? Would it not be possible,
without disrespect to the ministers of religion, to limit their powers as far
as building and repairs are concerned?[3]

But he relieved his pent-up feelings by penning long humorous
accounts of his misfortunes to friends like Jenny Dacquin or his fellow
civil servant Hippolyte Royer-Collard, and of course there were compensations. Sometimes he came across a kindred spirit in an unexpected
spot and would strike up a lasting friendship with him. In Avignon in
1834, for example, he was introduced to Esprit Requien, a botanist
and geologist who was curator of the local musum. Requien was a
jovial soul, rich, witty, intelligent and erudite, and like Mérimée a
confirmed bachelor with a taste for good food, the fair sex, and dirty

[1] *C.G.*, Vol. I, pp. 326–7.   [2] *Ibid.*, p. 338.
[3] *Notes d'un voyage en Auvergne*, Paris, Fournier, 1838, p. 168.

jokes. Requien's friends, who had been summoned to hear Mérimée give a reading of the recently composed *Ames du Purgatoire*, were surprised to find the great man sitting cross-legged on the floor greedily devouring green figs. To his host's warning of the dire effects likely to ensue, Mérimée replied complacently: 'They disagree with me, but I like them so much!'[4] Requien and Mérimée became bosom friends, visited each other whenever they could, and for many years kept up a regular exchange of often highly obscene letters. More respectable is the correspondence which passed between him and another provincial antiquary, François Jaubert de Passa, Prefect of Perpignan, whom he met on his way to the Pyrenees in 1834. Jaubert de Passa, too, was lively, genial and learned – he is honoured by a brief mention in *La Vénus d'Ille*.[5] Nor were all local architects quite such intolerable idiots as Mérimée sometimes made out. He got on very well with Joly-Leterne of Saumur, to whom he eventually entrusted many restorations, including that of St Savin, and whose only defect was an amiable reluctance to ask for payment.

Sometimes, too, Mérimée would have a travelling companion for all or part of his way. In 1834, Claude Fauriel, the specialist in folk-poetry, was with him in the South of France; in 1837 Stendhal accompanied him to La Charité-sur-Loire;[6] from 1840 onwards Viollet-le-Duc frequently travelled with him. 'M. Mérimée is the kindest and best travelling companion one could wish for, always in good humour, never complaining, caring little about the inconveniences of the journey and ready to take everything with a smile.'[7] Viollet-le-Duc not only enjoyed being with Mérimée but learnt much from him.

Every minute of the day is well filled, and entirely to my benefit, for there is little I can give him and there is a great deal that he gives me. He has that

---

[4] A. de Pontmartin, *Mes Mémoires. Seconde Jeunesse.* Vol. II, p. 61.

[5] 'I had been recommended to M. de Peyrehorade by my friend M. de P.' (*Romans et nouvelles*, Vol. II, p. 87). On the manuscript the reference had been even clearer: '. . . by my friend M. J. de P.' (cf. Roger Alexandre, *Le Manuscrit de 'La Vénus d'Ille' par Prosper Mérimée*, Paris, Techener, 1898 – from the *Bulletin du bibliophile* of the same year).

[6] Cf. M. Parturier, 'Stendhal et Mérimée à La Charité-sur-Loire', *Le Divan*, avril–mai 1933.

[7] Quoted by the editors in *C.G.*, Vol. III, p. 396, n. 2.

precious quality of those who do not readily confide in others: every day one discovers something new in his subtle mind and lofty intelligence.[8]

The sense of loneliness to which Mérimée was always prone, especially on his wanderings through France, was alleviated by such congenial company.

Even in Paris, Mérimée now led a quieter life. *Les Ames du Purgatorie*, the one work of imagination which he published in 1834, shows signs of a growing lassitude with debauchery, and though he continued to dine at Véry's restaurant with his old cronies, some of the zest seemed to be going out of their meetings. Increasingly he frequented men of learning, partly because his new occupations brought him inevitably into contact with them, partly because he was anxious to consolidate his qualifications as Inspector-General by learning from them, but most of all because his own tastes were undoubtedly developing in that direction. His father had familiarised him with the notion of exact scholarship, his school friends had furthered such dispositions in him, his early writings had been founded on serious documentation and wide reading. Increasingly he thought of himself above all as a scholar. In 1835, he told Charles d'Aragon, a lawyer and politician with whom he was friendly, 'my lot now is to do pure archaeology in France for a few years, then to go and die of fever in Persia while looking for forgotten subterranean passages in Persepolis',[9] and in 1838, he admitted to Esprit Requien: 'By profession I am a pedant, and I'm beginning to become one by taste too.'[10] At about the same time, he summed up his character thus: 'I've become very moral, very virtuous, an antiquary, a pedant; in the evenings, I sit working by my fireside.'[11] Of course, he was exaggerating for effect, but it remains true that he sobered down appreciably in the late 1830s and that his interests and activities changed accordingly.

This is manifested above all in the new direction which his writing took. Between his appointment as Inspector-General and 1840, only three tales appeared: *Les Ames du Purgatoire* in 1834, *La Vénus d'Ille* in 1837 (in which he caricatures himself as a dry-as-dust old fogey), and *Colomba* in 1840. But during the same period he published extensively on history and archaeology. His *Notes d'un voyage dans le Midi de*

[8] *C.G.*, Vol. IV, p. 158, n. 2.   [9] *C.G.*, Vol. I, p. 399.
[10] *C.G.*, Vol. II, p. 189.   [11] *Ibid.*, p. 200.

la France (1835), *Notes d'un voyage dans l'Ouest de la France* (1836), *Notes d'un voyage en Auvergne* (1838) and *Notes d'un voyage en Corse* (1840) form four substantial volumes in which he records and describes, often in highly technical language, the antiquities which he had visited on his travels. In addition, he wrote a learned *Essai sur l'architecture religieuse au moyen âge, particulièrement en France* (*Essay on Religious Architecture in the Middle Ages, especially in France*) (1837) and collaborated on an official manual about ancient monuments (1839) – to say nothing of all the detailed reports he sent to Vitet or to the Minister of the Interior, and a long series of letters on archaeological or architectural topics to correspondents all over France. As early as 1836, he announced that he was no longer concerned with imaginative literature:

> Many years ago I gave up writing for the general public. Now I turn out pretty obscure archaeological memoirs which are read by a handful of learned men, half of whom shrug their shoulders at them.[12]

One of the consequences of this change was the birth of a desire for election to the Academy of Inscriptions, the ultimate accolade for French archaeologists and ancient historians. Many of the scholars with whom Mérimée had to deal were already members, and, uncomfortably aware that his own antecedents in that line did not go back far, he no doubt wanted to give such men tangible proof that his standing was not inferior to theirs. The first glimmerings of this intention dawned in 1839. The previous year, Mérimée had become excited about the idea of writing a life of Julius Caesar, for whom he had conceived a great admiration, and he had put his idea to Félicien de Saulcy, an artillery officer and expert numismatist whom he had met at Metz in 1836:

> Do you think it would be fun to write the life of a man who, since he was never defeated, must have been the greatest general of all ages, the boldest lecher, a great orator, a fine historian, so good-looking that kings mistakenly took him for a woman, who cuckolded all the great men of his time, who changed the political and social constitution of his country, who this, who that, who thirty thousand different things, – the life of the late J. Caesar?[13]

For months he had worked away quietly at this project, but it gradually became in his mind a passport to the Academy, as he confessed to

---

[12] *Ibid.*, p. 39.   [13] *Ibid.*, p. 159.

Saulcy in April 1839[14] and to Sutton Sharpe a few weeks later, when he owned that for several months he had felt a 'great desire' to be a member.[15] The itch was to remain with him for several years, a constant source of irritation and expectation to someone of his nervous temperament. Despite his remarkable powers of sustained concentration, the completion of the book was continually adjourned, not so much from pressure of other occupations (heavy though it was) but because the subject itself required treatment on such a vast scale. By the spring of 1839, he had decided that his introductory study of the Social War was so long that it would have to be published separately; even then, he soon found that the first years of Caesar's political life would likewise necessitate a separate examination. For years his major preoccupation as a writer was thus a complicated set of researches into Roman history, so meticulous and so demanding that he sometimes yearned for those 'happy days when I used to make up cock-and-bull yarns!'[16]

Not that the irreverent, ironic side of Mérimée's nature had disappeared: it never did. The Inspector-General's treatises on architecture were enlivened by a straightfaced humour which must have puzzled the more naïve of his readers, as when he writes of an altar at Apt: 'none could be more respectable, for the Holy Ghost in person said mass there',[17] or when, with mock modesty, he lapses into the decent obscurity of a dead language to describe, in precise anatomical detail, obscene sculptures in churches.[18] Keenly alive to the absurd lengths to which archaeological speculation could go, he was not above practising the occasional mild hoax himself. Abetted by Saulcy, he once scratched a fake inscription with his penknife on a fragment of Roman pottery, then threw it into a field in the hope that some innocent enthusiast would have the joy of discovering it,[19] on another occasion at Aix, he solemnly persuaded a local antiquary that a broken butter dish was part of a Roman urn.[20] There is always an agreeable note of self-mockery when he talks to his friends about his own erudite preoccupations and ambitions, and his letters are full of amusing

[14] *C.G.*, Vol. I, p. 220.   [15] *Ibid.*, p. 249.   [16] *Ibid.*, p. 235.
[17] *Notes d'un voyage dans le Midi de la France*, p. 217.
[18] *Notes d'un voyage en Auvergne*, p. 273, n. 1, and p. 283; *Notes d'un voyage en Corse*, Paris, Fournier, 1840, pp. 130–1.
[19] *C.G.*, Vol. II, p. 72, n. 1.   [20] *C.G.*, Vol. IV, p. 461.

anecdotes. Here is one of them, couched in the somewhat bizarre English which Mérimée used for the edification of Fanny Lagden:

> I went up the day before yesterday the highest mountain of the department. I found there a lady who had climbed up I do not know how, but the great difficulty was to go down. On the summit of the Puy de Dome are the finest flowers in the world. This unfortunate lady had gathered a large nosegay which she held with both her hands. When she began to descend she wanted very much a kind hand, for it is continually necessary to take hold of the branches of a bush to try to find a firm ground. The consequence was a number of falls very alarming for our modesty. At each culbute her husband said: but why the devil did you not put on draws?[21]

Just as Mérimée's impish humour survived his transformation into an Inspector-General, so did his susceptibility to women. Céline Cayot was still his regular mistress in 1835, but with his characteristic fear of deep emotion, he tended to be frightened by the ardour of her attachment to him: 'that girl loves me too much, which sometimes makes me remorseful'.[22] Fanny Lagden appears to have come back into his life in 1836 – at least that is the date of the first of his extant letters to her, but their tone gives no hint than he then felt for her anything stronger than affectionate friendship. As for Jenny Dacquin, their postal flirtation continued apace, with Mérimée baring his heart to her as much as he did to anyone, doubtless hoping thereby (though evidently without success) to soften her adamant refusal to allow him any physical intimacy. Some of his letters show a delicacy of feeling surprising in one accustomed to disguising his most tender emotions beneath a veil of brusqueness and irony. The most outstanding example of this occurs after he had visited the Roman amphitheatre at Nîmes in 1834. There his attention had been struck by a strange silent bird, which followed him wherever he went, which reappeared on successive days in the same place and even flew down a dark, narrow passageway after him.

> Then I remembered that the Duchess of Buckingham had seen her husband in the shape of a bird on the day he was murdered, and the idea came to me that you were perhaps dead and had assumed that form in order to see me. In spite of myself, I was tormented by that stupid notion, and I can

---

[21] *C.G.*, Vol. II, p. 124.
[22] *C.G.*, Vol. I, p. 398.

F

assure you that I was delighted to see that your letter was posted on the day when I first saw my wondrous bird.[23]

However, in the late 1830s his interest in Jenny abruptly lapsed – he had at last realised his most cherished dream, the conquest of Valentine Delessert.

The elusive Valentine had for years been luring him on, only to rebuff him, and not even her coquettishness and the frequent disappointments he suffered had made him give up hope of winning her favours. For some time past, Mérimée had seen little of her, as her husband Gabriel had been appointed Prefect at Carcassonne early in 1834, and when he was transferred to Chartres later that year, Mérimée was already off on his first tour of inspection – on which, paradoxically, he had arranged to pass through Carcassonne. Sophie Duvaucel was mischievously amused at the thought of his discomfiture on discovering that the bird had flown.[24] But fortunately for him, Chartres was a town of great architectural interest, not too far from Paris, and he soon made it his business to pay an official visit there, staying over the New Year of 1835 at the Prefecture – as was only right and proper. Again, when he started out for the West of France in the summer of 1835, he took care to travel via Chartres and be, once more, the Prefect's guest. Valentine must have been impressed by the unwonted assiduity of a man reputed to be so inconstant; perhaps too the importance of his new status helped to melt her heart – she seems always to have chosen as her lovers men of high social distinction, and an Inspector-General was certainly a bigger prize than a Minister's private secretary. At all events, when Mérimée contrived to turn up in Chartres yet again early in 1836, she at long last yielded and on 16 February became his mistress.[25]

[23] *C.G.*, Vol. II, p. 357. Hippolyte Taine comments on this passage: 'That is how, even in someone sceptical, the heart and the imagination move; it is a "stupid notion"; nonetheless, he was on the threshold of dreams and on the high road of love' (*Lettres à une Inconnue*, Vol. I, pp. x–xi).

[24] 'It's a pity about this mishap, I agree, but I'll keep my pity for greater misfortunes, and anyway, I hope that the disappointment will bring the Inspector back to us a little sooner' (to Stendhal, 10 October 1834; in H. Martineau, *Cent Soixante-quatorze Lettres à Stendhal (1810–1842)*, Paris, Le Divan, 1947, pp. 88–9).

[25] For the details of this affair, cf. M. Parturier's edition of Mérimée's *Lettres à la famille Delessert*.

Mérimée made no attempt to hide his jubilation from his friends, and there is a rare note of profound emotion in his excitement. To Requien, he announced joyfully: 'I am in love, madly in love with the pearl of women, happy because she loves me, very unhappy because I can't prove my love to her as often as I should like.'[26] To Stendhal, with whom he was usually so bawdily flippant, he wrote solemnly: 'I am deeply and seriously in love.'[27] He referred to his feelings for Valentine as a 'great passion', crowned with success 'after long and agonising vicissitudes',[28] and for a long time his letters were free from the complaints of melancholia and loneliness so frequent in earlier years. There could of course be no question of marriage, but Gabriel Delessert, blind, indifferent or stoical, never constituted a real obstacle to their liaison, and indeed, Mérimée's rooted aversion to institutionalised domesticity[29] probably made him glad to be able to preserve what he wrongly thought of as his freedom. When the Delesserts returned to live in Paris on Gabriel's appointment as Prefect of Police in 1836, Mérimée was constantly to be seen in their *salon*, politely attentive to Madame and cordially intimate with Monsieur. To their children Cécile, born in 1825, and Édouard, born in 1828, he was a kind of unofficial uncle. His friends became friends of the Delesserts and theirs became his. In the circles in which they moved, it was an open secret that Mérimée was Valentine's lover; time came to lend their relationship a sort of respectability. None of Mérimée's letters to her from these years has survived, and to others he was discreetly silent on the details of their feelings. But he was certainly a thoughtful and assiduous lover, producing elaborate presents every year to mark their 'anniversary' on 16 February,[30] ceremoniously paying court to her, always anxious to please, and centring his emotional life on her more even than he knew.

[26] *C.G.*, Vol. II, p. 8.   [27] *Ibid.*, p. 60.   [28] *Ibid.*, pp. 23–4.

[29] This comes out strongly in the original text of *La Vénus d'Ille*: 'In a few seconds, a mayor with a tricolour sash and a priest with a stole put the most respectable girl in the world at the mercy of an animal . . . who will treat her like a courtesan [*or*: who will only teach her that side of love likely to disgust her with it].' But Mme Delessert objected to these strictures, and Mérimée crossed out the line with the mock-sorrowful note: 'Removed on superior orders'. Cf. R. Alexandre, *art. cit.*

[30] One such present was a valuable 1747 edition of *Gil Blas*, richly bound in morocco and with Valentine's name embossed in gold. It is described in the B.N. catalogue of the Mérimée exhibition, p. 107.

This warm and apparently settled affection constituted a vital stabilising element in Mérimée's life. Probably even more than his official position and his intellectual interest, it saved him from the desperate aimlessness of the early 1830s and made him for several years as near to being entirely happy as he could be with his disposition to pessimism and unease. What he wrote was written for Valentine first and foremost, for the public only as an afterthought. No doubt her thrustfulness spurred him on in his efforts to get elected to the Academy; certainly her influence is apparent in his greater restraint and dignity in those years. Admittedly he did not consider himself bound to remain physically faithful to her; as soon as he was away from Paris, he would resume his restless pursuit of sexual adventure, with the same determination as before. But his heart was never involved in such affairs, and the women who had hitherto claimed some share in his feelings, such as Céline Cayot or Jenny Dacquin, were largely eliminated from his life. What Mérimée did not realise was quite how dependent on Valentine he was becoming. Despite appearances, she was always the dominant and independent partner, and her lover's complete subjugation had been assured by the years of waiting and uncertainty which she made him endure. Her own needs, emotional, mental and physical, were for the time being adequately supplied by Mérimée, but in the end it was to become tragically clear that, if she thought she saw a more attractive match elsewhere, she would not scruple to sacrifice him. The combination of fickleness and hard-headedness which had characterised her early attitude towards him never wholly disappeared.

His dependence in itself helped to settle Mérimée's life from 1836 on a more solid emotional foundation than it had ever had before. Another cause of contentment was the arrival in Paris, in 1835, of the erstwhile Countess de Teba and her two daughters Paca and Eugenia, now aged ten and nine. The previous year, her husband had on the death of his brother acquired great wealth and the title of Count de Montijo, but the marriage was not a happy one, and the Countess decided to move to Paris so that her daughters could be educated there. Apart from a brief sojourn in England, they were to stay there until the death of the Count in 1839 called them back to Spain. Mérimée found great delight in the company both of the mother and of the daughters. He was not in love with Mme de Montijo, but he had the highest regard for her qualities of mind and character, and averred that there was nothing sweeter in the world than 'the society of an intelligent woman of whom you are not and cannot be the lover'.[31] As for the children, he came to dote on them both, taking them out to shooting galleries[32] (Mérimée was proficient at several non-strenuous sports such as shooting and billiards), buying them cream cakes, teaching them French, and telling them endless stories. In 1836, he introduced them to the fat and jolly M. Beyle, who instantly became a firm favourite – not least because they were allowed to stay up late when he visited them – and who, with fateful consequences, fired them with enthusiasm for Napoleon by dramatic accounts of his great campaigns. For them, Beyle was so much a family friend that, twenty years later, when Eugenia, now Empress of France, saw his picture in Grenoble Museum and was told that it was Stendhal, she replied: 'No, it isn't, it's M. Beyle – I knew him very well.'[33] It was with a heavy heart that Mérimée saw them leave in 1839, as he told their mother:

I loved those children so much that I cannot get used to the idea that I shall not see them again for a long time. They are going at that moment in a woman's life when a few months bring about a great change, and I have the feeling that I am going to lose them. When one is separated from a woman like yourself, one knows that some day one will find her again exactly as she was before, but I fear that in the place of our two little friends I shall see two *prim* and *stiff* young ladies who have completely forgotten me.[34]

The only event which darkened Mérimée's private life during these years was the death of his father. Though he had been deaf for some time, Léonor was a hale and hearty old man, regularly attending meetings at the School of Fine Arts, and delighted by his son's appointment, which he summed up with his usual perspicacity:

He is far from having the knowledge he needs to fulfil his mission properly; but he is young and a natural observer, and, if he can continue until our age in the career in which he has been placed, he will make a very respectable

---

[31] C.G., Vol. II, p. 471.

[32] Lettres familières de l'Impératrice Eugénie, ed. Duke of Alba, F. de Llanos de Torriglia and P. Josserand, Paris, Le Divan, 1935, Vol. I, p. 10: 'M. Mérimée has promised to take me pistol-shooting with real gunpowder' (April 1837).

[33] H. Martineau, Le Cœur de Stendhal, Paris, Michel, 1952, Vol. II, p. 334.

[34] C.G., Vol. II, p. 206.

antiquary, of whom the Winckelmanns of the future will speak with praise.[35]

However, early in 1836, he fell seriously ill with a stomach ailment and, despite a stay in the country with his friend Dr Régnier, his health did not return. With simple stoicism he told the painter Rochard: 'Unless I improve with the fine weather, I shall have to pack my bags.'[36] In the summer, after a few cautious experiments, he embarked on a course of homoeopathic treatment which momentarily cured him, but in September he caught bronchitis and died four days later. 'His death was gentle. He expired as a lamp goes out when there is no more oil, without visible suffering and preserving to the end that calmness and serenity which, as you know, were always his.'[37] The strong character of his widow kept her patient and resigned,[38] but Prosper, who had always felt very close to his father, was too moved to write to his friends and had to leave it to a cousin to spread the news.[39]

Henceforth, he was to live alone with his mother until her death, from 1838 in the Rue des Beaux-Arts and latterly in the Rue Jacob, but always in his favourite quarter of Paris on the Left Bank. They became even more devoted to each other. Mme Mérimée loved to talk about her son, whom she adored and admired and for whose everyday wants she catered with meticulous care – she said he was 'very particular about household things'[40] and always laid his fire herself, since he would not trust their maid to do it as he liked it. In return, Prosper treated his mother with great affection and never dined out if he had promised her to return home. Outspoken, eccentric and old-fashioned, the old lady would while away his long absences walking up and down her garden with the aid of her husband's stick, drinking tea with her inseparable friends the Lagdens, or stroking the numerous cats who inhabited the flat (one of them was allowed to sleep on

[35] G. Pinet, op. cit., p. 102.
[36] Ibid., p. 109.
[37] C.G., Vol. II, p. 37.
[38] According to Mérimée himself; C.G., Vol. II, p. 68.
[39] Ibid., p. 90.
[40] For this and some of the other details of Mérimée's home-life in the 1840s, see Marie-Louise Pailleron, François Buloz et ses amis. La vie littéraire sous Louis-Philippe, Paris, Calmann-Lévy, 1919.

Prosper's bed to keep his feet warm). Mérimée had not much time for
the remoter family ties – 'I don't like relatives,' he once told Jenny
Dacquin, 'you have to be familiar with people you have never set eyes on
simply because they are the sons of the same father as your mother'[41] –
but he was profoundly attached both to the material comforts of a home
and to the loving understanding which his parents always showed
towards him.

One might have thought that, with Mme Delessert and a carefully
tended home awaiting him in Paris, Mérimée would not be eager to
add to the already considerable travelling forced on him by his job.
But he frequently found occasion to leave the country on jaunts of his
own. In May 1835, he went off to London for three or four weeks,
ostensibly to look at English architecture and meet English antiquaries,
in fact to amuse himself with the incorrigible Sutton Sharpe. One place
to which he was taken vastly impressed him, as he told a colleague:

> My dear friend, I am writing to you seated in a wing-chair four feet wide
> in a room 120 feet long, heated, panelled, gilded, bedecked with tapestries.
> By my right hand is a bell-pull, and if I ring, a man in a brown tail-coat,
> velvet breeches and silk stockings will come upstairs and bring me tea in
> a silver tea-pot. Down below there is a dining-room as big as this room,
> with forty servants and every imaginable comfort. My dinner consisted
> of delicious fish with ten different sauces, a piece of roast beef carved by
> myself from a mountain of meat, two vegetables, cheese and sherry, with
> as much beer as one wanted: it all cost four shillings. Tipping is forbidden.
> The place where one sees all this luxury and enjoys all these conveniences
> is called the Athenaeum Club.[42]

Perhaps it was this delectable example which induced Mérimée the
following year to become a founder member of the Arts Club in Paris,
along with an array of illustrious friends including Stendhal, Bixio,
Chopin, Delacroix, Delécluze, Lenormant and Koreff.[43] Otherwise he
was not greatly excited by his stay in England: he thought the women
were less pretty than before and that radicalism in English politics was
beginning to look dangerous.

The following year, Mérimée took advantage of his tour of inspection in Eastern France to have a look at the Rhineland. But Speier,
Mainz, Cologne and their cathedrals left him unmoved; he declared

---

[41] *C.G.*, Vol. I, p. 310.   [42] *Ibid.*, p. 425.
[43] For further details, cf. *C.G.*, Vol. II, pp. 66, n. 2, and p. 75.

that Rhenish architecture was a lot of humbug,[44] and was more interested in experimenting with gambling systems in the German casinos, and in trying out the accomplishments of the local whores. Much more to his taste were the weeks he spent in Spain with the Montijos in the summer of 1840, partly at their estate at Carabanchel, partly at their great town house in the Plazuela del Angel in Madrid. In addition to the pleasure of seeing Spain again and being with the Countess and her daughters, he was entertained to find himself in the midst of one of the periodic revolutionary upheavals which troubled the reign of Isabella II, the more so as the Montijo mansion occupied a strategic position in the centre of the city. But though he professed himself pleased to have seen a new performance of the tragicomedy he had missed in 1789 and 1830, the sight of civil disorder awakened all his latent anxieties, and his parting letter to Mme de Montijo is full of foreboding: 'Will we never be able to laugh and talk together about the present without fear for the future?'[45]

The most significant of Mérimée's unofficial or semi-official journeys at this period was his voyage the previous year to Corsica and Italy.[46] Nominally this began as another tour of inspection, and in 1840 he published a volume of *Notes* on Corsican antiquities, though it is slimmer than its predecessors and padded out with disquisitions on local customs and appendices on folk-songs. In fact, when the visit to Corsica was arranged, both Mérimée and the then Minister of the Interior, Comte de Gasparin, knew perfectly well that the island was poor in archaeological interest, but both hoped that, with its reputation for wildness and lawlessness, it might provide inspiration for another *Mateo Falcone*. Gasparin proved that he knew his Mérimée when he wrote to the sub-prefect of Bastia: 'You have few monuments, but for a man like him, the island and its inhabitants will repay the trouble that he is taking to get to know them.'[47] When Mérimée arrived in August 1839, his first impressions of Bastia and the eastern side of the island were not especially remarkable, and he thought he would not stay very

[44] *C.G.*, Vol. II, p. 60.   [45] *Ibid.*, p. 448.

[46] On this journey, cf. especially M. Parturier, 'Itinéraire de Mérimée en Corse', *Mercure de France*, le 1er mars 1936, and G. Roger, *Prosper Mérimée et la Corse*, Algiers, Baconnier, 1945.

[47] Quoted by J.-B. Marcaggi, 'Les Sources de *Colomba*', *Revue de Paris*, le 15 juillet 1928.

long. But he was persuaded that on the western coast he had more chance of coming across those bandits and vendettas for which he had been looking in vain, and his expectations were soon amply fulfilled when in Olmeto he was introduced to Colomba Bartoli, a fierce old lady almost legendary for the relentless savagery with which she had sought revenge on the Durazzo family for killing her son François near Fozzano in 1833. His delight was increased by the fact that she had an attractive daughter by whom he confessed himself 'bewitched'.[48] In Sartène, he stayed for some days with a character scarcely less picturesque, one Jérôme Roccaserra, who boasted that a few years earlier, he had, despite a wounded left arm, shot two of his enemies stone dead.[49] It was with good cause that Mérimée exclaimed:

> What I liked best was pure nature [. . .] I mean the pure nature of MAN, who in these parts is really a very curious mammal.[50]

Even his insatiable taste for local colour was satisfied by Corsica: 'here local colour is almost as common as fleas'.[51]

Then, after seven stimulating weeks, Mérimée took ship for Leghorn and went on to Civitavecchia, where Stendhal was waiting to take him to Rome and thence to Naples. But while Italy was a revelation to him, relations with Stendhal were somewhat strained. Between May 1836 and the summer of 1839, the consul at Civitavecchia had been on extended leave in France, where he had frequently been in the company of Mérimée. However, the changes in the character of the Inspector-General were not greatly to the taste of Stendhal, who had kept all his old *brio* and who thought the new Mérimée pompous and pedantic. From about 1838, Stendhal stopped referring to him as 'Clara', choosing instead the unflattering appellation 'Academus' or even 'His Pedantry M. Academus'.[52] In Rome and Naples, they almost

---

[48] *C.G.*, Vol. II, p. 289. On Colomba Bartoli, one may consult Lorenzi di Bradi, *La Vraie Colomba*, Paris, Flammarion, 1922. But there is so much romancing in it that it is more entertaining than reliable.

[49] *C.G.*, Vol. II, pp. 288–9.

[50] *Ibid.*, p. 288.   [51] *Ibid.*, p. 290.

[52] This period of the friendship between Mérimée and Stendhal has been studied by H. Martineau and F. Michel in *Nouvelles Soirées du Stendhal-Club*, Paris, Mercure de France, 1950. Stendhal may have been irritated by Mérimée's display of archaeological erudition, but that did not prevent him from making use of it for his own purposes, especially in the *Mémoires d'un*

fell out. Mérimée wrote tartly to Requien: 'I hadn't been intending to see Rome and I allowed myself to be persuaded by M. Beyle. I couldn't be more delighted – I mean with Rome',[53] and after they had been to the South of Italy together, Stendhal noted savagely in one of his innumerable marginalia: 'the frightful vanity of Academus has spoilt this trip to Naples'.[54] Probably Mérimée, now that he was an important dignitary, had patronised Stendhal and lectured him on archaeology; Stendhal in turn had doubtless bored Mérimée by over-enthusiastic tourism and offended him by too obvious disapproval of his academic pretensions. Despite these irritations, Mérimée thoroughly shared in Stendhal's admiration for Italian life and character. To Saulcy he wrote rapturously on his return:

> Ah! my friend, what a country and how I should love to go back. It's the place to live when you are no longer bubbling over with youth. It's the place to find everything the mind and the body need, as King Moabdar would say. Life is so easy that I cannot imagine anyone ever dying there.[55]

Classical architecture, too, aroused him to unusual admiration, an opinion to be strengthened when he visited Greece a few years later and which increased his misgivings about Gothic:

> Poestum dumbfounded me. I should like to demolish all the modern rubbish and even the slightly less ancient rubbish called temples, churches and so on. I'd like to have the inventor of the Ionic order hung and the inventor of Corinthian broken on the wheel. Without Doric there is no salvation, most of all no base.[56]

It was not until November that Mérimée reluctantly set out on the return journey to Paris, consoled on his way only by some Pantagruelic repasts with Dr Cauvière, a gastronomically inclined physician in

---

touriste. On the subject of Stendhal's borrowings from Mérimée, see Adolphe Paupe, *La Vie littéraire de Stendhal*, Paris, Champion, 1914; P. Hazard, 'Les Plagiats de Stendhal', *Revue des Deux Mondes*, le 15 septembre 1921; and F. Gohin, 'Stendhal plagiaire de Mérimée', *Minerve française*, le 1er janvier 1920. According to Paupe, it was the learned Mérimée who provided Stendhal with epigraphs for 26 out of the 31 chapters of *Armance*.

[53] *C.G.*, Vol. II, p. 293.

[54] Stendhal, *Melanges intimes et marginalia*, Paris, Le Divan, 1936, Vol. II, p. 132.

[55] *C.G.*, Vol. II, p. 303.   [56] *Ibid.*, p. 295.

Marseille, to whom his friend Lenormant had recommended him.[57]
After six months' absence, he found a great accumulation of work
awaiting him, including the presentation of his reports to the Minister
and the Commission and the composition of his *Notes*, but this did not
stop him transforming his impressions of Corsica with remarkable
rapidity into one of his best-known tales – *Colomba*. Though it was
certainly not written and re-written sixteen times in a hotel room in
Marseille (as Du Camp absurdly pretends),[58] it was set down swiftly,
while the heat of excitement was still on him, and despite the innumerable preoccupations of a harassed civil servant who has just returned
after a long absence. It appeared in the *Revue des Deux Mondes* in July
1840 and was an immediate and outstanding success. As Sainte-Beuve
wrote to a friend a week or two later: 'Mérimée's *Colomba* is a masterpiece which has won universal acclaim here. For a fortnight it was the
sole subject of conversation everywhere. To my knowledge, he has
never written anything so beautiful, so perfect, so subtle.[59]

Happy in his love for Valentine Delessert, secure in his post as
Inspector-General, absorbed in his work and his intellectual interests,
fêted wherever he went, with an exceptionally wide circle of friends
all over France and a snug home in Paris, Mérimée was entering into
the 1840s with a confidence and a near-serenity which he was far from
having possessed a few years before. Though his hair was rapidly
turning grey and his taste for the social whirl diminishing, he was still
in excellent health, and his zest for what attracted him was perhaps
greater than it had ever been. In many ways, the late 1830s and the
beginning of the next decade were the most contented of his life; much
as he had achieved, there was still much on which he had set his heart,
and the future seemed full of promise. But before long, he was to
experience as much pain as pleasure, with failure and success meted
out to him in equal measure, the one poisoning the other.

[57] *Ibid.*, pp. 280–2. A few years later, Flaubert too was to experience Dr
Cauvière's overwhelming hospitality as he set out on his travels in the
Middle East.
[58] Maxime du Camp, *Souvenirs littéraires*, Paris, Hachette, 1882–3, Vol. I,
pp. 323 *et seq.*
[59] Sainte-Beuve, *Correspondance générale*, Vol. III (1938), p. 332.

Chapter 10

Psychologist

> En dépit des efforts de tant de philosophes et de réformateurs, le cœur humain n'a pas été modifié depuis le temps où le premier poète, le premier romancier eurent l'heureuse idée d'en faire l'étude.
>
> 'Lettre à M. Charpentier', in *Études de littérature russe*

Between 1830 and 1846, Mérimée wrote eight tales, which include his finest achievements; thereafter, he was to forsake fiction for twenty years until, in an access of what he professed to regard as senile euphoria, he was tempted again. Though there is a gap of three years between *La Partie de tric-trac*, the last of the stories collected in *Mosaïque*, and *La Double Méprise*, which appeared in 1833, there is no dramatic change in his methods as a narrator, but rather a gradual development of trends already apparent in the earlier works. These middle-period tales are less abrupt and schematic; they display a much richer and subtler understanding of psychology; they use his mastery of technique to produce effects more complex and more profound. Not all of them are equally successful – indeed, the last pair show disquieting signs of flagging inspiration – but the most outstanding are the best of Mérimée and constitute his clearest claim to be considered as something more than a brilliant literary technician.

The tales can roughly be divided into two groups, corresponding to Mérimée's two principal preoccupations in writing during these years. Into the first group, one may put those stories which deal with modern life in its falsity, its hypocrisy, its uncertainty – *La Double Méprise* (1833), *Arsène Guillot* (1844) and *L'Abbé Aubain* (1846), to which can be added *Les Ames du Purgatoire* (1834), since, although it is set in seventeenth-century Spain, its theme is closely connected with Mérimée's reactions to the life he was leading in the Parisian society of the 1830s. The second group comprises *La Vénus d'Ille* (1837), *Colomba* (1840), *Carmen* (originally composed in 1845) and *Il Viccolo di Madama*

Lucrezia (which, though only published posthumously, dates from 1846); these stories are primarily concerned with the darker, more mysterious forces of life, whose eruption can destroy the superficial façade of civilisation as most of us know it. There is of course nothing rigid in this classification, for just as *La Double Méprise* uses a refined and elegant setting to demonstrate the destructive power of emotion, so *La Vénus d'Ille* adds to its main preoccupation with phenomena outside rational control an attack on the misplaced values of a society which seeks to deny the existence of such phenomena. But it may at least serve to clarify the complex of themes which underlies all these tales and which Mérimée's brusque, blunt manner makes it easy to overlook.

La Double Méprise was written in the summer of 1833, at the time when Mérimée was still leading a life of dissipation as a self-confessed scamp and very shortly after his tragi-comic affair with George Sand. These circumstances have an unmistakable bearing on the sad, simple tale of Mme Julie de Chaverny who, married to an unbearable brute but still virtuously faithful, finds herself seduced in the space of nine hours by the cynical Darcy and then dies of remorse. It would be absurd to pretend that Julie as a person owes much to George Sand, far too idiosyncratic a model to be used with impunity; but Julie's situation with a coarse, thoughtless, philistine, philandering husband is undoubtedly akin to George Sand's deteriorating relationship with the deplorable Casimir Dudevant, with whom she was thoroughly disillusioned by the time she met Mérimée.[1] Likewise, Darcy, elegant but not rich, caustic, mildly misanthropic, highly experienced with women, full of a half-mocking predilection for exoticism, can hardly fail to recall Mérimée himself as a slightly jaundiced observer might have seen him at that time – and that Mérimée was eminently capable of turning an acutely critical gaze on his own person is made very plain by his letters. Moreover, the double misunderstanding of which the title speaks, the mutual failure of Julie and Darcy to understand each other's motives, is exactly what had characterised the George Sand–Mérimée débâcle, the one vainly hoping to find in it the great love of a broken life, the other seeing it as an adventure to be undertaken with deliberately cold detachment.

[1] Cf. for instance M. Regard, *L'Adversaire des Romantiques. Gustave Planche*, p. 122.

But the story is anything but a banal autobiographical transcription. Two things above all interested him. The first and more prominent of the two is that of demonstrating how a woman who has always prized her fidelity to her marriage vows can, in a matter of hours, ruin her whole life by committing adultery with someone whom she scarcely even knows, let alone loves. In one sense, this is a further variation on the theme already exploited in *Le Vase étrusque* and *La Partie de tric-trac*, where an emotion totally foreign to a character's normal habits of behaviour suddenly seizes control of him and causes his existence to collapse in ruins, and as one might expect, Mérimée pitilessly emphasises how unaccountably swift Julie's fall has been: 'It was at four o'clock that she had seen Darcy for the first time. – Yes, *seen* him, – she could not say seen him *again*. . . . She had forgotten his features, his voice; for her he was a stranger. . . . Nine hours later she had become his mistress!'[2] Once again, Mérimée has shown us the instability of feeling, the weakness of humanity, the impotence of principle or of conscious thought when an irrational desire flutters into the mind. The elements of his affair with George Sand have been selected and rearranged to show up an intuition which has little to do with that strange episode and which draws strength from its wider validity.

This theme, however, mingles with another which is perhaps even more poignant: the inability of two people to communicate with one another, the infinite possibilities of misunderstanding even in the tenderest relationship. After Darcy has seduced Julie in his carriage on the way back to Paris, she is overcome by a flood of conflicting emotions which eventually merge into a desperate resolve to sacrifice all for love and elope with him to some distant land; at that very moment, the unmoved Darcy 'was very calmly putting his glacé-kid gloves on again',[3] and Julie suddenly realises that, for him, she is no more than another conquest who will keep him pleasantly occupied during the winter. Her dying words, a few days later, are, significantly: 'Write to him that he doesn't know me . . . that I don't know him . . .'[4] Neither partner had been capable of seeing how the other was feeling: Julie had deluded herself into believing that Darcy was profoundly in love with her, whereas Darcy had supposed that she was simply

---

[2] *Romans et nouvelles*, Vol. I, pp. 509–10.
[3] *Ibid.*, p. 511.   [4] *Ibid.*

ready for a passing affair. The misunderstanding kills Julie, and leaves Darcy as ironically unperturbed as ever. In the original text published in 1833, that was as far as the story went; tragedy arose from the misunderstanding, but it was exclusively Julie's tragedy, since her impressionability had made her the victim of a Don Juan who remained unaffected by her misfortune. But when Mérimée revised the story for a new edition in 1842, he altered the emphasis so as to give a less harsh view of Darcy's attitude and to suggest that he might have lost almost as much as Julie by their failure to see into each other's minds. A sentence which had at first stated abruptly: 'Darcy was not in love'[5] now read more dubitatively: 'Darcy had been wrong about the nature of his feelings: it must be admitted that he was not in love.'[6] Darcy's reproaches of hard-heartedness, which finally decided Julie to succumb, were in 1833 uttered with 'his diabolical smile';[7] in 1842, he speaks 'in a voice so gentle that its tone was all the more moving'.[8] Above all, the end of the story is given a new twist, so that instead of finishing with Darcy's ironical smile, it goes on to the profound melancholy of: 'These two people, for all the misunderstanding between them, were perhaps made for one another.'[9]

That these changes are intended to add a new dimension to the tale is clear; that they succeed in doing so is less certain. The reader's general impression of Darcy remains what it was in 1833: a cynical seducer who may once have been capable of genuine feeling but who has become hardened by debauch. The lighter touches now added to the portrait seem to superimpose another image on it more than they modify the original physiognomy. Perhaps Mérimée wishes to alter the perspective because his own attitude to Darcy is no longer the same. In 1833, a Don Juan himself, he has presented a deliberately harsh, unsympathetic view of such a character – a man whose thoughtless search for pleasure can cause a woman's death. In 1842, less bitter, less inclined to self-reproach but still as pessimistic, he hints that Don Juan can frustrate his own chances of happiness just as much as those of the women he treats as his playthings. If the two themes had been equally prominent in the first conception of the tale, it might have been a

---

[5] *Ibid.*, p. 544.   [6] *Ibid.*, p. 508.
[7] *Ibid.*, p. 544.
[8] *Ibid.*, p. 508.
[9] *Ibid.*, p. 520.

more unified work; as it is, the suggestions of unrealised possibilities and missed opportunities do not marry perfectly with the idea of the mutability of human emotion.

The story thus remains primarily the account of Julie's succumbing in a few hours to the blandishments of a man who is in effect a stranger. In order to make this credible, Mérimée plans his narrative with quite extraordinary skill. He is not out for the facile enjoyment of satirising Julie's fallibility; he wants to make us understand it, believe in it, and feel for it, and to this end, he devotes meticulous care to the detailed motivation of her actions. Chaverny's unpardonable rudeness at the Opera, the assiduous but ineffectual courtship by young Châteaufort (who, by making her glimpse the possibility of adultery, unwittingly prepares the way for his rival), the memories of a past love and what might have been if it had led to marriage, the romantic adventures which the dashing Darcy had undergone in Cyprus, the alarm of the coach accident, Darcy's practised wooing of her in the long and fascinatingly organised conversation in his carriage – all these things are necessary preliminaries to Julie's fall. Nowhere else in Mérimée is there such delicacy and subtlety in the fine shades of psychological analysis. Moreover the analysis is carried out with more gentleness than acerbity, and for all the detachment of the style, *La Double Méprise* is, with *Arsène Guillot*, the best answer to those who would see in Mérimée only coldness and cruelty. In later years, he affected to disdain it: 'it's one of my wild oats, sown for money, which was given to someone of no great worth'.[10] (Céline Cayot is meant.) But posterity has been kinder, and it was with good reason that, a few years ago, a committee of distinguished French writers and critics voted it one of the twelve best novels of the nineteenth century.

If *La Double Méprise* has as one of its subordinate themes a critique of the Don Juan figure and a compassionate recognition of the ravages his selfishness can cause, that becomes the main point of *Les Ames du Purgatoire*, published the following year in 1834. Here, however, Mérimée is less concerned with the sufferings of the victim; his pre-occupation is now with the processes by which the debauchee starts on the downward path to damnation and with the agonising remorse which accompanies his downfall. This version of the Don Juan legend, according to Mérimée himself, is an attempt to separate those parts of

[10] *C.G.*, Vol. VIII, p. 345.

the story relating to Don Juan de Mañara (whom Mérimée for some unclear reason persists in calling Don Juan de Maraña) from those relating to Don Juan Tenorio, but in fact, like most adaptors of the legend, he has used elements from the lives of both men.[11] In this account of Don Juan's corruption by the demonic Garcia, his seduction and abandonment of the innocent Teresa after the murder of her father, his machinations to kidnap Teresa from her convent, his conversion after a vision of his own funeral, and his subsequent fall from the grace of repentance when he finds himself obliged to kill Teresa's vengeful brother in a duel, Mérimée observes an unwonted gravity; it is perhaps the only work he ever wrote from which humour is almost entirely banished.

This unusual seriousness makes the story seem – even in the absence of any explicit moralising – like a sombre warning. It was written at a time of weariness and increasing self-disgust, and when his anxious and superstitious temperament was probably making him wonder how long he could go on before his sins caught up with him. Don Juan's obsession with the painting of souls in torment, which gives the tale its title, points to an underlying but irrepressible fear of retribution, in this world or the next, and one remembers that, though Mérimée was an irreligious man, he could never rid himself of an uneasy and irrational attachment to talismans, magic formulae, fetishist precautions and the like. So the irony which he usually injects into his subjects is lacking here, though he preserves his detachment by making the events distant in time and space, by opening with some learned remarks on the sources of the legend, and by confining himself to a record of events free of commentary or analysis. But even these safeguards do not prevent the intrusion of the occasional personal note, as when his

[11] Cf. Gendarme de Bévotte, *La Légende de Don Juan*, Paris, Hachette, 1929. Mérimée saw Mañara's tomb at Seville in 1830 (cf. *Romans et nouvelles*, Vol. II, p. 10) and may well have based his story on oral tradition rather than written sources (which would explain the deformation of the name).

There has been a good deal of argument (beginning in Mérimée's lifetime – cf. *C.G.*, Vol. XIII, p. 21) about whether Mérimée borrowed the duel scene from a play by the Duque de Rivas entitled *Don Álvaro* or whether the borrowing was the other way round. There is a full if inconclusive discussion of the problem in F. Caravaca, '¿Plagió Mérimée el *Don Álvaro* del Duque de Rivas?', *La Torre*, Jan.–April 1965.

description of Don Juan's relations with Garcia seems to allude to his own attitude to Stendhal.[12]

> Don Juan mourned Don Garcia more than he would have mourned his own brother. Fool that he was, he told himself that he owed everything to him. He it was who had initiated him into the mysteries of life, and who had torn from his eyes the thick scales that were covering them. What was I before I knew him? he wondered, and his vanity assured him that he had risen above other men. In a word, all the harm that he had suffered from knowing the atheist was transformed into good, and he was as grateful for it as any disciple should be to his master.[13]

However, these individual undertones scarcely suffice to make Mérimée's story an outstanding contribution to the vast corpus of Don Juan legends. Expertly told though it may be, and full of incisive strokes of action, description or emotion, its interpretation of an archetypal myth has not the individuality which would raise it to the level of Tirso de Molina, Molière or Byron. The multiplication of incident tends to obscure the humanity of the hidden themes; Mérimée seems so remote from this untypical example of his art that it inevitably strikes many readers as coldly impersonal through to the very centre.

La Double Méprise, fairly obviously, and *Les Ames du Purgatoire*, more deviously, relate to Mérimée's feelings about the life he and others of his generation were leading in the early 1830s. *Arsène Guillot*, though not written until 1844, does so with even less attempt at disguise. In 1832, at the time of his escapade with Pauline,[14] Mérimée had noted: 'Thanks to her, I've made a lot of observations about the heart of Opera chorus-girls, and those girls known as *demi-castors*. I firmly intend to write a fine dissertation on them when I have time.'[15] That the dissertation, when it came, would defend these humble sinners against the strictures of the well-bred ladies of high society was also predictable, Mérimée having frequently inveighed against those who condemned them from the security of wealth and status: to Jenny Dacquin in 1832, after recounting the misfortunes of one such girl, he had exclaimed bitterly:

> Be so good as tell me whether that young girl isn't infinitely more meritorious for leading the life she leads than someone like yourself, who has

---

[12] The hypothesis comes from M. Parturier (*Romans et nouvelles*, Vol. II, p. 619).   [13] *Romans et nouvelles*, Vol. II, p. 54.

[14] Cf. p. 102.   [15] *C.G.*, Vol. XVI, p. 43.

the extraordinary good fortune to have an impeccable background and such a refined nature that for me it is almost the epitome of a whole civilisation.[16]

In the event, he is manifestly thinking of Céline Cayot when he comes to write his tale. Even the names are similar, and when Arsène Guillot complains that her lover cannot write her name correctly – 'Yes, I'm called Arsène Guillot, G, U, I, two L's and he spells it with a Y!'[17] – it is a direct reflection of Mérimée's own inability to remember the correct spelling of Céline's surname. The friendly affection he always felt for her is magnified here into a feeling of compassion for the heroine which almost verges on sentimentality. Nor can one doubt that his demonstration of the fundamental genuineness of the penniless Arsène is principally aimed at Valentine Delessert for whom he had abandoned Céline. Throughout the tale, he addresses himself with exaggerated respect to a supposed female listener who belongs to a higher social class than Arsène, and this can be none other than Mme Delessert, for whom, as he said himself, all that he ever wrote was destined. The engaging reprobate Max de Salligny, Arsène's ex-lover who is eventually stolen from her by the aristocratic Mme de Piennes, owes much to Mérimée himself: both are addicted to foreign travel, accustomed to high life as well as low life, elegant, humorous, modest, and zealous in their attentions to ladies.

But if the story has analogies with aspects of Mérimée's own life and opinions in the 1830s, its immediate cause is his fury with the neo-Catholic piety of the 1840s, which roused him to a peak of disgusted indignation about Easter 1843.[18] Convinced that the devoutness of fashionable society was nothing but a hypocritical sham, Mérimée plainly intends Arsène Guillot to draw an exemplary contrast between the honest and unselfish simplicity of Arsène, who has to have a lover to support herself and her ailing mother, and who tries to kill herself when she is abandoned, and the ostentatious and conventional religiosity of Mme de Piennes, who in the end finds herself going off with the lover of the girl she had tried to convert. Though the two women first meet in church, he shows a clear preference for the heartfelt superstitions of the one as compared to the superficial and meaningless

[16] C.G., Vol. I, p. 174.
[17] Romans et nouvelles, Vol. II, p. 296 (and also p. 280).
[18] Cf. p. 210.

unction of the other – Arsène, for him, has the spontaneity in her religious beliefs which enchanted him in Italy, whereas Mme de Piennes's devotions are those of a typical upper-class Frenchwoman.[19] In their feelings towards Max, Arsène is not ashamed to admit her love for him, while her easily shocked rival is too timorous to put a name to the emotions he arouses in her. Not that the portrait of Mme de Piennes is a satirical caricature: Mérimée is too interested in fathoming the contradictory workings of her mind to allow that. Nevertheless, the story mounts a most effective attack on those sanctimonious ladies in whom charity can easily be allied with adultery and reconciled with cruelty, and it is hard to take altogether seriously Mérimée's protestations of surprise at the scandal which its publication provoked.[20]

Ultimately more important than this polemical intent is the care and humanity Mérimée has shown in depicting the contrasting characters of Arsène and Mme de Piennes. The portrait of Arsène is not a complex one – by definition, that would have been impossible – but it is deliberately and intensely compassionate, so that the whole tale is bathed in an emotive atmosphere unique in Mérimée's work. Certainly the light, ironic style and the swift narration hold feeling in check; but its presence is no less clearly felt for being veiled. At the end, it even comes to the surface in an uncommonly obvious form, when Arsène on her deathbed suddenly and unconvincingly cries: 'I have loved!'[21] As one of Mérimée's critics has observed, if she were to say anything at all in those circumstances, it would have been: 'I have loved Max!' The greater psychological interest derives from Mme de Piennes, whose waverings between Christian charity and her inclination for Max are most adroitly analysed. Despite Mérimée's constant preoccupation with the notion of dupery and hypocrisy, he has not been content to portray Mme de Piennes as a two-faced deceiver. Instead, he has sought to understand how something which begins (however conventionally) as a charitable impulse gradually yields to the pressure of an

[19] 'I dislike the devoutness we have here in France; it is a sort of very mediocre philosophy which comes from the mind, not the heart. When you see popular devoutness in Italy, I hope you will agree with me that it is the only decent kind; but it isn't enough just to want to have it, and you can only believe in that way if you were born on the other side of the Alps or the Pyrenees' (to Jenny Dacquin, 22 June 1842; C.G., Vol. III, p. 179).
[20] Cf. pp. 210–11.   [21] Romans et nouvelles, Vol. II, p. 334.

emotion so unexpected that the person experiencing it cannot at first recognise it for what it is. When one thinks of the parallel with *La Symphonie pastorale*, it is no great surprise to discover that André Gide was very ready to except *Arsène Guillot* from his general dislike of Mérimée. The uncovering of hidden motives is one of Merimée's specialities; nowhere does he do it with more finesse than here.

When to these qualities of emotion and penetration is added a remarkable narrative dexterity, it is clear that *Arsène Guillot* deserves a high place in Mérimée's work. The last paragraphs are perhaps one of the most extraordinary foreshortenings of perspective in nineteenth-century fiction. Arsène has died, with Max and Mme de Piennes at her side. Mérimée turns to his imaginary female interlocutor to beg her not to jump to rash conclusions.

> Above all, never doubt the truth of my story. You do have doubts? Go to Père Lachaise cemetery; twenty paces to the left of General Foy's grave, you will find a very simple limestone tomb, always surrounded with fresh flowers. On the stone, you can read my heroine's name engraved in large letters: ARSÈNE GUILLOT, and, if you lean over the grave, you will see, unless the rain has already washed it off, a line delicately written in pencil: Poor Arsène! She is praying for us.[22]

With all this to recommend it, one can only echo André Gide's praise: 'I never knew there was anything like that in Mérimée. Why is it not better known? [. . .] Yes, it is better than anything I thought Mérimée was capable of writing. Truly excellent.'[23]

Two years later, Mérimée returned to an analogous theme with *L'Abbé Aubain*, in which, using the epistolary form, he tells how an ambitious young priest tricks a pious lady into obtaining his preferment for a better parish by pretending to be falling in love with her. It is a slight and anodyne work, which Mérimée claims is based on fact. In February 1846, he wrote to Mme de Montijo: 'I am sending you a little story which I published without signing it because if I so much as mention a priest, all the pious old women start screaming about irreligion. The adventure really happened, and I could name the people concerned.'[24] But whether or not the idea came to him from real life, it patently did not inspire him to anything more than the perfunctory relating of an amusing anecdote. Though there is a genially ironic

---

[22] *Ibid.*, p. 335.   [23] *Journal, 1889–1939*, p. 276.
[24] *C.G.*, Vol. IV, p. 422.

twist to the end, the worldly priest and the lady deliciously thrilled by the prospective scandal of a clerical love affair are no more than inoffensively lightweight caricatures. If *L'Abbé Aubain* appeared anonymously, it is perhaps less because Mérimée feared another uproar than because he was aware that no other story of his was quite so unsatisfyingly insubstantial.

These then are the stories in which Mérimée's chief concern is the human situation in civilised society. On the other side stands the group of stories in which he investigates the sombre and irrational fatality of passion. The first of these tales, *La Vénus d'Ille*, published in 1837, was Mérimée's own favourite among his works – twenty years later, he declared: 'In my opinion, it's my masterpiece.'[25] The outward form of this story of a statue of Venus which murders a bridegroom on his wedding-night because he has imprudently put his ring on its finger comes from Mérimée's activities as Inspector-General of Historic Monuments; indeed the first-person narrator is a mildly satirical self-portrait in which all the stress is on his erudition, his pedantry and his detachment from mundane considerations. Mérimée had twice in his travels commented on statues of Venus, and he had visited the region he describes here.[26] Moreover, M. de Peyrehorade, the enthusiastic if not very competent provincial antiquary in whose garden the statue is discovered, is a caricature of one Pierre Puigarri, who had taken Mérimée to task over some errors, real and supposed, in his *Notes d'un voyage dans le Midi de la France*,[27] and the M. de P. who is mentioned in passing is Jaubert de Passa.[28] The events recounted come from an age-old legend, which Mérimée might have come across in numerous sources – he claims to have found it in either Pontanus[29] or Marquard Freher, with some elements borrowed from Lucian's *Philopseudes*,[30] and commentators have pointed to others.[31] With his usual modesty, Méri-

---

[25] *C.G.*, Vol. VIII, p. 244.

[26] The two statues of Venus on which he comments are those of Vienne and Quinipili in Brittany; the latter is described at length in the *Notes d'un voyage dans l'Ouest de la France*, pp. 213–18.

[27] Cf. pp. 146, n.21. The bride's surname in the story in Puygarrig.

[28] Cf. p. 157.

[29] *C.G.*, Vol. VI, p. 233.   [30] *C.G.*, Vol. V, p. 200.

[31] M. Parturier, in 'Sur les sources de *La Vénus d'Ille*', *Le Divan*, avril-juin 1945, traces the legend back to William of Malmesbury in the twelfth century, and instances uses of it by Hermann Corner, quoted in Villemain's

mée made no pretensions to originality: 'I interlarded my plagiarism with little allusions to friends of mine and jokes which would be understood in the circle in which I was living when the story was written.'[32]

In reality, *La Vénus d'Ille* is something far more interesting than an ingenious and technically impeccable ghost-story (though it is perhaps one of the most successful ever written). Mérimée's aim is neither merely to entertain us by making our flesh creep, nor yet to convince us – as Balzac and Nodier seek to do in their fantastic tales – of the existence of supernatural agencies, in which he firmly declined to believe. What he sets out to do is to revivify myth because, in his view, that is the only form in which certain truths can be made accessible to the human mind.[33] Shortly after writing *La Vénus d'Ille*, he became passionately interested in the study of ancient mythology, and this is how he summarises one of the most significant conclusions which he reached:

> the general tendency of ancient mythologies is to leave first causes in what is perhaps a deliberate obscurity, while concentrating on some of their

---

Histoire de Grégoire VII, by Martin Delrio in his *Disquisitiones magicae*, by Vincent de Beauvais and by Heine. The list is further lengthened by Pierre Josserand in 'La Vénus d'Ille et La Mode', *Le Divan*, juillet–sept. 1949, who draws attention to a story published in *La Mode* in 1830 by Auger, which has much the same plot. Another contemporary possibility is Hérold's opera *Zampa*, first performed in 1831, as has been pointed out by Pierre Jourda, 'Zampa et La Vénus d'Ille', *Le Divan*, avril–juin 1945. Jean Decottignies notes, in 'Quelques rapprochements suggérés par *La Vénus d'Ille*', *Revue des sciences humaines*, juillet–sept. 1962, that Delrio's version of the tale is translated by an eccentric magnificently named Berbiguier de Terre-Neuve du Thym in the introduction to a book he wrote in 1821. Clearly, there is no shortage of possible sources; but the works of Pontanus and Freher cited by Mérimée himself do not appear to contain any reference to the legend.

[32] *C.G.*, Vol. V, p. 200. One such joke is the name 'Eutyches Myro' on the statue's arm, Eutyches being the Greek equivalent of Prosper (cf. Dr Parturier's note in *Romans et nouvelles*, Vol. II, p. 626). With the assonance Mérimée-Myro, Mérimée is – reasonably enough – giving himself the credit for the fabrication of the statue.

[33] An interesting interpretation of the story along these lines is offered by Frank Paul Bowman, 'Narrator and myth in Mérimée's *Vénus d'Ille*', *French Review*, April 1960.

effects. Incapable of elucidating mysteries above human understanding, these myths distract our thought as far as possible from the crux of the difficulty.[34]

La Vénus d'Ille, with its obvious allusions to Greek and Roman mythology, proceeds in exactly that way.

It is after all no accident that the statue involved is that of Venus, the goddess of love, and, more particularly, according to the inscription on her arm, *Venus turbulenta*, love in its strongest, most violent, most disruptive form. The dual nature of the statue, both attractive and frightening, symbolises the dual aspect of passion as Mérimée saw it, at once irresistibly fascinating and horribly dangerous. He stresses these two characteristics whenever he describes the statue's features. 'Disdain, irony and cruelty could be read on that face which was nevertheless incredibly beautiful.'[35] 'That expression of infernal irony',[36] 'her expression of ironic spite',[37] 'mischief almost shading into spitefulness'[38] – these are some of the terms he uses to characterise the ambivalence of its charm. At the end, the unfortunate Alphonse de Peyrehorade dies because, in the thoughtless gesture of putting his ring on the statue's finger, he has unwittingly committed himself to this sinister power, and the symbolic overtones are evident in Mérimée's comment on the statue as it stands impassively in the garden on the morning after the crime: 'I felt as though I were looking at some infernal divinity gloating over the misfortune which had descended on the household.'[39] At the centre of the tale is a conception of passion as a force at least as destructive as it is seductive – a conception never before propounded by Mérimée so forcefully as here.

But it is noteworthy, too, that the cruel goddess who represents this force comes from underground and from a far distant period of time. The milieu into which she is brought with such disastrous consequences is that of the provincial middle classes of early nineteenth-century France, and they are quite incapable of appreciating the real significance of the divinity of passion.[40] M. de Peyrehorade regards the statue

[34] 'Des Mythes primitifs', *Revue contemporaine*, 15 octobre 1855.
[35] *Romans et nouvelles*, Vol. II, p. 97.
[36] *Ibid.*, p. 98.   [37] *Ibid.*, p. 115.   [38] *Ibid.*, p. 97.   [39] *Ibid.*, p. 115.
[40] This view is developed convincingly by Ivan Nagel, 'Gespenster und Wirklichkeiten: Prosper Mérimées Novelle *La Vénus d'Ille*', *Die Neue Rundschau*, 1957, Drittes Heft.

simply as an archaeological find, a valuable piece of sculpture, and jovially trots out all the well-worn quotations about being 'wounded by Venus' without ever pausing to think of their true meaning. As for his son Alphonse, Mérimée deliberately makes him into a rather wooden young man, interested in his bride only because she has a large dowry and otherwise mainly concerned with his own prowess at *pelota*. Love and marriage for him are no more than convenient domestic arrangements; in his scale of values, amorous feeling comes a very poor second to the Hippolytus-like pursuit of sport. Both father and son live by a superficial and conventional set of values, which prevents them from seeing the more alarming forces to which humanity will always be subject. Just as the statue of Venus has by the passage of time become hidden by the accumulation of earth above it, so the primitive urges of the basic emotions have become overlaid by the trivial pretences of modern civilisation. When the statue is brought to light, it repels as much as it fascinates, and calamity ensues; so we are powerless victims once passion has broken down the shams and protections with which we seek to nullify its existence.

One of the reasons why *La Vénus d'Ille* makes such a powerful impact on the reader is that these symbolic intentions are only dimly hinted at in the narration, which moves forward with the implacable urgency characteristic of Mérimée. One is above all conscious of an overpowering sense of material reality, so convincingly conveyed that there is no option but to believe in the intrusion of the supernatural when it occurs – and with it all the vaguely adumbrated mythical implications. More than any other of his stories, *La Vénus d'Ille* demonstrates the validity of the principle Mérimée was to state later with reference to Gogol:

> the recipe for a good fantastic tale is well-known: begin with firmly de-lineated portraits of strange but possible characters, and give their features the most minutely observed reality. The transition from what is strange to what is marvellous is imperceptible, and the reader will find himself surrounded by the fantastic before he realises that the real world has been left far behind.[41]

Hence the relatively elaborate details of the narrator's arrival in Ille, the clear localisation of the events, the comic-grotesque description of M. de Peyrehorade, the deliberately pedantic discussion of the meaning

[41] *Études de littérature russe*, Vol. II, p. 10.

of the inscriptions on the statue. Stendhal felt that these erudite considerations go on too long and that the whole story is tainted with aridity,[42] but Mérimée was prepared to risk boring some readers in order to establish the impeccable academic qualifications of his narrator, a man so immersed in archaeology that he could never be suspected of romancing.

Into this realistically painted setting, there gradually spreads a sinister and uncanny mood, as strange, disturbing, but credible details mount up: the workman's broken leg, the broodingly ambiguous expression of the statue, the enigmatic inscriptions on it, the stone which rebounds from it to hit the thrower, the marriage on the ill-omened day of Venus, Peyrehorade's hollow jocularity about the power of Venus, finally Alphonse's account of how he had been unable to pull his ring off the statue's finger. As for the killing itself, that is only narrated at

---

[42] Stendhal's comments on *La Vénus d'Ille*, written down immediately after reading it at midnight on the day of its publication, are fascinating and deserve to be better known. They are reproduced by Louis Royer, 'La Vénus d'Ille appréciée par Stendhal', *Le Divan*, février–mars 1932. Here is a translation:

'1. Outlines extremely clearcut, even to the point of aridity.

2. Thing *existing in its own right*, and not in relation to things already known (means of producing this effect: things are related baldly as if the hearer was ignorant of everything, with no allusion to things already known. Less elegance with this method, but the reader's attention remains wholly fixed on what is narrated).

3. Strong dramatic sense, originality.

4. Neither depth nor originality (save in the way they are depicted) in the characters.

5. Horribly short sentences, style which looks as though it is imitated from Cousin (probably common imitation of the same models from the year 1600).

6. The author is becoming desiccated.

7. Admirable attention to small things, the mark of a good novelist, and boldness in emphasising these little things.

8. The author's great imprudence: he makes fun of his natural tool, his regular host, the provincial antiquary. This 25-page story is going to increase, and even to found with entirely reasonable people, his reputation for ill-nature. (Personal, *id est*, that no one will care about it in twenty years' time.)

There is a moment of aridity brought on by twenty or perhaps ten lines which are too erudite (15 May 1837. Read at midnight).'

second-hand, and we may have doubts about the sanity of the distracted bride. Indeed, the possibility of a natural explanation is not wholly excluded, since suspicion momentarily falls on a *pelota* player who had earlier been insulted by Alphonse. But in the end, while this intentional vagueness makes the tale more effective than a direct affirmation would be, we are likely to conclude that the statue is responsible, since Mérimée's ingenious arrangement of the circumstances makes that seem by far the most plausible explanation. The inevitability of the progression means that there is no head-on clash between incredulity and the incredible. Mérimée is indeed so far from abjuring his usual scepticism that, when a small boy naïvely asked him whether the statue had really killed Alphonse, he replied evasively: 'Goodness, child, I've no idea' – to which the boy, with sound common sense, objected: 'What, sir! You tell stories, and you don't even know them!'[43]

The theme of the conflict between passion and civilised values which gives *La Vénus d'Ille* its richness and its resonance is taken up again in *Colomba* (1840), the product of Mérimée's stay in Corsica in 1839.[44] Mérimée had always been fascinated by primitive societies. From the pirates of his childhood reading, through the hot-blooded Spaniards and Serbs of *Clara Gazul* and *La Guzla*, the brutal violence of life in the Middle Ages or the Renaissance, and the bandits of *Mateo Falcone* or the *Lettres d'Espagne*, to the frightening power of the statue of Venus, Mérimée had always been preoccupied with those modes of life based on strong feeling and which it was impossible to confine within the norms of polite convention. But his fascination had always been accompanied by an instinctive reluctance to give up those safeguards offered, however precariously, by the forms of advanced civilisation – social pressures, education, religion considered as a moral sanction and so forth. The authenticity of the man whose feelings run so high that he rejects the constraint of civilised rules and laws was something he admired and feared at one and the same time, as he was to admit in his 1851 article on Gogol:

I am one of those who have a strong liking for bandits, not that I have any desire to meet them on my travels; but, in spite of myself, the energy of

---

[43] M. Parturier, 'Sur les sources de *La Vénus d'Ille*'.

[44] The sources of *Colomba* have been studied many times and are now well known. One may consult on this subject the books and articles mentioned on pp. 168–9.

these men at war with the whole of society wrings from me an admiration of which I am ashamed.[45]

The observance of law and order might be hypocritical, but however seductive the alternative of unchecked passion appeared, it was also infinitely terrifying; perhaps it would have been better for the timorous bourgeois of La Vénus d'Ille if the statue had never been bared of its protective covering of earth. Nowhere is this hesitation in Mérimée's mind more clearly illustrated than in Colomba.

Mérimée had of course been delighted with all the tales of vendettas, outlaws and shootings which he had heard on the island, and which he incorporated into his story. Colomba Bartoli's feud with the Durazzos and Jérôme Roccaserra's famous coup double are of course the key elements in it, but innumerable other anecdotes, memories, facts and descriptions are worked into the tale – one of the reasons for the perennial popularity of Colomba is undoubtedly its excellence as a guide to Corsican mores. Mérimée makes no bones about admitting how much of it is borrowed from life, and tells his Corsican friend Étienne Conti: 'I have tried to make a mosaic with the stories I picked up here and there about your country.'[46] He even avers that only fear of the possible consequences made him refrain from being more specific in his references:

> if I weren't afraid of displeasing two or three bandits I know, I could have given you a few more touches of local colour, but here [in France] no one would have believed me, and when I returned to Corsica, I would have been made to die della mala morte.[47]

But more interesting than the factual sources of Colomba is the pattern into which Mérimée has arranged them, and which reveals more about its author than it was intended to.

The story has a readily apparent and symmetrical structure. Orso della Rebbia, after years of service as an officer in the French army, returns to his native Corsica to find himself torn between two women. On the one hand is his sister Colomba, who fanatically exhorts him to avenge his father's murder by pursuing a vendetta against the Barricini family whom she suspects of the crime; on the other hand is Lydia Nevil, the respectable young Englishwoman with whom he

---

[45] Études de Littérature russe, Vol. II, p. 9.
[46] C.G., Vol. II, p. 463.   [47] Ibid., p. 378.

has fallen in love and who would immediately disown him if he were to do anything so barbaric. Of the two, Colomba is infinitely the more impressive creation, with, significantly, something of the same ambivalent power of attraction as the statue of Venus. When she thinks she has persuaded Orso to kill the Barricinis, her eyes sparkle with 'a malign joy',[48] and as she sets out with him, Miss Lydia anxiously notices her 'sardonic smile':[49] 'it was as if she could see his evil genius dragging him away to destruction'.[50] Orso himself is all too conscious of the sinister side of his sister's lust for vengeance, and when she begs him to kill the Barricinis, 'he felt as though he were listening to some fatal, inevitable oracle demanding blood from him – innocent blood.[51] He even sees in her something diabolical, echoing so many other Mérimée characters in whom women inspire the terror of the devil: 'my sweet Colomba, I fear you are the devil himself'.[52] But the demure and correct Lydia acts as a counterpoise, and Orso finds himself unable to choose between the primitive violence which Colomba urges on him and the unadventurous conformity with civilised standards which Lydia would have him observe.

By far the greater part of the story (Mérimée's longest, apart from the *Chronique*) is concerned with Orso's hesitation between the forms of behaviour represented by the two women. Born a Corsican, he might by nature be inclined to follow the fierce practice of the vendetta; but years of contact with the life of metropolitan France have given him another and more sophisticated set of standards which he is powerless to ignore. Even Lydia is aware of the uncomfortable duality of his situation, and, comparing him with the hero of Byron's *Corsair*, she says: 'He was something between a Conrad and a dandy. . . . I've turned him into a complete dandy, and a dandy with a Corsican tailor!'[53] Orso's long indecisiveness, which is the real theme of the story, reflects Mérimée's inability to opt finally between the crude but genuine primitivism for which Colomba and Corsica stand, and the polite, superficial uniformity of that European civilisation exemplified by the prim and proper Lydia. *Colomba* is essentially the story of a dilemma, and in the end the dilemma remains unsolved. For Mérimée so arranges matters that the choice is eventually taken out of Orso's hands. Before he has made a decision, he is caught in an ambush in

[48] *Romans et nouvelles*, p. 177.   [49] *Ibid.*   [50] *Ibid.*
[51] *Ibid.*, p. 194.   [52] *Ibid.*, p. 229.   [53] *Ibid.*, p. 178.

which the Barricinis fire on him, and when, despite a broken arm, he kills them both with his return shots, he is simply saving his own life. As far as the real theme of the story is concerned, this is no more than an evasion of the issue. By a piece of dubious sleight-of-hand, Mérimée avoids having to conclude on the moral problem which has formed the whole basis of his tale.

Critics have often commented on the way in which *Colomba* fails to fulfil the expectations it arouses in us, without perhaps seeing quite what lies behind the sense of disappointment it leaves. Pierre Jourda for instance notes: 'he promised us a vendetta and tells us about an act of self-defence'.[54] Guy Michaut goes even further and suggests that Mérimée has, out of habit, hoaxed both the public and himself: 'the powerful, poetic drama has turned into a picturesque anecdote'.[55] The aesthetic effect of *Colomba* is notably weakened by this trick and its quality as a human document lessened. Mérimée has lacked the courage to face the tragic implications of the situation he has devised and wriggles out of it in what can only be described as a dishonest way. Orso never has to make up his mind and so can marry Lydia while keeping his sister's affection. The happy ending is contrived and as a result unsatisfying. But this is because Mérimée himself remains so uncertain over the basic issue underlying the whole story: primitivism or civilisation, passion or politeness – he refuses either to choose between them or to admit the impossibility of keeping both.

There are other reasons, too, why *Colomba* remains a relatively low-keyed work. One is that it is too visibly planned to show off representative antitheses, as was also the case with the *Chronique*. Every element in it is there for a fairly obvious reason of balance or symbolism.[56]

[54] *Colomba*, ed. P. Jourda, Paris, Droz, 1947, p. xxviii.

[55] G. Michaut, 'La Mystification de *Colomba*', *Annales de l'Université de Paris*, janvier–février 1933.

[56] Raymond Isay, in 'Une nouvelle interprétation de *Colomba*', *Revue des Deux Mondes*, 1er décembre 1953, suggests, plausibly if too schematically, that the underlying subject of the story is Corsica itself, personified as Colomba. The element of truth that there is in this reading goes some way to explaining the artificial effect which *Colomba* produces.

Colomba might have seemed an even more innocuous tale if Mérimée had not been deflected from his original intention. As it ran at first, after the death of the Barricini brothers, Mérimée had shown Colomba engineering matters so that Lydia was obliged to marry Orso; this was in his eyes typical

But where this method was reasonably effective in a work as diffuse and complex as the *Chronique*, the more tightly knit plot of *Colomba* reveals all too clearly the author manipulating his puppets for effect. It consequently never quite comes to life as an organic whole in the way that *La Vénus d'Ille* and *Carmen* do. Another flaw is Mérimée's slightly shamefaced but nevertheless very manifest predilection for local colour.[57] Whole episodes, scenes and characters are included because they are so typically and picturesquely Corsican – Colomba's slitting of the horse's ear, her improvisation at the wake, the appearance of the two outlaws and so on. Not even Mérimée's immense technical skill can quite disguise the fact that the whole work exists to excite us about Corsica; it may be the best of guide-books, but in essence a fictionalised Baedeker is what it remains. These flaws vitiate it as a work of art, and perhaps the highest praise it is fair to bestow on it is that few tales constitute a more successful imitation of a masterpiece.

If *Colomba* ultimately fails because Mérimée is unwilling to come to terms with the consequences of his own thoughts and feelings, *Carmen* succeeds magnificently because there, more than anywhere else, he takes his conception of passion to its logical – and intensely tragic – conclusion.[58] To appreciate *Carmen* at its true worth, it is of course necessary to forget all about Bizet; whatever the musical and dramatic merits of the opera, it is in its basic schema no more than an emascu-

---

of Corsican family loyalty. But Mme Delessert protested that this cast a suspicion of self-interest over a heroine otherwise only moved by noble passions, and Mérimée deferently changed his ending, leaving Colomba's views on the marriage unspoken, and exaggerating her venomous cruelty to old Barricini in the last scene, so as to nullify any hint of mercenariness on her part. But he admitted regretting his original idea, which struck him as more true to life (C.G., Vol. II, p. 463). In fact, it sounds as if this first intention might simply have given the story a rather insipid conclusion.

[57] At the beginning of the tale, Mérimée makes fun of Lydia Nevil's diligent search for local colour, 'whatever may be meant by these words, which I used to understand perfectly well a few years ago, but which are incomprehensible to me now' (*Romans et nouvelles*, Vol. II, p. 131). Yet as the story unfolds, it becomes plain that local colour is Mérimée's main interest too. As so often happens, Mérimée is afraid of being mocked for his own enthusiasm, and so affects to disdain it.

[58] The most complete study of *Carmen* is that by Auguste Dupouy, '*Carmen*' *de Mérimée*, Paris, SFELT, 1930.

lated and prettified version of Mérimée's tale. What Mérimée wrote has a savage power that the more conventional picturesqueness of Bizet's adaptation cannot match. The long gestation of the work may have something to do with this tautness of structure and incandescence of feeling. Though it only appeared in 1845, it is, on Mérimée's own admission, based on an anecdote about a young blood of Malaga which Mme de Montijo had told him in 1830,[59] and there are already suggestions of some of its thematic material in the *Lettres d'Espagne* of the early 1830s – the brigand José-Maria and the beautiful but disquieting Carmencita glimpsed at a wayside inn, for instance. But other elements are later accretions; the deep curiosity about gypsies is an interest of the 1840s, as is the preoccupation with Julius Caesar and the battlefield of Munda. Years of experience of Spain and things Spanish also contribute to the evocation of the setting, the characters and the atmosphere.[60] This lengthily prepared amalgam of a borrowed story and very personal feelings has far more inner unity than the hastily contrived mosaic-work of *Colomba*.

The 1845 text of *Carmen* is simple in its outlines (it was only in 1847 that a major revision brought in an entirely new section at the end). It begins with a leisurely account, in the first person, of the acquaintance-ship the narrator strikes up with the bandit Don José whom he meets during his archaeological researches in Spain, and of his subsequent encounter with Carmen herself. This leads into the main body of the tale, which is Don José's account, given to the narrator while awaiting execution for Carmen's murder, of how he had first set eyes on her, how he had deserted from the army and taken to banditry for love of her, how he twice killed men out of jealousy, and how he had finally murdered Carmen herself when he had realised that she could never be his alone. The function of the preamble, with its detached and pedantic narrator occupied only with ancient history, is similar to that of *La Vénus d'Ille*: to establish an atmosphere of normality in which the extraordinary figure of Don José will gradually but naturally take a

[59] *C.G.*, Vol. IV, p. 194. It was probably because his work on Don Pedro had brought him back into touch with Spain that Mérimée was moved to write the story in 1845.

[60] Some of these questions are examined in detail by Jean Pommier in 'Notes sur *Carmen*', *Bulletin de la Faculté des Lettres de Strasbourg*, novembre 1929, décembre 1929, février 1930, avril 1930.

5b Strendhal, a portrait by Sodermark

5a Sutton Sharpe, a portrait by Anne Mérimée

6b Valentine Delessert, from a portrait by Vernet

6a Jenny Dacquin

grip on our imagination. Don José's narration will thus be authenticated by the credentials of Mérimée himself, who at the same time absolves himself from responsibility for Don José's criminal aberrations. There is a good deal of irony in this part, most of it directed inwards against himself, even to the extent of hinting in advance that it is all very trivial compared with the serious business of locating Munda:

> until my dissertation at last solves the problem which is keeping all the learned men of Europe on tenterhooks, I am going to tell you a little story: it in no way prejudges the interesting question of the site of Munda.[61]

But once the narrator hands over to Don José, the irony vanishes. Mérimée has, as usual, protected himself by implying an ironic view of the whole proceedings; the irony is, however, confined to the preface and so enhances rather than detracts from the desperate sincerity of Don José's confession.

That confession itself, so rough-hewn, so terrifying, so monolithic that Charles du Bos has called it 'a literary menhir',[62] is the real centre of the tale. Undoubtedly, its bleak tragic power comes from the masterly description of Don José's jealous passion and from the taunting figure of Carmen herself. It is the only place in his works where Mérimée dares to give a full-scale depiction, from the inside, of the ravages of passion, and as one might expect, Carmen, the object of this irresistible and all-consuming force, has much in common with the statue of Venus. As a gypsy, she too stands outside the confines of normal contemporary society and cannot be peacefully integrated into it. Almost her last words are: 'Carmen will always be free.'[63] She too has associations with the supernatural, since she is a fortune-teller. Her hold over Don José is as absolute and as disastrous as that of Venus over Alphonse de Peyrehorade. Her beauty is as fierce and cruel as that of the statue:

> It was a strange and wild beauty, a face which at first called forth astonishment but which it was impossible to forget. Above all, her eyes had an expression both voluptuous and savage which I have never seen since in any other human gaze.[64]

---

[61] *Romans et nouvelles*, Vol. II, p. 345.
[62] *Notes sur Mérimée*, p. 59.
[63] *Romans et nouvelles*, Vol. II, p. 401.
[64] *Ibid.*, p. 360.

G

About her, as about the statue, there is something infernal, stated with
such terse, casual simplicity that it almost passes unnoticed – ' "You
are the devil," I said to her. "Yes," she replied.'[65] And like Colomba,
she represents the lure of a dangerously free and lawless existence,
which may liberate one from the shackles of society but also hurl one
headlong to destruction. Clearly, the concept of passion she embodies
is the same as that in *La Vénus d'Ille* and in *Colomba*, but because here
it appears in a more humanly comprehensible form than in the one
and is not subjected to the same devious evasiveness as in the other,
it is more effective than in either.

A large part of this effectiveness comes from the fact that Don José
speaks to us directly in his own words. There are no deflating comments,
no anticlimactic asides, no flippant badinage. Don José believes passionately in the love he has experienced and recounts events with all the
urgency and impact one might expect from a man under sentence of
death. The habitual straightforwardness and energy of Mérimée's style
are heightened here by the vivid speech of the soldier and bandit, in
which colourful metaphors abound. Mérimée always held that popular
speech had a pungency and vigour absent from more cultivated diction,
and particularly relished authors like Rabelais, Brantôme, d'Aubigné
and Molière in whose writings the popular element was well to the
fore. As he says in discussing Greek folk-poetry, 'nowadays, as in the
West, it is only in the mouths of unlettered people that bold and
ingenious metaphors are to be heard'.[66] Hence the images in this part
of *Carmen* are more frequent and more striking than in any of
Mérimée's other works – the scaffold is 'the wooden-legged widow',[67]
Carmen's mood is like the weather in the Basque country – 'the storm
is never so near as when the sun is shining most brightly',[68] and so on.
But despite the forceful images, Don José's normal speech is remarkably precise, exact statement of the barest, most immediate kind.
Perhaps the most outstanding example of this, haunting in its simple
affirmation of the cause of the tragedy, is what he reports Carmen as

[65] *Romans et nouvelles*, Vol. II, p. 387. Carmen herself says to Don José:
'You've met the devil, yes, the devil; he's not always black, and he didn't
wring your neck. I may be dressed in wool, but I'm not a sheep' (*ibid.*, p. 379).
[66] Preface to Marino Vreto, *Contes et poèmes de la Grèce moderne*, Paris,
Audois, 1855, p. 12.
[67] *Romans et nouvelles*, Vol. II, p. 379.   [68] *Ibid.*, p. 381.

saying to him just before the murder: 'I don't love you any more, but you still love me, and that's why you want to kill me.'[69]

Another result of allowing Don José to narrate is to make us go through all his hardships and torments with him. We too submit to the seductiveness of Carmen because we see her through his eyes – it is the same technique as Prévost uses to compel the readers of *Manon Lescaut* to acquiesce in Des Grieux's guilty passion for Manon. Indeed, the analogies between the works have not escaped the critics, and Sainte-Beuve described *Carmen* as 'a spicier *Manon Lescaut*, served in the Spanish style'.[70] But *Carmen* is superior to the earlier novel by its more incisive writing, its more concentrated plot and its more evocative descriptions. In each case, the outcome is inevitably tragic, for neither Manon nor Carmen can accept the constraints which their lovers would impose on them; they fascinate, because they are unpredictable, and conformity would rob them of the very quality which makes them so attractive. 'Carmen will always be free'; sensual, animal, unspoilt, untamed, she cannot bow to the laws José insists on, so from the moment when José first falls in love with her (characteristically just after she has tried to commit murder), their fate is sealed. The sense of fatality and the constant presence of danger characterise his passion for her, and it makes its full impact on us because we live through it with him.

The Spanish atmosphere moreover sets it off to perfection. Whereas *Colomba* was written as a deliberate showpiece for Corsican local colour, the Spanish setting is made into a part of the very fabric of *Carmen*. The basic theme is universal in its dramatic simplicity, but Spanish in its full though unobtrusive localisation.[71] The choice of detail here is particularly cunning; one may single out that gesture which so pleased Charles du Bos with its authenticity,[72] when Carmen has failed to persuade Don José to kill and rob the narrator: 'then the gypsy cast a glance of profound scorn at him, and sitting down cross-legged in a corner of the room, she selected an orange, peeled it and began to eat it.'[73] All these things are done with such rapid and economical dexterity that one scarcely realises all their implications and overtones.

[69] *Ibid.*, p. 401.   [70] *Mes Poisons*, p. 98.
[71] Though in order to avoid giving offence to his Spanish friends, Mérimée makes Carmen a gypsy and Don José a Basque.
[72] *Notes sur Mérimée*, p. 22.   [73] *Romans et nouvelles*, Vol. II, p. 362.

As Sainte-Beuve wittily commented, 'when Merimée achieves an effect, it is with such an abrupt, sudden blow that one always feels there may be a catch in it. It is like that Navarrese stance and the knife-thrust with which his bandit kills the one-eyed man. It hits you with a bang. There is no time to notice if it is well done.'[74] But it is the accumulation of these telling touches and the ability to say the most significant things in bare and sober terms that makes *Carmen* one of the world's finest tales.

One could almost wish that that were the end of the story of Mérimée's middle-period tales. But in 1846 he not only wrote *L'Abbé Aubain*, one of his slightest works, he also produced *Il Viccolo di Madama Lucrezia*, which displays a high degree of narrative skill but is otherwise almost entirely empty.[75] This tale of what appears to be a ghostly incident in Rome begins like another evocation of the dangers of passion, but in the end it mystifies us to no good purpose, since Mérimée supplies a natural explanation for all its mysterious events. It is a barefaced hoax on the reader, written apparently for no other reason than the unworthy pleasure of hoodwinking us. The ambiguity always present in Mérimée's attitude to imaginative literature seems now to have sapped his will to create seriously. Since all fiction involves deception, why not remove everything from it except deception? A few months later, he confirmed this view by adding an extra section to *Carmen*, which consists exclusively of a brief essay on the language of the gypsies, in which he had been taking a highly professional interest.[76] The last words of the story after this 1847 revision are these:

---

[74] *Mes Poisons*, p. 98.

[75] On this story, see Jean Decottignies, '*Il Viccolo di Madama Lucrezia*. L'élaboration d'une nouvelle de Mérimée', *Revue d'Histoire littéraire de la France*, oct.–déc. 1964. M. Decottignies explains the genesis of the story by suggesting that it arises from a combination of his own unhappiness in love in 1846, reminiscences of one of Hoffmann's tales, and a misadventure which had just befallen Walewski in Milan.

Mérimée did not deign to publish the story. He gave the manuscript to Mme Odier, Valentine Delessert's sister, and forgot about it until 1868, when he decided to try to remember enough of it to write it out again. This second manuscript presumably perished with the rest of his papers in 1871, and it was the 1846 text which was used for the first publication in 1873.

[76] In the early 1840s, Mérimée had been studying Borrow's *The Bible in Spain* and *The Zincali*, as well as Pott's *Die Zigeuner*, and it is Borrow who

That is quite enough to give the readers of *Carmen* a flattering idea of my studies of the Romany tongue. I shall end appropriately with a proverb: *En retudi panda nasti abela macha.* If you keep your mouth shut, the flies won't get in.[77]

Few readers can have felt this as anything other than a deliberate and provocative anticlimax.

Sainte-Beuve has defined the impression left by this appendix with his customary acumen:

> It is equivalent to saying, in salon society, and with that familiar smile: 'Of course! Don't be taken in by my brigand and my gypsy any more than you want to be.' After having indulged in so much local colour, the author, in his turn, does not want us to think he is more taken in than is proper.[78]

The canker of doubt about the value of imaginative creations which had scarred Mérimée's works from the earliest times has now grown to such proportions that it completely inhibits their life. The hints of aloofness, of disbelief, of irony detectable in the incongruous endings of the *Clara Gazul* plays, in the atmosphere of imposture surrounding *La Guzla*, in the off-hand conclusion of the *Chronique* or in various asides in the short stories, now coalesce in what comes close to a repudiation of any work of the imagination. Scepticism was always an essential ingredient in Mérimée's art; finally it destroys it. After 1847, Mérimée takes his own advice and fends off the flies of doubt by keeping his lips tightly closed. Having indicated by his wilfully perverse revision of *Carmen* that he scorns his own literature, he abandons it completely for twenty years, turning instead to history, which had been attracting him increasingly and which struck him as proof against the sort of corrosion which had eaten away his never very strong confidence in the validity of fiction. Novelists may be liars, but historians are not: henceforth Mérimée will make sure that no one can accuse him of duping himself or others. But the loss to art will be a sad one.

---

supplies a large proportion of the gypsy lore in *Carmen*. His philological curiosity about Romany was very professional, and he enlisted the help of friends all over Europe for the comparative study of different dialects.

[77] *Romans et nouvelles*, Vol. II, p. 409.

[78] *Les Grands Écrivains français, XIXᵉ siècle. Les romanciers*, Vol. II, p. 38.

Chapter 11

Academician

Si quelqu'un me demandait quel était le moment le plus
pénible de ma vie, au choix je ne dirais pas que c'est le jour
où je suis entré en prison . . . C'est celui où j'ai été reçu à
l'Académie.

Quoted by Ferdinand Bac, *Mérimée inconnu*

Corsica and Italy in 1839, Spain in 1840: one might think that Mérimée
would have welcomed a rest from his incessant voyaging. But in the
spring of 1841, several of his archaeological friends managed to persuade the government to sponsor an expedition to Italy, Greece and
Asia Minor and easily persuaded him to join them. The party was
composed of Charles Lenormant and Jean-Jacques Ampère, together
with a Belgian numismatist and expert on ceramography, Baron Jean
de Witte. As Mérimée was obliged to undertake his usual summer tour
of inspection, the others set off first, leaving him to make a perfunctory
round of Normandy and Touraine before taking ship at Marseille in
mid-August. In Naples he caught up with Lenormant and de Witte,
and a few days later, by way of Malta and Syra, they arrived in Athens,
where Ampère was waiting for them. A curious incident occurred in
Syra, revealing even to Lenormant, who had known Mérimée since
his schooldays, that one could never be sure what was going on behind
his façade of impassive detachment. They had gone to visit the village
church, but had found it in use for the funeral of a little boy, whose
flower-bedecked body lay in an open coffin. As the mourners took
leave of the corpse by kissing it on the forehead, Lenormant was
staggered: 'My companion the hard-boiled Mérimée broke down in
tears, which was no small surprise to me'.[1]

In Athens, the travellers were presented to the King of Greece, who
with confused amiability congratulated Mérimée first on his history

[1] Charles Lenormant, *Beaux-Arts et voyages*, Paris, Lévy, 1861, Vol. II,
pp. 283–4.

of French literature and then on his works about legislation.[2] A more fruitful meeting was with Théodose de Lagrené, the French Minister in Greece, and his wife, a Russian noblewoman named Barbe Doubenski, with whom Mérimée was perhaps near to falling in love and who was later to teach him Russian. As befitted men of learning on an officially subsidised mission, they were all active in studying Greek architecture, pottery, coins and inscriptions, with Mérimée energetically scrambling up to vantage points to sketch the illustrations for the books and articles the others were preparing.[3] Mérimée's impressions of Greek architecture were remarkably enthusiastic; he said that in Athens he 'spent three weeks in ecstasy before the most beautiful monuments the human mind could conceive'.[4] From Athens they went on to Eleusis, where Mérimée was smitten with colic, and thence to Delphi, where the same fate befell de Witte. Despite these mishaps, they were all in high good humour until a more serious accident happened on the way to Thermopylae. Many years later, Mérimée still remembered it vividly:

We were together in Greece, going to Thermopylae, and descending a very steep ravine on foot, holding the bridles of the horses. Suddenly, on the crest of the opposite slope of the ravine, we saw a man who, despite the drop and the rocks, was running as if he were falling. Yet he had a great white cloak, a long rifle and a dead deer slung across his shoulders. He reached the bottom of the ravine before us, and that was where we met him. I asked him if he would sell us his deer. He replied: 'I'm going to eat it with my friends.' In Greek, that is: *mè toûs filous mou*. The word *filous* made me laugh, for he was a very sinister-looking fellow.[5] With a couple of bounds he disappeared into the bushes. M. Lenormant asked me what I thought of the man. I told him that I thought he looked exactly like Samiel the wild hunter. – 'No' he said, 'I believe he's the devil.' 'Very likely', I answered and set off in front with Ampère. A moment or two later, surprised not to hear the sound of horses' hooves behind me, I turned round and saw M. Lenormant lying on the ground with a dislocated shoulder. It was very far from any help; we carried him to a village as best we could, and it was two days before we could find a doctor. For those two days he was more or less alone in the village, and later, he said

---

[2] *C.G.*, Vol. III, pp. 130–1.

[3] Cf. Jean-Jacques Ampère, *Une Course en Asie Mineure* in *La Grèce, Rome et Dante*, Paris, Didier, 1848.   [4] *C.G.*, Vol. III, pp. 161–2.

[5] Because the French word *filou* means 'rogue'.

that he had spent his time reflecting and had been converted. Since then, he has related in a lecture how he and I both saw the devil.[6]

After this mysterious misfortune, Mérimée and Ampère went on alone to Thermopylae, where even the 'prosaic' Mérimée had to admit to being moved by the thought of Leonidas and the Three Hundred.[7] He even picked a flower there as a memento for Jenny Dacquin.[8] But somehow melancholy was never far away, and as he rested with Ampère on a pile of straw in front of the gendarmerie guard-house, he reflected that he did not have a single tender memory of his youth that was not tinged with bitterness.[9] Then, while Lenormant convalesced in Athens, the others took ship to Asia Minor, visiting Smyrna, Ephesus and other archaeological sites before going on to Constantinople. Mérimée, usually clean-shaven, was now sporting a flowing moustache and savouring the pleasure of wearing pistols and a sabre in his belt in case of meeting brigands. He was also flattered that his Turkish passport described him as having 'hair like a turtle-dove and eyes like a lion'.[10] Artistically, he was disappointed by Constantinople and felt that nothing could approach the splendid purity of Doric.

In mid-November, Lenormant, now recovered, left on his own, with Mérimée and Ampère soon following. Mérimée was still full of praise for Greece: 'in these five months, I wasn't bored for five minutes'.[11] His only complaint was that it was impossible for him to satisfy his sexual appetites there – 'The one thing I find wrong with this country is its virtue, which is such that we shall doubtless leave as virgins and martyrs.'[12] But he was eminently pleased by its buildings, its art, its people, its picturesqueness, and even its landscapes, which almost weaned him from his usual preference for the works of man.[13] He regretted that he had been unable to visit Édouard Grasset, now French consul in the Albanian city of Janina,[14] but made no effort to

---

[6] C.G., Vol. IX, pp. 335–6.

[7] 'De l'Histoire ancienne de la Grèce' (an extended review of George Grote's book), in Mélanges historiques et littéraires, Paris, Lévy, 1855, p. 166.

[8] C.G., Vol. III, p. 154.   [9] Ibid.

[10] Ibid., p. 133.   [11] Ibid., p. 155.   [12] Ibid., p. 120.

[13] 'Art is always more beautiful than nature', he affirmed in 1843 (C.G., Vol. III, p. 365).

[14] C.G., Vol. III, p. 119.

see Stendhal in Italy. After a wearisome journey back, which included an unwelcome stay at the lazaret in Malta, he was at home in Paris early in December.

But Greece still occupied his thoughts so much that he spent much time that winter poring over Greek myths. He later said: 'I used to be very well up in mythology, which I studied with a sort of passion, and I had started a book which, like many others, I abandoned [. . .] I wanted to find the law of the human mind which makes it invent religious myths.'[15] Mérimée's meditations on mythology were at first something more than erudite curiosity; perhaps more affected than he realised by Lenormant's dramatic conversion, he wanted to investigate the religious impulse underlying all myth. But in the end, his scepticism got the upper hand, and he was forced to admit that, whatever the aesthetic and historic interest of mythology, it did nothing to assuage any deeper needs:

> it may well be that mythology leads nowhere. If one seeks in it a solution to the great problems about the beginning and the end of the world, I fear one will only find silliness and absurdity.[16]

A more lasting legacy of his voyage to Greece was an unbounded admiration for Greek civilisation. To Jenny Dacquin, he averred that it was from Greece that the taste for beauty came to the 'happy few',[17] and to Boissonade, one of the foremost classical scholars of the time, he wrote: 'the Greeks are our masters in everything'.[18] The erstwhile Romantic now stood revealed as an unashamed devotee of classicism.[19]

The winter of 1841-2 was an unusually busy one for Mérimée. His *Essai sur la Guerre Sociale* (*Essay on the Social War*) had appeared in May, shortly before he went to Greece, in a limited edition of 150 copies not intended for public sale, and he now settled down to work on the sequel *La Conjuration de Catilina* (*The Catilina Conspiracy*), in which he proposed to deal with Caesar's early political career. In addition, he had become fascinated by gypsy lore, was studying Borrow and Pott, and was soon pestering his friends in different countries for

[15] *C.G.*, Vol. VIII, p. 364.

[16] 'Des mythes primitifs', *Revue contemporaine*, 15 octobre 1855.

[17] *C.G.*, Vol. III, p. 229.   [18] *C.G.*, Vol. V, p. 33.

[19] There had always been strong classical elements in Mérimée's aesthetic. Cf. R. C. Dale, *op. cit.*, and Pierre Moreau, *Le Classicisme des Romantiques*, Paris, Plon, 1932.

examples of the local gypsy dialects. These intellectual pursuits, which took up long hours in the night after days of hard work on committees and in the office, made him increasingly weary of social obligations. When he did go to a ball, he felt like a fish out of water:

> it was as though I had landed in an unknown island. The women wear such deep *décolletés* that if you stand on the edge of their gowns, you undress them. The fashion is to talk at the top of one's voice, and I thought I was in a meeting of parrots.[20]

Some time later, he noticed that he had forgotten to go to a great ball, and sighed melancholically to Jenny Dacquin: 'What has become of the happy time when I used to enjoy such things? Nowadays it all bores me horribly. Don't I strike you as very old?'[21]

This impression of old age was suddenly made very vivid when within the space of a few months, two of his closest friends died. The first to go was Stendhal who, on the evening of 23 March, was laid low by a fatal stroke as he walked along the rue Neuve des Capucines, probably on his way to talk to Mme Ancelot about her proposed campaign to get him into the Academy. Mérimée was less distressed than one might have expected. Since their unfortunate meeting in Italy in 1839, their friendship had cooled off noticeably, and even when Stendhal was in Paris, they were no longer inseparable. Still, Mérimée at first thought of writing an obituary notice for the *Revue des Deux Mondes*, but then decided to leave it to Stendhal's cousin Romain Colomb, whose mediocre article was turned down by Buloz.[22] So it was not for several years that Mérimée paid his last tribute to the man who more than any other had been responsible for making him what he was. Much more of a shock to him was the stroke which Sutton Sharpe suffered on 31 December 1842. Sharpe had been on his usual visit to Paris in the summer, but had subsequently fallen ill from overwork and had been warned by his doctors to take things easy. This his energetic temperament refused to allow, with the inevitable result. He lingered on for six weeks, half paralysed and scarcely able to speak, while Mérimée hesitated about going to see him. Then, when he seemed to be convalescent, he sank into a coma and died on 22 February 1843. This time, there was no doubt that Mérimée was thoroughly shaken. 'I cannot tell you how painfully the poor chap's

[20] *C.G.*, Vol. III, p. 33.   [21] *Ibid.*, p. 313.   [22] *Ibid.*, pp. 163–5.

death has affected me. There used to be eight of us who dined together once a week. Three are already dead, and two of them, Beyle and Sharpe, in the same way.'[23] He found himself unable to get used to the idea that he would never see Sharpe again[24] and bitterly regretted his failure to visit him on his deathbed: 'it would have been some consolation to me to say goodbye to him'.[25]

In this grief, there was an unmistakable element of alarm for himself, even though he was only thirty-nine. Lord Brougham, who was in France at the time, told him that in England, people thought that Sharpe's Parisian friends were responsible for the excesses which had killed him,[26] and it was an idea he could not easily dismiss. First Stendhal, then Sharpe – which of the dining party at Véry's would go next? From this moment onwards his own health began to preoccupy him increasingly. He complained of headaches, of eye-strain, of difficulty in breathing, and always with the idea at the back of his mind that death might seize him without warning. 'Every day I am struck by my old age',[27] 'I'm in a pretty bad state of preservation, growing old little by little, and very annoyed to be growing old',[28] 'the blood is shooting to my head, and I'm very much afraid that one of these days the same will happen to me as did to poor Sharpe'[29] – the complaints in his letters grow ever more frequent, even though he was never ill enough to consult a doctor, at least on his own behalf, though when he sought medical advice for Hippolyte Royer-Collard, another of the Véry group, it was certainly to see if he could glean any comfort for himself.[30]

One new interest did, however, help to keep him young. That was the arrival in Paris, in 1842, of Jenny Dacquin, who, having inherited two large sums of money, had decided to come to live in the capital[31] – a decision at least in part prompted by the desire to see if closer contacts might not make Prosper less hostile to the idea of matrimony. Thus, after a decade of a largely epistolary friendship, they found themselves able to see each other almost daily. But the situation was a curiously false one. Jenny knew nothing of Mme Delessert, and Mérimée, never one to spoil his own chances with an attractive woman, saw no reason to tell her. So she regarded him as a free man and could not understand

[23] *Ibid.*, p. 330.   [24] *Ibid.*, p. 323.   [25] *Ibid.*, p. 322.
[26] *Ibid.*, p. 296.   [27] *Ibid.*, p. 345.   [28] *C.G.*, Vol. IV, p. 324.
[29] *Ibid.*, p. 435.   [30] *Ibid.*, p. 196.   [31] Cf. A. Lefèbvre, *op. cit.*

why, in view of his pressing interest in her, he was so adamant in refusing to think of marriage. Well aware too, that he had a highly compromising reputation as a philanderer, she took great care that he should never appear in her *salon*, and that their meetings should always have some decently reputable pretext – a walk in the forest of Vincennes, a visit to the Louvre, an evening at the Opera. Mérimée was keenly attracted by Jenny, excited by her reticence, frustrated by his inability to make her accept him on his own terms, and exasperated by her firmness.

The result was, inevitably, a stormy and unsatisfactory relationship. Mérimée's letters are in turn cajoling, sarcastic, conciliatory, angry, flattering and downright rude, but with that discreet elegance of style which he handled with such mastery. The burden of his reproaches always comes down to the same thing: 'each of us wants something impossible: you want me to be a statue, I want you not to be one'.[32] Whether he ever did make her descend from her pedestal is a moot point, but if he did, it must have been about this time. The text of Mérimée's letters to Jenny was meticulously doctored by her when she published them after his death, and the originals have never been found, but one ambiguous phrase seems to have escaped her censorship. This occurs in a letter written in October 1842: 'we began writing to each other by being witty, then what did we do? I shan't remind you.'[33] Suspicious though it may sound, it is perhaps rendered more innocuous by the following phrase: 'And now we are going in for erudition'. That Jenny omitted to excise the incriminating sentence may after all indicate that it is a perfectly innocent reference to some intellectual pastime similar to wit and erudition. Admittedly, some of those few friends of Mérimée who knew about Jenny were convinced that she was his mistress. Years later, Fanny Lagden, with aggrieved possessiveness, complained that, when she called on Mérimée, she was sometimes turned away by his servant with the words: 'Yes, Madam, Monsieur Mérimée is in, but Mademoiselle Dacquin is with him.'[34] But that insinuation could easily be ascribed to jealousy. Dr Maure, a friend and confidant of Mérimée's declining years in Cannes, was more categorical and said vehemently to Mme Juliette Adam:

[32] *C.G.*, Vol. III, p. 433.   [33] *Ibid.*, p. 230.

[34] M. Parturier, 'Jenny Dacquin, ou L'Inconnue mieux connue', *Le Figaro littéraire*, 14 février 1959.

You knew Mérimée's excellent qualities. Go on believing in them, but don't believe in his platonism. I can give you proofs which I shall leave with you when I next call. We are both friends of Mérimée, let us stop him being made grotesque![35]

But again, Maure was a hearty, pleasure-loving man who perhaps only saw one side of Mérimée's complex character and rejected what did not fit that image. In the absence of the proofs he refers to, his testimony too must be regarded as inconclusive. What is certain is that, if Jenny did in a moment of weakness yield to Mérimée, it was only a passing lapse; the tone of his letters makes it clear that she was never his regular mistress.

These skirmishes with Jenny did not interfere with the continuance of his affair with Valentine Delessert. Valentine herself, while spurring Mérimée on to more social and academic distinctions, seems to have begun once more to make him feel her domination by a return to her former coquettishness: that at least is the most likely explanation of a mysterious comment he made to Jenny Dacquin in December 1842: 'all suffering horrifies me, and for some time past I have believed in moral suffering. In a word, I try to forget my own person as much as I can.'[36] Probably she was tiring of a lover who was approaching middle age, whose hair was grey, and whose unquestioning devotion no longer satisfied that desire for power over men which she always felt.

For the time being, however, she was content to push him towards election to one or other Academy, an honour towards which he had been quietly moving for some time. His strategy was carefully prepared. The restriction of 150 copies of the first edition of his *Essai sur la Guerre sociale* was meant to demonstrate the seriousness of his pretensions as a historian: public success did not concern him so long as he pleased the specialists. The copies were distributed to selected archaeologists and classicists, accompanied by letters of becoming modesty: 'it is rash of a story-teller like myself to offer a man of learning a work on Roman history',[37] he wrote deferentially to one academician. But he had no intention of spoiling his chances by an over-hasty candidature, the more so as he was unwilling to stand against any of his friends. Thus he waited until Félicien de Saulcy had been elected in June 1842 before thinking seriously of campaigning; then, just as he was about to enter the lists in December, he decided to hold back on hearing that

[35] *Ibid.*   [36] *C.G.*, Vol. III, p. 36.   [37] *Ibid.*, p. 46.

Ampère was a candidate. In the meantime, he was sorely tempted to put his name forward not only for the Academy of Inscriptions and Belles-Lettres but also for the even more glittering prize of the French Academy itself. The trouble was that, while the French Academy was more desirable, the Academy of Inscriptions seemed more feasible, and he was afraid that he might ruin his hopes with one by trying too hard for the other. So he was even more circumspect with the French Academy, contenting himself with scanning the papers for news of the health of elderly members. Premature deaths were however no use to him, since he wanted to be sure of his ground before making a move: 'I am told that M. de Pongerville, the academician, is about to die; that upsets me greatly, for I shall not be his successor, and I should like him to wait until my time has come.'[38]

In the end, it was at the Academy of Inscriptions that a suitable vacancy occurred first, with the death in August 1843 of the Marquis de Fortia d'Urban, while Mérimée was in Burgundy on his annual tour of inspection. At once he started consulting his friends about the advisability of standing. To Vitet, he confessed his fear lest it should compromise his case with the French Academy:

> You know that though I have not officially come forward as one of the candidates for the French Academy, I am dancing attendance in distant hopes for the future. I cannot give up this situation, nor do I want to. So the question is this: will trying to be an academician do me any harm or not?[39]

Reassured by Vitet, Lenormant and Saulcy, he resolved to stake his claim, and began his round of compulsory visits as soon as he got back to Paris in September. His adversary was a historian called Charles-Henri Ternaux-Compans, whom he suspected darkly of currying favour by inviting people to expensive meals: 'I am very much afraid of the truffle man. People can rarely resist a good dinner. On the other hand it's in my favour if they happen to get indigestion.'[40] Having to call on all the academicians to solicit their votes was an acute embarrassment to him.

> At present I am doing the most vile and boring of jobs: I am canvassing for the Academy of Inscriptions. I keep running into the most ridiculous

---

[38] *C.G.*, Vol. III, p. 263.   [39] *Ibid.*, p. 400.   [40] *Ibid.*, p. 408.

scenes, and I am often gripped by a desire to laugh at myself, which I re-press so as not to shock the gravity of the academicians on whom I am calling.[41]

Though he did his best to make a joke of it, Mérimée was desperately anxious to be elected. A failure would have humiliated him beyond measure, which was why he had delayed so long before becoming a candidate. Now that he had publicly declared his desire for member-ship, his tender self-esteem would have been unbearably injured by an equally public rejection. So he spent his time nervously calculating the odds, debating tactics with his friends, and even resorting with an uneasy jocularity, to the antique practice of the *sortes virgilianae* – open-ing the pages of Virgil haphazardly and trying to read an oracular meaning into the passage on which he chanced.[42] The weeks of waiting were agonising, despite the assurances of his supporters that he was bound to succeed, and there was a last-minute alarm when a newspaper announced that he had written a five-act comedy, a false rumour that he viewed as an underhand trick by his opponent:

As I said in my letter to the Academy that I was only interested in works of erudition, the newspaper article is a very clever invention. I don't know if it's within the rules of the game, but I'm afraid it will do its work.[43]

But Mérimée's spade work with the academicians had been very thorough, and on 17 November 1843, he was triumphantly returned with 25 votes to Ternaux-Compan's 11, with one to a third candidate, and one blank paper. With immense relief, Mérimée ordered a cele-bration dinner at Véry's for a few close friends such as Vitet, Saulcy and Lenormant. Just over a week later, he was solemnly admitted to the Academy.

The permanent secretary, having put on gloves which I believe are only worn on such occasions, led me by the hand like a dancing-partner into the midst of the august assembly, which rose to its feet like one man. I bowed forty times, once for each member, I sat down, and it was all over.[44]

---

[41] *Ibid.*, pp. 421–2.

[42] *Ibid.*, p. 411. The pun on the name of Ternaux which resulted is un-translatable. The line which Mérimée hit on was: 'Dissultant ripae, refluitque exterritus amnis', which he proposed to render in French as: 'La porte s'ouvre, et Terne eau est refoulée'.   [43] *Ibid.*, p. 453.

[44] *Ibid.*, p. 463. But forty bows? Unless he did one for himself, there should only have been thirty-nine.

However, the respite and the relief were only temporary. Mérimée had tried to persuade himself and his friends that if he was successful at the Academy of Inscriptions, he would no longer care about the French Academy. In fact, when several academicians died almost simultaneously at the beginning of 1844, his ambitions immediately sprang to life again. The chair of the Romantic story-teller Charles Nodier seemed made for Mérimée. But here again there were complications caused by Mérimée's loyalty to his friends, since he did not want to stand until Sainte-Beuve was elected.[45] After much conferring, the two men eventually pooled their resources and, with a wealth of cunning, patience and subtlety, conducted a common campaign, Sainte-Beuve for Casimir Delavigne's seat, Mérimée for Nodier's. Once more, the tedious round of obligatory visits began, with Mérimée still secretly amused and irritated by the whole process.

> In the meantime, I am very conscientiously making my visits. I find people who are very polite, very much used to the parts they play and taking them most seriously; I do my best to take mine as earnestly, but I find it difficult. Don't you think it funny to say to someone: 'Sir, I believe myself to be one of the forty cleverest men in France, I'm just as good as you are', and similar witticisms. That has to be translated into decent and varied terms according to one's interlocutor.[46]

On 14 March 1844, Mérimée waited in Sainte-Beuve's flat as the votes were counted. Sainte-Beuve's fate was settled first, as he won an absolute majority on the second round of voting. Mérimée had to possess his soul in patience somewhat longer. There were seven candidates for the seat, including a minor dramatist called Casimir Bonjour, and Alfred de Vigny, who had just lost to Sainte-Beuve. From the outset, Mérimée was in the lead, and his vote rose with each successive round. After four votes, there were only three candidates left, with Mérimée slightly ahead of Bonjour and Vigny limping along behind. It took another three votes before Mérimée secured the absolute majority necessary for his election.

While the result was highly flattering to Mérimée, he had been uncomfortably aware throughout his two campaigns that it was most

[45] Cf. Jean Bonnerot, 'Les Dessous d'une élection à l'Académie française en 1844, Sainte-Beuve et Mérimée', *Revue universelle*, 1er juillet 1935.
[46] *C.G.*, Vol. IV, p. 39.

paradoxical for a man like himself, who prided himself on frank speaking and disdain for shams, to lend himself to so much hypocritical pretence. After all, nothing could be more false than paying scores of fulsomely complimentary visits in order to achieve an honour of the purely external kind which he professed to despise. It was as a natural corrective to this blatant infringement of his principles that in the early 1840s he took to being even blunter than usual and fulminating even more indignantly about the deceitfulness of modern society. He was particularly insistent with Jenny Dacquin that he had lost none of his usual honesty – she had touched him on a raw spot by accusing him of seeking election to the Academy out of vainglory.[47] 'As for me, I think I am neither better nor worse than I used to be; I am no more of a hypocrite, which is perhaps wrong of me. Certainly people don't like me any better for it,'[48] he told her firmly in 1842. To another lady he declared in 1845: 'my friends have very often told me that I didn't take enough trouble to show any goodness there may be in my nature, but I have always cared only about the opinion of a few people.'[49]

Not surprisingly, this affectation of aggressive sincerity won him many enemies, especially among those who, meeting him for the first time, were offended by his air of chilly indifference and his acid comments. Perhaps because of his assiduous cultivation of an 'English' manner, Mérimée was liable to have a particularly unfortunate effect on English travellers. Thomas Adolphus Trollope, historian and novelist, and elder brother of Anthony, met him in Mary Clarke's *salon* about 1840 and contrasted him unfavourably with the affable Fauriel:

> I find Fauriel [. . .] delightful, and am disgusted with Mérimée because he manifested self-sufficiency, as it seemed to my youthful criticism, by pooh-poohing the probability of the temple at Lanleff in Brittany having been aught else than a church of the Templars.[50]

The American literary critic and traveller George Ticknor also encountered Mérimée in the Clarke *salon* and was even less impressed: 'Mérimée [. . .] disappointed me. He is affected, and makes pretentions

[47] *C.G.*, Vol. III, p. 255.
[48] *Ibid.*, p. 159.
[49] *C.G.*, Vol. IV, p. 239.
[50] Thomas Adolphus Trollope, *What I remember*, London, Bentley, 1887, Vol. II, p. 58.

to exclusiveness. He ought to be above such follies.'[51] Like Molière's Alceste, Mérimée thus found himself charged with affectation for exaggerating his directness.

His most violent criticisms were directed against the Catholic revival which was a notable feature of society in the early 1840s. All his old anticlericalism was aroused. At Easter 1843, he waxed particularly sarcastic:

It was all very edifying here. Two hundred finely attired women went to Notre-Dame to shed tears over their sins before going for a drive at Long-champ. Fifteen hundred young men, with yellow beards, moustaches and gloves devoutly took communion at the hands of Reverend Father Ravignan, who is a roaring success. After which, the day before yesterday, Prince Belgiojoso eloped with the Duchess of Plaisance.[52]

To another militant anti-Catholic author, Jules Michelet, he expressed confidence that the fashion would soon pass: 'The moment it stops being *smart* to go to church, once the young ladies give up appearing there, religious enthusiasm will disappear.'[53] In the meantime, he was visibly irritated by what he condemned as hypocrisy, and began casting around for a way of making his displeasure public.

This was the mood in which he wrote *Arsène Guillot* early in 1843. In it he provocatively contrasts the pious duplicity of a society lady with the simple sincerity of a humble *grisette*. Mérimée's first intention was only to show it to his friends, and he gave the manuscript to Valentine as a present. But she talked about it to the Comtesse de Boigne, who persuaded him to give a reading of it to herself and some other female censors, and when they declared it unexceptionable, he decided to publish it. This was at the beginning of 1844, and Mérimée so calculated things that it appeared in the *Revue des Deux Mondes* the day after the elections to the French Academy so that if he was elected, it would show the world that he was keeping all his freedom of speech in his new dignity, and if he failed, he would be thumbing his nose at those high-minded people who had turned him down.

Arsène Guillot created a considerable scandal. There were those in the Academy who viewed Mérimée with grave disapproval for his

[51] *The Life, Letters and Journals of George Ticknor*, London, Low, Marston, Searle & Rivington, 1876, Vol. II, p. 125.

[52] *C.G.*, Vol. III, p. 362.   [53] *C.G.*, Vol. XVI, p. 196.

notorious anticlericalism and his almost equally notorious immorality –
the historian Villemain said disdainfully of his election: 'we needed a
man of letters and we've been given a stallion'[54] – and *Arsène Guillot*
confirmed all their worst fears about him. Two other academicians,
Count de Sainte-Aulaire and Prosper de Barante, sadly compared notes
on the terrible new arrival: 'I am very sorry about this latest tale by
our colleague Mérimée. There is a little talent in it, put to bad use.
Between ourselves I cannot remember having read a more thoroughly
bad frivolous production.'[55] Mérimée himself professed to be taken
aback by the storm which blew up over a story which had, as he said,
the imprimatur of 'a learned areopagus of old women'.[56] Though there
was some truth in his protestations of the innocence of his story, he
cannot have been entirely surprised that it stirred up trouble. What may
have disconcerted him was the violence of some of the attacks.

> People have become such bigots in Paris that unless you make yourself
> an illuminist, a Jesuit and a B.F., you are bound to be regarded as an atheist
> and a scoundrel. I continue to maintain that there's nothing in my story
> worth making a fuss about, yet the good souls are making a terrible to-do,
> opening their eyes and mouths like barn-doors.[57]

Resentful at so much criticism, Mérimée swore to get his own back
and to do something to stem the rising tide of religious fanaticism:

> all this fury of bigotry made me angry at first; now it amuses me. I've
> nothing more to fear and I snap my fingers at them. Indeed, some day I'll
> take my revenge, I hope, and I'll tell them what I think of them. You
> cannot possibly imagine what neo-Catholicism is like these days. We are
> heading fast for all manner of extravagance, and if things go on like that,
> we'll soon be right in the Middle Ages.[58]

In the event, though the quarrel served to lend new vigour to his anticlericalism, Mérimée, secure in his new dignity, could afford to laugh
at his critics. Only one painful task remained: that of pronouncing

[54] Auguste Barbier, *Souvenirs personnels et silhouettes contemporaines*, Paris,
Dentu, 1883, p. 293.

[55] *C.G.*, Vol. IV, p. 60, n. 1. Mérimée claimed to have been told that one
indignant lady, shortly after his election to the Academy, having heard that
in a police raid on a house of assignation several men had been arrested for
seducing girls under age, had asked eagerly: 'Did they get Monsieur Mérimée?' (F. Bac, *Mérimée inconnu*, p. 175).

[56] *C.G.*, Vol. IV, p. 75.   [57] *Ibid.*, p. 62.   [58] *Ibid.*, p. 67.

the ceremonial encomium of his predecessor Nodier. At the best of times, Mérimée detested public speaking, which made him excessively nervous and awkward; this was far worse, not only because it was such a gala occasion, but even more because he cordially detested Nodier's works.[59] A visit to Nodier's home town Besançon, where he interviewed those who had known the novelist in his youth, did little to alter his opinion:

> I have confirmed the truth of the adage that no man is a prophet in his own country. People said the most awful things about the great man, and I have come back with a fund of stories which would do excellently for a satire. Unfortunately it's a eulogy that I have to give.[60]

He was thoroughly bored with his enforced reading of Nodier's works, whose prolix sentimentality was altogether foreign to him: 'he was a very degenerate fellow who put on an air of simplicity and was always snivelling. In my exordium I am obliged to say that he was a dreadful liar.'[61]

It was in these inauspicious circumstances that on 6 February 1845, Mérimée was formally received into the Academy. Étienne, who was due to make the speech admitting him, had jaundice, and another academician had to read his text. Mérimée, in an acute state of nerves, then delivered his reply before a large audience, including Jenny Dacquin. It is anything but an inspired piece of work, full of embarrassed equivocation about Nodier's merits, and platitudinous when it tries to rise to general ideas, which were never Mérimée's *forte*. But Mérimée himself was not displeased with his performance:

> everything went off very well yesterday. I was scared stiff, and I've been told that I looked exactly like someone being led off to the scaffold to be hung. My face was the same colour as the green embroidery on my tail-coat. But the only thing I was concerned about was not to lose my voice. I read my speech quite well, in a firm and decisive tone. People seemed pleased.[62]

In reality, the press and public were unimpressed: Mérimée was so petrified that he read his text monotonously and quietly, in total im-

---

[59] As far back as 1830 he had disliked Nodier and said to Sophie Duvaucel: 'the Histoire du Roi de Bohème is certainly the stupidest thing in the world' (*C.G.*, Vol. I, p. 61).

[60] *C.G.*, Vol. IV, p. 102.   [61] *Ibid.*, p. 202.   [62] *Ibid.*, p. 239.

mobility, with soporific effect.[63] But at least the ordeal was over: he was a fully fledged member, he had not failed in his duty, and he could look forward to enjoying the prestige and privileges of one of the most august bodies of the nation.

[63] According to the *Iournal des Débats*, quoted in *C.G.*, Vol. IV, p. 240, n. 2.

Chapter 12

National Guard

Les révolutions, comme les maladies, s'annoncent par un
malaise vague dont on ne comprend rarement l'importance
que lorsqu'on en a vu les suites.
                Épisode de l'histoire de Russie. Les Faux Démétrius

In the early 1840s, Mérimée had been increasingly occupied with the
writing of history. The *Essai sur la Guerre Sociale* was finished by the
spring of 1840, then extended and revised on the advice of Lenormant,
to whom Mérimée had submitted the manuscript. After its publication
in the limited edition of 1841, he immediately set to work on *La
Conjuration de Catilina*, which he completed by February 1843. But he
was in no hurry to see it in print, and allowed it to rest for several
months, before appending it to the *Essai* and having both books published under a single cover as *Études sur l'histoire romaine* in March 1844,
this time in an edition available to the general public. One might have
expected him then to go on with the major part of the life of Julius
Caesar to which these works had been leading up. But his interest had
been distracted by another project which Mme de Montijo had been
urging on him for some time. This was a biography of Don Pedro the
Cruel, the fourteenth-century Castilian monarch and one of the key
figures in Spanish medieval history.

When the idea was first adumbrated is unknown – perhaps on
Mérimée's visit to Spain in 1840 – but as he neared the end of his
writing on Roman history in November 1843, he reminded Mme de
Montijo that she had promised him a manuscript on Don Pedro,
adding: 'I am still thinking very seriously about it.'[1] A month later,
his enthusiasm had grown: 'the more I study my subject, the more I
am delighted by it. I feel it is one of the great turning-points in the
constitution of nations, similar to those one sees in the lives of individuals.'[2] From then on he immersed himself in reading for his book,

[1] *C.G.*, Vol. III, p. 450.   [2] *Ibid.*, p. 472.

which was sketched out by the end of 1844. During 1845 and the first half of 1846, he was busy writing a first complete version, with a visit to Madrid in November and December 1845 to investigate sources there. On 7 July 1846, he wrote to Mme de Montijo in terms which do honour to his conscientiousness as a historian: 'I've finished my history of Don Pedro, but it has to be done all over again from the beginning [. . .] if I work long enough at my subject, I don't despair of making something tolerable out of it.'[3] A further visit to Spain in the winter of 1846 was much more fruitful than the first one, since he was given free access to the crown archives of Aragon, thanks to the good offices of the archivist Don Prospero de Bofarull, in whom he found a congenial companion and an able collaborator.[4] The new material was incorporated in the second version, the writing of which took until the summer of 1847. On 3 July, he proudly told Mme de Montijo: 'you should know that the day before yesterday I finished the last line of Don Pedro and that I wrote the word FINIS with inexpressible pleasure'.[5] The book, dedicated to Mme de Montijo, was serialised in the Revue des Deux Mondes in late 1847 and early 1848; publication as a separate volume was delayed by the Revolution until September 1848.

These lengthy and elaborate historical researches left Mérimée little time or inclination for fiction. Carmen, which he wrote in 1845 as relaxation from his work on Don Pedro, is related to the same Spanish interests, and Don Pedro is mentioned in it.[6] In February 1846, he gave L'Abbé Aubain to Le Constitutionnel for anonymous publication, and on 27 April 1846 finished an illustrated manuscript of Il Viccolo di Madama Lucrezia, which he presented to Mme Odier, Valentine Delessert's sister. But for him, none of this was anything more than a passing amusement. He had moved on to more serious forms of writing, and the promise he had made in 1843 to the Academy of Inscriptions to devote himself exclusively to erudition was henceforth to be

[3] C.G., Vol. IV, p. 470.

[4] See J. E. Martinez Ferrando, Prospero de Bofarull y Prospero Mérimée, una amistad ejemplar, Reus, Asociacion de estudios reusenses, 1954.

[5] C.G., Vol. V, p. 114. For a complete account of the composition of the Histoire de Don Pèdre, see Gabriel Laplane's introduction to his critical edition of it (Paris, Didier, 1961).

[6] Romans et nouvelles, Vol. II, p. 377.

scrupulously observed. In addition to his major historical studies, he was publishing extensively on art and archaeology, averaging some half-dozen articles and reviews a year, apart from the numerous reports he made to the Commission for Historic Monuments. The most important of these publications was his elaborately illustrated *Notice sur les peintures de l'Église de Saint-Savin*, which appeared at the end of 1845 and crowned his arduous achievement in carrying through the restoration of the wall-paintings.

Amid all the writing, the academic campaigns and the personal activities of the 1840s, Mérimée was still occupying the onerous post of Inspector-General, with its committee work, travelling, correspondence and administration. Though he had given up publishing regular notes on his journeys, he still had to undertake an annual tour of inspection: in 1844 he spent six weeks in the South-West, in 1845 he ranged through the Dordogne, Languedoc and Provence in August and September, in 1846 he went through Laon and Lyon to Provence again, in 1847 it was the turn of Picardy and Normandy. There were shorter trips, too: in May 1844, he was sent to Strasbourg to negotiate about preserving the church of St Étienne; in April 1845 he went with a committee to look at a church in Rouen, in October he had to inspect a Roman aqueduct near Metz; in the autumn of 1846, he returned to Metz, but instead of coming straight back to Paris, went on down the Rhine and the Moselle, and visited Brussels; in May 1847 he accompanied Lenormant to Angers and the day after his return was off again to see how the restoration of Vézelay was faring. A much more ambitious project, a visit to Algeria, had been planned for the same year in conjunction with Léon de Laborde, Valentine's brother, who was now Curator of Antiquities at the Louvre, but at the very last minute they had to cancel their voyage because the Ministry of the Army, which controlled Algeria, refused to sanction it.

One wonders how Mérimée found time to do so much. He was of course efficient, methodical, well organised; his business letters are models of economical lucidity, and he obviously wasted no time in his private life either. Moreover, he needed little sleep, and most of his writing, whether for publication or private correspondence, was done in the small hours of the morning. His mother looked after his home comforts for him, and there was no shortage of money to spend on servants and other conveniences. Léonor Mérimée had enjoyed a very reasonable income; now his son not only had a highly paid job, with substantial expenses for the long periods he had to spend away from Paris, but was also able to earn good money for his books and articles.[7] So he was completely free of material worries and able to devote all his considerable energy to things that interested him. Mme Mérimée, still lively and intelligent despite her seventy years, suffered somewhat from rheumatism (from which she was temporarily cured by the joy of her son's election to the Academy), but was very much in charge of the household. It was probably on her initiative as much as on Prosper's that in March 1847 they moved from the rue des Beaux-Arts to the nearby rue Jacob, where they had the precious privilege of the view of a few trees.

Mérimée added a few new hobbies about this time. For some years he had been collecting ancient stones and cameos, to some of which he attached superstitious veneration. As long ago as 1832, Édouard Grasset had made fun of the state he got into when he thought he had lost a talisman,[8] and in 1842, he was equally distressed when he lost an Etruscan stone representing Juno with a sickle.[9] But by then, his collection was large enough to excite Jenny Dacquin's admiration. Fine bindings were another concern. Now that he had wealth enough to indulge his tastes, he had his books elaborately bound by the most fashionable experts, and joined the Society of French Bibliophiles, of which Valentine was also a member. His part in their activities was not great, save that as a distinguished gastronome he was often consulted on the menu for their annual dinner. Billiards too amused him, and it was while he was playing billiards at Mme d'Arbouville's country house in 1846 that he said that he did not believe in providence because it would be too convenient if it did exist.[10] Drug-taking, on the other

[7] When Mérimée was living in the rue des Beaux-Arts, another flat in the same building was occupied by François Buloz, director of the *Revue des Deux Mondes*, so that the two men got to know each other well. Buloz was always eager to publish anything Mérimée wrote, and the *Revue* was a distinguished organ that paid its contributors handsomely. The various editions and re-editions of Mérimée's stories also brought him in a steady and substantial income.

[8] Grasset embodied it in a story he published in 1832. Cf. M. Parturier's introduction to Mérimée's *Lettres aux Grasset*.

[9] *C.G.*, Vol. III, p. 208.

[10] Cf. Sainte-Beuve, *Correspondance générale*, Vol. VI (1949), p. 523.

hand, merely disappointed him, and experiments with hashish did nothing to pull him out of a mood of black depression:

> I am dreadfully sad when I set out on my tours, and this time more than ever. Yet the weather is wonderful, and I have consumed hashish to make myself cheerful, but quite in vain. I had been told that I would see paradise and the Old Man of the Mountain's houris; but I saw nothing at all.[11]

Mérimée's sadness on this occasion was caused by something which was to distress him more and more: Valentine's fickleness. Since about 1844, she had been drawing ever closer to Charles de Rémusat, who was a contemporary of Mérimée's, a distinguished author and a brilliant social light. To placate Valentine, Mérimée did his best to get Rémusat into the Academy, and in January 1846 succeeded. But gratitude to the old love did not outweigh the charms of the new, and Valentine seems soon after to have become Rémusat's mistress. Rémusat commented on a photograph of Valentine in these revealing terms:

> I do not know how it comes about that features apparently lacking in grandeur and regularity can produce such a profound impression, a kind of grave delight which takes command of all one's soul and has nothing in common with the charm of a pretty face. I believe it is due to the height of the forehead, to the line of the nose, and above all to the penetrating sadness of the gaze in moments of seriousness. Her eyes seem to feel and understand everything, and emotion gives her features an expression which rises superior to their shape and her usual physiognomy which is no more than kind and intelligent. Her all-pervading gracefulness might hide many defects; in her case, it misleads one about her qualities. Those who do not know her (and to know a woman one must love her) can see no further than the incomparable gracefulness of her person. People simply find her charming. That is to misunderstand her.[12]

By Easter 1846 Mérimée had become aware that his rival was being preferred to him, and his letters to Mme de Montijo are full of pain and gloom. 'I am tormented by all the *blue devils*. If we were in Madrid, I would tell you about a lot of things that are happening to me, and you would give me some good advice',[13] he wrote on 4 April. A week later, the complaint was the same: 'for the last few days, I have been

[11] C.G., Vol. IV, p. 478.
[12] For this quotation and other details, see M. Parturier, 'Mérimée et Rémusat', *Revue de Paris*, 1er janvier 1939.
[13] C.G., Vol. IV, p. 441.

feeling a little better. Better physically, worse than ever morally. It's said that work is a great diversion, and I'm diverting myself a great deal, but nothing I do is any good.'[14] Unable to talk to Jenny Dacquin about Mme Delessert, he tried to persuade her that she was responsible for his being so downcast: 'every year I find the provinces more stupid and more unbearable. This time, I'm suffering from spleen and everything looks black to me, perhaps because you have forgotten me so shamefully.'[15] But whatever his suffering, Mérimée was too dependent on Valentine to break with her, and had to swallow his pride and accept the situation.

Pathetically, he tried to win his way back into her favour by ingratiating himself with her children. He took a keenly protective interest in her daughter Cécile, who as a rich and beautiful heiress was attracting the attentions of numerous suitors, and when in 1847 she married Count Alexis de Valon, he became a firm friend of the young man. As for Édouard Delessert, Cécile's younger brother, an intelligent but spoilt and debauched youth, Mérimée took him completely under his wing, advised him on his writing, encouraged him in his taste for pleasure, and introduced him to eminent acquaintances. Though this kept him in close touch with the Delesserts, it made little impression on Valentine's heart, and the relative happiness which Mérimée had known for ten years gradually drained out of his life.

There were of course other friends and other affections. Mérimée's worries about Valentine drew him closer than ever to Mme de Montijo, the only person in whom he confided about his private affairs. This intimacy was increased by their collaboration on the life of Don Pedro and by Mérimée's two visits to Spain in 1845 and 1846. Mérimée continued to follow the lives of her two daughters with sympathetic interest. Paca, the elder and her mother's favourite, had in 1844 made a brilliant marriage with the Duke of Alba; Eugenia, less fortunate, had had more than one unhappy love affair, and Mérimée was solicitously anxious to find a suitable match for her. Then there were the Lagrenés, whom he had met in Greece in 1841 and who, after a brief sojourn in China, had returned to Paris in 1846. From about 1844, he also became friendly with another couple where the wife was Russian: Comte Adolphe de Circourt, an ex-diplomat and traveller who had

[14] *Ibid.*, p. 443.   [15] *Ibid.*, p. 485.

married a Russian noblewoman named Anastasia de Klustine. These
Russian connections were shortly to have a profound effect in giving
a new orientation to his intellectual curiosity. The aged Chancellor
Pasquier and his friend Mme de Boigne had been known to Mérimée
for some years, but he took increasing pleasure in the company of the
old man, whose vast experience, impressive mind and sharp wit
delighted him[16] – Mérimée was beginning to show a noticeable preference for the society of the elderly, as the young reminded him
uncomfortably that he had passed irrevocably into middle age.

Among old friends, he still regularly saw Lenormant and Ampère,
whose circumstances changed in 1847. For years, Ampère had been
living with another bachelor intellectual, the German scholar Julius
Mohl, who had made his home in France and who became Professor
of Persian at the Collège de France in 1847. Everyone was astonished
when, the same year, Mohl suddenly announced that he was going
to marry Mary Clarke, whose long affair with Fauriel had been brought
to an end by the latter's death in 1844. The news was so unexpected
that when Mohl sent to ask Mérimée to give him his help the next
day at the wedding, Mérimée thought he must have been challenged
to a duel, and turned up saying anxiously; 'for heaven's sake, my dear
friend, who are you fighting?'[17] At the wedding itself, Mary Clarke
asserted her independence by replying to the mayor's regulation
question about her age: 'Sir, that is no business of yours, and if it were
your business, I'd jump out of the window sooner than tell you!'[18]
The departure of Mohl and the deaths of Chateaubriand in 1848 and
Mme Récamier in 1849 left Ampère a lonely and bereft man.

And there was still Jenny Dacquin. In later years, when asked why
they never married, Mary Clarke, who knew her Mérimée, said: 'he
had no desire for it; he was well off as a bachelor, but not rich enough
to have a family. Besides, he was probably attached to his freedom.'[19]
In reality, the prime obstacle was Valentine, and not even her faithless-

[16] Cf. M. Parturier, 'Mme de Boigne et Mérimée', Le Figaro, 6 mai 1933.
Pasquier too savoured Mérimée's irreverence and his incisive style, and had
his tales read to him over and over again. L'Abbé Aubain always brought to
his lips 'a mocking smile which only departed at the last phrase of this
delightful story' (C.G., Vol. III, p. 103, n. 1).

[17] K. O'Meara, Un Salon à Paris, Madame Mohl et ses intimes, Paris, Plon,
1886, p. 174.   [18] Ibid.   [19] Ibid., pp. 278–9.

ness would make Mérimée envisage a permanent tie with someone else. So his bitter-sweet relationship with Jenny went on from quarrel to reconciliation and back again, with neither partner able to accept the demands of the other, yet neither willing to break off relations altogether. Mérimée well knew what sort of gesture would help to ensure Jenny's continued devotion, and, at a solemn meeting of the French Academy in March 1846, while Comte Molé was welcoming the newly elected Ludovic Vitet, surreptitiously blew her a kiss[20] – only to complain afterwards that it was just like her to ignore it.[21]

During all these years, Mérimée had continued to follow political events in both France and Spain with intense curiosity but a large measure of detachment. His erstwhile liberalism had long since vanished, and he watched the frequent changes of government under Thiers, Molé and Guizot with an impartial if slightly apprehensive amusement. As a civil servant, he owed allegiance to the Orleanist régime which, in a small way, he had helped to bring into being, but his support had become very lukewarm. The sight of the constant civil disorders in Spain during the catastrophic reign of Isabella II had made him mistrustful of the effectiveness of any government which did not exert a measure of autocracy, and he had several times told Mme de Montijo that he thought the only hope for her country lay in a dictatorship, as when he affirmed in 1841: 'if you could have a Napoleonic government for eight or ten years, I think it would do you some good'.[22] He was keenly alive to the danger of a left-wing revolution, and in 1847 referred darkly to the intentions of the communists:

> now these gentlemen have got around to professing publicly that arson and theft are perfectly legitimate ways of correcting inequality in the distribution of property. This theory is unlikely to make many converts among those who own something, but in a great city like Paris, there are so many people who get up every morning without knowing what they will eat for lunch that ideas about sharing are sure to collect a few thousand fervent proselytes.[23]

What sympathy he had ever felt for the oppressed classes had evaporated, and however much he mocked Louis-Philippe, he preferred him to chaos. Even so, he found himself sickened by the growing odour of

[20] M. Parturier, 'Le Baiser à "L'Inconnue"', *Bulletin du bibliophile*, 20 octobre 1932.   [21] *C.G.*, Vol. IV, p. 433.
[22] *C.G.*, Vol. III, p. 29.   [23] *C.G.*, Vol. V, p. 131–2.

corruption given off by the régime, and he returned from his 1846 tour, which had coincided with a general election campaign, full of revulsion against the idea of representative government.

> How glad I am that I never had any taste for politics! As I travelled round, I was an unwilling witness to a certain amount of electoral filth, and I am still revolted by it. You need to be quite crazy and have a really low soul to go in for being a candidate as a deputy. If one has to have a master, I'd sooner have one than several.[24]

In the early weeks of 1848, Mérimée sensed that some upheaval was in the air, but could not quite convince himself that his fears were on the point of being realised. On 22 January, he wrote to Mme de Montijo:

> at the present time there is in Paris and, I believe, throughout France, a kind of instinctive terror of a revolution. Everyone is talking of it with horror, without being able to guess from what direction the storm will blow. Nobody has any doubt about it, yet one would bet against all foreseen or foreseeable odds.[25]

When on 22 February, the revolution did break out, Mérimée was as much stunned as everyone else. His immediate reaction was to try to save the works of art which he thought the revolutionaries would seek to destroy, and with Léon de Laborde did what he could to prevent the Tuileries from being looted. To his astonishment, the mob turned out to be well disciplined and innocuous, and workmen handed in at the Louvre priceless cameos which had been taken from the palace.[26] He expressed his surprise to Jenny Dacquin – in English, for fear of censorship:

> I begin to get accustomed to the strangeness of the thing and to be reconciled with the strange figures of the conquerors, who what's stranger still, behave themselves as gentlemen. There is now a strong tendency to order. If it continues, I shall turn a staunch republican.[27]

On 25 February, in the rue de Richelieu, he witnessed a strange spectacle which later convinced him that revolutions were caused by children, incompetence and indecision, rather than by skilful planning:

[24] C.G., Vol. IV, p. 513.   [25] C.G., Vol. V, p. 235.
[26] Ibid., p. 245.   [27] Ibid., p. 246.

a battalion was marching down the street. Three boys stood across it; they cried out that the troops should not pass without killing them. The men hesitated, the officers were afraid of responsibility, and, in fact the battalion halted for a quarter of an hour, and then retired.[28]

On 26 February, the Provisional Government placed Mérimée and Laborde in charge of the *objets d'art* in the Tuileries. But Mérimée was concerned about his post as Inspector-General. 'In the midst of such a vast catastrophe, one hardly thinks of one's private affairs. However, I am getting worried about what my poor mother and I will have to live on.'[29] To the architect Joly-Leterme he protested, with some justification, that he could not be accused of having abused his powers for political reasons:

> I don't have to reproach myself with having had unworthy churches restored under pressure from fat capitalists, and I've never even known the name of the deputy for St Savin. If I have to give up my job, I shall be sorry as anyone would be to have the bread taken out of his mouth, and I shall try to earn my living as best I can.[30]

Mme de Montijo even offered him asylum in Spain, but he decided that, as no one had interfered with him so far, it was worth staying on and doing what he could to save his monuments. His attitude was scarcely disinterested or courageous, but it was a perfectly reasonable one for a civil servant to take. He had after all been an Orleanist and owed his position to Thiers, and had some reason for thinking that he might be sacked out of vindictiveness. So long as that did not happen, however, it was certainly his duty to carry out his functions as Inspector-General; resignation would have been a pointless folly, since his allegiance was to the government of the day and not to the fallen Louis-Philippe.

The same was, however, not true of Gabriel Delessert, who as Louis-Philippe's chief of police – albeit a very inoffensive one – was clearly in jeopardy. A series of tragi-comic scenes ensued as his friends tried to ensure his escape to England. After Louis-Philippe's abdication, he took refuge in Mérimée's flat in the rue Jacob, and with the utmost

[28] Nassau William Senior, *Conversations with Distinguished Persons during the Second Empire from 1860 to 1863*, ed. M.C.M. Simpson, London, Hurst & Blackett, 1882, p. 245. The conversation is dated 14 April 1861.
[29] *C.G.*, Vol. V, p. 246.   [30] *Ibid.*, p. 250.

tranquillity was sleeping soundly within a few minutes of going to bed. Mérimée deemed it necessary to lie down outside his room to guard against possible intruders, and was kept awake all night by 'feverish terrors and continual worries'. The next morning, Alexis de Valon arrived to find his father-in-law calmly shaving at his usual hour, and had the greatest difficulty in persuading him to wear a cloak to hide his unmistakable figure. Valentine Delessert was next brought to the rendezvous by Mérimée; she too was unmoved, even though a rioter had aimed his rifle at her as they crossed the Place de la Concorde. Charles de Rémusat also arrived to see the Delesserts off into what might well have been permanent exile. Gabriel and Valentine remained stoical to the last; her two lovers on the other hand were unable to control their emotion. Rémusat's face was 'twisted with grief'; as for the usually impassive Mérimée, according to Alexis de Valon, *'he was sobbing like a child'*. One can imagine what torture this extraordinary farewell must have been for the sensitive Mérimée: he was losing Valentine, perhaps for ever, and he was not even sure whether he was the one she most regretted leaving.[31]

In the meantime, it gradually became apparent to him that the republican government had no intention of dismissing him, even if it did, to his dismay, remove his friend and superior Vitet from the Commission for Historic Monuments. As things momentarily settled down, Mérimée was able to take stock of the situation. The revolution, in his view, 'was brought about by less than six hundred men, most of whom knew neither what they were doing nor what they wanted'.[32] Louis-Philippe and his sons had been spineless beyond belief:

> the king and the princes were worse than their cousins of the elder branch in all that. They have brought about their own downfall and that of royalty in France. What the devil is the use of history if no one profits from it?[33]

Now the only hope lay in establishing the republic on a firm basis: 'here we are, in a republic, without any enthusiasm but determined to hang on to it, for it is our only remaining hope of salvation'.[34] But Mérimée had too poor an opinion of the French character to think

[31] For all this account of the Delesserts' flight, see Alexis de Valon, *Nos Aventures pendant les journées de février*, ed. A. de Laborde, Paris, Leclerc, 1910.

[32] *C.G.*, Vol. V, p. 258.

[33] *Ibid.*, p. 254.   [34] *Ibid.*, p. 252.

7a Adolphe Thiers, from a lithograph by
J. Lane, 1840

7b Eugène Viollet-de-Duc, from an
engraving of 1860

7c Ivan Turgenev

8a Victor Cousin, from an engraving by Maurin

8b Achille Fould, from an engraving after a
photograph of c. 1850

8c Antony Panizzi, from the portrait by G. F. Watts

it would work for long: 'before changing institutions, you have to change people's habits, and our habits are not republican.'[35] So he foresaw only the two alternatives of chaos and dictatorial repression:

> whatever happens, liberty is lost in this country. It will not stand up to anarchy, or to the fury for order which some day will perhaps follow.[36]

He even found himself deserting his normal anticlerical prejudices to regret that religion was no longer strong enough to hold popular passions in check:

> the only really deplorable thing is the weakening of religious feeling [. . .] It is certain that religion is the strongest and most effective form of police that exists. But how can one apply this form, how can one revive it today, now that the lower classes have caught the contagion of philosophy from us?[37]

Clearly, Mérimée's reactions in 1848 were archetypally bourgeois. If only there were a Napoleon, he sighed, all might yet be saved: 'but where is such a man?'[38]

Conscious of the need to preserve law and order, Mérimée once again took up service with the National Guard. There were frequent alarms and excursions in those uneasy months, and when on 18 May, Mérimée had the task of receiving Ampère into the Academy, he was horrified to hear the sound of drums during Ampère's speech. But it turned out to be only a passing regiment.[39] A few days earlier, there had been a more serious alert when the mob had burst into the Chamber of Deputies. Mérimée's battalion of the National Guard was the first to reach the spot, by which time the rioters were already making off, but he was grimly amused by the reaction of the parliamentarians: 'everyone had lost their head, I think, and the faces of the deputies were so decomposed by fear or indignation, to use noble and official terms, that people one meets every day were barely recognisable'.[40] When fighting did start again with the popular uprising of the *journées de juin* and the ensuing repression, Mérimée spent four days and nights on the streets in uniform. He never forgot the ghastly sights he saw then. Among the prisoners whom he had to escort were a woman who had just cut off a wounded officer's head with a kitchen knife and a

[35] *Ibid.*, p. 276. [36] *Ibid.*, p. 273. [37] *Ibid.*, pp. 359–60.
[38] *Ibid.*, p. 264. [39] *Ibid.*, p. 314. [40] *Ibid.*, p. 318.

H

man whose arms were covered with the blood of a soldier whose belly he had slit open.[41] The ferocity on the other side was almost as great, and a number of prisoners had been massacred. The horrors of civil war made Mérimée despair of the future: 'amid the pain I feel, I am above all conscious of the stupidity of this nation. It is unequalled. I don't know if it will ever be possible to divert it from the barbarism in which it is so inclined to wallow.'[42]

Mérimée was a patriotic man and deeply distressed by the sight of France torn by strife and suffering; his personal worries tortured him even more. He was still afraid of dismissal, and pulled all the strings he could to ensure that he kept his post. But what grieved him above all was the separation from Valentine. She wrote little to him from her exile in England, and though she made one or two brief trips to Paris, appeared less concerned with him than with Rémusat. When in June the Delesserts judged it safe to return permanently, it was again Rémusat who occupied her attention; in December, Mérimée mentioned sadly to Léon de Laborde that she was 'seeing a lot of M. de Rémusat'.[43] Powerless to tear himself away from her or to draw her back to him, Mérimée bore his distress in silence. Only to Mme de Montijo, who knew Valentine well, did he reveal something of the torments of jealousy he was undergoing.

It's a grim year that is about to end [he wrote in December 1848]. It has been worse for me and for many others, not that I have lost much in the material sense; but I feel discouraged, without hope for the future. In these last months I have experienced all the griefs of the heart that a human being can suffer. How I wish that I were beside you, my friend, so that I could tell you all my pain [. . .] Above all I would like to have two hours' conversation with you, to bare my heart to you to find out what is inside it. In truth, I have no idea what there is there and I would need your calmness and *sang-froid* to see clearly into that sorry abyss.[44]

From this time on, the peace of mind that Mérimée had known for a decade was gone. The discovery that he could no longer rely on Valentine's affection revealed to him the full extent of his love for her; it was as if the mainstay of his life had begun to crumble away. He tried with all his might to revive her waning interest in him, but to no avail; her indifference gradually hardened into callous distaste.

[41] *C.G.*, Vol. V, pp. 336 and 339. [42] *Ibid.*, p. 338.
[43] *Ibid.*, p. 422. [44] *Ibid.*, pp. 418–20.

To distract himself from all these public and private woes, Mérimée tried without much success to immerse himself in intellectual work. An attempt to resume his writing on ancient history helped him to while away the time, but soon petered out. Much more fruitful was his decision to start learning Russian with the help of Mme de Lagrené. Mérimée had had Russian friends for many years. In Mme Ancelot's *salon* in 1829 and 1830, he had met Alexander Turgenev, an ex-minister and historian (unrelated to the novelist),[45] and Sergei Sobolevski, another writer with whom he had instantly sympathised and with whom, especially after a second visit to Paris in 1837, he had struck up a warm friendship.[46] As a lover of the strange and the exotic and an accomplished linguist (apart from his fluent English and Spanish, and his professional knowledge of Latin and Greek, he also had a smattering of German, Italian, modern Greek, and Romany), it was natural for him to turn his insatiable curiosity to this new and exciting domain – especially when the charming Barbe Doubenski offered to guide him through it. The lessons began late in 1847. By the summer of 1848, on the advice of Sobolevski, who was passing through Paris, and a General Yermolov, he had moved on to Pushkin. Progress was slow and difficult, but the more Mérimée went on, the more he enjoyed the challenge and the rewards which the discovery of a new literature brought him. He once said: 'my quirk is only to get worked up about things which lie outside general interest'.[47] Knowledge of Russian language and authors in mid-nineteenth-century France was exceedingly rare, and Mérimée was delighted to have found a fascinating field in which he could work almost alone.

But this diversion did not fill the growing gap in his life left by Valentine's defection. By the end of 1848, Mérimée was a badly shaken man. The honours and distinctions of the preceding years were turning to ashes in his mouth. The future was sombre and uncertain, the present painful. From this time onwards, Mérimée's inner life was to grow ever darker.

[45] Henri Mongault, 'Mérimée, Beyle et quelques Russes', *Mercure de France,* 1er mars 1928; cf. also the same author's introduction to Mérimée's *Études de littérature russe*, Paris, Champion, 1931, Vol. I.

[46] A. Vinogradov, *Mérimée v pismakh k Sobolevskomou*, Moscow, 1928.

[47] F. Bac, *Mérimée inconnu*, p. 149.

Chapter 13

Historian

L'histoire, qu'est-ce, sinon un aveu interminable de la stupidité humaine?
Quoted by Ferdinand Bac, *Intimités du Second Empire*

Mérimée's abandonment of fiction for history was a gradual process.[1] From his earliest works onwards, he had shown a keen interest in history, and had frequently used it as the basis for his imaginative writing. The lost *Cromwell, Les Espagnols en Danemarck, La Jaquerie* and of course the *Chronique du règne de Charles IX* were all based firmly on historical episodes, on which Mérimée had documented himself more scrupulously than was usual with Romantic contemporaries like Hugo, Vigny or Dumas. Moreover, in both *La Jaquerie* and the *Chronique*, history was more than a mere background; it informed the whole fabric of the works, which were carefully constructed to give 'a faithful portrayal of manners and characters at a given period'.[2] This curiosity about the past was heightened by Mérimée's appointment as Inspector-General of Historic Monuments, a post which required him to become, in effect, a professional historian. His four volumes of *Notes de voyage* and the numerous archaeological articles which he published were the product of extensive personal research, and his constant examination of historic buildings familiarised him with a great deal of French local and national history.

At the outset of his career, like many other novelists of his generation, Mérimée did not make any rigid distinction between fiction and history. Many times he defined the nature of his concerns in writing, and always in terms which would be equally applicable to creations of the imagination and to factual reconstitutions of the past: what fascinated him above all was the understanding of the human heart.

[1] See A. W. Raitt, 'History and fiction in the works of Mérimée', *History Today*, April 1969, on which the first part of this chapter is based.
[2] *Romans et nouvelles*, Vol. I, p. 11.

In 1832, he laid claim to 'an insatiable curiosity about all the varieties of the human species',[3] and in 1855 he summed up his career as a writer in these words: 'all I have ever done is to paint portraits. When I was young, I used to love to dissect human hearts to see what was inside them.'[4] A few years later, he echoed the same idea when he described his writings as 'paintings of the human heart'[5] and asserted that the study of the human heart was still what interested him most.[6] In 1860, urging Jenny Dacquin to send him detailed accounts of her impressions of life in Algeria, he reminded her that 'everything to do with the history of humanity is full of interest for me'.[7] When the inexorable disintegration of his health had warned him that he was dying, he voiced one of his regrets: 'when one has a taste for the study of the human heart, it is very sad to die without having found the solution to some interesting problems'.[8] This incessant preoccupation with the vagaries of human behaviour puts Mérimée squarely in the tradition of the great French *moralistes*; he belongs to the same family of minds as lucid analysts of *mores* such as La Rochefoucauld, La Bruyère, Montesquieu or Chamfort.

But Mérimée differs from them in one essential respect: his ineradicable mistrust of generalisation. Where the *moralistes* of the seventeenth century and even of the eighteenth had been eager to deduce universal principles from specific observations, Mérimée's cautious scepticism led him to withhold credence from anything save precise, individual cases. Sainte-Beuve once said of him that 'in conversation, no one was ever more sparing of *ideas* in the proper sense of the word',[9] and the same is largely true both of what he wrote for publication and of his immense correspondence. What attracts him is the particular incident and that is why he is so incorrigibly attached to telling stories: each of them constitutes a unique specimen of the oddities of humanity. In the preface to the *Chronique*, he had declared: 'in history I only like anecdotes'.[10] In La Bruyère's *Caractères*, one finds the following dictum: 'One of the signs of a mediocre mind is to be always telling stories', and in the margin of his copy, Sainte-Beuve, perspicacious and

---

[3] C.G., Vol. I, pp. 174–5.   [4] C.G., Vol. VII, pp. 492–3.
[5] C.G., Vol. IX, p. 199.   [6] *Ibid.*, p. 78.
[7] C.G., Vol. X, p. 33.   [8] C.G., Vol. XIII, p. 443.
[9] Sainte-Beuve, *Le XIXe siècle. Les Romanciers II*, p. 286.
[10] *Romans et nouvelles*, Vol. I, p. 85.

uncharitable as ever, noted simply: 'Mérimée'.[11] Like many other
writers who have had a special affection for the 'short-story form,
Mérimée loved collecting examples of human idiosyncrasy while
prudently declining to offer explanations for them.

During the first half of his career, Mérimée satisfied this taste by
making up tales, cast in either narrative or dramatic form, the essential
interest of which lies in their exemplification of the paradoxes inherent
in human motives. But his attitude to fiction was equivocal. Always
sensitive to the danger of ridicule, he was uncomfortably aware that
story-telling could be represented as gratuitous invention, devoid of
any basis in reality; he would, one suspects, never have found it easy
to refute the proposition that novelists are liars. So, as we have
frequently noted, he tried to elude the reproach of gullibility by
indicating that he himself was fully conscious of the falsity of the tales
he was recounting. He emphasised the element of pretence inherent
in all art, taking the reader behind the scenes and inviting him to
inspect the mechanism of deception. *Cromwell* showed puppets taking
the parts of the historical characters. *Le Théâtre de Clara Gazul* was
supposedly the work of a Spanish actress. *La Guzla* was attributed to
the Illyrian bard-outlaw Hyacinthe Maglanovich. *La Famille de Carvajal* is preceded by two letters so patently faked that no one could
be taken in. The aesthetic illusion of the *Chronique* was shattered by a
Dialogue entre le lecteur et l'auteur, and the wry question with which the
novel ended served as a reminder that it was all make-believe. A casual
admission made at one point in the work summarises his doubts about
fiction: 'I wish I had the skill to write a history of France; I would not
bother with tales.'[12] Too respectful of historical method to adopt
Vigny's separation of the 'truth of art' from the 'truthfulness of fact',[13]
Mérimée was inclined to believe that the stuff of history was real, and
that of art merely fanciful.

In the 1830s, as Mérimée's output of fiction fell off and as he took
increasing pleasure in his new role of pedant, imaginative writing was
relegated to the status of an occasional and inferior diversion. As he
began his studies on Caesar, he announced to Esprit Requien: 'I am

[11] Cf. L. Pinvert, *Sur Mérimée*, Paris, Leclerc, 1907.
[12] *Romans et nouvelles*, Vol. I, p. 11.
[13] *Réflexions sur la vérité dans l'art* (preface to *Cinq-Mars*) in *Œuvres complètes*, Paris, Éditions du Seuil, 1965, p. 144.

working at something more serious than my old pranks',[14] and it is symptomatic of his changing interests that he campaigned for the Academy of Inscriptions before the French Academy, and that to attract votes there he was ready to declare that his only concern was with works of erudition. *La Vénus d'Ille* and *Carmen* both show their author as a dry-as-dust antiquarian, and the 1847 revision of *Carmen* bids a clear farewell to the practice of fiction. In 1856 Mérimée could say, with perfect sincerity, 'I wrote so many novels in years gone by that now I only like history.'[15]

But history fulfilled exactly the same need as fiction had done: the unslaked thirst for anecdotes. For him, historical writing consists above all of gripping linear narrative, demonstrating the variety of human eccentricity, satisfying a longing for exoticism and violence, and exploring the diversity of *mores*. Economics and sociology are of little moment to him; he is not much interested in tracing large-scale processes or movements; philosophising about history is shunned like the plague. As he told Edward Lee Childe,

> a philosophy of history is an absurd notion. Obviously when the same causes occur, the same effects are *likely* to follow, the heart of man being the same in every age and every land; but it is dangerous and narrow-minded to reduce everything to a system.[16]

For him, history should record not only political events, but also 'the facts which reveal the *mores* and characters of the men of past epochs'.[17] Great individuals loom very large in such a conception, and Mérimée has little sympathy for the school of thought which concentrates all its attention on mass movements:

> because all previous histories were wrongly conceived and paid no heed at all to the people, taking notice only of kings and important men, was that any excuse for rushing to the opposite extreme, for continually producing an apologia for the conquered, for always seeing racial issues where there is a conflict between temporal power and spiritual power?[18]

---

[14] *C.G.*, Vol. II, pp. 188–9.   [15] *C.G.*, Vol. VIII, p. 183.
[16] *Le Journal de Prosper Mérimée*, in *Lettres à Francisque Michel*, p. 159.
[17] *Histoire de Don Pèdre Ier roi de Castille*, ed. G. Laplane, Paris, Didier, 1961, p. 403.
[18] *Le Journal de Prosper Mérimée*, p. 157.

History seen in this light provides Mérimée with the same satisfactions as drama, according to a lengthy review of George Grote's *History of Greece* in 1847.

> Outside school, if by good fortune we remember something of what we were taught there, ancient history can become the most fascinating reading [. . .] No one can fail to take an interest in the interplay of passions, in portraits of those great characters who dominate whole peoples, in the alterations of glory and ignominy which, from close at hand, are known as chance, but which, seen together and from afar, appear as the embodiment of terrible and mysterious laws of humanity.[19]

Historical biography most clearly exemplifies this type of writing: 'for my part, I know of no more interesting problem than the complete dissection of an historical character'.[20] Passions, portraits, the understanding of humanity – this, for Mérimée, is the essence of history as it had been of imaginative literature, and his historical writings are invariably centred on outstanding individuals rather than critical periods or long evolutions: Julius Caesar, Don Pedro, Dmitri, Bogdan Chmielnicki, Stenka Razine and Peter the Great. He is speaking very much of his own practice when, commenting on W. H. Prescott's *History of the Reign of Philip II*, he writes:

> for an author as for the reader, it is a piece of great good fortune to come across one of those characters who dominate the times in which they live and who, like the protagonists of ancient tragedies, are at the centre of the peripateia and continually hold the stage.[21]

But if history can thus rival drama, it rises superior to all forms of fiction because it deals with facts and not fancies. Mérimée attributed supreme importance to respect for facts in history. With unusual solemnity, he affirmed in 1856: 'in my eyes, history is something sacred'.[22] The cardinal sin for a historian was to tamper with facts; neither morality nor abstract theory should be allowed to interfere with the judicious assessment of factual truth. The historian's prime aim is 'the discovery of the truth',[23] and his duty is to remain unswerv-

---

[19] *Mélanges historiques et littéraires*, Paris, Lévy, 1855, p. 110.
[20] *C.G.*, Vol. XIV, p. 312.
[21] *Mémoires historiques*, Paris, Bernouard, 1927, p. 14.
[22] *C.G.*, Vol. VIII, p. 160.
[23] *Mémoires historiques*, p. 47.

ingly 'detached and fair';[24] his function is not to prove a thesis but to 'collect numerous facts and subject them to impartial criticism'.[25] In 1848 he insisted that 'what one demands of history nowadays is sureness of critical evaluation and impartiality of judgement'.[26] He held that the great contribution which his own times had made to historiography lay in according primacy to the establishment of facts.

> The progress made by historical studies since the beginning of this century consists in having perfected methods of research and the art of criticism, and that is, to my mind, one of the claims to glory which the literature of our times will have in the sight of posterity.[27]

Naturally, the admixture of what is imagined to what is known is rigorously proscribed, and he is stern in his condemnation of German historians guilty of this offence: 'the Germans have committed the worst possible crime; they've brought imagination into a subject where it had no place: history'.[28]

Mérimée is most scrupulous in keeping history and fiction well apart in his later years. The only exception is *Les Débuts d'un aventurier*, and in this highly speculative account of the mysterious early years of the Dmitri impostor, the dramatic form makes it clear that he is not presenting a historical treatise. In 1859, after he had written nothing for several years, he said with truth: 'when I stopped writing, history was the only sort of literature that still interested me'.[29] The clearest instance of how he now saw the relative positions of history and fiction occurs when he congratulated Thiers on the latest volume of his *Histoire du Consulat et de l'Empire*: 'history, when it is written as you can write it, is as much superior to all poems and all plays as a diamond is to paste'.[30] History does not do more than fiction or drama; what it does is in essence the same, but with the inestimable advantage of provable authenticity. History is genuine; fiction is spurious.

All these attitudes are evident in Mérimée's *Études sur l'histoire romaine* and his *Histoire de Don Pédre Ier roi de Castille* (his works on Russian history fall into a somewhat different category and will be

[24] *C.G.*, Vol. VIII, p. 244.

[25] '*Edifices de Rome moderne*, par P. Letarouilly', *Revue des Deux Mondes*, 1er septembre 1841.

[26] *Mélanges historiques et littéraires*, p. 163.

[27] *Mémoires historiques*, p. 11.   [28] *Journal de Prosper Mérimée*, p. 140.

[29] *C.G.*, Vol. IX, p. 232.   [30] *Ibid.*, p. 421.

considered later, with his other activities as a Russophile). His research into Roman history may at first sight seem to be lacking in biographical interest, but it originated with a desire to write the life of Julius Caesar, and it was when he tried to understand the political situation at the moment of Caesar's arrival on the scene that Mérimée saw that he would have to begin far earlier. He then realised that the Social War, the long conflict between Rome and the allied Italian states in the first century B.C., was a singularly obscure episode which had never before been studied in detail. As this discovery coincided with the awakening of his ambition to be elected to the Academy of Inscriptions, he decided to expand his consideration of the Social War into a separate volume, a substantial work of history in its own right, as well as acting as prolegomena to a life of Caesar. The *Conjuration de Catalina* dealt with Caesar's political debut, and the continuation would have covered the remainder of his career. But though Mérimée went on working desultorily for some years, his attention was diverted first by Don Pedro and then by Dmitri, until in the end he turned over his material to Napoleon III, who had decided to write his own *Histoire de Jules César*.[31]

[31] There has been some argument about how much further Mérimée went with his life of Caesar. In 1850, he talked to Boissonade about 'une note prise, il y a bien des années quand je voulais écrire la vie de César' (*C.G.*, Vol. VI, p. 133), which might be taken to mean that by then he had given up the idea. But it might only signify that the plan is in temporary abeyance. At the other extreme, Louis de Loménie, in the speech he made on succeeding Mérimée in the French Academy, asserted that manuscript of the continuation had been found in the ruins of the Tuileries in 1870, and Maurice Tourneux (in *Prosper Mérimée, ses portraits, ses desseins, sa bibliothèque*, Paris, Charavay, 1879) inclines to the view that there may well be something in the story. It is more likely that what was found was an outline of Caesar's career sketched out by Mérimée for Napoleon III, which would explain its presence in the palace. There is clear evidence that Mérimée still had it in mind to resume work on Caesar between 1844 and the time when Napoleon III took up the idea in the late 1850s. In September 1855, for example, he wrote to Mme de Boigne: 'M. de Lamartine is poaching on my preserves. He is writing a *Life of Caesar*, naturally without having read anything except the biographical dictionary. He makes the most extraordinary howlers, but it vexes me and puts me off finishing my history' (*C.G.*, Vol. VII, pp. 526–7). Again, in September 1856, he told a friend: 'for a long time past I have been working on a life of Caesar' (*C.G.*, Vol. VIII, p. 121). The truth probably

This genesis has left its mark both on the *Essai sur la Guerre Sociale* and on the *Conjuration de Catilina*. The first of these works is unique among Mérimée's historical writings in that it does not have a central character; its avowed destination as a qualification for the Academy of Inscriptions also gives it an unusually stiff and circumspect tone. The second, though far from being a section of biography, tends to interpret the Catiline conspiracy very much as a stage in Caesar's rise to political power rather than as a happening significant in its own right. In both cases, the reader understandably has the feeling of watching *Hamlet* without the prince; we wait, in vain, for Caesar to occupy the centre of the stage. The absence of what ought to have been the culmination of these two volumes leaves the edifice uncrowned. This makes it difficult to provide a fair assessment of what remains: the two books stand as isolated 'studies' rather than as the parts of a grand whole which they were meant to be.

Of the two, the *Essai sur la Guerre Sociale* is the more original piece of scholarship. Mérimée was the first to attempt a complete and detailed account of an involved series of events, on which first-hand sources were fragmentary and unreliable, but which was of considerable importance in the history of Rome. He is frank about the difficulties and dangers:

> a full account of the events of the Social War presents more than one difficulty. Normally, when one is writing the history of some distant period, one has so to speak to restore a building which has been more or less damaged by time but which still has a recognizable shape that can be deduced from the remaining parts. Here on the contrary there are only ruins so scattered and so confused that in putting them together one is constantly afraid of changing their original layout.[32]

No precise chronology; no certainty about the battlefields; no reliable indication even of the main participants: such are the problems to be

---

is that Mérimée neither definitively abandoned work on Caesar after 1844, nor ever wrote any substantial part of the remainder. He seems to have continued desultory work on it at intervals, with less and less enthusiasm, until eventually Napoleon III, by announcing his desire to do the same thing, took matters out of his hands for good.

[32] *Études sur l'histoire romaine* (3rd edition), Paris, Lévy, 1876, p. 76.

resolved. Mérimée tackles them resolutely and systematically, but with the utmost caution:

> if awareness of the difficulties which arise at every step may keep me from some mistakes, I trust that I shall not fall into those to which I might be led involuntarily by prejudice or overconfidence in my own ability.[33]

With no axe to grind, a thorough training in the handling of archaeological evidence, a great willingness to accept the advice of expert friends like Lenormant,[34] an immense and patient capacity for hard work on arid texts, a strong sense of practical realities, and an uncompromising honesty which led him to admit freely the gaps which only intelligent speculation could fill, Mérimée was well equipped for such an arduous task, and from the specialist's point of view, he has carried it out admirably. He is becomingly modest about his achievement:

> I have no illusions about how bold my enterprise is, how far it is beyond my powers; but I should think that I had rendered some service to history if from my work there happened to emerge some neglected truth, if my very errors acted as a warning to those writers who will treat the subject after me.[35]

But the members of the Academy of Inscriptions were in no doubt about the merits of the book when they gave Mérimée such a handsome majority over his rival in 1843.

On the other hand, the *Essai* does not have a strong appeal for the general reader, despite the fact that Mérimée wanted it to be widely accessible. When he first decided to separate it from his biography of Caesar, he told his friend Saulcy: 'I am trying to make my book *exceedingly* comprehensible for the ignorant public. Perhaps I'll end

[33] *Études sur l'histoire romaine* (3rd Edition), Paris, Lévy, 1876, p. 77.

[34] When Mérimée submitted his first draft to Lenormant, the latter advised him, among other things, to add chapters on the history of the Samnite towns and on Italian coins of the period. Mérimée declined the first suggestion on the grounds that the materials were insufficient, but did accept the idea of a numismatic appendix, which appeared in the first edition. It was not included in the 1844 edition, but appeared in the *Revue numismatique*, mars–avril 1845, as 'Médailles italiotes de la Guerre sociale'.

[35] *Études sur l'histoire romaine*, p. 3. It is interesting to compare these words with what his father wrote at the beginning of his *Traité sur la peinture à l'huile* (cf. p. 18); the similarity of attitude is striking.

up by falling between the two stools of the Academy and the public.'[36] With the Academy, he succeeded; with the public at large, he did less well, probably through no fault of his own: the use of Greek and Latin is confined to footnotes, as are erudite discussions of detail, while the main text presents a narrative as clear and lively as is permitted by the confused intricacies of the subject. But what one misses is just what Mérimée himself most prized in history: the revelation of human truth, portraits of great characters, the dramatic clash of high interests. The sources on which Mérimée is forced to rely give him little opportunity for the utilisation of those touches of local colour, those picturesque anecdotes, those analyses of psychology which make his other historical works so vivid and gripping. Only in the third section of the book, when Mérimée describes the first civil war which followed the end of the Social War, is the drama brought to life by the conflict between Marius and Sulla. Elsewhere the sober relation of facts has insufficient human interest to make us relive past events with that immediacy which is otherwise one of the great qualities of Mérimée's historiography.

Mérimée was not unaware of the *Essai*'s shortcomings. When Pasquier's friend Mme de Boigne told him how much she had enjoyed reading it, he replied in these terms:

> You will make me conceited if you tell me that the *Guerre Sociale* did not strike you as boring. I assure you with absolute frankness that I thought it was, except for a dozen people like myself who have a liking for old Roman things. Moreover, when I was writing the book, all I had in mind was to ingratiate myself with the gentlemen in the Academy, and I had been told that to please them, one had to be boring. That wasn't very difficult, but there are so many ways of being boring. The one they prefer in history is that one should pass over everything connected with customs, with characters, with the human heart, and that one should discuss obscure and unknown texts, etc. [. . .] If you will allow me, I'll give you a comparison. Imagine a thousand little pieces of cloth more or less torn. I sew them together and make a carpet out of them. Admirers of sewing will appreciate the work, but the rest will think that a carpet made out of a single piece of material is better. The merit of my book is to have sewn a sentence of Appian to a fragment of Dion Cassius, a word of Orosus to a line of Diodorus Siculus. But who reads people like that?[37]

It would be unfair to blame Mérimée for this defect, since it is difficult

[36] *C.G.*, Vol. II, p. 235.   [37] *C.G.*, Vol. III, pp. 217–18.

to see what else, as a conscientious historian, he could have done. But the book is more forbidding than anything else he wrote, and its qualities are more appreciable to the expert than to the lay reader.

Oddly enough, the opposite is true of the *Conjuration de Catilina*, even though it is the sequel to the *Essai*. The conspiracy was more written about by the ancients than most episodes of Roman history – Sallust, Suetonius, Plutarch and Cicero, with a host of minor writers, all supply valuable material, a good deal of it at first hand. Nor was there any shortage of striking characters to place in prominent positions – Catilina himself, debauched, ambitious, unscrupulous, unreliable; Cicero, self-satisfied but a skilful politician and a superb orator; the un-bending Cato; and above all the young Julius Caesar, already wilier than the most experienced statesmen and gradually learning how to wield the power he was accumulating. The action of the story is unified and dramatic; the conflict of personalities fascinating; the insight into the *mores* of the Roman republic extraordinarily revealing. Of all this Mérimée makes excellent use, and as he unfolds the narrative of the formation of the conspiracy, its unmasking, and the subsequent trial of the conspirators, we are swept along by a masterly evocation of intrigue, rivalry, hatred and lust for domination. The writing has a strength and liveliness not often found in the *Essai*, and Mérimée's sources are detailed enough to justify him in those sudden close-ups at which he excels. Here for example is how he introduces Caesar:

Rome still knew nothing of the genius of Caesar; yet all eyes were already turning towards him as if drawn by a fatal presentiment. Everything about him seemed extraordinary and contradictory, his appearance no less than his behaviour. His dark eyes, flashing with a penetrating fire that was difficult to withstand, contrasted with the smile that played about the al-most feminine outlines of his mouth. In his youth, he was of a delicate disposition, and his white, softly rounded limbs did not bespeak great vigour; yet he excelled at all bodily exercises, and his health had suffered neither from excess of work nor excess of pleasure. Those who saw him in the morning in the Forum, draped in his ample toga every fold of which seemed to have been studied in a mirror, wondered if he was the same man who the day before had been taming a wild horse on the Campus Martius or raising his voice before the tribunal of the duumvirs to accuse a proconsul who had grown rich through Sulla's banishments. Proud of his birth, he liked to remind the Romans that he counted kings and gods among his ancestors, but no one knew if he was more proud of his mother

Venus or of his aunt's husband, Marius the plebeian with two names. Sometimes when he spoke in the Curia, the old senators trembled, thinking that Caius Gracchus had come to life again. A moment later the hot-headed tribune had disappeared, leaving only an elegant profligate more concerned with his latest mistress than with the affairs of the republic.[38]

This portrait is typical of that zest apparent on almost every page of the *Conjuration*, which makes it a remarkably exciting book.

But it has been subjected to much more criticism from specialists than has the *Essai*.[39] Mérimée is so obviously biased in Caesar's favour that the whole perspective in which he sees the conspiracy tends to be warped. The trial of Rabirius which preceded it is seen essentially as a chance for Caesar to test his strength; the possibility of Caesar having had anything to do with the conspirators is indignantly rejected; all parties are represented as keeping an anxious eye on Caesar throughout the proceedings. Complementary to this partiality is an equally obvious distaste for Cicero. Though Mérimée pays tribute to the eloquence of his orations against Catilina, he is visibly repelled by his vanity and tends to play down his part in events. This more than anything else led Sainte-Beuve to place the *Conjuration* below the *Essai*:

Mérimée has succeeded in his *Guerre sociale* and he has failed in his *Catilina*. In the first subject full of sudden actions and of wars, he quickly rushed off into the hills, and he brought it off. But in the other work, he had to hold the forum, which does not suit him. Above all he has not understood

---

38 *Études sur l'histoire romaine*, pp. 262–3.
39 Cf. notably Maurice Hily, 'Prosper Mérimée et l'histoire romaine', *Mélanges de la Société toulousaine d'études classiques*, I, 1946. M. Hily admits that Mérimée's method in going back to original sources was sound, but adds: 'to handle it properly, rigour, erudition and culture were needed. Mérimée only had curiosity and culture.' For him, Mérimée remains essentially a novelist when he writes about history: 'in his eyes, history and literature cannot be separated' – a view which is acceptable, though not in the sense in which M. Hily intended it. A more equitable assessment is provided by Emilio Gabba, 'Prospero Mérimée storico di Roma', *Rivista storica italiana*, LXVIII, 4, 1956; he compares the *Essai sur la Guerre sociale* with the only other modern work on the subject, Adolf Kiene's *Der römische Bundes-genossenkrieg* (1845), and the comparison is to Mérimée's advantage. On the other hand, he does not regard the *Conjuration* as a very outstanding contribution to its subject.

the first thing about Cicero, about that man of whom it has been magnificently said that he was *the only genius the Roman people ever had to equal their empire*.[40]

Mérimée's argument is that the trial of the conspirators marks the last twitch of the dying Senate, leaving the way open for Caesar and Pompey; the real victor of the whole Catilina affair is, in his eyes, Caesar. Whatever the merits of this case, it is not a new one, and he does not adduce any fresh evidence to support it. Judged as a contribution to historical scholarship, the *Conjuration de Catilina* is inferior to the *Essai sur la Guerre Sociale*; judged as literature, it is superior.

After completing the *Conjuration*, Mérimée did not go on, as he had planned, to deal with the rest of Caesar's career; his place as an ancient historian might be more secure if he had. Instead, he allowed Mme de Montijo to persuade him to turn to Don Pedro. But in the *Conjuration* there are already signs of the historical problem which was to obsess him throughout his work on medieval Spain: is a cruel and ruthless character like Caesar or Don Pedro to be assessed and condemned by modern standards of morality, or ought one to make allowances for the habits of the time and admire him for the unflagging energy with which he pursues his ends? In the *Conjuration*, Mérimée is very severe in his judgement of the debauchery, the dishonesty, the selfishness of public men in Rome, and in one place demands that we make no concessions to a different way of life: 'we are too much accustomed to judging the ancients with the prejudices and sophisms of their history'.[41] Yet elsewhere he warns us 'how difficult it is to judge the ancients with the ideas of our own times'.[42] The reason for these apparent contradictions is revealed when he replied to criticisms by Charles de Rémusat:

> you have very justifiably taxed me with the excess of the reproaches I levelled at Roman *mores*. On reflection I think you are right and that we are no better. If we are less savage, that perhaps just comes from the fact that we have novels and theatres every day, and that the Prefect of Police forbids gladiatorial combats. My mistake comes from the fact that, being too fond of the Romans and in particular Caesar, I wanted to guard against what I regarded as partiality. I fell over backwards to be fair to the other side, as often happens.[43]

---

[40] *Les Cahiers de Sainte-Beuve*, Paris, Lemerre, 1876, pp. 54–5.

[41] *Études sur l'histoire romaine*, p. 402.

[42] *Ibid.*, p. 285, n. 1.   [43] *C.G.*, Vol. IV, p. 125.

The hesitation is identical with that which plagued him in *Colomba* and *Carmen*. The life of Don Pedro was to confront him with the same dilemma in unusually acute form.

Don Pedro was king of Castille from 1350, when he was a boy of sixteen, until 1369, when he was killed by his half-brother Don Enrique of Trastamara. The reign was marked by almost incessant civil wars between Don Pedro's supporters, and those who preferred Don Enrique; in addition there were bloody conflicts with Aragon and Granada. At one time, Don Pedro, betrayed by his mother and his brothers, was imprisoned by his enemies; after his escape, he avenged himself on his great vassals with extraordinary ferocity, starting the series of tortures and murders which earned him the name of 'the Cruel'. Having with the help of the Black Prince and his troops defeated Don Enrique and Du Guesclin at the battle of Najera in 1367, Don Pedro treated his allies with such ingratitude that they left him to his own devices. The country then rose against him and it was after an ignominious rout at Montiel that he died at his brother's hands. From the beginning, Mérimée was attracted by the ruthless energy of Don Pedro, as well as by his uninhibited passions and his defiance of the Church, and he was also intrigued by the paradox of Don Pedro being known as 'the Cruel' to historians but as 'el Justiciero' in popular tradition. The question which most exercised him was whether or not it was legitimate to condone Don Pedro's orgies of blood-letting, in the name of the establishment of royal power, in the light of medieval behaviour generally, or in consideration of the overriding rights of passion.

Mérimée's letters to Mme de Montijo make it clear that his instinctive reaction was one of admiration for Don Pedro, with as its corollary a strong desire to exculpate him for his sanguinary excesses. In 1845 he wrote to her:

> The more I study your history, the more excuses I find for Don Pedro. It is absurd to judge him with our modern ideas. To understand him, one has to bear in mind the opinions and political necessities of the Middle Ages. Murdering someone in 1350 was a quite different thing from doing it in 1800.[44]

The following year, he explained that 'I am trying to demonstrate that in the middle of the fourteenth century it was not so wrong to kill

[44] *Ibid.*, p. 291.

someone as it is to write a slanderous newspaper article in 1846'.[45]
But in the book itself, tempering his enthusiasm with caution, he is
much less affirmative. In the opening pages he withholds his verdict:

> today we must take account of the customs of his times and of the diffi-
> culties which he encountered. We have to assess his intentions and the plans
> of his adversaries. Such is the examination one must undertake before
> delivering judgement; such is the aim of the work I have set out to write.[46]

He protests that he has no wish to produce an apology:

> for my part, I have in no wise undertaken to defend Don Pedro; but I
> believe that his character and his actions deserved to be better known, and
> that the struggle between a vigorous genius like his and the *mores* of the
> fourteenth century was worthy of a historical study.[47]

When it comes to specific incidents, Mérimée hesitates. Don Pedro
was often accused of poisoning his innocent and maltreated wife
Blanche de Bourbon: the crime is so appalling that Mérimée clearly
could not excuse Don Pedro if he had committed it, and so he embarks
on a contrived and inconclusive attempt to clear his hero of complicity
in it.[48] After capturing Toro in 1356, Don Pedro had several of his
opponents slaughtered as they threw themselves on his mercy. Here
Mérimée admits the crime but rather half-heartedly seeks to lessen its
enormity and the degree of Don Pedro's guilt.

> It is wrong to judge this bloodthirsty execution with our modern ideas;
> one must bear in mind the customs of the Middle Ages, not in order to
> justify it, but to see whether the horror of the massacre should fall on the
> prince who ordered it or on the times which witnessed so many similar
> scenes. There is no doubt whatever that, according to the laws and usages
> of Castille in the fourteenth century, rebellious vassals were considered as
> traitors and that any loyal subject was allowed and indeed obliged to kill
> them when he recognised them [. . .] Certainly, in 1356, nobody would
> have denied Don Pedro the right to inflict exemplary punishment on the
> rebels of Toro; but what is one to think of this butchery of defenceless
> people who, led by two women, were coming to implore his pity?[49]

---

[45] *C.G.*, Vol. IV, p. 430.   [46] *Histoire de Don Pèdre Ier*, p. 10.
[47] *Ibid.*, p. 19.
[48] *Ibid.*, pp. 423–6. Later in the book, Mérimée tacitly admits that there
must have been good grounds for thinking Don Pedro to be guilty (pp. 447
and 515).   [49] *Ibid.*, pp. 263–4.

The fullest examination of this problem comes about half-way through the book, and is hedged about with so many qualifications, so many reservations, so many evasions, that it is easy to see that Mérimée was no more able to make up his mind about Don Pedro's passions than he was about passion in general in his works of fiction.

> Whatever the indignation, whatever the disgust one feels at the recital of these continual executions, it is impossible to attribute them to heedless ferocity, to that cruelty of temperament which most historians ascribe to Don Pedro in order to explain the number of murders he ordered and carried out in quick succession. I see them rather as the inevitable consequence of the king's ambition at odds with the customs of his time. The outstanding trait of his character is a violent love of power, always suspicious, always uneasy, perhaps to some extent excusable in a medieval prince who, after witnessing for years the evils of anarchy, had in the end come to regard his despotism as a superhuman mission to regenerate his country [. . .] Everywhere one sees only perfidy and shameless treachery. Is it any wonder that a prince brought up amid civil war, constantly surrounded by revolts and conspiracies, whom his brothers and his cousins had played false, who had been betrayed by his mother and his aunt, should have sought to turn against his enemies those arms which had wounded him so grievously? It is not an apologia for Don Pedro that I am writing; all I want to establish is the difficulty of judging men of past ages with our modern ideas.[50]

Even where Mérimée's sympathy for Don Pedro and his contemporaries shines through, it is liable to be suddenly retracted:

> the men of the fourteenth century lived in isolation, and that energy, that will-power which nowadays we admire too much in them, perhaps derives from the awareness of their own wickedness, which constantly showed them that they could and should rely only on themselves.[51]

The major question posed by the *Histoire de Don Pèdre* thus in the end goes unanswered, which could scarcely surprise anyone who has studied *Colomba*. But the fact that Mérimée is so intimately concerned with it gives a rare humanity to a book that might easily have become a monotonous catalogue of wars and murders. Mérimée passionately wants to understand Don Pedro and shows as much psychological acumen as antiquarian skill in trying to do so. Nor is it a foolhardy

[50] *Ibid.*, pp. 382–5. Whatever Mérimée may say, his book does come close to being an attempted rehabilitation of a man often regarded as being one of the great villains of history.   [51] *Ibid.*, p. 58.

enterprise. The sources for the life and reign of Don Pedro are unusually rich, even if they had not been fully utilised before Mérimée's time. The richest was the *Chronicle of Don Pedro* by Lopez de Ayala, a familiar of the king and an active participant in many of the events he describes, though Mérimée never made use of its data without subjecting them to vigilant critical scrutiny. His own researches into the Aragonese archives enabled him to add many original discoveries, some of them of considerable importance – the pact which the king of Aragon imposed on his rival lieutenants Don Enrique and Don Fernando after the battle of Najera, for instance, the details of the Peace of Terrer in 1361, the Treaty of Monzon between Don Enrique and the king of Aragon in 1362, the Treaty of Benifar in 1363 and so on. Mérimée's painstaking researches transformed knowledge of the subject, and his book remains an essential work on Spanish medieval history. Little that he could have known in the 1840s escaped him, and his scrupulous scholarship enabled him to avoid almost all save the most venial errors.

This abundant documentation is most dexterously handled by Mérimée. He never seeks to highlight what he has himself discovered, and never overburdens his narration with irrelevant quotation. What interests him is the unfolding of a story, and to this task he brings not only the professional accomplishments of a palaeographer, an archaeologist, a linguist and a historian, but also the superb art of the author of *La Vénus d'Ille* and *Carmen*. Thanks to Gabriel Laplane's excellent critical edition of the *Histoire de Don Pèdre*, it is possible to see in minute detail how Mérimée has combined meticulous respect for facts with the gifts of a born story-teller. With great discretion, he has used his original sources to provide the essentials of his narrative, enlivening it by bringing out all the concrete touches they supply, and adding to it only those assumptions about motive and about the visual aspect of the scenes which the circumstances seem to render inevitable. Here for instance is how Mérimée describes the slaughter of Don Pedro's enemies at Toro:

> Carpentero and Castañeda were each bearing up the queen by one arm. Castañeda was holding aloft the letter of amnesty open and unfolded. The others clustered around the two women, whom they regarded as their safeguard, clinging to their clothes. All were looking for some great lord, some leader of the royal army, whose protection they might implore. To reach the king, this mournful procession had to pass through a serried mass

of men at arms who were awaiting them on the edge of the moat, bared swords in their hands. They were obliged to cross the drawbridge and walk between two lines of soldiers. Castañeda, displaying the parchment and the king's seal, cried that he had obtained his pardon, forgetting that he had passed the time limit allowed for his surrender. They moved slowly forward amid the jeers and insults of the mob, and still there was no sign of the king. A few paces from the drawbridge, a squire of Diego de Padilla, recognising Carpentero by the insignia of Calatrava, forced his way through the crowd and with his mace struck him a blow on the head that stretched him out at the feet of the queen. He was then stabbed to death. It was the signal for the massacre. An instant later Castañeda, Martin Telho and Tellez Giron fell to the ground, run through again and again, their blood soaking the clothes of the two women who had fainted at the awful sight. When she regained consciousness, the first thing the queen saw, as she was held up in the arms of a few fierce soldiers, her feet in a pool of blood, was the four mutilated corpses, already despoiled and naked. As despair and fury brought her strength back, in a voice broken by screams and sobs, she cursed her son and accused him of having for ever dishonoured her.[52]

The outlines of this tragic scene are directly borrowed from Ayala. Mérimée has confined himself to the addition of a few plausible details (the 'serried mass' of men at arms, the drawbridge, the two lines of soldiers, the pool of blood), the insertion of one or two dramatic epithets ('mournful', 'awful'), the heightening of suspense by the occasional interpretative phrase ('still there was no sign of the king'), the increase of tension and vividness by the untranslatable use of the historic present. In this way he remains faithful to his sources while giving the reader the startling impression of being an eye-witness.

The vigour and precision of Mérimée's style do much to enhance this dynamism and vividness. Shunning abstract reflections, forgoing, save on rare occasions, rhetorical flourishes, Mérimée concentrates on action and character. No one has given a better definition of Mérimée as a historian than Sainte-Beuve:

the way in which M. Mérimée writes history is sane, simple, full of concision and firmness [. . .] In our times, excessive play has been made with general ideas and considerations, with diverse influences, which are arbitrarily set in motion down the centuries. M. Mérimée, who likes only what is certain, keeps strictly clear of them; he approaches history through

---

[52] *Histoire de Don Pèdre Ier*, pp. 262–3.

its most authentic monuments and its most precise pieces of evidence, never goes far away from them, only arranges them so far as he thinks the facts admit of it, and stops the moment there is nothing positive to work on.[53]

The narrative is stripped down to its essentials, but even where Mérimée is doing no more than repeating his sources, he has an eye to holding the reader's attention. So for example when he reproduces Spanish medieval documents, he does so in an imitation of the language of Froissart; he does not allow his judgement to be affected by popular legends, but he adds sparkle to the story by quoting them; and he is ever on the lookout for the significant detail recorded by some four-teenth-century chronicler. There are few historical works of the period which remain both such essential and enjoyable reading.

Mérimée's reputation as a historian deserves to be a high one. If he is sometimes underestimated, it is largely because his detestation of the beaten track led him far away from his native land to ancient Rome, medieval Spain, and later to seventeenth-century Russia. This diversity is not a sign of dilettantism, since his writings are almost all the work of a highly skilled and conscientious professional. But it shows how very personal his approach was, with its emphasis on certain topics and characters to the exclusion of others as dull or irrelevant. Mérimée never sought to erect one of those massive monuments so characteristic of contemporary historians like Thiers, Michelet, Taine or Renan. Just as he prefers the isolated episode of the short story to the rounded construction of the novel, so, in his historiography he keeps to single, unrelated subjects, and is never tempted by the grand design. Within his chosen confines, he is a first-rate scholar, and his *Histoire de Don Pèdre* comes close to being a masterpiece.

[53] *Le XIXe siècle. Les Romanciers II*, pp. 31–2.

Chapter 14

Gaolbird

Lorsque vous serez trahi à 45 ans, vous trouverez que ce que
vous avez souffert à vingt ans était peu de choses.
To Achille Vogue, 18 September 1857

In the second half of 1848, as the political situation attained a precarious
stability under the military government of General Cavaignac, Mérimée was able to carry out the duties of his inspectorship as he had been
doing for fourteen years. His annual tour in 1848 did not take place
until late September and consisted only of a brief trip to Alsace, but
at least it indicated that the situation was returning to normal. Unfortunately for him, people were still very preoccupied with politics, so
that the publication of his *Histoire de Don Pèdre* in the summer passed
almost unnoticed in France, though it attracted sufficient international
attention for it to be translated into Spanish the same year, into English
in 1849 and into German in 1852. Mérimée himself watched the
evolution of republican politics with anxious concern. Not that he
took any active part in them, nor even had any very clear idea which
of the various conservative factions – Legitimists, Orleanists, Bonapartists or moderate Republicans – was most likely to avert the chaos of a
second revolution. Never a Bonapartist, he showed nothing more than
curiosity at the return of Louis-Napoleon, whom he disrespectfully
referred to as 'old Bonaparte',[1] though he came grudgingly to admit
that after his election as Prince-President in December 1848, the new
man was at least showing vigour and artfulness. The first time he met
him was in January 1849, and the impression was neutral:

he struck me as small, with a head made for a far bigger body, looking
very much the gentleman, with almost a foreign accent of some un-
identifiable kind. He talks very little, and what he says is sensible, but he

---

[1] E.g. *C.G.*, Vol. V, p. 411.

doesn't put himself to much trouble. He has the manners of a legitimate ruler, *cold, distant and self-conscious*.[2]

But as Louis-Napoleon held at bay the spectre of further upheavals, Mérimée felt that he had at any rate the merit of tenacity.

Too disturbed by the 1848 revolution to settle down to any large-scale work, Mérimée pursued his Russian studies with the diligence of a gifted schoolboy. The discovery of Pushkin delighted him, and with the help of Mme Doubenski, who was sometimes more willing than efficient, he set about translating *The Queen of Spades*. His version appeared in the *Revue des Deux Mondes* in July 1849 and created something of a sensation – there were those who, in view of the similarity with Mérimée's usual narrative manner, suspected him of being its author as well as its translator. Having also read Pushkin's *Boris Godunov*, Mérimée's interest was aroused by Russian history and he started casting around for historical works about the false Dmitri who succeeded Boris as Tsar at the beginning of the seventeenth century, and by the middle of 1850, by dint of pestering his Russian friends, notably the helpful Sobolevski, he had become immersed in recondite Russian source-books.

In 1850 Mérimée did unexpectedly publish a short play entitled *Les Deux Héritages* (*The Two Inheritances*), but it is not a very distinguished work, and one wonders quite what impelled him to write this mild domestic comedy. The political satire in it is out of date, since the July Monarchy was no more, the characters are not very substantial, and the action is scarcely convincing. It reminds one rather of the earlier playlet, *Les Mécontents*, though more human and less caricatural, but it comes nowhere near to equalling the best plays of Mérimée's youth. Only an undertone of sadness in the depiction of the raffish hero's middle-aged uncle who returns to the army after failing to win the woman he loves shows some personal interest in what is otherwise indifferent material.[3] It is not surprising that *Les Deux*

[2] *C.G.*, Vol. V, p. 434. The italicised words are in English in the original.
[3] Writing to Adolphe de Circourt: 'It has the fault of our times, that of being neither pathetic nor gay, but I am very pleased that you found a grain of truth in it' (*C.G.*, Vol. VI, p. 75). Ernest Legouvé, who later made a one-act adaptation of *Les Deux Héritages*, gives us this tantalising half-confidence about the character of the Marquise de Montrichard in the play: 'Mérimée told me that the part was simply the portrait of a very great lady, whom he

Héritages has always been largely ignored. In contrast, another short work which appeared in 1850 has always attracted more than its fair share of notoriety. This is Mérimée's anonymous pamphlet on Stendhal, *H.B. par un des Quarante* (*H.B. by one of the Forty*), only twenty-five copies of which were printed and given by Mérimée to his friends. It is a deliberately provocative work, which emphasises Stendhal's atheism and licentiousness, and says little about his qualities as a novelist. But it is an extraordinarily living and intimate portrait of an exceptional man, and it is written with such verve and humour that one can easily forgive its shortcomings. Whatever the coolness which had arisen between the two men in the later years of Stendhal's life, Mérimée has found again for this sketch the affectionate camaraderie of their earlier friendship, and though it has none of the solemnity usually associated with a funeral oration, its irreverent wit makes it a memorial of which Stendhal himself would have appreciated the savour.

There is a certain nostalgia for lost youth in both *Les Deux Héritages* and *H.B.* Mérimée's gloomy preoccupation with what he felt ever more keenly as his own decrepitude was growing. When Édouard Grasset was coming to France in 1849, Mérimée warned him that things had changed for the worse: 'I'm perhaps the best preserved of those who used to dine at Véry's, and you may have difficulty in recognising me.'[4] His sexual needs had abated, and he joked sadly about his declining powers: 'I am too old, and it's rare these days that I do it more than 120 times a month.'[5] When on some special occasion he did try to revive the Véry dinners, the result was only to depress him.

The tradition has gone, and I cannot tell you how sad I felt to be back again in that room where we had so many riotous meals with friends who are

named and whom I shall not name, because he did so. I guessed too, at a certain reticence on his part, that there was in this comedy an implication which was a memory, a painful memory which for me explained why the work lacked charm. I shall not say what this implication is because I divined it and he did not tell me' (quoted in *C.G.*, Vol. XIII, p. 297, n. 1). But while we may accept that Saqueville's frustrated love for the Marquise relates to some disappointment in Mérimée's life, there are so many possible identifications for the character that there is not much point in speculating about it.

[4] *C.G.*, Vol. V, pp. 466–7.
[5] *C.G.*, Vol. VII, p. 133.

now under the earth. It was as if I were returning from some great battle in which half my regiment had been killed.[6]

The casualty rate among old friends was alarmingly high. In December 1850, Hippolyte Royer-Collard died, followed in May 1851 by Dr Koreff. Esprit Requien too died in May 1851, and of his death Mérimée said bitterly: 'it afflicts me all the more cruelly as I have no doubt that it was due to his temerity which age had done nothing to lessen'.[7] Of all these men, Mérimée could have said, as he did of Sutton Sharpe, 'he died because he worked too hard and made love too much'[8] – a diagnosis which was anything but reassuring.

In 1850 Mérimée returned to England for the first time since 1835. He was accompanied by Viollet-le-Duc, and their mission was to look at English architecture. But England without Sutton Sharpe was a dull place. The English Sunday drove Mérimée to contemplate suicide, the English attitude to art moved him to derision, and after a week or two he could stand it no longer: 'I have had just about enough of this country. I am fed up with perpendicular architecture and the equally perpendicular manners of the natives.'[9] His anticlericalism was violently offended by Oxford and Cambridge, the dons of which he defined witheringly as 'Protestant canons enjoying an income of £4000 or £5000, on the pretext that they know some Greek, which they have forgotten, and spending their time singing litanies and drinking old port wine'.[10] Dining at High Table in Balliol did nothing to improve his humour:

> there was a fish four inches long on one great silver platter and a lamb chop on another, all served in magnificent style, with potatoes in a carved wooden dish. But I've never been so hungry. It's all the fault of the hypocrisy of those people. They like showing foreigners that they are abstemious, and on the grounds that they have a *luncheon*, they do without dinner.[11]

---

[6] *C.G.*, Vol. VI, p. 159.   [7] *Ibid.*, p. 199.
[8] *C.G.*, Vol. XI, p. 163.   [9] *C.G.*, Vol. VI, p. 57.
[10] *Ibid.*, p. 71.
[11] *Ibid.*, p. 58. Mérimée does not specify which college he dined in. But the only don whose name he mentions is a Mr Lake (*C.G.*, Vol. VI, p. 68), who can be identified as the Rev. William Charles Lake, Fellow and Senior Tutor of Balliol (cf. *Oxford University Calendar* for 1850). So it is probably not a calumny to suppose that Balliol was the guilty institution.

Another official visit in the summer of 1851, to see the Great Exhibition in the company of Léon de Laborde, was only marginally more palatable. Despite his adoption of English clothes and an anglicised manner, Mérimée never felt drawn to England as he did to Spain: there was an absence of wildness in the English landscape and character which he found boring.

But this did not stop him having many close English friends. Among those whom he began to see more regularly at this time were Lord and Lady Ashburton whose house was a celebrated meeting-place for politicians and men of letters, and Monckton Milnes (later Lord Houghton), M.P., poet, philanthropist, traveller and giver of lavish dinners – it was he who in 1848 had with accidental tactlessness invited Mérimée and George Sand to the same lunch. He also made the acquaintance of the political economist Nassau William Senior,[12] whose insatiable appetite for conversation and copious diaries provide a valuable picture of French life in the 1850s and 1860s. From about 1848 onwards, Mérimée and the Seniors saw a good deal of each other in Paris. But as always happened, for every new friend he made, there was someone else who was irretrievably alienated by his aggressive bluntness or his aloof indifference. The impression he made on Thomas Carlyle was violently unfavourable. They had met first in London, with little mutual sympathy; the second explosive encounter came in Paris in September 1851. They were both the guests at dinner of the Ashburtons, and though Carlyle had to admit that Mérimée was 'linguistically and otherwise of worth', he condemned him as 'a hard, logical, smooth but utterly barren man'.[13] Two days later, after a dinner given by Lady Sandwich, the ill-feeling came to a head. No doubt with the intention of provoking the irascible Scot, particularly tetchy

[12] One of the very few errors in Dr Parturier's remarkable edition of Mérimée's correspondence is the statement (*C.G.*, Vol. VII, p. 232, n. 2) that Senior first mentions Mérimée in 1854. In reality they had met several years before. In his *Journals kept in France and Italy from 1848 to 1852*, ed. M. C. M. Simpson, London, King, 1871, Senior mentions hearing Mérimée's speech welcoming Ampère to the Academy on 17 May 1848 (Vol. I, p. 101). The first meetings he records took place in May 1851. On the 12th, Mérimée was one of those who drank tea with the Seniors (Vol. II, p. 185), and on the 20th, he was one of their guests at a breakfast party (*ibid.*, p. 207).

[13] *Last Words of Thomas Carlyle*, London, Longmans, Green, 1892, pp. 171–2.

at the time because he was suffering from insomnia, Mérimée set about a systematic denigration of German literature – Jean-Paul was 'a hollow fool of the first magnitude', Goethe 'an inferior French apprentice', 'a paltry kind of Scribe *manqué*'.[14] Carlyle, unable to contain his rage at these sallies, rammed a cigar into his mouth and fumed out into the street, muttering: 'you impertinent blasphemous blockhead!'[15] Even when he had had time to cool down in Chelsea, his verdict on Mérimée was categorical: 'wooden pedant, not without conciseness, pertinency, and a certain sarcastic insight – on the whole, no mortal of the slightest interest or value to me'.[16]

In the course of 1850, Mérimée had one unusual diversion: the production of *Le Carrosse du Saint-Sacrement*. As early as 1827 *L'Amour africain* had been included in a composite entertainment at the Théâtre des Nouveautés[17] – but this was the first time Mérimée himself had consented to have anything to do with a production. In 1848, Augustine Brohan, one of a pair of famous actress sisters, had approached Mérimée for permission to act the part of the heroine, La Périchole, but though flattered, he had refused to sanction the production. The satire in the play, he said, was unlikely to succeed now, and in any case he thought it was a bad work which he was incapable of adapting. 'I am not in the least used to the stage, and I feel particularly unsuited to writing for the theatre.'[18]

However, in 1849 Théophile Gautier suggested in an article that it should be put on at the Comédie française, and in the end, Mérimée, who had a weakness for Augustine Brohan, agreed to allow Arsène

[14] The printed text says 'scribe *manqué*', which makes poor sense. Clearly, the reference is to the popular dramatist Eugène Scribe.

[15] *Last Words of Thomas Carlyle*, pp. 181–2.

[16] J. A. Froude, *Thomas Carlyle. A History of his Life in London*, London, Longmans, Green, 1884, Vol. II, p. 84. Another famous English author who met and disliked Mérimée at about the same time was Thackeray. On 2 July 1855, he was visiting Lord and Lady Ashburton: 'Mérimée came in – it's very odd, admiring his writing as I do, what an antipathy I have to him' (*Letters of Anne Thackeray Ritchie with 42 additional Letters from her Father William Makepeace Thackeray*, ed. Hester Ritchie, London, Murray, 1924, p. 69).

[17] Emile Bouvier, 'Les Débuts de Mérimée au théâtre (juillet 1827)', *Mélanges Lanson*, Paris, Hachette, 1922.

[18] *C.G.*, Vol. V, p. 393.

Houssaye, the director, to produce it. Typically, Mérimée affected to be unconcerned about the outcome and declined to give the reading to the Committee which was customary with new plays, but began to grow secretly excited about the prospect of being a famous dramatist. He came to one or two rehearsals and seemed vaguely pleased with the way things were going, while in reality understanding little of what was happening. Houssaye on the other hand was worried lest it should fail and wanted Mérimée to withdraw it. 'But Mérimée was like a child playing with a kite for the first time and already imagining it in the clouds; there was no turning back.'[19] On the first night, Mérimée arrived late, and hearing booing as he slipped into his box, inquired innocently what unfortunate work was being so thoroughly scorned – only to be told that it was Le Carrosse. At this, he tactfully joined in the booing himself.[20]

But Mérimée was not as indifferent to criticism as he liked to pretend. He used to claim that he had learnt from Stendhal that it was always wrong to be annoyed by adverse notices of one's works, a precept he once stated in these terms:

> My principles are that a man of letters should never get angry, whatever is said about him, provided he is not called either a coward or a thief. If someone calls you a bugger, then you must take counsel and decide in what sense it's meant.[21]

He was inordinately sensitive to the opinion of others, and usually contrived to be away from Paris when one of his major works was published, so that his friends should not see how he reacted to its reception. So one can be sure that the dismal failure of Le Carrosse was an acute disappointment. Indeed, Houssaye affirmed that Mérimée never forgave him for having allowed the play to be staged.[22]

Another blow was the accidental death through drowning in August 1851 of Alexis de Valon, Cécile Delessert's husband. Mérimée was as distressed by his death as if it had been his own son-in-law. He felt under an obligation to commemorate him by an obituary article in

[19] Arsène Houssaye, Les Confessions, Paris, Dentu, 1885, Vol. III, pp. 86–7.
[20] This at least is Houssaye's story. But, as Dr Parturier has pointed out, there is a Mérimée letter from which one may infer that the author was not present at the first night (C.G., Vol. VI, pp. 24–5).
[21] C.G., Vol. VI, p. 469.   [22] Les Confessions, Vol. III, p. 87.

the *Revue des Deux Mondes*,[23] but, not for the first time, found that his personal grief was too deep for public expression and so produced something stiff and impersonal. To Léon de Laborde he confessed his impotence to say what he felt:

> I cannot tell you how much I suffered writing those two pages [. . .] I did not say half of what there was to be said, but I was thinking on the one hand of his family and on the other of the public, and I arrived at a compromise with which I am anything but pleased.[24]

At least their common sorrow brought him momentarily closer to Valentine. Rémusat was less in evidence, and though Mérimée cannot have felt very confident of Valentine's loyalty, he was not at that time as painfully aware of her disaffection as he had been.

In fact, Mérimée had inadvertently prepared the way for their final break-up. His avuncular interest in the career of Valentine's son Édouard had led him to arrange in 1850 for the young man to visit the Dead Sea on an archaeological expedition with Félicien de Saulcy, with much waggish advice about the sexual customs of the East. During this voyage, Saulcy's party had met two other French travellers, Gustave Flaubert and his friend Maxime du Camp.[25] Both were then unknown young writers, but Du Camp, an ambitious, intelligent socialite not overburdened with moral scruples, had cultivated his acquaintance with Édouard Delessert in the hope that this might give him a footing in Valentine's influential *salon*. Du Camp succeeded and became a frequent visitor to Passy. When Alexis de Valon was drowned, he entertained high hopes of marrying the attractive young widow, but soon found that she preferred another suitor, whom she married in December 1852. Once it was clear that the way to the daughter's heart was barred, he turned his attention to the mother and was courting her pressingly in the latter part of 1852. Valentine, now in her forties and dissatisfied with both Mérimée and Rémusat, saw in Du

[23] 'Alexis de Valon', *Revue des Deux Mondes*, 1er septembre 1851; reproduced in *Portraits historiques et littéraires*.

[24] *C.G.*, Vol. VI, p. 241.

[25] On the relations between Du Camp and Valentine Delessert, see M. Parturier's edition of Mérimée's *Lettres aux Delessert*; M. Parturier, 'Autour de Mérimée. *Les Forces perdues* et *L'Éducation sentimentale*', *Bulletin du Bibliophile*, 1931; Dr André Finot, *Maxime du Camp*, Paris, 1949.

Camp a highly eligible replacement, and by the end of 1852 had become his mistress. The whole affair was conducted with the utmost discretion, and while Mérimée certainly had a fairly clear idea of the relations between Rémusat and Valentine, he equally certainly never suspected that Du Camp was anything more than a casual friend. It is true that until Valentine was sure of Du Camp, she took good care to keep Mérimée in thraldom, on the principle that even an old lover is better than none at all; only in 1853 did she once more allow him to see how little he meant to her. In the meantime, things went on between between them much as usual: with small enthusiasm on Valentine's part and suppressed anxiety on Mérimée's. It was one more subject for unease in a very uncertain period of his life.

Another matter, in which he eventually became far more inextricably enmeshed than he would have wished, began in a relatively small way. Among Mérimée's acquaintances in the world of learning in the 1840s was one Guillaume Libri-Carucci, a mathematician of remarkable brilliance, Italian by origin, whose liberal opinions had caused his exile from Italy in 1830 and whose talents had won him such acclaim in France that by 1840 he had a chair at the Sorbonne and by 1843 was a professor at the Collège de France. Mérimée had corresponded with him about bibliophily and they had been drawn together by a common anticlericalism. But Libri, for all his outstanding gifts, was a man of very dubious character. In 1816, his father had been convicted of forgery, in 1831 he himself had been suspected of theft and only cleared by the energetic intervention of Hortense Allart de Méritens, his mistress and subsequently Chateaubriand's, and in the 1840s it was noticed with alarm that his visits to famous libraries in France tended to coincide with the disappearance of precious books and manuscripts. A confidential investigation was started, and the so-called Boucly report, made public just after the February Revolution in 1848, formally accused him of numerous thefts. But by this time, Libri had taken refuge in London, carrying with him a whole cargo of rare books. He strenuously denied his guilt, began publishing a series of violent pamphlets charging his accusers with ignorance, prejudice and bad faith, and claiming that the forces of corruption arrayed against him were so powerful that it would be folly for him to return to Paris to stand trial.

From the outset, Mérimée was convinced of Libri's innocence, as were many other eminent Frenchmen including Sainte-Beuve and the bibliophile Paul Lacroix. There is nothing surprising in this. The least one can say about Libri is that he was possessed of exceptional intellectual qualities, and that, if he was a rogue, he was one of the most plausible rogues ever. Moreover, Mérimée shared many of his opinions: like Libri, he had no love for the École des Chartes, the official institute of palaeography, and he too knew what it was to be falsely accused of the theft of a manuscript. Always the most staunch of friends, Mérimée was bound to join Libri's active defenders. At first, his part was confined to assisting in the distribution of propaganda in France and advising the exile on the conduct of his affairs. But when he was in England in 1850, his zeal for Libri's cause was given a new impetus. This was partly due to a meeting with him but even more to the fact that, while Mérimée was in London, Libri married Mélanie Double, whose hand Mérimée had vainly sought in the 1820s. Since then she had been married to a famous lawyer, Athénodore Collin; on his death in 1849, she resolved to throw in her lot with Libri, who had long been a friend of her family. Mérimée now flung himself into the struggle with reckless zeal. He appealed to Baroche, vice-president of the Council of State; he wrote anonymous articles in the press; he collected the documents Libri needed to justify himself; he organised the printing of Libri's numerous diatribes. So great was his eagerness to help that in October 1850, a few months after Libri had been sentenced in absence to ten years' imprisonment, he gave him this assurance:

> although I am pretty busy, *I shall do all that is required, and if necessary I shall jettison everything else.* I am too anxious to see you out of this awful situation to do anything other than offer you every help I can. As for the matter of money, let us say no more about it.[26]

For some time he remained a close and devoted collaborator. Then in 1852 he resolved to throw the whole weight of his reputation openly into the conflict on Libri's side. This was no sudden impulse, as he himself liked to maintain, but the culmination of a carefully planned strategy. So, with the connivance of Buloz, another of Libri's supporters, he wrote a long, detailed and extremely cutting refutation of the case against Libri, which appeared in Buloz's journal, the *Revue*

---

[26] Giuliana Colajanni, 'Mérimée e "L'Affaire Libri" ', *Rivista di letterature moderne e comparate*, 1968, settembre, Vol. 21, No. 3.

des Deux Mondes, in April 1852. The tone of the article is one of vitriolic sarcasm, as one can judge from the climax of his attack on the lawyer who drew up the charges:

> to prove that the accused man's books are identical with the volumes lost, he takes no account of format, of titles, or of dates; he does not even know if the books have been lost, since he does not bother to check the simplest matters; he puts his own construction on phrases in a correspondence in Italian, and he is incapable of quoting three words of Italian without getting them hopelessly wrong; he accepts the wildest charges against the accused and does not mention the evidence in his favour; he is ignorant of facts known to everyone; he neglects to open books which are accessible to any specialist. What is there that he does not neglect to do? He neglects to re-read his own text, and often refutes himself when he thinks he is adducing some new proof of guilt.[27]

It never occurred to him that, being an Officer of the Legion of Honour (since January 1852), a member of the French Academy, a member of the Academy of Inscriptions, Inspector-General of Historic Monuments, he was not above the law. So when rumblings of grave official displeasure were heard, he reacted with alarm. The experts whose report he had criticised so scathingly counter-attacked in the *Revue des Deux Mondes*,[28] and Mérimée was obliged to produce a reply, in which he back-pedalled furiously, while still maintaining that Libri was the victim of a miscarriage of justice.[29] He also wrote a letter to Baroche, in which he humbly begged forgiveness:

> I very much regret, Sir, that you should have found my little pamphlet too hot-tempered, but I trust that someone of your generous character will be good enough to pardon any involuntary excess in the impulsive actions which I may have committed when I saw so many imputations contrary to the truth piled on the head of a former colleague, abandoned by everyone, just because in times gone by he was bold enough to speak ill of M. Arago, the École des Chartes and the Jesuits.[30]

But it was all too late. In May 1852, Mérimée was sentenced to a fortnight's imprisonment, with a fine of 1,000 francs, for having insulted the officers of the court, and Buloz was fined for publishing the offending article.

[27] 'Le Procès de M. Libri', *Revue des Deux Mondes*, 15 avril 1852.
[28] *Revue des Deux Mondes*, 1er mai 1852.
[29] *Ibid.*   [30] *C.G.*, Vol. VI, p. 318.

I

Mérimée had been extremely nervous at the thought of a public appearance in such embarrassing circumstances. Once the brief trial was over, he accepted his punishment philosophically: 'for my part, I was expecting the worst, and the only thing I regret is that my friends took advantage of the state of despondency I was in to make me take steps to disarm the authorities'.[31] He offered to pay Buloz's fine,[32] and in turn received an offer from Libri to pay his;[33] in the end each paid his own. He also submitted his resignation as Inspector-General; this was refused.[34] So, having declined to countenance the idea of an appeal, he settled down to prepare for his enforced stay at the prison of the medieval Conciergerie.[35] As luck would have it, Valentine's brother-in-law Édouard Bocher had also just received a light sentence for distributing Orleanist leaflets, and, with the amiable co-operation of the officers of the law, the two gentlemen arranged to purge their crimes together in July, when business was slack and it was uncomfortably hot outside. Mérimée went into prison on 6 July, equipped with a large supply of books and papers, two cushions, and a Persian carpet, and was given a commodious cell with a view over the exercise-yard; Bocher joined him there on the 10th. By now, Mérimée had decided to make it all into a joke, penned amusing descriptions of prison life, and encouraged his numerous friends to visit him there – which, since he was treated more as an honoured guest than as a prisoner, they were allowed to do in such numbers that he was unable to get on with his writing. But he was astute enough to realise that most of them came out of curiosity: 'there are lots of people who bring you sweets. It's in order to see what sort of face you are putting on the situation.'[36]

Though Mérimée's stay in prison in some ways resembled a holiday in unusual surroundings, and though his reputation was untarnished by it, the episode left a bitter taste in his mouth. His defence of Libri was less of a spontaneous impulse than he claimed, but it was nevertheless

[31] *C.G.*, Vol. VI, p. 347. [32] *Ibid.*, p. 340.

[33] Cf. M.-L. Pailleron, *François Buloz et ses amis. La Vie littéraire sous Louis-Philippe*, p. 287.

[34] *C.G.*, Vol. VI, p. 345.

[35] Mérimée was amused that, as Inspector-General of Historic Monuments, he should be incarcerated in a medieval monument.

[36] F. Bac, *Mérimée inconnu*, p. 59.

an unselfish action, for which he had been publicly condemned and punished. This convinced him more than ever that it was best to be cautious:

I embarked on a chivalrous task on impulse, and you know that that is something one should never do. I regret it sometimes [. . .] There are more kicks than ha'pence if you do a thing like that, but sometimes you get so revolted by injustice that you do silly things.[37]

His faith in Libri's innocence remained unshaken for many years; for the ignorance and touchiness of judges he had only contempt.

The impact of the case was greatly increased by the fact that, in the middle of the furore which it caused, his mother was taken ill, and a week later, on 30 April, died. This was a terrible blow to him. He had been extremely close to his mother, whose caustic and unorthodox intelligence so much resembled his own, and having never when in Paris lived anywhere other than with her, found her sudden absence a yawning gap in his life. 'I lived for so long on my mother's devotion that I feel all the time like a child on his first day at school',[38] he confessed to one friend. He regretted that he had not done enough to show his affection for her:

all her life she never thought of herself. I was used to relying on her for everything, and today I reproach myself very bitterly for having only made her share in my griefs. I wish I could begin my life with her over again.[39]

A feeling of utter solitude came over him as he contemplated what his life now was: there seemed no longer to be any centre to his existence. It occurred to him that he could now go to Spain to see Mme de Montijo whenever he liked:

but there is something extremely sad about the idea that one is no longer attached to anything, and that one is completely free. So long as my mother was alive, I had duties and prior commitments. Now the world belongs to me as it did to the Wandering Jew, and all my enthusiasm and activity have gone.[40]

Perhaps it was in order to shake himself out of his gloom and get away from memories which had become painful that he decided to

[37] C.G., Vol. VI, p. 295.   [38] Ibid., p. 384.
[39] Ibid., p. 327.   [40] Ibid., p. 342.

move out of the flat in the rue Jacob where he and his mother had
lived since 1847. His cousins the Fresnels owned a building in the rue
de Lille in which there was a vacant apartment, so he moved in there
towards the end of August. It was a spacious flat, on the second floor.
Édouard Grenier, a young man of letters who lived on the third floor,
occasionally visited him there:

> he was usually to be found reading, with a cigarette between his lips, or
> smoking a long cherry-wood pipe, Turkish babouches on his feet, and
> draped in a magnificent Japanese or Chinese dressing gown with a large
> floral pattern. One first went through the dining room, which was very
> simple, though decorated with remarkable pictures, almost all Spanish,
> then one entered a large drawing-room which had been turned into a
> study; that was where Mérimée generally sat, as I have just described him.
> The walls of this very high room were covered to the ceiling with old oak
> bookshelves, filled with the rarest books; few ornaments, if any, apart
> from some mementoes of his travels, and two superb Japanese flower vases
> on the mantelpiece; enormous upholstered armchairs, on which no wood
> was visible, a divan at the far end in a sort of alcove, scattered everywhere
> a mass of embroidered cushions; in the middle, a rosewood desk in Louis
> XV style decorated with fine brasses and covered with brochures and a
> few paperweights, nearly all of which were exquisite *objets d'art* or curio-
> sities, among them an admirable ancient bronze representing a young faun
> half turning round to play with his tail.[41]

It was the flat of a wealthy and much-travelled man, a lover of comfort
and of beauty, more homely than imposing, but in which everything
contributed to an atmosphere of quiet luxury and of relaxed study,
and it was to be Mérimée's home for the rest of his life.

The *coup d'état* by which Louis-Napoleon seized power on 2 December 1851 did not at first much affect Mérimée. He knew a number of
Louis-Napoleon's ministers, notably his half-brother the Duc de
Morny, whose guardian had at one time been Gabriel Delessert, and
for whose supple intelligence he felt some respect. Indeed, on 28
November, Mérimée had dined in Morny's company. But Mérimée
was in no sense an active Bonapartist and was patently not in the closely
guarded secret of the Prince-President's intentions. Nor was he sufficiently identified with Louis-Napoleon's cause for it to be in the least
likely that there is any truth in Victor Hugo's story of meeting him

[41] Édouard Grenier, *Souvenirs littéraires*, Paris, Lemerre, 1894, pp. 128-9.

on 4 December and refusing to shake hands with him.[42] It is true that he was pleased when it was clear that Louis-Napoleon had won the day, but that was because he saw his victory as a defeat for the reds: 'they were given a good hiding, which can count as revenge for 1848. Let us hope they remember it.'[43] In view of his chronic fear of a popular revolution, such an attitude was entirely predictable, as was his lack of sympathy for the agitators and recalcitrants who were exiled. According to him, Hugo had had great difficulty in becoming a martyr, the police inspector having declared that he would only arrest serious people.[44]

There was, inevitably, some cooling-off in relations with those of his Orleanist friends who were opposed to Louis-Napoleon, among them Thiers, Ludovic Vitet and even the Delesserts, but the break with Hugo merely confirmed a mutual distaste which had been apparent for years. Apart from Morny, there was only one member of the Bonaparte family with whom Mérimée was at all friendly at this time; that was Princess Mathilde, Louis-Napoleon's intelligent, unorthodox, outspoken and artistic cousin who constituted the main if not the only link between the imperial household and the world of literature and painting. Her lover the sculptor Comte de Nieuwerkerke was Director-General of National Museums and consequently a colleague of Mérimée, but the latter had a low opinion of him: 'his genius came roaring up like a locomotive. But now all one can see is the smoke.'[45] He professed to be astonished that Princess Mathilde had such good taste in pictures and such bad taste in lovers. Being a friend of Princess Mathilde was not in any case an automatic passport to favour at court, since Mathilde had never quite forgiven Louis-Napoleon for not wishing to marry her and allowing her instead to drift into a disastrous match with Anatole Demidoff, a brutal Russian nobleman.

But circumstances soon changed dramatically. When Mme de

[42] Victor Hugo, *Histoire d'un crime*, Paris, Hetzel-Quantin, s.d., Vol. II, p. 41: 'at one moment I was in the street. I had just left that brave and honest man; I saw coming towards me someone who was the exact opposite, M. Mérimée. "Hello", said M. Mérimée, "I was looking for you." I replied: "I hope you won't find me." He held out his hand to me; I turned my back on him. I have never seen him again. I believe he is dead.'

[43] *C.G.*, Vol. VI, p. 266.   [44] *Ibid.*, p. 271.

[45] F. Bac, *Mérimée inconnu*, p. 60.

Montijo had visited Paris in 1849, she and Eugenia had been introduced to the Prince-President. Eugenia, recently disappointed in love, always romantically inclined, and still full of the adulation of Napoleon she had learned from 'Monsieur Beyle', wanted to offer him all her fortune, but was with difficulty restrained. Then, in 1852, when she and her mother returned to Paris, they began to receive regular invitations to galas given by Louis-Napoleon, and it soon became obvious that, impressionable as he was with women, he had fallen deeply in love with her. There can be little doubt that mother and daughter consulted Mérimée in this situation; there can be little doubt too that he was opposed to the idea of a possible marriage, though the letters he must have written to Mme de Montijo at that time were later destroyed by the Empress.[46] That in itself strongly suggests that they were unfavourable to Louis-Napoleon as a prospective husband, and one can easily understand why. Mérimée was far from convinced of the long-term stability of the régime; he was by nature disposed to avoid tempting fate; and like everyone else, he knew that Louis-Napoleon was a notorious womaniser, whose current mistress Miss Howard was installed in quasi-royal pomp at Saint-Cloud. What chance of happiness would there be for the little girl he had known and loved for over twenty years if she joined her life to that of such a man?

At a house-party in Compiègne in December 1852, only a few days after he had been proclaimed Emperor, Louis-Napoleon secretly declared his love to Eugenia. His ministers were almost all aghast at the idea that he might make the Spanish girl his Empress, and did all they could to dissuade him. But his passions were tumultuous, and on 15 January 1853, he formally asked for her hand. By this stage, Mérimée was resigned to letting Eugenia have her way, and placed himself at her disposal for the diplomatic and social negotiations.[47] These were

[46] According to the Duke of Alba. But there is no reason to think that the numbers are anywhere near so large as those suggested by Ferdinand Bac (*Intimités du Second Empire*, Paris, Hachette, s.d., Vol. I, p. 54, n. 1), who maintains that there were originally 1,200, of which 800 were destroyed. Admittedly the *Correspondance générale* includes 431 letters to Mme de Montijo, which is quite close to the figure for surviving letters given by Bac. However, the sequence of letters makes it clear that no very substantial part of the correspondence can have been burnt.

[47] It has often been alleged that Mérimée drafted the letters Eugénie wrote at this time to Napoleon III, and it may well be true.

very rapidly completed, and, to a mixture of acclamation at the triumph of true love and groans at the neglect of dynastic prudence, they were married on 30 January 1853 in Notre-Dame, specially decorated for the occasion by Viollet-le-Duc. The only slightly discordant note was struck when it was made clear to Mme de Montijo that she would not be welcome to reside permanently in Paris with her daughter. She had the reputation of being an intriguer and in 1847 had had a brief period as *camerara mayor* to the Queen of Spain before being ousted. Napoleon III, as he now was, feared (in which he may have been right) that she hoped to become a power behind the throne, and with his predilection for the solitary exercise of authority, he would have none of that. So in March, she returned, hurt and disappointed, to Madrid, accompanied as far as Poitiers by the faithful Mérimée.

From the moment she became Empress, Eugénie (to give her the name under which the French knew her) was determined to find some high office for Mérimée which would bring him close to the Imperial house. There was talk of his becoming her private secretary, but that came to nothing; then the Emperor asked him to accept the post of Keeper of the Imperial Archives, but Mérimée declined. However, in June, Napoleon decided to make him a Senator. Mérimée's first reaction was astonishment, then dismay. Even though the Senate was more of a decorative than a functional body, with its members appointed for life by the Emperor himself, Mérimée had little taste for politics or public life, and besought Eugénie to get her husband to change his mind. But she had been so delighted by the proposal that she would hear nothing of a refusal.[48] She said that if Mérimée loved her, he had to accept; he replied that, if she had any affection for him, she would leave him alone. 'But you won't have anything to do', she insisted. 'But I have nothing to do anyway and I'm happy', he countered. 'But in any case you'll be hung when we are.'[49] In the end she produced the decisive argument: 'be our enemy or accept'.[50] At this Mérimée capitulated, and on 23 June his nomination was officially announced.

His own feelings were very mixed. Only a short time before, he had been telling Mme de Montijo how world-weary he was:

I am thinking very seriously of going off somewhere very far away, to leave my bones in some sun-drenched land, as old cats do who leave home

---

[48] *C.G.*, Vol. VII, p. 78.   [49] *Ibid.*, p. 74.   [50] *Ibid.*, p. 88.

when they feel ill. I've lost nearly all my friends, I'm perfectly useless to other people, and I'm bored. It's only out of old habit that I care for Paris, and Paris doesn't care for me. There's something very bitter about this feeling, yet I can tell that I'm getting hardened to it. The only trouble is that with the life I lead, I give myself fits of spleen and rage several times a week, which I might avoid if I went to live all alone in a forest.[51]

In this mood of discouragment, the evidence of Eugénie's attachment to him moved him profoundly: 'Since I have been living alone with a cat and a tortoise, I am happy to feel that someone loves me. That probably means that my end is drawing near.'[52] His acceptance of the position was thus very much a personal matter. In addition, Mérimée was of course secretly flattered by the magnitude of the honour: 'it would be a lie if I told you I was sorry about it; but I'm not pleased either [. . .] I've already seen so much of the seamy side of human nature that I neither needed nor wanted a front seat to see more.'[53] Mérimée never despised the outward marks of distinction, and though this one was more compromising than most in that it committed him irrevocably to an imperial régime in which he had no great confidence, it was nevertheless too imposing to be lightly cast away.

Then there was the question of his Inspector-Generalship. One reason for the failure of the earlier approaches was that they would have entailed abandoning the post. Being a Senator, however, was not incompatible; it would even be an advantage – 'I have more freedom and more authority to speak to people about the arts and about collapsing churches.'[54] The annual tours would have to be left to his deputy the architect Émile Boeswillwald, but Mérimée would continue to officiate in Paris; he insisted, however, that he would no longer accept any salary for his work. He was still an indispensable committee man in the world of art and architecture – in 1849 he boasted to Horace de Viel-Castel that he was on nine committees,[55] and the number was even higher[56] – so that he would have ample opportunity to influence policy-making on the things that were dear to his heart. For all these reasons (to say nothing of the considerable financial rewards which

[51] C.G., Vol. VII, p. 60.   [52] Ibid., p. 78.
[53] Ibid., p. 77.   [54] Ibid., p. 88.
[55] Horace de Viel-Castel, Mémoires, Vol. I, p. 70.
[56] Cf. C.G., Vol. V, p. 515, where Mérimée claims to sit on eleven committees.

probably did not sway him anyway), Mérimée's show of reluctance was more assumed than real.

Thus, within a few months, Mérimée had been pitchforked from prison into the Senate, which no doubt appealed to his sardonic humour. He had gone to prison unwillingly; he was not very much more enthusiastic about entering the Senate. But he knew that he could not refuse without causing grave offence to someone whom he loved and for whose happiness he was much concerned – and he was curious to see what this strange twist of fate would bring in the way of fresh interest to a life that was perceptibly losing its savour.

Chapter 15

Senator

Il y a des moments où les âmes les plus fortes et les plus.
habituées à cacher leurs sentiments les trahissent sous l'empire
d'une grande émotion.
'*Histoire de Jules César*, par Napoléon III',
in *Mémoires historiques*

As Mérimée was not sworn in as a Senator until March 1854, the
appointment did not immediately change his life. In fact, he affirmed:
'I'd like to establish that I'm still a teller of tales, and if I had one ready,
I'd publish it straightaway.'[1] Though no longer composing fiction, he
had been writing a lot in the last few years. Since 1850, he had been
immersed in the strange history of the Dmitri impostors, but had
decided to divide his work on it into two sections: a fictional recreation
of the first impostor's early years, then a historical account of his later
career. Constructed like *Le Jaquerie* as a series of dramatic scenes, *Les
Débuts d'un aventurier* (*The Beginnings of an Adventurer*) is an unsatisfactory work, loose in composition, unconvincing in local colour.
When Mérimée published it in the *Revue des Deux Mondes* in December
1852, it aroused little comment, save on its too blatant advertisement
for his *Episode de l'histoire de Russie*. *Les Faux Démétrius* (*Episode from
the History of Russia. The Dmitri Impostors*), which came out immediately afterwards. A more substantial work altogether, this was a
notable success, with translations into English and German in 1853,
a pirated Belgian version, and a second edition by 1854.

Mérimée had also been pursuing his Russian translations and critical
studies. Pushkin was still occupying him in 1852, with two renderings
of poems,[2] but his attention had also been drawn to Gogol, perhaps
by Buloz, who commissioned an article on him for the *Revue des Deux*

[1] *C.G.*, Vol. VII, p. 79.

[2] *Les Bohémiens* and *Le Hussard*, published in an edition of Mérimée's
Nouvelles in May 1852.

Mondes in November 1851. However, while Mérimée's affinities with
Pushkin had led to a sympathetic understanding of his writings, he
never came to terms with Gogol, even though he produced a complete
if inaccurate translation of *The Inspector-General* in 1853. In addition to
these Russophile activities there were the usual technical articles on
archaeological and architectural topics,[3] as well as a long review, in
Le Moniteur universel, of 'Le Salon de 1853', the annual painting exhibition. In this he expressed his displeasure with the growing school of
realism, a tendency which had offended him in Gogol (as it had years
before in Stendhal).

> Out of detestation of conventional nobility, people have plunged into the
> trivial; out of disgust with ideal beauty, they have deliberately sought
> ugliness. Oh, gentlemen, do not look for it; it is found all to easily without
> trying. Look rather for what is beautiful and do not lose heart, for it is
> only after long and patient effort that you may chance upon it.[4]

The more literature and art moved towards an unembellished rep-
resentation of a sordid reality, the more Mérimée took refuge in a
conservative canon of selection and omission.

A good deal of what Mérimée wrote at this time was second-hand
or superficial. The political uncertainties of the Second Republic, the
anxieties of the Libri case (some of his work on Dmitri was done in
prison), the death of his mother, above all the torment of Valentine's
ever more obvious estrangement – all these worries preyed on him,
interfering with the tough-minded concentration that had characterised
his earlier works, preventing him from finding that coherency of form
he valued so highly. His health too was preoccupying him. In September 1852, while in the South on his annual tour, he suffered severe
sunstroke. For the first time since his duel with Félix Lacoste, he was
convinced that his life was about to end:

> I thought it a bit of a bore to move on into a better world, but it struck me
> as even more of a bore to put up any resistance. I believe that it's through
> this animal resignation that one leaves this world, not because one is over-

---

[3] Details of these articles, which are more numerous than important, can
be found in Trahard and Josserand, *Bibliographie des œuvres de Prosper
Mérimée*, pp. 217-24.
[4] 'Le Salon de 1853', *Le Moniteur universel*, 16-17 mai 1853.

come by malady, but because one has grown indifferent to everything, and because one abandons one's defences.[5]

Intellectual work during this period was thus very much a distraction and its quality was correspondingly lower.

Even his nomination as Senator brought only fleeting relief. By July 1853 he had sunk back into depression: 'I'm bored and I rather hate myself',[6] 'I'm disillusioned and fed up with a lot of men, women and things',[7] 'I feel as if I were constantly on the balance of an electrical machine, and when I come out of total prostration, it is only to find my nerves on edge and to get furious with nature and myself. I've no heart for anything and I can't do a hand's turn.'[8] However, when he went to Spain to spend September and October with Mme de Montijo, his mood changed. Accompanied by his friend Louis de la Saussaye, otherwise known as 'La Sauvage', he lazed around in the sun at Carabanchel, eating grapes, surrounded by a bevy of attractive young ladies, and feeling like Apollo among the nine muses. Occasionally he would rouse himself to explore Madrid, sometimes to see churches, museums and libraries, but mostly in search of low life. At an establishment run by a Mme Violante, he found a girl called Maruja who was very much to his taste, and whom he was tempted to take back to Paris with him. But he preferred not to perturb his euphoria by thoughts of the future: 'I long ago gave up making plans, and I live from day to day in splendid sloth.'[9] Sometimes he would even contemplate getting married and settling in Spain for good – Mme de Montijo had no doubt insinuated into his mind the idea of a match with one of the dark-eyed beauties of Carabanchel. 'I am in love in several different ways at the moment. Sentimentally, and then I say to myself: *quid*, if I never went back to France?'[10] In all this idyll, there was something of the agonising sweetness of a moment of happiness bound to come to an end, and Mérimée kept on prolonging his stay so as not to break the charm. 'I am hanging on to this country because I have a foreboding that this is the last good year that remains for me.'[11] But the Senate, his job, his long-ingrained habits, even the tortures of his love for Valentine called him back to Paris, and he reluctantly set off home at the beginning of December.

[5] *C.G.*, Vol. VI, p. 432.   [6] *C.G.*, Vol. VII, p. 108.
[7] *Ibid.*, p. 123.   [8] *Ibid.*, p. 130.
[9] *Ibid.*, p. 203.   [10] *Ibid.*, p. 206.   [11] *Ibid.*

The flat in the rue de Lille had been redecorated in his absence, and there he took up his life where he had left it in the summer. Fortunately, there was still Eugénie's affection to console him, and the interest of becoming acquainted with the Emperor. He had already dined with them once before leaving for Spain, and had been happy to discover an atmosphere of relaxed informality at their table – they had even amused themselves by putting on false noses. 'As I came away, I reflected that I had just seen two people who were perfectly *natural*.'[12] Napoleon III had the gift of putting people at their ease, a quality which appealed to Mérimée, and the two men liked each other. But Napoleon, while he appreciated Mérimée's erudition and wit, had no intention of confiding state secrets to him, nor had Mérimée any desire to wield political power, so that their friendship remained a purely personal affair. There is perhaps a grain of truth in Hugo's malicious description of how Mérimée became a Senator:

> a literary ornament was needed for the Élysée Palace. A brigands' cavern is improved by something from an academy. M. Mérimée happened to be available. It was written in his destiny that he would sign himself: *the Empress's Jester*. Madame de Montijo presented him to Louis Bonaparte, who took him on and completed his court with this fawning man of talent.[13]

It is notable that in the first few years of the Second Empire Mérimée only offered three pieces of advice to his sovereigns: that Eugénie would be unwise to introduce bull-fighting in Paris, that her husband ought to buy a bullet-proof waistcoat, and that it would be very rash of him to lead his troops in the Crimea. His political influence was non-existent.

Physically Mérimée had not changed much in the last decade. At fifty, his hair was grey, but he was erect and vigorous, with a disconcerting stare and a bitter twist to his mouth. This is how Edmond Grenier, his neighbour, saw him:

> Mérimée was tall, thin and *svelte*; there was nothing remarkable about his clean-shaven face, except a vast forehead and two deep-set grey eyes, under bushy eyebrows already turning grey. This bony countenance, with its prominent cheekbones and rather large-ended nose, was anything but aristocratic; nevertheless, his dress, which was always immaculate, gave

---

[12] *Ibid.*, p. 91.   [13] *Histoire d'un crime*, Vol. II, p. 24.

him an air of distinction. He received people with the utmost courtesy, but somewhat coolly; one was faced by a perfect gentleman. There was in fact something slightly anglicised about him; he spoke slowly, in a monotone, almost hesitantly, without liveliness or emphasis; he rarely laughed, even when he was telling the most comical or spicy stories. A veneer of reserve and chilly distinction never left him, even among men and with close friends. The contrast of his demeanour with his speech, especially when he started on the most scabrous subjects, gave to what he said a singular piquancy.[14]

Neither the passage of time nor the accumulation of honours had made Mérimée any less vulnerable, but he had become more adept at hiding and doctoring his wounds.

Maxime du Camp, who had of course reasons of his own for detesting Mérimée, has left a portrait of him similar to Grenier's, but much more acidly etched:

> in society he bore himself well, though with some constraint and deliberation; he spoke little, as if he did not trust himself [. . .] He was of middle height and well-built; the upper part of his face was very handsome; the broad forehead and magnificent eyes showed intelligence and lofty aspirations; but the snout-like nose, the sensual mouth, the thickness of the jawbones betrayed the coarseness of appetites to which he had often succumbed.[15]

Du Camp, like Grenier, commented on Mérimée's habit of telling obscene stories, amid a wealth of disgusting detail, without a hint of a smile: 'he wallowed serenely in filth'.[16] This was perhaps partly a need to compensate for his failing sexual powers; but it was much more a way of baffling others, of jolting them out of their composure while preserving his own equanimity. Thus he revenged himself on society for the constrictions which it imposed on him.

His taste for obscenities was one which he indulged a good deal in his correspondence with Francisque-Michel, with whom he regularly exchanged letters in the early 1850s. Francisque-Michel, professor of foreign literature at the University of Bordeaux, was a prolific polygrapher, pouring out works on the gypsies, on medieval crafts, on silk, on slang, on the Basques, on Franco-Scottish relations, and on trade

[14] *Souvenirs littéraires*, pp. 129–30.
[15] *Souvenirs littéraires*, Paris, Hachette, 1882–3, Vol. II, pp. 327–8.
[16] *Ibid.*, p. 328.

in Bordeaux, to say nothing of numerous editions of medieval texts and translations from Shakespeare, Sterne, Goldsmith and Tennyson.[17] He was an ambitious intriguer, not above mischievous gossip about his friends behind their back (he even told someone that Mérimée was secretly married to Mme de Montijo),[18] and though Mérimée enjoyed his company, as he usually did that of hedonistic intellectuals, Francisque-Michel pestered him so much with queries for his endless publications that their friendship languished and eventually died. Much more durable were Mérimée's connections with Antonio Panizzi (later Sir Antony) of the British Museum.[19] Though their friendship did not fully blossom until later in the 1850s, Mérimée met him in London in 1850 to discuss the Libri affair since Panizzi, also an exiled Italian liberal, was another of Libri's supporters. They later corresponded about matters of erudition, and in the course of time became inseparable.

But when one reads the letters of these years, it is obvious that underlying all the forced gaiety, all the political gossip, all the learned discussions, all the ribald jokes, there is one constant preoccupation: Valentine's coldness. In May 1853 he confessed to Mme de Montijo, always the person in whom he most readily confided: 'I have endured every possible misfortune – I mean of the heart, for my life is running with the greatest smoothness, on the *material* side.'[20] After the momentary relief of his Spanish interlude, he was soon back at his gloomy brooding, and even had a transient intuition of the truth when he told Francisque-Michel:

> I am very sad and I'm suffering from spleen. I wish I had got married ten years ago so that I should be quite used to being a cuckold. The fact is that

---

[17] On Francisque-Michel, see P. Trahard's introduction to Mérimée's *Lettres à Francisque-Michel 1848–1870*.

[18] *C.G.*, Vol. VII, p. 87, n. 3. Inevitably, there was much gossip about Mérimée's relations with the Empress's mother. The malicious Du Camp echoes some of this slander when he says there were those who alleged that Mérimée was Eugénie's father: 'he would modestly lower his eyes, and, without conviction, deny the paternity that was attributed to him; he should have repudiated it fairly and squarely, for it cannot be his responsibility' (*Souvenirs d'un demi-siècle*, Paris, Hachette, 1949, Vol. I, p. 149).

[19] See Edward Miller, *Prince of Librarians. The Life and Times of Antonio Panizzi of the British Museum*, London, Deutsch, 1967.

[20] *C.G.*, Vol. VII, p. 60.

I'm dreadfully bored and that I can't find anything to interest me. *Man delights me not nor woman neither,* except for a girl called Maruja whom I was silly enough to leave in Madrid.[21]

But his natural reticence got the better of him when the inquisitive professor wanted to know what was the matter with him:

you ask me why I am sad and you talk to me about wealth and greatness. I thought those words were only used in comic opera style, and I shall reply in the same style that they are both chimeras. If I am sad, it's not for nothing. I have very good reasons, but it would give you no pleasure to hear them, and it would make me wince to write them down.[22]

Gradually he was forced against his will to recognise that Valentine no longer loved him.

My state of mind is still below zero. If a sorcerer had taken it into his head ten years ago to tell me that in 1854 I would be as free as air and that I would think myself very unhappy I would have taken him for a great fool. But I think I'm the biggest fool in the whole business, since I placed all my happiness in finding a white crow, far too rare a bird.[23]

Valentine, totally immersed in her affair with Du Camp, held back from an open break with Mérimée, hoping by cold-shouldering him to compel him to take the initiative; she wanted the odium of a final separation to fall on him. However, Mérimée found it impossible to believe that she wished this separation, and went on desperately trying to win his way back into her good graces. By July 1854, at his wit's end, he resolved to force a showdown, but was unable to face the thought of a direct confrontation and used the excuse of a letter on some trivial subject. The impeccable formality of the note does little to hide his anguish:

I believe I have noticed that for some time you have been treating me with great coldness, to say the least. I am sure I have done nothing to deserve it. On the contrary, *I think* that for a year I have done all I can to avoid anything which might displease you. If I have been wrong, Madam, I should be infinitely grateful if you would tell me.[24]

But still Valentine temporised evasively, and Mérimée, half-reassured, ignored all the hints that he would do well to withdraw.

Then, at the end of 1854, perhaps pushed by Du Camp, she at last

[21] *C.G.*, Vol. VII, p. 257.
[22] *Ibid.*, p. 290.
[23] *Ibid.*, p. 312.   [24] *Ibid.*, p. 318.

decided to take the decisive step herself. So she sent back to him the letters he had written to her and the presents he had given her, on the pretext that, if she died, she would not want her heirs to find anything compromising. Among the trinkets was an Etruscan ring that Mérimée had lost and found again so often, as if by a miracle, that he had come to the superstitious belief that his fate was attached to it, and had given it to Valentine as his most treasured possession.[25] The shock of opening this packet dazed Mérimée.[26] He realised the speciousness of the excuse Valentine proffered, as he was meant to, and felt himself obliged to return to her all her letters and presents.[27] But for all his cynical perspicacity, he was unable to divine the reason for her gesture, which left him as bewildered as he was wounded.

> I cudgel my brains to try to understand what lies behind her conduct. Sometimes I feel she hates me, but I cannot guess why. There are no priests mixed up in it. Although in the last few years I have had to steel myself to a lot from that direction, I cannot tell you how much this has pained me. There is nothing sadder than finding oneself more and more alone as the years go by and one feels an ever greater need for confidence and friendship![28]

Inexplicably the idea that he had a rival never crossed his mind.

In the ruins of his love, even the past seemed to have been annulled.

> The outcome of a liaison which lasted more than twenty years drives me to despair, and I have come to the point where the past saddens me and where I think all the happiness I have had was false. Even my memories have gone.[29]

Mme de Montijo was as puzzled by Valentine's desertion as Mérimée; Valentine herself took good care to avoid finding herself alone with him, and in any case he was so frightened of a scene that he did not dare to try too hard to elicit an explanation. Even his customary distraction through hard work failed him, since it had always been with Valentine in mind that he had written before. 'Up to now I have never done anything for myself, and I no longer have anyone to work for. That is what puts so many black clouds on my horizon.'[30] '... In the days when I wrote, I had an aim. Now I haven't any longer. If I wrote, it

[25] *C.G.*, Vol. XVI, p. 357.   [26] *C.G.*, Vol. VII, p. 412.
[27] *Ibid.*   [28] *Ibid.*
[29] *Ibid.*, p. 418.   [30] *Ibid.*, p. 426.

would be for me, and I should bore myself even more than I do at present.'[31] So he worked only at mechanical tasks like finishing off the annotations to *Les Aventures du Baron de Faeneste* (*The Adventures of Baron de Faeneste*) by d'Aubigné, one of his favourite sixteenth-century authors.[32] This only half engaged his attention, and in the evenings, he would sit around hopelessly, trying to read and moping about his fate.

There were few people to whom Mérimée could talk openly. Only Mme de Montijo was fully in the secret, but he was so much in need of sympathy that to various other female correspondents he told part of the story, suppressing names and details. With Mrs Senior, for instance, the wife of the Oxford economist, he used the transparent device of pretending that it had all happened to someone else.

> Imagine two people who have been very really in love for a long time, for such a long time that nobody ever thinks about it any more. One fine day the woman takes it into her head that what had for ten years made her happiness and that of another person is wrong. 'Let us separate. I still love you, but I don't want to see you again.' I do not know, madam, if you realise all that a man can suffer when something to which he has entrusted all the happiness of his life is thus suddenly removed from him. The story I've told you is true: it happened to one of my friends.[33]

With men on the other hand, he was reticent, doubtless for fear of ridicule; what he needed was compassionate understanding. But though he received good advice from Mme de Montijo and from Mme Xifre, one of her Spanish friends, nothing did any good.

> The dream is over. It is rather a rude awakening. All I have to console myself is the thought that I have done nothing to deserve being treated in that way. The more I think about it, the less I understand it [. . .] I am experienced enough to know that one can get over anything, but I wish the time had come when I shall be able to think about it all with no more grief than one feels at a novel with a sad ending.[34]

For months Mérimée remained in a state of prostration. True, there were moments when he considered desperate measures to alleviate his

---

[31] *C.G.*, Vol. VII, p. 511.
[32] The book was published in January 1855.
[33] *C.G.*, Vol. VII, p. 441.   [34] *Ibid.*, p. 436.

sufferings. One unexpected idea which recurred again and again was the adoption of a little girl. Mostly he talked about it in a jocular tone:

> I'm too old to get married, but I should like to find a little girl already grown to bring up. I've often thought of buying a child from a gypsy woman, because, if my educational system went wrong, I probably wouldn't have made the little creature I adopted any more unhappy. What do you think? And how can one get hold of a little girl?[35]

But sometimes an involuntary earnestness in his style showed how anguished was his longing for love and companionship:

> I am right in the dumps and horribly bored. Society makes me fed up to the teeth and I don't know what I am going to do. I haven't a friend in the world, I think. I have lost all those I loved, because they have died or changed. If I could, I would adopt a little girl; but this world and especially this country are so uncertain that I dare not allow myself such a luxury.[36]

Even as late as 1857 he was still turning the possibility over in his mind. Marriage, he told Mme de Montijo, was out of the question:

> I should prefer, if I were sure of leaving anything when I die, to have a little girl whom I should bring up to the best of my ability. But it is a very chancy lottery. The best thing, I think, is to get used to living like a tree and resign oneself.[37]

At the bottom of his heart, Mérimée knew that, for all his love of children, he would never take the risks involved in adopting a girl. The nearest he came to it was developing an avuncular interest in the Lagrenés' younger daughter Olga, a pretty and delicate girl in her early twenties, who was often ill and with whom he started a gravely tender correspondence. Maybe he even entertained romantic notions of marrying her, but he always held back from the revealing word. To allow himself to hope for such unlikely happiness would have been folly, and he knew it all too well.

Another distraction, almost equally improbable, was a new friendship with Mme de la Rochejaquelein, an elderly and devout lady of monarchist opinions. He had first met her at a ball early in 1854, when, to his great surprise, she had urged him to join the Church.[38] At first, Mérimée fobbed her off with flippancy. When she tried to persuade

[35] *Ibid.*, p. 442.   [36] *Ibid.*, p. 455.
[37] *C.G.*, Vol. VIII, p. 376.   [38] *C.G.*, Vol. VII, pp. 293-4.

him to be christened, he replied politely: 'very well, madam, I agree, but on one condition: you must be my godmother, I'll be dressed all in white, and you'll carry me in your arms'.[39] But Mme de la Roche-jaquelein was not discouraged, and when she sent him a medallion of the Virgin Mary, accompanied by a prayer, instead of being scornful at her naïveté he was touched by her solicitude.[40] At most other times, he would no doubt have brushed her off; now, in his miserable lone-liness, he found himself drawn into a long correspondence of unusual solemnity. In response to her earnest attempts at conversion, he for-sook his habitual aggressive anticlericalism, and consented to examine his attitude to Christianity without frivolity or prejudice. But he frankly admitted that he regarded his conversion as a cause lost in advance:

> I have the misfortune to be a sceptic, but it's not my fault. I have tried to believe, but I have no faith. Though I'm not insensitive to poetry, I've never been able to write verse. I am too much of *a matter of fact man*'. It's not a question of the way I was brought up, but the way I'm made.[41]

Mérimée assured her that belief in any supernatural agency was utterly impossible for him:

> you cannot imagine, madam, since you were born with the mind of a poet, the difficulty I have in *believing*, and the difference there is between the things I enjoy postulating, and those which I accept as true. I like imagining ghosts and fairies, but, despite the purely physical impression I experience, that doesn't stop me not believing in ghosts, and on that point my in-credulity is so great that if I saw a spectre I still shouldn't believe in them. It is in fact much more likely that I am mad than that a miracle should happen.[42]

Mérimée nevertheless for some years continued a courteous discussion in letters which are unique in his correspondence for their serious attempt to come to grips with the vast questions which exercise mankind about its destiny. If Mérimée's attitude is in the end that such questions fall outside his competence, at least he does not seek to elude them in this critical period of his life.

There were of course occasional diversions too – a visit to Chinon in June 1855 to inspect the castle, a short stay at Trouville in August

[39] Comte d'Haussonville, *Prosper Mérimée. Hugh Elliot.*
[40] *C.G.*, Vol. VII, p. 293.
[41] *Ibid.*, p. 426.   [42] *C.G.*, Vol. VIII, p. 182.

with Chancellor Pasquier and Mme de Boigne, dinners with the Seniors, Lord and Lady Holland, Delacroix or Monckton Milnes, a handful of learned articles and reviews, the start of a plan to publish, with the assistance of one Louis Lacour, an annotated edition of the sixteenth-century memorialist Brantôme. Moreover, he never ceased to maintain a watchful interest in political events, the more so as he was reporting regularly to Mme de Montijo on his meetings with her daughter and Napoleon III. The Crimean War worried him, in view of the evident lack of preparation among the allies, and he was horrified when the Emperor showed signs of wanting to lead his army into battle. Napoleon's confidence in his own star was diametrically opposed to Mérimée's anxious temperament: 'he likes chance, he has often been lucky, and he trusts in his good fortune'.[43] After the failure of Pianori's attempt at assassination in April 1855, Mérimée was staggered by the Emperor's calm:

> it was a narrow escape for us. I have just left the Tuileries where there were a great many people. He thanked us and told us 'not to worry, that Providence would watch over him so long as his mission was unfinished'. His voice was perfectly steady and clearer than usual; he smiled more and looked more cheerful. The Empress was very upset and very pale. As she passed in front of me she clasped my hand tightly, and her eyes spoke volumes.[44]

Mérimée suspected that Napoleon was not cautious and mistrustful enough, and that he had 'the defect of being too lazy and too kind-hearted'.[45] But like everyone else he found him singularly difficult to penetrate, and ruefully admitted to Mme de Montijo, 'your son-in-law, as you know, is not a man whose thoughts one can ask about or guess'.[46]

Still, nothing could make him forget for long the pain of having lost Valentine. The lack of any real will to go on living began to take its toll of his already fragile health, and early in 1856, he was forced to see a doctor. For many years, Mérimée had led an extremely strenuous life, but despite the alarms his health had sometimes given him in the last few years, he had refused to admit to himself that he should seek medical advice, both because he suspected doctors of being charlatans and because he had a sneaking suspicion that if he did he

[43] *C.G.*, Vol. VII, p. 466.
[45] *Ibid.*, p. 477.
[44] *Ibid.*, p. 472.
[46] *Ibid.*, p. 228.

might be told he was really ill. When he could postpone it no longer, the outcome was almost as discouraging as he had feared. Somewhat reluctantly he told Mme de Montijo of his weakness:

> a short while ago, I was stupid enough to consult a doctor, and naturally he discovered I had three or four fatal diseases [. . .] I'm not very pleased with my health, but I don't believe in all the predictions I've been given. I have no desire to move on to a better world any sooner than I have to, but I don't object to leaving when I have to. There are only two things I am afraid of: pain and an illness which would make me a burden to others, and I'm told that I must take a few precautions to avert this misfortune.[47]

However he may have tried to make light of it, the doctor's pessimism profoundly affected Mérimée. To his moral collapse was added an impending physical collapse. In some ways, Mérimée was a broken man now: still stoical, still humorous, still fighting to hide his decline and to make his remaining days bearable, but irremediably aware that, little by little, he would be defeated.

[47] *C.G.*, Vol. VIII, pp. 61–2.

Chapter 16

Russophile

On connaît à peine de nom les auteurs russes et ils mériteraient
plus d'attention de notre part.
To Charles Lenormant, 17 April 1856

It has often been said, following Paul de Saint-Victor,[1] that for over
twenty years Mérimée went into literary emigration in Russia. From
the early 1850s until his death, Mérimée's prime intellectual preoccupation was with the study of Russian literature and Russian history,
publishing books, articles, essays and reviews in such number and
quality that in both domains he ranks as a pioneer. Knowledge of
Russian authors spread very slowly in France in the first half of the
nineteenth century. There had been occasional translations of Pushkin
and Gogol, but they had not touched a wide public,[2] and apart from
a few expatriate Russians[3] and one or two Frenchmen who happened
to have travelled or lived in Russia,[4] there were few people in France
who could pretend to any real competence. This was in itself an attraction for Mérimée, who never liked to find himself only one of many,
and it meant that with his inquisitive mind, his linguistic facility, his

[1] Quoted by H. Mongault in P. Mérimée, *Études de littérature russe*, Paris,
Champion, 1931, Vol. I, p. vii.

[2] Cf. V. Boutchik, *La Littérature russe en France*, Paris, Champion, 1947.

[3] It was of course through such people that Mérimée had become involved
with Russian literature, notably Mme de Lagrené and Mme de Circourt. He
had also met numerous Russian visitors to Paris, from Alexander Turgenev
and Sobolevski in 1829 to Ivan Turgenev in 1857.

[4] Among them was Mérimée's cousin Henri Mérimée, who was in Russia
in 1839–40 and who in 1847 published a book on his experiences under the
title *Une Année en Russie* (*A Year in Russia*). Though Prosper was never on
very good terms with his cousin, he may have been spurred on to emulation
by this publication. On this and other matters concerning Mérimée's knowledge of Russian literature, see Henri Mongault's authoritative introduction
to the *Études de littérature russe*, Vol. I, pp. vii–cxli.

lucid intelligence and his established reputation, he was in an especially favourable position to play a leading part in the new movement. He worked under handicaps: he never read or wrote Russian with complete fluency (he was nearly fifty when he began learning it), his knowledge of the country and its customs was second-hand and imperfect, and his reading was not wide enough for him to fit the topics with which he was familiar into a broader context. But his intellectual brilliance and his determination enabled him to produce work of durable merit.

In the early stages of his initiation, Mérimée had to depend on his mentors for guidance. He first spent months on a laborious word-for-word deciphering of Zhukovski's *Ondine*, itself a verse translation from the German. It is remarkable that Mérimée, who liked neither poetry nor Germans, should have persevered with this. When various friends urged him to read Pushkin, however, the effect was electric; he immediately recognised a kindred spirit in the Russian poet who had himself liked *La Guzla* so much that he had rendered parts of it into Russian. His first publications in the field of Russian studies were a rendering of *The Queen of Spades* for the *Revue des Deux Mondes* in July 1849, followed in 1852 by versions of two Pushkin poems, *The Gypsies* and *The Hussar*, which appeared in a re-edition of some of Mérimée's short stories, and it was probably about the same time that he translated three other poems which he only published in 1868.[5] In 1856, *Le Moniteur universel* printed *The Pistol Shot*, perhaps the most successful of his Pushkin texts. In no case was Mérimée the first to translate these, but the prestige of his name and the sober elegance of his style helped to give Pushkin a permanent place in the affections of the French literary public.

Mérimée's championing was all the more effective in that he was

[5] The poems are *Antchar*, *The Privileged One* and *The Prophet*, and the translations were used by Mérimée in his 1868 article on Pushkin. Mérimée's predilection for *The Gypsies* is in part due to the analogies which its poignant theme of lost love presented with his own case. He was fond of quoting a line from it: 'Ce qui a été ne sera plus' ('what once has been will be no more'). A manuscript text of his translation given to Mme Odier in 1852 shows by its many differences from the printed version how much care he took over it (M. Parturier, 'Un Manuscrit des *Bohémiens*', *Bulletin du Bibliophile*, 20 mai 1933).

convinced that Pushkin was one of the great poets of European literature. Turgenev said that Mérimée thought him the greatest poet of
the nineteenth century,[6] and in 1864, Mérimée declared: 'Pushkin's
lyric poems are the most perfect things I know since the Greeks'[7] –
praise indeed, as Mérimée averred that he was incapable of appreciating
poetry and affirmed that 'everything that is grand, beautiful, nay
sensible, has a Grecian origin'.[8] But it was only in 1868, in the *Moniteur
universel*, that he publicly explained the grounds for his admiration
(though he had been intending to write the article at least since 1860).[9]
But, afraid of being carried away, Mérimée keeps his feelings on such
a tight rein that one might be excused for not noticing how strong they
are. Only in his eulogy of the tense and moving *Gypsies* does he allow
himself some freedom of expression:

> I know of no work more *taut*, if it is permissible to use the term as one of
> praise; not a line, not a word is superfluous; each one has its place, each
> one has its purpose, yet it all appears simple and natural; the art of it is
> only visible in the total absence of any vain decoration.[10]

The nature of the compliment in itself betrays how close Mérimée felt
to Pushkin – it applies with equal force to his own best work.

The second Russian author on whom Mérimée chose to write was
Gogol, who was the subject of his first critical essay on Russian literature, suggested and published by Buloz in the *Revue des Deux Mondes*
in November 1851. But the tenor of the article is in general stern
and disapproving. Gogol's language is too luxuriant, his choice of
details too indiscriminate, his effects too facile. Above all, like other
realists, he concentrates too much on the sordid for Mérimée's taste:

> his studies of human behaviour show a certain preference for what is ugly
> and grim. Admittedly these two unfortunate elements exist all too prom-
> inently in reality; it is for the very reason that they occur so frequently that
> it is wrong to insist on ferreting them out with insatiable curiosity.[11]

Substantial specimens of Gogol's art are provided from *Dead Souls* and
The Inspector-General, but the accompanying commentaries as often as

---

[6] Quoted by H. Mongault, *Études de littérature russe*, Vol. I, p. xliv.
[7] *C.G.*, Vol. XII, p. 109.   [8] *C.G.*, Vol. XVI, p. 269.
[9] *C.G.*, Vol. X, p. 75.
[10] *Études de littérature russe*, Vol. I, p. 19.
[11] *Ibid.*, Vol. II, p. 6.

not denote exasperated incomprehension, mitigated by lukewarm praise of individual scenes. Visibly, Mérimée is baffled by Gogol, and can only appreciate him by placing him inappropriately in the tradition of the English humorists. Under the circumstances, it is incongruous that Mérimée should have laboured so hard to produce a complete translation of *The Inspector-General*, which he published in 1853. It is a mediocre piece of work, inaccurate, incompetent, colourless and heavy. One can only suppose that, as an Inspector-General himself, with a predilection for practical jokes, his fancy was taken by the idea of a large-scale hoax carried out by a trickster posing as an Inspector-General. If his feeling for Gogol's manner had been adequate to rendering the nuances of the situation, he might have been more successful in bringing out the full flavour of the comedy.

Even as early as 1852, Mérimée privately admitted that his opinion of Gogol was not high:

I think there is some exaggeration in the praise bestowed on Gogol in these obituaries [. . .] For me, Gogol is a sort of untutored Sterne. He cannot distinguish between the ugly and the ridiculous, and doesn't know how to choose his models.[12]

By 1859, his antipathy was undisguised, and he wrote to the French translator of *Dead Souls:* 'I do not like Gogol who strikes me as an imitator of Balzac with a decided liking for ugliness. I am sorry that you should have done him the honour of translating him.'[13] Nowhere are Mérimée's defects as an interpreter of the Russian soul more in evidence than in his writings about Gogol. The most one can say is that, however unwillingly, he did at least help to draw attention to Gogol's works at a time when they were largely unknown outside Russia.

Ivan Turgenev was the only other Russian author on whom Mérimée wrote publicly.[14] Though Mérimée first came into contact with him through a translation of the *Sketches from a Hunter's Notebook*, which he reviewed under the title *La Littérature et le servage en Russie* (*Literature and Serfdom in Russia*) in July 1854, he met Turgenev in 1857 and struck up a close friendship with him which lasted until Mérimée's death in

---

[12] *C.G.*, Vol. VI, pp. 333–4.   [13] *C.G.*, Vol. IX, p. 95.
[14] On Mérimée and Turgenev, see M. Parturier, *Une Amitié littéraire: Prosper Mérimée et Ivan Turguéniev*, Paris, Hachette, 1952.

1870. In numerous letters and conversations, they kept up a regular interchange of ideas on literary and artistic topics, and though they did not always see eye to eye, each developed a sympathetic affection for the other. Turgenev helped Mérimée with his translations and historical studies; Mérimée not only translated several of Turgenev's stories into French and wrote critical studies of his works, but also advised him when his novels were published in French. Mérimée was far from being Turgenev's only literary friend in France; he was perhaps not even his best friend (there was his long intimacy with Flaubert). But Mérimée's original high assessment of Turgenev's talents were reinforced by his respect for the man, and for the last ten years of his life, Turgenev was the Russian author in whom he took the keenest interest and for whom he had the warmest admiration.

Mérimée translated *Apparitions* (1866), *The Jew*, *Petushkov* and *The Dog* (1869), and *Strange Story* (1870).[15] In addition he read the proofs for the French translation of *Fathers and Sons* in 1862, and collaborated closely with Turgenev in revising the defective version of *Smoke* produced by Prince Augustin Galitzin in 1867[16] – Galitzin had moral scruples which infuriated Mérimée, so there was a constant struggle between them: 'Prince Galitzin takes out the slightly scabrous passages, and I put them back in.'[17] Mérimée substantially improved these versions and his own renderings are generally faithful and attractive. On the other hand, his choice of works to translate is suspect; he preferred the fantastic tales, which were closest to a tradition which he favoured, and was less impressed by some of Turgenev's most characteristic stories, which remain closer to a poetic evocation of everyday life in Russia.

Mérimée's three essays on Turgenev are of uneven value. The 1854 article on the *Sketches from a Hunter's Notebook* is sensible and laudatory, despite some reservations on Turgenev's liking for detail. The preface he wrote for *Fathers and Sons* in 1863 is disappointingly brief and superficial; one feels that Mérimée is insufficiently familiar with the intellectual background of the novel to assess it with any confidence. Only

[15] In fact, not all of these are Mérimée's own work. Turgenev himself translated *The Jew* and *Petushkov*, and Mérimée revised his rendering.

[16] At one time, Mérimée had thought of doing the translation himself, but decided he was too busy (cf. Parturier, *Une Amitié littéraire*, p. 161, n. 2).

[17] *C.G.*, Vol. XIII, p. 611.

the last examination of Turgenev's work, published in 1868 and intended as an introduction to *Smoke*, is a representative view of his
true stature. Mérimée gives unstinted praise to his gifts of observation,
his impartiality, his simplicity, his understanding of psychology and
society, his descriptive ability, and the conclusion is eloquent:

> without prejudice, without affecting any banal philanthropy, he is the
> defender of the weak and the disinherited. In the most degraded natures,
> it is his pleasure to discover some redeeming feature. He often reminds me
> of Shakespeare. He has the same love of truth; like the English poet, he is
> capable of creating figures of astonishing reality; but, despite the art with
> which he hides behind the characters he invents, one may still divine his
> personality, and that is perhaps not the least of his claims to our sym-
> pathy.[18]

Though it is arguable that Mérimée missed something of Turgenev's
genius, that he failed to react to the poetic overtones of the novels,
that he ignored the mysterious hinterland of this apparently realistic
writing, it is nevertheless clear that he recognised in him a writer of
the first magnitude.

Mérimée published nothing else on Russian authors. On the whole,
his off-hand comments cause no regret that he did not. On Lermontov,
for example, he simply wrote that his poems were 'not up to their
reputation'[19] and that reading them 'produces a marvellous predis-
position to sleep'[20] (admittedly he changed his mind later and helped
Turgenev translate *The Novice*).[21] On Dostoevsky, his verdict was
even more eccentric: 'I must tell you frankly,' he said after reading
Crime and Punishment, 'that in spite of his great talent, I don't care for
this author; there is some kind of tension about him, some exaltation
of feelings, and that damages the artistic vision. He owes more to
Hugo than to Pushkin. With such a model to hand, is there any reason
why a Russian writer should follow in the footsteps of Hugo?'[22] The
truth is that, especially in his latter years, Mérimée's literary tastes
were narrow. He read voraciously, but was little impressed by most
of the books which helped him pass his time. Moreover, he was not

---

[18] *Études de littérature russe*, Vol. II, pp. 254–5.

[19] *C.G.*, Vol. VIII, p. 215.   [20] *C.G.*, Vol. IX, p. 18.

[21] *Études de littérature russe*, Vol. I, pp. lxxxviii and 133–54.

[22] Mérimée is supposed to have said this in a lost letter to a Mme Long-
hinoff (cf. Mongault, *Études de littérature russe*, Vol. I, p. cxxxviii).

a good literary critic: 'I am particularly ill-suited for literary criticism. All I can say is "good" or "bad"; I am embarrassed by the question "quo modo".'[23] He was not good at putting himself in other people's shoes, and was excessively chary in praising others, lest his vigilance should be surprised by something unworthy. His critical essays, even on authors whom he liked, therefore appear constrained and ungenerous; measured by absolute standards, what he wrote on Pushkin, Gogol and Turgenev is not outstanding.

But the significance of Mérimée's writings on Russian literature, as of his translations, lies less in their intrinsic value than in their contribution to the appreciation of Russian authors in France. It is reasonable to give him pride of place among those who paved the way for what has been called 'the invasion of French literature by the Russians'[24] in the 1880s. This movement would have occurred even without Mérimée, but he contributed much in creating a state of receptivity towards Russian novelists. It was left to other advocates, more persuasive and more highly qualified, to press home the case; at least his authority and his seriousness proved that interest in Russian literature was intellectually respectable.

When Mérimée began studying Russian, he was already at least as much preoccupied with history as with imaginative literature, and it was natural that his curiosity should soon turn in the direction of Russian history. Pushkin's *Boris Godunov* induced him to start his own investigations:

> I've just been reading Pushkin's *Boris Godunov* which I thoroughly enjoyed, even though it's rather too obvious an imitation of *Goetz von Berlichingen*. It made me want to read in Karamzin the story of the false Dmitri, which struck me as very badly told.[25]

From Karamzin he went on to other texts, including a vast collection of diplomas and charters, and by early 1851 had decided to produce his own version. By July, he had acquired Oustrialov's *Contemporary Memoirs on the False Dmitri*, which he reviewed at length in the *Journal*

---

[23] *C.G.*, Vol. VII, p. 490.
[24] F. W. J. Hemmings, *The Russian Novel in France 1884–1914*, London, O.U.P., 1950, p. 1. Professor Hemmings (p. 5) rightly calls Mérimée 'the first French man of letters to take a serious interest in Russian literature.'
[25] *C.G.*, Vol. V, p. 497.

des Savants at the beginning of 1852,[26] expounding his own thesis that the impostor was not the same person as the monk Otrepief, also involved in the uprising of 1604, but was probably a Ukrainian Cossack of low extraction but some education. What most intrigued Mérimée was the immense and inexplicable success with which the impostor hoodwinked so many people. Unfortunately, in writing about this vast confidence trick he was faced with the problem that its early stages were virtually unknown, which excluded the possibility of a proper historical treatment, whereas the later stages were too well documented to admit of a fictional re-creation (at least for someone as attached to the sanctity of historical truth as Mérimée then was). Hence the division into a series of dramatic scenes giving concrete form to plausible hypotheses about the impostor's early years in *Les Débuts d'un aventurier*, and a conventional history of his public career in *Les Faux Démétrius*. Mérimée explained to Sobolevski how the division had come about:

> after having thoroughly studied my subject, I had the idea of writing the story *as it must have happened*. I produced a few scenes on this theme which took me as far as Poland. There, as I came up against Pushkin, I gave up my project (what a shame!) and wrote a common or garden history.[27]

A similar account was given to Circourt a few months later: 'at first I'd thought of turning the whole story into dialogue, but, fortunately for the dear public, I didn't have the strength. Once the story becomes clear, there's no point in making a melodrama out of it.'[28]

The historical interest of *Les Débuts d'un aventurier* is obviously small. It shows that Mérimée has devoted much thought to the sequence of events he postulates for the critical phase during which the impostor was establishing his bogus credentials, but it does not make the postulates inherently any more convincing. As for *Les Faux Démétrius* itself, Mérimée has documented himself as conscientiously as he could at such a distance from the sources, and he has not merely accepted what other historians have affirmed. But inevitably there is no original research as there was for the *Histoire de Don Pèdre*. *Les Faux Démétrius* is more akin to his studies of Roman history, since in both cases he was

---

[26] Reproduced in Mérimée, *Mémoires historiques*, Paris, Bernouard, 1927, pp. 161–206.

[27] *C.G.*, Vol. VI, p. 306.   [28] *Ibid.*, p. 472.

obliged to rely on a review of existing evidence to see if any new conclusions could be drawn from it. Mérimée's own reassessment is confined to denying that the impostor and Otrepief were one and the same person, and to arguing that he was likely to have been of Ukrainian Cossack origin. The case is subtly presented, but remains no more than an attractive possibility.

Where Mérimée was unique is in his vigorous narration. The story is unfolded clearly, convincingly, dramatically and picturesquely. Mérimée was fascinated by the enigmatic figure of the trickster who managed to seize absolute power in one of the world's great empires, only to die murdered and reviled a few months later. The sense of ironic paradox is increased by the fact that he almost turned out to be a ruler of genius: 'this impostor was a great man'.[29] His rise and fall are for Mérimée full of strange lessons on politics and human nature. In his eyes, the false Dmitri's mistake was to have been too optimistic in his view of mankind: 'Dmitri was not cruel; he was even gentle by nature, a rare thing in his time and perhaps misplaced in a usurper, for it is the punishment of those who achieve power by violence that they can only keep it by terror.'[30] Had he seen more clearly how to hang on to power, he might have been spared to carry out his vast designs; but 'with the presumptuousness of youth, he wanted to reform a nation which was still rough and wild before he had assured himself of either its love or its fear'.[31] This is Mérimée's summing-up of his life:

> that is how I see the impostor who contrived to win a throne and who perished in the midst of his triumph, perhaps solely because instead of having all the attributes of a usurper, he had some of those endearing qualities which one sees with pleasure in a legitimate prince.[32]

Such drastic changes of fortune on such an uncertain foundation were made to delight Mérimée's sardonic mind, and he communicates the delight to the reader.

It is only a pity for the artistic unity of the book that Mérimée did not terminate it after the false Dmitri's death, which occurs about

[29] P. Mérimée, *Les Deux Héritages. Les Débuts d'un aventurier*, ed. E. Marsan, Paris, Le Divan, 1928, p. 153.

[30] P. Mérimée, *Épisode de l'histoire de Russie. Les faux Démétrius* (2nd edition), Paris, Lévy, 1854, p. 197.

[31] *Ibid.*, p. 289.   [32] *Ibid.*, p. 305.

three-quarters of the way through. Instead, he included an account of the second Dmitri impostor, who succeeded in carrying off the first impostor's widow. The pace of narration gradually speeds up, as though Mérimée himself were conscious that he had drifted into irrelevance and wanted to get it all over before his audience grew restive: the last pages of the book are little more than a summary of events with none of the brilliant psychological insights that had characterised the earlier sections. Mérimée confessed to friends that he ought to have taken more care over the ending, which occurs for no better reason than that Marine, Dmitri's widow, has died; when he sent his manuscript to his friend Circourt, he wrote: 'I am sorry to be sending you a sort of rough draft on which there is still a lot to be done, but once I got to Marine's death, I felt so discouraged that I couldn't bring myself to give it the polishing up it so badly needs.'[33] The book is neither one thing nor another. If it was meant as a biography, it should have stopped with Dmitri's death. If it was meant as an analysis of a historical period, it should have gone on to discuss the third Dmitri impostor, who was of more consequence than the second. The final impression is weakened by the presence of the last quarter, so that, aesthetically as well as historically, the work is inferior to the *Histoire de Don Pèdre*. Even so, it is a grippingly readable book, and the only one among Mérimée's studies of Russian history which deserves to rank as an original contribution to the subject.

In the barren period when his distress at Mme Delessert's defection left him unable to write, Mérimée did little more than keep a mild interest going by reviewing a couple of books on Russia: Haxthausen's *Études sur la Russie* in *Le Moniteur universel* in October 1852[34] and Villebois's *Mémoires secrets* in the *Athenaeum français* in January 1853[35]. Somewhat more ambitious was an essay, published in 1854, on *Les Cosaques de l'Ukraine et leurs derniers Atamans* (*The Ukrainian Cossacks and their last Hetmans*)[36] in which he turned his attention for the first time to the notorious Cossack leader Bogdan Chmielnicki. Mérimée had been intrigued by Cossacks ever since as a child he had seen them among the occupying forces of the Champs-Élysées, and his studies on

[33] *C.G.*, Vol. VI, pp. 273–4.
[34] Reproduced in *Mémoires historiques*, pp. 207–22.
[35] Reproduced in *Mémoires historiques*, pp. 223–32.
[36] Reproduced in *Mélanges historiques et littéraires*, pp. 59–89.

the false Dmitri had increased his respect for their ruthless energy and
savage love of freedom – it was the same sort of attraction as he had
already experienced towards Spanish smugglers, Corsican brigands, or
gypsies in general. Chmielnicki was a popular hero with a sanguinary
reputation, somewhat in the same vein as Don Pedro. The 1854 article
is however based only on a French *Histoire des Cosaques*, published by
Lesur in 1814,[37] so it has no claim to authority.

It was not until the 1860s that Mérimée returned to his Cossacks. It
was probably his friend Sobolevski who recommended to him the
works of the Russian historian Kostomarov, in which he found not
only a more elaborate account of Chmielnicki but also a highly
picturesque life of another popular Cossack hero, Stenka Razine. So
in the late spring and early summer of 1861, he did a rapid translation
and abridgement of Kostomarov's researches. Kostomarov's technique
was well calculated to please a man with Mérimée's liking for folklore:

> he has taken into account local traditions and popular songs, which are
> often more use than official evidence in revealing the feelings and passions
> of the masses. It is easy to see that M. Kostomarov is a disciple of Macaulay.
> Like his illustrious model, he believes that the historian, without losing his
> judicial gravity, can and should borrow from drama and poetry. The
> deliberate, skilful use of these decorations does no harm to truth, which
> on the contrary gains from them when they are chosen with art and
> discernment, just as in a portrait the clever and accurate execution of
> accessories adds to the lifelikeness of the main figure.[38]

That Mérimée is prepared to accept such a view of history shows how
far he has travelled from the stern rigour of the *Études sur l'histoire
romaine* or the *Histoire de Don Pèdre*. There, though he did not hide his
interest in the legendary aura of history, he relegated it to footnotes
and parentheses; here, since he is simply repeating someone else's conclusions, he allows it to invade the narrative itself. Mérimée's *Stenka
Razine* is a stirring piece of writing, full of movement and excitement,
and with the additional allurement of folk-poetry, even if it is really
little more than a shortened translation of someone else's work.

After Stenka Razine, Mérimée returned to Bogdan Chmielnicki,

[37] On this as on other points connected with Mérimée's studies on Russian
history, see H. Mongault's thorough investigation of 'Mérimée et l'histoire
russe', *Le Monde slave*, août, septembre, octobre 1932.

[38] *Les Cosaques d'autrefois*, Paris, Lévy, 1865, pp. 296–7.

K

again following and adapting Kostomarov. The articles first appeared in the *Journal des Savants* between January and July 1863, forming a much more substantial whole than *Stenka Razine*. It is more sober in its colouring, and its greater length makes it a little tedious in its catalogues of wars, murders, tortures and treachery, as Mérimée himself had to admit; 'the defect of my book is that it lacks diversity. All the Cossacks the Poles catch are impaled. All the Poles the Cossacks catch are flayed alive. It's a bit monotonous. I wish I could vary it, but I'm held back by historical truth.'[39] However, Chmielnicki's character emerges very vividly from the sequence of horrors he provoked. From the outset, Mérimée defines the reasons which drew him to this 'unknown great man'.[40]

> The elected leader of a small nation surrounded by powerful neighbours, he devoted his whole life to the struggle for independence. As skilful at dividing his enemies as at preserving unity among the savage bands he commanded, an intrepid warrior, a resourceful politician, cautious in success, unshakably resolute after reverses, all Chmielnicki needed to win European fame was a less barbaric people and, perhaps, a name less difficult to pronounce.[41]

A similar admiration is evident in the conclusion to the recital of Chmielnicki's bloodthirsty exploits:

> nations like to find in their chosen leader the qualities and even the defects of their national character. Bogdan Chmielnicki was as it were the perfect type of the Cossack. He was brave, cunning, enterprising; he had an instinctive understanding of war. His intemperance, his real or assumed brutality were no more discreditable to him among Russians than Henri IV's love-affairs were shocking to the French. Few rulers have been more absolute; none observed more carefully the laws and customs of his country.[42]

Yet whatever art Mérimée may have shown in presenting Kostomarov's conclusions to his countrymen, it is again clear that the effort of conducting his own research is now beyond him.

What is true of the essays on Razine and Chmielnicki, collected in 1865 as *Les Cosaques d'autrefois* (*The Cossacks of Bygone Times*), remains true of the lengthy articles he published on Peter the Great between

---

[39] *C.G.*, Vol. XI, pp. 349–50.   [40] *Ibid.*, p. 46.
[41] *Les Cosaques d'autrefois*, pp. 1–2.   [42] *Ibid.*, pp. 291–2.

1864 and 1867. Since 1852 Mérimée had been eagerly awaiting the promised publication of a massive work on Peter the Great by Oustrialov, whose collection of documents he had used for his study on the false Dmitri. When he eventually (and belatedly) received the sixth volume of Oustrialov's book in 1864, he decided to summarise it for the readers of *Le Journal des Savants* under the title of *Le Procès du Tsarévitch Alexis* (*The Trial of Tsarevitch Alexis*). Oustrialov himself was flattered by Mérimée's adaptation and thanked him in person while on a visit to Paris in 1865; his gratitude then extended to sending Mérimée the earlier volumes in 1866, which were in turn summarised as *Jeunesse de Pierre le Grand* (*The Youth of Peter the Great*) in 1867 and 1868. Mérimée's success in condensing into digestible form the enormous mass of documents provided by Oustrialov should not be underestimated. As he himself says of Oustrialov's work, 'it is not even a connected story that is set before us, but a series of documents joined together by a few very brief sentences. One feels that the erudite archivist is afraid of being considered a historian.'[43] Mérimée's patience with Oustrialov's unselective conscientiousness later wore so thin that he exclaimed that the Russian was 'an ass'.[44] The incisiveness, the clarity, the psychological acumen of Mérimée's articles are attributable to him alone, as is the unobtrusive ease with which he puts a French audience in a position to appreciate the background to Peter's life.

Mérimée's last contribution to Russian historiography was his *Histoire de la fausse Élisabeth II* (*History of the False Elizabeth II*), an account of the extraordinary impostor who somehow duped so many experienced, intelligent statesmen and courtiers in Russia before dying in prison in 1775. In no more than forty pages, he produces some of his liveliest prose, detailing with immense gusto the rise and fall of the adventuress's fortunes, and watching with malicious pleasure the unfailingly entertaining spectacle of human gullibility. It is curious and instructive that the theme of deception should run through so many of Mérimée's Russian studies – the fake Inspector-General, the Dmitri impostor, the false Elizabeth II. As in his stories, Mérimée is obsessed by the contrast between appearance and reality, by the inability of humanity to see through even the most impudent pretences. Nowhere is this

[43] P. Mérimée, *Histoire du règne de Pierre le Grand*, ed. H. Mongault and M. Parturier, Paris, Conard, 1947, p. 137.
[44] *C.G.*, Vol. XIII, p. 301.

idea more richly developed than in the *Histoire de la fausse Élisabeth II.*
Though Mérimée wrote it in a few weeks in 1869, when he was
already very sick, it has the sharpness of style and analysis which
characterises the best of his earlier work. It is a fitting conclusion to his
contributions to Russian history.

> Three or four articles of quite sagacious criticism, with here and there
> some interference from politics; a book, which, despite a somewhat over-
> bold thesis, marks the beginning in France of serious monographs on
> Russian history; a less happy attempt at a theatrical evocation of the past;
> a few good adaptations; such is the sum total of his studies in Russian his-
> tory.[45]

That is how Henri Mongault sums up Mérimée's achievement in this
field. It is a less substantial addition to historical knowledge than his
Spanish and Roman studies made. His choice of topics is haphazard,
dictated largely by personal predilections for a certain type of hero and
by the accessibility of particular works of original scholarship. His
materials are never new, and though he handles them with practised
craftmanship, he adds little to them save coherence and an occasional
intelligent hypothesis. With Russian history, unlike the literature,
Mérimée was practically alone in trying to introduce it to his countrymen, and his writings widened the intellectual horizons of the cultivated
public in France. Moreover, his historical essays have stood the test
of time better than either his attempts at literary criticism or his translations: they remain stimulating, thoroughly readable, full of action
and passion, composed with that meticulousness of observation and acid
humour which are the hallmarks of his style.

[45] H. Mongault, 'Mérimée et l'histoire russe'. The same conclusion is used
in the introduction to the Mongault-Parturier edition of the *Histoire du
règne de Pierre le Grand*.

Chapter 17

Courtier

If y a un fantôme devant lequel je fuis volontiers, c'est moi-
même.

To Mme de Montijo, 15 July 1858

By the spring of 1856, the wound that Valentine Delessert had inflicted
was slowly beginning to scar over. Mérimée had kept up his social
obligations by continuing to appear in her *salon*, but the pain of seeing
her was diminishing, as he confided to Mme de Montijo: 'at Passy, the
lady is well: still the same attitude, rather cold. The last time I had
the feeling that it hurt me less.'[1] But Mérimée was not sure that this
increasing indifference made him any happier:

> at first I didn't feel my misfortune too keenly. I felt that I was the victim
> of injustice, and that kept me going. I was like Galileo in prison with his
> energy. Little by little, I suffered more, then I grew *callous*, and very truly
> unhappy.[2]

Still, by the end of the year, he was able to persuade himself that he was
'on the way to being cured':[3]

> on my side, there isn't the slightest enmity, not even anger, which would
> after all be quite a natural reaction. For some time I thought she hated me.
> Now I don't believe it. She doesn't even do me that honour. It's like a
> lamp that burnt for a while, then went out through some mischance.[4]

To Mme de Montijo, he confirmed this: 'as for my heart, I feel much
better than I did a year ago. I no longer have any deep regrets or
emotions when I see her. I am gradually coming to indifference.'[5]
Every now and then, the old despair would sweep back over him
and he would take up his pen to express his distress to Mme de la

---

[1] *C.G.*, Vol. VIII, p. 51.
[2] *Ibid.*, p. 149. The word 'callous' is in English in the original.
[3] *Ibid.*, p. 161.   [4] *Ibid.*, p. 167.   [5] *Ibid.*, p. 278.

Rochejaquelein; in veiled terms, he explained that he had loved a woman for fifteen years, that he still loved her, but that she no longer loved him and perhaps never had done.

> The result is that I have to cut fifteen years out of my life, which were not only wasted, but the very memory of which is now poisoned for me. Not that I am sorry about the wasted time – that would be more than I could cope with; but there are memories which were a superhuman world for me, into which I used to be able to pass, and which is now closed to me.[6]

If he had succeeded in becoming indifferent to his own suffering, the indifference extended to most other things too. The idea of writing still repelled him. To Mrs Senior he ascribed his inability to write entirely to Valentine's defection:

> There was once a madman who thought he had the queen of China (you know she is the fairest princess in the world) shut up in a bottle. He was very happy to own her, and he took great pains to ensure that the bottle and its contents should have no cause for complaint against him. One day he broke the bottle, and, since you don't come across a Chinese princess twice in a lifetime, he changed from being mad to being stupid.[7]

He worked desultorily on the annotated edition of Brantôme which he was producing in collaboration with Louis Lacour, and which appeared in 1858. He sat on an official committee for the publication of Napoleon I's correspondence, collecting letters, checking texts and correcting proofs, but without much enthusiasm, and he also took part in the preparation of an edition of Victor Jacquemont's letters. Otherwise, only a handful of reviews and learned articles reminded the reading public that he was still alive.

Writing for Mérimée had never been an imperious calling, and now it had become another distraction from boredom. Anything that involved thinking ahead was anathema; all he cared about was getting through one day after another as painlessly as possible. Always an assiduous letter-writer, he now grew even more prolific, lessening his loneliness by constant correspondence, especially with sympathetic female friends to whom he could talk, openly or covertly, about his unhappiness. For more intellectual sustenance, he had Francisque-Michel, though he was growing weary of the Bordeaux professor's importunate desire to pick his brains, and Count Arthur de Gobineau,

---

[6] *C.G.*, Vol. VIII, p. 165.   [7] *Ibid.*, p. 511.

whose gloomily misanthropic temperament and immense if disordered researches into the history of humanity were analogous to his own preoccupations. His emotions were more involved in his prolonged exchanges with Jenny Dacquin; by now, quarrels were less frequent, since he no longer tried to seduce her and she had given up hope of inveigling him into marriage. A more serene friendship had taken the place of the tumultuous relations of earlier years, and each found satisfaction in the understanding affection of the other – even if habit still made the tone of their letters waspish. Olga de Lagrené, too, aroused in him feelings which were not simply those of an old family friend or an unofficial uncle, and when he bantered with her about their eventual marriage, it was not without a tinge of wistfulness for what could never be.

Mme de Montijo still wanted Mérimée to get married, but though marriage attracted him in some ways, he refused to countenance the idea.

I'm old and I have such ingrained habits of independence that they couldn't be changed. I think there are only two ways of living. The first is (if one can) to avoid doing anything silly. The second, when one has done something silly, is to bear the consequences as philosophically as possible. You know how I've spent the better part of my life. Very probably that was a piece of romantic silliness. The romance had a pretty sad ending for me. All the arrangements I had made for a future which turned out to be only an illusion have been overthrown. I have neither the courage nor the strength to try to arrange my life differently. The only advantage that marriage could offer me now would be some consolation in illness and at that very disagreeable moment when one has to set off for the other world. Perhaps on a purely selfish basis that advantage would be worth thinking about. But on the other hand, the responsibility of a wife, all the looking after she would need, the future she would be left with – all that is frightening.[8]

But the advice he gave to a young American friend, Edward Lee Childe, betrayed his regrets:

if you marry young, you can marry pretty well whom you like; you can assure your own happiness. You have enough wit and intelligence to choose well. When you have an aim in life, you'll find that life isn't as bad as you think, and that you aren't either. In your existence you've never

---

[8] *C.G.*, Vol. VIII, pp. 375-6.

worried about anything except how to fill in the week ahead. Think of the years to come, and heed the example of a very elderly man, a complete *old bachelor*, who is giving you the benefit of his own experience, which is very sad.[9]

There were of course things to keep him busy; often too much so. Though he had handed over active direction of ancient monuments to his deputy Émile Boeswillwald he still retained the title of Inspector-General and took part in the committee work and policy-making in Paris. Then there was the Academy, with its constant intrigues over new elections, complicated now by the fact that because of its largely Orleanist complexion, it was inclined to act in opposition to Napoleon III. Not even loyalty to the Emperor could make him cast his vote other than as an anticlerical, and when pressed by his Imperial master, he would reply firmly: 'No, Sire, I cannot vote for a clerical candidate.'[10] The power of the church among his colleagues disgusted him:

the French Academy will only look at candidates who have proved their Catholicism. I have no desire to take part in the next election. I would be powerless to prevent the worst happening, so I wash my hands of it.[11]

At the Senate, there was less disagreement, since it was a docile body composed exclusively of the Emperor's nominees, but its meetings were mortally boring, and Mérimée told Senior: 'I have heard peers complain that the atmosphere of your House of Lords is benumbing; it is warm and exciting compared with our Senate [. . .]; it is a moral ice-house.'[12]

In addition, there were the duties of court life. The Empress was always anxious to have Mérimée among her guests at the lengthy official house parties she and her husband gave throughout the summer at Compiègne or Fontainebleau, and he was expected to take a leading part in organising entertainment for the assembled dignitaries. Neither Eugénie nor Napoleon liked a formal atmosphere on these occasions, so charades and amateur dramatics were usually included with Méri-

[9] *C.G.*, Vol. X, pp. 209-10. The italicised phrase is in English in the original.

[10] André Billy, *Sainte-Beuve. Sa vie et son temps*, Paris, Flammarion, 1952, Vol. II, p. 351.   [11] *C.G.*, Vol. VIII, p. 418.

[12] Nassau William Senior, *Conversations with Distinguished Persons during the Second Empire from 1860 to 1863*, p. 247.

mée functioning as author, producer and actor. Sometimes these trivial occupations amused him; more often they left him exhausted and satiated with futility. At Fontainebleau in 1858, he wrote plaintively to Jenny Dacquin:

> I'm quite out of sorts and half poisoned through having taken too much laudanum. Moreover, I have written verses for Her Netherlandish Majesty, played charades and *made a fool of myself.* That's why I'm completely worn out. What can I tell you about the life we lead here? We took a deer yesterday, we ate out of doors; the other day we got soaked and I caught a cold. Every day we eat too much; I'm half dead. Fate did not intend me to be a courtier. I wish I could stroll with you in this beautiful forest and talk of a fairy world. I have such a headache that I can't see a thing. I'm going to sleep for a while, until the fatal time when I have to spring to arms, that is to say, put on tight breeches.[13]

Sometimes the proceedings came close to offending his sense of decorum, as when the whole court indulged in a 'romp' at Villeneuve-l'Étang in 1847.

> The Empress and her ladies occupied a hill with a steep slipping slope, the gentlemen tried to mount it, and were repulsed with nosegays and parasols, till at last the Emperor threw himself, when half-way up, on all fours, scrambled to the top, made way for himself and his followers, and established himself 'maître de la position'. The display of pretty feet was charming, all the more so to us who have not seen a lady's foot for the last four years.[14]

Mérimée had mixed feelings about court life. On the one hand, he complained bitterly about the necessity for dressing up, for sitting through pointless ceremonies, for listening to dreary speeches, for discoursing amiably to strangers, for participating in childish games. As the only writer and intellectual in the Imperial circle, he was sometimes acid and petulant about the low level of conversation and thought there. On the other hand, he felt that Eugénie needed his support, the more so as Napoleon's roving eye had fallen on Comtesse de Castiglione whose boastful indiscretions left few people in doubt about their relations.

[13] *C.G.*, Vol. VIII, pp. 529–30. The italicised phrase is in English in the original.
[14] Nassau William Senior, *Conversations with M. Thiers, M. Guizot and Other Distinguished Persons during the Second Empire*, ed. M. C. M. Simpson, London, Hurst & Blackett, 1878, Vol. II, p. 141.

In addition, there were compensations in observing the absurdities of human behaviour in such unnatural conditions. So he put up with the inconveniences of etiquette and loyally responded whenever he was pressed into service. Only if the responsibilities seemed likely to be too onerous did he decline them. In November 1855, Hippolyte Fortoul, the Minister of Public Instruction, offered Mérimée a chair of comparative literature at the Sorbonne or the Collège de France, but he turned it down,[15] just as he turned down overtures from Eugénie to take Fortoul's place as Minister on his death in July 1856.[16] General support for Napoleon's government was acceptable but he had no intention of becoming involved in running it.

Even the round of official and semi-official entertainments was such a strain on his shaken health in winter-time that by mid-1856 he was wondering how he could decently withdraw: 'I have been so bored by the pleasures of this winter that I am looking for a place where I can take shelter,' he admitted to Mrs Senior.[17] So when Lord and Lady Ashburton invited him to their villa at Nice in December, he accepted with alacrity. Emma Lagden and Fanny Ewer had for some time been exercising general supervision over his domestic staff, which consisted of a housekeeper, a cook and a manservant, and he persuaded them to go and set up house for him in Cannes, so that he could join them there after leaving the Ashburtons.

Cannes in 1856 was a small resort, difficult of access, with very few hotels, but already a favourite winter haunt of the English and Russian aristocracy. Lord Brougham had started the vogue for it, and among the colony of distinguished visitors there, Mérimée had soon made friends with Lord Londesborough, the Marquis of Conyngham, Sir David Brewster, the Duke of Hamilton and Richard Cobden. Mérimée was delighted with the climate and with the life he led. The warm sunshine relieved his asthma; the absence of constraint relaxed his mind; the change of habits distracted him from his self-pity. He spent the days visiting the environs, painting, chatting with friends, drinking tea, cultivating a praying mantis as a pet, writing letters, or simply lazing around. Emma and Fanny saw to all the practical details of his life, and both morally and physically, he soon began to feel stronger. In 1856, they all stayed at the Hôtel de la Poste; in subsequent years,

---

[15] C.G., Vol. VII, p. 545.   [16] C.G., Vol. VIII, p. 71, n. 1.
[17] Ibid., p. 70.

Mérimée rented part of a house in the rue du Bivouac-Napoléon. His first stay there lasted nearly two months, and he enjoyed it so much that he resolved to return every year.

Dividing his time between Paris and Cannes was only one aspect of Mérimée's incorrigible restlessness. His circle of English acquaintances had widened considerably in the 1850s, and visits to England consequently attracted him more than they had done at any time since the heyday of his relations with Sutton Sharpe. He was now more intimate than ever with Panizzi, who was in 1856 appointed Principal Librarian of the British Museum, in the teeth of violent opposition from those on whose toes he had trodden heavily during his turbulent ascent to eminence, and he had also got on to excellent terms with Edward Ellice, Whig M.P. for Coventry, known as 'the Bear' because of his connections with the Hudson Bay Company, and whose munificent hospitality left him subject to regular attacks of gout. In July 1856 he used the pretext of an antiquarian conference to travel to Edinburgh, then going on a triumphal progress round the stately homes of Scotland, staying successively with the Duke of Hamilton, John Balfour of Balbirnie and the Marquis of Breadalbane, before coming to rest at Ellice's property at Glenquoich, near Inverness. The picturesque scenery and feudal manners of Scotland were greatly to his liking, even if the Scottish Sabbath provoked his irony – he related the following anecdote to Jenny Dacquin on that much-maligned institution:

> an Englishman is walking beside the henhouse in a Scottish castle on a Saturday evening, when he hears a great squawking from the cocks and hens. Thinking that some fox has got in, he raises the alarm. But he is told that it's nothing, that it's just the cocks being separated from the hens so that they should not pollute *the Lord's Day*.[18]

Drinking whisky toddy, eating great meals to the sound of bagpipes, inspecting deer on vast estates, attending Sunday evening prayers in the presence of the domestic staff assembled in the drawing-room,[19] Mérimée was both entertained and intrigued by the experience of a new way of life – even if he did feel 'mildly shocked at such an uneven

[18] *Ibid.*, p. 90.
[19] As they left the room after prayers, Ellice turned to Mérimée and said: 'A very good auxiliary to the Police, sir' (*C.G.*, Vol. XV, p. 6).

distribution of worldly goods'.[20] After a final stop with the Ashburtons at Kinloch Luichart, and a tour which took in Elgin and Aberdeen, he set off back to London, breaking his journey to look at the cathedrals in Durham and York. At Durham he spent a rowdy evening swapping dirty stories with a group of commercial travellers, while at York he made sociological observations of a different kind: 'I suppose that York is a town where virtuous women run very few risks. According to my calculations, there are non-virtuous women in the proportion of two to every male inhabitant.'[21]

The following year, in 1857, though he did not get as far as Scotland, he did return to England on a semi-official visit with Achille Fould, one of Napoleon III's ministers, to see an exhibition in Manchester. This journey produced three articles, one on the exhibition,[22] another, highly laudatory, on Panizzi's great new reading-room at the British Museum,[23] and a third on art in England, in which he ineptly berated the Preraphaelites for trying to give an exact reproduction of reality.[24] In London, he stayed with Ellice, but missed the chance of dining with Lord Brougham because his invitation went astray.[25] Mérimée was much intrigued by the puzzling figure of Lord Palmerston:

he is the real king of England. He struck me as a very strange mixture of statesman and imp. He has the poise of an old minister and a schoolboy's taste for adventure. I think he is very scatterbrained, full of confidence in his star and totally unscrupulous. He would turn the world upside down for the pleasure of hearing one of his speeches applauded in Parliament. He has all the prejudices and ignorance of John Bull, with his pigheadedness and his pride. In a word, I believe he is one of the evil geniuses of our time.[26]

---

[20] C.G., Vol. VIII, p. 119.

[21] Ibid., p. 104.

[22] 'Exposition de Manchester', Le Moniteur universel, 9 juillet 1857. This article, like the two following, is reproduced in P. Mérimée, Études anglo-américaines, ed. Georges Connes, Paris, Champion, 1930.

[23] 'Nouvelle Salle de lecture au British Museum', Le Moniteur universel, 26 août 1857.

[24] 'Les Beaux-Arts en Angleterre', Revue des Deux Mondes, 15 octobre 1857.

[25] See unpublished letter in Appendix A.

[26] C.G., Vol. VIII, p. 327.

Mérimée's stay in England lasted for a month; a few weeks later, on 10 August, he was off again, this time to Switzerland, where he discovered that he was still fit enough to do some climbing.

1857 also found Mérimée indirectly involved in a literary *cause célèbre*, the judicial condemnation of Baudelaire's *Fleurs du Mal*. Exactly what prompted Mérimée to join in the poet's defence is uncertain, but when it became known that Baudelaire was going to be prosecuted for the alleged immorality of his poems, Mérimée quietly went to the Minister of Justice in an unsuccessful attempt to persuade him to drop the case.[27] Mérimée was given to acts of disinterested charity (he regularly interceded with Eugénie's private secretary for some indigent old ladies), but liked to do them as stealthily as possible, for fear of being thought sentimental. So when Mme de la Rochejaquelein mentioned that she had heard he had intervened on Baudelaire's behalf, he immediately bristled, denigrated *Les Fleurs du Mal*, and invented contorted excuses for his own kindness:

> I have taken no steps to stop the author to whom you refer being burnt, except for telling a minister that he would do better to burn others first. I presume you are alluding to a book entitled *Fleurs du Mal*, a very mediocre work, not in the least dangerous, where there are a few sparks of poetry in a young fellow who knows nothing about life and who is tired of it because he's been deceived by a *grisette*. I don't know the author, but I would bet that he is naïve and honest: that's why I don't want to see him burnt.[28]

Baudelaire was deeply grateful and thereafter assumed Mérimée to be one of his supporters, expecting his assistance in obtaining a post as a theatre manager and even in securing election to the Academy.[29] During the poet's last illness Mérimée willingly helped Sainte-Beuve and the poet Banville in trying to get government funds to support him, expressing great esteem for his writings and his talent.[30] Yet a year or two later he was declaring that the same writings made him

[27] *C.G.*, Vol. XIII, p. 193.   [28] *Ibid*, pp. 364–5.
[29] Charles Baudelaire, *Correspondance générale*, Paris, Conard, Vol. II (1957), p. 80: 'on my side I have [. . .] *M. Mérimée* (who is not only a celebrated man of letters, but the only one who represents literature in the Senate)', 27 April 1857; Vol. IV (1958), p. 21: 'Mérimée, with whom I am on good terms . . .'; p. 75: Mérimée had once given Baudelaire 'evidence of close interest'.   [30] *C.G.*, Vol. XIII, pp. 190, n. 3, and 191.

'furious', that Baudelaire was 'mad', and that immorality was the only merit of his poetry.[31] These apparent contradictions are easy to understand. He was always sensitive to real suffering, and so was perfectly willing to alleviate the hardships of Baudelaire's life while remaining utterly unmoved by his works.

In 1857 Mérimée was made chairman of a committee set up by the government to consider the reorganisation of the Bibliothèque Impériale, which has since become the Bibliothèque Nationale. He did not greatly relish the task, for it involved, so he said, tormenting colleagues and sometimes pointing out to them that they were lying to him, but he was well aware of the need for change, especially after he had seen the effects of Panizzi's reform of the British Museum.

> For very many years, posts as librarians have been distributed and accepted as sinecures; [. . .] disorder there has reached a point which passes belief; [. . .] from the buildings which are collapsing in ruins to the books which are all over the place, everything needs reorganising.[32]

The only compensation was a closer collaboration with Panizzi. Sometimes Panizzi came to stay with him in Paris; sometimes he went over and lodged in Panizzi's apartments at the British Museum. The committee's report was not in the end adopted by the government, as is the way with such things, but Panizzi and Mérimée were henceforth as inseparable as Stendhal and Mérimée had once been, united by similar political views, by rabid anticlericalism, by great unwillingness to suffer fools gladly, by detestation of cant, by love of comfort and good living, by iconoclastic humour, by the shared loneliness of elderly bachelors. In the spring of 1858, Mérimée stayed with Panizzi for nearly a month, meeting Panizzi's numerous and influential Whig political friends and conferring with Libri about a possible reopening of his case. The only disagreeable event of this stay was the sudden obligation to make a speech at the Royal Literary Fund dinner.[33] Like most of Mérimée's public utterances, it was almost ruined by nervousness. Turgenev, who had met Mérimée the previous year at the Circourts' house in Paris but found him 'cold, with a taste for coarseness',[34]

[31] C.G., Vol. XIV, p. 531.   [32] C.G., Vol. VIII, p. 477.
[33] The text of this speech has never been found, probably because it was improvised.
[34] M. Parturier, Une Amitié littéraire, p. 12.

was present and noted the contrast between the speaker's supposed impassibility and his obvious stage-fright:

> Mérimée has a very shrewd face, intelligent, almost immobile. He has the reputation of being an epicurean and a sceptic whom nothing can disturb, who does not believe in anything, and who in the face of any movement of enthusiasm observes a polite but slightly scornful mistrust. He is a senator and in favour at the French Court. Yet this sceptic turned pale when in reply to Milnes's amiable remarks he had to make a little speech which he had learned by heart. Mérimée's English is not very good, his voice was trembling, and he broke down twice.[35]

Later in 1858, Panizzi and Mérimée were together again in Northern Italy, during the course of a tour through Switzerland and the Tirol which Mérimée had undertaken with the Lagdens in tow.

At about the same time, both of them became aware that their respective situations put them in a unique position for improving understanding between France and England. Mérimée was a personal friend of the Imperial family and of several of Napoleon III's ministers; Panizzi was intimate with many of the most prominent liberal politicians of the day – Palmerston, Gladstone, Russell, Clarendon and Devonshire. Franco-British relations in the 1850s and 1860s were not very good; there was suspicion and resentment on both sides, which alarmed both Panizzi and Mérimée. So Mérimée regularly passed on to Panizzi unofficial information about French policies and intentions, in order that Panizzi could explain and defend them to his powerful Whig friends; he tended to do much the same with Ellice, with whom he was also in regular correspondence. These calculated indiscretions, which were obviously encouraged by Napoleon himself, may not have done as much as Panizzi liked to believe to modify British attitudes – as Filon aptly remarks, he was half Machiavelli and half Punch,[36] and was perhaps not always taken as seriously in politics as he would have wished, but they undoubtedly kept open a useful avenue of informal communication.

Not that Mérimée was in Napoleon III's confidence. Like most other people, he had the utmost difficulty in penetrating behind the enigmatic mask; the heavy lids, the gentle caress of the moustache, the evasive speech were as baffling to him as they were to most of the Emperor's acquaintances. As he had to admit to Panizzi, one could talk to Napo-

[35] *Ibid.*, p. 15.   [36] Augustin Filon, *Mérimée et ses amis*.

leon *de rebus omnibus et quibusdam aliis,* but it was never easy to guess what was going on in his mind.[37] Moreover, Mérimée was treated as a personal friend and not as a political associate. Though he knew most of the members of the government, he was only on really good terms with one of them: Achille Fould, a banker by trade, Jewish by birth but Protestant by conversion, a practical, intelligent and astute man who had been in politics since 1842 and who at various times was Napoleon's Minister of the Imperial Household and Minister of Finance. Mérimée occasionally stayed in his house at Tarbes and accompanied him on official journeys. In any case the Emperor always played a lone hand, and as Mérimée said to Senior: 'I believe there is only one person who knows anything about his intentions, the Empress, and I doubt whether she knows much.'[38]

Still, even if he was only a privileged spectator, Mérimée followed political events with keenness. His great anxiety was that red revolution would seize on some international upheaval to overthrow the Second Empire. Mérimée viewed the instability of European politics with the greatest trepidation. When in 1859 Napoleon III decided to send French troops into Italy against the Austrians, Mérimée reacted with a characteristic mixture of patriotic fervour and nervous agitation:

> this war has upset me dreadfully. I wish I had been young so that I could have gone off to it, even though not everything has turned out as I would have liked. I am very sorry for the wounded but not in the least for the dead. I feel there is no better end than a good bullet on a battlefield.[39]

Popular enthusiasm for the war struck him as both 'magnificent' and 'frightening',[40] and though Napoleon's departure to lead his armies in person greatly worried him, he was convinced that knowing the Emperor was watching would make the French fight 'like lions'.[41]

Internal politics likewise kept him in a state of perpetual worry. His habitual pessimism made him very unsure of the durability of the Napoleonic régime.

> I ought not perhaps to amuse myself with the vision that I shall live to see anything permanent in France. I believe that we are too enlightened to

---

[37] C.G., Vol. IX, p. 322.
[38] *Conversations with M. Thiers, M. Guizot and Other Distinguished Persons during the Second Empire,* Vol. II, p. 246.   [39] C.G., Vol. IX, p. 170.
[40] *Ibid.,* p. 103.   [41] *Ibid.,* p. 110.

submit permanently to a despotism, and every other form of government seems to require what we have lost, an aristocracy,[42]

he perspicaciously told Senior. The Empress was well aware of Mérimée's doubts and is reputed to have said. 'My husband had a high regard for his qualities and used sometimes to remark: "your Mérimée is a very pleasant fellow, but in my eyes he has one serious defect: he's not a Bonapartist".'[43] When towards 1860 Napoleon began contemplating the liberalisation of the Empire, Mérimée was aghast. 'Sometimes I have heard him say things so liberal they made me tremble',[44] he confided to Léon de Laborde. To Mme de Montijo, he was just as gloomy: 'I know how incorrigible this country is and I'm always frightened when I see the reins being slackened. Like children, it loves playing with firearms, and despite several accidents it's always ready to start again.'[45] All he was able to do himself was to try to win over the recalcitrant Thiers to qualified support for the régime; encouraged by Napoleon himself, who saw in the Orleanist ex-minister the one man who might rally the non-socialist opposition in his favour. Mérimée assiduously and tactfully cultivated the wily little lawyer's favours, visiting him regularly, praising his books, discreetly hinting at the importance of the role he could play if he wished. But Thiers held back, and Mérimée's efforts seemed doomed to failure. Sometimes Napoleon himself behaved in a way which offended Mérimée, as when in 1860 he abruptly dismissed Fould and replaced him by the conceited and incompetent Walewski. Mérimée was hurt: he felt that Fould had been unjustly treated, he detested Walewski for his stupidity, and he resented the fact that the real reason for the new appointment was that Walewski's wife was the Emperor's current mistress.

On this and on other occasions Mérimée found himself involved in the domestic affairs of the Imperial family. He was Eugénie's oldest friend in France, and his loyalty was much more to her than to the Emperor, so that, when she chose to confess her domestic troubles to him, as she sometimes did, he was always on her side. He was all the more drawn into their home life as at about this time Napoleon took

[42] *Conversations with M. Thiers, M. Guizot and Other Distinguished Persons during the Second Empire*, Vol. II, p. 157.

[43] Ferdinand Bac, 'L'Impératrice Eugénie au Cap Martin', *Revue universelle*, 15 mars 1927.

[44] *C.G.*, Vol. X, p. 118.   [45] *Ibid.*, p. 144.

it into his head to write a life of Julius Caesar and enlisted Mérimée's help as technical adviser. Mérimée's own biography of Caesar had been in abeyance for some years, and he was not in the least unwilling to place his services at the Emperor's disposal, the more so as it provided him with a way of resuming writing without the full burden of authorial responsibility. 'I am working and writing as I did in the good old days,'[46] he told Jenny Dacquin, and something of his former pleasure in historical composition soon returned:

> I've started scribbling again, and at ancient history. Modern stuff has never had much attraction for me. In general, what I reproach the moderns with is never having had the frankness or, if you prefer it, the audacity of the ancients.[47]

Mérimée now saw much more of Napoleon, and his respect for the Emperor's mind grew accordingly. To Mme de Montijo, he described the draft of the introduction as 'very remarkable for its ideas and its style',[48] and to Jenny Dacquin he professed himself 'astonished' at the ease with which Napoleon had taken to matters of erudition.[49] Mérimée was to provide detailed material for the Emperor's perusal and to produce memoirs on aspects of Roman history which might be necessary for an understanding of Caesar's career. It was not an exalted function, and there were those who accused Mérimée of servility, notably the spiteful Du Camp, who commented that Mérimée 'was always on hand, when someone was required to do service'.[50] In fact, Mérimée was helping himself as much as the Emperor. Without the devilling for Napoleon III, Mérimée might never have returned to serious writing.

In the autumn of 1859, Mérimée went to Spain for some six weeks. He realised that he was not going to savour the atmosphere of the country as he had done: 'happily one becomes more humane as one grows older. I remember with what delight I saw my first bull-fights. Now I hardly care for them at all.'[51] Once he was there, he wrote politely to Valentine (as he had done at intervals since their break) in a tone of distant amiability which scarcely hid a bitter sadness: 'but what

---

[46] *C.G.*, Vol. IX, p. 479. [47] *Ibid.*, p. 482.
[48] *C.G.*, Vol. X, p. 72. [49] *Ibid.*, p. 46.
[50] *Souvenirs d'un demi-siècle*, Vol. I, p. 139.
[51] *C.G.*, Vol. IX, p. 195.

could I say that would be of the slightest interest to you? Either I have grown very old, or this country has changed; the fact is that I am not as happy here as I used to be.'[52] Perhaps indeed he was mellowing with age and no longer appreciated the more savage aspects of life in Spain. Certainly some people who had known him for years found him less cuttingly sharp-tongued. When over dinner one evening in 1856 Mérimée affirmed that he admired Dumas more than Walter Scott, Eugène Delacroix was surprised by his generosity: 'perhaps he is growing more kind-hearted as he gets older; perhaps he bestows praise all round for fear of making enemies of his favoured position'.[53] Mérimée himself detected some change in his character. As early as 1857, no doubt mindful of his own sufferings, he told Mrs Senior: 'I've never been ill-natured, but as I've grown older, I've tried to avoid hurting people, and it's more difficult than one might think.'[54] In 1859, he explained to Mme de la Rochejaquelein that 'in times past, I used to go to great lengths to puncture the good opinion which people had of themselves. Now I'm very tolerant.'[55]

The fact was that Mérimée had still not recovered his zest for living, and what had once roused him to fury now provoked only a disdainful grimace. In 1859 he told Mme de la Rochejaquelein that he was feeling more and more a stranger among men.[56] Now that the purpose had irrevocably gone out of his life, there was no point in exerting himself:

> if nowadays I saw the most beautiful diamonds at my feet, I wouldn't bend down to pick them up, since I've no one to give them to.[57]

Even the discovery towards the end of 1857 that Valentine had a lover had failed to jolt him out of his insensibility:

> I have found, or I think I have, the answer to a riddle which had greatly puzzled me. This hasn't consoled me, but it has given a new form to my grief. Now I feel more pity than anger, and I regard myself as having been above all stupid. As I haven't too much vanity, for *a man of my weight*, I

---

[52] *Ibid.*, p. 289.

[53] E. Delacroix, *Journal*, ed. André Joubin, Paris, Plon, 1932, Vol. II, p. 422.

[54] *C.G.*, Vol. VII, p. 511.   [55] *C.G.*, Vol. IX, p. 74.

[56] *Ibid.*, p. 44.   [57] *C.G.*, Vol. VIII, p. 633.

am perhaps less sad at this discovery than others might be. Even so, I wish I could have my life over again from the age of twenty.[58]

In 1858, he assured Mme de Montijo that in his black moods, he scarcely ever thought of Valentine,[59] and by 1860, he was able to tell Mme de la Rochejaquelein:

> for five or six years I had been haunted by a phantom, or to use less poetic terms, I had a memory (not a regret) which used to make me very unhappy. The other day I noticed that it was only by chance that this memory returned to my mind, and that it no longer hurt so much. Have I become philosophical or am I beginning to turn into a mummy? Unfortunately the latter explanation is more likely.[60]

So the 1850s drew to a close with Mérimée still bereft and lonely, but gradually accommodating himself to a situation he had given up hope of altering. Provided he could stop himself thinking too much about either the past or the future, he found his existence bearable. 'The older I get, the more I believe one should live in solitude and like a lizard in its hole,'[61] he wrote to Olga de Lagrené. Not a very inspiring philosophy, but following it was the only way in which Mérimée could keep going.

[58] C.G., Vol. VIII, p. 407. The italicised phrase is in English in the original.
[59] Ibid., p. 586.   [60] C.G., Vol. IX, p. 389.
[61] Ibid., pp. 375–6.

Chapter 18

Observer

Everything is degenerating.
To Fanny Lagden, 24 October 1864

By 1860, age and suffering had begun to mark Mérimée's appearance, whitening his hair, furrowing his brow and tightening his lips. Members of the Court often saw Eugénie accompanied by this old gentleman with a big, square-ended nose of curious shape, with a forehead crossed by four deep wrinkles, with round, cold and rather beady eyes behind a 'flashing pince-nez. His meticulous, even coquettish dress, consisting of a tail-coat and grey trousers, a white waistcoat and an old-fashioned cravat, gave him the stiff and studied air of an English diplomat.[1] His English friends too were struck by his anglicised manner, and Nassau William Senior's daughter was one of those who commented on it:

> he affected the *flegme Britannique*, in which he was assisted by his appearance. Tall, rather gaunt, studiously quiet in voice and manner, stately and good-looking, he was much more like an Englishman than a Frenchman. But there the resemblance ended; the turn of his mind, his cynical *esprit* were essentially French. He had, however, a way of saying the most caustic things in his calm, gentle voice that reminded us of Kinglake; it was only after a moment's reflection that it occurred to his hearers how pointed and amusing his paradoxes were. Some people never found it out at all, and wondered why he was considered so entertaining.[2]

---

[1] That is how Augustin Filon saw him a few years later – see *Mérimée et ses amis*, pp. vii–viii.

[2] M. C. M. Simpson, *Many Memories of Many People*, London, Arnold, 1898, p. 292. Mary Senior, as she then was, used to go and drink *thé jaune* in Mérimée's rooms in the rue de Lille: 'he was more charming than ever in his character as host, showing us all sorts of interesting and beautiful things' (*ibid.*, p. 293). The nature of some of these 'interesting things' may be guessed from an anecdote which Mérimée retails somewhere about 'a friend'

One such person was a man called Paul Lanfrey, who met Mérimée in 1856 and was bewildered by the contrast between man and reputation:

> I find that he is not in the least like the portraits people paint of him. They pretend he is a sort of Don Juan, a haughty, perverse man of the world. As far as I am concerned, there is nothing of that about him: a dry, cold, common nature, devoid of charm, unless it lie in that reserve and that immobility which often exercise a hypnotic attraction over the weak.[3]

As usual, Mérimée only unbent when he felt himself among friends; with strangers, he adopted a pose of indifference and hostility.

At this time, Mérimée's health was an ever more constant source of worry. Though wintering at Cannes saved him from the worst of the Parisian climate, his asthma, complicated with emphysema, was becoming more and more harassing. Shortness of breath, incessant coughing, violent pains in the chest and stomach were the worst of the symptoms, which seemed to come and go without reason, but there were other complaints, too: insomnia, loss of appetite, eye-strain, and lumbago. These ailments preyed on Mérimée's mind, and his anxiety increased them. It was not only the regular pain and discomfort which obsessed him, but also the thought that these were the advance signs of death. 'As I grow older, I cannot acquire a proportionate supply of philosophy. That's the great trouble,' he confessed to the dramatist Émile Augier.[4] He tried to keep his worries to himself, but every now and then, beneath a disguise of flippancy, they would slip out, as when in July 1859, with a comic metaphor which was to become a habit with him, he confided to Jenny Dacquin:

> sometimes I have the impression that I am hastening rapidly towards the monument. This notion sometimes gets on my nerves, and I wish there were a way of taking my mind off it.[5]

His friend Dr Maure looked after him at Cannes; in Madrid, he sought advice from Mme de Montijo's physician Dr Seoane; in Paris, he consulted Dr Trousseau. But while they reassured him about his heart,

---

(obviously himself) who mentioned to some ladies that he had a collection of erotica in a secret drawer, gave in, rather reluctantly, to their desire to see it, and was then vastly amused to find them full of enthusiastic acclaim.

[3] Quoted in Sainte-Beuve, *Correspondance générale*, Vol. X (1960), p. 531.
[4] *C.G.*, Vol. IX, p. 385.   [5] *Ibid.*, p. 180.

which he feared was giving out, they could do little for his asthma, which they said was largely of nervous origin.

Apart from this, the early 1860s were a period of relative tranquillity. His life had now fallen into a routine which varied little from year to year, and which enabled him to combine the maximum of rest and freedom with the punctilious observance of his court and social duties. As early in the winter as he could, sometimes in November but more often in December, he would take the train to Cannes, whither the Lagdens had been dispatched in advance to prepare his lodgings in the Maison Sicard. There he would remain, savouring the sunshine, the sea air and the pleasures of idleness until late February or early March, when he would reluctantly return to the capital, sometimes slipping back to Cannes for a few more days at Easter if he could get away. The spring and early summer would be spent in Paris, attending the meetings of the Senate and showing his face in various official *salons*. Then he would go off to London to stay with his beloved Panizzi for a month or six weeks, usually in July and August; this would be varied by visits to his numerous other English friends in their country estates. The late summer tended to find him involved in attendance at Court, sometimes at Compiègne, sometimes at Fontaine-bleau, sometimes at the Villa Eugénie at Biarritz, which could usually be arranged so as to allow him also to spend a few days at Achille Fould's house at Tarbes. By then, after a brief return to his flat at 52 rue de Lille, it would be time for him once more to head southwards to Cannes. Over the first half of the 1860s, he lived in Paris on average for less than six months in the year; a further three months or so would be devoted to Cannes; between one and two months were spent at Court, and the remaining time in England.

Cannes was where Mérimée now felt happiest. His occupations there were varied but all had the attraction of being voluntary and undemanding. He painted and sketched when his eyes were not troubling him too much, and even now that he was approaching sixty, delighted in technical innovations and discoveries. 'I have started trying pastels,' he announced in 1864. 'Up to now, all I've managed to do is cover myself in all the colours of the rainbow, but if I dirty enough paper, I haven't given up hope of doing a sunset in ten minutes. As for the sunrise, I have little interest in it.'[6] Nature too excited his

[6] *C.G.*, Vol. XII, p. 594.

curiosity. Early in 1862, he started botanising: 'I'm studying botany
in a book and with the plants I come across; but every few seconds I
curse my bad eyesight.'[7] The habits of the hermit-crab intrigued him,
and he experimented with trying to get one to take over a new shell
he provided for it. Sometimes he would go out into the country to
stay with Dr Maure at St Césaire. On his walks in 1862, he befriended
a stray cat who lived in a hut in the woods, and was touched when the
animal would come bounding out of the distance to greet him. In 1860,
while researching into Roman customs on behalf of Napoleon III,
he decided that the only way he could satisfy himself about the Roman
technique of javelin-throwing was to try it out. A more lasting pastime
was archery, which he took up in 1862 on medical advice as a way of
stretching his chest muscles. He became President of the Cannes
Archery Club, and, accompanied by the Lagdens, used to go out
shooting down pine cones for his fire. Mme Juliette Adam, a young
writer devoted to the republican cause, used to watch him at work.

> I would see Mérimée from afar, followed by his old English women
> friends in light-coloured dresses, one carrying a quiver and the other a large
> bag, each slung on a strap. Mérimée held a bow, like a god, as Homer
> would have said. At a certain moment, one Englishwoman would pass
> him an arrow. Mérimée drew his bow, the arrow flew off and struck some
> pine cone specially selected for its ripeness. One of the English women ran
> to pick up the cone which she slipped into the bag, while the other re-
> covered the arrow if it fell to earth. As he shot, there was silent excitement,
> followed by cries of joy and exclamations, or rather acclamations, which
> only ceased when Mérimée once more drew the bow and shot his arrow.

Lord Brougham, now in his eighties but as pungent as ever in his
epigrams, commented mischievously to Mme Adam that the Lagdens
were scarcely appropriate Psyches for such a large Cupid.[8]

There were also many friends at Cannes. The already extensive
English colony was growing steadily. Lord Brougham of course remained faithful to the resort whose fame he had launched. Among
new visitors was Henry Bellenden Ker, former Recorder of Andover,
law reformer and botanist, who had decided to grant himself the luxury
of a premature retirement on the Côte d'Azur; Mérimée soon found

[7] C.G., Vol. XI, p. 5.

[8] Juliette Adam, Mes Premières Armes littéraires et politiques, Paris, Lemerre,
1894, pp. 356–7.

him a congenial companion. Edward Ellice's son also took up his quarters on the Côte, as did Edward Lee Childe, and one of Achille Fould's nephews. The historian Alexis de Tocqueville came to die there. Viollet-le-Duc passed that way whenever Mérimée could tempt him, and sometimes Émile Boeswillwald, who had succeeded Mérimée as Inspector-General in 1860, would come too, though more often he contented himself with sending a magnificent Strasbourg pâté. But the most prominent new member of Cannes society was the philosopher Victor Cousin. Cousin, who was some ten years older than Mérimée, had been the object of public adulation since the 1820s as orator, moralist and politician, and Mérimée had first met him in 1825 in inauspicious circumstances, noted with amusement by Delécluze.

> Coming up to Mérimée with every appearance of ceremonious and ironic affectation, he eulogised the plays of the theatre of Clara Gazul with such exaggeration that the author (Mérimée) thought himself the victim of a practical joke.[9]

In the intervening decades, they had seen little of one another, especially since Cousin, a friend of Thiers, was an unrepentant Orleanist. When in the late 1850s Cousin's state of health compelled him to take up winter residence at Cannes, he and Mérimée somewhat surprisingly became close friends, and spent hours together every day. At one time, Mérimée would probably have had nothing but scorn for Cousin's lofty metaphysical excursions, his newlyfound Catholic leanings, his florid oratorical prose and his slightly pompous presence. Now, more tolerant, he saw in him a witty, intelligent and entertaining associate, a man who could be gently teased but whose opinions deserved respect. Moreover, there was always the hope of converting him to wholehearted approval of the Second Empire and, through him, of influencing Thiers, still potentially a vital figure in the broadening of Napoleon's popular support.

Their conversations were diverting affairs. The one, prolix and rhetorical, would hold forth by the hour on any topic under the sun; the other, caustic, reserved, irreverent, would puncture the philosophical bubble with some needle-sharp comment. Juliette Adam has left a delightfully vivid picture of an encounter over lunch at Dr Maure's house. Maure, a lover of good food, kept on pressing fresh dishes on

[9] Étienne Delécluze, *Journal 1824–1828*, p. 227.

Cousin, saying: 'Even if you've never *really* loved, at least have something real to eat for once', at which Mérimée mischievously reminded
the company that for years Cousin had been the lover of Flaubert's
Muse, the irascible poetress Louise Colet. 'Mérimée, you have a sharp
tongue,' sighed the philosopher, 'and you say things which hurt me.'
'Very well, I withdraw them – reluctantly, since it was a good subject
for dirty stories.' Then religion was mentioned, and Mérimée once
again started goading the 'Orator of Philosophy', as he called him.
'Oh yes, *you* go to Mass, Cousin, but you're just a hypocrite; you don't
believe in it any more than I do.' 'Hush!' whispered Cousin, 'the
servants might hear: be as shameless as you like with people of standing,
but never in front of the lower orders.' 'Would you go to Mass for
your maidservants?' asked Mérimée pursuing his advantage. 'To set an
example, yes, and even if you like, for my maidservants.' Then Cousin
changed his ground and counter-attacked by asking Mérimée if he
read the Catholic critic Pontmartin, to which Mérimée replied that he
preferred Sainte-Beuve. Cousin seized on this: 'a witty remark interests
you a hundred times more than an idea, so naturally Sainte-Beuve
delights you.' 'Better than that, he stops me being bored.' At this,
Cousin bridled: 'Is that an allusion?' But Mérimée answered blandly:
'*You* never bore me, my dear Cousin, but I confess that I am sometimes
submerged by your eloquence.' 'Being submerged is not much better
than being bored,' grumbled the philosopher, but Mérimée was not
finished: 'I beg your pardon, boredom sterilises, whereas a flood
fertilises . . . when it subsides.' Cousin then touched Mérimée on a
sore spot by paying him a double-edged compliment in return: 'You
are an admirably accomplished ironic courtier.' 'What, a courtier, me,
a courtier!' cried the other indignantly.' Yes, yes,' went on Cousin,
'and there are many people who, when they refer to you as one of our
most famous writers, add: the man who made the Empress's fortune.
I know the story of Mme de Montijo's correspondence with the
Emperor, at Compiègne, and I know too much about it for you to
be able to deny it.' At this, Mérimée, who, like many wags, resented
being mocked himself, almost took serious offence, and the situation
was only saved by Mme Adam suddenly introducing a new topic.

   This in turn had unexpected consequences, since she mentioned that
the exiled Hugo had called the motherland 'an idea'. Mérimée at once
grew very excited:

The motherland an idea! It is the image of what is most tangible in the world, it is the flesh of our flesh, the spirit of our spirit, the heart of our heart. It is the living amalgam of our ancestors, of our fathers, of ourselves; it is the vibration of the voices of us all. Language, tradition, science, art, literature – she it is who sorts them out to make them French. I'm so overflowing with patriotism that I could talk about it for five hours on end, like Cousin can about philosophy. People say I don't believe in anything. I believe in 'Her', in our France, I am her idolatrous son, I worship her fanatically!

A stupefied silence greeted this unwonted outburst. Then Mérimée added brusquely:

That's how it is. I love the Empire, I believe it is a necessity in order to keep revolutionary upheavals in check, but with the Empire I know that France runs the risk of European coalitions against her, and of invasion; that's why my patriotism is so vigilant and so violent. If ever France were invaded, I should die.[10]

Coming from such a reticent and cynical man, this emotional declaration of faith was like a bombshell; events were to prove that he meant every word of it.

Not that their conversations were always so inflammatory. More typical is the exchange recorded by Count d'Haussonville. 'I remember that one day Cousin had become very animated while talking about the thirteenth century: "That century", he cried, "which witnessed God's finest creation, St Louis, and men's finest creation, Notre-Dame, that century which . . . " – "Excuse me, Cousin," Mérimée interrupted coldly, "but Notre-Dame was begun in 1163." – "You're quite right, Mérimée," Cousin went on after a moment of embarrassment, "but it makes no difference . . . " – and he shot off even more strongly in his enthusiasm for the thirteenth century.'[11] These clashes cemented a friendship built on mutual esteem and something even approaching affection. Cousin used to say: 'There is nothing of which Mérimée's knowledge is imperfect';[12] he is also reported to have passed the Olympian remark: 'M. Mérimée is a gentleman, M. Sainte-Beuve is not.'[13]

[10] Juliette Adam, *Mes Premières Armes littéraires et politiques*, pp. 392 *et seq.*
[11] Comte d'Haussonville, *Prosper Mérimée. Hugh Elliot*, pp. 176–7.
[12] *Ibid.*
[13] Auguste Barbier, *Souvenirs personnels et silhouettes contemporaines*, p. 320.

Mérimée, though he was amused by Cousin's patent love of the sound of his own voice, showed the tenderest solicitude as the philosopher's health gradually worsened.

In Paris, Mérimée's main occupation was attendance at the Senate. He spoke rarely and badly, and his interventions usually produced an effect opposite to the one he intended. In 1861 he made two speeches. The first was to urge the government to provide more funds to encourage art, but to his amazement, when an amendment in that sense was moved, Walewski, the minister responsible for fine arts, spoke against it – no doubt because Mérimée had bestowed praise on his predecessor Fould. Mérimée was so incensed that he said in an undertone which was unfortunately overheard: 'You can take a . . . minister to water, but you can't make him drink.'[14] There had never been any love lost between the two men; now they openly detested each other.

Mérimée's second speech was just as ineffectual. Mme Libri, who was now a very sick woman,[15] had petitioned the Senate to have her husband's case reopened, and Mérimée, who had remained in touch with them, deemed it his duty to speak on their behalf, stressing the fact that Libri was a naturalised Frenchman. In reply, the government spokesman merely demonstrated that Libri had forged the documents which had secured him his naturalisation. The petition was then of course rejected. For form's sake, Mérimée put on a show of disgust; in reality, though he never went so far as to admit Libri's guilt, he had for long been so disillusioned with the exile's eccentricities that the outcome was no surprise. As he said dolefully to Panizzi a few months later: 'In all this business, M. Libri has never given a fig for his friends and has thought only of himself. If the idiotic things he has done affected him alone, it wouldn't matter quite so much.'[16] Mérimée's continued interest was now motivated solely by pity for the dying Mélanie Libri, who had clung to her husband with admirable and ill-rewarded devotion. He visited her whenever he could, in Bath or in Paris, wrote to her regularly, and did his best for this woman whom he had once loved so desperately.

As for the Academy, Mérimée continued to favour anticlerical candidates in elections but found himself ever more out of sympathy with

[14] C.G., Vol. X, p. 262.

[15] She died in 1865. Libri then married again, but himself died in Italy in 1869.   [16] C.G., Vol. XI, p. 238.

contemporary literary developments. Among his fellow-Immortals, he was most closely associated with Émile Augier, the comic dramatist and apostle of the *école du bon sens*, whom he seems to have regarded, at least potentially, as a modern Molière. Mérimée had given himself a great deal of trouble to secure Augier's election in 1857,[17] and regularly corresponded with him about his plays, published or still in gestation. But while he read widely among new publications, he found little to take his fancy. In 1857, he had thought there were signs of talent in Flaubert's *Madame Bovary*, though in his eyes they were outweighed by a doctrinaire attachment to realism. In 1863, however, *Salammbô* enraged him with what he regarded as its amateurish archaeology and its pseudo-Hugolian lyricism.[18] Hugo himself, needless to say, was treated with even greater scorn. 'The world is getting stupider every day. On that topic, have you read *Les Misérables* and heard what people are saying about it? That's another of the subjects on which I regard the human species as lower than the gorilla.'[19] Modern music was no more to his taste than modern novels. Wagner's *Tannhäuser*, on its ill-starred performance at the Paris Opera in 1861, struck him as 'an infernal racket',[20] which he could easily equal by copying the sound of his cat walking up and down a piano keyboard. On the other hand, while he had some reservations about the realistic elements in Turgenev's works, he willingly exempted them from his general condemnation of current fiction. After their first cool contacts in February 1857, they gradually got to know each other better, and

[17] Cf. *C.G.*, Vol. VIII, p. 281, n. 3.

[18] *C.G.*, Vol. XI, pp. 250–1. According to Ferdinand Bac (*Intimités du Second Empire*, Vol. III, pp. 10–11), Sainte-Beuve let it be known that Eugénie had quarrelled with Mérimée because of the latter's rudeness about *Salammbô*. Only when the Empress reverted to her normal taste for the novels of Octave Feuillet did Mérimée feel reassured.

[19] *C.G.*, Vol. XI, p. 177. Hugo in exile, if he loathed Mérimée's political opinions, had evidently not abandoned all respect for his literary talent, and is reported to have said in 1867, with his usual grandiloquent vanity: 'There's only one classic in this century, do you hear? It is I. I am the man with the best knowledge of French today. After me come Sainte-Beuve and Mérimée . . . . But he's a very short-winded writer. *Sober*, they call him. What fine praise to bestow on an author! . . .' (quoted by André Maurois in *Olympio ou la Vie de Victor Hugo*, Paris, Hachette, 1954, p. 468).

[20] *C.G.*, Vol. X, p. 256.

were frequently together during the Russian writer's prolonged visits to Paris in the early 1860s. Mérimée helped Turgenev over the translation of his works into French; in turn, he called on Turgenev's assistance in his own researches into Russian history. An active and interesting exchange of letters took place over the years; it is one of the few places where Mérimée expounds his views on the nature and function of the novel.

In the autumn of 1861, Mérimée introduced Turgenev to Valentine Delessert, who gave him valuable advice on the upbringing and marriage of his daughter. By now, Mérimée was able to appear at the Delessert *salon* without embarrassment. Gabriel Delessert had died in 1858, and Valentine had committed the indiscretion of allowing Du Camp, now a man of letters of some standing, to see too clearly that she expected him to marry her. By 1860, their liaison was breaking up under the pressure of Valentine's jealous possessiveness and Du Camp's incorrigible egotism. But even if Mérimée knew about this, it was rare for him now to give her more than a passing thought. Of his other amorous friendships, the affair with Jenny Dacquin ran on what had become its appointed course. On the other hand, in the early 1860s, his correspondence with Mme de la Rochejaquelein ground to a halt, in a slow realisation that they had said to each other all that they could say.

In the ranks of Mérimée's male friends, death caused several gaps. In 1859, Charles Lenormant had died suddenly in Athens; in 1864 he was followed by Mérimée's other old schoolmate and travelling companion Jean-Jacques Ampère. It is remarkable that Ampère was the only person among the recipients of the thousands of extant Mérimée letters to be addressed by the familiar *tu*, which gives some idea of the closeness of their association. Once, in Ampère's presence, someone described Mérimée as 'mediocre'. Ampère exclaimed angrily: 'Mediocre! In the first place, there are no mediocre men; there are many who are very bad and a few who are excellent: Mérimée is one of those who are excellent.'[21] In 1862 Théodose de Lagrené died; Mérimée immediately helped his widow and daughters straighten out their affairs. In July 1862 Chancellor Pasquier died, aged ninety-six, but lucid and calm to the end. 'Bear' Ellice died in his sleep in September 1863; in 1864 Lord Ashburton, Nassau William Senior and Horace

[21] Comte d'Haussonville, *Prosper Mérimée. Hugh Elliot.*

de Viel-Castel all went. It is small wonder that the ailing Mérimée dwelled so obsessively on the imminence of his own death.

Fortunately, whether he was in Paris or Cannes, there was one fixed point in Mérimée's existence: the devotion of Fanny Lagden and Emma Ewer. It is possible to infer from his letters to them that they were simple, unsophisticated and not very intelligent. Even allowing for the rather approximate nature of Mérimée's English, the level was not elevated. The letters, which are very numerous, give a fascinating picture of the day-to-day trivia of Mérimée's life in the 1860s, but they rarely rise above mundane matters. Nor are they particularly affectionate in tone. That Mérimée cared about Fanny is shown only by the trouble he took to keep her informed about his doings and by a rather spinsterly concern for her physical well-being: otherwise he wrote coolly and undemonstratively. This was also his way with the two sisters in conversation. Hippolyte Taine noted how his deep feeling for them was hidden by ostensible brusqueness:

> towards the end of his life, one would meet two elderly English ladies with him, to whom he spoke little and about whom he seemed not to care much; a friend of mine saw him with tears in his eyes because one of them was ill.[22]

Sometimes Mérimée himself realised that his unintentional rudeness could cause real hurt, and in one letter, written in August 1860 after he had accidentally offended Fanny, he comes close to baring his heart to her:

> I hate to hear you speak of pecuniary obligations, as if you did not know that in money matters I think like my friend Ellice, viz. . . . that I do not

---

[22] Hippolyte Taine, preface to *Lettres à une Inconnue*, Paris, Lévy, 1883 (2nd ed.), p. viii. There one can also find this description of Mérimée, whom Taine had occasionally met in society: 'He was a tall, erect, pale man, and who had the appearance of an Englishman, apart from the smile; at least he had that cold, *distant* air which discourages any familiarity. As soon as one saw him, one could feel in him natural or acquired impassiveness, self-control, will-power, and a habitual reluctance to give himself away. Especially on ceremonial occasions his features were immobile. Even in private, when he was telling some ridiculous story, his voice remained monotonous, completely calm, with no sudden changes of tone, no enthusiasm; he would repeat the most extraordinary details, without mincing words, in the tone

care a damn. Secondly because you know very well that in this occasion
you really oblige me. If I was alone at Cannes I should be dead in a short
time. I am very poorly and my health is gone. I know that sometimes I am
very nervous and impatient, that I cannot control my dark humours. But
at the same time I thought you knew truly I loved you and depended on
your kindness. I shall do all I can to make you happy and comfortable.
But never imagine suppositions and bad intentions in me. When I am saucy
believe that I suffer very much. That is often the case and perhaps will be.
I dare say that with a little care and forgiveness on every side all will be
right at Cannes and elsewhere.[23]

As for Mérimée's court obligations, his poor health made him feel
them more and more onerous. He was often summoned to Fontainebleau or Compiègne and it was impossible for him to refuse. Had the
atmosphere of the Court been more intellectual or even less easy-going,
he could have borne it more stoically. But he was made uncomfortable
by the feeling that slightly drunken charades were scarcely fitting
pastimes for the Emperor's guests. From Fontainebleau he wrote to
Fanny Lagden in June 1864: 'we have been very gay all this time, that
is to say killing time in a very foolish way',[24] and a few days later he
admitted to Mme de Montijo: 'the fact is that we weren't sufficiently
kept in order'.[25] The same discreet complaint was made in January 1865
to Viollet-le-Duc: 'Is it true that things have been more formal than
usual at Compiègne? There's no harm in that.'[26] Towards the end of
the same year, Panizzi was told the same about another party at
Compiègne: 'people are behaving respectably, and I'm in favour of
that for our hosts, who often allow those whom they invite to enjoy
themselves to excess'.[27] Not even his illness excused Mérimée from
writing, producing and acting in fatuous little playlets. Their level can
be gauged by what Mérimée told Fanny Lagden in November 1863:

---

of a man asking for a cup of tea. In him sensibility was so far tamed that it
appeared absent; not that it was; quite the opposite' (pp. i–ii).
   [23] C.G., Vol. IX, pp. 538–9. The impatient, cutting tone Mérimée sometimes adopted towards the meek Fanny is illustrated by this excerpt from a
letter he wrote in 1863: 'I hope you will remember my recommendations to
take care of yourself and not shut up yourself like a fool. It is absurd and to
me very disagreeable' (C.G., Vol. XI, p. 505).
   [24] C.G., Vol. XII, p. 162.   [25] Ibid., p. 168.
   [26] Ibid., p. 314.   [27] Ibid., p. 580.

9a Napoleon III, Empress Eugénie and the Prince Imperial

9b Madame Mérimée with Mrs Ewer (Emma Lagden) and Fanny Lagden, a photograph taken in 1850. Mrs Ewer standing, on her right Mme Mérimée, on her left Fanny Lagden

10a Unpublished caricature by Mérimée of an unidentified dignitary
10b Unpublished drawing by Mérimée of an imaginary statue of Macadam, supported by crossing-sweepers, who had good reason to be grateful to the inventor of macadamized roads

10c Unpublished page of sketches by Mérimée. Mérimée used to draw and doodle a great deal during the many meetings he attended. This is one such page, which formerly belonged to Baron de Nieuwerkerke. The Arabic script at the top means: 'do you want any hunting dress?' Three of the drawings are based on puns. The helmeted character at the top left is evidently the Marquis de Cascaret, transformed into the 'Marquis de Casque à raies' (the marquis with the striped helmet). The mantled ape ('Singe en Baptiste' means 'ape in a clown's cloak') is a word play on 'Saint Jean Baptiste'. As for the electoral urn, 'vase d'élection' means 'chosen vessel' but is here wilfully misinterpreted

10d Unpublished caricature by Mérimée of Horace de Viel-Castel, drawn between 1852 and 1863, when Viel-Castel was successively Conservateur du Musée des Souverains français and Conservateur du Moyen Age et de la Renaissance at the Louvre. The legend and surrounding figures presumably relate to private jokes not now comprehensible.

I was interrupted by orders to prepare a charade. I have just written one but the end and am much embarrassed. One of the principal characters having swallowed a medal of Caesar, I am at a loss to find an honest and elegant way to get it out.[28]

But there were compensations, and when he played opposite Morny, he relished the insight into human nature which the experience gave him: 'De M[orny] who acted with me was a little intimidated, but I was not at all, and while speaking I contrived to observe the effect of the epigrams upon the people.'[29]

Apart from such futilities, Mérimée was still working hard to supply material for Napoleon's *Life of Caesar*. As the project neared completion, Mérimée started to worry about publication. So long as it had seemed to be merely a way of keeping the Emperor occupied, Mérimée had co-operated willingly; when it became apparent that it was meant to be a major work of erudition, he had serious misgivings. It would have been better, he thought, if Napoleon had ordered him to write the whole book and had restricted himself to crossing out what displeased him.[30] But to try to do it all himself, even with expert help, and then to offer the result to a sceptical public was, in Mérimée's eyes, folly for a ruling sovereign.

> One shouldn't write books when one is in a certain position. Moreover, I have more than one objection to the plan of the work, and, taking everything into consideration, it would have been better not to print anything.[31]

When the first volume appeared in the early spring of 1865, Mérimée resigned himself to the worst. With Panizzi, he did not hide his doubts: 'the book's great defect, in my opinion, is that it gives the impression that the author has posed in front of a mirror to draw the portrait of his hero'.[32] With these reservations, it was indiscreet of Mérimée to allow the *Journal des Savants* to persuade him to review it, which he did in October 1865.[33] His article is not obsequious, but equally, it is something less than frank, and on this if on no other occasion, Mérimée is open to the charge of being too obliging a courtier.

[28] *C.G.*, Vol. XI, p. 512.   [29] *Ibid.*, p. 235.
[30] *C.G.*, Vol. XII, p. 15.   [31] *Ibid.*, pp. 317–18.   [32] *Ibid.*, p. 405.
[33] The article is reproduced in Mérimée's *Mémoires historiques*, Paris, Bernouard, 1927, together with another on the second volume which appeared in July 1866.

L

Still, his contribution to Napoleon's labours had revived his taste for writing, and the early 1860s were relatively fertile years after the barren 1850s, with his writings on Russian literature or history.[34] The collaboration led also to a closer involvement in politics. It was inevitable that their conversation should sometimes range over the burning topics of the day. This was all the more natural as Mérimée, a rabid anticlerical, held strong views on the Roman question in which Napoleon had become embroiled, when, after the Italian campaign of 1859, he had left a French corps stationed in Rome to safeguard the papal government. Mérimée could not conceal his indignation that French troops should find themselves guaranteeing the temporal power of the Pope, and was eager to see them withdraw and 'Mastai', as he disrespectfully called Pius IX, left to his own devices. On 28 September 1862, there was what Mérimée called 'a pitched battle' between himself and the Emperor. 'I think I was as firm as I could be, but keeping very calm, without holding anything back. I'm told I behaved decently', he told Panizzi the next day.[35]

Mérimée noted with disquiet about this time that Napoleon seemed to be losing his grip on the direction of affairs. What had once been enigmatic secretiveness was now turning to chronic indecision; what had been confidence in Providence had degenerated into fatalistic resignation. In March 1862, Mérimée disclosed his fears to Viollet-le-Duc: 'the real trouble, between ourselves, is that one wonders whether he [the Emperor] really knows what he wants, whether he has an aim and a fixed plan'.[36] At the beginning of April, he repeated his complaint to Mme de Montijo: 'the real trouble is that no initiative is coming from the usual place. No one knows where we are heading or what the intentions are.'[37] Neither prefects nor ministers had any idea what Napoleon's projects or even wishes might be, and in the absence of any clear lead from above, all sorts of divisions were appearing among the Bonapartists: 'people are using the Empress's name for certain views. They make her responsible for lots of things of which she has never even thought.'[38] Since Mérimée now ranked as a close personal friend of Napoleon, there were even attempts by ministers

[34] For details of Mérimée's publications on Russian subjects, see Chapter 16.

[35] C.G., Vol. XI, p. 191.   [36] Ibid., p. 54.
[37] Ibid., p. 71.   [38] Ibid., p. 230.

to employ him to put pressure on the Emperor, as he confided to
Panizzi in April 1862:

> I dined yesterday with three ministers, all three very upset and despairing
> of making any impression. One of them, and he's the most eloquent of
> the lot, took me aside to ask me to talk to the master and tell him how
> things are. 'How do you expect him to take any notice of me when I have
> no official standing?' – It's precisely for that reason, I was told, that he
> may take some notice of you.[39]

Perhaps it was also because Mérimée was supposed to wield some influence that, when there was a government reshuffle in June 1863,
Fould tried yet again to induce him to join the cabinet as Minister of
Education. Fanny Lagden was the only person whom Mérimée took
into his confidence: 'M. Fould asked me if I should accept the Instruction publique? I answered by no means. He insisted a little and I told
him I was determined to live a free man.'[40] For the rest of his life, he
grew more pessimistic about the future of France and the survival of
the Empire; but he did not regard it as his business to put matters to
rights.

As Napoleon became more sluggish and more apathetic, so Eugénie
acquired a greater taste for power – especially as her marriage was
subject to intolerable strains. After Miss Howard, Comtesse de Castiglione; after the Comtesse, Mme Walewska; after Mme Walewska,
the plebeian Marguerite Bellanger: the Emperor's infidelities were
unending and ostentatious. Mérimée was still Eugénie's chosen confidant on these painful occasions, as when in October 1864, she poured

[39] *Ibid.*, p. 74.
[40] *Ibid.*, p. 419. Mérimée might well have been a good Minister of Education. Apart from his brilliance as an administrator, he had taken a close
interest in educational problems, especially in English public schools, on
which he reported to the French government in 1864. In 1867, he wrote to
Mme de Beaulaincourt: 'I should have loved to have a daughter to bring up.
I am full of ideas on education, particularly for girls, and I believe I have
talents which unfortunately will never be applied. All I have ever brought
up is cats, who have reflected great credit on me. I always tried to develop
their individual genius, without seeking to give them any other ideas than
those which were native to them, according to the conformation of their
brain. What strikes me as absolutely deplorable in present-day education is
that, by teaching girls all sorts of things, we disgust them with everything
elevated and truly interesting' (*C.G.*, Vol. XIII, p. 674).

out to him her anguish at Marguerite Bellanger's ascendancy. In veiled terms, he reported the incident to Panizzi:

> before I left Paris, last Friday, I saw our friend from Biarritz. I had a little conversation, four hours long, of which you can guess the subject. She needed to *sfogarsi*. It's all very sad, even more than you can imagine, but not a word to anyone. I think I gave some good advice, without forgetting what the proverb says about not interfering in family quarrels, but I'm not sure it will be followed.[41]

In May 1865, Mérimée added: 'In the last year, I think she has learnt a lot about men and things'.[42] By September, there had been some kind of reconciliation: 'This is the summary of what is proposed. Eugénie no longer exists, there is only an Empress. I am full of pity and admiration. In addition, on both sides, more confidence and friendship.'[43] Mérimée's own past was too chequered for him not to have some sympathy with Napoleon's compulsive philandering, but he also had too clear an insight into Eugénie's sufferings to condone its consequences. A further sorrow which bound them together was the death in 1860 of Paca, Duchess of Alba. This occurred while Eugénie and Napoleon were visiting Algiers, but the Emperor withheld the news from her until their return to France. It was years before she forgave him. Mme de Montijo too was dreadfully shaken; her health began to give way, and as late as July 1862, Mérimée was telling Jenny Dacquin: 'she has completely changed and looks pitiful. Nothing can console her for the loss of her daughter, and I find her less resigned than she was on the first day.'[44]

In public Mérimée's relations with the Empress combined irreproachable formal dignity with a smiling and ambivalent irreverence. Despite his anticlericalism, he respected Eugénie's piety, but he could not resist scandalising her and her ladies-in-waiting by remarks which skirted sacrilege or anecdotes which only just avoided outright indecency. 'You know that in families the girls are sent out when someone is telling an improper story. But at Compiègne, I'm the one who gets sent out when I'm about to tell one. After which everyone nearly dies of boredom. . . .'[45] Eugénie herself never quite knew how to take this

[41] *C.G.*, Vol. XII, p. 252. *Sfogarsi* means 'to pour her heart out'.
[42] *Ibid.*, p. 436.   [43] *Ibid.*, p. 518.
[44] *C.G.*, Vol. XI, p. 159.
[45] F. Bac, *Mérimée inconnu*, p. 98.

sort of talk, the more so as Mérimée was careful to cast over it a veneer of verbal respectability. 'When he starts on things of that kind, one doesn't dare look at one's reflection in a mirror,' she used to say.[46] If she thought he was sailing too close to the wind, she would jokingly say to him: 'You're a silly old thing!'[47] Sometimes, since she never gave up hope of seeing him forswear his atheism, she would try to be more earnest in her reproaches. On one occasion at Fontainebleau, she affirmed that her greatest desire was to see him converted. Mérimée, who was seated sketching at a table, pursed his lips in displeasure, said: 'Ah, Madam, always making personal remarks!' picked up his hat, and left the room.[48]

With other members of the Bonaparte family, Mérimée remained cautiously friendly. When Louis-Napoleon had first come to power, Mérimée had been drawn to the intellectual and artistic *salon* of Princess Mathilde, whose independence of mind and unorthodox character were greatly to his liking.[49] But after the Imperial marriage, he was obliged to be circumspect, since Mathilde and Eugénie were at daggers drawn. He continued to visit Mathilde, and by dint of dexterity and discretion, contrived to offend neither lady. In Mathilde's *salon*, he was liable to throw up a protective smoke-screen of erudition around his personality, so that his hostess was perplexed to know what manner of man he really was. Sometimes she would interrupt his learned disquisitions with characteristic bluntness: 'No, you know too much! Keep the rest for the next time.'[50] Mérimée was equally reserved in his contacts with Mathilde's brother Prince Napoleon, otherwise 'Plon-Plon', the *enfant terrible* of the Imperial family. He approved of the Prince's militant anticlericalism and his robust insistence on speaking his mind, but was alarmed by his unpredictable irresponsibility. At a banquet at Compiègne in November 1863, Plon-Plon, who detested Eugénie, gruffly refused the Emperor's invitation to propose her health; Mérimée was deeply shocked that such dissensions should be made

[46] F. Bac. *Intimités du Second Empire*, Vol. II, p. 204.

[47] F. Bac, 'L'Impératrice Eugénie au Cap Martin'.

[48] H. Blaze de Bury, preface to *Lettres à une autre Inconnue*, Paris, Lévy, 1875, pp. xlvii–xlviii.

[49] On Princess Mathilde, see Joanna Richardson's recent biography *Princess Mathilde*, London, Weidenfeld & Nicolson, 1969.

[50] F. Bac, *La Princesse Mathilde. Sa vie et ses amis*, Paris, Hachette, 1928.

public when the future of the dynasty was so uncertain. He used to say: 'When I have an enemy, I send him to see Prince Napoleon when he's in a bad mood. Afterwards, I'm avenged for ever. . . .'[51]

The first half of the 1860s saw something like a return to the stability which Valentine's desertion had shattered a decade earlier. If only anxiety about the decline of his health and about the future of his country had not plagued him, it might even have been a contented time. As it was, only by filling his life with minor occupations could he keep the *blue devils* at bay. 'Growing old is a sorry business!'[52] he admitted to Jenny Dacquin in 1860. But only the body grew old; his emotional vulnerability remained as great as it had been in his adolescence. 'I believe that I still feel all I felt when I was twenty-five. What a pity that the soul does not grow old at the same time as the body.'[53] The stoicism he had always sought to cultivate was as hard to maintain now as when he was a young man.

[51] F. Bac, *Mérimée inconnu*, p. 64.
[52] *C.G.*, Vol. IX, p. 381.
[53] *C.G.*, Vol. VIII, p. 555.

Chapter 19

Entertainer

La recrudescence de cette maladie de jeunesse m'alarme, et
ressemble beaucoup à une seconde enfance.
To Jenny Dacquin, 3 September 1868

At intervals since his last venture into fiction in 1846, Mérimée had
toyed with the idea of writing another novel or short story. On 12 July
1860, he told Jenny Dacquin: 'sometimes I would like to produce a
novel before I die; but either I haven't the energy, or, if I am in form,
people give me stupid administrative jobs to deal with.'[1] But these
vague aspirations never came to anything, and there is no knowing
what type of work he had in mind. Perhaps it would have been a social
satire of the kind he was thinking about at the end of 1867:

> A man has a wife with every possible quality, and a confessor. He is silly
> enough to be in love with his wife. The wife is very virtuous; the con-
> fessor is very pious and very virtuous, with the result that, in the end, the
> husband comes to strangle the wife, and the reader will have no option
> but to agree that he was right, so long as he admits the truth of what the
> proverb says about not interfering in family quarrels.[2]

A variation on this anti-Catholic plot tempted him a week or two later:
'given on the one hand a wife, a husband and a priest, all respectable;
on the other hand, a husband, a wife and a lover; demonstrate the
profound misery of the first triad and the perfect bliss of the second'.[3]
But these passing notions, perhaps inspired by his admiration for
Augier's social comedies, never came to anything, and when, from
1866 onwards, Mérimée belatedly returned to imaginative literature,
he wrote in a quite different vein.[4]

---

[1] *C.G.*, Vol. IX, p. 524.   [2] *C.G.*, Vol. XIII, p. 703.
[3] *C.G.*, Vol. XIV, p. 4.
[4] On this group of late tales, see especially P. Mérimée, *Derniers Contes*,
ed. Léon Lemonnier, Paris, Champion, 1929; P. Trahard, *La Vieillesse de*

In the last four years of his life, Mérimée produced three stories: *La Chambre bleue* (*The Blue Room*) in September 1866, *Lokis* in the latter part of 1868, and *Djoûmane* early in 1870. In addition, in the winter of 1868–9, he tried to reconstitute *Il Viccolo di Madama Lucrezia*, of which the original manuscript, dating from 1846, had been given to Valentine's sister Mme Odier. But this new version, if it was ever completed, disappeared, and the text of the story as we know it is that of 1846. None of these late tales was intended for publication, and it was only at the insistence of Buloz that *Lokis* appeared in the *Revue des Deux Mondes* on 15 September 1869. *La Chambre bleue* and *Djoûmane* were published only after Mérimée's death.[5] This hesitancy does not mean that Mérimée was in doubt about their quality – he took great pains over *Lokis* and had a surprisingly high opinion of the mediocre *Chambre bleue*. But he was mildly bemused by his sudden recrudescence of interest in story-telling, apprehensive about the effect on public opinion of scabrous subjects treated by a senator, and generally disinclined to advertise works conceived as entertainments for his friends. In fact, these last stories, despite the twenty-year gap, retain the narrative skill of the earlier tales but their themes break new ground.

The first of them, *La Chambre bleue*, is the least impressive. With a series of knowing sniggers, Mérimée tells the banal story of a couple who go to a country hotel for an illicit weekend, find their bliss interrupted by sinister nocturnal noises in the next-door room occupied by an English lord, see with horror what appears to be blood seeping underneath the door – only to discover the following morning that the bibulous lord had upset his bottle of port. It is a strangely pointless

---

Prosper Mérimée (*1854–1870*), Paris, Champion, 1930, Chapter XIV; and of course M. Parturier's edition of the *Romans et nouvelles*.

[5] The manuscript of *La Chambre bleue* was found among the Imperial papers in the Tuileries after the overthrow of the Empire in 1870. The official commission appointed to deal with these papers hesitated to publish it because of its frivolity, and it appeared, somewhat mysteriously, in *L'Indépendance belge* in September 1871. It aroused bitter controversy, republicans arguing that it showed the degeneracy of the fallen régime, and even insinuating that the lovers in the story were Mérimée and Eugénie, and imperialists protesting that Mérimée would not have written such filth, nor the Empress read it. *Djoûmane* was published in *Le Moniteur universel* in January 1873, by the editor Paul Dalloz who had been given the manuscript by Mérimée.

story, creating tension only to dissipate it with the announcement that it was all a misunderstanding. What Mérimée told his friends about the genesis of *La Chambre bleue* helps to explain the impression of gratuitousness which it leaves. According to the account he gave later to Jenny Dacquin, while he had been staying with the Empress at Biarritz in the summer of 1866, the guests had amused themselves by discussing how to behave in difficult situations, such as that of Rodrigue torn between his father and Chimène in Corneille's *Le Cid*. 'That night, having drunk too much strong tea, I wrote about fifteen pages on a situation of that kind.'[6] For Turgenev's benefit, he went into more detail.

> I had intended my subject to be very tragic, and I had written the pre-liminaries to it in a facetious style so as to surprise the reader even more. As the thing was dragging on and boring me, I rounded it off with a joke, which is bad.[7]

He also boasted of its immorality.[8] The manuscript which he subsequently presented to Eugénie, is signed: 'Composed and written by Pr. MÉRIMÉE, jester to Her Majesty the Empress'.[9]

But if Mérimée wanted to involve the reader in the moral dilemma of two lovers afraid to report an apparent murder lest their relationship be made public, he has sadly miscalculated. The problematic aspect of their situation is only touched on. What seems to have interested him most is the evocation of the emotions of the guilty couple as they arrive at the hotel, as they find their solitude disturbed by an officers' dinner, as they gradually come to suspect that some dreadful crime is being committed in the adjoining room. All this is done skilfully, with a light touch, but even more than *Il Viccolo di Madama Lucrezia*, it builds up its effects for no other purpose than the meretricious pleasure of a deliberately bathetic anticlimax. It is no more than an irritatingly childish hoax; perhaps it is significant that the two stories which stand on either side of the twenty-year period during which Mérimée devoted himself to history should demean fiction to the lowest level of deception. If Mérimée had given the tale the tragic ending he originally planned, maybe the lovers' dilemma would have been more dramatic and more gripping. Maybe too the latent association of

[6] *C.G.*, Vol. XIII, p. 278.   [7] *Ibid.*, p. 229.
[8] *Ibid.*, p. 242.   [9] *Romans et nouvelles*, Vol. II, p. 514.

eroticism with scenes of bloodshed and death which marks the other late stories would have been more forcibly expressed and would have given it something of that sinister, enigmatic and slightly repellent fascination which characterises *Lokis* and *Djoûmane*. But one can only marvel at the self-delusion which led Mérimée to remark with satisfaction to Jenny Dacquin: 'it is not, I think, the worst thing I've produced, even if it was written in a great hurry'.[10]

Lokis is very different. Relatively long, carefully planned, scrupulously documented, it is a work to which Mérimée from the outset attached some importance. Like *La Chambre bleue*, it was written for the Empress, and, if we are to believe the author, was meant to outdo in sensationalism the extravagant fantastic novels which in 1868 formed the staple diet of the Court at Fontainebleau.[11] But it turned out more seriously: 'the trouble is that I immediately started to find it attractive, and instead of drawing a caricature, I tried to do a portrait'.[12] First roughed out in August 1868, it was not finished until the following summer, and when Buloz pressed Mérimée to allow the *Revue des Deux Mondes* to print it, his resistance soon wilted. The story of the Lithuanian count whose mother was violated by a bear, and who had consequently always had bearish traits in his nature, which culminate in the murder of his bride on their wedding-night, is not original. Like the legend on which *La Vénus d'Ille* is based, it is an ancient story,[13] retold, revivified and localised by Mérimée, which had often crossed his mind. The subject was clearly mapped out in 1867 when he had written to the young and pretty Lise Przezdziecka:

> you talk to me about hunting with such enthusiasm that I imagine you would rather like to find yourself face to face with a wolf, or even a bear. The first of these dreadful animals is all right, but I absolutely forbid you to have anything to do with bears; they are much too ill-bred to show respect to huntresses.[14]

---

[10] *C.G.*, Vol. XIII, p. 279.   [11] *C.G.*, Vol. XIV, pp. 233 and 245.
[12] *Ibid.*, p. 248.
[13] The legend occurs in the works of the twelfth-century historian Saxo Grammaticus, as well as in the tales of Bandello. A modern version which Mérimée had almost certainly read was printed in the *Revue de Paris* in July 1833. On *Lokis*, see the critical edition by R. Schmittlein, Baden, Art et Science, 1949, which is full of information but sometimes inaccurate.
[14] *C.G.*, Vol. XIII, p. 529.

In 1850 he wrote to Mme de Montijo about a girl who was going to live in Sweden: 'if one gets married in that sort of country, it is a great stroke of luck, I think, if one doesn't give birth to a polar bear'.[15]

Mérimée decided to locate the story in Lithuania because when he wrote it, he was studying a Lithuanian grammar, Schleicher's *Handbuch der litauischen Sprache*.[16] Moreover, as he had been zestfully translating some of Turgenev's fantastic tales, he was tempted to try his own hand at giving a fantastic anecdote an Eastern European colouring. Mickiewicz's *Pan Tadeusz*, which he had been reading in French, supplied some of the detailed documentation,[17] as did *La Pologne captive et ses trois poètes* (*Enslaved Poland and its three poets*) by Charles Edmond, otherwise Choiecki, a Polish émigré living in Paris, whom Mérimée knew and consulted in person about *Lokis*.[18] Turgenev too was put to work, and eventually provided the title.[19] The local colour is on the whole accurate and convincing – remarkably so for someone who had never been within hundreds of miles of Lithuania. It is the same kind of imaginative divination which had enabled Mérimée to write *Mateo Falcone* without visiting Corsica.

The theme of the story is bizarre and disturbing. In his first draft, Mérimée had made it clear that Countess Szémioth was raped by the bear when it dragged her off into a thicket. But when he read *Lokis* to Jenny Dacquin, she objected to this scandalous postulate, and in deference to her wishes, he made the incident more vague,[20] so that, as he remarked to Mme Delessert, 'timorous people who would refuse to believe in cross-breeding between *plantigrades* will be at liberty to assume that the hero's eccentricities derive from a pregnant woman's fright or fancy'.[21] This decent obscurity does not alter the zoological prodigy on which the story rests: Michel Szémioth *is* the son of the bear. Various small touches hint at this relationship in the early part of the tale – his propensity for tree-climbing, the terror he inspires

[15] *C.G.*, Vol. VI, p. 54.   [16] Cf. Schmittlein, *op. cit.*, pp. 58–9.
[17] *Ibid.*, pp. 45–52. The poem of *Les Trois Fils Boudrys* with which the mischievous Ioulka hoaxes the narrator and which is by Mickiewicz, had originally been rendered into French by Mérimée from Pushkin's Russian translation, in the belief that it was an original Pushkin poem.
[18] See notably Letter 4407 in *C.G.*, Vol. XIV.
[19] See Mérimée's letters to Turgenev, *C.G.*, Vol. XIV, pp. 262 and 311.
[20] *C.G.*, Vol. XIV, p. 255.   [21] *Ibid.*, p. 264.

in domestic animals, the mysterious remarks of the witch-like old woman he meets in the forest, his crushing embrace of the girl he eventually marries, his sudden accesses of savage violence, his mother's madness. But the climax is reached when, after the wedding-night, the corpse of his bride Ioulka is found with teeth-marks in her throat. For Mérimée, there was in this gruesome theme something more than the arbitrary evocation of horror. To Turgenev, he made an uncharacteristic admission: 'if I were any good at writing verse, I would have made a poem out of it; I find something poetic in this mixture of humanity and bestiality'.[22] In the story itself, this aspect of the action is made explicit when, in a conversation with the narrator and a doctor, the count asks for an explanation of 'the *duality* or the *duplicity* of our nature'.[23] How does it come about, he wonders, that our passions can make us commit acts which our reason abhors? The implied answer is that, in all of us, there is a latent animal nature which is normally held in check by reason and morality, but which is liable to escape if reason momentarily loses its vigilance.

I believe that if all *your* thoughts, professor – and I consider you a wise man – ,were written out, they would form a folio volume perhaps, on the evidence of which any lawyer could easily get you declared legally incapable, any judge would have you locked up in prison or a madhouse.[24]

So the idea of Szémioth having been fathered by a bear is ultimately used as a means of heightening dramatically the theme that there is a beast in all of us. Clearly, this is related to the treatment of the destructive force of passion to be found so often in Mérimée's work. In particular, *Lokis* resembles *La Vénus d'Ille*. In both stories a pedantic narrator arrives in an out-of-the-way spot, witnesses a variety of more or less disquieting incidents, is present at a wedding, and the morning

[22] *C.G.*, Vol. XIV, p. 262.
[23] *Romans et nouvelles*, Vol. II, p. 480.
[24] *Ibid.*, M. Schmittlein (*op. cit.*, pp. 39–40) claims that Mérimée had met the real Count Szémioth and heard from him of the legend of the bear's son which was current in his family. That this is not so is proved by a letter from Mérimée to Charles Edmond on 14 October 1869, in which he says: 'I am very sorry I used the name of Szémioth which I thought had been extinct since the time of Jagellon' (*C.G.*, Vol. XIV, p. 638). No doubt it was only after the publication of *Lokis* that the Szémioth family started finding bears in its lineage.

after discovers that one of the spouses has been the victim of a brutal and mysterious slaughter. This pattern emphasises the extent to which both works are concerned with the dangers of unleashed erotic passion. But whereas *La Vénus d'Ille* treats this theme on the level of mythology, *Lokis* transfers it to that of pathology. The murder in the first story is the work of a statue symbolising Venus; in the second, it springs from the instinctive lusts of a young man. Whatever the implausible explanation for these lusts proffered by Mérimée, they are something which well up inside a human being, and which, it is suggested, any of us may feel. Sex, the most primitive of urges, releases the bestiality underlying even the most civilised of natures (Szémioth is presented as an affable, cultured and distinguished man in ordinary circumstances), and the woman, like Mlle de Puygarrig in *La Vénus d'Ille*, has a white-skinned, childlike innocence that marks her out as a predestined victim. The sexual implications are underlined both by the account of Szémioth's mother's experience with the bear, and by the overtly phallic imagery of the encounter with the old woman and her snake.

Nowhere has Mérimée penetrated further into the dark recesses of the human mind than in *Lokis*. One is forced to envisage unpleasant possibilities about one's own constitution, which are all the more disquieting for being only half-spoken. If in the end *Lokis* remains distinctly inferior to *La Vénus d'Ille*, that is partly because it comes too close to repeating the effects of the earlier story, and partly because it is difficult to overlook the physical impossibility on which it depends. We are required to believe, not in the supernatural, but in a misstatement of the laws of physiology.[25] Perhaps there are some obsessional undertones in this choice of a subject involving a sexual prodigy – Ioulka resembles Lise Przezdziecka, with whom Mérimée was conducting a platonic flirtation, and there must have been something frustrating in such a situation for a man of his once voracious sexual appetites. He has not succeeded in giving *Lokis* the same air of general human truth as *La Vénus d'Ille*. The impression it gives is ultimately one of eccentricity, of abnormality; in the literal sense, it is a monstrous tale.

Djoûmane was the last story Mérimée wrote, begun in January 1870

[25] Mérimée had doubts about the wisdom of this: 'how can one depict something impossible?' he complained to Mme Delessert on 22 September 1868 (*C.G.*, Vol. XIV, p. 248).

and finished in March of the same year.[26] It is supposedly related by
a French officer fighting against the Arabs in Algeria. Exhausted by
a long ride, he and his troops are obliged to set out again without sleep,
but they first witness a performance by a snake-charmer, in which a
little girl is bitten but recovers as if by miracle. The officer is then
involved in a skirmish at a ford, becomes separated from his men, sees
an extraordinary scene in which a magician apparently drowns a girl
in a well with some sort of serpent swimming in its waters, wanders
through passages cut in a rocky hillside, is welcomed into a luxurious
chamber by a raven-haired beauty . . . and then awakes to realise that
he had been dreaming while riding out in accordance with his orders.
At first sight, one might be tempted to consider the final revelation
as yet another instance of Mérimée's taste for anticlimactic deceptions,
in the manner of *La Chambre bleue*. But it does not cancel out the
strangely fascinating quality of the dream sequences, so that one is
forced to seek some profounder meaning in it.

Raoul Roche[27] has provided a Freudian reading of the tale, regarding
it as a reproduction of one of Mérimée's own dreams, and seeing in it
the disguised expression of a passing desire for a young Jewish girl,
figured by a recurrent association of a snake with the girl's death and
intensified by the oppression caused by his asthma. This reading is
marred by the critic's failure to realise at what point in the story the
dream begins;[28] it is only when the officer, after the snake-charming
incident, rides out with his troop towards the ford that his fatigue
causes him to fall asleep on horseback. The dream thus opens with the
arrival at the ford and the fight with the Arab leader: the rest is presented as part of the officer's waking experience. But that does not
altogether disqualify M. Roche's theory, since Mérimée's sexual obses-
sions might just as much be translated by the images of what he states
to be reality as by those which he specifically attributes to a dream –
the more so as the two parts of the tale are thematically very closely

---

[26] He mentioned to Viollet-le-Duc on 26 January 1870 that he had started
it (*C.G.*, Vol. XV, p. 16). On 21 March, he told Charles Edmond that it was
finished except for the title (*C.G.*, Vol. XVII, p. 63).

[27] Raoul Roche, 'Un rêve de Mérimée: *Djoûmane*', *Grande Revue*, octobre
1928.

[28] As has been pointed out by P.-G. Castex in *Le Conte fantastique en
France*, Paris, Corti, 1951, p. 281.

related. In support of his opinion, one might add that not only is the
'-mane' of *Djoûmane* the phonetic equivalent of the termination
'-mann' common in Jewish surnames, but that the first syllable 'Djoû'
is almost a transcription of the English word 'Jew'. Moreover, Mérimée
must often have fallen asleep while looking at his father's picture
Innocence feeding a serpent, which hung in his bedroom. The inconsequential flow of images, the almost surrealistic illogicality of the
action, the obvious sexuality of certain scenes, Mérimée's own casual
remark to Jenny Dacquin that in *Djoûmane* 'there is a lot about love',[29]
which is not an immediately noticeable feature, all legitimise a psycho-
analytic approach to the story.

Not that one need follow M. Roche in diagnosing its origins in a
guilty fancy for a little Jewish girl. In the latter years of his life, Mérimée
sought the company of attractive young women with whom he
bantered about love – Olga de Lagrené, Lise Przezdziecka, the Duchesse
de Castiglione-Colonna. Superficially, these amorous friendships were
innocent; beneath the surface, they undoubtedly offered the ageing
Mérimée a somewhat shame-faced compensation for his vanished sexual
powers. The idea of real sexual contact with one of these girls would
have been unthinkable, given his age, his ill-health and his loss of
potency. But it must always have been there as a culpable temptation,
and this seems to be one of the reasons for the hints that the girl in
Djoûmane is Jewish. Like many Frenchmen of his class and generation,
Mérimée had been vaguely and as it were automatically anti-semitic –
in 1849, for instance, he had recommended a bookseller to Sobolevski
with the words: 'he's a Jew, but he has a good stock',[30] and in 1854,
he joked that Jews repelled him 'as much for their conduct under the
government of Pontius Pilate as for their love of money'.[31] Yet he
appreciated the charms of Jewish prostitutes, and in 1830 had happily
announced to Sutton Sharpe that the cargoes of newly arrived whores
included some 'splendid Jewesses with fine large black eyes, and delicate
feet'.[32] In this way, Mérimée associated illicit sexual pleasure with a

[29] *C.G.*, Vol. XV, p. 34.
[30] *C.G.*, Vol. V, p. 430.
[31] *C.G.*, Vol. VII, p. 379. Admittedly, he says there that the Jews he has
just met in Vienna are so delightful that he has lost his prejudices. But old
habits die hard.
[32] Unpublished letter to Sutton Sharpe in Appendix A.

taboo on Jewishness,[33] and no doubt this comes out in the Semitic references in *Djoûmane*, rather than any specific attraction to a young Jewess.

The preoccupations of *Djoûmane* are highly personal, which is possibly why Mérimée kept it for himself and a few intimate friends. It has much less relevance to the human situation in general than *Lokis*, and in any case contains much less narrative substance. The gratuitousness of the sequence of events militates against dramatic tension, and there is not much inducement for the reader to delve below its surface. It is only if one takes the trouble to decode the perhaps inadvertent symbolism with which it is strewn that it appears as a work of any cogency or inner necessity. Even then, its interest scarcely extends beyond that of being a curious and slightly sinister document on the subterranean workings of Mérimée's emotions.

Though this isolated outcrop of stories at the end of Mérimée's life includes no masterpieces, it does represent an interesting new departure in his art. The style and the narrative techniques are still those he had used twenty years earlier. But they serve different purposes. More clearly than he had ever done before, Mérimée tries to penetrate the mysteries of the subconscious. That the result is wholly satisfactory in literary terms may be doubted, even though these stories are nowadays more highly rated by critics than they used to be. They are too strange, too disconnected, too individual to be accessible even to a sympathetic public. Nevertheless, without them, something would be missing in our image of Mérimée: a direct glimpse into the steamy, tangled undergrowth of his mind. He was taken aback by this sudden return of an imaginative inspiration he believed to be long dead, and attempted to dismiss it as a manifestation of senility.

> When you are young, you can call on women of easy virtue in broad daylight; a venerable old man like myself, if he still thought about such women, would only visit them in secret. I'm reaching the stage of second childhood, and I may be weak enough to go on writing stories, but I have sense enough to show them only to my friends.[34]

---

[33] He was not alone in this. Maupassant, in *La Maison Tellier*, notes that in Mme Tellier's establishment, one Raphaële 'played the indispensable role of the *beautiful Jewess*' (*Contes et nouvelles*, Paris, Albin Michel, 1956, Vol. II, p. 1180). Some of things Proust says about Saint-Loup's Rachel are in a similar vein.   [34] *C.G.*, Vol. XIV, p. 271.

He only agreed to the publication of *Lokis* when readings of it at Court had convinced him that most people would misunderstand it, and chance alone assured the survival of the other tales. This sense of shame betokens a fear that he is exposing himself without defence. That he did so is both their strength and weakness. They initiate us into the most secret parts of his personality, and the protective structures so prominent in his earlier fiction have largely collapsed. But the constraint and reticence, always essential to his art, have also been damaged, and the result, if more revealing, is also less telling.

Chapter 20

Invalid

Qu'est-ce qu'est pour moi l'éternité? Ce qui est important
pour moi, c'est un petit nombre de jours. Pourquoi me les
donne-t-on si amers?

To Jenny Dacquin, 2 January 1866

In 1864, Mérimée visited Spain for the last time, spending several
weeks with Mme de Montijo at Carabanchel and Madrid. The weather
was cold and wet, the bull-fights disappointing, and the general character of the country less original, so without great regret he went
on to Cannes. After that, he rarely disturbed the regular rhythm of his
life: Cannes in the winter, Paris in the Spring, London in summer,
Paris and the Court in the autumn, then back to Cannes.

In 1866, Mérimée stayed at Cannes until 7 April, even longer than
usual. The fine weather had made him feel stronger than he had done
a year before, but he took care never to go out after sunset for fear
of colds and chills, to which he had become very susceptible and which
increased the discomforts caused by his asthma. Back in Paris, he set
to work on a speech he had to deliver in the Senate opposing a law
exempting mechanical musical instruments from copyright restrictions.
Behind the apparent triviality of the subject, Mérimée saw an important
principle at stake: 'at bottom, what is under attack is the ownership
of things of the mind,'[1] he told Turgenev. But as usual, his public
performance was ineffectual; he saved up his epigrams for a reply to
the debate which he was never asked to make, and the law went
through without difficulty. In fact, Mérimée showed considerable foresight in realising the implications of the law for possible new inventions; had his eloquence been equal to his insight, many later complications might have been avoided.

Otherwise he occupied his time in Paris much as he had done in
previous years: helping Turgenev with the translation of his works

[1] *C.G.*, Vol. XIII, p. 28.

into French, pursuing his own studies of Peter the Great, keeping up his voluminous correspondence, observing with anxious interest the changing political scene in Italy, Spain, England and France. Now that Napoleon III's book on Caesar was finished (Mérimée reviewed the second volume in July 1866 for the *Journal des Savants*), contacts between the two men were less close and less frequent. In any case, Mérimée had privately begun to lose confidence in the Emperor as he saw his energy waning, and had now acquired a new idol in the person of Bismarck, whom he had met in Biarritz one Sunday morning in 1864 when the Chancellor had arrived at the Villa Eugénie while everyone except Mérimée was at Mass. Mérimée had immediately conceived a great admiration for the aura of ruthless strength which emanated from him. To Panizzi he averred that Bismarck was his hero,[2] to Mme de Montijo that Bismarck was 'a great man',[3] to Mme de Beaulaincourt that 'there is unfortunately only one great man every century, and M. de Bismarck occupies the post'.[4] Henceforth, Mérimée regarded him, with a mixture of awe and trepidation, as the arbiter of the fate of Europe. In internal politics, he had long since abandoned hope of making Thiers useful to the Imperial cause. Thiers had been elected to the National Assembly in 1863, but instead of adopting a conciliatory attitude, had allied himself, to Mérimée's chagrin, with the republican opposition. This led to a break between them, and in 1866 Mérimée said angrily: 'for a long time now I haven't been seeing him. He has told me so many lies and made so many fine promises that I don't want anything more to do with him.'[5] The slow return to a form of parliamentary government which the Emperor was introducing alarmed and depressed him: 'the greatest misfortune which can befall a nation is, I believe, to have institutions more advanced than its intelligence', he wrote sadly to Panizzi in February 1866.[6] All this meant that he viewed politics with growing distaste and detachment; powerless to influence events, he watched with deepening gloom the portents of revolution which he detected everywhere.

A visit to Panizzi in July 1866 helped to revive his flagging spirits. But Panizzi himself was now ailing; he had lost some of the boisterous joviality which had so much amused Eugénie when, on an excursion into the mountains from Biarritz where he had stayed with Mérimée in 1864,

---

[2] *Ibid.*, p. 163.   [3] *Ibid.*, p. 164.
[4] *Ibid.*, p. 310.   [5] *Ibid.*, p. 51.   [6] *Ibid.*, pp. 47-8.

he had decided that his corpulence prevented him from getting off his horse and had remained in the saddle to eat the lunch which the Empress handed up to him. Now he was all too eager to retire as he had unsuccessfully tried to do in 1865, and Mérimée had regretfully to bid farewell to the British Museum, where he had become such a part of the institution that the policemen always saluted him. On his return to Paris, Mérimée was whisked off to St Cloud, where Eugénie had decided to receive her guests so as not to be too far from Paris while the international crisis caused by the Austro-Prussian war remained unresolved. The party was small and intimate, which pleased Mérimée, and he took advantage of this to read Turgenev's story *The Dog* to the Emperor and Empress. Then, at the beginning of September, the Court, with Mérimée still in attendance, set off for Biarritz, where they remained for almost two months. Though Mérimée preferred Biarritz to Paris, he found such a long stay tedious, deplored the Empress's tendency to indulge in futile parlour-games, and became so bored that he was reduced to writing *La Chambre bleue* to pass the time. That he was at last able to return to original composition is evidence of his relative equanimity at this time,[7] but the product is regrettably mediocre.

From Biarritz, Mérimée went back briefly to Paris before his annual hibernation in the South. On 31 October he called on Valentine Delessert, and to his astonishment found, for the first time for more than twelve years, that she greeted him affectionately and seemed disposed to resume their former close friendship. Now that her other lovers had faded out, that she felt herself growing old, that loneliness was weighing heavily on her, and that the unscrupulous Du Camp had capitalised on their romance by using it as the basis for his auto-

[7] It is often stated that it was his reconciliation with Valentine that enabled Mérimée to start writing fiction again (e.g. R. Baschet, *Mérimée*, p. 247). But the dates give the lie to this. *La Chambre bleue* was written at Biarritz in September 1866; Mme Delessert did not welcome him back as a friend until 31 October. The fact is that by 1866 Mérimée had so far forgotten Mme Delessert that he was for the first time able to write a story for someone else – in this case the Empress Eugénie. Admittedly, the restoration of Valentine's friendship may have helped him to go on writing other tales; as in his youth, he always had to write with some specific person in mind. But it is going too far to see a causal connection between Valentine's affection and his ability to produce works of the imagination.

biographical novel *Les Forces perdues* (*Lost Energy*) which had just appeared,[8] Valentine had begun to realise the true worth of Mérimée's stubborn fidelity. For both of them, the age of passion was past, but each knew how much friendship could mean, and for the last few years of his life it was balm for Mérimée's troubled soul to know that, after all the betrayals and estrangements, he could once more rely on Valentine's affection. With typical restraint it was not until almost a month later, writing to her from Cannes, that he trusted himself to thank her without breaking down. At the end of a long letter full of indifferent news and gossip, with a quiet dignity that overlay the profoundest feeling, he said:

> the last time I saw you, you made me very happy. You restored to me, I hope I am right in saying, a friendship which had been extremely precious to me and yet which I had sometimes doubted, with the greatest possible distress. I felt that you were taking a thorn out of my heart. Let us speak no more of that, Madame; allow me simply to thank you.[9]

Those who find Mérimée cold would do well to ponder the degree of self-control needed to speak with such moving simplicity of a love which had filled his whole life, which had almost destroyed him when it was broken, and which now, as he neared death, was given back to him. There is not the slightest trace of 'literature' in his reaction: only an unassuming allusion to something which meant more to him than words could ever express. True to his promise, he never spoke of it again, but it must have been a constant comfort to him.

In the meantime, the winter sunshine of Cannes failed to produce its usual curative effect, and Mérimée's health and spirits drooped accordingly. When he arrived in November, he wrote: 'I have the feeling that in this part of the world, I am *at home*, which I scarcely am in Paris.'[10] But by the end of December, his thoughts had once more turned to death:

> when I have difficulty in breathing, that is, very often, I produce all sorts of fine arguments to convince myself that this world is not worth caring about. I can find no reason for regretting it; yet I do regret it much more than I hope in the next one. I am in the position of someone getting ready

---

[8] See M. Parturier, 'Autour de Mérimée. *Les Forces perdues* et *L'Éducation sentimentale*'.

[9] *C.G.*, Vol. XIII, p. 302.   [10] *Ibid.*, p. 285.

for a troublesome journey; the preparations are even more troublesome than the journey.[11]

It was in this depressed frame of mind that on 13 January 1867 he was struck by sudden disaster. Victor Cousin, who in the morning had seemed perfectly fit, suffered a stroke as he slept after lunch. Mérimée was sent for, and arrived to find Cousin unconscious. The death agony continued in his presence until five o'clock the next morning, when the philosopher died. This harrowing sight seared Mérimée's mind: in the next few days, he described it at length no fewer than ten times in his letters.

M. Cousin's death has hit me hard, and I can still see his death agony. I wonder what is better, to die like him with a bolt from the blue, or to pass on gradually in prolonged suffering.[12]

As if this blow were not enough, a few days later Mérimée was aghast to learn that Napoleon III had dismissed Fould, who had been Minister of Finance since 1861. Though his loyalty to the Empire held him back from saying all he felt, there is little doubt that he thought the Emperor's conduct both crass and ungentlemanly. Fould was more than merely the only minister with whom Mérimée was on terms of close friendship, he was the only one in whom he had any confidence, and to see him sacked for the second time was a cruel disappointment. Shortly afterwards, Panizzi, now retired, arrived to keep Mérimée company, followed by Fould himself, apparently resigned to his return to private life and the pleasures of racehorse ownership. But even these welcome companions were unable to bring Mérimée out of his dejection. Another friend, Henri Courmont, once a colleague at the Historic Monuments commission and now a member of the Cannes colony, informed Viollet-le-Duc in March how low he had sunk:

he is more silent than ever, and, far from having recovered his former cheerfulness, is only in a good mood when he is forced to be by the presence of someone who impresses him and when his two petticoats are out of the way [. . .] Since M. Fould and Panizzi left, he has fallen back into apathy.[13]

---

[11] C.G., Vol. XIII, pp. 351–2.
[12] Ibid., p. 402.   [13] Ibid., p. 448, n. 2.

He was unable to hide his melancholy even from the Empress:

> I've never felt weaker, more discouraged, more *avvilito* as the Italians say.
> I long ago gave up any expectation of being cured, but I still cannot
> accustom myself to suffering; above all I am irritated and indignant to see
> my mind following the same path of decadence as my body. I despise and
> loathe myself for no longer being master of my own person.[14]

Still, at the beginning of April, he plucked up his courage and forced
himself to return to Paris. Inevitably this did not improve his health,
and he spent the summer in gloom-ridden contemplation of his own
decrepitude. For the first time since 1859, he failed to cross the Channel
to visit Panizzi, and was obliged to decline the Empress's invitation to
join the Court at Biarritz. He managed to attend a few debates in the
Senate but otherwise went out rarely, and spent his evenings at home
reading or playing backgammon with his cousin Léonor Fresnel. He
was still able to work on Russian history and had widened the circle
of his numerous correspondents to include two elegant and attractive
young ladies. One was Lise Przezdziecka, wife of a Polish count and
very much *persona grata* at Court, where she presided over a 'Court of
Love' of which Mérimée was secretary. Between them there reigned
an ambivalent atmosphere of *marivaudage* which was always on the
verge of becoming more serious. 'The fact is that I'm afraid of you',
Mérimée confided to her in August 1866. 'I'm not enough of a philosopher to allow myself to love you, as I might be tempted to do.
I do my best to think of you as a pretty fairy who appears to me from
time to time, who charms and delights me by her grace and her kindness. Then I tell myself there are no fairies nowadays, that this sub-
lunary world is serious and boring, that one should enjoy visions of
another world when they come, but not believe too much in their
reality.'[15] The other new quasi-amorous interest was the Duchesse de
Castiglione-Colonna, the young Swiss-born widow of an Italian nobleman, who had established her reputation as a sculptor under the
pseudonym Marcello.[16] Mérimée knew her by 1864, and as she travelled
regularly, met her as often in Cannes or Nice as he did in Paris. A
third new partner with whom he began to exchange letters in the late
1860s was an older woman, Mme de Beaulaincourt, twice widowed

[14] *Ibid.*, p. 454.   [15] *Ibid.*, p. 177.
[16] See P. Trahard's edition of Mérimée's *Lettres à la duchesse de Castiglione-
Colonna*, Paris, Boivin, 1938.

and possessor of a lurid past which did not stop her being a friend of the Empress.[17] Mérimée had known and disliked her mother, though he later felt he had been unfair to her, and he found Mme de Beaulaincourt an agreeably frank and unorthodox friend. Some idea of her character can be gained from the fact that she was Proust's model for the picturesque Mme de Villeparisis.

Friendships of this kind, always important to Mérimée, now helped to keep him alive. He was so desperate at his inability to find any relief from his asthma that by December of 1867 he had even been driven to vain experiments with towels manufactured by nuns at Tarascon and designed to be applied to the chest. But nothing did any good, especially as his morale was deplorable, aggravated by Achille Fould's sudden death in October 1867. He was sure that Fould's dismissal was responsible for his death: 'he wore himself out with inward emotions that he hid with care. Those who were close to him know how sensitive he was.'[18] He admitted to Lise Przezdziecka that Fould's death had affected him more than he could say and that he had become a permanent victim to the blue devils.[19] To make matters worse, the moment he arrived in Cannes, the weather, which had been magnificent there for seven months, suddenly broke, and he found only torrential rain.

1868 thus began with Mérimée more ill than ever, despairing of any improvement, obsessed with his own ailments save when he cast a pessimistic glance at political developments. Remote now from the centre of events, he had to rely for news on the papers and on gossip from his friends, but in any case he was more certain than ever that the Empire was heading for disaster. Napoleon seemed to have lost his authority, clumsy concessions to parliamentarianism had opened the door to anarchy, left-wing agitation was only awaiting a favourable opportunity to raise the standard of revolt. Occasional visitors momentarily interrupted his brooding, as when Edward Lear called on him on his way to paint in Corsica, but normally he was reduced to the company of Fanny and Emma, who were far from being scintillating conversationalists. On 10 February, he complained bitterly to Jenny Dacquin that his melancholy and dark humours were intensifying: 'I

[17] See M. Parturier's edition of *Lettres de Prosper Mérimée à Madame de Beaulaincourt (1866–1870)*, Paris, Calmann-Lévy, 1936.

[18] *C.G.*, Vol. XIII, p. 623.   [19] *Ibid.*, p. 627.

still haven't got used to suffering and it irritates me, which gives me
two ills instead of one.'[20] Ten days later, he told Boeswillwald that
he had had to rest three times while dressing and had only managed
to finish after drugging himself.[21] The situation was 'unbearable' and he
saw no remedy for it, he wrote to another friend.[22] When he could,
he went out for short walks, and cultivated the society of a squirrel and
a lame seagull, but often he was so weak he could not leave his house.

Then came unexpected relief. A lawyer in Marseille wrote to tell
Mérimée that he had been cured of his asthma by compressed air treatment given by a Dr Bertin at Montpellier and advised him to experiment with it. By now, as Mérimée himself admitted, he was even
ready to try charlatans. It was not until mid-April that he felt strong
enough to travel to Montpellier, and he strove not to expect too much.
'I am going without hope. I don't see how such a treatment can repair
broken-down lungs, and you know that one must believe if one is to
be cured. I am totally lacking in faith.'[23] But once he had settled down
at the Hôtel Nevet and started the treatment, he found his breathing
notably easier. Every other day he went to Bertin's clinic, entered a
metal chamber fitted with portholes, ensconced himself in an armchair
with a copy of the *Revue des Deux Mondes*, waited while a steam
machine pumped in compressed air, and then usually fell asleep for
a couple of hours. Apart from a slight cracking of the ears, the treatment was not disagreeable, and almost at once the emphysema began
to diminish. After a month, he wrote triumphantly in English to his
friend Bellenden Ker: 'I am a great deal better from my baths of
compressed air. The emphysema of the lungs has disappeared and I
breathe a great deal better than I did.'[24]

On 17 May he was able to return to Paris, stronger and healthier
than he had been for well over a year. On 16 June, he even spoke in
the Senate against a petition denouncing materialism, a subject on
which, as the 'last Voltairean',[25] he held strong views. Sainte-Beuve,
who was present, recorded his impressions when he returned home:

> people were expecting something stimulating from him; he disappointed
> them by producing an arid and insignificant report. Through fear of

---

[20] *C.G.*, Vol. XIV, p. 30.   [21] *Ibid.*, p. 39.
[22] *Ibid.*, p. 44   [23] *Ibid.*, p. 97   [24] Unpublished letter in Appendix A.
[25] Mérimée claimed to have been given this nickname by a bishop (*C.G.*,
Vol. VI, p. 439).

falling into rhetoric, he too often goes to the opposite extreme and comes dangerously near to sterility. He likes awakening the attention of his admirers, then letting them down. It is a mistake [. . .] Decidedly, Mérimée keeps himself on too tight a rein; he deliberately set out to be too detached; in the end, it has become natural to him.[26]

But if Mérimée's public speaking was as unimpressive as ever, at least he was taking an interest in life, and throughout the summer remained positively gay. At the beginning of July, he spent ten days in London with Panizzi, and dined out several times without ill effects. One of his dinners was with Gladstone, whom he had known for several years and with whom he had stayed at Hawarden Castle in 1865. Then his feelings about the future Prime Minister had been mixed: 'Mr Gladstone struck me in some respects as a man of genius, in others as a child. He is part child, part statesman, part lunatic.'[27] Now he was surprised by Gladstone's rashness in scholarship: 'he's a very intelligent and talented man, but I have doubts about his wisdom. He is ruthlessly logical. As a passionate admirer of Homer, he cannot admit that he was not a Christian, so supposes that he was the recipient of a special revelation.'[28]

On his return to Paris, Mérimée was still reasonably fit and went off with the Empress to Fontainebleau, where he wrote *Lokis* and was able to go on several excursions.[29] But he complained that the cooking tasted of old pans, and as his shortness of breath was tending to return sporadically, he decided that it would be prudent to undertake a second course of treatment at Montpellier. He spent almost the whole of October there, accompanied by Panizzi, who was also in very poor shape, but this time the results were less satisfactory. The emphysema

[26] Sainte-Beuve, *Mes Poisons*, p. 100.

[27] *C.G.*, Vol. XII, p. 508.   [28] *C.G.*, Vol. XIV, p. 193.

[29] Mérimée is often said to be the author of a famous dictation, of diabolical difficulty, set to the Court at Compiègne. In fact, it has been shown – conclusively, it would seem – that the dictation happened at Fontainebleau in 1868 at a time when Mérimée was in England. One of the various extant texts of this dictation can be found in the Marquis de Luppé's *Mérimée*, Paris, Albin Michel, 1954, pp. 193–4. The attribution to Mérimée has been refuted by Charles Samaran, 'Une énigme pseudo-littéraire: la dictée de Mérimée', *Le Monde*, 18–19 avril 1954, and M. Parturier, 'La célèbre "dictée" de Compiègne n'est en rien l'œuvre de Mérimée', *Le Figaro littéraire*, 7 juin 1958.

was alleviated, but he caught a heavy cold which turned to persistent bronchitis.

For the last fortnight I've been coughing incessantly, day and night. I'm very ill and very fed up, and I spend all my time brooding. Particularly at night, as I can't sleep, I have *blue devils* all round me. I wonder if this will be my last cold or only the one before the last.[30]

By the time he had gone to Cannes with Panizzi in November, his spirits were as low as they had ever been. Even with people in whom he had hitherto been reluctant to confide, he now waxed plaintive. To Princess Mathilde, he wrote on 5 November:

unfortunately, for the short time I still have to live, I am condemned to a solitary existence. I think I could resign myself to suffering if I had a few intervals of calm and respite which I could spend with my friends. But day by day I can feel myself growing weaker, more morose, more useless, more of a nuisance. Since I left Paris, I have been coughing and suffocating all the time. I never sleep now. I'm disgusted with everything, especially myself.[31]

The weather was bad, and as the winter wore on, his condition worsened. Then, to his dismay, in January 1869 Fanny Lagden fell dangerously ill with what looked like typhoid. Though the crisis soon passed, the worry and the extra work reduced Mérimée to a state of near-collapse. On 17 February 1869, his friend Du Sommerard told Viollet-le-Duc that the outlook was bleak. 'I found him changed and weakened beyond expression. He still gets up, but has such attacks of breathlessness that one cannot but fear the worst. He has no interest in anything, can hardly walk, and eats nothing.'[32] The following day, Dr Maure examined him and took Du Sommerard aside to tell him that Mérimée's heart was seriously affected. The news of his illness filtered back to Paris, and by early March the press was persistently reporting his death. This rumour afforded Mérimée some grim amusement: 'if I weren't such a sceptic, I'd end by believing it myself', he told Turgenev.[33] Indeed, it may have helped to revive him, such was his inveterate reluctance to do what was expected of him. The Empress did her best to cheer him up by inviting him to edit the archives of the House of Alba, and a visit from Prince Napoleon in April helped to put some spirit in him.

[30] *C.G.*, Vol. XIV, p. 274.
[31] *Ibid.*, p. 287.
[32] *Ibid.*, p. 394, n. 1.
[33] *Ibid.*, p. 415.

But no one expected to see him in Paris again. In March, Viollet-le-Duc told Princess Mathilde and the Goncourt brothers that he was dying of heart disease, and the Goncourts, as always uncharitably anxious to pick up tittle-tattle, noted in their diary:

> the end of this man who always acted the part of someone insensitive is apparently as grisly as one could imagine, dying without a friend, shut up with two old *governesses* who keep him short of food and drink so that there will be more pickings for them after his death.[34]

They were totally unmoved by the sufferings of a man whom they had disliked on the rare occasions when they had met him at Princess Mathilde's house at Saint-Gratien in 1865.

> He listens to his own voice as he talks, which he does slowly, with mortal silences, word by word, drop by drop, as if he were distilling his effects, causing a sort of icy chill to fall all round him. No wit, no epigrams; just a recherché turn of phrase, the diction of an old actor taking his time, with a hint of the impertinence of a spoiled conversationalist, an affected disdain for all illusion, modesty, social convention. For decent-minded people, there is something hurtful in this dry and spiteful irony, deliberately evolved to startle and dominate women and other weak creatures.[35]

But against all expectations (and perhaps to the Goncourts' secret disappointment), he began to recover, and early in April started to go out again. When the weather was warm enough, he would set out with Fanny and Emma, one carrying his paint-box, the other with a folding stool on which he rested every few yards until he found a suitable place in which to set up his easel. In the evenings he stayed indoors and played patience, but as the shock of Fanny's illness receded, his own health picked up, and at the end of April, he returned to Paris.

There he was able to see his friends, to catch up on his reading (with characteristic vigour, he dismissed Hugo's *L'Homme qui rit* as 'false and stupid'[36] and declared that Renan's *Saint-Paul* suffered from a 'monomania for landscape'[37]), to get on with writing his *Histoire de la fausse Elisabeth II*, and even, for the last time, to attend a meeting of the Commission for Historic Monuments. In July, he accepted the Empress's invitation to go to St Cloud with the Court. While they

[34] Edmond and Jules de Goncourt, *Journal*, ed. Robert Ricatte, Paris, Fasquelle-Flammarion, 1959, Vol. II, p. 501.

[35] *Ibid.*, p. 211.

[36] *C.G.*, Vol. XIV, pp. 490-1.   [37] *Ibid.*, p. 530.

were there, he gave a reading of *Lokis* to the assembled ladies, largely
to see if the scurrilous aspects of the story were sufficiently obscure for
it to be published. Among those present was Augustin Filon, the
Empress's young reader, later to become one of Mérimée's first and
best biographers. This is how he remembered the scene in the great
drawing-room overlooking the courtyard:

> It was a warm evening, but out of consideration for the reader, someone
> closed the windows. The doors of the adjoining rooms, brightly lit but
> deserted, remained open, and soon there was only the voice of Mérimée
> echoing in the calm stillness of the sleeping palace. The Empress was
> seated at a round table in a corner of the room, in front of a marble bust
> of the King of Rome at the age of twenty. On her left was Mérimée.
> Around the table sat the two ladies-in-waiting who were on duty that
> week, the maids of honour, Mlle de Larminat and Mlle d'Elbée, and finally
> the Empress's nieces Marie and Louise, with that very amiable and dis-
> tinguished lady who was at the time in charge of their education. A heavy
> lamp cast its light over the white exercise book in which *Lokis* was written
> out in a large, firm hand, over the slowly fluttering fans, over the em-
> broidery noiselessly moving through slender, agile fingers, over all these
> bent heads, over these girls whose eyes would sometimes be raised towards
> the reader with an expression of meditative curiosity. Two or three men,
> sitting further back, completed the little group. Mérimée read in his in-
> different, monotonous voice, interrupted only by smiles or slight murmurs
> of approval led by the Empress [. . .] A moment after he had finished, he
> stood up and said to me abruptly, in an undertone: 'Did *you* understand?'
> I must have looked rather foolish. Perhaps in the end I would have found
> an even more foolish answer, but he gave me no time. 'You didn't under-
> stand, that's fine!' And he left me utterly bewildered.[38]

At the beginning of August, Mérimée returned to Paris, but life
at 52 rue de Lille was far from restful: Léonor Fresnel, Mérimée's
cousin and landlord, had died the previous March, and his widow had
now gone mad, dismissing servant after servant for imagined thefts
and barricading herself in her flat. A compressed air clinic had opened
in Paris and Mérimée started treatment again. He was in fair condition
when he went off to Cannes in mid-October, and an illness of Mrs
Ewer, the fatigue of the journey, and the simultaneous news of Sainte-
Beuve's death cast him down less than might have been expected.
Lokis had been published on 15 September, and Mérimée was now

[38] Augustin Filon, *Mérimée et ses amis*, pp. 303–5.

working on a biography of Cervantes to serve as a preface for a new translation of his works.[39] At first, it seemed that the Mediterranean sun would hold his illness at bay, but by early December he was once more a querulous invalid – 'very poorly, very weak and very discouraged'.[40] Weariness had almost made him give up the struggle to prolong a life filled with so much pain. Nor can he have been much cheered by reading Flaubert's newly published *Éducation sentimentale*. His first reaction was lukewarm, but as he studied it, he grew ever more irritated. One wonders if it had begun to dawn on him that Mme Dambreuse was based on Mme Delessert, Frédéric in part on Du Camp, and Martinon, the lover supplanted by Frédéric, on himself.[41]

By January, he was thinking darkly and incessantly of death, asking Panizzi which of its forms would be least disagreeable,[42] telling him that it was 'a difficult voyage to a country which is perhaps not particularly pleasant',[43] confessing to Jenny Dacquin: 'I am certain that I am drawing near to a slow and very painful death.'[44] Somehow he finished his study on Cervantes and wrote *Djoûmane*, but as he said: 'Sometimes I'm surprised to be still alive; if I continue to suffer as I am doing, one must hope that it won't be for long.'[45] He retained a desperate hope that the return of fine weather might bring an improvement, but spring merged into summer and he was no better. In the meantime, Napoleon's creation of the 'liberal Empire' had thrown him into dismay; Émile Ollivier, the new Prime Minister, was, he thought, an untried apprentice, and universal suffrage likely to destroy any form of sensible government. He felt that duty called him back to the capital, but when he tested his strength by going to Nice, 'I thought I was going to be so indiscreet as to die in the house of someone whom I did not know well enough to take such a liberty.'[46] Bronchitis kept him in bed almost throughout April, and it was only on 1 June that he finally arrived in Paris, prostrate with exhaustion. Soon three doctors were around his bed, and his friends were convinced that the end was near. The Empress offered to visit him, but he declined

[39] Published in the *Revue des Deux Mondes*, 15 décembre 1877.
[40] *C.G.*, Vol. XIV, p. 674.
[41] See M. Parturier, 'Autour de Mérimée. *Les Forces perdues* et *L'Éducation sentimentale*'.
[42] *C.G.*, Vol. XIV, pp. 688–9.   [43] *C.G.*, Vol. XV, p. 5.   [44] *Ibid.*, p. 8.
[45] *Ibid.*, p. 74.   [46] *Ibid.*, p. 84.

on the pretext that, as a good courtier, he would be obliged to die afterwards. So instead she secretly dispatched one of her maids of honour to a priest to arrange for prayers to be said for his conversion.[47]

At the beginning of July, Mérimée was out of bed again, but his legs were swelling, and everyone knew that he was doomed. Oddly, he was not greatly alarmed by the announcement of the Hohenzollern candidacy for the Spanish throne, and said that he did not believe it would lead to war. A few days later, events gave the lie to one of the few optimistic predictions he had ever made. France and Prussia were at war. Perhaps it was the stimulus which this gave to his patriotic feelings that momentarily revived him. For the first few days, he was able to delude himself, as everyone else was doing, that Prussia would be unable to resist the military might of France. He subscribed generously to funds for the wounded and for armaments, and averred that he had so far lost his feelings of humanity that he wanted to see the Prussians destroyed by any means whatever. On 27 July, when Édouard Grenier, who was leaving Paris, went to pay his respects, he found Mérimée, calm and resigned, sitting by an open window finishing a water-colour. They talked for a while about the Academy and the war; Mérimée was by then pessimistic about the eventual result. Then Grenier said 'Au revoir'. Mérimée smiled gently, held on to the younger man's hand, and replied: 'No, you should say adieu; I shan't be here when you come back'. To Grenier's protests he merely shrugged, adding: 'no, it's all over; I can see death approaching and I am ready for it. Adieu!'[48]

Then on 4 August, the series of catastrophic French defeats began, and Mérimée at once fell into black despair, consoling himself only with the bitter thought that he would not live to suffer long from the desecration of his country. On 16 August, he went to the Tuileries to see Eugénie, who had remained behind in Paris as Regent while Napoleon was at the front. He found her 'as steady as a rock' and imagined he could see a martyr's halo round her head.[49] 'I left heart-broken and more exhausted by the efforts I had made not to break down in tears than if I had let myself go.'[50] Eugénie was later to say

[47] *Ibid.*, p. 128, n. 1. The same story is told by F. Bac, *Intimités du Second Empire*, Vol. I, p. 112.

[48] Édouard Grenier, *Souvenirs littéraires*.

[49] *C.G.*, Vol. XV, p. 153.

[50] *Ibid.*, p. 152.

that this was the only time she ever saw Mérimée lose control of himself.[51] On the 18th, by a last desperate resolve to do something to save the situation, he dragged himself out in carpet slippers to beg Thiers to collaborate with the Empress in staving off final defeat. But Thiers simply talked of abdication and refused to commit himself.[52] Hopelessly, helplessly, Mérimée went back to the rue de Lille and wrote sadly to Panizzi: '*Finis Galliae!*'[53] He gathered together as much money as he could lay his hands on, and sent it off to England, but decided to await the outcome of the war in Paris. 'I'm not too keen to see the end, but I don't think I shall.'[54] Then, on 2 September, came the capitulation of the Emperor and his army at Sedan, and on the 4th the overthrow of the Empire and Eugénie's flight to England. Once again it was the faithful Panizzi who was the recipient of Mérimée's incoherent and horror-stricken reactions. 'The blackest fancies that the most lugubrious imagination could invent have been overtaken by events. It is a general collapse. A French army surrendering; an emperor taken prisoner.'[55] To Mme de Montijo he poured out his heart about Eugénie:

> how I wish I could spend a few more hours with her and persuade her to write three hundred pages that will appear when God is willing, and make future generations fall in love with her.[56]

---

[51] J.–N. Primoli, 'L'enfance d'une souveraine'.

[52] Thiers claimed that this visit took place after Sedan on 3 September, but his account is manifestly doctored, and there is good evidence that it was on 18 August that Mérimée called on him, though there may have been another visit a day or two earlier or later (cf. *C.G.*, Vol. XV, p. 153, n. 2). That Mérimée should have undertaken such a desperate mission is wholly in character. He had always regarded Thiers as a vital figure in French politics, and when he had last seen him in Cannes in November 1869, had thought there were signs that 'he is beginning to return to the fold' (*C.G.*, Vol. XIV, p. 655). Whether the Empress was apprised of Mérimée's intentions is another matter. The evidence quoted above about the conversation between Thiers and Mérimée suggests that she was, but she later vehemently denied it (Maurice Paléologue, *Les Entretiens de l'Impératrice Eugénie*, Paris, Plon, 1929, p. 211). Mérimée had seen her shortly before, so she could have entrusted him with an unofficial approach. Or he may have suggested it and not been overtly discouraged. Or, of course, it may have been a quixotic initiative of his own.   [53] *C.G.*, Vol. XV, p. 155.

[54] *Ibid.*, p. 165.   [55] *Ibid.*, p. 166.   [56] *Ibid.*, p. 167.

11a Mérimée in 1853, a portrait
by Rochard, his art teacher

11b Mérimée in 1860
11c Mérimée in 1868

12 The house where Mérimée lived, after destruction during the Commune

Now that everything he loved in Paris had disappeared, Mérimée went back to Cannes on 10 September to die. When he arrived at Cannes station, Dr Maure happened to be there. Mérimée, wearing a house-jacket and slippers, was 'mad with grief', according to Maure, and could only say: 'France is dying, I want to die with her. Come and say goodbye to me tomorrow. Try to get Thiers to save what he can of France.' The violence of Mérimée's despair was unspeakable.

His features, his gestures, his manner had changed. He had turned into a bent, dyspeptic old man with a ravaged face and tears always in his eyes. His lips, normally sternly closed, were trembling with an expression I shall never forget. No one in France suffered more from the defeat than Mérimée.[57]

All he had with him was a packet of stocks and shares and an enormous bundle of letters he was going to burn.

The last few days of his life were inexpressibly miserable. He was too enfeebled now even to write more than a few lines, but one letter to Mme de Beaulaincourt showed the depth and genuineness of his attachment to France.

All my life I have tried to be free of prejudice, to be a citizen of the world before being a Frenchman, but all these philosophic cloaks are useless. Today I bleed from the wounds of these fools of Frenchmen, I weep at their humiliations, and, however ungrateful and absurd they may be, I still love them.[58]

For ten days he was unable to write to anyone else. Then, on 23 September, he found enough strength to scrawl three brief notes, one to the Duchesse de Castiglione-Colonna, one to Turgenev, and the last to Jenny Dacquin, to offer her his copies of Shakespeare and Mme de Sévigné's letters as a memento. Worn out by the effort, he had to dictate a fourth note for Du Sommerard to Fanny Lagden. When Dr Gimbert, his physician in Maure's absence, called that evening to visit his patient, he found him sitting in an armchair, bathed in a cold sweat, and immediately sent him to bed. Fanny, who had sat up with him every night for over three weeks, was so exhausted that Gimbert insisted she should retire too. So Emma Ewer sat with the invalid while he played patience on a sheet of cardboard laid across his bed.

[57] Juliette Adam, *Mes Angoisses et nos luttes*, pp. 65-6.
[58] *C.G.*, Vol. XV, p. 170.

M

At about 9 o'clock, Mérimée said to her: 'Goodnight now, I want to go to sleep.' Emma went out of the room for a few moments, then looked in again. Mérimée had turned on his side. He was dead.[59]

Two days later, he was buried in the Protestant cemetery at Cannes. As long ago as 1865, talking of people's tendency to conform with convention, he had written to Viollet-le-Duc:

> Is there any man in the world who would not have his children baptised, who would not have his dead parents taken to church? I declare in my will that I belong to the Augsburg confession, and I'll ask you to make sure that I am not taken to the Church of St Thomas Aquinas.[60]

Such a declaration was included in the will he made in 1869,[61] no doubt to ensure that some sort of ceremony would occur at his funeral and that it would not pass off with that casualness which he had deplored when Stendhal was buried.[62] So a local Protestant minister made a graveside speech, in which he tactlessly insulted the Catholic Church. Dr Maure, an atheist, suspecting that the service was all the work of the Lagdens whom – in common with many of Mérimée's male friends – he disliked, interrupted angrily and brought the proceedings to an abrupt close.[63] Mérimée's body still lies there. In the same grave, there also rests Fanny Lagden, who died in 1879. Mérimée left her the bulk of his considerable fortune, which amounted to some 365,000 francs.[64] During the Commune in 1871, the house in the rue de Lille in which he had lived was burnt down after being three times soaked in petrol by the *pétroleuses*, the Communist women arsonists, either because of his associations with the defunct Imperial régime or because there were government offices next door. All his books, papers and belongings were destroyed. When Édouard Grenier, who had a flat on the floor above, came to pick through the ruins, the only recognisable object he could find was the little statuette of the faun playing with its tail. It was as if the same fatality which had destroyed

---

[59] These details are taken from M. Parturier, 'Mérimée sur la Côte d'Azur', *Annales du Centre universitaire méditerranéen*, Vol. II, 1958.

[60] *C.G.*, Vol. XII, p. 315. [61] *C.G.*, Vol. XV, p. 171, n. 1.

[62] *Portraits historiques et littéraires*, p. 154.

[63] Juliette Adam, *Mes Angoisses et nos luttes*, p. 66.

[64] *C.G.*, Vol. XV, p. 171, n. 1.

the Empire and the writer who had been so closely identified with it, were now hounding him beyond the grave.

Few obituary notices appeared. Everyone was too preoccupied with the chaos of war and defeat to pay much attention to the disappearance of an individual. Moreover the ignominious downfall of the Empire discredited those who had supported it, so that there was little incentive to mark his passing. The only worthy memorial was an article by Turgenev in a St Petersburg paper.

Beneath an outward show of indifference and coldness, he had the most affectionate of hearts; right to the end, he was indefatigably devoted to his friends[. . .] No one who knew him will ever forget the light and witty elegance of his conversation in the old French style. His knowledge was wide and varied [. . .] During our friendship, I never met a man *plus impersonnel*, as the French say, more hostile to the first person pronoun. Nor have I ever known anyone less conceited: Mérimée was the only Frenchman who did not wear in his buttonhole the rosette of the Legion of Honour (he was a Commander of that order).[65] As the years went by, – there had developed in him a more and more mocking and sensitive character, in reality profoundly human in his way of looking at life, a character peculiar to sceptical but kindly minds, constantly peering into human behaviour with all its weaknesses and passions.[66]

---

[65] In fact, Mérimée had been promoted to Grand Officer some years before his death.

[66] M. Parturier, *Une Amitié littéraire*, pp. 54–5.

Conclusion

Si je pouvais recommencer ma vie avec l'expérience que j'ai
(malheureusement), je me conduirais d'une tout autre manière.
Je crois que je n'en serais pas plus mauvais et que je serais plus
heureux.

To Mrs Senior, 16 February 1856

Judgements on Mérimée as a man and an artist have always been
diverse and contradictory. During his lifetime, there were those who
came near to hating him, but there were also those who defended him
passionately. Since his death, critics have similarly tended to divide
into two camps: those who are repelled by his personality and the tone
of his works, and those for whom he can do no wrong. Very few
remain indifferent to him. That is in itself an indication of vitality.
There has never been any danger that Mérimée would simply drop
quietly into oblivion, or that he would be safely relegated to a fixed
position in manuals of literary history. A century after his death, people
still react as violently to him as they did when he was alive.

This is at least in part due to the unusual complexities of a character
much profounder, much more subtle, much less easy to define than is
apparent at first glance. Mérimée himself went to great lengths to keep
the innermost chamber of his heart locked, even to his most intimate
friends. The use of the familiar *tu* is all but unknown in his vast correspondence, and to each correspondent he presented a different face.
With Stendhal he was a brazen cynic; with Jenny Dacquin a pressing
suitor or a pettishly disappointed admirer; with Thiers, Gobineau and
sometimes Panizzi, an erudite intellectual; with Francisque-Michel and
Esprit Requien a lubricious satyr; with Mme de la Rochejaquelein an
earnest if pessimistic seeker after the truth; with Eugénie, Princess
Mathilde or Princess Julie a respectful and ceremonious courtier; with
innumerable others a highly disrespectful commentator on men and
events. No one of these faces represents the true Mérimée more than
do the others. They are all manifestations of a temperament rich in
paradox and full of unexpected vagaries.

There are of course constants in these multifarious images. The quality of Mérimée's intellect is everywhere apparent: sharp, incisive, independent, vigilant, industrious, always seeking to clarify involved problems, treating every concept with critical lucidity, and above all firmly refusing to abnegate its responsibilities. Likewise, humour is never absent. In conversation, in private letters, or in published writings, Mérimée's sense of the ridiculous was unfailingly in evidence. It would be no exaggeration to say that every page of his works, every brief note that he ever penned, has somewhere in it a joke or a wry smile. Even in the darkest days, even on the most aridly unpromising subjects, Mérimée could not help exercising his ironic wit: he was constitutionally incapable of being dull. The presence of contained emotion is also consistently detectable, once one is attuned to the reticence of his style and the affectation of stoicism in his manner. Whether it be in the veiled confidences of his letters to Jenny Dacquin or Mme de Montijo, in the strong passions invoked by his tales, in the sudden outbursts of indignation and the occasional muted lyricism of his architectural treatises, or in the rare moments of self-revelation which occur at intervals throughout all he wrote, Mérimée regularly if involuntarily revealed the depths of his own sensibility – the efforts he makes to disguise and repress it serve only to show how powerful it was.

It would be legitimate to argue that the Protean variety of Mérimée's character is primarily the result of the multiple means he adopted to regulate a sensitivity so exacerbated that, unchecked, it would destroy him. His subjection to the 'blue devils', his incessant worries about the future, his preoccupation with illness and death, his incorrigible insomnia, his touchy irritability, the moral prostration which always followed his numerous disappointments in love, the obsession, so visible in his stories and historical writings, with passion as an untamable and destructive force – all these things are evidence of a keenness of feeling which is little short of morbid. To counteract this morbidity, Mérimée assiduously cultivated impassibility of speech, expression, dress and bearing, in the hope that imitation of insensibility would enable him to acquire its reality. Irrational anxieties were passed off with self-deprecatory irony or transferred to the plane of intellect, where they could be coldly dissected and thereby rendered at least temporarily innocuous. Mérimée's humour and his razor-sharp intelligence were thus both used as defensive devices to palliate the ill-effects of his turbulent emotional life.

Much of Mérimée's life consists of a struggle for self-control. At critical moments, his show of indifference was liable to break down – at the news of Julia Garnett's marriage, at the sight of a dead child in Syra, at Valentine Delessert's defection, at the French defeat in 1870. At other times, he kept such an iron hand on his feelings that their growth was stunted and their expression stultified. That is why his relations with women were so stormy and in the end so unsatisfactory. On the one hand, his sexual appetites were voracious and his emotional needs intense; on the other, his fear of passion and mistrust of effusiveness were so acute that he shunned the commitments to which he might otherwise have been drawn. Over five thousand letters attest his desperate longing for communication, yet at the same time demonstrate an invincible reluctance to emerge from the isolation of his protective shell. Torn between a fervent desire for amorous companionship and a dread of alienating his liberty or his supposed dominance over his own feelings, he could only fleetingly attain the illusion of happiness in love. In the absence of any direct evidence, it will never be known exactly what sort of relationship he had with Valentine Delessert during the first years of their liaison, but to judge by their later letters, it was a strangely formal one for a lover and his mistress. Certainly the twists and turns of his long correspondence with Jenny Dacquin show a bewildering mixture of hesitancy, duplicity, insistence, genuine affection, sulky withdrawal and specious flippancy. Even his attitude to the meek Fanny Lagden is compounded of feelings more intense than friendship, of a rather patronising form of banter, and of snappish impatience. Love never afforded him whole-hearted bliss when it was requited; but it caused him unspeakable pain when it was thwarted.

Friendship with women was a much more stable factor in his life. Mme de Montijo, Mme de la Rochejaquelein, Mrs Senior, the Duchesse de Castiglione-Colonna, Mme de Beaulaincourt, Lise Przezdziecka, even the Empress, all meant much to him at different times, and helped to provide him with that feminine comradeship for which he craved but which his inhibitions prevented him from finding in love. Mérimée was always a loyal and reliable friend, whether with women or with men, and the number and diversity of his friendships is a notable tribute to his character. No one whose nature was banal or second-rate could have maintained close and lasting relations with men as different as Stendhal, Sainte-Beuve, Turgenev, Victor Cousin, Viollet-le-Duc, Panizzi, Thiers and Napoleon III. If those who met him casually in society were often disconcerted by his scornful cynicism and his icy reserve, those who got to know him well found him exceptionally responsive, reliable, warm-hearted and sympathetic. Few people have cultivated the art of friendship more successfully than Mérimée.

In this way, he alleviated his essential loneliness. An only child of elderly parents, shy, nervous and susceptible, Mérimée never integrated himself into any group, either at school or later. He preferred to select individuals as his associates; mass movements displeased him, and as soon as any cause which he favoured became popular, he abandoned it. Nor was he ever impelled by strong conviction to subordinate his individuality to an idea or a principle. Too sceptical, too mistrustful, too much afraid of ridicule to commit himself without reserve, he remained aloof, detached and mocking. In the literal sense of the word, Mérimée was an unprincipled man. Such was the ironic bent of his mind that he dismissed any abstraction as meaningless, and subjected every emotion, every assertion to a ferociously hostile examination. Even his rabid anticlericalism is more instinctive than reasoned, which is why Paul Bourget accused him of spiritual anaemia and why Barbey d'Aurevilly refused to accord to him the right to be anti-Catholic which he allowed to Stendhal. Neither in literature nor in politics did Mérimée attach any real importance to fidelity to general lines of conduct. His opinions were dictated by temperament, by empirical, pragmatic considerations, or by expediency, never by ethical, aesthetic or philosophic rules. This of course left him wide open to the charge of time-serving, the more so as he never disdained to collect all the worldly honours to which he could lay claim. The July Monarchy, the Second Republic and the Second Empire successively found in him a faithful and efficient servant, and it was with some misgivings that he eventually allowed his fortunes to become irrevocably associated with those of the Bonaparte dynasty. But what others took for materialistic ambition was for him no more than another bulwark against an ineradicable insecurity.

Mérimée was not a happy man – even at the height of his affair with Valentine, his letters show few signs of exaltation; they simply become less querulous. The seat of his dissatisfaction lay within himself. The constant exercise of the precept engraved and incorporated by Viollet-le-Duc in his book-plate: Μὲμνησο ἀπιστεῖν (remember to be mistrustful), made him so suspicious of everything that even that which might have pleased and excited him was automatically devalued. As Taine said of him, 'for fear of being duped, he was mistrustful in life, in love, in learning, in art, and he was duped by his own mistrustfulness'.[1] Mérimée himself used to tell a story to illustrate his view of life. A man falls off a tall building. As he hurtles downwards, someone asks him how he is getting on. 'Not too bad so far', he replies: '*pourvu que ça dure . . .*' The presentiment of imminent disaster rarely left him, and tainted every joy he knew. Stendhal was right to leave on Mérimée's desk a large card on which he had printed in English: 'BEWARE OF IRONY'.[2] Irony may have saved Mérimée from some ills, but it threw him headlong into others which proved perhaps even more insidious.

It is pointless to try to sum up in a few words a man whose life and character are so full of paradoxes; it is even more pointless to seek to apportion moral praise and blame for the different features of his personality. It is legitimate for some people to feel offended by his irreligiousness, his obscenity, his philandering, his selfishness, his lack of beliefs or his cynicism. But these traits are inextricably commingled with those qualities of mind and heart which caused Charles du Bos to say that the *Lettres à une Inconnue* are 'a manual of true courage and authentic delicacy'.[3] What is best and most characteristic in Mérimée only fully reveals itself after long and intimate acquaintance: even with all the evidence available today, it is difficult to get to know him well. But there is much in his complex temperament that amply repays close study. His weaknesses, his failings, his limitations should not obscure the fundamental humanity of his character.

The same may be said of his works. That sagacious critic Albert Thibaudet wrote that 'the name of Mérimée evokes for us at one and the same time the rare quality of the contents and the nearness of its limits',[4] and it would be doing Mérimée a disservice to put him on the

[1] *Preface to Lettres à une Inconnue*, p. xxxii.
[2] Mérimée recalls this in a letter to Léon Godard in 1858 (*C.G.*, Vol. XVI, p. 395), and adds: 'it was good advice'.   [3] *Notes sur Mérimée*, p. 100.
[4] Albert Thibaudet, *Histoire de la littérature française de 1789 à nos jours*, Paris, Stock, Delamain & Boutelleau, 1936, p. 213.

same level as the giants of the French nineteenth-century novel. Inevitably, he suffers from the comparison with Balzac, with Flaubert, or,
more significantly, with his friend Stendhal. Walter Pater had some
reason to conclude his Taylorian lecture on Mérimée with the words:
'there are masters of French prose whose art has begun where the art
of Mérimée leaves off'.[5] There is something lacking in Mérimée as
an artist: a certain generosity of spirit, a willingness to take risks, that
ardent ambition to achieve the impossible which characterises the
greatest creators. If art is controlled madness, as some people have
argued, Mérimée controlled his all too well. He once said: 'you have
to be a bit stupid to spend all your time doing one thing, and you can
only excel in the arts by devoting yourself absolutely to them'.[6] That
devotion was missing in his own case. Though he was anything but a
dilettante, his versatility partly sprang from a lack of commitment. Art
was one of many agreeable ways of passing the time, and while it
filled one of his most pressing psychological needs, it was never an
overriding compulsion.

Evidence of this can be seen in the self-defeating irony which
Mérimée so often injected into his artistic creations, and it is also apparent in his gradual abandonment of fiction for history. Perhaps too,
Mérimée's predilection for the short story form is symptomatic of
reluctance to venture into the wider fields of the novel, to which artists
endowed with greater creative vitality are so readily drawn. To quote
Thibaudet again, the tale is 'a genre which is shorter, which makes its
points more rapidly than the novel, a genre which corresponds, not
to a widening and a discovery of the world, but to a reduction, a
classification and a utilisation of the world'.[7] The reader cannot move
into Mérimée's imaginative universe and inhabit it as he can with that
of the outstanding masters of fiction. Likewise in Mérimée's historical
works: there is no grand design, no desire to recreate the whole of a
past epoch or trace some vast historical process, but only relatively
small, well-defined fragments that do not fit together into any coherent
pattern. There is much truth in Pater's remark that 'what Mérimée
gets around his singularly sculpturesque creations is neither more nor
less than empty space'.[8]

[5] *Studies in European Literature*, p. 53.   [6] *C.G.*, Vol. VII, p. 512.
[7] *Histoire de la littérature française de 1789 à nos jours*, p. 212.
[8] *Studies in European Literature*, p. 34.

But while these reservations must be made, it would be wrong to imply that Mérimée is devoid of greatness. In some respects, his very qualities have militated against full recognition of his stature. For instance, it is generally agreed that Mérimée is one of the most consistently readable of all authors, whatever the subject he is writing about, and from this it is sometimes falsely inferred that he is no more than an accomplished story-teller. The rapidity of narration, the excitement of action, the incisiveness of style are thereby debased to the level of meretricious technical tricks, and because they have become the common currency of much unpretentious modern thriller and detective-story writing, it is too easy to assume that there is no more to Mérimée than that. Equally, because his style is laconic, direct and unassuming, there are critics who dismiss it as grey and characterless. In fact, both in language and in subject-matter, Mérimée relies on the impact of economy and density to do more than he appears to be doing. As Henry James said of him: 'he seldom or never describes; he conveys'.[9] If he does not ostentatiously emphasise the profundity of his intentions or the originality of his inspiration, it is because he prefers to efface himself and allow events to speak for themselves, which is one reason why his works have stood the test of time so well while the attitudes so self-consciously struck by many of his Romantic contemporaries have now become painfully dated. Once the reader realises that readability is not synonymous with superficiality, that swiftness of movement is not incompatible with subtlety of vision, that simplicity of outline and clarity of expression do not exclude contacts with the mysterious underworld of the human personality, he will be well on the way to a true appreciation of Mérimée.

Mérimée's insight into human nature, for all that it is couched in terms of individual cases rather than high-sounding theories, is in fact rich and penetrating. Stories like La Double Méprise and La Vénus d'Ille are the product of something much more complex than mastery over form: they bear witness to a highly personal conception of humanity as frail, threatened, uncertain, contradictory, striving in vain for control

---

[9] Quoted by P. R. Grover, 'Mérimée's influence on Henry James', *Modern Language Review*, Vol. 63, No. 4, Oct. 1968. James had a high admiration for Mérimée's tales, of which he said in 1878: 'it is a capital offence in a young story-teller to put pen to paper without having read and digested them'.

over the dark forces within it, and desperately seeking to maintain a pretence of civilised superiority. In his historical writings, too, Mérimée shows the same unobtrusive skill as an interpreter of men and *mores*: the best of his historiography – the *Histoire de Don Pèdre Ier* and the incomplete study of Julius Caesar – marks him out not only as a determined and conscientious researcher, but also as a remarkably clear-sighted analyst of hidden motives and unsuspected impulses. Nor is Mérimée quite so easily satisfied with the idea of man as a finite creature as his hostility to revealed religion might make one think. The recurrent intervention of the supernatural in his fiction, even if he would himself have passed it off as mere fancy, indicates an uneasy suspicion that all may not be as it seems and as, for his peace of mind, he would like it to be. He is a much less assertive writer than he appears on the surface (perhaps if he were more visibly problematical, intellectual critics would take him more seriously nowadays), and there are in his works secret depths that a casual reading is unlikely to reveal.

Moreover, the quality of mind manifest in all Mérimée wrote is unusually high. Always provocative, always intelligent, Mérimée as an author cannot be lightly shrugged off. Whether we like it or not, he compels us to re-examine our own ideas and our own emotions. The delicate ambivalence of his irony insinuates itself into our reactions to him, so that accepted attitudes, conventional ideas and standard moral assumptions are regularly being called into question – more than we normally notice and more perhaps than he himself would have wished. This makes him anything but a comfortable author to study, but that is his strength: by gouging into our intellect and our sensibility, he changes us. To follow Mérimée uncritically might be to become as unhappy as he was; but to ignore the lessons of his work would be to opt for false security, vagueness, facile optimism. Whether one finds Mérimée attractive or repellent, reading him is a salutary experience. One might well apply to him Mallarmé's symbolic description of Baudelaire: 'un poison tutélaire à respirer si nous en mourons'.

Mérimée's place in the history of French culture is a lonely one. The date of his birth and his first literary affiliations make him a member of the great Romantic generation, but his adherence to the movement was never unreserved, and he had little of the expansive lyricism which characterises Hugo, Vigny and Musset, or of the vast creative urge of prose writers like Balzac. Equally, he held aloof from the early stages of Realism, which offended his fastidious temperament by its concentration on the sordid and the trivial: Stendhal's audacity alarmed him, and his mind remained obstinately closed to the greatness of Flaubert and Baudelaire. No doubt *Le Théâtre de Clara Gazul*, alongside Musset's plays, remains the most viable attempt at Romantic drama in France; no doubt *La Guzla*, in its idiosyncratic way, constitutes a significant experiment in the poetic utilisation of folk themes and prose rhythms; no doubt the *Chronique du règne de Charles IX* is the most readable French historical novel of the early nineteenth century. But ultimately none of these works has quite the spark of genius to lift Mérimée into the first rank of authors. Nor can he be accounted pre-eminent among historians: his interests were too dispersed, his conception of history too personal, to entitle him to comparison with Tocqueville or Taine. As a mediator between France and Russia, he was unquestionably a pioneer; there too, however, later students have surpassed him in competence and penetration. Only in the evolution of the short story can he be said to occupy a key position, since he not only developed a new technique of concision and concentration, copied by most subsequent practitioners of the art, but also produced some of the finest tales in any language.

When one takes all these achievements together and adds to them Mérimée's incalculable contribution as Inspector-General of Historic Monuments to the preservation of his country's architectural treasures, it becomes clear that he is of major importance in the artistic heritage of France. Above all, he is himself: an individual and unmistakable voice, sometimes harsh and startling, sometimes deceptively subtle, but always powerful, always distinctive. Today Mérimée is as much a living force as any writer of his time.

Appendices

Un ouvrage parfait, me disait Mérimée, ne devrait pas comporter de notes.

Eugène Delacroix, *Journal*

Appendices

Appendix A

Unpublished Letters

During research for this book, thirteen unpublished letters from Mérimée to English correspondents have come to light; the text[1] is reproduced here.

The two earliest letters, addressed to Sutton Sharpe, are in the Sutton Sharpe papers given to University College London by Professor Egon Pearson, and I am grateful to the Librarian of University College London and Professor Pearson for permission to print them. The first of them, written on 2 January 1830, has recently appeared in the *Modern Language Review*,[2] where a more detailed commentary can be found.

Paris Jany 2d. 1830

Will you be so kind as to throw (or cause to be thrown) the inclosed letter in the twopenny postbag.[3]

You promised to write to me; you promised to come at Christmas, and you neither wrote nor came. I ought to leave you to your coalfire and give you no news, however as I am good I shall give you a brief bulletin of proper food for your wicked mind i.e. scandal. I° de Mar^e. is still in high favour with Mrs Azur. She is desperately in love with him. Mar^e. is so proud of it that he becomes every day more unmerciful for Stendhal[4] who is in love too and extremely jealou[s]. Stendahl will not see her any more; he confirmed to me the story of the grand tr[io in] which he played his part so well, and says that he never knew before what pl[easure?] was. Mar^e. will play only solos. Do you remember a stupid looking tiresome little physician whom you saw at Mrs Azur? He was jealous too. He did not take the dagger or cushion of Othello but he revenged himself in a way worthy of an apothecary. Mrs Azur had something on the cheek. Her skin was not smooth enough for Mar. She asked a drug to smoothe it and the said physician gave her a certain pomatum which would have burned her to the bones had she kept it on her face. She had only her head swelled as a pumpkin for three days, and lost a good quantity of epiderm. After all she is still very handsome. – Ancilla has decidedly left her baron. Beyle and I we received separately broad hints to take his place; we refused unless we would partake.[5] You see that he is fond still of trios. In the meantime came a tall russian M^r.

---

[1] I have so far as possible reproduced faithfully all the eccentricities of Mérimée's spelling and punctuation in these letters, but without inserting *sic* wherever by accident or design he departs from the norm. In the first letter, a few words have been mutilated by the removal of the seal.

[2] *Modern Language Review*, April, 1970.

[3] Mérimée often used Sharpe to forward letters to other friends in England, but there is no means of knowing for whom this letter was intended.

[4] *Sic*; Mérimée varied unpredictably over the orthography of his friend's name, so that in addition to Stendahl, one finds Stendalh and even the correct Stendhal.

[5] 'Partake' is evidently a bad guess at an English equivalent for 'partager'. This is the only letter Mérimée wrote to Sharpe in English.

Sobolewsky, who has beseiged the place and is ready to storm it. – Mᵉ. de Villanova has cashiered two lovers after having learned that her husband was going to inherit a large sum of money. So she is very decent now, having only her husband, Tromelin, and a Mʳ. Langsdorff. *Excusez du peu.* The winter has brought us a new provision of beautiful whores fresh from Alsace and Franche comté. Amongst them are some splendid Jewesses, with fine large eyes and delicate feet. Where are you?? Good bye I must run to the garden of plants. Give me some news and let me hear from you more often.

Pr. M.

P.S. If the address of the inclosed letter appears to you too funny, will you have the goodness to wrap it in an enveloppe.

[address] Sutton Sharpe Esqre
Lincoln's Inn
London.

This letter deals with a series of inter-related unhappy love affairs. The first is Stendhal's brief but intense passion for Alberthe de Rubempré (nicknamed Mme Azur because she lived in the rue Bleue), whom he had taken over from Eugène Delacroix in June 1829, briefly consti-tuting with them a trio which evidently afforded him great satisfaction. But soon after, Stendhal's friend Baron Adolphe de Mareste (the 'Marᵉ.' of this letter) had also fallen in love with Alberthe and, when Stendhal unwisely absented himself from Paris for several months, rapidly succeeded in taking his place. Mérimée's letter is written shortly after Stendhal's return, at a time when re-lations between Stendhal and Mareste were extremely strained. Indeed, when on the following day, 3 January 1830, Mareste made a tactless remark on politics, Stendhal seized on the pretext to break off their friendship. 'Ancilla' is Mme Ancelot, to whom Stendhal had paid ostentatious

court in the summer of 1829 in order to attract Alberthe's attention and whom he and Mérimée were now treating with equally visible derision. It is impossible to identify the baron whom she is said to have left, but Sobolevski is the Russian novelist who had recently arrived in Paris, who assiduously frequented Mme Ance-lot's salon, and who later became one of Mérimée's closest Russian friends. Mme Villanova is an unknown quantity, but Baron Émile de Langsdorff was a young diplomat and Comte W. de Tromelin was a nobleman who later helped Mérimée on his architectural tour of Brittany in 1835. At this time Sharpe himself was deliberately staying away from Paris because he had reached a crisis in his long-standing unofficial engagement to Sophie Duvaucel, Cuvier's stepdaughter, who felt unable to leave her parents after the sudden death in 1827 of Cuvier's daughter Clémentine. In September 1829, Sharpe had offered to marry Sophie on any con-ditions she cared to impose, but, reluctant to take advantage of his rash generosity, she had insisted that he think it over. Back in England, he had consulted his friends and regretfully decided to withdraw his proposal. Mérimée knew of all this through Stendhal, but out of consider-ation for Sharpe's feelings, feigned ignor-ance, contenting himself with recom-mending the dissipation he regarded as an infallible remedy for melancholy and only alluding obliquely to the Cuviers when he comically says he must 'run to the garden of plants' (the Jardin des Plantes being the zoological gardens of which Cuvier was director). Mérimée himself was no less miserable at this period than Sharpe, since he was in the throes of his ill-starred love for Mélanie Double – but with typical reticence he says nothing of this to Sharpe.

The second letter to Sharpe was written only a few days later, on 19 January 1830, but is on totally different topics.

Paris 19 J^r. 1830

Mr Jacquemont père malgré son affectation d'insensibilité est en ce moment très inquiet de son fils. Il n'en a pas reçu de nouvelles depuis Pondichery, c'est à dire depuis la fin d'Avril ou le commencement de Mai. Vous connaissez l'exactitude de Victor à écrire (en quoi vous lui ressemblez si peu!) Il aurait pu donner trois ou quatre fois de ses nouvelles. D'autre part Mareste a reçu une lettre du consul de France à Yamaon auprès de Calcutta, lequel dit en PS. 'J'ai reçu hier une lettre de votre ami M^r. V^r. J^t. Il se disposait à quitter Calcutta'. Ladite lettre est datée des premiers jours d'aout ou de la fin de Juillet. Mr Jacquemont pense que quelque anicroche qu'il ne peut deviner arrete ses lettres à la poste de Londres. Cela ne me parait guères probable cependant pour le satisfaire ladessus, j'ai promis de vous écrire pour vous prier de passer à la poste et de demander s'il n'y a point quelque lettre pr [?] France⁶ 'arrêtée faute d'affranchissement'.⁷

Pour votre peine voici deux anecdotes qui sont vieilles mais que peut-être vous ne savez pas plus que je ne les savais il y a deux heures. I°. A propos du tableau de David représentant les Spartiates aux Thermopyles, Napoléon Buonaparte dit: Pauvres fous! Ils ont été tournés.

2°. Après la bataille d'Eylau, Berthier, major général de l'empereur tint ce discours à ses aides de camp. 'Foutre Foutre! messieurs, qu'est-ce que cela veut dire. Est-ce ainsi qu'on sert l'Empereur. Comment Foutre! Il n'y en a pas un de vous de tué'.

Croyez fermement que Mad. Malibran est enfoncée par la Sontag. Elle en crève de jalousie. Dernierement elle a pleuré assez publiquement en voyant jeter des couronnes à Mlle Sontag. Pelot en est b^t. content: car il ne craint plus maintenant que cette F.B. là avec ses S.F. mines de mijaurée (F!) fasse oublier la petite mère.

Mes amis (qui sont les votres) du *National* veulent apparement jeter quelques fleurs sur la tombe de sir Thomas Lawrence. Ils desireraient avoir une notice sur sa vie et ses ouvrages, et m'ont prié de m'en procurer une. Je sais trop que les lois et les petits pieds vous occupent exclusivement, aussi j'ai chargé mon ami Mr Vulliamy, de deterrer la notice en question. Voulez vous etre assez bon pour lui envoyer la lettre ci-incluse par la petite poste, et s'il vous envoie la notice, pour me la faire passer par l'entremise et sous le couvert de Mlle Sophie? Bien entendu qu'il existerait une notice, et que cette notice ne serait pas trop volumineuse.

Adieu. Vous qui etes si fier des petits pieds de vos maîtresses, envoyez moi donc la mesure de la votre (j'entends de celle de ce mois-ci.) Je parie vous riposter par une mesure encore plus petite.

[no signature]
[address] Sutton Sharpe Esqre
Lincoln's Inn.

The explorer Victor Jacquemont set off for India in 1828, and his father had

---

⁶ This part of the letter is difficult to decipher. The word apparently written as 'pr' might be taken as an abbreviation of 'pour', but then one would expect the definite article 'la' before 'France'. The sense seems clear enough; the actual formulation remains somewhat conjectural.

⁷ Here again there is a problem of decipherment. What I have tentatively reproduced here as inverted commas looks like a Greek alpha with an apostrophe above it: two of these signs occur before the words 'faute d'affranchissement' and one after. I have not encountered them elsewhere, and they do not in fact re-

become alarmed when no letters arrived in the latter part of 1829. As letters from India to Paris had to travel via London, Mérimée was asked to find out through Sharpe whether some error might have prevented their transmission from there. In the event Jacquemont proved to be safe and well, his correspondence was resumed, and it was only in 1832 that he died.

As for Maria Malibran (1808–1836) and Henriette Sontag (1806–1854), these two famous singers were at the height of their rivalry in 1829. The Pelot who was so pleased to see La Malibran's stock falling is a Président Pelot (or Pellot), to whom both Mérimée and Stendhal occasionally refer in the 1820s and 1830s. He was an ardent admirer of Giuditta Pasta (1798–1864), another *prima donna* of a slightly earlier vintage, whose glory had been dimmed by La Malibran's debut in 1828, which explains Pelot's grudge against the younger woman. Pelot was notorious for his swearing (see F. Michel, *Fichier stend-halien*, Vol. III, p. 111), which is why Mérimée lists the oaths used about La Malibran; these can doubtless be read as: 'cette foutue bougresse-là avec ses sacrées foutues mines de mijaurée (foutre!)'. 'La petite mère' is of course La Pasta. Mérimée himself preferred La Sontag to La Mali-bran; the former he described as 'charm-ante' (*C.G.*, Vol. I, p. 16), whereas he was soon to be violently and obscenely rude about the latter (*C.G.*, Vol. XVI, pp. 25–6).[8]

Evidently either Benjamin Vulliamy or Sharpe did find the obituary notice Mérimée wanted on Sir Thomas Law-rence, who had died on 7 January, since his own article on Lawrence, which appeared on 24 February in *Le National*,

founded by Thiers on 3 January, clearly draws on printed sources as well as on Mérimée's personal reminiscences and gossip from his painter friends. It may have been this English obituary that supplied him with the erroneous information that Lawrence was born in Birmingham in 1773 – it should be Bristol in 1769. Un-fortunately, I have not been able to find the article in question.

Also in the library of University College London among the Brougham Papers are three letters from Mérimée to Lord Brougham and two to Mrs William Brougham, Lord Brougham's sister-in-law, and I thank the Librarian for his kind permission to print them. Mérimée had known Brougham at least since the 1830s – Sharpe and Brougham were friends – and saw him frequently in the 1850s and 1860s, mostly at Cannes, but also in London. The first letter to Lord Brougham, dated 1857 on the back, presumably by the recipient, was written while Mérimée was in Lon-don in June with Achille Fould, staying with Edward Ellice at 18 Arlington Street.

Mylord,

Je suis désolé d'avoir appris que vous m'avez fait l'honneur de m'inviter à dîner *hier soir* à 11ʰ par M. Fould. Je n'avais reçu aucune lettre. On a fait des recherches dans le monceau de cartes amassé sur la table, et jusqu'à présent on n'a rien découvert. J'espère Mylord que vous voudrez bien pardonner à mon ignorance involontaire et agréer avec mes excuses l'expression de tous mes sentiments dévoués.

Pr. Mérimée

18 Arlington St.
mercredi.

semble the orthodox inverted commas Mérimée uses round the earlier quotation from the French consul's letter. But if they are not quotation marks, I am at a loss to explain them.

[8] To Stendhal in December 1831: 'elle perd une note à chaque coup de cul qu'elle donne, et elle en donne beaucoup'.

The next letter was written in Cannes at the end of 1861.

Pr. Mérimée présente ses compliments empressés à Lord Brougham at aura l'honneur de se rendre à l'invitation qu'il a bien voulu lui adresser.

29 Dec^re. 1861

The most interesting of these letters dates from February 1861 and is written to thank Lord Brougham for his gift of *The British Constitution*, which had just been published.

Paris 20 Fév.

Mylord,

Le volume que vous avez eu la bonté de me donner est bien 'The British Constitution'. J'attendais pour vous en remercier que je l'eusse lu entièrement. Il m'a fait passer très agréablement le temps si long d'ordinaire dans l'express train de Toulon à Paris. Je n'ai lu cependant encore que la moitié environ du volume, mais j'en sais déjà plus long que vingt autres ouvrages ne m'auraient appris. Je crains Mylord d'offenser un peu votre patriotisme, si je vous dis ce que je pense; c'est que vous devez peutêtre à vos relations avec nous autres français, et à votre connaissance si approfondie des hommes et des choses de ce pays, l'art de faire des livres didactiques. Assurément ce n'est pas faute de penser que tant d'autres anglais sont illisibles; mais ils ne savent pas coordonner leurs pensées et chez eux l'instruction ne peut s'allier à la méthode. Ils nous donnent des diamants bruts, et tout le monde n'a pas la patience ou l'adresse de les tailler. Chez vous au contraire Mylord, j'ai été frappé tout d'abord par la méthode et la clarté, j'ose dire toute française.

Je n'ai encore vu que peu de monde ici, cependant il me semble que l'on est moins papiste et légitimiste que je ne le craignais à distance. Le petit roi de Naples a été déclaré héros, et il est inutile de contredire les enthousiastes, qui veulent bien ne plus demander qu'on lui envoye une armée pour le remettre sur le trône. Quant au Pape les belles dames et les beaux messieurs continuent à penser qu'il n'y aura de paix, de tranquillité et d'*élégance* sur cette terre que lorsque S. Sainteté aura recouvré son temporel, y compris le comtat Vénaissin. On prétend d'ailleurs qu'il se refuse à toute concession. Les Italiens disent que Garibaldi se tiendra tranquille. J'en doute un peu, autant au moins que du catholicisme de nos amis orléanistes.

Veuillez agréer Mylord avec tous mes remercîments l'expression de tous mes sentiments dévoués.

Pr. Mérimée

The political comments of the second paragraph relate to the recent capitulation (on 13 February) of Francis II of Naples at Gaeta to the armies of Garibaldi and Victor Emmanuel, which put an end to the rule of the Bourbons in Naples and established Victor Emmanuel as King of Italy. French forces had up to then prevented the final attack on Gaeta; it was their withdrawal which had precipitated the fall of the town and the Bourbon monarchy, much to the indignation of right-wing opinion in France. One of the reasons for Mérimée's return from Cannes to Paris (it was on this long train journey that he had been reading *The British Constitution*) was to vote in favour of Napoleon III's policies in the Senate, which, he had confided to Jenny Dacquin on 16 February, was so 'papiste et légitimiste' (*C.G.*, Vol. X, p. 220) that his vote might be needed to save a government defeat. The problem of the Papal States remained of course unresolved, and Mérimée, as is clear here, was torn between anticlericalism and fear of the disturbances which might ensue in Europe if Garibaldi went on to lead his revolutionary forces against Rome.

Mrs William Brougham was the wife of Lord Brougham's younger brother, who succeeded to the title in 1868; she and her husband were frequent visitors to Cannes. There is no indication of the date of the first letter, save that it must be later than 1859, when Mérimée met her for the first time.

Cannes 21 Février

Madame,

Voici l'intéressant voyage que vous avez eu la bonté de me prêter et qui m'a fait tant de plaisir, que je soupire après le second volume. Permettez moi de venir vous le demander un de ces jours. Nous sommes des gens trop philosophes pour aller au bal, et nous vous remercions bien humblement de votre aimable invitation.

Veuillez agréer Madame l'expression de tous mes respectueux hommages.

P^r. Mérimée

A pencilled note on the second letter gives the date as 1867.

Cannes 29 Janvier

Madame,

J'espérais avoir l'honneur de me rendre à votre charmante soirée, mais je suis si souffrant depuis deux jours qu'il m'est impossible de sortir le soir. Veuillez agréer Madame l'expression de tous mes vifs regrets et de mes respectueux hommages.

P^r. Mérimée

The Gladstone Papers in the British Museum contain one letter from Mérimée to W. E. Gladstone.[9] The existence of this letter is mentioned by M. Parturier in

C.G., Vol. VIII, p. 623, n. 1, following Morley's *Life of Gladstone*. Édouard Grasset had asked Mérimée for an introduction to Gladstone, and in the covering letter which Mérimée sent with this note (and which M. Parturier publishes in C.G., Vol. VIII, p. 623), Mérimée said: 'mes relations avec M. Gladstone consistent à avoir fait un assez mauvais déjeuner chez lui et un bon dîner chez je ne me rappelle plus qui. Ce serait un grand hazard s'il se souvenait de moi.' The two men got to know each other better in later years, but no more correspondence seems to have passed between them. James (later Sir James) Lacaita, a friend of Panizzi and like him of Italian birth, was Gladstone's secretary at the time.

Paris 52 rue de Lille
10 décembre 1858

Monsieur,

Il y a peut-être beaucoup de présomption de ma part à supposer que vous vous souvenez de moi. J'invoquerai le nom de nos amis communs Mr Panizzi & Mr Lacaïta pour vous demander la permission de vous présenter officieusement un de mes amis intimes, qui sans doute a déjà eu l'honneur de vous faire sa cour *officiellement*. C'est Mr E. Grasset consul de France à Corfou, qui en sa quantité de philhellène et d'Helléniste désire ardemment connaître le docte & éloquent commentateur d'Homère. Il a longtemps pratiqué les descendants du grand poëte, et il y a peu de parties de la Grèce qu'il n'ait visitées. Après avoir pris part à la guerre de l'Indépendance, il a été successivement consul à Iannina & à Thessalonique. Si vous aviez besoin de renseignements sur la Grèce moderne ou la Turquie, peu de personnes je crois pourraient vous en

---

[9] Gladstone Papers, 44390, f. 243.

donner de plus exacts. Quant à la Grèce antique il est digne de vous entendre.

Veuillez agréer Monsieur l'expression de tous mes sentiments de la plus haute considération.

Pr. Mérimée

Among the Holland Papers in the British Museum are to be found four letters from Mérimée to Panizzi's great friend, that eminent hostess the fourth Lady Holland. The first of these letters bears a tentative pencil dating '11 March or 11 November 1856', but these dates do not fit with Mérimée's punning remark that he has just returned from Sens. As he visited that town in late October 1849, one might suggest early November of that year.

Mylady,

J'arrive de Sens et j'en ai assez pour me rendre avec grand plaisir à votre aimable invitation.

Veuillez agréer l'hommage de tous mes respectueux sentiments.

Pr. Mérimée

mardi

[address] Lady Holland.

The next letter has a conjectural dating 'June 1850 just before 23', which is entirely plausible, since in early June of that year Mérimée did visit several cathedrals in the North of England, as well as going to Oxford – though it must have been written before the 21st, when Mérimée returned to Paris. The possible dates are consequently Tuesday 11th or Tuesday 18th. The Mr Milnes whom Mérimée mentions is of course his friend Monckton Milnes.

Madame

Je plains bien plus ce pauvre Tantale depuis que je connais son supplice. Etre si près de Holland's house & n'y pas aller. Ce matin au retour d'un petit voyage dans le Nord, je suis allé chez Mr Milnes pour le prier de vouloir bien me mener chez vous. – Mais le traître était en compagnie de trois dames sans compter je ne sais combien d'hommes. Il était impossible de l'arracher à cette séduisante compagnie. J'ai voulu le prier de se charger de mes excuses auprès de vous & de Lord Holland ce qu'il n'a pas voulu faire. Il faut donc que je vous dise moi même par quelle concomitance d'accidents je n'aurai pas l'honneur de vous voir cette fois. Je suis le cornac de deux de mes compatriotes qui se perdent dès que je les abandonne. De plus j'ai trouvé ici un ancien ami qui part aujourd'hui & qui m'a engrossé comme disait une dame anglaise de l'abbé Maury dont elle avait entendu un sermon. Demain je vais fouiller un MS de la bibliothèque Bodliene à Oxford. Si comme je l'espère je repasse par votre Babylone, permettez moi Madame de venir prendre vos commissions pour Paris, & de vous exprimer en personne tous mes respectueux hommages.

Pr. Mérimée

Mardi.

The third letter was written while Mérimée was staying with Panizzi at the British Museum, and a pencilled dating of 1862 is acceptable: Mérimée was at that time in London. St Anne's (rather than Ann's) Hill, near Chertsey, was one of the Holland family residences.

British Museum
May 19th

Mylady,

Mon maître, M. Panizzi, voudrait aller à St Ann's Hill après demain mercredi, si vous l'aviez pour agréable. Il vous prie dans ce cas, de l'envoyer chercher à Chertsey à 5 heures 25 minutes, ainsi que son serviteur qui vous

prie d'agréer ses respectueux hommages.
                        Pʳ. Mérimée.
Nous partirons de Londres par le train
de 4,30 après midi.

The last of these letters also has a tentative dating of May 1862.

Mylady
    Vous connaissez mon obéissance. Si
j'avais cru que vous étiez à Londres je
serais accouru aussitôt vous présenter
mes hommages. J'avais été trompé par
des rapports mensongers et l'on pré-
tendait que vous étiez au bord de la mer.
    Veuillez agréer mylady l'expression
de tous mes respectueux sentiments.
                        Pʳ. Mérimée
Vendredi soir.

Finally, here is a letter from Mérimée
to the lawyer and botanist H. Bellenden
Ker, one of his friends in Cannes. This is
in the John Rylands Library, Manchester
(Ryl. Eng. MS. 381/1386), and I am indebted to the Librarian for his kind permission to publish it.

                Montpellier Hotel Nevet
                        14 May
Dear Mr Ker
    So poor lord Brougham is dead with-
out suffering, as my friend A. Fould
died. I wish the same would happen to
me.
    I am a great deal better from my
baths of compressed air. The emphysema of the lungs has disappeared and I
breathe a great deal better than I did.
    I have written to you but you
scorned to answer. It does not prevent

me from wishing to hear from you and
Mrs Ker & the Woolfields whom we
left rather ill. Is the water come at
length to the monumental fountains of
the Cours?[10] Is there anything to eat
where you are besides the ham of Mr
Eustis? and do you know the address of
that gentleman's mother in Paris?
    I should have many more questions
to ask, but I shall have the discretion to
reserve them for next autumn. However if you have any decided opinion
about the fine pickle the House of
Commons and the Cabinet are in, I
should be very happy to have a communication of the same.
    I leave Montpellier the day after to-
morrow, so if you are kindhearted
enough to write, direct your letter to
Rue de Lille 52, Paris.
    Miss Lagden & Mrs Ewer who had
the kindness to keep me company in
this nasty town, send you & Mrs Ker
their love. So they say. Proh pudor!
    Believe me dear Mr Ker
                yours very sincerely,
                        Pr. Mérimée

The reference to Lord Brougham's death
makes it certain that the letter was written
in 1868 while Mérimée was undergoing
his first course of compressed air treatment
at Montpellier. 'The Woolfields' were Mr
and Mrs Thomas Robinson Woolfield,
owners of a large house at Cannes; 'Mr
Eustis' was another member of the Cannes
colony: George Eustis, an American
lawyer. Four days later Mérimée was still
trying to discover his mother's address in
Paris (C.G., Vol. XIV, p. 133).

---

[10] There had been much talk about this time about the improvement of the water supply to
Cannes.

Appendix B

Mary Shelley's article on Mérimée

This is the text[1] of the article on Mérimée's works which Mary Shelley published in the *Westminster Review* for January 1829, and which, to the best of my knowledge, has never been reprinted. It is enthusiastic and well informed, and in general constitutes a judicious critique of his writings – though Mary's spirited defence of the rights of the romantic imagination in *La Famille de Carvajal* is obviously affected by thoughts of her late husband's play *The Cenci*. As for the translations of *L'Amante de Dannisich*, *La Flamme de Perrussich* and *Maxime et Zoé*, they are accurate and sensitive, conveying the strong, rough flavour of the original.

Several years ago, the *Comedies de Clara Gazul* appeared in Paris, and excited a great deal of attention. They were hardly less known and praised in England. It was soon understood that they were imitations of the Spanish drama, the production of a very young Frenchman, (M. Mérimée) and that 'Clara Gazul' was altogether a fictitious personage. They were, in every way, striking and interesting productions, possessing at once the faults and beauties of their models, full of spirit, originality and fire. They were introduced by an account of their feigned authoress, which, as well as the dramas themselves, is remarkable for its utter freedom from affect-

ation. There are to be found in them none of those defects, too generally attributed to French imaginative works; there is no circumlocution, no parade, and their very hyperbole, as being common to the Spanish drama, is natural and in its place. The first of these comedies is founded on a circumstance that occurred during the last war; when a woman, brought up in infamy, was bribed to spy and betray, through their officers, a Spanish detachment to the French authorities in Finland.[2] The gradual softening and repentance of the girl, when she discovers the worth, and learns to love the man she is about to lead to the scaffold, contrasted with the obduracy of her mother, is finely drawn; and the scene in which she confesses her guilt to her lover is touching from its simplicity and truth. Energy is the characteristic of these pieces, mingled with a display of knowledge in the lighter touches of humanity; such as the sweet gracefulness of Iñez, and the struggles between a Catholic woman's religion and her love in *Le Ciel et l'Enfer*. This drama is one of the best in the book; it is founded on the stormy passion of jealousy, the most terrible and selfish of human emotions, and the most interesting, from its being the most universal. As Clara Gazul was a Liberal, inquisitors and priests are attacked in her productions, and there

---

[1] The text is reproduced exactly as it stands in the *Westminster Review*. The article is unsigned, but Mary Shelley's correspondence makes it clear that she is the author.

[2] This is obviously a slip for Denmark, probably caused by the fact that the play is set in the island of 'Fionie'.

375

reigns through all of them the spirit of freedom from political and religious servitude.

The author's next work was in a very different style, resembling the first in one particular only, that it is an imitation. It is entitled the *Guzla*, and imports to be a translation of a collection of Illyrian national poems. We have in the preface some account of the players on the Guzla (a single-stringed guitar) and their mode of reciting to music, much in the manner of the Italian *improvisatori*. We are introduced also to an imaginary person, Hyacinth Maglanovich, who is supposed to be the author of the greater number of the poems in the volume before us. They are warlike, pathetic, and amatory – and, above all, whatever is their theme, they are characterised by the utmost simplicity, while a vein of sweetness runs throughout, that lends to each a particular charm. By a strong effort of the imagination, the young Parisian writes as if the mountains of Illyria had been the home of his childhood; the rustic and barbarous manners are not softened, nor the wild energy of the people tamed; and, if we trace any vestige of civilisation, it merely arises from the absence of all that would shock our tastes or prejudices. We are induced to give a few specimens from this extraordinary production, glad of an opportunity to introduce it to the lovers of poetry in this country.

We select, in the first place, a love poem, entitled, *The Beloved of Dannisich*. To render it intelligible, we are informed in a note, that the Illyrian girl is in the habit of receiving gifts from her various suitors, and that after she has collected a sufficient number, her chosen lover requests permission to carry her off; and she consenting, always names the place and hour for flight.

THE BELOVED OF DANNISICH

I.

'Eusebius has given me a ring of chased gold; I have received from Vladimir a red toque adorned with coins; but I love thee, Dannisich, better than both.

2.

'Eusebius has dark and curled hair: Vladimir has a complexion fair as that of a young woman from the mountains; but Dannisich, thou art to me more beautiful than either.

3.

'Eusebius kissed me and I smiled: Vladimir kissed me, and his breath was sweet as violets; but when Dannisich kissed me, my heart thrilled with pleasure.

4.

'Eusebius knows many old songs. Vladimir can play upon the guzla; I love songs and the guzla, but they must be the songs and guzla of Dannisich.

5.

'Eusebius has commissioned his godfather to ask me in marriage. Vladimir will send to morrow the priest to my father; but come thou under my window, Dannisich, and I will fly with thee.'

Another of the poems is founded on the oaths of friendship which it is usual for the Illyrian warriors to take one with the other. Two men thus united are called *Pobratimi*, or half brothers; they often sacrifice their lives for each other, and any quarrel between them is as scandalous as if, among us, a son ill-treated his father.

THE FLAME OF PERRUSSICH

I.

'Why is the bey Janco Marnavich never seen in his own country? Why does he wander among the rugged mountains of Vergoraz, never sleeping two nights under the same roof? Do his enemies pursue him, and have they sworn that the price of blood shall never be received?

2.

'No. The bey Janco is rich and powerful. No one dares call himself his enemy, for at his voice two hundred swords will leap from their scabbards. But he seeks solitary spots, and hides himself in the caverns which the Heydukes inhabit, for his heart is a prey to sorrow, since the death of his *pobratim*.

3.

'Cyril Pervan died in the midst of feasting. Brandy flowed in torrents, and men became mad. A dispute arose between two renowned beys, and the bey Janco Marnavich shot at his enemy; but drinking caused his hand to tremble, and he killed his *pobratim*, Cyril Pervan.

4.

'They swore to live and die together in the church of Perrussich; but two months after they had interchanged this vow, one of the *pobratimi* died by the hand of his brother. Since that day the bey Janco drinks neither spirits nor wine; he eats roots only, he wanders hither and thither, like an ox pursued by a gadfly.

5.

'At length he returned to his own country, and he entered the church of Perrussich; there, during one whole day, he prayed lying on the pavement with outspread arms, shedding bitter tears. But when night came, he returned home, he appeared calmer, and he supped, waited on by his wife and children.

6.

'When he was in bed, he called his wife and said, "Can'st thou see the church of Perrussich from the mountain of Pristeg?" she looked from the window, and replied, "The Morpolatza is covered with mist, and I can see nothing beyond it." The bey Janco said, "Good; rest again beside me"; and he prayed in his bed for the soul of Cyril Pervan.

7.

'And when he had prayed, he said to his wife, "Open the window and look again towards Perrussich." His wife immediately arose and said, "Beyond the Morpolatza, in the midst of the mist, I see a pale and flickering light." Then the bey smiled and said, "Good; lie down again"; and he took his rosary and continued to pray.

8.

'When he had told his beads, he called his wife, saying, "Pascorra, once again open the window and look." She rose and said, "My lord, I see a brilliant light in the middle of the river, which is advancing rapidly hither." Then she heard a deep sigh, and something fell on the floor. The bey Janco was dead.'

Another poem is founded on the superstition attached to an evil eye, which, whomsoever it looks on, it kills. There are various kinds of evil eyes, one consists in having two pupils in each eye.

MAXIMUS AND ZOE

1.

'O Maximus Duban! O Zoe, daughter of Jellavich! May the holy Mother of God reward your love! May you be happy in heaven!

2.

'When the sun had set in the sea, and the *vaivode*[3] had gone to rest, a sweet

---

[3] '*Vaivode* – governor'. (Mary Shelley's note, following Mérimée. But several longer notes by Mérimée have been omitted by her, no doubt because they were not essential to the comprehension of the text.)

guzla was heard beneath the windows of the fair Zoe, the eldest daughter of Jella-vich.

3.

'And quickly fair Zoe rose on tiptoe, she opens the window, and a tall youth is seated on the ground, who sighs and sings his love on the guzla.

4.

'He prefers the darkest nights; when the moon is at its full, he hides himself in the shade, and the eye of Zoe only could discern him under his mantle of black lamb's skin.

5.

'Who is this youth with so sweet a voice? Who can tell? He is come from a distance, but he speaks our language; no one knows him, Zoe alone is acquainted with his name.

6.

'But neither Zoe, nor any other person has seen his face; for when morning dawns, he raises his gun on his shoulders, and he penetrates the woods in pursuit of game.

7.

'He always brings back the horns of the little goat of the mountains, and he says to Zoe: "Carry these horns with thee, and may Mary preserve thee from the evil eye!"

8.

'He binds his head in a shawl like an Arnaut, and the wandering traveller who meets him in the woods has never beheld his face beneath the many folds of the gold-enwoven muslin.

9.

'But one night Zoe said: "Approach, that my hand may touch thee" – She felt his features with her white hand; and when she touched herself, she felt not a more lovely face.

10.

'Then she said: "The young men of this village tire me; they all court me, but I love only thee: come to-morrow at noon, while they are all at mass.

11.

' "I will mount behind thee on thy horse, and thou shalt carry me as thy wife to thy own country – I have long worn the *opanke*[4] – I wish to wear em-broidered slippers."

12.

'The young player on the guzla sighed and said: "What dost thou ask? I cannot see thee in the day time, but descend to-night, and I will carry thee to the beautiful valley of Knin: and there we will marry."

13.

'She replied: – "No, I wish thee to take me to-morrow, for I will carry with me my richest dresses; my father has the key which keeps them. I will steal it to-morrow, and then I will come with thee."

14.

'Then once again he sighed and said: – "As thou desirest, so it shall be." Then he embraced her; but the cocks crew, and the sky reddened, and the stranger departed.

15.

'When the hour of noon came, he was at the *vaivode's* door, mounted on a courser white as milk, and on the crupper there was a velvet cushion, that the soft Zoe might ride more gently.

16.

'The stranger had his face covered with a thick veil – his mouth and his mous-tachios were hardly seen. His dress

---

[4] 'Large shoes, the token of virginity – they are changed to slippers at the time of nuptials' (Mary Shelley's note).

glittered with gold, and his girdle was embroidered with pearls.

17.

'The fair Zoe leapt lightly on the crupper, the courser white as milk neighed, proud of his burthen, and he galloped off, leaving whirlwinds of dust behind him.

18.

' "Zoe, tell me, have you brought with you the beauteous horn I gave thee" – "No," she replied, "what have I to do with such trifles? I have brought my gold embroidered garments, my neck-laces and my coins."

19.

' "Tell me, Zoe, hast thou brought the fair relic I gave thee" – "No," she replied, "I hung it round the neck of my little brother, who is ill, to cure him of his sickness."

20.

'The stranger sighed sorrowfully. "Now that we are far from my home," said the lovely Zoe, "rein in thy horse, remove that veil, and permit me to embrace thee, dear Maximus."

21.

'But he replied: – "We shall be more at our ease to-night at my home; there are satin cushions there, and we shall repose to-night under damask curtains."

22.

' "How," exclaimed fair Zoe, "is this thy love for me? Why turn your head from me? Why treat me with disdain? Am I not the fairest girl in our village?"

23.

' "Ah Zoe," said he, "some one passing might see us, and thy brothers pursuing us, might take thee back to thy father." And speaking thus he spurred on his courser.

24.

' "Stop, stop, O Maximus," cried she, "I see that thou lovest me not; if thou turnest not thy face towards me, I will throw myself from the horse, should I die from my fall."

25.

'Then with one hand the stranger reined in his horse, and with the other he threw his veil on the ground, and then he turned to embrace Zoe. Holy Virgin, he had two pupils in each eye!

26.

'Deathly, deathly was his look! Before his lips touched those of fair Zoe, the young girl leant her head on his shoulder, and she fell from the horse pale and lifeless.

27.

' "Cursed be my father," cried Maximus Duban, "who gave me this fatal eye. It shall be the cause of no more ill!" And he tore out his eyes with his hanzar.[5]

28.

'He caused the fair Zoe to be interred with pomp, and for himself, he entered a cloister: but he survived not long, for soon they opened the grave of Zoe, and placed her Maximus beside her.'

One of the most interesting parts of this book is an account of Vampyrism, and a detail of the death of a girl, the victim of a vampire. But the above specimens are sufficient to recommend it to the reader; and every lover of nature in its wildness and its freedom, will find pleasure in these emanations of a mind, imbued with grand and unsophisticated imagery, true as the echo in giving back the voice of the imaginative and simple mountaineer.

The last production of this author,

---

[5] 'Hanzar – handschaar. (Teutonic)' (Mary Shelley's note).

recently published, is now before us. It is
ushered in as no dramatic attempt. *La
Jaquerie* consists of a series of dramatic
scenes, developing with those in our own
country which occurred under Richard
II. The author observes in his short preface, that similar tumults broke out almost
at the same time in France, Flanders,
England and the north of Germany. They
all arose from the same cause: – the
peasantry, long trampled on by the iron
heel of feudal tyranny, endured such
matchless privations and cruelties, that in
spite of the prejudices that degraded them
in their own eyes, beneath the rank of
their fellow men; in spite of the arms and
strongholds of their adversaries, they rose
against them and loosened, though they
could not break, their feudal chains. The
plan of the author of *La Jaquerie* is, to give
a faithful picture of the manners of those
times, bringing together under one point
of view the many and successive scenes
and personages that formed the then state
of society. A history written with this
view would develop a new and terrible
page of human experience. To present this
to us in the form of dialogue merely is a
difficult undertaking; individual character
is lost in the infinite variety of persons
made to pass before us, and we have the
ideal instead of the real being presented to
us. We are introduced to the factious
priest, murmuring because, in the choice
of an abbot, the monks prefer the noble
blood of another to his learning. We have
the knights of France, whose very names
awaken all the delusive associations of
romance; the English captains of adventurers, whose trade was war; the burgess
grasping and cowardly; the robber driven
to outlawry by the cruelty of his superiors,
and nourishing vengeance as a duty; the
peasant first sinking beneath, and then
rising to throw off oppression; and finally

the lord of the castle, the feudal chief, the
suzerain of the surrounding country, his
daughter and her betrothed lover, and the
baron's men[6] at arms, who though, in the
language of the day, a villain, joins the
gifts of poetry to those of valour.

These scenes may be divided into three
parts. The first consisting of a development of the causes that led to rebellion.
The picture of arbitrary power, un-
softened by any tinge of humanity, is
frightful and true; ingratitude, pride and
cruelty exercised over the poor and un-
armed, produce at last hatred and desire of
vengeance: the peasantry, incited to open
rebellion by a priest, rise in arms: they
take a band of English adventurers into
their pay, they besiege the castle of their
lord, march to Beauvais, which, admitted
by the lower orders, they take and sack,
defeat the regular forces sent against them,
and spread terror and devastation around.
The lord of Apremont defends himself
long, and is willing to endure any ex-
tremity, rather than submit to his rebel-
lious vassals. Among these is one, late a
favourite in the castle, Pierre, the minstrel
and the man at arms. He had saved the life
of the lady Isabel, and her father bestowed
him on her as a page. Her beauty awakens,
her gracious kindness fosters, his love, and
he dared hope. Called on by her in an
hour of ennui, to recite a tale for her
amusement, he feigns to read one in which
a noble girl becomes the bride of a serf.
She discovers the deceit and guesses the
cause – she dismisses him from the castle
with blighting disdain, while his temerity
even degrades her in her own eyes. Pierre
is seized on by the grand mover of the plot,
the monk, who gives him hope of triumph, and a chance of winning his lady,
if he should join the insurgents, and he is
now the chief of those who besiege the
castle. Poor Isabel, her father wounded,

---

[6] *Sic*, but it is patently a misprint for 'man'.

every hope lost, asks her betrothed to give her back her faith, and then offers herself a sacrifice to Pierre, if he will save her parent. The end is tragical – he is too generous to accept the victim, and endeavours to provide for the escape of her and her family; but the miseries of civil discord in all its most hideous results, envelope the fugitives in one mighty ruin. The peasantry are victorious, and now begins the third part of the drama, their downfall – schism among themselves, a wish to return to their native fields and humble homes, a confidence in the word of their enemies, an incapacity to submit to discipline, joined to the treachery of their English allies, bring on the catastrophe. Such is a slight sketch of the progress of these scenes. We feel the want of one prominent character to concentrate the interest, without which a dramatic composition is never perfect. But the author has not aimed at a regular tragedy, and he has succeeded in giving us in a series of interesting scenes, a forcible picture of our ancestors, and of the crimes and misfortunes resulting from the feudal system, from which our state of civilization preserves us.

To the *Jaquerie* is added a drama, entitled the *Family of Carvajal*. This is a tremendous domestic tragedy, founded on the same story as the Cenci. In this production the author is no longer a painter of manners only, but he becomes a depictor of passion, an observer and a narrator of the secret motives that influence our nature, and the dread events that are the result of unlawful indulgence. It is a question whether certain combinations of circumstances, though it is allowed that they have existence, should be recalled to our memory and represented to our imaginations. But it is difficult for the author, whose impulse is a gift of his nature, whose talent is spontaneous, who can no more repress the yearning of his mind to trace the boundaries of the unknown intellectual world, than he can rule the pulsations of his heart; it is difficult for him to submit to rules imposed by those whose tamer thoughts never emerge from the narrow bounds of their personal experience; who repose in a windless atmosphere, and who fear to have their downy slumbers broken by the war of elements. Columbus, anticipating the discovery of the unknown shores that pale our western progress over the wild and distant waves of the Atlantic, felt the old world, extended in latitude and longitude so far and wide, a narrow prison – and thus the imaginative writer, who deems that beyond the usual track he may find a fresh and untried ground, courageously launches forth, leaving the dull every-day earth behind him. If his discoveries do not interest us, do not let us vituperate his adventurous spirit, and thus degrade ourselves to the level of all detractors from the fame attendant on intellectual enterprise. Let us remember that the poets of Greece, whose names are as a part of our religion, and the highly-gifted dramatists of our own country, have been prone to select as subjects for their tragedies, events grounded on the direst passions and the worst impulses.

The Family of Carvajal has given rise to these reflections: they may be received as applying to every similar production which seeks to interest by new and strange combinations, and which are vivid in their conception and strong in their delineation of what they only know through force of the imagination. The author before us has shewn no lack of boldness in his treatment of the subject, while he has never overstepped those boundaries which must be observed for our tastes not to be shocked, instead of our interest excited. He has made the father and daughter equally impetuous and resolute, but one is the oppressor, the other the victim. The scene is laid in an unpopulated province of New Granada, and the father is represented as a despot over his wife, a cruel tyrant to his slaves, a man grown old in crime. His hapless daughter was brought up in a rustic semi-barbarous convent, and she returns home to find herself an associate of guilt, while love for another adds to her vehemence and misery. This meeting of two fierce natures in unnatural discord presents a new and terrible source for dramatic interest. Each scene transcends the one before in its appalling horror; and the last, in which the miserable girl poignards her father, completes the dark picture, spreading over the canvas the lurid hues of whirlwind and volcano. We turn trembling from the contemplation, while we confess the force of the genius that presents it to our eyes.

Appendix C

French Originals of translated quotations in text and notes

CHAPTER I

p. 13, l. 12: C'était l'air de ce ciel sans tache, où brillait tant de gloire, où resplendissait tant d'acier, que les enfants respiraient alors. Ils savaient bien qu'ils étaient destinés aux hécatombes; mais ils croyaient Murat invulnérable, et on avait vu passer l'empereur sur un pont où sifflaient tant de balles, qu'on ne savait s'il pouvait mourir. Et, quand même on aurait dû mourir, qu'était-ce que cela? La mort elle-même était si belle alors, si grande, si magnifique dans sa pourpre fumante! Elle ressemblait si bien à l'espérance, elle fauchait de si verts épis, qu'elle en était comme devenue jeune, et qu'on ne croyait plus à la vieillesse. Tous les berceaux de France étaient des boucliers, tous les cercueils en étaient aussi; il n'y avait vraiment plus de vieillards, il n'y avait que des cadavres ou des demi-dieux.

p. 14, l. 21: Fort honnête et fort intéressant.

p. 16, l. 6: J'ai été un peu froissé en 1815, un homme qui possédait une place de mille écus d'appointements devait être dénoncé, je le fus. Je perdis ma place de professeur à l'École Polytechnique.

p. 17, l. 10: Je suis constamment occupé et ne fais point de peinture; il n'y a pas de mal à ça, comme je n'ai point d'ambition, je ne suis pas mécontent de mon sort.

p. 17, l. 14: Une belle épitaphe en lettres d'or.

p. 17, l. 27: L'École romantique perd un peu de son crédit. On revient toujours aux bonnes gens qui sont vrais.

p. 17, l. 30: Quand je vois le peuple de Paris massacrer une douzaine de personnes parce qu'il croit que le gouvernement veut diminuer la population en empoisonnant le vin; quand je le vois se persuader que les médecins sont les auteurs du choléra, je ne me fie pas au gouvernement de la multitude.

p. 17, l. 35: Mon père n'était pas crédule et (. . .) il avait pour habitude d'examiner toute chose avant de la regarder comme vraie.

p. 18, l. 4: Si je n'ai pas atteint le but que j'avais en vue, je l'aurai du moins signalé. J'aurai tracé une route utile, dans laquelle d'autres pourront s'avancer avec plus de succès (. . .) Je me suis borné à expliquer ce qui a été fait sans prétendre donner de préceptes.

p. 19, l. 1: Capable d'attendrissement une fois par an.

p. 19, l. 17: Mon mari est toujours gras et frais, toujours bon et calme (. . .) Je suis pour le moment aussi heureuse qu'on peut l'être quand on n'a ni ambition ni goûts à satisfaire.

p. 20, l. 23: Il était né avec un cœur tendre et aimant; mais, à un âge où l'on prend trop facilement des impressions qui durent toute la vie, sa sensibilité trop expansive lui avait attiré les railleries de ses camarades. Il était fier, ambitieux; il tenait à

383

l'opinion comme y tiennent les enfants. Dès lors, il se fit une étude de cacher tous les dehors de ce qu'il regardait comme une faiblesse déshonorante. Il atteignit son but; mais sa victoire lui coûta cher. Il put celer aux autres les émotions de son âme trop tendre; mais, en les renfermant en lui-même, il se les rendit cent fois plus cruelles. Dans le monde, il obtint la triste réputation d'insensible et d'insouciant; et, dans la solitude, son imagination inquiète lui créait des tourments d'autant plus affreux qu'il n'aurait voulu en confier le secret à personne.

p. 21, l. 11: Il a force ambition; mais *il est mauvais et goilleur à taper* [*sic*]; sa santé n'est pas mauvaise; cependant il est maigre comme une garenne.

p. 21, l. 24: Prosper a toujours la fantaisis de faire du barbouillage d'après nature, et il se flatte d'arriver un jour à faire des pochades qui rappelleront les vôtres et celles des artistes anglais (...) L'objet essentiel est que Prosper acquière, sans y employer beaucoup de temps, assez de pratique pour pouvoir s'amuser.

p. 21, l. 29: L'impulsion que Prosper a reçu de vous subsiste dans toute sa force et son plus grand plaisir est de mettre de la couleur sur du papier. Malheureusement il n'a pas comme vous de fondations solides; il ne sait pas dessiner un œil; de sa vie il n'a pas étudié l'attache d'un poignet.

p. 22, l. 10: Au mois de juin 1810 où diable étiez-vous? Dans les bras de Mml Régnier la médecine.

p. 22, l. 31: Je m'en doutais, mais je n'en avais jamais été sûre!

p. 23, l. 1: Dans mon cœur, dans mon âme, dans ma chair tu es toute, ma Fanny bien aimée. Maintenant tu es mienne et je suis à toi pour toujours. Je t'en ai fait le serment hier et je te redis: Je t'aime, je t'adore pour la vie.

p. 23, l. 23: Il y a bien longtemps, lorsque je sortais du collège, j'ai lu des livres de magie, et pendant six mois j'ai étudié cela comme j'aurais dû étudier les mathématiques. Malgré toute mon ardeur à me plonger dans ce chaos de niaiseries, je n'ai jamais pu y trouver autre chose qu'un amusement d'esprit (...) Je me montais assez l'imagination après un quart d'heure de lecture pour entrer tout à fait dans les idées de l'auteur; mais un quart d'heure après avoir posé le livre, je le tenais pour un fou et moi pour un imbécile.

p. 24, l. 5: Mérimée ne croit pas que Dieu existe, mais il n'est pas bien sûr que le diable n'existe pas.

p. 24, l. 18: Très vif, violent même, très décidé en toute chose.

p. 24, l. 22: Il est venu au monde avec les dispositions les plus viriles et (...) une vieille coquette l'a châtré.

p. 24, l. 35: Je continue à apprendre avec Mérimée la langue d'Ossian, nous avons une grammaire. Quel bonheur d'en donner en français une traduction exacte avec les inversions et les images naïvement rendues!

p. 26, l. 4: Nous avons été bien mystifiés par cet Écossais-là. C'est un financier pour tout potage.

CHAPTER 2

p. 27, l. 11: J'ai un grand fils de 18 ans dont je voudrais bien faire un avocat (...) Toujours élevé à la maison, il a de bonnes mœurs et de l'instruction.

p. 28, l. 24: D'une témérité saisissante.

p. 30, l. 3: Mérimée, âgé de vingt-deux à vingt-trois ans, avait déjà les traits forte-ment caractérisés. Son regard furtif et pénétrant attirait d'autant plus l'attention que le jeune écrivain, au lieu d'avoir le laisser-aller et cette hilarité confiante propre à son âge, aussi sobre de mouvements que de paroles, ne laissait guère pénétrer sa pensée que par l'expression, fréquemment ironique, de son regard te de ses lèvres (. . .) Mérimée a naturellement la parole brève, aussi prenait-il peu de part aux discussions qui se développaient régulièrement, si ce n'est en lançant un mot, une réflexion, ordinairement spirituels et bouffons, qu'il accompagnait de ce coup d'œil et de ce sourire ironique qui forment un contraste si frappant avec l'immobilité habituelle de ses traits.

p. 31, n. 8: Un fond de *fashionable* chez Mérimée qui retient et glace l'artiste.

p. 31, n. 8: Mérimée, trop homme du monde pour être entièrement artiste.

p. 31, n. 9: Mérimée eût été un homme de premier ordre s'il n'eût pas eu d'amis. Ses amis se l'approprièrent.

p. 32, l. 21: Ce pauvre jeune homme en redingote grise et si laid avec son nez retroussé. Ce jeune homme avait quelque chose d'effronté et d'extrêmement déplaisant. Ses yeux, petits et sans expression, avaient un air toujours le même et cet air était méchant.

p. 33, l. 15: J'ai vu souvent moins de charme dans sa personne que dans l'omnibus qui conduit chez elle.

p. 33, l. 17: Je ne suis pas trop sûr de son cœur, mais je suis sûr de ses talents.

p. 34, l. 1: Singulièrement déteint [sur les miennes].

p. 35, l. 29: Riait sous cape et sans mot dire, des harangues brusques de Beyle.

p. 36, l. 12: N'observant donc plus que les repos strictement indiqués par la coupe des phrases, mais sans élever ni baisser le ton, il lut ainsi tout son drame sans modifier ses accents, même aux endroits les plus passionnés. L'uniformité de cette longue cantilène (. . .) rendit cette lecture assez froide.

p. 39, l. 30: Avec Walter Scott, l'écrivain moderne le plus éminemment vrai.

p. 40, l. 7: Grosse Talente, die ein Fundament in sich selber haben und sich von der Gesinnungsweise des Tages frey erhalten.

p. 40, l. 11: Beaucoup d'admiration.

p. 40, l. 14: Un grand *humbug*, qui n'excelle qu'à donner des énigmes sans mot.

p. 40, l. 30: J'avoue que s'il eût commencé plus tôt, je le verrais barbouiller du papier avec plaisir; mais puisqu'il s'est lancé dans la littérature et qu'il a débuté avec quelque succès il me semble, quand je le vois employer une matinée entière à peindre, qu'il perd son temps. Mais il y a un charme indicible à faire ce qu'on n'est pas obligé de faire.

p. 41, l. 16: La passion veut toujours le mot propre, fût-il vulgaire, et la distinction impérieusement exigée chez nous entre les mots poétiques et ceux qui ne le sont point, ne produit-elle pas souvent des contre-sens aussi ridicules que les pointes dont nous venons de parler?

p. 42, l. 2: Voici deux volumes de poésies serbes qu'on m'envoie; apprenez le serbe.

p. 43, l. 12: Hommage de l'auteur du théâtre de Clara Gazul.

CHAPTER 3

p. 47, l. 6: Je ne vais pas m'informer, pour juger une pièce, si l'événement se passe dans vingt-quatre heures, et si les personnages viennent tous dans le même lieu, les uns pour comploter leur conspiration, les autres se faire assassiner, les autres se poignarder sur le corps mort, comme cela se pratique de l'autre côté des Pyrénées.

p. 47, l. 19: Et s'ils n'étaient morts que depuis trois cent cinquante ans, est-ce que la comédie ne pourrait pas être bonne?

p. 47, l. 24: Certaines expressions dans le rôle d'Antonio pourront peut-être scandaliser les dames. L'auteur les supplie de songer que ce pauvre jeune homme n'avait jamais vu le monde, et n'avait lu d'autre livre que l'Écriture, où chaque chose est appelée par son nom.

N

p. 47, l. 32: Il faut lui savoir gré de ne pas avoir copié aussi le style *culto*, si fatigant pour les lecteurs de ce siècle.

p. 47, l. 35: Clara Gazul affecte de se servir du mot *comédie, comedia,* employé par les anciens poètes espagnols pour exprimer tout ouvrage dramatique, ou bouffon ou sérieux.

p. 48, l. 3: COMÉDIE ou, si vous voulez, TRAGÉDIE, comme l'on dit maintenant.

p. 49, l. 7: En France, c'est toujours à un grand seigneur que l'on donne les ministères; tandis que chez nous maintenant . . .

p. 49, l. 37; Le véritable patriotisme, celui qui refuse de faire la patrie complice du crime.

p. 50, l. 14: Je ne suis plus bourreau!

p. 50, l. 20: Cette comédie étrange fut composée par Clara Gazul à la requête d'une dame de ses amies, passionnée pour les romans larmoyants et improbables.

p. 50, l. 25: Leurs défauts ordinaires, tels que le trop de rapidité dans l'action, le manque de développements, etc.

p. 52, l. 23: Il est le seul de ses contemporains à l'avoir vraiment compris [le génie espagnol].

p. 53, l. 15: Ah! cela est différent.

p. 53, l. 20: Je ne bougerai pas, attendu que la comédie est finie. Oui, mesdames et messieurs, c'est ainsi que finit la seconde partie d'INÈS MENDO, OU LE TRIOMPHE DU PRÉJUGÉ.

p. 53, l. 23: L'auteur m'a dit de ressusciter pour solliciter votre indulgence: et vous pouvez vous en aller avec la satisfaction de penser que vous n'aurez pas de troisième partie.

p. 53, l. 33: Fusillez! fusillez! fusillez! tous les hommes sont des faquins qui valent tout au plus la cartouche qui les envoie dans l'autre monde.

p. 54, l. 1: En une heure je suis devenu fornicateur, parjure, assassin.

p. 54, l. 20: Il aura besoin d'un déguisement pour oser être lui-même.

p. 55, l. 19: Un petit roman bien noir, bien terrible, avec beaucoup de crimes et de l'amour à la lord Byron.

p. 55, n. 26: L'étude pathologique d'un cas de perversité morbide.

p. 58, l. 29: 1º Deviner le goût et les susceptibilités du public, les effets de théâtre, comme on dit; 2º Avoir une patience, une fermeté, une résignation à toute épreuve, pour faire marcher les acteurs. Eussé-je le nº 1, qui me fait complètement défaut, je me sens incapable de supporter l'ennui d'une répétition.

p. 59, l. 17: Une seconde mystification greffée sur celle de 1827.

p. 59, l. 23: Me moquer de la couleur locale dans laquelle nous nous jetions à plein collier vers l'an de grâce 1827.

p. 59, l. 28: Je ne conteste pas le plaisir qu'une mystification peut procurer à son auteur; mais la première condition pour qu'elle soit bonne, complète, c'est qu'elle ne lui coûte pas trop de peine.

p. 60, l. 15: Se contentera de sons au lieu de pensées, et croira avoir atteint le but lorsqu'il aura réjoui les oreilles par une certaine mélodie appréciable par un petit nombre de connaisseurs. Il n'est pas rare que la perfection d'un instrument entraîne celui qui sait le manier à une recherche minutieuse et puérile. Plus d'un poète prend pour des idées des images confuses, et à force de raffiner devient inintelligible.

p. 60, l. 25: J'aime les chants populaires de tous les pays et de tous les temps, depuis l'Iliade jusqu'à la romance de Malbrouk. A vrai dire, je ne conçois pas, et c'est peut-être une hérésie, je ne conçois guère de poésie que dans un état de demi-civilisation, ou même de barbarie, s'il faut trancher le mot. C'est dans cet heureux état seulement que le poëte peut être naïf sans niaiserie, naturel sans trivialité. Il ressemble alors à un charmant enfant qui bégaye des chansons avant de construire une phrase. Il est toujours amusant, parfois sublime;

il m'émeut, parce qu'il croit tout le premier les contes qu'il débite.

p. 61, l. 9: La grande crainte que j'ai du
ridicule en ma qualité de Français.

p. 62, l. 15: Es fehlt freilich diesen Gedich-
ten nicht an allerlei schauerlichen Motiven
von Kirchhöfen, nächtlichen Kreuzwegen,
Gespenstern und Vampyren; allein alle
diese Widerwärtigkeiten berühren nicht

das Innere des Dichters; er behandelt sie
vielmehr aus einer gewissen objectiven
Ferne und gleichsam mit Ironie. Er geht
dabei ganz zu Werke wie ein Künstler, dem
es Spass macht auch einmal so etwas zu ver-
suchen (. . .) Mérimée ist freilich ein gan-
zer Kerl! wie dann überhaupt zum objectiven Behandeln eines Gegenstandes mehr
Kraft und Genie gehört als man denkt.

CHAPTER 4

p. 63, l. 20: On s'amusait fort, on causait
bien et beaucoup, et on ne se grisait pas.

p. 64, l. 9: Des exercices de gymnastique
par 6 filles in naturalibus.

p. 64, l. 24: Il gagnait en dix mois cent
cinquante mille francs, puis il passait deux
autres mois parmi les rats de l'opéra.

p. 65, l. 26: Alors vieillard à cheveux
blancs, négligé de mise, visage vénérable
et fatigué.

p. 66, l. 26: Quel chagrin pour un cœur
sensible!

p. 66, n. 14: Une jeune Anglaise dont il a
été fort épris, mariée dernièrement et qui
lui laisse dans la mémoire des souvenirs
qui le rendent jaloux.

p. 67, l. 3: 'Vous savez que Mlle J[ulie]
G[arnett] va épouser M. P[ertz]?' 'Du tout'.

p. 68, l. 1: Avec quelqu'un qui n'aimait
pas ma prose.

p. 68, l. 5: Un affreux cocu me visait avec
un pistolet qu'il maniait fort bien.

p. 68, l. 7: Tomber dans de la merde, parlant par respect, car il y en avait beaucoup
dans ce fossé.

p. 68, n. 19: Au bras gauche, si cela vous
est égal.

p. 69, l. 1: M. Mérimée a bien le bonheur
le plus triste du monde.

p. 71, l. 11: Dont, par parenthèse, il est,
je crois, un peu féru.

p. 72, l. 4: V^r Jacquemont est un des
hommes les plus remarquables que j'aie
rencontrés, celui qui me représentait le
mieux le stoïcien grec, aimable avec cela

et plein de gaîté et de grâce. Je pense
toujours à lui lorsque je me trouve dans
quelque situation difficile et au conseil
qu'il pourrait me donner.

p. 72, l. 11: Je n'ai jamais connu de cœur
plus vraiment sensible que celui de Jacquemont. C'était une nature aimante et tendre,
mais il apportait autant de soin à cacher ses
émotions que d'autres en mettent à dis-
simuler de mauvais penchants. Dans notre
jeunesse, nous avions été choqués de la
fausse sensibilité de Rousseau et de ses
imitateurs. Il s'était fait une réaction,
exagérée, comme c'est l'ordinaire. Nous
voulions être forts, et nous nous moquions
de la sensiblerie. Peut-être Victor cédait-il
involontairement à cette tendance de sa
génération.

p. 73, l. 17: Un méchant roman qui
m'ennuie, mais que je veux finir parce que
j'ai d'autres plans en vue.

p. 73, n. 37: Il y a dans le caractère de
Julien des traits atroces dont tout le monde
sent la vérité, mais qui font horreur. Le
but de l'art n'est pas de montrer ce côté de
la nature humaine. Rappelez-vous le portrait de Delia par Swift, et l'abominable
vers qui le termine: *But Delia pisses and
Delia shits.* Certes, mais pourquoi le dire?
Vous êtes plein de ces odieuses vérités-là.

p. 74, l. 4: Mérimée, (. . .) qui est fort
de mes amis, a publié un charmant livre,
mi-roman, mi-chronique, sur la Cour de
Charles IX.

p. 74, l. 7: Plein d'esprit à la Voltaire.

p. 74, l. 11: Le Mazeppa d'une armée dont
M. Hugo est le Charles XII.

p. 74, l. 13: A M. Prosper Mérimée, notre
maître à tous.

p. 75, l. 21: Comme deux chats sauvages,
de deux gouttières opposées, sur la défensive,
les poils hérissés et ne se faisant la patte
de velours qu'avec des précautions infinies.

p. 77, l. 1: La jalousie ne tue l'amour que
dans un cœur froid de quarante ans, qui
désespère. Cette jalousie vous grave à
jamais dans le cœur de M ... Cette
cristallisation peut être lente. Vous pouvez
la hâter de six mois (+ ou −), en lui
disant: 'Depuis trois ans je vous adore,
mais je n'ai que dix-sept cents francs de
rente et ne puis vous épouser. Je n'ai pas
voulu mourir fou'. Ni plus ni moins.
Laissez le développement à son cœur.

p. 78, l. 4: Je ne pourrais plus être amoureux,
parce que mes illusions m'ont procuré bien
des *desengaños* sur l'amour. J'allais être
amoureux lorsque je suis parti pour
l'Espagne. C'est une des belles actions de
ma vie. La personne qui a causé mon
voyage n'en a jamais rien su. Si j'étais
resté, j'aurais peut-être fait une grande
sottise: celle d'offrir à une femme digne
de tout le bonheur dont on peut jouir sur
terre, de lui offrir, dis-je, en échange de la
perte de toutes les choses qui lui étaient
chères, une tendresse que je sentais moi-
même très-inférieure au sacrifice qu'elle
aurait peut-être fait. Vous vous rappelez
ma morale: 'L'amour fait tout excuser,
mais il faut être bien sûr qu'il y a de
l'amour'.

p. 79, l. 9: Les antiquités, surtout les antiquités romaines, me touchent peu (...)
Je ne voyage pas dans un but déterminé;
je ne suis pas antiquaire.

p. 79, l. 33: – Mauvaise maison! disait-il.
 – Mauvaise! pourquoi? Le gazpacho
était excellent.
 – Cela n'est pas extraordinaire, c'est
peut-être le diable qui l'a fait.
 – Le diable! Dites-vous cela parce

qu'elle n'épargne pas le piment, ou bien
cette brave femme aurait-elle le diable
pour cuisinier?
 – Qui sait?
 – Ainsi . . . elle est sorcière?

p. 80, l. 12: En vérité, j'aime les cérémonies
catholiques, et je voudrais y croire.

p. 80, l. 17: J'entendis une voix douce prononcer à côté de moi avec émotion:
Amen; je tournai la tête, et je vis une de
mes jolies Valenciennes dont les joues
étaient un peu plus colorées, et qui agitait
son éventail précipitamment. Elle regardait avec beaucoup d'attention du côté de la
potence. Je dirigeai mes yeux de ce côté:
le moine descendait l'escalier, et le condamné était suspendu en l'air, le bourreau
sur ses épaules, et son valet lui tirait les pieds.

p. 80, l. 28: J'avais quatre filles en activité
de service, appelées toutes les quatre
Vicenta, Saint Vincent est le patron de la
ville. Pour m'y reconnaître, j'avais Vicenta
1, et V 2, puis Vicentita 1 et Vta 2, classification commode pour la mémoire.

p. 81, l. 3: La première fois que j'entrai
dans le cirque de Madrid, je craignis de ne
pouvoir supporter la vue du sang que l'on
y fait libéralement couler; je craignais surtout que ma sensibilité, dont je me défiais,
ne me rendît ridicule devant les amateurs
endurcis qui m'avaient donné une place
dans leur loge.

p. 81, l. 9: Maintenant j'éprouve un
indicible plaisir à voir piquer un taureau,
éventrer un cheval, culbuter un homme. A
une des dernières courses de Madrid, j'ai
été scandaleux. On m'a dit, mais j'ai peine
à le croire, que j'ai applaudi avec fureur,
non le matador, mais le taureau au
moment où il enlevait, sur ses cornes,
cheval et homme.

p. 81, l. 17: Aucune tragédie au monde ne
m'avait intéressé à ce point.

p. 81, l. 19: Monsieur Maïquez, voyez-
vous, ce ne sont pas ici des menteries
comme sur vos planches.

p. 82, l. 13: C'est une admirable amie,

mais il n'a jamais été question de chair entre nous.

p. 82, l. 31: Le sombre et profond Mérimée.

p. 82, l. 32: Le jeune homme mélancolique.

p. 83, l. 26: Je ne me console pas d'avoir manqué un spectacle qui ne se donne que tous les mille ans. Voilà deux représentations que je manque, la première pour être né un peu trop tard, et l'autre (représentation extraordinaire à notre bénéfice) pour ce malheureux voyage d'Espagne.

CHAPTER 5

p. 87, l. 4: J'ai tâché de donner une idée des mœurs atroces du quatorzième siècle, et je crois avoir plutôt adouci que rembruni les couleurs de mon tableau.

p. 87, l. 16: Voilà comme ils sont, tous ces Français. Toujours ils se plaignent, et jamais ils n'ont le courage de se rendre libres.

p. 90, l. 4: Il est curieux, ce me semble, de comparer ces mœurs avec les nôtres, et d'observer dans ces dernières la décadence des passions énergiques au profit de la tranquillité et peut-être du bonheur.

p. 90, l. 7: Je suis assez porté à croire que la masse de vices et de vertus a été la même à toutes les époques; aussi, je ne pense pas que nous valions beaucoup mieux que nos pères, bien que nous n'assassinions plus. L'assassinat était une forme de leurs passions; leurs passions sont encore les nôtres, mais elles ont d'autres formes; seulement je crois que nous devons nous féliciter de vivre dans un temps où ces formes sont sensiblement adoucies.

p. 90, l. 15: Nous ne sommes pas de ceux qui croient que nos aïeux valussent beaucoup mieux que nous; nous ne pensons pas non plus que nous leur soyons très supérieurs en moralité.

p. 90, l. 24: Je venais de lire un assez grand nombre de mémoires et de pamphlets relatifs à la fin du XVIe siècle. J'ai voulu faire un extrait de mes lectures, et cet extrait, le voici.

p. 91, l. 30: Un voltairien qui se trompe de siècle.

p. 91, l. 35: – Papistes! huguenots! superstition des deux parts. Je ne sais point croire ce que ma raison me montre comme absurde. Nos litanies et vos psaumes, toutes ces fadaises se valent. Seulement, ajouta-t-il en souriant, il y a quelquefois de bonne musique dans nos églises, tandis que chez vous c'est une guerre à mort aux oreilles délicates.

– Belle supériorité pour ta religion, et il y a là de quoi lui faire des prosélytes!

– Ne l'appelle pas ma religion, car je n'y crois pas plus qu'à la tienne. Depuis que j'ai su penser par moi-même, depuis que ma raison a été à moi . . .

– Mais . . .

– Ah! trêve de sermons. Je sais par cœur tout ce que tu vas me dire. Moi aussi j'ai eu mes espérances, mes craintes. Crois-tu que je n'ai pas fait des efforts puissants pour conserver les heureuses superstitions de mon enfance? J'ai lu tous nos docteurs pour y chercher des consolations contre les doutes qui m'effrayaient, et je n'ai fait que les accroître. Bref, je n'ai pu et je ne puis croire. Croire est un don précieux qui m'a été refusé, mais pour rien au monde je ne chercherais à en priver les autres.

p. 92, l. 22: Pratiquement parlant il me semble que le doute a moins d'inconvénients que la croyance. Il n'y a rien de plus terrible qu'un homme convaincu quand il est logicien et qu'il part d'une donnée fausse.

p. 93, l. 7: Je n'aime dans l'histoire que les anecdotes, et parmi les anecdotes je préfère celles où j'imagine trouver une peinture vraie des mœurs et des caractères à une époque donnée. Ce goût n'est pas très noble; mais, je l'avoue à ma honte, je donnerais volontiers Thucydide pour des mémoires authentiques d'Aspasie ou d'un esclave de Périclès; car les mémoires, qui sont des causeries familières de l'auteur avec son lecteur, fournissent seuls ces portraits de l'*homme* qui m'amusent et qui m'intéressent.

p. 94, l. 25: Devant une table de chêne, noircie par la graisse et la fumée, était assis le capitaine des reîtres. C'était un grand et gros homme de cinquante ans environ, avec un nez aquilin, le teint fort enflammé, les cheveux grisonnants et rares, couvrant mal une large cicatrice qui commençait à l'oreille gauche, et qui venait se perdre dans son épaisse moustache. Il avait ôté sa cuirasse et sa casque, et n'avait conservé qu'un pourpoint de cuir de Hongrie noirci par le frottement de ses armes, et soigneusement rapiécé en plusieurs endroits. Son sabre et ses pistolets étaient déposés sur un banc à sa portée; seulement il conservait sur lui un large poignard, arme qu'un homme prudent ne quittait que pour se mettre au lit.

p. 95, l. 9: Vous vous accoutumerez bien vite à exprimer vos idées facilement et naturellement. Sans ces deux adverbes là on n'écrit pas en Français.

p. 95, l. 10: Écrivez tout comme vous écrivez une lettre, et soyez sûr qu'entre le style élevé et le familier la différence la plus grande n'est pas dans les mots mais dans les idées.

p. 95, l. 22: Le capitaine à la plume rouge tourna la tête, et Mergy reconnut son frère. Il étendit la main vers l'arquebuse de son voisin pour la détourner; mais, avant qu'il pût la toucher, le coup était parti. Les cavaliers, surpris de cette décharge inattendue, se dispersèrent fuyant dans la campagne; le capitaine George tomba percé de deux balles.

p. 96, l. 4: Ah! je m'aperçois que je ne trouverai pas dans votre roman ce que j'y cherchais.

p. 96, l. 6: Je le crains.

p. 96, l. 8: Mergy se consola-t-il? Diane prit-elle un autre amant? Je le laisse à décider au lecteur qui, de la sorte, terminera toujours le roman à son gré.

CHAPTER 6

p. 100, l. 4: Mon fils désirait courir la carrière diplomatique (. . .) Voilà ses occupations littéraires interrompues; mais il acquerra dans l'administration des idées nouvelles que plus tard il mettra en œuvre.

p. 100, l. 12: M. Prosper Mérimée, auteur du Théâtre de Clara Gazul et de plusieurs productions distinguées, vient d'être nommé chef du bureau du Secrétariat général de la Marine. Il vaque, dit-on, une place à la division des lettres, au Ministère de l'Intérieur. Nous espérons qu'on la donnera à un officier de marine.

p. 101, l. 8: De s'en foutre carrément, de ne pas forniquer après dîner et de se tenir le ventre chaud.

p. 101, l. 10: Je hais et méprise toute cette racaille autant qu'elle me hait elle-même.

p. 101, l. 13: Mourant d'ennui et de rage.

p. 101, l. 28: Mon antique philosophie de *nil admirari*.

p. 102, l. 27: C'était une personne très-singulière, ayant de la vertu à sa façon, et qui a laissé des souvenirs aux nombreux heureux qu'elle a faits.

p. 102, l. 32: Je me propose bien de faire là-dessus une belle dissertation, lorsque j'aurai du loisir.

p. 103, l. 6: Je ne supporte la mauvaise société qu'à de rares intervalles, et par une curiosité inépuisable de toutes les variétés de l'espèce humaine (. . .) J'aime simplement à voir d'autres mœurs, d'autres figures, à entendre un autre langage.

p. 103, l. 13: Et je m'ennuie.

p. 103, l. 15: Ce qu'il y a de singulier dans

ma vie, c'est qu'étant devenu un très-grand vaurien, j'ai vécu deux ans sur mon ancienne bonne réputation, et qu'après être redevenu très-moral, je passe encore pour vaurien. En vérité, je ne crois pas l'avoir été plus de trois ans, et je l'étais, non de cœur, mais uniquement par tristesse et un peu peut-être par curiosité.

p. 105, l. 3: Allons, je le veux bien, qu'il soit fait ainsi que vous le désirez, puisque cela vous fait tant de plaisir, car en ce qui me concerne je dois vous déclarer que je suis très sûre de n'en avoir aucun.

p. 105, n. 29: Je suis plus résignée que vous ne pensez. J'ai fait beaucoup de progrès depuis hier. Non, je ne suis pas folle, je m'en défends. Je ne rougirais pas de l'être, mais je sens que je ne suis même pas très exaltée.

Dans une belle soirée d'été.

Seul parmi les adorateurs de la chaude saison, Mérimée, au bout de deux ou trois jours, avait pris l'initiative de la rupture, et les femmes qui aiment ne peuvent souffrir qu'on les quitte.

p. 106, l. 6: Comment, Madame, pouvez-vous avoir aucune intimité avec Mme Dorval?

p. 106, l. 9: P.M. a 5 pieds 5 pouces.

p. 107, l. 10: Elle n'avait rien, mais rien de ce que je croyais trouver en elle. Sensible, soumise, elle s'offrit à l'esclavage.

p. 107, l. 13: Mais là encore, au lieu de la malédiction, de la haine, je n'eus en face de moi qu'une femme désabusée une fois de plus et pleurant son rêve.

p. 107, l. 19: Un de ces jours d'ennui et de désespoir je rencontrai un homme qui ne doutait de rien, un homme calme et fort, qui ne comprenait rien à ma nature et qui riait de mes chagrins. La puissance de son esprit me fascina entièrement, pendant huit jours je crus qu'il avait le secret du bonheur, qu'il me l'apprendrait, que sa dédaigneuse insouciance me guérirait de mes puériles susceptibilités. Je croyais qu'il avait souffert comme moi et

qu'il avait triomphé de sa susceptibilité extérieure. Je ne sais pas encore si je me suis trompée, si cet homme est fort par sa grandeur ou par sa pauvreté. Je suis toujours portée à croire le premier cas (. . .) Enfin je me conduisis à trente ans comme une fille de quinze ans ne l'eût pas fait, et je commis la plus incroyable sottise de ma vie, je fus la maîtresse de P.M. (. . .) L'expérience manqua complètement. Je pleurai de souffrance, de dégoût et de découragement. Au lieu de trouver une affection capable de me plaindre et de me dédommager, je ne trouvai qu'une raillerie amère et frivole.

p. 107, n. 31: Le plus haut magistrat du Royaume.

p. 108, l. 21: Une femme débauchée à froid par curiosité plus que par tempérament.

p. 108, l. 25: Bon, mais il est ordurier. Alors il est tout à fait comme M.

p. 108, l. 28: Ne me parlez pas de cet homme, son souvenir m'est odieux.

p. 111, l. 14: A tout prendre, je crois avoir été un grand jobard avec elle, mais je crois avoir plus gagné à faire ce que j'ai fait qu'à la traiter comme une aiguille.

p. 111, l. 20: J'avais une pierre superbe, bien taillée, brillante, scintillante, admirable sur tous points. Je la croyais un diamant que je n'aurais pas troqué pour celui du Grand Mogol. – Pas du tout! voilà qu'il se trouve que ce n'est qu'une pierre fausse. Un chimiste de mes amis vient de m'en faire l'analyse. Figurez-vous un peu mon désappointement. J'ai passé bien du temps à penser à ce prétendu diamant et au bonheur de l'avoir trouvé. Maintenant il faut que je passe autant de temps (encore plus) à me persuader que ce n'était qu'une pierre fausse.

p. 112, l. 11: Lorsque le cœur est préoccupé on ne peut agir sur la partie brutale qu'au moyen d'espèces de monstres. Les mulatresses sont excellentes. Le plaisir qu'elle font ne s'élève pas au-dessus de la région épigastrique.

p. 113, l. 8: Je serais désespéré pourtant que ce fût cela dont le siècle voulût.

p. 113, l. 15: J'ai eu d'abord, tout jeune, quelque estime pour Mérimée. Mon mépris pour lui a commencé le jour où je l'ai vu venir à la sonnette de M. d'Argout. Tiens! me suis-je dit, c'est un laquais!

p. 114, l. 3: Sa momie, avant de descendre dans sa crypte, a été exposée un moment à Londres, comme représentant de la royauté-cadavre qui nous régit.

p. 114, l. 10: Oh! très sale, très sale.

p. 114, l. 17: C'est ce qui est en effet arrivé, Messieurs. Anvers est à nous depuis hier.

p. 116, l. 7: J'aimerais mieux qu'il fût mon égal. La société de Paris est, je le crains, mortelle pour un jeune écrivain; il voit qu'il est peut-être plus dangereux de s'écarter de la médiocrité *en dessus* qu'en dessous. Le dégoût le saisit. Pour le dégoût, Clara a déjà 45 ans; donc, consul à Cagliari ou Salonique.

p. 116, l. 26: Déchirante.

p. 117, l. 13: Épargnez-moi.

p. 117, l. 23: Personne peut-être n'a éprouvé une volupté plus secrète à décevoir que Mérimée.

p. 118, l. 3: Il a beau se ganter étroitement, faire faire ses habits en Angleterre, il n'arrivera jamais à être un parfait dandy, il aura toujours le derrière de tête d'un paysan et les abatis canailles.

p. 118, l. 13: Je n'ai pas assez de prudence pour cela. J'aime trop mes aises et je suis devenu un peu cynique par paresse.

p. 118, l. 32: Attendez encore un peu. Quand vous aurez un cœur pour tout de bon, vous m'en direz des nouvelles. Vous regretterez ce bon temps où vous ne viviez que par la tête, et vous verrez que les maux que vous souffrez maintenant ne sont que des piqûres d'épingles en comparaison des coups de poignard qui pleuvront sur vous, quand le temps des passions sera venu.

CHAPTER 7

p. 120, n. 2: Cela est exactement vrai. L'homme aux poissons a plutôt diminué la beauté du caractère de Rondino. Il lui a ôté un peu de son élan.

p. 123, l. 15: La vue d'ensemble ne lui sied pas, il est trop positif pour y croire; il croit au fait bien défini, bien circonstancié, poursuivi jusqu'au bout dans sa spécialité de passion et dans son expression matérielle; le reste lui paraît fumée et nuage.

p. 126, l. 15: Ainsi que Reynolds, il pensait que le *lâché* du fond faisait ressortir le *fini* des têtes.

p. 126, l. 17: Choisissez un trait dans la figure de votre modèle; copiez-le fidélement.

p. 126, l. 20: Il ne faut pas oublier que lorsqu'on raconte quelque chose de surnaturel, on ne saurait trop multiplier les détails de réalité matérielle. C'est là le grand art de Hoffmann dans ses contes fantastiques.

p. 126, l. 25: En effet, un peu d'obscurité est toujours nécessaire dans une histoire de revenants. Remarquons encore qu'il y a dans toutes un trait qui frappe et qu'on n'oublie plus: trouver le trait qu'il faut, c'est là le problème à résoudre. (. . .) Tout gros mensonge a besoin d'un détail bien circonstancié moyennant quoi il passe. C'est pourquoi notre maître Rabelais a laissé ce beau précepte: '*qu'il faut mentir par nombre impair*'.

p. 127, l. 5: Cependant la montre oscillait, tournait, et quelquefois lui heurtait le bout du nez. Enfin, peu à peu, sa main droite s'éleva vers la montre: le bout de ses doigts la toucha; et elle pesait tout entière dans sa main sans que l'adjudant lâchât pourtant le bout de la chaîne . . .

Le cadran était azuré . . . la boîte nouvelle-
ment fourbie . . . au soleil, elle paraissait
toute de feu . . . La tentation était trop
forte.

p. 127, l. 33: Au lieu de conter son affaire,
il décrit les bois et les prés.

p. 128, l. 3: Qu'on dise à mon gendre
Tiodoro Bianchi de venir demeurer avec
nous.

p. 128, l. 20: Je ne pus savoir comment
mourut le pauvre lieutenant Roger.

p. 128, n. 17: Un de mes étonnements, et
j'en ai quelques uns dans cet ordre, est la
réputation de styliste conquise par Mérimée. De sa sécheresse, de son étisie, ne
parlons pas, c'est hideux mais défendable,
mais de cette prose inerte, de cette composition lourde et mal cuite; ah, oui! La
composition compte dans le style. Dans
La Double Méprise, le caractère de Julie est
inexistant avant la scène de la loge et l'on
pourrait croire que Cheverny fût le principal rôle. C'est du style dépouillé, oui,
comme un lapin est dépouillé.

p. 129, l. 6: J'ai tant d'antipathie pour le
style brillant que je ne lui fais grâce nulle
part.

p. 130, l. 19: 'Car enfin, disait Ledoux à
son armateur pour justifier cette mesure

libérale, les nègres, après tout, sont des
hommes comme les blancs.'

p. 130, l. 23: Ils se sauvèrent, qui deçà,
qui delà, fort embarrassés de retourner
dans leur pays à deux cents lieues de la
côte.

p. 132, l. 8: Mateo fit feu, et Fortunato
tomba roide mort.

p. 133, l. 16: Une insupportable impression
de perfection inutile et de devoir réussi.

p. 134, l. 12: Le colonel du 75e le vit et
le prit pour en faire un cymbalier dans la
musique de son régiment. Il apprit un peu
d'anglais; mais il ne parlait guère. En
revanche il buvait avec excès du rhum
et du tafia. – Il mourut à l'hôpital d'une
inflammation de poitrine.

p. 136, l. 4: Quand j'ai triché ce Hol-
landais, je ne pensais qu'à gagner vingt-
cinq napoléons, voilà tout. Je ne pensais
pas à Gabrielle, et voilà pourquoi je me
méprise . . . Moi, estimer mon honneur
moins que vingt-cinq napoléons! . . .
Quelle bassesse!

p. 136, l. 9: Une baleine? s'écria le capitaine transporté de joie et laissant là son
récit. Vite, la chaloupe à la mer! la yole
à la mer! toutes les chaloupes à la mer! –
Des harpons, des cordes! etc., etc.

CHAPTER 8

p. 137, l. 8: Elle convient fort à mes
goûts, à ma paresse et à mes idées de
voyage.

p. 140, l. 20: Votre tombeau de Richard
Cœur de Lion est une véritable farce qui
ne valait pas la peine qu'un pauvre diable
s'y enrhumât.

p. 142, l. 29: Il m'a demandé si St. Savin
était une église gothique, et il m'a paru
croire pieusement que le gothique et le
roman étaient contemporains, quelque
chose comme l'ordre ionique et l'ordre
corinthien; que l'on bâtissait tantôt d'une
manière tantôt de l'autre suivant le goût
des personnes.

p. 142, l. 36: Il devient tous les jours plus
évident que nous n'avons que trois ou
quatre architectes sur lesquels nous puis-
sions compter.

p. 144, l. 3: Malheureusement je puis dire
que, si j'ai rencontré partout le patriotisme
provincial, je ne l'ai vu que rarement
se manifester par le soin et l'intérêt
portés aux ouvrages qui font honneur au
pays.

p. 144, l. 14: Je suis déjà en guerre avec
je ne sais combien de villes et une de plus
ou de moins ne m'effraye pas.

p. 144, l. 26: Mérimée avait au plus haut
degré le don de captiver – quand il voulait

s'en donner la peine, – et il était admirablement doué pour se faire écouter. Sa voix mesurée, avec des intonations graves, ses grands yeux doux auxquels l'abondance des sourcils et la profondeur du regard donnaient une importance extraordinaire, son regard où la bonté se confondait avec l'ironie, sa façon câline d'interroger, tout cela vous enveloppait et vous prenait. L'interlocuteur, sans même s'en apercevoir, était conduit à lui fournir tous les renseignements, à lui faire tous les aveux. Il eût fait le juge d'instruction le plus aimable qu'on puisse rêver. Avec cela, bon diplomate et habile politique (. . .) Bien que Mérimée fût excellemment bon (il l'a maintes fois prouvé), il avait pour règle de ne jamais laisser entamer, si peu que ce fût, l'autorité qu'il représentait, et malheur à celui, quel qu'il fût, qui commettait une incorrection à son égard; il était rappelé à l'ordre avec une sûreté de main qui lui laissait une impression durable.

p. 145, n. 19: M. Guizot, à la première séance, nous dit que nous devons faire un catalogue de *tous* les monuments de la France actuellement existants. Je me récriais, il me dit: 'Figurez vous que ni le temps ni l'argent ne vous manqueront'. Je fus réduit au silence, et mon voisin, homme au pis, m'écrivit sur un morceau de papier: 'Le temps? il ne sera pas ministre dans trois mois. L'argent? il n'a déjà plus un sou des 120.000 francs votés pour 1835'.

Déjà un ministre à qui les études historiques devront une reconnaissance éternelle nous avait invités à ne nous préoccuper nullement de la question de temps et d'argent.

p. 146, l. 18: Le mauvais goût qui a présidé à la plupart des réparations faites depuis deux siècles à nos monuments du moyen âge, a laissé des traces peut-être plus funestes que les dévastations, suites de nos guerres civiles et de la révolution. Les Protestants et les Terroristes se sont contentés de mutiler les statues, de détruire quelques ornements tandis que souvent les réparateurs ont complètement changé l'aspect des édifices qu'ils ont voulu restaurer.

p. 146, n. 21: Le pire des critiques, c'est qu'elles sont justes.

p. 146, n. 22: Mais, je n'hésite point à le dire, ni les fureurs iconoclastes du protestantisme, ni le vandalisme stupide de la Révolution, n'ont imprimé sur nos monuments des traces aussi déplorables que le mauvais goût du XVIIIe et du XIXe siècle. Les barbares laissaient au moins des ruines: les prétendus réparateurs ne nous ont laissé que leurs tristes ouvrages.

p. 147, l. 2: Lorsqu'il reste quelque chose de certain, rien de mieux que de réparer, voire même de refaire, mais lorsqu'il s'agit de *supposer*, de suppléer, de recréer, je crois que c'est non seulement du temps perdu mais qu'on risque de se fourvoyer et de fourvoyer les autres. Observez que l'archéologie est une science qui commence à peine (. . .) En refaire de toutes pièces à présent, ce n'est pas prudent, je crois.

p. 147, l. 13: Après être demeuré stupide pendant un grand quart d'heure, j'ai retrouvé la voix pour entrer dans une colère telle que Leduc craignait à chaque instant de me voir disparaître par un des trous de l'échaffaud.

p. 147, l. 36: Le temps n'est pas éloigné où les ressources ordinaires se trouveront tout-à-fait insuffisantes pour rémédier aux dommages que le temps et une funeste imprévoyance accumulent tous les jours. Alors il faudra se demander s'il convient de laisser périr à la fois tous les souvenirs de notre histoire, tous les monumens crées par nos ancêtres, tous ces nobles édifices qui attestent le génie et la splendeur des siècles passés. Quelques-uns les verront disparaître d'un œil indifférent, et diront qu'on peut prier Dieu aussi bien dans un grand hangar que dans une cathédrale gothique, et que, pourvu que nous ayons des canaux et des chemins de fer, il importe peu que tous les ouvrages d'art périssent. Mais j'ai trop bonne opinion de notre pays pour croire qu'il se résigne ainsi froidement à l'abandon d'une si grande partie de sa gloire. Des sacrifices énormes, devenus nécessaires, seront consentis, j'aime à le penser; mais aujourd'hui, à moins de frais, on pourrait retarder indéfiniment l'époque de ruine universelle qui s'approche rapidement. Il est encore temps de le prévenir, et des secours prompts, immédiats, seraient moins onéreux que des restaurations tardives commandées par une impérieuse nécessité.

p. 148, l. 31: Si, en entrant dans une église gothique, nous admirons la hardiesse des voûtes, l'élancement des colonnes, en un mot, sa fabrique tout aérienne, pour me servir de l'expression si juste de M. Dusommerard, on éprouve, en la contemplant de loin le sentiment pénible qu'excite la vue d'une ruine chancelante et soutenue par des étais.

p. 148, n. 26: J'ai une querelle avec Viollet au sujet des arcs-boutants. Élever des murs à une telle hauteur pour être obligé de les soutenir par des béquilles, c'est une démence. Mais cette querelle est un reproche que je fais au style gothique. Viollet veut le justifier, mais il se heurte contre mon bon sens.

p. 149, l. 5: Je ne puis voir ces feuilles de chardon, ces dais gothiques, ces pinacles si minces, si délicats, si détachés de la pierre, sans éprouver une certaine émotion en pensant au chagrin que l'artiste aurait éprouvé si, par une distraction il avait donné un coup de marteau plus fort que les autres. Mais les artistes de ce temps-là n'avaient pas de distractions, et j'aime à croire qu'ils prenaient plaisir à ces merveilleuses bagatelles. Mais est-ce là le but de l'art?

p. 149, l. 13: Le mur de la façade porte les traces d'une réparation très maladroite dont j'ignore la date, et qui peut-être aurait eu lieu sous le règne de Louis XIV; mais je ne hasarde cette conjecture qu'avec

timidité, car, détestant l'architecture de cette époque, je suis peut-être trop porté à lui attribuer tous les traits de barbarie qui ont défiguré tant de beaux monumens du moyen-âge.

p. 149, l. 19: Mérimée admire les beaux monuments, mais il n'a jamais senti ses yeux se mouiller à l'aspect de leurs ruines.

p. 149, l. 28: De l'archéologie sentimentale.

p. 149, l. 29: Je suis absolument sceptique en fait de tels monumens, et je ne crois pas même aux théories de mon invention.

p. 150, l. 12: Le Gardon, grossi par des averses prodigieuses, était débordé et roulait, avec un bruit affreux, ses eaux, couleur de café, sous les arches de l'aqueduc; le ciel était à l'orage, mais une éclaircie dorait le monument qui paraissait étincelant de lumière; le site sauvage, la solitude complète du lieu, le bruit du torrent, ajoutaient une poésie sublime à l'architecture imposante qui s'offrait à mes yeux.

p. 150, n. 37: Je crois indispensable d'ôter à toutes les petites villes de province leurs manuscrits dont elles n'ont que faire et qui n'y restent que jusqu'à ce qu'un amateur passe et les vole.

p. 151, l. 4: La Bibliothèque de Tournus est dans le plus grand désordre. Autrefois, elle avait un assez grand nombre de livres rares; la plupart ont été perdus. On ne tient point note des livres prêtés et depuis quelques années plusieurs volumes précieux ont disparu (. . .) Il serait à désirer que ce ms. que personne à Tournus ne peut lire fût envoyé à Paris. S'il doit rester dans cette bibliothèque, on peut le considérer comme perdu.

p. 151, l. 20: Mérimée est susceptible.

p. 152, l. 2: Mérimée et Viollet-le-Duc, qui sont inséparables, portent l'écrasante responsabilité de ces faux témoignages que profèrent, à leur insu, les monuments les plus vénérables de l'art français.

p. 152, l. 30: Cela a dû coûter beaucoup et n'ajoute rien au mérite de la restauration.

396   PROSPER MÉRIMÉE

p. 153, l. 8: C'est une œuvre devant laquelle je reste comme anéanti... – Merci! vous êtes un bon ami.

p. 154, l. 22: Il a bien mérité de l'ancienne France; il a droit à la gratitude de la France d'aujourd'hui.

CHAPTER 9

p. 155, l. 26: Au fait, la vie que je mène est abrutissante. Quand je ne vais pas en voiture, je me lève à neuf heures, je déjeune et je donne audience aux bibliothécaires, archivistes et autres espèces. Ils me mènent voir leurs masures. Si je dis qu'elles ne sont pas carlovingiennes on me regarde comme un scélérat et on ira cabaler auprès du député pour qu'il rogne mes appointements. Pressé entre ma conscience et mon intérêt, je leur dis que leur monument est admirable et que rien dans le Nord ne peut y être comparé. Alors on m'invite à dîner, et on dit dans le journal du département que j'ai bougrement d'esprit. On me prie de déposer une pensée sublime sur un album. J'obéis en frémissant. Le soir on me reconduit à mon hôtel en cérémonie, ce qui m'empêche d'aller au vice. Je rentre excédé et je broche des notes, des dessins, des lettres officielles etc. Je voudrais que mes envieux me vissent alors.

p. 156, l. 15: Un monument druidique.

p. 156, l. 16: Une inscription *syriaque*.

p. 156, l. 24: Jusques à quand laissera-t-on aux évêques et au clergé la faculté de gâter nos plus beaux édifices, par des restaurations ou des additions maladroites? Ne pourrait-on pas, sans manquer aux égards dus aux minstres du culte, borner leur pouvoir en matière de réparations et de constructions?

p. 157, l. 5: Elles me font mal; mais elles me font tant plaisir.

p. 157, l. 22: M. Mérimée est le meilleur et le plus aimable compagnon de route qu'on puisse avoir, toujours de bonne humeur, ne se plaignant jamais, se souciant peu des inconvénients du chemin et disposé à bien prendre toute chose.

p. 157, l. 27: Il n'y a pas de minute dans la journée qui ne se trouve remplie, tout à fait à mon avantage, car je ne puis guère donner et lui me donne bien des choses à prendre. Il a cette qualité précieuse des gens qui ne se livrent que très difficilement, c'est que tous les jours on découvre de nouvelles choses parmi cet esprit fin et cette intelligence élevée.

p. 157, n. 5: J'étais recommandé à M. de Peyrehorade par mon ami M. de P.

p. 158, l. 20: Mon lot maintenant c'est de faire de l'archéologie pure, pendant quelques années en France, puis d'aller crever de la fièvre en Perse en découvrant des souterrains ignorés de Persépolis.

p. 158, l. 23: Je suis cuistre par profession et je commence à le devenir par goût.

p. 158, l. 25: Je suis devenu très moral, très vertueux, antiquaire, cuistre, je travaille le soir au coin de mon feu.

p. 159, l. 14: Depuis bien des années j'ai renoncé à écrire pour les gens du monde. Maintenant je fais des mémoires archéologiques passablement obscurs et qui sont lus par une demi douzaine de doctes dont la moitié hausse les épaules.

p. 159, l. 29: Croyez-vous que la vie d'un homme qui a été le plus grand capitaine de tous les siècles puisqu'il n'a jamais été battu, le plus intrépide paillard, grand orateur, bon historien, si joli garçon que les rois s'y trompaient et le prenaient pour femme, qui a fait cocus tous les grands hommes de son temps, qui a changé la constitution politique et sociale de son pays, qui, qui, trente mille qui, que la vie de feu J. César en un mot soit amusante à écrire?

p. 160, l. 2: Un grand désir.

p. 160, l. 15: O heureux temps où j'écrivais des contes à dormir debout!

p. 160, l. 21: On n'en peut trouver de

plus respectable; car le Saint-Esprit en personne y a dit la messe.

p. 161, l 17. Cette fille m'aime trop et il m'en vient des remords de temps en temps.

p. 161, l. 32: Je me souvins alors que la duchesse de Buckingham avait vu son mari sous la forme d'un oiseau le jour de son assassinat, et l'idée me vint que vous étiez peut-être morte et que vous aviez pris cette forme pour me voir. Malgré moi, cette bêtise me tourmentait, et je vous assure que j'ai été enchanté de voir que votre lettre portait la date du jour où j'ai vu pour la première fois mon oiseau merveilleux.

p. 162, n. 23: Voilà comment, même chez un sceptique, le cœur et l'imagination travaillent; c'est une 'bêtise'; il n'en est pas moins vrai qu'il était sur le seuil du rêve et dans le grand chemin de l'amour.

p. 162, n. 24: Le contre-temps est fâcheux, j'en conviens mais je garde ma pitié pour de plus grandes infortunes et d'ailleurs je me flatte que cette déconvenue nous ramènera M. l'inspecteur un peu plus tôt.

p. 163, l. 3: Je suis amoureux, amoureux fou de la perle des femmes, heureux parce que je suis aimé, très malheureux parce que je ne puis prouver mon amour aussi souvent que je voudrais.

p. 163, l. 6: Je suis grandement et gravement amoureux.

p. 163, l. 8: Une grande passion.

p. 163, l. 8: Après de longues et poignantes péripéties.

p. 163, n. 29: Un maire avec une écharpe tricolore, un curé avec une étole mettent dans un instant la plus honnête fille du monde à la merci d'un animal . . . qui va la traiter comme une courtisane [ne lui fera connaître de l'amour que ce qui pourrait l'en dégoûter].

Effacé par ordre supérieur.

p. 165, l. 3: L'intimité d'une femme d'esprit dont vous n'êtes ni pouvez être l'amant.

p. 165, l. 15: Mais non, c'est M. Beyle, je l'ai bien connu.

p. 165, l. 18: Ces enfants me plaisaient tellement que je ne puis m'accoutumer à l'idée de ne les plus revoir de longtemps. Elles partent à une époque de la vie des femmes où quelques mois les changent beaucoup et il me semble que je vais les perdre. Quand on se sépare d'une amie comme vous on a la certitude de la retrouver un jour absolument telle qu'on l'a quittée, mais au lieu de nos deux petites amies je crains de voir deux demoiselles *prim* et *stiff* m'ayant tout à fait oublié.

p. 165, l. 3: Il s'en faut de beaucoup qu'il ait les connaissances qui seraient nécessaires pour bien remplir sa mission; mais il est jeune, naturellement observateur et s'il peut suivre jusqu'à nos âges la carrière dans laquelle on l'a fait entrer, il sera un antiquaire d'une force respectables dont les futurs Winckelmann parleront avec éloges.

p. 165, n. 32: M. Mérimée m'a promis de me faire tirer des coups de pistolet avec de la poudre.

p. 166, l. 6: Si je suis pas remis durant la belle saison, il faudra que je plie bagages.

p. 166, l. 10: Sa mort fut douce. Il expira comme une lampe qui s'éteint faute d'huile, sans souffrance apparente et conservant jusqu'au dernier moment ce calme et cette sérénité que vous lui connaissiez.

p. 166, l. 22: Difficile pour la maison.

p. 167, l. 2: Je n'aime pas les parents. On est obligé d'être familier avec des gens qu'on n'a jamais vus parce qu'ils se trouvent fils du même père que votre mère.

p. 167, l. 16: Mon cher ami, je vous écris assis dans un fauteuil à oreilles de quatre pieds de large, dans une salle de 120 pieds de long, chauffée, lambrissée, dorée, tapissée. A ma droite est un cordon de sonnette, et si je le tire, un homme en habit brun, culotte de velours et bas de soie, montera et m'apportera du thé dans une théière d'argent. En bas salle à manger aussi grande que le salon, quarante domestiques, conforts de toute espèce. Mon dîner s'est, composé d'un plat de poisson délicieux, sauces de dix espèces, un morceau de roast-beef coupé par moi dans une montagne de viande, deux plats de légumes, du fromage et du vin de Xerez; bierre à discrétion, le tout m'a coûté 4 shillings. Défense de rien donner aux domestiques. L'endroit où l'on voit tout ce luxe et où l'on jouit de toutes ces commodités s'appelle le club de l'Athenæum.

p. 168, l. 15: Ne nous verrons-nous donc jamais pour causer et rire du présent sans crainte pour l'avenir?

p. 168, l. 28: Vous avez peu de monuments, mais pour un homme comme lui, l'île et ses habitants valent la peine qu'il veut se donner pour les connaître.

p. 169, l. 8: Ensorcelé.

p. 169, l. 13: C'est la pure nature qui m'a plu surtout (. . .) je parle de la pure nature de l'HOMME. Ce mammifère est vraiment fort curieux ici.

p. 169, l. 15: On trouve ici de la couleur locale presque aussi souvent que des punaises.

p. 170, l. 1: Je ne comptais pas voir Rome et je me suis laissé entraîner par M. Beyle. J'en suis on ne peut plus content. Je dis de Rome.

p. 170, l. 5: L'affreuse vanité d'Ac gâte ce voyage à Naples.

p. 170, l. 13: Ah! mon ami, quel pays et que j'y voudrais retourner! C'est là qu'il faut vivre quand on n'est plus bouillant de jeunesse. C'est là qu'on trouve tout ce qu'il faut pour l'esprit et le corps comme disait la roi Moabdar. La vie y est tellement facile que je ne conçois pas que l'on y meure.

p. 170, l. 20: Poestum m'a stupéfait. J'éprouve le besoin de démolir toutes les infamies modernes et même un peu moins anciennes qu'on appelle temples, églises, etc. Je voudrais que l'inventeur de l'ordre ionique fût pendu, et l'inventeur du corinthien roué vif. Il n'y a point de salut hors du dorique, surtout point de base.

p. 171, l. 13: La *Colomba* de Mérimée est un chef-d'œuvre qui a réuni ici tous les suffrages. On n'a parlé que de cela durant 15 jours en tous lieux. Je ne connais rien de lui de si beau, de si parfait, de si fin.

CHAPTER 10

p. 174, l. 12: C'était à quatre heures qu'elle avait vu Darcy pour la première fois. – Oui, *vu*, – elle ne pouvait dire *revu* . . . Elle avait oublié ses traits, sa voix; c'était un étranger pour elle . . . Neuf heures après, elle était devenue sa maîtresse!

p. 174, l. 29: Remettait ses gants glacés avec beaucoup de sang-froid.

p. 174, l. 33: Écrivez-lui qu'il ne me connaît pas . . . que je ne le connais pas . . .

p. 175, l. 10: Darcy n'était pas amoureux.

p. 175, l. 11: Darcy s'était trompé sur la nature de son émotion: il faut bien le dire, il n'était pas amoureux.

p. 175, l. 14: Son sourire diabolique.

p. 175, l. 15: D'une voix dont la douceur

même rendait l'expression plus poignante.

p. 175, l. 18: Ces deux cœurs qui se méconnurent étaient peut-être faits l'un pour l'autre.

p. 176, l. 24: C'est un de mes péchés, faits pour gagner de l'argent, lequel fut offert à quelqu'un qui en valait pas grand'chose.

p. 178, l. 3: Don Juan regretta don Garcia plus qu'il n'aurait fait son frère. Il se disait, l'insensé! qu'il lui devait tout. C'était lui qui l'avait initié aux mystères de la vie, qui avait détaché de ses yeux l'écaille épaisse qui les couvrait. 'Qu'étais-je avant de la connaître?' se demandait-il, et son amour-propre lui disait qu'il était devenu un être supérieur aux autres hommes. Enfin tout le mal qu'en réalité lui avait fait la connaissance de cet athée, il le changeait en bien, et il en était aussi reconnaissant qu'un disciple doit l'être à l'égard de son maître.

p. 178, l. 25: Par son moyen j'ai fait de grandes observations sur le cœur humain de l'opéra et des filles nommées demi-castors. Je me propose bien de faire là-dessus une belle dissertation, lorsque j'aurai du loisir.

p. 178, l. 34: Veuillez me dire si cette petite fille n'a pas infiniment plus de mérite à mener la vie qu'elle mène, que vous n'en avez, vous qui jouissez du bonheur singulier d'un entourage irréprochable et d'une nature si raffinée, qu'elle résume un peu pour moi toute une civilisation.

p. 179, l. 7: Oui, je m'appelle Arsène Guillot, G, U, I, deux L; il m'écrit par un Y.

p. 180, l. 22: J'ai aimé!

p. 180, n. 19: Notre dévotion en France me déplaît; c'est une espèce de philosophie très-médiocre, qui vient de l'esprit et non du cœur. Lorsque vous aurez vu la dévotion du peuple en Italie, j'espère que vous trouverez, comme moi, que c'est la seule bonne; seulement, ne l'a pas qui veut et il faut être né au delà des Alpes ou des Pyrénées pour croire ainsi.

p. 181, l. 14: Surtout, ne doutez pas que mon histoire ne soit vraie. Vous en douteriez? Allez au Père-Lachaise: à vingt pas à gauche du tombeau du général Foy, vous trouverez une pierre de liais fort simple, entourée de fleurs toujours bien entretenues. Sur la pierre, vous pourrez lire le nom de mon héroïne gravé en gros caractères: ARSÈNE GUILLOT, et, en vous penchant sur cette tombe, vous remarquerez, si la pluie n'y a déjà mis ordre, une ligne tracée au crayon, d'une écriture très fine: Pauvre Arsène! elle prie pour nous.

p. 181, l. 22: Je ne connaissais rien de pareil dans Mérimée. Pourquoi cela n'est-il pas plus connu? [. . .] Oui; cela est meilleur que tout ce que je supposais que Mérimée pût écrire. Excellent vraiment.

p. 181, l. 30: Je vous envoie une petite historiette que j'ai faite sans la signer, parce qu'il suffit que je parle de curé pour que les vieilles dévotes crient à l'irréligion. L'aventure est vraie et je pourrais nommer les personnages.

p. 182, l. 12: C'est suivant moi mon chef-d'œuvre.

p. 183, l. 1: J'ai entrelardé mon plagiat de petites allusions à des amis à moi, et de plaisanteries intelligibles dans une coterie où je vivais lorsque cette nouvelle a été écrite.

p. 183, l. 17: La tendance générale des mythologies antiques est de laisser les causes premières dans une obscurité, peut-être cherchée à dessein, pour mettre en évidence quelques-uns de leurs effets. Hors d'état d'interpréter des mystères au-dessus de l'intelligence humaine, elles éloignent autant qu'elles peuvent la pensée du nœud de la difficulté.

p. 184, l. 12: Dédain, ironie, cruauté, se lisaient sur ce visage d'une incroyable beauté cependant.

p. 184, l. 14: Cette expression d'ironie infernale.

p. 184, l. 14: Son expression de méchanceté ironique.

p. 184, l. 15: La malice arrivant jusqu'à la méchanceté.

p. 184, l. 22: Il me sembla voir une divinité infernale applaudissant au malheur qui frappait cette maison.

p. 185, l. 29: On sait la recette d'un bon conte fantastique: commencez par des portraits bien arrêtés de personnages bizarres, mais possibles, et donnez à leurs traits la réalité la plus minutieuse. Du bizarre au merveilleux, la transition est insensible, et le lecteur se trouvera en plein fantastique avant qu'il se soit aperçu que le monde réel est loin derrière lui.

p. 186, n. 42: 1. Contours extrêmement nets et même secs.

2. Chose *existante de par soi* et non avec relation à des choses déjà connues (moyen de cet effet: les choses sont racontées nettement comme si l'auditeur était ignorant de tout, sans allusion aux choses déjà connues. Moins de grâce par ce système, mais toute l'attention du lecteur reste à la chose narrée).

3. Bien le cachet dramatique, l'originalité.

4. Ni profondeur ni originalité (autre que dans la façon d'être montrés) dans les caractères.

5. Phrases horriblement courtes, style qui a l'air imité de Cousin (probablement imitation commune des mêmes originaux de l'an 1600).

6. L'auteur tourne au sec.

7. Admirable attention aux petites choses, trait du bon romancier, et hardiesse d'appuyer sur ces petites choses.

8. Grande imprudence de l'auteur: il se moque de son instrument naturel, de son hôte de tous les jours, l'antiquaire de province. Ce conte de 25 pages va augmenter et meme fonder aux yeux des purement raisonnables sa réputation de *méchanceté*. (Personnel, *id est*, dont on se moquera dans vingt ans).

Il y a un moment de sécheresse causée par vingt lignes ou peut-être dix trop savantes. (15 mai 1837. Lu à minuit).

p. 187, l. 12: Ma foi, mon enfant, je n'en sais rien. – Comment, Monsieur? Vous écrivez des histoires et vous ne les savez même pas.

p. 187, l. 33: Je suis de ceux qui goûtent fort les bandits, non que j'aime à les rencontrer sur mon chemin; mais, malgré moi, l'énergie de ces hommes en lutte contre la société tout entière m'arrache une admiration dont j'ai honte.

p. 188, l. 18: J'ai tâché de faire une mosaïque avec les récits que j'ai recueillis à droite et à gauche sur votre pays.

p. 188, l. 22: Si je n'avais crainte de déplaire à trois ou quatre bandits de mes amis, j'aurais pu vous donner encore quel-ques touches de couleur locale, mais ici on ne m'aurait pas cru, et quand je serais retourné en Corse, on m'aurait fait mourir *della mala morte*.

p. 189, l. 5: Une joie maligne.

p. 189, l. 7: Un sourire sardonique.

p. 189, l. 7: Elle crut voir son mauvais génie l'entraînant à sa perte.

p. 189, l. 10: Il lui semblait entendre un oracle fatal, inévitable, qui lui demandait du sang, et du sang innocent.

p. 189, l. 14: Ma douce Colomba, tu es, je le crains, le diable en personne.

p. 189, l. 27: C'était quelque chose entre un Conrad et un dandy . . . J'en ai fait un pur dandy, et un dandy qui a un tailleur corse!

p. 190, l. 10: Il a promis une vendetta et conte un acte de légitime défense.

p. 190, l. 12: Le drame puissant et poétique se tourne en une anecdote pittoresque.

p. 191, n. 57: Explique qui pourra le sens de ces mots, que je comprenais fort bien il y a quelques années, et que je n'entends plus aujourd'hui.

p. 193, l. 7: En attendant que ma dissertation résolve enfin le problème qui tient toute l'Europe savante en suspens, je veux vous raconter une petite histoire; elle ne préjuge rien sur l'intéressante question de l'emplacement de Munda.

p. 193, l. 16: Un menhir littéraire.

p. 193, l. 25: Carmen sera toujours libre.

p. 193, l. 30: C'était une beauté étrange et sauvage, une figure qui étonnait d'abord, mais qu'on ne pouvait oublier. Ses yeux surtout avaient une expression à la fois voluptueuse et farouche que je n'ai trouvée depuis à aucun regard humain.

p. 194, l. 2: Tu es le diable, lui disais-je. – Oui, me répondait-elle.

p. 194, l. 22: Aujourd'hui de même qu'en Occident, les métaphores hardes et in-génieuses ne se trouvent plus guère que dans la bouche des gens illettrés.

p. 194, l. 26: Une veuve à jambes de bois.

p. 194, l. 27: Jamais l'orage n'est si près

dans nos montagnes que lorsque le soleil est le plus brillant.

p. 194, n. 65: Tu as rencontré le diable, oui, le diable; il n'est pas toujours noir, et il ne t'a pas tordu le cou. Je suis habillée de laine, mais je ne suis pas mouton.

p. 195, l. 1: Je ne t'aime plus; toi, tu m'aimes encore, et c'est pour cela que tu veux me tuer.

p. 195, l. 9: Une *Manon Lescaut* plus poivrée et à l'espagnole.

p. 195, l. 30: Alors la bohémienne lui lança un regard de profond mépris; puis, s'asseyant à la turque dans un coin de la chambre, elle choisit une orange, la pela et se mit à la manger.

p. 196, l. 1: Quand Mérimée atteint son effet, c'est par un coup si brusque, si court, que cela a toujours l'air d'une attrape. C'est comme cette garde navarraise et ce fameux coup de couteau par lequel son bandit tue le borgne. On reçoit cela . . . *vlan!* On n'a pas le temps de voir si c'est beau.

p. 197, l. 1: En voilà bien assez pour donner aux lecteurs de Carmen, une idée avantageuse de mes études sur le Rommani. Je terminerai par ce proverbe qui vient à propos: *En retudi panda nasti abela macha.* En close bouche, n'entre point mouche.

p. 197, l. 9: Cela revient à dire, en présence des salons, et avec le sourire que vous savez: 'Bien entendu! ne soyez dupes de mon brigand et de ma bohémienne qu'autant que vous le voudrez'. Après s'être si fort avancé en fait de couleur locale, l'auteur, à son tour, ne veut pas qu'on le croie plus dupe qu'il ne faut.

CHAPTER II

p. 198, l. 20: Mon compagnon Mérimée, *le dur à cuire*, s'est mis à fondre en larmes, ce qui ne m'a pas médiocrement étonné.

p. 199, l. 10: Passé trois semaines en extase devant les plus beaux monuments que l'esprit humain puisse concevoir.

p. 199, l. 17: Nous étions ensemble en Grèce, allant aux Thermopyles et descendant un ravin très roide à pied, tenant nos chevaux par la bride. Nous vîmes tout à coup, sur la crête de la pente opposée dudit ravin, un homme qui, malgré l'escarpement et les rochers, allait courant comme s'il tombait. Il avait pourtant un grand manteau blanc, un long fusil et un daim mort sur les épaules. Il fut au fond du ravin avant nous et là nous nous rencontrâmes. Je lui demandai s'il voulait nous vendre son daim. Il me répondit: 'Je veux le manger avec mes amis'. Cela se dit en grec: *mè toûs filous mou*. Ce mot de *filous* me fit rire, car cet homme avait très mauvaise mine. Il disparut dans les broussailles en un bond ou deux. Au moment de remonter à cheval, M. Lenormant me demanda ce que je pensais de cet homme. Je lui répondis qu'il m'avait tout l'air de Samiel le chasseur sauvage. – Non, dit-il, je crois que c'est le diable. – C'est très probable, lui dis-je, et je partis en avant avec Ampère. Au bout d'un instant, surpris de ne pas entendre de pas de chevaux derrière moi, je me retournai et je vis M. Lenormant par terre, avec l'épaule démise. C'était très loin de tout secours; nous le portâmes comme nous pûmes dans un village, et il se passa deux jours avant que nous pussions trouver un médecin. Pendant ces deux jours il resta à peu près seul dans le village, et plus tard, il a dit qu'il avait employé son temps à réfléchir et qu'il s'était converti. Il a raconté depuis dans son cours qu'il avait vu le diable et moi aussi.

p. 200, l. 16: Cheveux de tourterelle et yeux du lion.

p. 200, l. 22: Dans ces cinq mois, je ne me suis pas ennuyé cinq minutes.

p. 200, l. 24: La seule faute que je trouve à ce pays-ci, c'est sa vertu. Elle est telle que nous en sortirons sans doute vierges et martyrs.

p. 200, n. 13: L'art est toujours plus beau que la nature.

p. 201, l. 5: J'ai été très fort dans mon temps sur la mythologie, que j'ai étudiée avec une espèce de passion, et j'avais commencé un livre que j'ai laissé là (. . .) Je voulais trouver la loi de l'esprit humain qui lui fait inventer les mythes religieux.

p. 201, l. 16: Il se pourrait bien que la mythologie ne fût qu'une impasse. Si l'on y cherche une solution aux grands problèmes sur l'origine et la fin de ce monde, je crains qu'on n'y trouve que niaiseries et absurdités.

p. 201, l. 23: Les grecs sont nos maîtres en tout.

p. 202, l. 5: Il m'a semblé que j'étais débarqué dans une île inconnue. Les femmes sont décolletées de telle sorte que si l'on marche sur le bas de leur robe on les déshabille. La mode est de crier très haut en parlant et je me croyais dans une réunion de perroquets.

p. 202, l. 10: Où est le bon temps où j'y prenais plaisir? Maintenant, tout cela m'ennuie horriblement. Ne vous semblé-je pas bien vieux?

p. 202, l. 36: Je ne puis vous dire combien la mort de ce brave garçon m'a douloureusement affecté. Nous étions autrefois huit qui dînions ensemble une fois par semaine. Trois sont morts déjà et deux, Beyle et Sharpe, de la même manière.

p. 203, l. 5: J'aurais eu quelque consolation à lui dire adieu.

p. 203, l. 16: Tous les jours je suis frappé de ma vieillesse.

p. 203, l. 17: Je me conserve assez mal, vieillissant doucement et fort irrité de vieillir.

p. 203, l. 18: Le sang me monte à la tête, et je crains fort qu'il ne m'arrive un de ces jours comme au pauvre Sharpe.

p. 204, l. 14: Tous les deux, nous faisons

l'impossible: vous, que je sois une statue; moi, que vous n'en soyez pas une.

p. 204, l. 21: Nous avons commencé à nous écrire en faisant de l'esprit, puis nous avons fait quoi? je ne vous le rappellerai pas.

p. 204, l. 24: Voilà que nous faisons de l'érudition.

p. 204, l. 31: Oui, Madame, Monsieur y est, mais Mlle Dacquin est avec lui.

p. 205, l. 1: Vous avez connue les excellentes qualités de Mérimée. Croyez-y toujours, mais croyez peu à son platonisme. Je puis vous mettre en main des preuves que je vous laisserai à ma première visite. Nous sommes tous deux amis de Mérimée, défendons-le d'être grotesque!

p. 205, l. 18: J'ai horreur de toutes les souffrances et je crois aux souffrances morales depuis quelque temps. Enfin, je tâche d'oublier mon *moi* le plus possible.

p. 205, l. 30: Il y a de la témérité à un faiseur de contes comme moi d'offrir à un savant un travail sur l'Histoire romaine.

p. 206, l. 11: On me dit que M. de Pongerville, l'académicien, va mourir: cela me désole, car je ne le remplacerai pas, et je voudrais qu'il attendît jusqu'à ce que mon temps fût venu.

p. 206, l. 20: Vous savez que bien que je ne me sois pas mis officiellement sur les rangs des candidats pour l'Académie française, je fais antichambre avec une espérance éloignée. Je ne puis ni ne voudrais quitter cette situation. La question est donc celle-ci: chercher à être académicien me nuira-t-il ou non?

p. 206, l. 29: Je crains fort l'homme aux truffes. On boude rarement contre un bon dîner. La chance des indigestions par exemple m'est favorable.

p. 206, l. 34: Je fais en ce moment le métier le plus bas et le plus ennuyeux: je sollicite pour l'Académie des inscriptions. Il m'arrive les scènes les plus ridicules, et souvent il me prend des envies de rire de moi-même, que je comprime pour ne pas choquer la gravité des académiciens que je vais voir.

p. 207, l. 18: Comme j'ai dit dans ma lettre à l'Académie, que je ne m'occupais que de travaux d'érudition, l'article du journal est bien inventé. Je ne sais si c'est de bonne guerre, mais je crains que le coup ne porte.

p. 207, l. 28: Le secrétaire perpétuel ayant mis des gants, dont il n'use je crois qu'à cette occasion, m'a conduit par la main comme sa danseuse au milieu de l'auguste assemblée qui s'est levée en pieds comme un seul homme. J'ai fait quarante saluts, un pour chaque membre, je me suis assis et tout a été dit.

p. 208, l. 15: En attendant, je fais des visites fort consciencieusement. Je trouve des gens fort polis, fort accoutumés à leurs rôles et les prenant très au sérieux; je fais de mon mieux pour prendre le mien aussi gravement, mais cela m'est difficile. Ne trouvez-vous pas drôle qu'on dise à un homme: 'Monsieur, je me crois un des quarante hommes de France les plus spirituels, je vous vaux bien', et autres facéties? Il faut traduire cela en termes honnêtes et variés, suivant les personnes.

p. 209, l. 11: Quant à moi, je crois ne valoir ni plus ni moins qu'autrefois; je ne suis pas plus hypocrite et j'ai peut-être tort. Il est certain qu'on ne m'en aime pas davantage.

p. 209, l. 15: Mes amis m'ont dit bien souvent que je ne prenais pas assez de soin pour montrer ce qu'il peut y avoir de bon dans ma nature, mais je ne me suis jamais soucié que de l'opinion de quelques personnes.

p. 270, l. 8: Ce fut fort édifiant chez nous. Deux cents femmes bien parées allaient verser des larmes sur leurs péchés à Notre-Dame avant de se promener à Longchamp. Quinze cents jeunes gens à moustache, barbe et gants jaunes ont communié dévotement par les mains du révérend père Ravignan, lequel fait fureur.

A la suite de quoi, avant-hier, le prince Belgiojoso a enlevé la duchesse de Plaisance.

p. 210, l. 15: Dès qu'il ne sera plus de *bon air* d'aller au sermon, lorsque les jeunes femmes ne s'y montreront plus, l'enthousiasme religieux disparaîtra.

p. 211, l. 2: Nous avions besoin d'un lettré, on nous a donné un étalon.

p. 211, l. 6: J'ai grand regret à cette dernière *Nouvelle* de notre confrère Mérimée. Il y a là un peu de talent mal employé. Entre nous je ne me souviens pas d'avoir lu une production frivole plus radicalement mauvaise.

p. 211, l. 11: Un docte aréopage de vieilles femmes.

p. 211, l. 15: On est devenu tellement cagot à Paris qu'à moins de se faire illuminé, jésuite et j.–f., il est impossible de ne pas passer pour athée et scélérat. Je persiste à trouver qu'il n'y a pas de quoi fouetter un chat dans ma nouvelle et pourtant les bonnes âmes crient au scandale, ouvrant des yeux et des bouches comme des portes cochères.

p. 211, l. 22: Tout ce déchaînement de cagotisme m'a mis d'abord en colère, maintenant cela m'amuse. Je n'ai plus rien à craindre et je me moque d'eux. Je me vengerai même un jour je l'espère et les traiterai comme ils le méritent. Vous ne pourrez jamais vous figurer ce que c'est aujourd'hui que le néo-catholicisme. Nous marchons à grands pas à toutes les extravagances et si cela dure nous serons avant peu en plein moyen âge.

p. 211, n. 55: Est-ce que Monsieur Mérimée est pris?

p. 212, l. 8: J'ai bien trouvé la vérité que nul n'est prophète en son pays. On m'a dit pis que pendre de ce grand homme et je suis revenu avec une provision d'anecdotes excellentes pour une satire. Malheureusement c'est un éloge que je dois faire.

p. 212, l. 13: C'était un gaillard très taré qui faisait le bonhomme et avait toujours la larme à l'œil. Je suis obligé de dire dès mon exorde que c'était un infâme menteur.

p. 212, l. 26: Tout s'est fort bien passé avant hier. J'avais la plus belle peur du monde, et l'on m'a dit que j'étais la vraie peinture d'un pendu qu'on mène à la potence. Mon visage était de la même couleur que les broderies vertes de mon habit. Mais je ne m'étais appliqué qu'à un point, c'est à conserver ma voix. J'ai lu mon discours assez bien, d'un ton ferme et décidé. On a paru content.

p. 212, n. 59: L'histoire du Roi de Bohème est bien ce qu'il y a de plus bête au monde.

CHAPTER 12

p. 214, l. 21: J'y pense toujours fort sérieusement.

p. 214, l. 22: Plus j'étudie mon sujet plus j'en suis charmé. Il me semble que c'est une de ces grandes époques de travail dans la constitution des peuples, semblables à celles qu'on observe dans la vie des individus.

p. 215, l. 5: J'ai fini mon histoire de don Pedro, mais il faut que la recommence depuis le premier mot (. . .) A force de travailler mon sujet, je ne désespère pas d'en faire quelque chose de tolérable.

p. 215, l. 15: Vous saurez que j'ai fini avant-hier la dernière ligne de don Pedro et que j'ai écrit le mot FIN avec un indicible plaisir.

p. 218, l. 3: Je suis horriblement triste quand je pars pour mes tournées, et cette fois plus que jamais. Cependant, il fait un temps superbe et j'ai mangé du *haschisch* pour me donner de la gaieté, mais fort inutilement. On m'avait dit que j'allais voir le paradis et les houris du Vieux de la Montagne; mais je n'ai rien vu du tout.

p. 218, l. 16: J'ignore comment des traits qui n'ont, ce semble, ni grandeur, ni régularité, arrivent à produire l'impression la plus profonde, une sorte de ravissement sérieux qui prend toute l'âme, et qui ne ressemble en rien à la séduction d'un joli visage. Je crois que cela tient à la grandeur du front, à la ligne du nez, et surtout à la tristesse pénétrante du regard quand il est sérieux. Les yeux semblent tout sentir et comprendre, et l'émotion donne à ses traits une expression supérieure a leur forme et à sa physionomie ordinaire, qui n'est que bonne et spirituelle. Sa grâce qui couvre tout pourrait cacher bien des défauts; chez elle, elle trompe sur ses qualités. Ceux qui ne la connaissent pas (et pour connaître une femme il faut l'aimer) ne croient et ne savent d'elle que cette grâce incomparable de la personne. On ne la trouve que charmante. C'est la méconnaître.

p. 218, l. 31: Je suis tourmenté par tous les *blue devils*. Si nous étions à Madrid, je vous conterais un tas de choses qui m'arrivent et vous me donneriez un bon conseil.

p. 218, l. 34: Je suis un peu mieux depuis quelques jours. Mieux au physique, pis que jamais au moral. On dit que le travail est une grande distraction, je me distrais beaucoup, mais je ne fais rien qui vaille.

p. 219, l. 5: Chaque année, je trouve la province plus sotte et plus insupportable. Cette fois-ci, j'ai le spleen et je vois tout en noir, peut-être parce que vous m'avez oublié si indignement.

p. 220, l. 20: Pour Dieu, mon cher ami, avec qui vous battez-vous?

p. 220, l. 23: Monsieur, cela ne vous regarde pas, et si cela vous regardait, je sauterais par la fenêtre plutôt que de vous le dire!

p. 220, l. 28: Lui ne s'en souciait pas, il était à l'aise comme garçon, mais pas assez riche pour avoir un ménage. Probablement aussi il tenait à sa liberté.

p. 220, n. 16: Un sourire moqueur qui ne finissait qu'à la dernière phrase de ce charmant récit.

p. 221, l. 22: Si vous pouviez avoir un

gouvernement napoléonien pendant huit ou dix ans, je crois que vous ne vous en trouveriez pas plus mal.

p. 221, l. 26: Maintenant, ces messieurs en sont venus à professer publiquement que l'incendie et le vol sont des moyens fort légitimes de rémédier à l'inégalité dans la répartition de la propriété. La théorie n'est pas faite pour gagner des adeptes parmi ceux qui possèdent quelque chose, mais dans une grande ville comme Paris, il y a tant de gens qui se lèvent tous les matins sans savoir comment ils déjeune-ront que les idées de partage sont sûres de trouver toujours quelques milliers de fervents prosélytes.

p. 222, l. 4: Combien je me félicite de n'avoir jamais eu de goût pour la politique. En courant, j'ai vu, bien malgré moi, quel-ques-unes des saletés électorales, et j'en suis encore révolté. Il faut avoir le diable au corps et l'âme bien basse pour faire le métier de candidat à la députation. Tant qu'à avoir un maître, j'en aime mieux un seul que plusieurs.

p. 222, l. 13: Il y a dans ce moment à Paris et, je crois, dans toute la France, une espèce de terreur instinctive d'une révolu-tion. Chacun en parle avec effroi, sans deviner de quel côté l'orage viendra. Il n'y a personne qui en doute, et cependant on parierait contre toutes les chances prévues ou à prévoir.

p. 223, l. 7: Au milieu d'une si grande catastrophe, on ne pense guère à ses affaires particulières. Cependant, je com-mence à être en peine comment je vivrai et ferai vivre ma pauvre vieille mère.

p. 223, l. 13: Je n'ai pas à me reprocher d'avoir fait restaurer des églises, à la re-commandation des ventrus, et je n'ai jamais su même le nom du député de St Savin. S'il faut quitter la place, j'en serai fâché comme quelqu'un à qui l'on ôte son dîner, et je tâcherai de gagner mon pain de mon mieux.

p. 224, l. 4: Les terreurs fébriles et des préoccupations constantes.

p. 224, l. 13: Le visage bouleversé.

p. 224, l. 15: *Il sanglotait comme un enfant.*

p. 224, l. 24: La révolution a été faite par moins de six cents hommes qui, la plupart, ne savaient ce qu'ils faisaient, ni ce qu'ils voulaient.

p. 224, l. 27: Le roi et les princes ont été au-dessous de leurs cousins de la branche aînée, dans tout cela. Ils se sont perdus, et ont perdu la royauté en France. A quoi diable sert l'histoire, que personne n'en profite?

p. 224, l. 32: Nous voilà en république, sans enthousiasme, mais déterminés à nous y cramponner, car c'est la seule chance de salut qui nous reste.

p. 225, l. 1: Avant de changer les institu-tions il faut changer les mœurs, et les nôtres ne sont pas des mœurs républi-caines.

p. 225, l. 4: Quoi qu'il arrive, la liberté est perdue dans ce pays-ci. Elle ne résistera pas à l'anarchie ou bien à la fureur de l'ordre qui lui succédera peut-être un jour.

p. 225, l. 9: La seule chose vraiment regret-table, c'est l'affaiblissement du sentiment religieux (. . .) Il est certain que la religion est le plus fort et le plus efficace moyen de police qui existe. Mais ce moyen comment l'appliquer, comment le faire revivre aujourd'hui, maintenant que les classes inférieures ont gagné de nous la contagion philosophique?

p. 225, l. 15: Mais cet homme où est-il?

p. 225, l. 27: Tout le monde avait perdu la tête, je crois, et les figures des députés étaient si décomposées par la peur ou l'in-dignation, pour parler noblement et offici-ellement, qu'on avait peine à reconnaître les gens qu'on rencontre tous les jours.

p. 226, l. 4: Au milieu de la douleur que j'éprouve, je sens par-dessus tout la bêtise de cette nation. Elle est sans égale. Je ne sais s'il sera jamais possible de la détourner de la barbarie sauvage où elle a tant de propension à se vautrer.

p. 226, l. 17: Voit souvent M. de Rémusat.

p. 226, l. 22: Voici une triste année qui va finir. Elle a été pire pour moi et pour bien d'autres, non que j'y aie perdu beaucoup matériellement; mais je me sens découragé, sans espoir pour l'avenir. J'ai éprouvé dans ces derniers mois toutes les misères de cœur qu'il est donné à un être humain se souffrir. Que je voudrais être auprès de vous, mon amie, et vous conter toutes mes douleurs (. . .) Je voudrais surtout avoir deux heures de conversation avec vous, vous ouvrir mon cœur pour savoir ce qu'il y a dedans. C'est en vérité ce que je ne sais guère et il me faudrait du calme et du sang-froid comme vous en avez, pour voir clair dans ce triste abîme.

p. 227, l. 22: Mon travers a toujours été de me passionner pour des sujets étrangers à l'intérêt général.

CHAPTER 13

p. 228, l. 10: Une peinture vraie des mœurs et des caractères à une époque donnée.

p. 229, l. 1: Une curiosité inépuisable de toutes les variétés de l'espèce humaine.

p. 229, l. 3: Je n'ai jamais cherché qu'à faire des portraits. Quand j'étais jeune, j'aimais beaucoup à disséquer des cœurs humains pour voir ce qu'il y avait dedans.

p. 229, l. 6: Peintures du cœur humain.

p. 229, l. 9: Tout ce qui se rapporte à l'histoire de l'humanité est plein d'intérêt pour moi.

p. 229, l. 12: Quand on a du goût pour l'étude du cœur humain, c'est bien triste de mourir sans avoir obtenu la solution de quelques problèmes intéressants.

p. 229, l. 24: Jamais personne en causant n'a fait moins de dépense d'*idées* proprement dites.

p. 229, l. 30: Dans l'histoire, je n'aime que les anecdotes.

p. 229, l. 32: Une des marques de la médiocrité d'esprit est de toujours conter.

p. 230, l. 26: Je voudrais bien avoir le talent d'écrire une Histoire de France; je ne ferais pas de contes.

p. 230, l. 28: La Vérité de l'art. Le Vrai du fait.

p. 230, l. 34: Je travaille en ce moment (. . .) à quelque chose de plus sérieux que mes anciennes fredaines.

p. 231, l. 8: J'ai tant fait de romans autre- fois que je n'aime plus maintenant que l'histoire.

p. 231, l. 18: Une philosophie de l'histoire est une absurdité. Évidemment quand les mêmes causes se présentent, les mêmes effets *probablement* suivront, le cœur de l'homme étant partout et toujours le même; mais réduire tout en système est dangereux et étroit.

p. 231, l. 22: L'histoire ne doit pas se borner, ce me semble, au récit des événe- ments politiques; mais elle doit encore enregistrer les faits qui font connaître les mœurs et les caractères des hommes d'autrefois.

p. 231, l. 27: Parce que toutes les histoires précédentes étaient conçues dans un esprit faux, que l'on n'y tenait nullement compte des peuples, mais que c'était aux rois et aux grands seuls que l'on faisait attention, était-ce une excuse pour se jeter dans l'extrême opposé, pour faire sans cesse l'apologie des vaincus, pour voir toujours des questions de races là où il y a lutte entre le pouvoir temporel et le pouvoir spirituel?

p. 232, l. 4: Hors du collège, si par fortune nous avons retenu quelque chose de ce qu'on nous y a montré, l'histoire ancienne pourra devenir pour nous la plus attach- ante lecture. Tout le monde n'est pas roi ou ministre pour avoir besoin des enseigne- ments de l'histoire, mais il n'est personne qui ne prenne intérêt au jeu des passions, aux portraits de ces grands caractères qui dominent des peuples entiers, à ces alternatives de gloire et d'abaissement que de près on nomme la fortune, mais qui, vues de loin et d'ensemble, deviennent la révélation de terribles et mystérieuses lois de l'humanité.

p. 232, l. 12: Pour moi, je ne connais pas de problème plus intéressant que la dissection complète d'un caractère historique.

p. 232, l. 21: Pour l'auteur comme pour le lecteur, c'est une bonne fortune que de rencontrer un de ces personnages qui dominent leur époque, et qui, de même que le protagoniste des tragédies antiques, est le centre de toutes les péripéties et tient sans cesse la scène occupée.

p. 232, l. 28: L'histoire est à mes yeux une chose sacrée.

p. 232, l. 32: La découverte de la vérité.

p. 233, l. 1: Froid et juste.

p. 233, l. 2: Rassemblent des faits nombreux et les soumettent à une critique impartiale.

p. 233, l. 3: Ce qu'on exige de l'histoire aujourd'hui, c'est la sûreté de la critique et l'impartialité des jugements.

p. 233, l. 7: Perfectionnement dans les méthodes de recherche, perfectionnement dans l'art de la critique, voilà les progrès que les études historiques ont faits depuis le commencement du siècle, et c'est, je pense, un des titres de gloire qui recommandera à la postérité la littérature de notre époque.

p. 233, l. 13: Les Allemands ont fait ce qu'il y a de pire; ils ont mis de l'imagination dans un sujet qui n'en comportait pas, l'histoire.

p. 233, l. 21: Lorsque j'ai cessé d'écrire, l'histoire était la seule chose qui m'intéressât encore en fait de littérature.

p. 233, l. 25: L'histoire, quand elle est écrite comme vous savez faire, l'emporte sur tous les poëmes et tous les drames comme le diamant sur le strass.

p. 234, n. 31: Monsieur de Lamartine chasse sur mes terres. Il écrit une *Vie de César*, bien entendu sans avoir lu autre chose que la biographie universelle. Il fait les coqàlanes les plus extraordinaires, mais cela me vexe et me dégoûte de finir mon histoire.

Il y a longtemps que je travaille à une vie de César.

p. 235, l. 22: Un récit complet des événements de la guerre sociale offre plus d'une difficulté. D'ordinaire lorsqu'on écrit l'histoire d'une époque ancienne, on a pour ainsi dire à restaurer un édifice plus ou moins mutilé par le temps, mais dont les formes restent encore reconnaissables et se peuvent déduire des parties qui ont subsisté. Ici, au contraire, ce ne sont que des ruines tellement éparses et confuses, qu'en les rassemblant on a toujours la crainte d'en altérer la disposition primitive.

p. 236, l. 3: Si la conscience des difficultés qui se présentent à chaque pas peut me préserver de quelques erreurs, j'ai l'espérance de ne point tomber dans celles où l'esprit de système et la confiance dans mes forces pourraient m'engager involontairement.

p. 236, l. 15: Je ne me dissimule pas combien cette tentative est hardie, combien elle est au-dessus de mes forces; mais je croirais avoir rendu service à l'histoire, si de mon travail pouvait ressortir quelque vérité négligée, si mes erreurs mêmes servaient d'avertissement aux écrivains qui traiteront le même sujet après moi.

p. 236, l. 26: Je tâche de faire mon livre *excessivement* compréhensible pour le public ignorant. Peut-être, entre l'Académie et le public, resterai-je le cul à terre.

p. 237, l. 22: C'est vous qui me donnerez de l'orgueil en me disant que la Guerre sociale ne vous a pas paru ennuyeuse. Je vous assure avec la plus parfaite *franchise* que je la croyais telle, excepté pour une douzaine de personnes qui ont comme moi le goût des vieilleries romaines. En outre lorsque je faisais ce livre, je ne pensais qu'à être agréable à Messieurs de l'Académie des Inscriptions et l'on m'avait dit que pour leur plaire, il fallait être ennuyeux. Cela n'était pas trop difficile, mais encore il y a tant de manières d'être ennuyeux. Celle qu'ils préfèrent en matière d'histoire, c'est qu'on glisse sur tout ce qui tient aux mœurs, aux caractères, au cœur humain, par contre que l'on approfondisse les petits faits indifférents, qu'on discute les textes obscurs et inconnus, etc. (. . .) Si vous le permettez 'je m'en vais vous bailler une comparaison'. Supposez mille petits morceaux d'étoffe plus ou moins déchirés. Je les couds ensemble et j'en fais un tapis. Les admirateurs de couture apprécieront ce travail, mais les autres trouveront qu'un tapis d'une seule pièce est préférable. Le mérite de mon livre c'est d'avoir recousu une phrase d'Appien à un fragment de Dion Cassius, un mot d'Orose à une ligne de Diodore de Sicile. Mais qui lit ces gens-là?

p. 238, l. 24: Rome ignorait encore le génie de César, et déjà cependant tous les regards se tournaient vers lui comme attirés par un pressentiment fatal. Tout en lui semblait extraordinaire et contradictoire, son extérieur aussi bien que sa conduite. Ses yeux noirs, dont on avait peine à soutenir le feu pénétrant, contrastaient avec le sourire habituel d'une bouche aux contours presque féminins. Dans sa jeunesse il était d'une complexion délicate, et ses membres blancs et mollement arrondis n'annonçaient pas la vigueur; cependant il excellait dans tous les exercices du corps, et sa santé n'était altérée ni par l'excès du travail, ni par l'excès des plaisirs. En le voyant le matin au Forum, drapé dans sa toge flottante dont tous les plis semblaient étudiés au miroir, on se demandait si c'était le même homme qui la veille au Champ de Mars domptait un cheval fougueux, ou qui devant le tribunal des duumvirs élevait la voix au nom du peuple pour accuser un proconsul enrichi par les proscriptions de Sylla. Orgueilleux de sa naissance, il aimait à rappeler aux Romains qu'il comptait parmi ses ancêtres des rois et des dieux, mais on ne savait s'il était plus fier de Vénus, sa mère, que du mari de sa tante, Marius le plébéien à deux noms. Quelquefois, lorsque dans la curie il prenait la parole, les vieux sénateurs tremblaient, croyant revoir C. Gracchus. L'instant d'après le tribun fougueux avait disparu, il ne restait plus qu'un élégant débauché plus préoccupé de sa nouvelle maîtresse que des affaires de la république.

p. 239, l. 20: Mérimée a réussi dans sa *Guerre sociale*, et il a échoué dans son *Catilina*. Dans le premier sujet plein d'actions coupées et de guerres, il s'est vite jeté dans les montagnes, il s'en est tiré. Mais dans l'autre ouvrage, il lui a fallu tenir le *forum*, ce qui ne lui va pas. Il n'a surtout rien compris à Cicéron, à cet homme dont a dit magnifiquement qu'il était *le seul génie que le peuple romain ait eu d'égal à son empire.*

p. 239, n. 39: Il fallait, pour le manier, de la rigueur et de l'érudition et de la culture Mérimée n'avait que de la curiosité et de la culture.

En lui, histoire et littérature ne se séparent pas.

p. 240, l. 23: Nous sommes trop habitués à juger les anciens avec le préjugés ou les sophismes de leur histoire.

p. 240, l. 25: Combien il est difficile de juger les anciens avec les idées de notre temps.

p. 240, l. 28: Vous m'avez très justement repris de l'excès de mes reproches contre les mœurs romaines. En y réfléchissant je crois que vous avez raison et que nous ne valons pas mieux. Si nous sommes moins féroces cela tient peut-être seulement à ce que nous avons des romans et des théâtres tous les jours, et à ce que le Préfet de Police défend les combats de gladiateurs.

Mon erreur vient de ce que, aimant trop les Romains et César en particulier, je voulais me mettre en garde contre ce qui me semblait de la partialité. J'ai versé du côté où je ne penchais pas, cela arrive bien souvent.

p. 241, l. 31: Plus j'étudie votre histoire et plus je trouve d'excuses à D. Pedro. Il est absurde de le juger avec nos idées modernes. Pour le comprendre il faut se reporter aux opinions et aux nécessités politiques du moyen âge. Assassiner en 1350 était tout autre chose qu'en 1800.

p. 241, l. 36: Je tâche de démontrer qu'au milieu du XIVᵉ siècle il était moins mal de tuer un homme que de faire un article calomnieux dans un journal, en 1846.

p. 242, l. 4: Aujourd'hui nous avons à tenir compte des mœurs de son temps et des difficultés qu'il rencontra. Nous devons apprécier ses intentions et les projets de ses adversaires. Tel est l'examen auquel il faut se livrer avant de porter un jugement; tel est le but du travail que j'ai entrepris.

p. 242, l. 9: Pour moi, je n'ai point entrepris de défendre don Pèdre; mais il me semble que son caractère et ses actions méritaient d'être mieux connus, et que la lutte d'un génie énergique comme le sien contre les mœurs du quatorzième siècle était digne d'une étude historique.

p. 242, l. 22: On ne doit point juger cette sanglante exécution avec nos idées modernes; il faut se reporter aux mœurs du moyen âge, non pas pour la justifier, mais pour examiner si l'odieux de ce massacre doit retomber sur le prince qui le commanda ou sur l'époque qui vit tant de scènes semblables. Il n'est point douteux que, suivant les lois et les usages de la Castille au quatorzième siècle, des vassaux rebelles ne fussent considérés comme des traîtres, que le premier sujet fidèle pouvait et devait tuer en les reconnaissant (. . .) Assurément, en 1356, personne n'eût contesté à don Pèdre le droit de tirer un châtiment exemplaire des rebelles de Toro; mais que

penser de cette boucherie de gens sans défense qui venaient, conduits par deux femmes, implorer sa pitié?

p. 243, l. 6: Quelque indignation, quelque dégoût qu'on éprouve au récit de ces exécutions continuelles, il est impossible de les attribuer à une férocité irréfléchie, à cette cruauté de tempérament que la plupart des historiens prêtent à don Pèdre pour expliquer tant de meurtres ordonnés, exécutés coup sur coup. Ils me semblent plutôt la conséquence fatale de l'ambition du roi aux prises avec les mœurs de son époque. Le trait principal de son caractère est un violent amour de la domination, oujours soupçonneux, toujours inquiet, excusable peut-être jusqu'à un certain point dans un prince du moyen âge, qui, longtemps témoin des maux de l'anarchie, avait fini par ériger son despotisme en une mission surhumaine pour régénérer son pays (. . .) Partout on ne rencontre que trahisons, parjures éhontés. Faut-il s'étonner qu'un prince élevé au milieu de la guerre civile, toujours entouré de révoltes et de conspirations, trahi par ses frères et ses cousins, vendu par sa mère et par sa tante, ait cherché à tourner contre ses ennemis les armes dont il avait éprouvé lui-même les dangereuses blessures? Je ne fais point ici l'apologie de don Pèdre, je veux seulement établir combien il est difficile de juger les hommes d'autrefois avec nos idées modernes.

p. 243, l. 26: Les hommes du quatorzième siècle vivent isolés comme les animaux de proie, et cette énergie, cette force de volonté que nous admirons trop aujourd'hui en eux, ils la doivent peut-être à la conscience de leur propre méchanceté, leur démontrant sans cesse qu'ils ne peuvent et ne doivent compter que sur eux-mêmes.

p. 244, l. 33: Carpentero et Casteñeda soutenaient chacun d'un côté la reine tremblante. Ce dernier élevait en l'air la lettre d'amnistie toute déployée. Les autres se serraient autour des deux femmes, qu'ils considéraient comme leur sauvegarde, et s'attachaient à leurs vêtements. Tous cherchaient quelque seigneur de marque, quelque chef de l'armée royale dont ils pussent implorer la protection. Pour arriver jusqu'au roi, ce lugubre cortège avait à traverser une masse compacte d'hommes d'armes qui les attendaient l'épée nue à la main sur le revers du fossé. Il fallut passer le pont-levis et s'engager entre deux haies de soldats. Castañeda, montrant le parchemin et le sceau du roi, s'écriait qu'il avait sa grâce, oubliant qu'il avait laissé expirer le délai fixé pour sa soumission. On s'avançait lentement au milieu des huées et des injures de la foule, et le roi ne paraissait point. A quelques pas du pont-levis, un écuyer de Diego de Padilla, reconnaissant Carpentero aux insignes de Calatrava, fend la presse et lui assène sur la tête un coup de masse qui l'abat aux pieds de la reine. On l'achève à coups de poignard. Ce fut le signal du massacre. En un instant Castañeda, Martin Telho et Tellez Giron tombent percés de mille coups, et inondent de leur sang les vêtements des deux femmes évanouies à cet horrible spectacle. En reprenant connaissance, la reine, soutenue entre les bras de quelques soldats farouches, les pieds dans une mare de sang, vit d'abord les quatre cadavres mutilés, déjà dépouillés nus. Alors le désespoir et la fureur lui rendant des forces, d'une voix entrecoupée par des cris et des sanglots, elle maudit son fils et l'accusa de l'avoir à jamais déshonorée.

p. 245, l. 34: La manière dont M. Mérimée écrit l'histoire est saine, simple, pleine de concision et de fermeté (. . .) De nos jours, on a fort abusé des idées et des considérations générales, des influences diverses qu'on a fait jouer à travers les siècles; M. Mérimée, qui n'aime que ce qui est sûr, s'en abstient strictement; il aborde l'histoire par ses monuments les plus authentiques et ses témoignages les plus précis, s'en écarte peu, ne les combine qu'autant qu'il lui semble que les faits s'y prêtent, et s'arrête dès que la donnée positive fait défaut.

CHAPTER 14

p. 247, l. 18: Le Bonaparte.

p. 247, l. 22: Il m'a paru petit, avec une tête faite pour un corps beaucoup plus grand, l'air très gentleman, un accent presque étranger sans qu'on puisse lui assigner une origine. Il parle fort peu, et ce qu'il dit est convenable, mais il ne fait pas de frais. Il a les manières d'un légitime, *cold distant and self-conscious*.

p. 248, n. 3: Elle a le défaut de notre temps, c'est de n'être ni pathétique ni gaie, mais je suis bien heureux que vous y ayiez trouvé un peu de vérité.

Mérimée m'apprit que le rôle n'était pas autre chose que le portrait d'une fort grande dame, qu'il me nomma et que je ne nommerai pas, parce qu'il me l'a nommée. Je compris aussi, à de certaines réserves de sa part, qu'il y avait dans cette comédie, un sous-entendu qui n'était qu'un souvenir, souvenir pénible qui m'expliqua le manque de charme de l'ouvrage. Je ne dirai pas quel est ce sous-entendu parce que je l'ai deviné et qu'il ne me l'a pas dit.

p. 249, l. 21: Je suis peut-être le mieux conservé des dîneurs de Véry, et vous aurez peut-être de la peine à me reconnaître.

p. 249, l. 24: Je suis trop vieux, et il est rare à présent que je le fasse plus de 120 fois par mois.

p. 249, l. 27: La tradition s'en est perdue et je ne saurais vous dire combien je me suis senti triste en me retrouvant dans ce salon où nous avons fait tant de joyeux dîners avec des amis qui sont maintenant sous terre. Il me semblait revenir d'une grande bataille où la moitié de mon régiment serait restée.

p. 250, l. 6: Elle m'afflige d'autant plus cruellement que je ne doute pas qu'elle ne soit due à sa témérité que l'âge n'avait pu abattre.

p. 250, l. 9: Il est mort (. . .) pour avoir trop travaillé et trop fait l'amour.

p. 250, l. 16: Je commence à avoir assez de ce pays-ci. Je suis excédé de l'architecture perpendiculaire et des manières également perpendiculaires des natifs.

p. 250, l. 20: Des chanoines protestants jouissant de 4 ou 5.000 livres sterling de revenu, sous prétexte de grec, qu'ils ont oublié, et passant leur vie à chanter des litanies et à boire du vieux vin de porto.

p. 250, l. 25: Il y avait un poisson de quatre pouces dans un grand plat d'argent et une côtelette d'agneau dans un autre. Tout cela servi dans un style magnifique, avec des pommes de terre dans un plat de bois sculpté. Mais jamais je n'ai eu si faim. C'est la suite de l'hypocrisie de ces gens-là. Ils aiment à montrer aux étrangers qu'ils sont sobres, et, moyennant qu'ils font un *luncheon*, ils ne dînent pas.

p. 252, l. 20: Je n'ai pas la moindre habitude de la scène, et je me sens particulièrement impropre à écrire pour le théâtre.

p. 253, l. 8: Mais Mérimée était comme un enfant qui joue pour la première fois au cerf-volant et qui le voit déjà dans les nues: il n'y avait pas à rebrousser chemin.

p. 253, l. 19: Mes principes sont qu'un homme de lettres ne doit jamais se fâcher, de quelque façon qu'on le traite, pourvu qu'on ne l'appelle ni lâche, ni voleur. Si enculeur, il faut en délibérer et savoir comment on l'entend.

p. 254, l. 5: Je ne puis vous dire combien j'ai souffert en écrivant ces deux pages (. . .) Je n'ai pas dit la moitié de ce qu'il y avait à dire, mais je pensais d'un côté à sa famille de l'autre au public et j'ai fait

un juste milieu dont je ne suis pas content.

p. 256, l. 25: Quoique j'aie pas mal d'occupations, *je ferai tout ce qui sera nécessaire et j'enverrai au besoin promener le reste.* Je suis trop anxieux de vous voir enfin sortir de ce coupe-gorge pour ne pas vous tendre à pleines mains les deux mains. Quant à la question d'argent, n'en parlons pas.

p. 257, l. 4: L'auteur, pour prouver l'identité des livres de l'accusé avec des volumes perdus, ne tient compte ni du format, ni des titres, ni des dates; il ne sait pas même si les livres sont perdus, car il ne prend pas le peine de faire les vérifications les plus faciles; il interprète des phrases d'une correspondance italienne, et il ne peut citer trois mots d'italien sans les estropier; il accepte les témoignages les plus absurdes contre l'accusé et ne mentionne pas les dépositions à décharge; il ignore des faits connus de tout le monde; il néglige d'ouvrir des livres qui sont dans les mains de tous les amateurs. Que ne néglige-t-il pas? Il néglige de se relire, et se réfute souvent lui-même, croyant alléguer une présomption nouvelle.

p. 257, l. 25: Je regrette beaucoup, Monsieur, que vous ayez trouvé trop de vivacité dans mon petit factum, mais j'ose espérer qu'un caractère généreux comme le vôtre voudra bien excuser les mouvements involontaires excessifs qui me seraient échappés en voyant entasser les imputations les plus contraires à la vérité, contre un ancien confrère, abandonné de tout le monde, parce qu'il s'est permis autrefois de mal parler de Mr Arago, de l'école des Chartes et des Jésuites.

p. 258, l. 3: Quant à moi, je m'attendais au pire, et je n'ai qu'un regret, c'est que mes amis aient profité de l'accablement où j'étais pour me faire faire des démarches à l'effet de désarmer messieurs.

p. 258, l. 25: Il y en a beaucoup qui vous apportent des bonbons. C'est pour voir la tête que vous faites dans cette position.

p. 259, l. 4: J'ai entrepris une œuvre chevaleresque dans un premier mouvement, et vous savez qu'il faut se garder de cela. Je m'en repens parfois (. . .) Il n'y a que des coups à gagner à ce métier-là; mais quelquefois on se sent si révolté par l'injustice, qu'on devient bête.

p. 259, l. 16: J'ai vécu si longtemps par le dévouement de ma mère, que je crois être tous les jours comme un enfant le jour de son entrée au collège.

p. 259, l. 20: Pendant toute sa vie elle n'a amais pensé à elle-même. J'étais habitué à compter sur elle pour tout, et je me reproche bien amèrement aujourd'hui de l'avoir associée à toutes mes peines seulement. Je voudrais pouvoir recommencer ma vie avec elle.

p. 259, l. 28: Il y a quelque chose de bien triste cependant dans l'idée qu'on ne tient plus à rien, et qu'on est absolument libre. Tant que ma pauvre mère a vécu, j'avais des devoirs et des empêchements. Aujourd'hui le monde est à moi comme au Juif errant, et je n'ai plus ni enthousiasme ni activité.

p. 260, l. 7: On le trouvait d'ordinaire lisant, une cigarette aux lèvres, ou fumant une longue pipe en mérisier, les pieds dans des babouches turques, et drapé dans une magnifique robe de chambre japonaise ou chinoise à grands ramages. On traversait d'abord la salle à manger qui était fort simple, quoique ornée de tableaux remarquables, presque tous espagnols, et l'on entrait dans un grand salon transformé en cabinet de travail, où se tenait Mérimée, tel que je viens de le décrire. Les parois de ce salon très élevé étaient tapissées jusqu'au plafond de rayons en vieux chêne, garnis des livres les plus rares; peu ou point de bibelots, sauf quelques souvenirs de voyages, et deux cornets du Japon superbes sur la cheminée; de vastes sièges, tout capitonnés, sans bois apparent, un divan dans le fond d'une espèce d'alcôve, une foule de coussins brodés dans tous les coins; au milieu, un bureau en bois de rose, style Louis XV, orné de cuivres fins et couvert de brochures, avec quelques presse-papiers, presque tous d'exquis objets d'art ou de curiosité, entre autres un bronze antique admirable, représentant un jeune Faune se retournant à demi pour jouer avec sa queue.

p. 261, l. 3: La raclée a d'ailleurs été vigoureuse et peut compter comme une revanche de 1848. Il faut espérer qu'on s'en souviendra.

p. 261, l. 21: Son génie s'est annoncé comme une locomotive. Mais on ne voit plus que la fumée.

p. 261, n. 42: A un certain moment j'étais dans la rue. Je quittais cet honnête et courageux homme; je vis venir à moi tout le contraire, M. Mérimée. – Tiens! me dit M. Mérimée, je vous cherchais. Je lui répondis: J'espère que vous ne me trouverez pas. Il me tendit la main, je lui tournai le dos. Je ne l'ai plus revu. Je crois qu'il est mort.

p. 263, l. 28: Mais vous n'aurez rien à faire. – Mais je ne fais rien et je suis heureux. – Mais vous serez pendu avec nous de toutes façons.

p. 263, l. 31: Soyez notre ennemi, ou laissez-vous faire.

p. 263, l. 35: Je songe très sérieusement à m'en aller quelque part bien loin, laisser mes os dans quelque pays favorisé du soleil, comme les vieux chats qui abandonnent la maison quand ils se sentent malades. J'ai perdu presque tous mes amis, je suis parfaitement inutile aux autres, et je m'ennuie. Je ne tiens à Paris que par un reste d'habitude, et Paris ne tient plus à moi. Ce sentiment a quelque chose de fort amer, mais cependant je sens que je me blase là-dessus. Le seul mal, c'est que menant la vie que je mène, je me procure plusieurs fois par semaine des accès de *spleen* et de fureur que j'éviterais peut-être en allant vivre au fond d'un bois.

p. 264, l. 8: Depuis que je vis seul avec

un chat et une tortue, je suis heureux de me sentir aimé. Cela veut dire probablement que je suis près de mes fins.

p. 264, l. 12: Vous dire que je sois fâché de la chose ce serait mentir; content, non . . .) J'ai déjà vu tant de vilains côtés de la nature humaine que je n'avais ni besoin ni envie d'entrer aux premières loges pour en voir davantage.

p. 264, l. 23: J'ai plus de liberté et d'autorité pour parler aux gens des arts et églises qui dégringolent.

CHAPTER 15

p. 266, l. 3: Je voudrais bien établir que je suis toujours un faiseur de contes, et si j'en avais un de prêt je le donnerais aussitôt.

p. 267, l. 11: En haine de la noblesse de convention, on s'est jeté dans le trivial; en dégoût du beau idéal, on a recherché le laid de parti pris. Eh! messieurs, ne le cherchez pas, il se trouve trop facilement sous vos pas. Cherchez plutôt le beau et ne vous découragez pas, car ce n'est qu'après de longs et patients efforts que vous pourrez le rencontrer.

p. 267, l. 30: Je sentais bien quelque ennui de passer dans un monde inconnu, mais ce qui me semblait encore plus ennuyeux, c'était de faire de la résistance. C'est par cette résignation brute, je crois, qu'on quitte ce monde, non pas parce que le mal vous accable, mais parce qu'on est devenu indifférent à tout, et qu'on ne se défend plus.

p. 268, l. 6: Je m'ennuie et me déteste assez.

p. 268, l. 7: Je suis désabusé et ennuyé de quantité d'hommes, de femmes et de choses.

p. 268, l. 8: Je crois être sans cesse sur le plateau d'une machine électrique et je ne passe de la prostration la plus complète que pour avoir les nerfs agacés et devenir furieux contre la nature et contre moi. Je n'ai courage à rien, et je ne puis écrire une panse d'A.

p. 268, l. 22: J'ai renoncé depuis longtemps à faire des projets, et je vis au jour le jour dans une fainéantise magnifique.

p. 268, l. 26: Je suis amoureux de plusieurs manières en ce moment. Sentimentalement, et puis je me dis: quid, si je ne revenais jamais en France?

p. 268, l. 30: Je me cramponne à ce pays, parce que j'ai le pressentiment que c'est la dernière bonne année qui me reste.

p. 269, l. 7: En m'en retournant je me disais que je venais de voir deux personnes parfaitement naturelles.

p. 269, l. 16: Il fallait à l'Élysée un ornement littéraire. Un peu d'académie ne messied pas à une caverne. M. Mérimée était disponible. Il était dans sa destinée de signer: le Fou de l'Impératrice. Madame de Montijo le présenta à Louis Bonaparte qui l'agréa, et qui compléta sa cour par ce plat écrivain de talent.

p. 269, l. 32: Mérimée était grand, maigre et svelte; sa figure, toujours soigneusement rasée, n'avait rien de remarquable, si ce n'est un vaste front et deux yeux gris, enfoncés sous l'arcade sourcilière, qui était surmontée de sourcils épais et déjà grisonnants. Cette tête osseuse, aux pommettes saillantes, au nez un peu gros du bout, n'était rien moins qu'aristocratique; mais une tenue toujours très soignée lui donnait, malgré tout, un air de distinction mondaine. Son accueil était d'une courtoisie parfaite, quoiqu'un peu froide: on se trouvait devant un gentleman accompli. Il avait en effet dans son abord quelque chose de légèrement anglaisé; sa parole était lente, le ton égal, le débit presque hésitant; rien de vif, d'accentué; il riait à peine, même quand il contait les histoires les plus drolatiques ou les plus croustilleuses. Un vernis de réserve et de froide distinction ne le quittait jamais, même entre hommes et avec des intimes. Le contraste de sa tenue avec sa parole, surtout quand il abordait les sujets les plus scabreux, donnait un piquant singulier à ce qu'il racontait.

p. 270, l. 16: Dans le monde, il avait bonne tenue, quoique un peu contrainte et préparée; il ne parlait guère, comme s'il se fût méfié de lui (. . .) Il était de taille moyenne et bien bâti; le haut du visage était très beau; le front ample et des yeux magnifiques révélaient l'intelligence et les aspirations élevées; mais le nez en groin, la bouche sensuelle, les maxillaires épais indiquaient la grossièreté des appétits auxquels il n'a pas toujours résisté.

p. 270, l. 25: Il se vautrait dans l'immondice avec sérénité.

p. 271, l. 19: J'ai eu tous les chagrins possibles, de cœur s'entend, car ma vie va comme sur des roulettes pour la partie *matérielle*.

p. 271, l. 25: Je suis fort triste et j'ai le spleen. Je voudrais m'être marié il y a dix ans afin d'être tout habitué à être cocu. Le fait est que je m'ennuie horriblement et que je ne sais à quoi m'intéresser. *Man delights me not nor woman neither*, excepté une Maruja que j'ai été assez bête pour laisser à Madrid.

p. 271, n. 18: Il baissait modestement les yeux et niait sans conviction la paternité qu'on lui attribuait; il aurait dû la répudier nettement, car elle ne peut remonter jusqu'à lui.

p. 272, l. 6: Vous me demandez pourquoi je suis triste et vous me parlez de l'or et de la grandeur. Je croyais que ces mots n'étaient employés qu'en style d'opéra-comique, et je vous répondrai dans le même style que l'un et l'autre sont une chimère. Si je suis triste ce n'est pas pour des prunes. J'ai de très bonnes raisons, mais elles ne vous amuseraient pas à entendre et me crisperaient à écrire.

p. 272, l. 13: Quant au moral il est toujours au-dessous de zéro. Si un sorcier s'était avisé de me dire, il y a dix ans, que je serais en 1854 libre comme l'air et que je me trouverais très malheureux, je l'aurais pris pour un grand sot. Le plus grand c'est, je crois, moi-même qui ai fait consister le bonheur à trouver un merle blanc, oiseau infiniment trop rare.

p. 272, l. 27: J'ai cru remarquer que depuis quelque temps vous me traitez avec une grande froideur pour ne pas dire plus. J'ai la conscience de n'avoir rien fait pour mériter cela. *Je crois* au contraire m'être appliqué depuis un an à éviter en tout ce qui pourrait vous déplaire. Si je me suis trompé, Madame, je vous serais on ne peut plus reconnaissant de me le dire.

p. 273, l. 13: Je me creuse la tête pour comprendre ce qui la fait agir. Quelquefois, il me semble qu'elle m'a pris en haine, mais je ne puis deviner le pourquoi. Il n'y a pas de prêtre dans cette affaire. Bien que depuis plusieurs années j'aie eu beaucoup à m'endurcir de ce côté, je ne puis vous dire combien cela m'a fait de peine. Il n'y a rien de plus triste que de se trouver de plus en plus isolé à mesure que les années viennent et qu'on sent davantage le besoin de la confiance et de l'amitié!

p. 273, l. 22: Le résultat d'une liaison de plus de vingt ans me désespère, et j'en suis à m'attrister pour le passé et à penser que tout le bonheur que j'ai eu était faux. Mes souvenirs ne me restent plus.

p. 273, l. 31: Je n'ai rien fait jusqu'à présent, et je n'ai plus personne pour qui travailler. Voilà ce qui me met beaucoup de nuages noirs à mon horizon.

p. 273, l. 33: Lorsque j'écrivais, j'avais un but. Maintenant je n'en ai plus. Si j'écrivais, ce serait pour moi, et je m'ennuierais encore plus que je ne fais.

p. 274, l. 14: Figurez-vous deux personnes qui s'aiment très réellement, depuis longtemps, depuis si longtemps que le monde n'y pense plus. Un beau matin la femme se met en tête que ce qui a fait son bonheur et celui d'un autre pendant dix ans est mal. 'Séparons-nous. Je vous aime toujours, mais je ne veux plus vous voir'. Je ne sais pas, madame, si vous vous représentez ce que peut souffrir un homme qui a placé tout le bonheur de sa vie sur quelque chose qu'on lui ôte ainsi brusquement. L'histoire que je vous raconte est vraie et arrivée à un de mes amis.

p. 274, l. 26: C'est un rêve fini. Le réveil est assez triste. Je n'ai, pour me consoler, que la pensée de n'avoir rien fait pour être de la sorte. Plus j'y pense, et plus je m'y perds. (. . .) J'ai assez d'expérience pour savoir qu'on se console de tout, mais je voudrais bien être au temps où je ne penserai plus à cela qu'avec le chagrin que laisse un roman qui finit mal.

p. 275, l. 3: Je suis trop vieux pour me marier, mais je voudrais trouver une petite fille toute faite à élever. J'ai pensé souvent à acheter un enfant à une gitana, parce que, si mon éducation tournait mal, je n'aurais probablement pas rendu plus malheureuse la petite créature que j'aurais adopté. Qu'en pensez-vous? Et comment se procurer une petite fille?

p. 275, l. 10: Je suis triste comme un bonnet de nuit et horriblement ennuyé. Le monde m'assomme et je ne sais que devenir. Je n'ai plus un ami au monde, je crois. J'ai perdu tous ceux que j'aimais, qui sont morts ou changés. Si j'avais le moyen, j'adopterais une petite fille; mais ce monde et surtout ce pays-ci est si incertain que je n'ose me donner ce luxe.

p. 275, l. 17: J'aimerais mieux, si j'étais sûr de laisser quelque chose après ma mort, avoir une fille que j'élèverais le mieux qu'il me serait possible. Mais c'est une loterie bien chanceuse. Le mieux, je crois, c'est de s'accoutumer à vivre comme un arbre et à se résigner.

p. 276, l. 1: Eh bien, Madame, j'y consens, mais à une condition: c'est que vous servirez de marraine; je serai habillé de blanc et vous me porterez dans vos bras.

p. 276, l. 14: J'ai le malheur d'être sceptique, mais ce n'est pas ma faute. J'ai tâché de croire, mais je n'ai pas la foi. Bien que je ne sois pas insensible à la poésie, je n'ai jamais pu faire de vers. Je suis trop *a matter of fact man*. Cela ne tient pas à mon éducation mais à mon organisation.

p. 276, l. 20: Vous ne pouvez pas comprendre, Madame, vous qui êtes née avec le cerveau d'un poète, la difficulté que j'éprouve à *croire*, et la différence qu'il y a entre les choses qui me plaisent à supposer et celle que j'admets comme vraies. Je me plais à supposer des revenants et des fées. Je me ferais dresser les cheveux sur la tête en me racontant à moi-même des histoires de revenants, mais, malgré l'impression toute matérielle que j'éprouve, cela ne m'empêche pas de ne pas croire aux revenants, et sur ce point mon incrédulité est si grande que si je voyais un spectre je n'y croirais pas davantage. En effet, il est beaucoup plus probable que je sois fou qu'il ne l'est qu'un miracle se fasse.

p. 277, l. 12: Il aime les hasards, il a été souvent heureux et il se fie à sa fortune.

p. 277, l. 16: Nous l'avons échappé belle. Je sors des Tuileries où il y avait beaucoup de monde. Il nous a remerciés et nous a dit 'de ne rien craindre, que la Providence veillerait sur lui tant que sa mission ne serait pas achevée'. Il avait la voix parfaitement calme et plus claire que d'ordinaire, l'air plus souriant et plus gai. L'impératrice était très émue et très pâle. En passant devant moi, elle m'a serré la main fortement et j'ai lu mille choses dans ses yeux.

p. 277, l. 24: Le défaut d'être trop paresseux et d'être trop bon.

p. 277, l. 26: Votre gendre, vous le savez, n'est pas de ces gens qu'on questionne ni qu'on devine.

p. 278, l. 4: J'ai eu la bêtise de consulter un médecin il y a peu de temps, et bien entendu il m'a trouvé trois ou quatre maladies mortelles (. . .) Je suis assez mécontent de ma santé, mais je ne crois pas toutes les prédictions qu'on m'a faites. Je n'ai pas envie de passer plus tôt que mon temps dans un monde meilleur, mais je n'ai pas d'objection à m'en aller lorsqu'il le faudra. Je crains seulement deux choses, la douleur et une maladie qui me rendrait à charge aux autres, et on me dit qu'il faut prendre quelques précautions pour que ce malheur ne m'arrive pas.

CHAPTER 16

p. 281, l. 3: Les poésies lyriques de Pouchkine sont ce que je connais de plus parfait depuis les Grecs.

p. 281, l. 14: Je ne connais pas d'ouvrage plus *tendu*, si l'on peut se servir de cette expression comme d'un éloge; pas un vers, pas un mot ne s'en pouvait retrancher; chacun a sa place, chacun a sa destination, et cependant en apparence tout cela est simple, naturel, et l'art ne se révèle que par l'absence complète de tout ornement inutile.

p. 281, l. 27: Ses études de mœurs dénotent une certaine préférence pour le laid et le triste. Sans doute ces deux fâcheux éléments n'existent que trop dans la nature, et c'est précisément parce qu'ils se rencontrent si souvent qu'il ne faudrait pas s'appliquer à leur recherche avec une insatiable curiosité.

p. 282, l. 16: Je trouve un peu d'exagération dans les éloges qu'on donne à Gogole dans ces articles (. . .) Gogole est pour moi un Sterne un peu sauvage. Il ne distingue pas le laid du ridicule et ne choisit pas ses modèles.

p. 282, l. 21: Je n'aime pas Gogol qui me paraît un imitateur de Balzac avec un goût décidé pour la laid. Je regrette que vous lui ayez fait l'honneur de le traduire.

p. 283, l. 20: Le prince Galitzine supprime les passages un peu scabreux et moi je les rétablis.

p. 284, l. 6: Sans parti pris, sans affecter une philanthropie banale, il est le défenseur des faibles et des déshérités. Jusque dans les natures les plus dégradées, il aime à découvrir quelque trait qui les relève. Il me rappelle souvent Shakespeare. Il a son amour de la vérité; comme le poète anglais, il sait créer des figures d'une étonnante réalité; mais, malgré l'art avec lequel l'auteur se dissimule sous les personnages de son invention, on devine pourtant son caractère, et ce n'est peut-être pas son moindre titre à notre sympathie.

p. 284, l. 21: Ne valent pas leur réputation.

p. 284, l. 22: Prédispose merveilleusement au sommeil.

p. 284, l. 25: Je vous dirai tout franc qu'en dépit de son grand talent cet auteur ne me plaît pas: il y a en lui je ne sais quelle tension, quelle exaltation des sentiments et cela nuit à la vision artistique. Il relève plus de Hugo que de Pouchkine. Possédant un pareil modèle, un écrivain russe devrait- il suivre les traces de Hugo?

p. 285, l. 1: Je suis particulièrement impropre à la critique littéraire. Je ne sais que dire bien ou mal, mais la question quo modo m'embarrasse.

p. 285, l. 25: Je viens de lire Boris Godounof de Pouchkine, qui m'a plu fort bien que cela sente un peu trop son imitation de Goetz de Berlichingen. Cela m'a donné envie de lire dans Karamzine l'histoire du faux Démétrius qui m'a paru bien mal conté.

p. 286, l. 17: Après avoir bien étudié mon affaire, l'idée m'était venue d'écrire l'histoire *comme elle a dû se passer*, affirmant au lieu de présenter une hypothèse. J'ai fait sur ce thème quelques scènes qui m'ont conduit jusqu'en Pologne. Là rencontrant Pouchkine, j'ai abandonné mon projet (grand dommage) et j'ai écrit une vulgaire histoire.

p. 286, l. 21: J'avais pensé d'abord à mettre en dialogue toute l'histoire mais le courage m'a manqué heureusement pour le respectable public. Du moment que l'histoire devient claire, il n'y a plus lieu à faire du mélodrame.

p. 287, l. 13: Cet imposteur était un grand homme.

p. 287, l. 16: Démétrius n'était pas cruel, il avait même une douceur naturelle rare de son temps, et peut-être déplacée dans un usurpateur, car c'est le châtiment de ceux qui parviennent au pouvoir par la violence, de ne s'y maintenir que par la terreur.

p. 287, l. 21: Avec la présomption de la jeunesse, il voulut réformer un peuple encore sauvage et grossier, avant de s'en être fait aimer, ou de s'en être fait craindre.

p. 287, l. 24: Voilà comme je me représente l'imposteur qui sut conquérir un trône, et qui succomba au milieu de son triomphe, seulement peut-être parce qu'au lieu d'avoir toutes les parties d'un usurpateur, il avait quelques-unes des qualités aimables qu'on chérit dans un prince légitime.

p. 288, l. 11: Je regrette de vous envoyer une espèce de brouillon où il y a encore fort à faire, mais arrivé à la mort de Marine, je me suis senti si découragé que je n'ai pas pu prendre sur moi de donner un coup de rabot, bien nécessaire pourtant.

p. 289, l. 16: Il a consulté les traditions locales et même les chansons populaires, qui souvent, mieux que les témoignages officiels, font connaître les sentiments et les passions des masses. On s'aperçoit que M. Kostomarof est un élève de Mac-Aulay. De même que son illustre modèle, il croit que l'historien, sans rien perdre de sa gravité de juge, peut et doit faire des emprunts au drame et à la poésie. L'emploi réfléchi et habile de ces ornements ne nuit point à la vérité; elle y gagne, au contraire, lorsqu'ils sont choisis avec art et discernement, de même que, dans un portrait,

l'exécution habile et fidèle des accessoires ajoute à la ressemblance de la figure principale.

p. 290, l. 6: Le défaut de mon œuvre, c'est qu'elle manque de diversité. Autant de Cosaques que les Polonais peuvent attraper, autant ils en empalent. Autant de Polonais pris par les Cosaques, autant d'écorchés vifs. Cela est un peu monotone. Je voudrais varier, mais la vérité historique me retient.

p. 290, l. 12: Grand homme inconnu.

p. 290, l. 13: Chef élu d'une petite nation entourée de puissants voisins, il consacra toute sa vie à combattre pour son indépendance. Aussi habile à diviser ses ennemis qu'à maintenir l'union parmi les bandes sauvages qu'il dirigeait, guerrier intrépide, politique plein de ressources, prudent au milieu des succès, d'une constance inébranlable après les revers, il ne manque à Chmielnicki, pour obtenir une renommée européenne, qu'un peuple moins barbare, et peut-être un nom moins difficile à prononcer.

p. 290, l. 22: Les peuples aiment à trouver dans le chef qu'ils se sont choisi les vertus et jusqu'aux défauts de leur caractère national. Bogdan Chmielnicki fut comme le type accompli du cosaque. Il était brave, rusé, entreprenant; il avait l'instinct de la guerre. Son intempérance, sa brutalité réelle ou de commande ne lui nuisaient pas plus auprès des Russiens que les galanteries de Henri IV ne choquaient les Français. Peu de souverains furent plus absolus, aucun n'observa avec plus d'attention les lois et les usages de son pays.

p. 291, l. 14: Ce n'est pas même un récit suivi qu'il nous offre, mais une série de documents liés les uns aux autres par quelques phrases fort courtes. On dirait que le savant archiviste a peur de passer pour un historien.

p. 291, l. 19: Une bête.

p. 292, l. 6: Trois ou quatre articles d'une critique assez sagace, mais contrariée de-ci

o

de-là par la politique; un livre qui, en dépit d'une thèse un peu aventureuse, inaugure en France les monographies sérieuses d'histoire russe; une tentative moins heureuse d'évocation scénique du passé; quelques bonnes adaptations de travaux russes contemporains: tel est le bilan des *Études d'histoire russe*.

CHAPTER 17

p. 293, l. 4: A Passy, on se porte bien: toujours même mine, un peu grise. Il m'a semblé la dernière fois que cela me faisait moins de peine.

p. 293, l. 8: D'abord je n'ai pas senti trop fort mon malheur. Il me semblait que j'étais comme Galilée en prison avec son énergie. Petit à petit, j'ai souffert davantage, puis je suis devenu *callous*, et très véritablement malheureux.

p. 293, l. 13: En voie de guérison.

p. 293, l. 14: De ma part, il n'y a pas la moindre inimitié, pas même de la colère, ce qui serait cependant assez naturel. J'ai cru assez longtemps qu'on me haïssait. Maintenant je ne le crois plus. On ne me fait même pas cet honneur. C'est une lampe qui a brillé quelque temps, puis qui s'est éteint je ne sais par quel accident.

p. 293, l. 18: Je me sens beaucoup mieux de cœur que je n'étais il y a un an. Je n'ai plus ni vifs regrets, ni émotions en la voyant. Petit à petit, j'arrive à l'indifférence.

p. 294, l. 4: Le résultat, c'est qu'il faut que je retranche quinze ans de ma vie, non seulement perdus, mais dont le souvenir même est empoisonné pour moi. Je ne regrette pas le temps perdu, car j'aurais trop à faire, mais il y a des souvenirs qui étaient un monde surhumain pour moi, où j'avais autrefois accès et qui m'est fermé.

p. 294, l. 13: Il y avait une fois un fou qui croyait avoir la reine de Chine (vous n'ignorez pas que c'est la plus belle princesse du monde) enfermée dans une bouteille. Il était très heureux de la posséder et il se donnait beaucoup de mouvement pour que cette bouteille et son contenu n'eussent pas à se plaindre de lui. Un jour il cassa la bouteille, et, comme on ne trouve pas deux fois une princesse de la Chine, de fou qu'il était il devint bête.

p. 295, l. 17: C'est que je suis vieux et que j'ai pris des habitudes d'indépendance tellement invétérées que ce serait impossible de les changer. Il me semble que dans la vie il y a deux choses à faire. La première, c'est (lorsqu'on le peut), d'éviter de faire des sottises. La seconde, lorsqu'on les a faites, d'en subir les conséquences le plus philosophiquement qu'on pourra. Vous savez comment j'ai passé la meilleure partie de ma vie. Très probablement c'était une sottise romanesque. Le roman a eu un dénouement assez triste pour moi. Tous mes arrangements pris en vue d'un avenir qui n'était qu'un brouillard se sont trouvés renversés. Je n'ai ni le courage ni la force d'essayer un nouvel arrangement de vie. Le seul avantage, maintenant, que le mariage pourrait m'offrir, c'est quelque douceur pendant les maladies et surtout au moment très désagréable où il faut partir pour l'autre monde. Peut-être en ne faisant qu'un calcul égoïste, cet avantage mériterait-il réflexion. Mais d'un autre côté, la responsabilité d'une femme, les soins qu'il lui faut, l'avenir qu'on lui laisse, tout cela est effrayant.

p. 295, l. 34: Si vous vous mariez jeune, vous avez le moyen de vous marier à peu près à qui vous voudrez, vous pouvez assurer votre bonheur. Vous avez de l'esprit et de l'intelligence pour choisir. Lorsque vous avez un but dans la vie, vous verrez qu'elle vaut mieux que vous ne croyez et que vous-même valez mieux. Vous n'avez jamais considéré dans la vie que l'emploi de la semaine devant vous. Pensez aux années et prenez exemple d'un très vieux et très old bachelor qui vous offre ici son expérience personnelle, expérience très triste.

p. 296, l. 14: Non, Sire, jamais je ne voterai pour un clérical.

p. 296, l. 16: L'Académie française ne veut plus que des candidats ayant fait preuve de catholicisme. Je ne me soucie pas de prendre part à la prochaine élection. Je ne pourrais rien empêcher et je m'en lave les mains.

p. 297, l. 5: Je suis très-contrarié et à moitié empoisonné pour avoir pris trop de laudanum. En outre, j'ai fait des vers pour Sa Majesté Néerlandaise, joué des charades et *made a fool of myself*. C'est pourquoi je suis absolument abruti. Que vous dirai-je de la vie que nous menons ici? Nous prîmes un cerf hier, nous dînâmes sur l'herbe; l'autre jour nous fûmes trempés de pluie, et je m'enrhumai. Tous les jours, nous mangeons trop; je suis à moitié mort. Le destin ne m'avait pas fait pour être courtisan. Je voudrais me promener à pied dans cette belle forêt avec vous et causer de choses de féerie. J'ai tellement mal à la tête que je n'y vois goutte. Je vais dormir un peu, en attendant l'heure fatale où il faudra se mettre sous les armes, c'est-à-dire entrer dans un pantalon collant.

p. 299, l. 25: Un Anglais se promène le long d'un poulailler, dans un château d'Écosse, un samedi soir. Grand bruit, cris de coqs et de poules. Il croit que quelque renard est entré et il avertit. On lui répond que ce n'est rien, et qu'on sépare seulement les coqs des poules pour qu'ils ne polluent pas the *Lord's day*.

p. 299, l. 34: Un peu choqué de voir un partage si inégal des biens de ce monde.

p. 300, l. 6: Je suppose que York est une ville où les femmes vertueuses ont fort peu de risques à courir. D'après mes supputations, il y a des femmes non vertueuses

dans la proportion de deux par habitant mâle.

p. 300, l. 20: Il est le véritable roi d'Angleterre. Il m'a paru un mélange très bizarre d'homme d'État et de gamin. Il a l'aplomb d'un vieux ministre et le goût des aventures d'un écolier. Je le crois très étourdi, confiant dans son étoile et parfaitement sans scrupules. Il bouleverserait le monde pour avoir un petit succès d'éloquence au Parlement. Il a tous les préjugés et toute l'ignorance de John Bull, avec son opiniâtreté et son orgueil. Bref, je crois que c'est un des mauvais génies de notre époque.

p. 301, l. 17: Je n'ai fait aucune démarche pour empêcher de brûler le poëte dont vous me parlez, sinon de dire à un ministre qu'il vaudrait mieux en brûler d'autres d'abord. Je pense que vous parlez d'un livre intitulé: *fleurs du mal*, livre très médiocre, nullement dangereux, où il y a quelques étincelles de poésie dans un pauvre garçon qui ne connaît pas la vie et qui en est las parce qu'une grisette l'a trompé. Je ne connais pas l'auteur, mais je parierais qu'il est niais et honnête; voilà pourquoi je voudrais qu'on ne le brûlât pas.

p.301, n. 29: J'ai pour moi (. . .) M. Mérimée (qui est non seulement un littérateur illustre, mais le seul qui représente la littérature au *Sénat*).

Mérimée, avec qui je suis lié.

Le signe d'une vive sympathie.

p. 302, l. 1: Furieux.

p. 302, l. 1: Fou.

p. 302, l. 13: Depuis un très long temps on donne et l'on reçoit les places de Bibliothécaire comme des sinécures; (. . .) le désordre y est arrivé à un point qui passe toute croyance; et (. . .) depuis les bâtiments, qui tombent en ruines, jusqu' aux livres qui se cachent dans tous les recoins, il faut tout réorganiser.

p. 302, l. 33: Froid, qui aime les grossièretés.

p. 303, l. 3: Mérimée a un visage très intelligent, peu mobile. Il a la réputation d'un épicurien et d'un sceptique que rien au monde ne peut troubler, qui ne croit à rien et qui observe devant tout élan d'enthousiasme une défiance polie, mais un peu méprisante. Il est sénateur et bien vu à la cour de France. Et pourtant ce sceptique pâlit au moment où il dut répondre par un petit 'speech' appris par cœur aux aimables paroles de Milnes. Mérimée sait mal l'anglais, sa voix tremblait et il s'interrompit deux fois.

p. 304, l. 21: Cette guerre m'a remué horriblement. J'aurais bien voulu être jeune pour y aller, bien que tout n'ait pas tourné précisément comme je l'aurais désiré. Je plains beaucoup les blessés, mais pas du tout les morts. Il me semble qu'il n'y a pas de fin meilleure qu'une belle balle sur un champ de bataille.

p. 304, l. 25: Magnifique; effrayant.

p. 304, l. 28: Comme des lions.

p. 305, l. 4: Mon mari appréciait beaucoup ses qualités et il me disait parfois: 'Votre Mérimée est bien agréable, mais il a un grand défaut à mes yeux, c'est qu'il n'est pas bonapartiste'.

p. 305, l. 8: Quelquefois je lui ai entendu dire des choses d'un libéralisme à faire trembler.

p. 305, l. 11: Je connais ce pays-ci pour incorrigible et j'ai toujours peur lorsque je vois qu'on lui lâche la bride. Il aime à jouer avec les armes à feu comme les enfants et il a beau avoir essuyé plusieurs accidents, il recommencera toujours.

p. 306, l. 6: Je travaille et (. . .) j'écris comme dans mon bon temps.

p. 306, l. 8: Je me suis remis à écrivailler, et de l'histoire ancienne. Le moderne n'a jamais eu pour moi beaucoup de charmes. En somme, le reproche que je fais aux modernes c'est de n'avoir jamais eu la franchise, ou, si vous voulez, l'audace des anciens.

p. 306, l. 15: Très remarquable pour les idées et le style.

p. 306, l. 16: Il m'étonne.

p. 306, l. 22: Était toujours là quand il s'agissait de servir.

p. 306, l. 29: Heureusement on devient plus humain en vieillissant. Je me rappelle avec quel ravissement j'ai vu les premiers combats de taureaux. Maintenant ils ne me plaisent presque plus.

p. 306, l. 33: Mais que vous dirai-je qui soit du moindre intérêt pour vous? Je suis devenu très vieux, ou ce pays-ci a changé; le fait est que je ne m'y trouve plus aussi heureux qu'autrefois.

p. 307, l. 8: Peut-être en vieillissant se fait-il meilleur; peut-être loue-t-il beaucoup, de peur d'avoir des ennemis de sa faveur.

p. 307, l. 13: Je n'ai jamais été méchant, mais en vieillissant j'ai tâché d'éviter de faire du mal, et c'est plus difficile qu'on ne croit.

p. 307, l. 15: Autrefois (. . .) je me mettais en quatre pour détromper les gens sur la bonne opinion qu'ils avaient d'eux-mêmes. A présent, je suis très tolérant.

p. 307, l. 24: Maintenant je recontrerais sous mes pieds les plus beaux diamants que je ne me baisserais pas pour les ramasser, faute d'avoir quelqu'un à qui les offrir.

p. 307, l. 28: J'ai découvert, ou j'ai cru découvrir le mot d'une énigme qui m'était demeurée tout à fait obscure. Cela ne m'a pas consolé, mais cela a donné une nouvelle forme à mon chagrin. J'ai maintenant plus de pitié que de colère, et je trouve que j'ai été surtout bête. Comme je n'ai jamais eu trop d'amour-propre, *for a man of my weight*, je suis peut-être moins triste de cette découverte-là que ne le serait un autre. Cependant je voudrais bien recommencer ma vie à partir de vingt ans.

p. 308, l. 6: Depuis cinq ou six ans j'étais poursuivi par un fantôme, ou pour parler moins poétiquement j'avais un souvenir (non pas un remords) qui me rendait très malheureux. Je me suis aperçu l'autre jour que ce souvenir ne m'était rappelé que par accident, et qu'il n'était plus aussi pénible. Est-ce que je suis devenu philosophe ou que je commence à me momifier? Le dernier est malheureusement le plus probable.

p. 308, l. 15: Plus je vais et plus je trouve qu'il faut vivre dans la solitude et comme le lézard dans son trou.

CHAPTER 18

p. 310, l. 4: Je trouve qu'il ne ressemble en rien aux portraits qu'on fait de lui. On a voulu voir en lui une espèce de Don Juan, homme du monde, hautain et pervers. Rien de tout cela, selon moi; nature sèche, froide et vulgaire, séduction aucune, à moins qu'elle ne réside dans cette réserve et cette immobilité qui souvent attirent et magnétisent les faibles.

p. 310, l. 21: En prenant des années je ne puis prendre une dose proportionnelle de philosophie. C'est là le grand mal.

p. 310, l. 27: Il me semble quelquefois que je marche à grands pas vers le monument. Cette idée est quelquefois assez importune et je voudrais bien m'en distraire.

p. 311, l. 33: Je me mets à faire du pastel. Jusqu'à présent je n'ai réussi qu'à me barbouiller de toutes les couleurs de l'arc-en-ciel, mais j'espère, à force de salir du papier, d'arriver à faire un soleil couchant en dix minutes. Quant au soleil levant, je ne m'en soucie guere.

p. 312, l. 1: J'étudie la botanique dans un livre et avec des herbes qui me tombent sous la main; mais à chaque instant je maudis ma mauvaise vue.

p. 312, l. 17: J'y voyais de loin Mérimée, suivi de ses vieilles anglaises en robe claire, dont l'une portait un carquois et l'autre un grand sac, attachés tous deux par une courroie en bandoulière. Mérimée tenait un arc, tel un Dieu, eût dit Homère. A certain moment, une Anglaise passait une flèche. Mérimée tendait l'arc, la flèche sifflait et atteignait une pomme de pin choisie fort mûre. L'une des Anglaises courait après la pomme de pin qu'elle glissait dans son sac, l'autre reprenait la flèche si elle tombait. C'était un émoi silencieux pendant le tiré, des cris de joie

ensuite, des exclamations, ou pour mieux dire des acclamations qui ne finissait qu'au moment où de nouveau Mérimée tendait l'arc et tirait.

p. 313, l. 13: S'approchant de Mérimée avec tous les dehors d'une affectation cérémonieuse et ironique, il a fait des éloges outrés des pièces de théâtre de Clara Gazul, au point que l'auteur (Mérimée) a cru qu'on voulait lui faire une mystification.

p. 314, l. 1: Si vous n'avez jamais aimé pour de *vrai*, mangez au moins une fois pour de vrai.

p. 314, l. 4: Mérimée, vous êtes méchant et me dites des choses qui me sont pénibles. – Bon, je les retire à regret, car il y avait là matière à gaudrioles.

p. 314, l. 8: L'orateur en Philosophie.

p. 314, l. 9: Ah oui! vous allez à la messe, vous, Cousin, mais vous n'êtes qu'un hypocrite et ne croyez pas plus que moi. – Chut! prenez garde aux domestiques: soyez cynique entre gens d'importance, mais point vis-à-vis des gens de peu. – Iriez-vous à la messe pour vos servantes? – Pour l'exemple, oui, et même, si vous voulez, pour mes servantes.

p. 314, l. 17: Une pensée vous intéresse cent fois moins qu'un trait d'esprit, et naturellement Sainte-Beuve vous ravit. – Mieux que cela, il me désennuie. – Est-ce une allusion? – Vous ne m'ennuyez jamais, vous, mon cher Cousin, mais je confesse que parfois votre éloquence me submerge. – Submerger ne vaut guère mieux qu'ennuyer. – Pardon, l'ennui stérilise, le flot féconde . . . en se retirant. – Vous êtes un courtisan ironiste parfait. – Courtisan, moi, courtisan! – Oui, oui, et il y a beaucoup de gens qui, en parlant de vous comme de l'un de nos plus célèbres écrivains, ajoutent:

l'auteur de la fortune de l'Impératrice. Moi, je sais l'histoire de la correspondance de Mlle de Montijo avec l'Empereur, à Compiègne, je la sais de façon à ce que vous ne puissiez la nier.

p. 315, l. 1: La Patrie, une idée! quand c'est l'image de ce qu'il y a de plus tangible au monde, c'est la chair de notre chair, l'esprit de notre esprit, le cœur de notre cœur. C'est l'amalgame vivant de nos ancêtres, de nos pères, de nous; c'est la vibration de toutes nos voix. Langue, tradition, science, art, lettres, c'est elle qui les triture pour les faire français. Je pourrais parler cinq heures durant patriotisme comme Cousin peut parler philosophie, j'en déborde. On dit que je ne crois à rien. Je crois en 'Elle', en notre France, je suis son fils idolâtre, j'ai son culte jusqu'au fanatisme!

p. 315, l. 12: Voilà. J'aime l'Empire, je crois à sa nécessité pour mater la poussée révolutionnaire, mais avec l'Empire je sais que la France court le danger des coalitions européennes, d'invasion, c'est pourquoi mon patriotisme toujours en éveil est violent. Si la France était jamais envahie, je mourrais.

p. 315, l. 21: Je me souviens qu'un jour Cousin s'était animé en parlait du XIIIᵉ siècle: 'Ce siècle, s'écriait-il, qui a vu la plus belle création de Dieu, saint Louis, et la plus belle création des hommes, Notre-Dame, ce siècle qui . . .' – 'Pardon, Cousin, interrompit froidement Mérimée, mais Notre-Dame a été commencée en 1163. – Vous avez raison, Mérimée, reprenait Cousin après un instant d'embarras, mais cela n'empêche pas . . .' et il repartit de plus belle dans son enthousiasme pour le XIIIᵉ siècle.

p. 315, l. 31: Mérimée ne sait rien imparfaitement.

p. 315, l. 33: M. Mérimée est un gentilhomme. M. Sainte-Beuve ne l'est pas.

p. 316, l. 12: Qu'on ne pouvait faire boire un ministre qui n'a pas soif.

p. 316, l. 26: Dans toute cette affaire, M. L. ne s'est jamais mis en peine de ses amis et n'a songé qu'à lui-même. Si les sottises qu'il a faites ne retombaient que sur lui, ce ne serait que demi-mal.

p. 317, l. 13: Le monde devient tous les jours plus bête. A propos de cela, avez-vous lu les *Misérables* et entendu ce qu'on en dit? C'est encore un des sujets sur lesquels je trouve l'espèce humaine au-dessous de l'espèce gorille.

p. 317, l. 19: Cet infernal vacarme.

p. 317, n. 19: Il n'y a qu'un classique en ce siècle, un seul, entendez-vous bien? C'est moi. Je suis l'homme de nos jours qui sait le mieux le français. Après moi viennent Sainte-Beuve et Mérimée . . . Mais celui-ci est un écrivain de courte haleine. *Sobre*, comme ils disent. Bel éloge d'un auteur, vraiment! . . .

p. 318, l. 31: Médiocre! D'abord, il n'y a pas d'hommes médiocres; il y en a beaucoup de très mauvais et quelques-uns d'excellents: Mérimée est parmi les excellents.

p. 319, l. 17: A la fin de sa vie, on trouvait chez lui deux vieilles dames anglaises auxquelles il parlait peu, et dont il ne semblait pas se soucier beaucoup; un de mes amis le vit les larmes aux yeux parce que l'une d'elles était malade.

p. 319, n. 22: C'était un homme grand, droit, pâle, et qui, sauf le sourire, avait l'apparence d'un Anglais; du moins, il avait cet air froid, *distant*, qui écarte d'avance toute familiarité. Rien qu'à le voir, on sentait en lui le flegme naturel ou acquis, l'empire de soi, la volonté et l'habitude de ne pas donner prise. En cérémonie surtout, sa physionomie était impassible. Même dans l'intimité et lorsqu'il contait une anecdote bouffonne, sa voix restait unie, toute calme; jamais d'éclat ni d'élan; il disait les détails les plus saugrenus en termes propres, du ton d'un homme qui demandait une tasse de thé. La sensibilité chez lui était domptée jusqu'à paraître absente; non qu'elle le fût; tout au contraire.

p. 320, l. 20: Le fait est que nous n'étions pas assez morigénés.

p. 320, l. 22: Est-il vrai qu'on ait été plus en cérémonie à Compiègne que de coutume? Il n'y a pas de mal à cela.

p. 320, l. 25: On est sérieux, ce qui me plaît assez pour nos hôtes, qui souvent laissent trop s'amuser les personnes qu'ils invitent.

p. 321, l. 21: Il ne faut pas faire des livres quand on est dans une certaine position. En outre, j'ai plus d'une objection contre le plan de l'ouvrage et je crois que, tout considéré, il eût mieux valu ne rien imprimer.

p. 321, l. 26: Le grand défaut du livre à mon avis c'est qu'on dirait que l'auteur se place devant un miroir pour faire le portrait de son héros.

p. 322, l. 14: Une bataille en règle.

p. 322, l. 15: Il me semble que j'ai été aussi ferme que possible, mais me maintenant très calme sans rien ménager. On m'a dit que j'avais été convenable.

p. 322, l. 23: Le grand mal, entre vous et moi, c'est qu'on se demande souvent s'il veut réellement, s'il a un but et un plan arrêté.

p. 322, l. 26: Le grand mal, c'est qu'il n'y a pas d'initiative du côté d'où elle vient ordinairement. Personne ne sait où l'on va et ce qu'on veut.

p. 322, l. 31: On se sert du nom de l'impératrice pour je ne sais quelles vues. On la rend responsable de bien des choses auxquelles elle n'a jamais songé.

p. 323, l. 3: J'ai diné hier avec trois ministres, tous les trois désolés et désespérant de se faire écouter. Un d'eux, et c'est le plus éloquent de la bande, m'a pris à part pour me prier de parler au maître et de lui dire l'état des choses. Comment voulez-vous qu'on m'écoute, lui ai-je dit, moi, qui n'ai pas qualité pour être écouté. – C'est précisément à cause de cela, m'a-t-il répondu, que peut-être on vous écoutera.

p. 323, n. 40: J'aurais beaucoup aimé à avoir une fille et à l'élever. J'ai beaucoup d'idées sur l'éducation, particulièrement sur celle des demoiselles, et je me crois des talents qui resteront malheureusement sans application. Je n'ai élevé que des chats en grand nombre qui m'ont fait beaucoup d'honneur. Je me suis toujours appliqué à développer leur génie particulier, sans chercher à leur donner des idées autres que celles qu'ils avaient apportées, selon la conformation de leur cerveau. Ce qui me paraît parfaitement déplorable dans l'éducation actuelle, c'est qu'on parvient, à force d'apprendre toutes sortes de choses aux demoiselles à les dégoûter de tout ce qu'il y a d'élevé et de vraiment intéressant.

p. 324, l. 3: En quittant Paris, vendredi dernier, j'ai vu notre amie de Biarritz. J'ai eu une petite conversation de quatre heures, dont vous pouvez deviner le thème. Elle avait besoin de sfogarsi. Tout est fort triste, plus même que vous ne pouvez l'imaginer, mais n'en dites mot à personne. J'ai donné de bons conseils, je crois, tout en me rappelant le proverbe, ne pas mettre le doigt entre l'arbre et l'écorce; mais je ne sais trop si on les suivra.

p. 324, l. 9: Je crois que, depuis un an, elle en a appris beaucoup sur les choses et sur les hommes.

p. 324, l. 11: Le résumé du plan de conduite qu'on s'était tracé était celui-ci. Il n'y a plus d'Eugénie, il n'y a plus qu'une Impératrice. Je plains et j'admire. D'ailleurs, renouvellement de confiance et d'amitié de part et d'autre.

p. 324, l. 23: Elle est bien changée et fait peine à voir. Rien ne la console de la mort de sa fille, et je la trouve moins résignée qu'au premier jour.

p. 324, l. 31: Vous savez que dans les familles on fait sortir les jeunes filles quand on raconte une gaudriole. Mais à Compiègne, c'est moi que l'on fait sortir quand je m'apprête à en conter une. Après quoi tout le monde s'embête à crever.

p. 325, l. 2: Quand il se met sur ce chapitre, on n'ose plus se regarder dans une glace.

p. 325, l. 5: Vous n'êtes qu'une bête!

p. 325, l. 10: Ah! madame, toujours des personnalités.

p. 325, l. 23: Non, vous en savez trop! Gardez-nous le reste pour la prochaine fois.

p. 326, l. 2: Quand j'ai un ennemi, je l'envoie chez le prince Napoléon, un jour où il est mal embouché. Quand il en sort, je suis vengé pour la vie . . .

p. 326, l. 9: C'est une triste chose que de vieillir!

p. 326, l. 12: Il me semble que je sens tout ce que je sentais à vingt-cinq ans. Quelle triste chose que l'âme ne vieillisse pas en même temps que la corps.

CHAPTER 19

p. 327, l. 3: J'ai quelquefois envie de faire un roman avant de mourir; mais tantôt le courage me manque, tantôt, quand je suis en bonne disposition, on me donne des bêtises administratives à arranger.

p. 327, l. 9: Un mari a une femme ornée de toutes les vertus et un confesseur. Il est assez bête pour être amoureux de sa femme. La femme est très vertueuse; le confesseur est très dévot et très vertueux; d'où il arrive que, de fil en aiguille, le mari étrangle sa femme, et le lecteur devra trouver qu'il a raison, pourvu qu'il reconnaisse la vérité du proverbe qu'entre l'arbre et l'écorce il ne faut pas mettre le doigt.

p. 327, l. 16: Étant donné une femme, un mari et un prêtre, tous honnêtes, d'une part; d'autre part, un mari, une femme et un amant; montrer la misère profonde de la première triade et la félicité de la seconde.

p. 329, l. 8: La nuit, ayant pris un thé trop fort, j'écrivis une quinzaine de pages sur une situation de ce genre.

p. 329, l. 12: J'avais conçu mon sujet très tragique, et j'avais fait une préparation en style à quinze pour mieux surprendre le lecteur. Comme la chose tirait en longueur et m'ennuyait, j'ai terminé par une bouffonnerie, ce qui est mauvais.

p. 329, l. 17: Composé et écrit par Pr Mérimée fou de S. M. l'Impératrice.

p. 330, l. 6: Ce n'est pas, je pense, ce que j'ai écrit de plus mal, bien que cela ait été écrit fort à la hâte.

p. 330, l. 14: Le malheur est que j'y ai trouvé aussitôt quelque charme, et qu'au lieu de faire une caricature j'ai voulu faire un portrait.

p. 330, l. 26: Vous me parlez de chasse avec tant d'ardeur, que vous voudriez déjà, je pense, vous trouver en face d'un loup, voire même d'un ours. Passe pour la première de ces vilaines bêtes, mais je vous interdis absolument les ours: ils sont trop mal élevés pour avoir du respect pour les chasseresses.

p. 331, l. 2: Quand on se marie dans un pays pareil on est bien heureux je trouve, de ne pas accoucher d'un ours blanc.

p. 331, l. 24: Les personnes timorées qui n'admettraient pas le croisement entre *plantigrades*, pourront supposer que les bizarreries du héros, tiennent à une peur ou une fantaisie de femme grosse.

p. 332, l. 8: Si je savais faire des vers, j'aurais fait un poème, et il me semble qu'il y a quelque chose de poétique dans ce mélange d'humanité et de bestialité.

p. 332, l. 12: La *dualité* ou la *duplicité* de notre nature.

p. 332, l. 18: Je crois que si toutes *vos* pensées, monsieur le professeur, que je tiens pour un sage, étaient écrites, elles formeraient un volume in-folio peut-être, d'après lequel il n'y a pas un avocat qui ne plaidât avec succès votre interdiction, pas un juge qui ne vous mît en prison ou bien dans une maison de fous.

p. 332, n. 24: Je suis bien fâché d'avoir pris

ce nom de Szémioth que je croyais éteint depuis Jagellon.

p. 333, n. 25: Mais comment faire un portrait d'une impossibilité?

p. 335, l. 9: Il est fort question d'amour.

p. 335, l. 26: C'est un juif mais bien approvisionné.

p. 335, l. 27: Tant à cause de leur conduite sous le gouvernement de Ponce Pilate, qu'à cause de leur amour pour l'argent.

p. 336, l. 29: Lorsqu'on est jeune on peut aller voir des cocottes en plein jour; un vénérable vieillard comme moi, s'il pensait encore aux cocottes, se cacherait pour leur faire visite. J'entre dans la période de la seconde enfance, et je puis avoir la faiblesse de faire encore des nouvelles, mais j'ai le bon sens de ne les montrer qu'à mes amis.

CHAPTER 20

p. 338, l. 16: Au fond la question est la propriété intellectuelle qui est attaquée.

p. 339, l. 14: Un grand homme.

p. 339, l. 15: Il n'y a malheureusement qu'un grand homme par siècle et c'est M de Bismark qui occupe la place.

p. 339, l. 23: Il y a longtemps que je ne le vois plus. Il m'a dit tant de mensonges et fait tant de belles promesses que je ne veux plus le voir.

p. 339, l. 27: Le plus grand malheur qui puisse arriver à un peuple est, je crois, d'avoir des institutions plus avancées que son intelligence.

p. 341, l. 12: La dernière fois que je vous ai vue, vous m'avez fait un très grand bonheur. Vous m'avez rendu, j'aime à le croire, une amitié qui m'était bien précieuse, et dont j'ai cependant douté quelquefois, avec le plus grand chagrin de ma part. Il m'a semblé que vous m'ôtiez une épine du cœur. Ne parlons plus de cela Madame, permettez-moi seulement de vous en rendre grâces.

p. 341, l. 27: J'ai dans ce pays-ci le sentiment que je suis at home, que je n'éprouve guères à Paris.

p. 341, l. 31: Lorsque je respire mal, c'est à dire, très souvent, je me fais de beaux raisonnements pour me prouver que le monde ne vaut pas la peine qu'on y tienne. Je ne trouve pas d'arguments pour le regretter et cependant je le regrette beaucoup plus que je n'espère dans l'autre. Je

P

suis dans l'état de quelqu'un qui se prépare à un voyage ennuyeux; les préparatifs sont encore plus ennuyeux que le voyage.

p. 342, l. 11: Cette mort de M. Cousin m'a vivement frappé et j'ai toujours sous les yeux le spectacle de son agonie. Je me demande ce [qui] vaut mieux, ou mourir comme lui d'un coup d'assommoir ou bien s'en aller doucettement dans des souffrances prolongées.

p. 342, l. 30: Il est plus silencieux que jamais, et ne trouve plus, je ne dirai pas sa gaieté d'autrefois, mais au moins sa bonne humeur, que quand il y est forcé par la présence de quelque personne qui lui en impose, et que ses deux cotillons sont absentes (. . .) Depuis le départ de M. Fould et de Panizzi il est retombé dans l'apathie.

p. 343, l. 2: Jamais je ne me suis senti plus faible, plus découragé, plus *avvilito*, comme disent les Italiens. Il y a longtemps que je n'ai plus la prétention de guérir, mais je ne m'accoutume pas encore à souffrir, surtout je m'irrite et je m'indigne de voir chez moi le moral suivre la décadence du physique. Je me méprise et me prends en horreur de n'être plus maître chez moi.

p. 343, l. 21: Au fond, j'ai peur de vous. Je ne me trouve pas assez philosophe pour me laisser aller à vous aimer, comme j'y serais peut-être porté. Je m'applique à vous considérer comme une jolie fée qui

m'apparaît de temps en temps, qui me
charme et me ravit par sa grâce et sa
bienveillance. Puis je me dis qu'il n'y a
plus de fées, que ce monde sublunaire est
sérieux et ennuyeux, qu'il faut se réjouir
des visions d'un autre monde quand elles
viennent, mais ne pas les croire trop réelles.

p. 344, l. 14: Il s'est usé par des émotions
intérieures qu'il cachait avec soin. Ceux
qui l'ont bien connu savent à quel point il
était sensible.

p. 344, l. 35: Je n'ai pas encore pu m'accoutumer à souffrir et je m'en irrite, ce qui
me donne deux maux au lieu d'un.

p. 345, l. 4: Insupportable.

p. 345, l. 14: J'y vais sans espoir. Je ne vois
pas comment un pareil traitement peut
remettre à neuf des poumons détraqués,
et vous savez que, pour guérir, il faut
croire. La foi me manque absolument.

p. 345, l. 33: On s'attendait de sa part à
quelque chose de piquant: il a trompé
l'attente, il a fait un rapport sec et in-
signifiant. La peur de tomber dans la
rhétorique le jette aussi trop souvent dans
l'excès contraire qui frise la stérilité. Il se
plaît à déjouer l'attention en éveil de ses
admirateurs. C'est un tort (. . .) Décidé-
ment, Mérimée se retient trop; il est trop
exempt par système: il l'est, à la longue,
devenu par nature.

p. 346, l. 12: M. Gladstone m'a paru, sous
quelques aspects, un homme de génie,
sous d'autres un enfant. Il y a en lui de
l'enfant, de l'homme d'État et du fou.

p. 346, l. 15: C'est un homme de beaucoup d'esprit et de talent mais je doute de
sa prudence. Il a une logique impitoyable.
Admirateur passionné d'Homère, il n'ad-
met pas qu'il ne fût pas chrétien et il
suppose qu'il a été l'objet d'une révélation
spéciale.

p. 347, l. 3: Voilà quinze jours que je
tousse sans arrêter, le jour et la nuit. Je suis
très souffrant, très découragé et je passe
mon temps à broyer du noir. La nuit surtout, ne pouvant dormir, j'ai les *blue devils*

autour de moi. Je me demande si je suis
à mon dernier rhume ou seulement
l'avant-dernier.

p. 347, l. 11: Malheureusement, je suis
condamné à une vie solitaire pour le peu
de temps qui me reste à vivre encore. Je
m'abonnerais, je crois, assez facilement à
souffrir, si j'avais quelques intervalles de
tranquillité et de repos que je pusse con-
sacrer à mes amis. Mais je me sens devenir
tous les jours plus faible, plus morose, plus
inutile et plus ennuyeux. Depuis mon
départ de Paris, je n'ai pas cessé de tousser,
d'étouffer. Je ne dors plus. Je suis dégoûté
de tout et surtout de moi-même.

p. 347, l. 23: Je l'ai trouvé changé et
affaibli au delà de ce que je pourrais dire.
Il est toujours debout mais de temps en
temps il éprouve des crises d'étouffement
telles qu'il est impossible de n'en pas
concevoir les plus sérieuses inquiétudes. Il
ne prend plus goût à rien, marche à peine
et ne mange pas du tout.

p. 347, l. 31: Si je n'étais pas sceptique, je
finirais par le croire.

p. 348, l. 5: Une des plus tristes fins, du
reste, paraît-il, que celle de ce comédien
de l'insensibilité, qui meurt, à ce qu'il
paraît, sans un ami, claquemuré entre deux
vieilles *governesses* lui rognant le boire et
le manger, pour grossir les restes qu'il leur
laissera.

p. 384, l. 12: Il cause en s'écoutant, lentement, avec de mortels silences, mot à mot,
goutte à goutte, comme s'il distillait ses
effets, faisant tomber peu à peu, autour de
lui, une sorte de froideur glaciale. Point
d'esprit, point de trait; mais un tour
cherché, une façon de dire de vieil acteur
qui prend ses temps, avec un fond d'im-
pertinence de causeur gâté, un mépris
affecté de tout ce qui est illusion, pudeur,
convenance sociale. Je ne sais quoi de
blessant, pour les gens bonnement cons-
titués, s'échappe, de cette sèche et
méchante ironie, travaillée pour étonner et
dominer la femme et les faibles.

p. 348, l. 29: Faux et bête.

p. 348, l. 31: La monomanie du pays-age.

p. 349, l. 7: La soirée était chaude, mais on ferma les fenêtres par égard pour le lecteur. Les portes des salles voisines, éclairées, mais désertes, demeurèrent ouvertes, et bientôt il n'y eut que la voix de Mérimée qui résonnât dans cette quiétude et ce recueillement du grand palais ensommeillé. L'impératrice était assise à une table ronde placée dans un coin de la pièce, devant un buste en marbre du roi de Rome à vingt ans. A sa gauche, Mérimée. Autour de la table, les deux dames du palais, qui faisaient le service de semaine, les demoiselles d'hon-neur, Mlle de Larminat et Mlle d'Elbée, enfin les nièces de l'impératrice, Marie et Louise, avec la femme très aimable et très distinguée qui dirigeait alors leur éduca-tion. Une lourde lampe éclairait le cahier blanc où *Lokis* était écrit d'une écriture large et ferme, les éventails qui battaient l'air lentement, les broderies qu'agitaient sans bruit des doigts agiles et menus, tous ces fronts penchés et ces yeux de jeune filles qui se levaient quelquefois vers le lecteur avec une expression de curiosité et de rêverie. Deux ou trois hommes, assis un peu plus loin, complétaient le petit cercle. Mérimée lut de sa voix indifférente et monotone, interrompu seulement par des sourires ou par de légers murmures d'approbation dont l'impératrice donnait le signal (. . .) Un peu après avoir fini, il se leva et me dit à demi-voix, d'un ton brusque: 'Avez-vous compris, vous?' Je dus avoir l'air assez niais. J'aurais peut-être fini par trouver une réponse encore plus niaise, mais il ne m'en donna pas le temps. 'Vous n'avez pas compris, c'est parfait!' Et il me laissa complètement abasourdi.

p. 350, l. 4: Très souffreteux, très faible et fort découragé.

p. 350, l. 14: Un voyage difficile vers un

pays qui n'est peut-être pas des plus agréables.

p. 350, l. 15: J'ai la certitude que c'est une mort lente et très-douloureuse qui s'approche.

p. 350, l. 18: Je m'étonne parfois de vivre encore; si je continue à souffrir ainsi, il faut espérer que ce ne sera pas pour longtemps.

p. 350, l. 27: J'ai cru un instant que je commettrais l'indiscrétion de mourir chez quelqu'un que je ne connaissais pas assez intimement pour prendre cette liberté.

p. 351, l. 22: Non, c'est adieu qu'il faut dire; vous ne me retrouverez pas.

p. 351, l. 24: Non, c'est bien fini: je vois venir la mort et j'y suis préparé. Adieu!

p. 351, l. 31: Ferme comme un roc.

p. 351, l. 32: Je suis sorti navré et plus fatigué des efforts que j'avais faits pour ne pas sangloter que si je m'étais abandonné complètement.

p. 352, l. 9: Je ne suis pas curieux de voir la fin, mais je ne pense pas la voir.

p. 352, l. 14: Tout ce que l'imagination la plus lugubre pourrait inventer de plus noir est dépassé par l'événement. C'est un effondrement général. Une armée fran-çaise qui capitule; un empereur qui se laisse prendre.

p. 352, l. 19: Que je voudrais passer quelques heures encore auprès d'elle et lui persuader d'écrire trois cents pages qui paraîtront quand il plaira à Dieu et qui feront que les gens qui ne sont pas encore nés deviendront amoureux d'elle.

p. 352, n. 52: Il commence à revenir au bercail.

p. 353, l. 4: Fou de chagrin.

p. 353, l. 5: La France meurt, je veux mourir avec elle. Venez demain me dire adieu. Tâchez que Thiers sauve ce qu'il peut de la France.

p. 353, l. 8: Il avait changé de physionomie, de gestes, d'allure. C'était un vieillard cacochyme, courbé, ravagé de visage, qui avait constamment des larmes dans les

yeux. Ses lèvres sévères et pincées d'ordinaire s'abandonnaient avec une expression
que je n'oublierai jamais. Nul en France
n'a plus souffert de la défaite que Mérimée.
p. 353, l. 19: J'ai toute ma vie cherché à
être dégagé de préjugés, à être citoyen du
monde avant d'être Français, mais tous ces
manteaux philosophiques ne servent à rien.
Je saigne aujourd'hui des blessures de ces
imbéciles de Français, je pleure de leurs
humiliations, et, quelque ingrats et
absurdes qu'ils soient, je les aime toujours.
p. 354, l. 1: Maintenant bonsoir, je veux
dormir.
p. 354, l. 8: Quel est l'homme du monde
qui ne fasse baptiser ses enfants, qui ne
fasse porter ses parents morts à l'église?
Je déclare dans mon testament que
j'appartiens à la confession d'Augsbourg,
et je vous prierai de veiller à ce qu'on ne
me porte pas à Saint-Thomas-d'Aquin.
p. 355, l. 9: Sous un extérieur d'indifférence et de froideur, il cachait le cœur le
plus affectueux; pour ses amis il a été

jusqu'au bout d'un dévouement à toute
épreuve (. . .) Qui l'a connu n'oubliera
jamais le tour spirituel, léger et élégant
de sa conversation, à l'ancienne manière
française. Il possédait des connaissances
étendues et variées (. . .) Au cours de nos
relations je n'ai jamais connu d'homme
'plus impersonnel', comme on dit en français, plus grand ennemi de la particule:
je. Je n'ai jamais connu non plus d'homme
moins vaniteux: Mérimée était le seul
Français à ne pas porter à sa boutonnière
la rosette de la Légion d'honneur (il était
commandeur de cet ordre). Avec les
années, s'était developpé chez lui un
caractère de plus en plus moqueur et
sensible, en réalité profondément humain
dans sa façon de voir la vie, caractère
propre aux esprits sceptiques mais bons,
fouillant constamment les mœurs humaines
dans leurs faiblesses et dans leurs passions.
Il a clairement compris même ce qui ne
s'accordait pas avec ses convictions, et en
politique aussi il était sceptique.

CONCLUSION

p. 360, l. 6: Par crainte d'être dupe, il s'est
défié dans la vie, dans l'amour, dans la
science, dans l'art, et il a été dupe de sa
défiance.
p. 360, l. 23: Un manuel de courage
véritable et d'authentique délicatesse.
p. 360, l. 31: Le nom de Mérimée nous
évoque en même temps la rare qualité du
contenu et la proche présence des limites.
p. 360, n. 2: Le conseil était bon.

p. 361, l. 10: Il faut être un peu bête pour
ne faire qu'une chose, et dans les arts
on n'excelle qu'en s'y consacrant d'une
manière absolue.
p. 361, l. 24: Il s'agit d'un genre plus court
et plus tôt arrivé que le roman, d'un genre
qui n'est pas un monde, et qui coïncide
non avec un élargissement et une découverte du monde, mais avec une réduction,
un classement et une utilisation du monde.

Bibliography

i – *Works by Mérimée*

Mérimée's published writings, collected and uncollected, are very voluminous; for that reason, this bibliography is necessarily selective. Included in it are the main editions of his major works, together with those of his uncollected articles to which reference is made in the text. Further details will be found in P. Trahard and P. Josserand, *Bibliographie des œuvres de Prosper Mérimée*, Paris, Champion, 1929.

a) *Works of imagination*

An unfinished series of *Œuvres complètes* published in the 1920s and 1930s includes the following editions, all of which are worth consulting:

Premiers Essais (1823–1824). Théâtre de Clara Gazul (1825–1830), ed. P. Trahard, Paris, Champion, 1927.
La Jaquerie, suivie de la Famille de Carvajal, ed. P. Jourda, Paris, Champion, 1931.
Mosaïque, ed. M. Levaillant, Paris, Champion, 1933.
Carmen, Arsène Guillot, L'Abbé Aubain, ed. A. Dupouy, preface by Gérard d'Houville, Paris, Champion, 1927.
Dernières Nouvelles, ed. L. Lemonnier, Paris, Champion, 1929.

There is also a ten-volume edition of Mérimée's works of imagination, without critical apparatus but with stimulating prefaces by Eugène Marsan, published by Le Divan from 1927 to 1931: this contains works such as *La Guzla* not easily found elsewhere.

For individual works, out of the many available editions, the following may be specially recommended:

Romans et nouvelles, ed. M. Parturier, Paris, Garnier, 1967 (this authoritative two-volume edition is obviously destined to become standard for all Mérimée's narrative fiction).
Romans et nouvelles, ed. H. Martineau, Bibliothèque de la Pléiade, 1951.
Chronique du règne de Charles IX, ed. G. Dulong, Paris, Les Textes français, 1933.
Le Théâtre de Clara Gazul, ed. P. Salomon, Paris, Garnier-Flammarion, 1968.
Colomba, ed. P. Jourda, Paris, Droz, 1947.
Lokis, ed. R. Schmittlein, Baden, Art et Science, 1947.

The following works by Mérimée are currently to be found in English translation:

Carmen and Colomba, translated and introduced by E. Marielle, Penguin Classics.

Carmen and other stories, translated by G. Chapman, Blackie.

Carmen (with *Manon Lescaut*), translated by E. H. Garrett, Dent (Everyman Series).

Carmen, Colomba and selected stories, translated by W. J. Cobb, introduced by G. Steiner, Signet Books.

The Pearl of Toledo, translated by C. C. H. Fenton, 10 Dowry Square, Bristol.

A Slight Misunderstanding (*Une Double Méprise*), translated by D. Parmée, Calder (*European Classics Series*).

Tales of Love and Death, Yoseloff (Perpetua Paperbacks).

The Venus of Ille and other stories, translated by Jean Kimber, introduced by A. W. Raitt, Oxford University Press.

b) Other works

There are modern editions of several of Mérimée's other works. The following are all noteworthy:

Études anglo-américaines, ed. G. Connes, Paris, Champion, 1930.

Études de littérature russe, ed. H. Mongault, Paris, Champion, 1931–2.

Portraits historiques et littéraires, ed. P. Jourda, Paris, Champion, 1928 (it should be noted that the article 'Gentilshommes de lettres' included in this volume is probably not by Mérimée – cf. *C.G.*, Vol. V, p. 436, n. 1).

Mémoires historiques, Paris, Bernouard, 1927.

Pages retrouvées de P. Mérimée, ed. H. Malo, Paris, Émile-Paul, 1929.

Histoire du règne de Pierre le Grand, ed. H. Mongault and M. Parturier, Paris, Conard, 1947.

Histoire de Don Pèdre Ier roi de Castille, ed. G. Laplane, Paris, Didier, 1961.

Études sur les arts du Moyen-Age, ed. P. Josserand, Paris, Flammarion (Images et Idées), 1967 (the title should be *Études sur les arts au Moyen-Age* but is misprinted everywhere except in the introduction).

The main scholarly works by Mérimée which have not been reprinted in modern times are:

Notes d'un voyage dans le Midi de la France, Paris, Fournier, 1835.

Notes d'un voyage dans l'Ouest de la France, Paris, Fournier, 1836.

Notes d'un voyage en Auvergne, Paris, Fournier, 1838.

Notes d'un voyage en Corse, Paris, Fournier, 1840.

Études sur l'histoire romaine, Paris, Lévy, 1845.

Épisode de l'histoire de Russie. Les Faux Démétrius, Paris, Lévy, 1852.
Mélanges historiques et littéraires, Paris, Lévy, 1855.

Other articles and shorter works by Mérimée which have not been collected include the following:

'Notice historique et littéraire sur la vie et les ouvrages de Cervantès', preface to Filleau de Saint-Martin's translation of the *Histoire de Don Quichotte de la Manche*, Paris, Sautelet, 1826.
'Le Salon de 1839', *Revue des Deux Mondes*, 1er et 15 avril 1839.
'*Édifices de Rome moderne*, par. P. Letarouilly', *Revue des Deux Mondes*, 1er sept. 1841.
'Le Procès de M. Libri', *Revue des Deux Mondes*, 15 avril 1852.
'Réponse aux experts', *Revue des Deux Mondes*, 1er mai 1852.
'Salon de 1853', *Le Moniteur universel*, 16–17 mai, 5 juin, 8 juillet 1853.
Introduction to Marino Vreto, *Contes et poèmes de la Grèce moderne*, Paris, Audois, 1855.
'Des Mythes primitifs', *Revue contemporaine*, 15 oct. 1855.
'Ballades et chants populaires de la Roumanie', *Le Moniteur universel*, 17 janvier 1856.
'La Vie et l'œuvre de Cervantès', *Revue des Deux Mondes*, 15 déc. 1877.

c) Correspondence

Mérimée's *Correspondance générale* has been magnificently edited by Maurice Parturier in seventeen volumes, between 1941 and 1964. The first six volumes, on which J. Mallion and P. Josserand collaborated with M. Parturier, were published in Paris by Le Divan, the remainder in Toulouse by Privat. This constitutes by far the most complete, reliable and informative edition of Mérimée's letters, no matter to whom they are addressed. But though textually it supersedes all the previous partial editions, many of these are still of interest because of their prefaces and other critical material. The following are particularly valuable:

Lettres à une Inconnue, preface by H. Taine, Paris, Lévy, 1874.
Lettres à une autre Inconnue (Lise Przezdziecka), preface by H. Blaze de Bury, Paris, Lévy, 1875.
Lettres à M. Panizzi, ed. L. Fagan, Paris, Calmann-Lévy, 1881.
Une Correspondance inédite (Mme de la Rochejaquelein), preface by F. Brunetière, Paris, Calmann-Lévy, 1897.
Lettres à Viollet-le-Duc (1839–1870), ed. P. Trahard, Paris, Champion, 1927.
Lettres aux Grasset, ed. M. Parturier, Paris, La Connaissance, 1929.
Lettres à Francisque-Michel (1848–1870). Journal de Prosper Mérimée (1860–1868), ed. P. Trahard, Paris, Champion, 1930.
Lettres à la famille Delessert, ed. M. Parturier, preface by E. Henriot, Paris, Plon, 1931.

Lettres à la comtesse de Boigne, ed. L. de Sercey, Paris, Plon, 1933.

Lettres à Ludovic Vitet, ed. M. Parturier, Paris, Plon, 1934.

Lettres à Mme de Beaulaincourt (1866–1870), ed. M. Parturier, Paris, Calmann-Lévy, 1936.

Lettres aux antiquaires de l'Ouest, ed. J. Mallion, preface by M. Parturier, Poitiers, 1937.

Lettres à la duchesse de Castiglione-Colonna, ed. P. Trahard, Paris, Boivin, 1938.

Une Amitié littéraire: Prosper Mérimée et Ivan Tourguéniev, ed. M. Parturier, Paris, Hachette, 1952.

Lettres à Edward Ellice (1857–1863), ed. Marianne Cermakian and France Achener, Paris, Grasset, 1963.

ii – Other Works

It would obviously be impossible to give here a complete bibliography oꓲ works relating to Mérimée; the following list consists only of those books and articles which have been quoted in the present volume or which have been useful in writing it. Those interested in further details should consult the Mérimée bibliography by Trahard and Josserand already mentioned, which is invaluable for the period up to 1929, and for subsequent publications, in addition to the book-list given by M. Baschet in his excellent book on Mérimée, general bibliographies such as *The Year's Work in Modern Language Studies*.

ADAM, Mme Juliette: *Mes Premières Armes littéraires et politiques*, Paris, Lemerre, 1904.

——*Mes Angoisses et nos luttes 1871–3*, Paris, Lemerre, 1907.

ALEXANDRE, R.: 'Le manuscrit de *La Vénus d'Ille* de Prosper Mérimée', *Bulletin du Bibliophile*, 1898.

AMPÈRE, J.-J.: *La Grèce, Rome et Dante*, Paris, Didier, 1848.

AMPÈRE, A.-M. and J.-J.: *Correspondance et souvenirs de 1805 à 1864*, Paris, Hetzel, 1875.

ANCELOT, Mme V.: *Les Salons de Paris, foyers éteints*, Paris, Tardieu, 1858.

——*Un Salon de Paris 1824–64*, Paris, Dentu, 1866.

ARAGON, L.: *La Lumière de Stendhal*, Paris, Denoël, 1954.

ARBELET, P.: *Trois Solitaires (Courier, Stendhal, Mérimée)*, Paris, Gallimard, 1934.

——*Deux Vauriens: Mérimée et Sutton Sharpe*, Paris, Giraud-Badin, 1932.

ARRIGHI, P.: 'Centenaire et jeunesse de *Colomba*', *Hommage au doyen E. Gros*, Gap, 1959.

BAC, F.: 'L'Impératrice Eugénie au Cap Martin', *Revue universelle*, 15 mars 1927.

——*La Princesse Mathilde, sa vie et ses amis*, Paris, Hachette, 1928.

——*Le Mariage de l'Impératrice Eugénie*, Paris, Hachette, 1928.

——*Intimités du Second Empire*, Paris, Hachette, 1931–2.

——*Mérimée inconnu*, Paris, Hachette, 1939.

BALDENSPERGER, F.: 'Les années 1827 et 1828 en France et au dehors', *Revue des Cours et Conférences*, 1928–9.

BARBIER, A.: *Souvenirs personnels et silhouettes contemporaines*, Paris, Dentu, 1883.

BARDÈCHE, M.: *Stendhal romancier*, Paris, La Table Ronde, 1947.

BASCHET, R.: *E.-J. Delécluze témoin de son temps (1781–1862)*, Paris, Boivin, 1942.

——*Du Romantisme au Second Empire. Mérimée*, Paris, Nouvelles Éditions Latines, 1959.

——'Vitet, Mérimée, Musset,' *Revue des Sciences humaines*, oct.–déc. 1962.

BATAILLON, M.: 'L'Espagne de Mérimée d'après sa correspondance', *Revue de Littérature comparée*, janv.–mars 1948.

——'Mérimée et l'américanisme d'il y a cent ans', *Bulletin hispanique*, No. 4, 1954.

BÉQUIGNON, Y.: 'Mérimée et César', *Revue d'Histoire littéraire de la France*, janv.–mars 1930.

BERNARD, Suzanne: *Le Poème en prose de Baudelaire jusqu'à nos jours*, Paris, Nizet, 1959.

BERTAUT, J.: 'La Jeunesse de l'Impératrice Eugénie', *Figaro littéraire*, 6 novembre 1954.

——*L'Impératrice Eugénie et son temps*, Paris, Dumont, 1956.

BIANQUIS, Geneviève: 'Le thème de la Vénus fatale chez Eichendorff et Mérimée', *Revue universitaire*, mars–avril 1942.

BILLY, A.: *Sainte-Beuve, sa vie et son temps*, Paris, Flammarion, 1952.

——'L'Amitié de Stendhal et de Mérimée', *Revue de Paris*, oct. 1956.

——*Mérimée*, Paris, Flammarion, 1959.

BLAZE DE BURY, H.: Avant-propos des *Lettres à une autre Inconnue*, Paris, Lévy, 1875.

BONNEFON, P.: 'Victor Jacquemont annoté par Stendhal et par Mérimée', *Revue d'Histoire littéraire de la France*, 1921.

BONNEROT, J.: 'Les dessous d'une election à l'Académie française en 1844, Sainte-Beuve et Mérimée', *Revue universelle*, 1er juillet 1935.

BOULENGER, J.: . . . *Mais l'art est difficile*, 2e série, Paris, Plon, 1921.

——*Candidature au Stendhal-Club*, Paris, Le Divan, 1926.

BOURGET, P.: *Nouvelles pages de critique et de doctrine*, Paris, Plon, 1922.

——*Essais de psychologie contemporaine*, Paris, Plon, 1901.

BOUTCHIK, V.: *La Littérature russe en France*, Paris, Champion, 1947.

BOUVIER, E.: 'Les Débuts de Mérimée au théâtre', *Mélanges Lanson*, Paris Hachette, 1922.

BOWMAN, F. P.: 'Narrator and myth in Mérimée's *Vénus d'Ille*', *French Review*, 1960.

——*Prosper Mérimée. Heroism, Pessimism and Irony*, Berkeley and Los Angeles, University of California Press, 1962.

BRÄUER, R.: 'Der Stilwille Mérimées', *Archivum romanicum*, aprile–giugno 1930.

BRUNETIÈRE, F.: Ed. *Lettres de Mérimée à Mme de la Rochejaquelein*, Paris, Calmann-Lévy, 1897.

CARAVACA, F.: '¿Plagió Mérimée el Don Álvaro del Duque de Rivas?', *La Torre*, XIII, 49, Jan.–April 1965.

CARLYLE, T.: *The Last Words of Thomas Carlyle*, London, Longmans, Green, 1892.

CASTEX, P.-G.: *Le Conte fantastique en France*, Paris, Corti, 1951.

CERMAKIAN, M.: 'Treize lettres inédites de Prosper Mérimée (1862–70)', *Revue d'Histoire littéraire de la France*, juillet–sept. 1965.

CHAMBON, F.: *Notes sur Prosper Mérimée*, privately printed, 1902.

——*Pro Memoria*, Paris, Journal des Débats, 1907.

CHARLIER, G.: 'La source principale de *Mateo Falcone*', *Revue d'Histoire littéraire de la France*, juillet–sept. 1921.

CHRIST, Y.: 'Chronique du règne de Mérimée', *La Table Ronde*, mars 1962.

COLAJANNI, Giuliana: 'Mérimée e "l Affaire Libri" ', *Rivista di letterature moderne e comparate*, settembre 1968.

COMBES, Marguerite: *Pauvre et aventureuse bourgeoisie. Roulin et ses amis, 1796–1874*, Paris, Peyronnet, 1929.

CORDIER, H.: *Stendhal et ses amis*, Évreux, Hérissey, 1890.

COURTILLIER, G.: 'L'inspiration de *Mateo Falcone*', *Revue d'Histoire littéraire de la France*, avril–juin 1920.

DALE, Hilda: 'Note sur Fanny Lagden', *Revue de Littérature comparée*, avril–juin 1954.

DALE, R. C.: *The Poetics of Prosper Mérimée*, The Hague and Paris, Mouton, 1966.

DECOTTIGNIES, J.: '*Il Viccolo di Madama Lucrezia*. L'élaboration d'une nouvelle de Mérimée', *Revue d'Histoire littéraire de la France*, oct.–déc. 1964.

——'Quelques rapprochements suggérés par *La Vénus d'Ille*', *Revue des Sciences humaines*, juillet–sept. 1962.

DELACROIX, E.: *Journal*, ed. A. Joubin, Paris, Plon, 1932.

——*Correspondance générale*, ed. A. Joubin, Paris, Plon, 1935–8.

DELÉCLUZE, E.-J.: *Souvenirs de soixante années*, Paris, Lévy, 1862.

——*Journal*, ed. R. Baschet, Paris, Grasset, 1948.

DIVERSE: *Jacquemont*, Paris, Muséum d'Histoire naturelle, 1959.

——'Mérimée et l'Espagne', *Bulletin de l'Institut français en Espagne*, No. 78, déc. 1954.

——*Mérimée*, Catalogue de l'exposition de la Bibliothèque Nationale.

DOLLOT, R.: *Stendhal journaliste*, Paris, Mercure de France, 1948.

DU BOS, C.: *Notes sur Mérimée*, Paris, Messein, 1920.

DU CAMP, M.: *Souvenirs littéraires*, Paris, Hachette, 1882–3.

——*Souvenirs d'un demi-siècle*, Paris, Hachette, 1949.

DUGAS, L.: 'La timidité de Prosper Mérimée', *Mercure de France*, oct. 1920.

DULONG, G.: 'La *Chronique du règne de Charles IX* et les Registres-Journaux de Pierre de L'Estoile', *Mélanges Lanson*, Paris, Hachette, 1922.

DUPOUY, A.: '*Carmen*' de Mérimée, Paris, Malfère, 1930.

DUTOURD, J.: *Le Fond et la forme*, Paris, Gallimard, 1958.

ECKERMANN, J. P.: *Gespräche mit Goethe in den letzten Jahren seines Lebens*, ed. H. H. Houben, Wiesbaden, Brockhaus, 1949.

ESTÈVE, E.: *Byron et le romantisme français*, Paris, Hachette, 1907.

EUGÉNIE: *Lettres familières de l'Impératrice Eugénie*, ed. Duke of Alba, F. Llanos y Torriglia and P. Josserand, Paris, Le Divan, 1935.

FAHLIN, C.: 'Mérimée et ses amis espagnols: la comtesse de Montijo et Estébanez Calderon', *Studia neophilologica*, No. I, 1959.

FALKE, E.: *Die romantischen Elemente in Prosper Mérimées Romanen und Novellen*, Halle, Romantische Arbeiten, 1914.

FILON, A.: *Mérimée et ses amis*, Paris, Hachette, 1894.

——*Mérimée*, Paris, Hachette, 1898.

——*Souvenirs sur l'Impératrice Eugénie*, Paris, Calmann-Lévy, 1920.

FINOT, DR A.: *Maxime du Camp*, Paris, 1949.

FROUDE, J. A.: *Thomas Carlyle. A History of his Life in London 1834–1881*, London, Longmans, Green, 1884.

FRUTON, C.: *Mérimée et la médecine*, Paris, Tournan, 1938.

GABBA, E.: 'Prospero Mérimée storico di Roma', *Rivista storica italiana*, fasc. IV, 1956.

GALLAS, M. K. R.: 'Mérimée et la théorie de l'art pour l'art', *Neophilologus*, V, 1919–20.

GAULMIER, J.: 'Mérimée, Gobineau et les bohémiens', *Revue d'Histoire littéraire de la France*, oct.–déc. 1966.

GEORGE, A. J.: 'Prosper Mérimée and the short prose narrative', *Symposium*, Spring, 1956.

——*Short Fiction in France 1800–50*, New York, Syracuse University Press, 1964.

GIROD DE L'AIN, G.: 'Une muse romantique: Émilie Lacoste', *Revue des Deux Mondes*, 15 sept. 1954.

GOETHE, J. W. von: *Serbische Gedichte*, *Werke*, 41 II and 42 I, Weimar, Böhlaus Nachfolger, 1903–4.

GONCOURT, E. and J. DE: *Journal*, Paris, Flammarion/Fasquelle, 1959.

GOURVIL, G.: 'Voleur sans le savoir. Prosper Mérimée et Gwenchlan en 1835', *Nouvelle Revue de Bretagne*, mars–avril, mai–juin–juillet–août 1949.

GOUT, P.: *Viollet-le-Duc*, Revue de l'art chrétien, Supplément 3, 1914.

GRENIER, E.: *Souvenirs littéraires*, Paris, Lemerre, 1894.

GROVER, P. R.: 'Mérimée's influence on Henry James', *Modern Language Review*, Vol. 63, No. 4, Oct. 1968.

GUNNELL, Doris: *Sutton Sharpe et ses amis français*, Paris, Champion, 1925.

HAINSWORTH, G.: 'West African local colour in *Tamango*', *French Studies*, Jan. 1967.

HALLAYS, A.: 'Mérimée Inspecteur des monuments historiques', *Revue des Deux Mondes*, 15 avril 1911.

HAUSSONVILLE, O. D': *Prosper Mérimée. Hugh Elliot*, Paris, Calmann-Lévy, 1885.

HAYWARD, A.: *A Selection from the Correspondence of Abraham Hayward Q.C.*, ed. H. E. Carlisle, London, Murray, 1886.

HAZARD, P.: 'Énigmes stendhaliennes', *Revue d'Histoire littéraire de la France*, 1914.

——'Les plagiats de Stendhal', *Revue des Deux Mondes*, 15 sept. 1921.

HEALY, D.MCN.: 'Mary Shelley and Prosper Mérimée', *Modern Language Review*, July 1941.

——*Mérimée et les Anglais*, Paris, André, 1947.

HEMMINGS, F. W. J.: *The Russian Novel in France 1884–1914*, London, Oxford University Press, 1950.

HILY, M.: 'Prosper Mérimée et l'histoire romaine', *Mélanges de la Société toulousaine d'études classiques*, I, 1946.

HOUSSAYE, A.: *Les Confessions*, Paris, Dentu, 1885.

HOVENKAMP, J. W.: *Mérimée et la couleur locale*, Paris, Les Belles Lettres, 1928.

HUGO, V.: *Histoire d'un crime*, t. II, Paris, Calmann-Lévy, 1877–8.

HYTIER, J.: *Les Romans de l'individu*, Paris, Les Arts et le Livre, 1928.

IBROVAC, M.: *Claude Fauriel et la fortune européenne des poésies populaires grecque et serbe*, Paris, Didier, 1966.

ISAY, R.: 'Une nouvelle interprétation de *Colomba*', *Revue des Deux Mondes*, 1er déc. 1953.

JACQUEMONT, V.: *Lettres à Stendhal*, Paris, Poursin, 1933.

JOHNSTONE, G. H.: *Prosper Mérimée. A Mask and a Face*, New York, Dutton, 1927.

JOSSERAND, P.: Ed. *Lettres à la comtesse de Montijo*, Paris, Le Divan, 1936.

——'Le Manuscrit de l'*Alexandre Pouchkine* de Mérimée', *Revue de Littérature comparée*, janvier–mars 1937.

——'Le chapelet de Mérimée', *Le Divan*, oct.–déc. 1946.

——'*La Vénus d'Ille* et *La Mode*', *Le Divan*, juillet–sept. 1949.

——'H.B.', *Le Divan*, juillet–sept. 1950.

——'Encore *H.B.*', *Le Divan*, oct.–déc. 1950.

JOURDA, P.: *Stendhal raconté par ceux qui l'ont vu*, Paris, Stock, 1931.

——'A propos de la *Jaquerie*', *Le Divan*, fév.–mars 1933.

——'*Zampa* et la *Vénus d'Ille*', *Le Divan*, avril–juin 1945.

KING, R.: 'Prosper Mérimée: attempts at Romantic drama', *Nottingham French Studies*, Oct. 1967.

KOSKO, Maria: *Le Thème de Mateo Falcone*, Paris, Nizet, 1960.

KRAPPE, A. H.: 'Notes sur les sources de Mérimée', *Revue d'Histoire littéraire de la France*, avril–juin 1928.

KURTZ, H.: *The Empress Eugénie*, London, Hamilton, 1964.

KUTTNER, M.: 'Die korsischen Quellen von Chamisso und Mérimée', *Archiv für das Studium der neueren Sprachen*, Vol. CXI, 1903.

LAUNAY, L. DE: *Un Amoureux de Mme Récamier. Le Journal de J.-J. Ampère*, Paris, Champion, 1925.

LEDOUX, A.: 'Situation de Mérimée', *Stendhal-Club*, No. 7, 16 avril 1960.

LEFÈBVRE, A.: *La célèbre Inconnue de Prosper Mérimée*, Paris, Sansot, 1908.

LELARGE, A.: 'Duranty, Mérimée et Mme Lacoste', *Intermédiaire des chercheurs et des curieux*, 10 janvier 1929 and 10 mars 1929.

——'Une amie de Mérimée: Mme Lacoste', *Bulletin de la Société de l'histoire de Paris et de l'Île-de-France*, 1935.

LENORMANT, C.: *Beaux-Arts et voyages*, Paris, Lévy, 1861.

LÉON, P.: *La Vie des monuments français*, Paris, Picard, 1951.

——*Mérimée et son temps*, Paris, P.U.F., 1962.

LORENZI DI BRADI: *La vraie Colomba*, Paris, Flammarion, 1922.

LUPPÉ, Marquis de: *Mérimée*, Paris, Michel, 1945.

LYON, Sylvia: *The Life and Times of Prosper Mérimée*, New York, The Dial Press, 1948.

MAES, P.: *Un Ami de Stendhal. Victor Jacquemont*, Paris, Desclée de Brouwer, 1936.

MAIGRON, L.: *Le Roman historique à l'époque romantique*, Paris, Champion, 1912.

MAIXNER, R.: 'Quelques victimes de la *Guzla* de Mérimée', *Revue de Littérature comparée*, juillet–sept. 1956.

——'La retraite parisienne d'Antoine Sorgo-Sorkoćevič', *Revue de Littérature comparée*, juillet–sept. 1966.

MARCAGGI, J.-B.: 'Les sources de *Colomba*', *Revue de Paris*, 15 juillet 1928.

MARIX-SPIRE, T.: *Les romantiques et la musique. Le cas George Sand (1804–1838)*, Paris, Nouvelles Éditions Latines, 1955.

MARKIEWICZ, S.: 'La Pologne dans l'œuvre et la vie de Mérimée', *Revue de Littérature comparée*, avril–juin, 1953.

MARSAN, E.: *Instances*, Paris, Éditions Prométhée, 1930.

MARSHALL, J. F.: 'Les Dames Garnett amies de Stendhal', *Le Divan*, oct.–déc. 1949.

MARTIN, Marietta: *Un aventurier intellectuel, le docteur Koreff*, Paris, Champion, 1925.

MARTINEAU, H.: *Stendhal et le salon de Mme Ancelot*, Paris, Le Divan, 1932.

——Ed. *174 Lettres à Stendhal*, Paris, Le Divan, 1947.

——*Petit dictionnaire stendhalien*, Paris, Le Divan, 1948.

——*Le Calendrier de Stendhal*, Paris, Le Divan, 1950.

——*Nouvelles Soirées du Stendhal-Club*, Paris, Mercure de France, 1950.

——*Le Cœur de Stendhal*, Paris, Michel, 1952–3.

MARTINENCHE, E.: *L'Espagne et le romantisme français*, Paris, Hachette, 1932.

MARTINEZ FERRANDO, J. E.: *Prospero de Bofarull y Prospero Mérimée, una amistad ejemplar*, Asociacion de estudios reusenses, Reus, 1954.

MEYNIEUX, A.: *Mérimée, Tourguénev–Flaubert traducteurs de Pouchkine*, Librairie des Cinq Continents, 1962.

MICHAUT, G.: 'La mystification de *Colomba*', *Annales de l'Université de Paris*, janvier 1933.

MICHEL, F.: *Études stendhaliennes*, Paris, Mercure de France, 1957.

——*Fichier stendhalien*, Boston, Hall, 1964.

MICKEL, E. J., Jr: 'Some sources for Mérimée's Charles IX', *Modern Language Quarterly*, June 1968.

MILLER, E.: *Prince of Librarians. The Life and Times of Antonio Panizzi of the British Museum*, London, Deutsch, 1967.

MONGAULT, H.: 'Mérimée, Beyle et quelques russes', *Mercure de France*, 1er mars 1928.

——'Mérimée et l'histoire russe', *Le Monde slave*, août, sept., oct. 1932.

MOREAU, P.: 'Deux remarques sur la phrase de Mérimée', *Revue d'Histoire littéraire de la France*, juillet–sept. 1924.

——*Le Classicisme des romantiques*, Paris, Plon, 1932.

MOREL-FATIO, A.: 'Mérimée et Calderon', *Revue d'Histoire littéraire de la France*, janvier–mars 1920.

MORGAN, Lady: *France in 1829–30*, London, Saunders & Otley, 1830.

MUSSET, R.: '*Tamango*', *Annales de Bretagne*, t. xxxviii, 1928–9.

NAAMAN, A.: '*Mateo Falcone*' de Mérimée, Paris, Nizet, 1967.

NAGEL, I.: 'Gespenster und Wirklichkeiten: Prosper Mérimées Novelle *La Vénus d'Ille*', *Neue Rundschau*, Drittes Heft, 1957.

O'MEARA, K.: *Un Salon à Paris, Mme Mohl et ses amis*, Paris, Plon, 1886.

PAILLERON, Marie-Louise: *François Buloz et ses amis*, Paris, Calmann-Lévy, 1919.

——*François Buloz et ses amis*, *Le Second Empire*, Paris, Perrin, 1924.

PALÉOLOGUE, M.: *Les Entretiens de l'Impératrice Eugénie*, Paris, Plon, 1928.

PARTURIER, M.: 'Notes bibliographiques sur Prosper Mérimée', *Bulletin du Bibliophile*, août–sept. 1929 and 20 nov. 1930.

——'Précisions sur Mérimée', *Revue de Paris*, 1er and 15 sept. 1932.

——'Le Baiser à l'Inconnue', *Bulletin du Bibliophile*, 20 oct. 1932.

——*Autour de Mérimée. 'Les Forces perdues' et 'L'Éducation sentimentale'*, Giraud-Badin, 1932.

——'Autour de Mérimée. L'aventure Mary-Grasset et *Le Rouge et le Noir*', *Bulletin du Bibliophile*, 20 mai 1932.

——'Stendhal et Mérimée à la Charité-sur-Loire', *Le Divan*, avril–mai 1933.

——'Mme de Boigne et Mérimée', *Le Figaro*, 6 mai 1933.

——'Un manuscrit des *Bohémiens* de Pouchkine', *Bulletin du Bibliophile*, 20 mai 1933.

——*Une Expérience de Lélia, ou le fiasco du Comte Gazul*, Paris, Le Divan, 1934.

——'La fin du *Rouge* et le problème de Mary', *Le Divan*, mai–juin 1935.

——'Deux lettres de Mérimée à George Sand', *Le Divan*, juillet–sept. 1935.

——'Itinéraire de Mérimée en Corse', *Mercure de France*, 1er mars 1936.

——'Stendhal, *le Masque de fer* et la famille Cenci', *Le Divan*, avril 1936.

——Ed. 'Épisode d'un roman inédit', *Revue de Paris*, 15 janvier 1937.

——'Une version inédite de la *Dame de Pique* par Mérimée', *Revue de Littérature comparée*, janvier–mars 1937.

——'Chronologie mériméenne', *Bulletin du Bibliophile*, 20 février–20 mars 1938.

——'Rémusat et Mérimée, lettres inédites', *Revue de Paris*, 1er janvier 1939.

——'Pour le centenaire de *Colomba*', *Le Divan*, avril–juin 1941.

——'Sur les sources de *La Vénus d'Ille*', *Le Divan*, avril–juin 1945.

——'Précision sur Céline Cayot', *Le Divan*, janvier–mars 1946.

——'Ivan Tourguéniev et Maxime du Camp', *Revue de Littérature comparée*, oct.–déc. 1947.

——'Les secrets de la pièce *Les Espagnols en Danemarck*', *Figaro littéraire*, 8 mai 1948.

——Ed. (with J. Mallion) Mérimée, *Morceaux choisis*, Paris, Didier, 1952.

——'Rendez-vous espagnols de Prosper Mérimée', *Revue de Paris*, déc. 1953.

——'Trois aspects de Mérimée', *Figaro littéraire*, 19 déc. 1953.

——Ed. *Nouvelles moscovites* (translated by Mérimée), Paris, Club des libraires de France, 1955.

——'La célèbre "dictée" de Compiègne n'est en rien l'œuvre de Mérimée', *Figaro littéraire*, 7 juin 1958.

——'L'amour de Mérimée et de Jenny Dacquin', *Figaro littéraire*, 14 février 1959.

——'Mérimée sur la Côte d'Azur', *Annales du Centre universitaire méditerranéen*, Vol. 11, 1958.

——'Une lettre inédite de Mérimée', *Revue des Sciences humaines*, oct.–déc. 1965.

PARTURIER, M. and LUPPÉ, A. DE: *La Naissance de Duranty (fin d'une légende)*, Paris, Giraud–Badin, 1947.

PATER, W.: 'Prosper Mérimée', in *Studies in European Literature*, Oxford, Clarendon Press, 1900.

PAUPE, A.: *La Vie littéraire de Stendhal*, Paris, Champion, 1914.

PAUPHILET, A.: 'Mérimée critique d'art en 1839', *Annales romantiques*, IV, 1907.

PEYRE, R.: 'A propos de *La Vision de Charles XI* de Mérimée', *Revue d'Histoire littéraire de la France*, janvier–mars 1914.

PINET, G.: *Léonor Mérimée (1757–1836)*, Paris, Champion, 1913.

PINVERT, L.: *Sur Mérimée, à propos d'ouvrages récents*, Paris, Leclerc, 1906.

——*Sur Mérimée, à propos d'une cérémonie récente*, Paris, Leclerc, 1907.

——*Sur Mérimée, notes bibliographiques et critiques*, Paris, Leclerc, 1908.

——*Un post-scriptum sur Mérimée*, Paris, Leclerc, 1911.

——'*L'Enlèvement de la redoute*', *Revue des études historiques*, mai–juin 1914.

PLANCHE, G.: *Portraits littéraires*, Paris, Charpentier, 1883.

POLIKOWSKY, J.: *Prosper Mérimée. Le caractère et l'œuvre littéraire*, Berne, 1910.

POMMIER, J.: 'Notes sur *Carmen*', *Bulletin de la Faculté des Lettres de Strasbourg*, nov., déc. 1929, fév., avril 1930.

——*Variétés sur Alfred de Musset et son théâtre*, Paris, Nizet, 1944.

PONTMARTIN, A. DE: *Mes Mémoires. Seconde Jeunesse*, t. II, Paris, Calmann-Lévy, 1886.

——*Souvenirs d'un vieux critique*, 3e série, Paris, Calmann-Lévy, 1883.

POULET-MALASSIS, A.: *Le Portrait de Prosper Mérimée . . .*, Paris, Baur, 1876.

PRIMOLI, Comte de: 'L'enfance d'une souveraine', *Revue des Deux Mondes*, 15 oct. 1923.

RAITT, A. W.: 'History and fiction in the works of Mérimée', *History Today*, April 1969.

——'An unpublished letter from Mérimée', *Modern Language Review*, April 1970.

RATERMANIS, J. B.: 'La perspective temporelle dans *La Vénus d'Ille* de Mérimée', *Le Français moderne*, juillet 1963.

REGARD, M.: *L'Adversaire des Romantiques. Gustave Planche*, Paris, Nouvelles Éditions Latines, 1955.

RICHARDSON, Joanna: *Princess Mathilde*, London, Weidenfeld & Nicolson, 1969.

RITCHIE, Anne T.: *Letters of Anne Thackeray Ritchie with 42 Additional Letters from William Makepeace Thackeray*, London, Murray, 1942.

ROBERT-DUMAS, C.: 'Prosper Mérimée', *Die neueren Sprachen*, Jan. 1930.

ROCHE, R.: 'Un rêve de Mérimée: *Djoûmane*', *Grande Revue*, oct. 1928.

ROGER, G.: *Prosper Mérimée et la Corse*, Alger, Baconnier, 1945.

ROUSSEAUX, A.: *Le Monde classique*, t. I, Paris, Michel, 1941.

ROYER, L.: *Stendhal au Jardin du Roi*, Grenoble, Arthaud, 1930.

——'*La Vénus d'Ille* appréciée par Stendhal', *Le Divan*, février–mars 1932.

SAINTE-BEUVE, C.-A. DE: *Portraits contemporains*, t. II and III, Paris, Didier, 1846.

——*Causeries du lundi*, t. VII.

——*Lettres à la Princesse*, Paris, Lévy, 1873.

——*Les Cahiers de Sainte-Beuve*, Paris, Lemerre, 1876.

——*Mes Poisons*, Paris, Les Œuvres representatives, 1926.

——*Correspondance générale*, ed. J. Bonnerot, Paris, Stock, 1935-.

SAISSET, F.: 'Mérimée et les sources de la *Vénus d'Ille*', *Revue bleue*, 6 février 1932.

SAMARAN, C.: 'Une énigme pseudo-littéraire: la dictée de Mérimée', *Le Monde*, 18–19 avril 1954.

SAND, George: *Correspondance*, ed. G. Lubin, Paris, Garnier, 1964-.

——*Lélia*, ed. P. Reboul, Paris, Garnier, 1960.

SCHINZ, A.: 'Notes sur le vocabulaire de Maupassant et de Mérimée', *Revue des Langues romanes*, mai–déc. 1909.

SENIOR, N. W.: *Journals kept in France and Italy from 1848–52*, London, King, 1871.

——*Conversations with M. Thiers, M. Guizot and other distinguished persons*, London, Hurst & Blackett, 1878.

——*Conversations with Distinguished Persons during the Second Empire from 1860–63*, London, Hurst & Blackett, 1882.

SHELLEY, Mary W.: 'Illyrian Poems – Feudal Scenes', *Westminster Review*, Vol. X, Jan. 1829.

——*The Letters of Mary Shelley*, ed. F. L. Jones, Norman, University of Oklahoma Press, 1944.

SIMPSON, M. C. M.: *Many Memories of Many People*, London, Arnold, 1898.

SMITH, Marion E.: *Une Anglaise intellectuelle en France sous la Restauration, miss Mary Clarke*, Paris, Champion, 1927.

SÖDERGÅRD, Ö.: 'George Sand et Prosper Mérimée', *Revue des Sciences humaines*, oct.–déc. 1959.

SORVILLO, G.: *Mœurs et coutumes de la Corse dans l'œuvre de Prosper Mérimée*, Naples, L' Arte tipografica, 1954.

SOURIAU, M.: 'Les variantes de *Mateo Falcone*', *Revue d'Histoire littéraire de la France*, avril–juin 1913.

SPAZIANI, M.: *Gli amici della principessa Matilde*, Rome, Edizioni di storia e letteratura, 1960.

SPOERRI, T.: 'Mérimée and the short story', *Yale French Studies*, No. 4.

STENDHAL: *Courrier anglais*, Le Divan, 1935-6.

——*Œuvres intimes*, ed. H. Martineau, Paris, Bibliothèque de la Pléiade, 1961.

——*Correspondance*, ed. V. del Litto, Paris, Bibliothèque de la Pléiade, 1964.

STEUBER, E.: 'Carmen. Eine psychologisch-ästhetische Betrachtung der Novelle von Prosper Mérimée', *Zeitschrift für französische Sprache und Literatur*, XLVIII, 4–5–6, 1926.

STRYIENSKI, C. and ARBELET, P.: *Soirées du Stendhal-Club*, 2e série, Mercure de France, 1908.

SUZANNET, A. DE: 'Le portrait de Clara Gazul', *Bulletin du Bibliophile*, 20 janvier 1932.

SYMONS, A.: *The Symbolist Movement in Literature* (2nd ed. 1919), New York, Dutton, 1958.

TAINE, H.: Preface to *Lettres à une Inconnue*, Paris, Lévy, 1874.

THEIS, O.: *Sprache und Stil Mérimées in seinen Novellen*, Frankfurt, 1929.

THIBAUDET, A.: *Histoire de la littérature française de 1789 à nos jours*, Paris, Stock, Delamain & Boutelleau, 1936.

THOMAS, L.: *Curiosités sur Mérimée*, Paris, Aux Armes de France, 1944.

TICKNOR, G.: *The Life, Letters and Journals of George Ticknor*, London, Sampson Low, Marston, Searle & Rivington, 1876.

TOCQUEVILLE, A. DE: *Souvenirs*, Paris, Gallimard, 1942.

TOURNEUX, M.: *Prosper Mérimée, ses portraits, ses desseins, sa bibliothèque*, Paris, Charavay, 1879.

——*Prosper Mérimée, comédienne espagnole et chanteur illyrien*, Paris, Monnier, 1887.

TRAHARD, P.: *Prosper Mérimée et l'art de la nouvelle*, Paris, P.U.F., 1923.

——*La Jeunesse de Prosper Mérimée (1803–1834)*, Paris, Champion, 1925.

——*Prosper Mérimée de 1834 à 1853*, Paris, Champion, 1928.

——*La Vieillesse de Prosper Mérimée (1854–1870)*, Paris, Champion, 1930.

——'A propos de Mérimée', *Revue d'Histoire littéraire de la France*, avril–juin 1934.

TROLLOPE, T. A.: *What I remember*, London, Bentley, 1887–9.

TROTAIN, Marthe: *Les Scènes historiques*, Paris, Champion, 1923.

VALON, A. DE: *Nos Aventures pendant les journées de février*, Paris, Leclerc, 1910.

VERDIER, P.: 'Le Service des monuments historiques', *Congrès archéologique de France*, 97, Vol. I, Picard, 1936.

VIEL-CASTEL, H. DE: *Mémoires*, Paris, Le Prat, 1942.

VIGNERON, R.: 'Stendhal et Sanscrit', *Modern Philology*, mai 1936.

VIGNOLS, L.: 'Une version remaniée et inconnue du *Tamango* de Mérimée', *Revue d'Histoire littéraire de la France*, 1927.

——'Les sources du *Tamango* de Mérimée et la littérature "négrière" à l'époque romantique', *Mercure de France*, 15 déc. 1927.

VIOLLET-LE-DUC, E.: 'Prosper Mérimée et les monuments historiques', *Revue de Paris*, 15 nov. 1895.

YOVANOVITCH, V. M.: *La Guzla de Prosper Mérimée*, Paris, Hachette, 1911.

YU-HOUO-JOKI: *Prosper Mérimée romancier*, Lyon, 1936.

Index

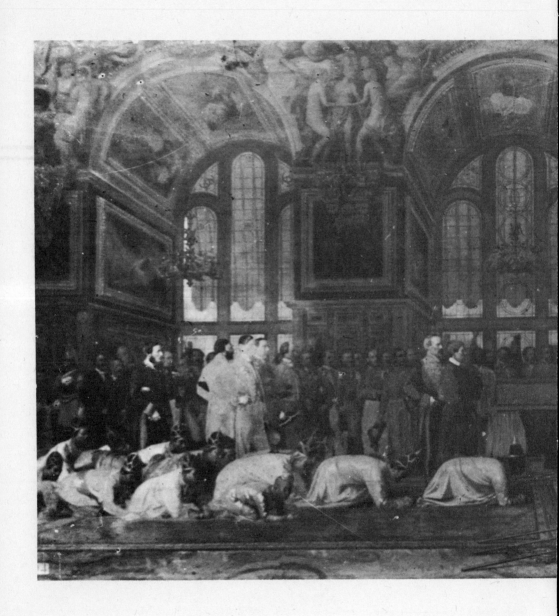